# *Advances in Altered States of Consciousness & Human Potentialities, Volume I.*

**A PDI RESEARCH REFERENCE WORK**

# *Advances in Altered States of Consciousness & Human Potentialities,* Volume I.*

**A PDI RESEARCH REFERENCE WORK**

*Editor*

**THEODORE X. BARBER**

*FIRST EDITION—1976*

PDi

**PSYCHOLOGICAL DIMENSIONS, INC.**
**500 FIFTH AVENUE, NEW YORK, N.Y. 10036**

* THE PREPUBLICATION TITLE OF THIS VOLUME WAS *"ALTERATIONS IN AWARENESS & HUMAN POTENTIALITIES"*

LIBRARY OF CONGRESS CATALOG CARD NUMBER : 76-42132

ISBN: 0-88437-002-X

0987654321

PRINTED IN THE UNITED STATES OF AMERICA

# Preface

Interest in alterations in awareness associated with psychedelic drugs, meditation, yoga, religious experiences, hypnosis, and biofeedback is fast increasing and research on these topics is beginning to accumulate. Undergraduate majors in psychology are typically eager to learn about these phenomena. Some of the brightest graduate students would like to carry out research in this area. A substantial number of teachers of psychology have personally explored either meditation, self-hypnosis, or the effects of 'mind-altering' drugs. An increasing number of courses are being taught in our colleges and universities which pertain to alterations in awareness and to human potentialities. Many signs point to a shift in emphasis in psychology toward a greater probing of these topics. We venture to predict that, during the next decade, the area we are labeling as *Altered States of Consciousness and Human Potentialities* will become one of the most important areas of psychology.

These volumes, which will be published every two or three years, will cover this new emphasis in psychology. Each volume will reprint the 40 to 50 most important papers that were published during the preceding years. The papers will focus on modes of experience or awareness that differ from our ordinary or 'normal' experience. The topics that will be considered include: hypnosis, biofeedback, meditation, yoga, Zen, autogenic training, and acupuncture; fantasy, daydreams, nocturnal dreams and sleep; religious and mystical experiences; parapsychology and psychic research; psychological effects of cannabis and psychedelic drugs; and methods for heightening human capabilities and fulfilling human potentialities.

The task of the editorial board is to select material published during the preceding two or three years that is both important and stimulating. Excerpts from books will be included as well as journal articles. Empirical studies will be published but priority will be given to reviews that summarize and integrate a series of experimental studies. We hope that the volumes will be informative, readable, and interesting and that they will serve as the basic archives for work in this area.

We shall include papers that are relevant and provocative even though we might disagree with the ideas they contain. This area of inquiry is still at an early hypothesis-forming stage and the selections are intended to stimulate further thinking and research and are not to be viewed as definitive. Of course, we shall include critical reviews of the various topics when they are available.

To attain a broader overview of the kinds of material that will comprise these volumes, let us glance briefly at the papers that have been chosen this year.

## Awareness, Consciousness, and Mental Functions

The first section begins with an overview of the field by Robert M. Nideffer. His paper summarizes relevant literature pertaining to altered states of consciousness, includes original material on dreaming and mind-altering drugs, and attempts a theoretical integration of the data.

The second selection by Charles T. Tart, "States of Consciousness and State-Specific Sciences," is required reading for anyone interested in this area. Tart proposes that the significance of altered states of consciousness will be missed if scientists only try to understand them from the perspective of their normal awareness. He argues that the scientific method can and should be used to study altered states of consciousness when scientists themselves are experiencing the altered states. To what extent this provocative thesis will influence research remains to be seen. Although it has already aroused controversy (see *Science,* June 8, 1973, Vol. 180, pp. 1005-1008) it appears certain that investigators in this area will have to consider Tart's thesis seriously.

Whether one adopts a monistic or dualistic position with regard to the mind-brain relationship, there is no doubt that what we see as brain and what we conceptualize as "mind" are intimately interrelated. R.W. Sperry's important work, which supports the conclusion that each hemisphere of the brain "has its own separate domain of conscious awareness," is summarized in this section. The dominant left hemisphere in man specializes in speech, writing, calculation, and other verbal activities whereas the non-dominant right hemisphere specializes in non-verbal activities and spatial relations. It appears that the work of Sperry and his collaborators is relevant to understanding the processes that occur during both normal awareness and during alterations in awareness and we look forward to future studies that will elucidate these relationships.

Formal training programs that aim to produce alterations in awareness are not new. The followers of Gurdjieff, for example, have been working along these lines for many years. Recently, there has been a marked increase in formal courses that aim to teach individuals to produce alterations in their own awareness. One such training program, the Arica course, is critically analyzed in Adam Smith's "Alumni Notes—Altered States University." We also present the Epilogue from John C. Lilly's book, *The Center of the Cyclone,* in which he discusses his own self-directed attempts to produce alterations in awareness.

## Biofeedback

Biofeedback has been a prolific and important area of investigation in recent years. The basic principle of biofeedback is that the subject is given information concerning moment-to-moment variations in his physiological functions—e.g., variations in his blood pressure, muscle tension, or alpha brain waves—which the subject then utilizes to change, or control, the physiological function. The technical research in this area is presented in another series of volumes on *Biofeedback & Self-Control,* Aldine, Chicago. In the present volume we include general papers which indicate the possibilities of biofeedback for control of physiological functions and its ramifications for a broader understanding of human potentialities.

Al Berger's "Biofeedback in Action" and Turin and Nideffer's annotated bibliography on the clinical applications of biofeedback introduce this section. These are followed by a report of ground-breaking research by Thomas H. Budzynski "Some Applications of Biofeedback-Produced Twilight States" which aims to induce and prolong hypnagogic phenomena by means of biofeedback. The paper by Elmer E. Green and his collaborators covers two phases of their recent research, one phase pertaining to the feats of Swami Rama and the other to utilizing biofeedback for "mind-body self-regulation." The stimulating paper which follows, by Johann Stoyva, attempts to explain how biofeedback can be used to study introspection, thought processes, and hypnagogic imagery.

Although biofeedback research has helped to stimulate a new era of psychology, some aspects of it, particularly the use of biofeedback training to produce more alpha brain waves, have been misinterpreted by the popular press and by lay organizations. We include a paper by Thomas B. Mulholland that discusses this important topic "Can You Really Turn on With Alpha?" and a brief paper by Charles Muses that attempts to place biofeedback research in broader perspective.

## Mind-Altering Drugs

The widespread use of ''mind-altering'' drugs, such as marihuana, hashish, and LSD, has been largely responsible for the expansion of interest in altered states of consciousness. In these volumes we shall include papers which formulate descriptions and explanations of the psychological effects of these drugs. In the present volume we include a paper by F.L. DeLong and B.I. Levy which attempts to integrate the available data pertaining to the cognitive effects of marihuana.

## Hypnosis

Hypnosis has traditionally been viewed as an altered state of consciousness. In this volume we include three papers that cast a new light on this old topic. T.X. Barber's ''Suggested ('Hypnotic') Behavior: The Trance Paradigm versus an Alternative Paradigm'' integrates data indicating that the ''good hypnotic subject'' has positive attitudes, motivations, and expectancies toward the test situation, and, consequently, allows himself to think with and vividly imagine those things that are suggested. The paper which follows by Louise H. Kidder ''On Becoming Hypnotized: How Skeptics Become Convinced: A Case of Attitude Change?'' shows how individuals learn to behave like ''good hypnotic subjects'' and how they learn to accept new definitions of their own feelings and of the term ''hypnosis.'' The final paper in this section, by N.P. Spanos and T.X. Barber ''Cognitive Activity during 'Hypnotic Suggestibility: Goal-Directed Fantasy and the Experience of Nonvolition'' pinpoints the importance of cognition and ''goal-directed fantasy'' in determining the experiences of the hypnotic subject.

## Acupuncture

There are at least two reasons why acupuncture is a relevant topic for this volume. First, the dramatic effects of acupuncture have been attributed to a ''life energy'' (Qi or Ch'i) which maintains a balance between two forces, Yin and Yang. If this hypothesized ''life energy'' actually exists, it would, of course, be very relevant for understanding human potentialities. Second, it appears that the success of acupuncture in attenuating pain during surgery is important in understanding the human potential for controlling pain. J.F. Chaves and T.X. Barber's ''Needles and Knives: Behind the Mystery of Acupuncture and Chinese Meridians'' attempts to explain how and why acupuncture is effective in reducing pain during surgery. These authors discuss the effectiveness of acupuncture in surgery in terms of six factors that are already known but usually overlooked by Western medicine.

In order to integrate acupuncture into a general understanding of human potentialities, it is first necessary to determine whether the claims for its effectiveness in relieving a wide variety of illness and ailments are valid. The critical analysis by Arthur S. Freese ''What Acupuncture Won't Do'' indicates that its effectiveness has been highly exaggerated.

## Meditation, Yoga, and Religious Experience

The first selection in this section, from Robert E. Ornstein's book *The Psychology of Consciousness,* discusses the effects of meditation in terms of our present-day psychological knowledge. The following three papers by Victor F. Emerson, A.N.D. Frederick and T.X. Barber, and Beverly Timmons et al. focus on the psycho-physiological concomitants of training in meditation or in hatha yoga. The scholarly paper by Daniel Goleman, which presents a detailed description of Hindu Bhakti, Sufism, Christian Hesychasm, Yoga, Zen, and related disciplines is required reading for all students of the area. This section also includes a selection from Alan Watt's autobiography *In My Own Way* which helps to clarify the usefulness of Zen; and a selection on psychedelic drugs, mysticism, and the counterculture from Walter Houston Clark's book *Religious Experience: Its Nature and Function in the Human Psyche*.

## Dreams and Sleep

From the rapidly accumulating literature on dreams and sleep we have selected a scholarly paper by Allan Rechtshaffen which integrates many studies pertaining to the nature of and the correlates of mental activity during sleep. We have also included an experimental investigation by T.X. Barber, P.C. Walker, and K.W. Hahn which indicates that individuals can influence their dreams and mental activity during sleep by thinking about a specified topic prior to falling asleep.

## Parapsychology and Psychic Research

This section includes three 'tight' papers that are within the ''hard-headed'' scientific tradition; two somewhat ''far-out'' papers that discuss topics which are not typically considered in ''hard-headed'' journals; and two critiques of ''far-out'' topics.

The first set of three "tighter" papers include Gertrude Schmeidler's integration of empirical investigations on ESP and psychokinesis; a striking seet of replicated experiments by William and Lendell Braud indicating that deep relaxation can markedly enhance ESP performance; and selections from John Palmer's theoretical integration of the empirical studies pertaining to the effect of belief in ESP on ESP performance.

The two somewhat "far-out" papers are by Charles T. Tart. In one paper he analyzes the methodological problems in studying the "human aura;" and in the other he presents stimulating data pertaining to "out-of-the-body experiences."

This section also includes a brief summary of a Master's thesis by R. V. Johnson II which indicates that Cleve Backster's contentions concerning "primary perception in plants" may be due to artifacts (failure to control for changes in temperature and humidity). The section ends with an interesting article by E. Lester Smith which suggests an answer to the question, How can we explain the data in Raudive's recent book, *Breakthrough*? (Raudive presented a mass of data which seemed to indicate that the dead are still 'alive' and can communicate with us.)

## Toward a Broader Awareness in Science

This section includes two selections: Charles Muses' "Altered States of Consciousness in Science," and Alfred Taylor's "Meaning and Matter." The latter paper presents cogent data to support the following important conclusion:

> *Scientific knowledge has revealed a universe of meaning, plan, ideation, intelligence. The more that scientists are able to translate the book of nature, the more astounding is the wisdom revealed. We can be confident that the previous emphasis on materialism will soon be discarded. Further, it will in fact be through science that the strange aberration of materialism will be removed from human affairs, leaving man that much more able to develop his intelligence in ways far beyond our present scope.*

## Human Potentialities

In the final section, we present reports by David M. Rorvik and by Erik Peper which describe individuals who have learned to "feel no pain" by detaching themselves mentally from pain-producing stimulation. In the next selection, John Brodie (quarterback for the San Francisco 49ers) discusses with Michael Murphy how the effectiveness of football players is directly related to their ability to be in the here and now—"to be right there, doing that thing, in the moment." The following selection, which summarizes Harold Saxton Burr's life-time work indicating that all living things are moulded and controlled by measurable "electrodynamic fields," has vast implications for our understanding of human potentialities. The "plateau experience," in which the individual continuously perceives the miraculous elements in ordinary existence, is the focus of the next paper by Stanley Krippner. Brewster Smith then re-examines Maslow's concept of "self-actualization" and the volume concludes with a contribution by Carl Rogers, "Some New Challenges," which urges psychologists to move toward a more human science and to be open to other "realities."

Theodore X. Barber, *Editor*

# Contents

## SECTION IX. TOWARD A BROADER AWARENESS IN SCIENCE



## SECTION X. HUMAN POTENTIALITIES

# Contributors

Theodore X. Barber, Ph.D — *Research Department, The Medfield Foundation, Inc., Medfield State Hospital, Medfield, Mass. 02052*

Al Berger — *Senior Writer, Medical World News, 1221 Avenue of the Americas, New York, N.Y. 10020*

L.W. Braud, Ph.D. — *Department of Psychology, Texas Southern University, Houston, Texas 77004*

W.G. Braud, Ph.D. — *Department of Psychology, University of Houston, Houston, Texas 77004*

John Brodie — *Quarterback, San Francisco 49ers*

Thomas H. Budzynski, Ph.D. — *Assistant Professor of Clinical Psychology, University of Colorado Medical Center, Denver, Colorado 80210*

Harold Saxton Burr, Ph.D. — *Department of Anatomy, Yale University School of Medicine, New Haven, Conn. 06520*

J.F. Chaves, Ph.D. — *Senior Research Psychologist, The Medfield Foundation, Inc., Medfield State Hospital, Medfield, Mass. 02052*

Walter Houston Clark, Ph.D. — *750 Commonwealth Avenue, Newton, Mass.*

Fonya L. DeLong, M.S. — *Psychology Department, George Washington University, 2029 G, N.W., Washington, D.C. 20006*

Victor F. Emerson, Ph.D. — *Department of Psychology, Queens University, Kingston, Ontario, Canada*

A.N.D. Frederick, M.A. — *Psychology Department, The Medfield Foundation, Inc., Medfield State Hospital, Medfield, Mass. 02052*

Arthur S. Freese, D.D.S. — *137 East 36th Street, New York, N.Y. 10016*

D. Girton — *Langley Porter Neuropsychiatric Institute, 401 Parnassus Avenue, San Francisco, Calif. 94122*

Daniel Goleman, Ph.D. — *Department of Social Relations, William James Hall, Harvard University, Cambridge, Mass. 02138*

A.M. Green, Ph.D. — *Psychophysiology Lab, Research Department, Menninger Foundation, Topeka, Kansas 66601*

E.E. Green, Ph.D. — *Psychophysiology Lab, Research Department, Menninger Foundation, Topeka, Kansas 66601*

K.W. Hahn, Jr., M.D. — *The Medfield Foundation, Inc., Medfield State Hospital, Medfield, Mass. 02052*

Rex V. Johnson II, M.A. — *1102 North 46th Street, Seattle, Washington 98103*

J. Kamiya, Ph.D. — *Langley Porter Neuropsychiatric Institute, 401 Parnassus Avenue, San Francisco, Calif. 94122*

Louise H. Kidder, Ph.D. — *Department of Psychology, Temple University, Philadelphia, Pa. 19102*

Stanley Krippner, Ph.D. — *Department of Psychology, California State University, Sonoma, Calif. 95476*

Bernard I. Levy, Ph.D. — *Psychology Department, George Washington University, 2029 G, N.W., Washington, D.C. 20006*

| | |
|---|---|
| John C. Lilly | *℅ Human Software Corp.*<br>*33307 Decker School Road*<br>*Malibu, Calif. 90265* |
| Thomas B. Mulholland, Ph.D. | *Perception Laboratory*<br>*Veterans Administration Hospital*<br>*Bedford, Mass. 01730* |
| Michael Murphy | *President, Esalen Institute*<br>*Big Sur, Calif.* |
| Charles Musès, Ph.D. | *Journal for the Study*<br>*of Consciousness*<br>*844 San Ysidro Lane*<br>*Montecito*<br>*Santa Barbara, Calif. 93108* |
| Robert M. Nideffer, Ph.D. | *Department of Psychology*<br>*University of Rochester*<br>*Rochester, N.Y. 14627* |
| Robert E. Ornstein, Ph.D. | *Langley Porter Neuro-*<br>*psychiatric Institute*<br>*401 Parnassus Avenue*<br>*San Francisco, Calif. 94122* |
| John Palmer, Ph.D. | *Department of Psychiatry*<br>*University of Virginia*<br>*Charlottesville, Va. 22901* |
| Erik Peper | *Berkeley, Calif.* |
| Allan Rechtschaffen, Ph.D. | *Department of Psychiatry*<br>*and Psychology*<br>*University of Chicago*<br>*Chicago, Ill. 60637* |
| Carl R. Rogers, Ph.D. | *Center for Studies*<br>*of the Person*<br>*1125 Torrey Pines Road*<br>*La Jolla, Calif. 92037* |
| J. Salamy | *Langley Porter Neuro-*<br>*psychiatric Institute*<br>*401 Parnassus Avenue*<br>*San Francisco, Calif. 94122* |
| Gertrude Schmeidler, Ph.D. | *Department of Psychology*<br>*City University of New York*<br>*New York, N.Y. 10031* |
| 'Adam Smith' | |
| B. Smith, Ph.D. | *University of California*<br>*Santa Cruz, Calif. 95060* |
| E. Lester Smith, Ph.D. | *715 Washington Ave.*<br>*Wilmette, Ill. 60091* |
| N.P. Spanos, Ph.D. | *Research Department*<br>*The Medfield Foundation, Inc.*<br>*Medfield State Hospital*<br>*Medfield, Mass. 02052* |

| | |
|---|---|
| R.W. Sperry, Ph.D. | *Division of Biology<br>California Institute<br>of Technology<br>Pasadena, Calif. 91109* |
| Johann Stoyva, Ph.D. | *Department of Psychiatry<br>School of Medicine<br>University of Colorado<br>Denver, Colorado 80220* |
| Charles Tart, Ph.D. | *Department of Psychology<br>University of California<br>Davis, Calif. 95616* |
| Alfred Taylor, Ph.D. | *University of Texas<br>Austin,. Texas* |
| B. Timmons, D.Ed. | *Langley Porter Neuro-<br>psychiatric Institute<br>401 Parnassus Avenue<br>San Francisco, Calif. 94112* |
| Alan Turin, Ph.D. | *Department of Psychology<br>University of Rochester<br>Rochester, N.Y. 14627* |
| P.C. Walker, Ph.D. | *Research Department<br>The Medfield Foundation, Inc.<br>Medfield State Hospital<br>Medfield, Mass. 02052* |
| E.D. Walters, M.A. | *Psychophysiology Lab<br>Research Department<br>Menninger Foundation<br>Topeka, Kansas 66601* |
| Alan Watts | *Sausalito, Calif.* |

# Acknowledgments

The publisher acknowledges with appreciation the following permissions to reprint from copyright holders and others for the articles appearing in this volume:

Chapter 1. R. M. Nideffer, "Altered States of Consciousness." Reprinted from L. Wheeler, R. Goodale, and J. Deese, *General Psychology*. 1975 Allyn and Bacon Inc., Boston, Mass. 02210.

Chapter 2. C. T. Tart, "States of Consciousness and State-Specific Sciences." *Science*, Vol. 176, pp. 1203-1210, June 16, 1972. Copyright 1972 by the American Association for the Advancement of Science.

Chapter 4. J. C. Lilly, M.D. *The Center of the Cyclone*. New York, Julian Press, 1972; Bantam paperback, 1973. Copyright 1972 by John C. Lilly, M.D.

Chapter 5. W. W. Sperry. "Hemispheric Specialization of Mental Faculties in the Brain of Man." 36th Yearbook, Claremont Reading Conference, Claremont, California, 1972, pp. 126-136.

Chapter 6. A. Berger. "Biofeedback in Action." Reprinted from *Medical World News*. Copyright 1973, McGraw-Hill, Inc.

Chapter 7. A. Turin and R. M. Nideffer. "Biofeedback: Clinical Applications." Used by permission from the authors.

Chapter 8. T. S. Budzynski. "Some Applications of Biofeedback-Produced Twilight States." Dr. Budzynski is an Assistant Professor of Clinical Psychology, University of Colorado Medical Center.

Chapter 9. E. E. Green, with A. M. Green and E. D. Walters. "Biofeedback for Mind-Body Self Regulation: Healing and Creativity." Published in *Fields Within Fields... Within Fields*, 1972, *5*, No. 1, pp. 131-144.

Chapter 10. J. Stoyva. "Biofeedback Techniques and the Conditions for Hallucinatory Activity." Published in *The Psychophysiology of Thinking*, New York: Academic Press, 1973.

Chapter 11. T. B. Mulholland. "Can You Really Turn On With Alpha?" Reprinted from *The Newsletter-Review,* Vol. V, Spring 1972. pp. 32-40. R. M. Bucke Memorial Society for the Study of Religious Experience. 4453 Maisonneive Blvd. W., Montreal 215, Canada.

Chapter 13. F. L. DeLong and B. I. Levy. "Cognitive Effects of Marijuana, Described in Terms of a Model of Attention." *Psychological Reports*, 1973, 33, 907-916.

Chapter 14. T. X. Barber. "Suggested ('Hypnotic') Behavior: The Trance Paradigm Versus an Alternative Paradigm." Reprinted from Erika Fromm and Ronald E. Shor, editors, *Hypnosis:Research Developments and Perspectives*. (Chicago: Aldine-Atherton Inc., 1972); pp. 115-182. Copyright 1972 by Erika Fromm and Ronald E. Shor. Reprinted by permission of the author and Aldine Publishing Co.

Chapter 15, L. N. Kidder. "On Becoming Hypnotized: How Skeptics Became Convinced—A Case of Attitude Change?" *Journal of Abnormal Psychology*, 1972. Vol. 80, No. 3, pp. 317-322. Copyright 1962 by the American Psychological Association, Inc. Reprinted by permission.

Chapter 16. N. P. Spanos and T. X. Barber. "Cognitive Activity During 'Hypnotic' Suggestability: Goal-Directed Fantasy and the Experience of Non-Volition." Reprinted from *Journal of Personality*, December 1972, 40.

Chapter 17. J. F. Chaves and T. X. Barber. "Needles and Knives: Behind the Mystery of Acupuncture and Chinese Meridians." Copyright 1973 by *Human Behavior Magazine.* Reprinted by permission.

Chapter 18. A. S. Freese. "What Acupunture Won't Do." Reprinted from *Science Digest*, December 1973.

Chapter 19. R. E. Ornstein. "Selections from the Psychology of Consciousness." From *The Psychology of Consciousness* by Robert E. Ornstein. W. H. Freeman and Company. Copyright 1972.

Chapter 20. V. F. Emerson. "Can Belief Systems Influence Neurophysiology? Some Implications of Research on Meditation." Reprinted from the *Newsletter-Review*, Vol. V, Spring 1972. pp. 20-32. R. M. Bucke Memorial Society for the Study of Religious Experience. 4453 Maisonneuve Blvd. W., Montreal 215, Canada.

Chapter 21. A. N. D. Frederick and T. X. Barber. "Yoga, Hypnosis and Self-Control of Cardiovascular Functions." Published in the Proceedings, 80th Annual Convention, American Psychological Association,

1972, pp. 859-860. Copyright 1972 by the American Psychological Association. Reprinted by permission.

Chapter 22. B. Timmons with J. Salamy, J. Kamiya and D. Girton. "Abdominal-Thoracic Respiratory Movements and Levels of Arousal." Published in *Psychonomic Science*, 1972, Vol. 27, No. 3, pp. 173-175. Copyright 1972 by The Psychonomic Society, Inc.

Chapter 23. D. Goleman. "The Budha on Meditation and States of Consciousness." Reprinted with permission for the *Journal of Transpersonal Psychology*, Vol. 4, No. 2, 1972; 2637 Marshall Drive, Palo Alto, Calif. 94303. Copyright 1973.

Chapter 24. A. Watts. "Selections from In My Own Way: An Auto-biography, 1915-1965." Reprinted by permission from the Estate of the late Alan Watts and Jonathan Cape.

Chapter 25. W. H. Clark. "Selections from Religious Experience: Its Nature and Function in the Human Psyche." Published in *Religious Experience: Its Nature and Function in the Human Psyche.* Courtesy of Charles C. Thomas, Publisher.

Chapter 26. A. Rechtschaffen. "The Psychophysiology of Menial Activity During Sleep." Reprinted from *The Psychophysiology of Thinking*, ed. by F. J. McGuigan and R. A. Schoonover. New York: Academic Press 1973. pp. 153-192, 200-205.

Chapter 27. T. X. Barber. "Effect of Hypnotic Induction and Suggestions on Nocturnal Dreaming and Thinking." With P. C. Walker and K. W. Hahn, Jr. Reprinted from *Journal of Abnormal Psychology,* 1973, *82*, 414-427.

Chapter 28. G. Schmeidler. "Respice, Adspice, Prospice—on ESP." Reprinted with permission from *Proceedings of the Parapsychological Association*, No. 8, 1971, pp. 117-143. Copyright 1972 by the Parapsychology Association.

Chapter 29. W. G. Braud and L. W. Braud. "Preliminary Explorations of Psi-Conductive States: progressive Muscular Relaxation." Reprinted with permission from the *Journal of the American Society for Psychical Research*, 1973, 67, 26-46. Copyright 1973, The American Society for Psychic Research.

Chapter 30. J. Palmer. "Scoring in ESP Tests as a Function of Belief in ESP." Reprinted with permission from the *Journal of the American Society for Psychical Research*, 1972, 66, 1-26. Copyright 1972, The American Society for Psychic Research.

Chapter 31. C. T. Tart. "Concerning the Scientific Study of the Human Aura." Published in the *Journal of the Society for Psychical Research*, March 1972, Vol. 46, No. 751, pp. 1-21.

Chapter 32. C. T. Tart. "Out-of-the-Body Experiences." A paper presented at the 1973 Festival of the International Cooperative Council, Los Angeles, January 13, 1973.

Chapter 33. R. V. Johnson, II. "Letter to the Editor—On Cleve Backster and Plant Perception." Reprinted from the *Journal of Parapsychology*, March 1972, Vol. 36, No. 1, pp. 71-72, by permission of the editors and the author.

Chapter 34. E. L. Smith. "The Raudive Voices—Objective or Subjective?" Reprinted from the *Journal of the Society for Psychical Research*, Vol. 46, No. 754, December 1972, pp. 192-200.

Chapter 35. C. Muses, M.A., Ph.D. "Altered States of Consciousness in Science." Copyright 1971 and 1972 by Dr. C. Muses. Reprinted by permission from the anthology sources *Consciousness and Reality,* edited by Charles Muses and Arthur M. Young. E. P. Dutton, 2nd printing, December 1972.

Chapter 36. A. Taylor. "Meaning and Matter." First appeared in *Consciousness and Reality*, C. Muses and A. M. Young eds., published by Outerbridge and Lazard, New York, 1972 and distributed by E. P. Dutton.

Chapter 37. M. Rorvik. "Jack Schwarz Feels No Pain." First published in *Esquire Magaine,* December 1972. Copyright 1972 by David M. Rorvik.

Chapter 38. E. Peper. "Voluntary Pain Control: Psychological and Physiological Correlates." Paper presented at Biofeedback Research Society Meeting, St. Louis, 1971.

Chapter 29. M. Murphy and J. Brodie. "I Experience A Kind of Clarity." Published in *The Intellectual Digest*, January 1973, Vol. 3, No. 5, pp. 19-22.

Chapter 40. H. S. Burr. "An Adventure in Science." Reprinted by permission of Neville Spearman Ltd., 112 Whitfield Street, London W.1. England, from *Blueprint for Immortality* by Dr. Harold Saxton Burr. Copyright 1972 by Harold Saxton Burr.

Chapter 41. S. Krippner. "The Plateau Exerience: A. H. Maslow and Others." Reprinted with permission frfom the *Journal of Transpersonal Psychology*, 1972, Vol. 4, No. 2, pp. 107-120.

Chapter 42. B. Smith. "On Self-Actualization: A Transambivalent Examinatioon of A Focal Theme in Maslow's Psychology." Reprinted with permission from the *Journal of Humanistic Psychology*, Spring 1973, pp. 17-33.

Chapter 43. C. R. Rogers. "Some New Challenges." Reprinted with permission from *American Psychologist*, May 1973, Vol. 28, No. 5, pp. 379-387.

## SECTION I

# AWARENESS, CONSCIOUSNESS, AND MENTAL FUNCTIONS

# 1

# NIDEFFER, R. M.

# *Altered States of Consciousness*

The past few years have witnessed a growing interest, from all levels of society, in those "cognitive" and "affective" awarenesses that fall beyond our "normal" day to day experience. These changes in mental and physical perception, regardless of their derivation, have been lumped together under the label "Altered States of Consciousness: (ASC). The increasing interest in ASC phenomena, both from research and experiential points of view, justifies including them in an introductory text of psychology. The present chapter represents an attempt to first provide an overview of some selected means of developing Altered States. Following this presentation, a hypothetical formulation will be offered in an attempt to provide an integrated understanding of consciousness.

Individuals have been attempting to alter their level of awareness for thousands of years. Almost every religious discipline has sanctioned means of achieving "revelatory experiences." Methods have included meditation, pain, fasting, sensory deprivation, suggestion, and drugs including marijuana, mescaline, and psilocybin. In spite of the continuing interests of a few people, until quite recently such experiences were avoided and punished by the majority of western society.

Through the 1960's large numbers of America's youth were exposed to ASC at both a philosophical and biological level. Our third war in Asia brought hundreds of thousands of troops face to face with different religious philosophies and with mind altering chemical substances, such as marijuana and hashish. Soldiers returned home and went back to school though not without being influenced by their confrontation with the orient. Colleges and Universities proved to be fertile grounds for both the new ideas and for the drugs that returned with the troops. As more students became interested in oriental philosophy and religion, and as they experimented with an ever increasing range of mind altering drugs, society at large became more frightened. To the conservative elements of society the behavior of the young threatened to destroy everything they believed in. The result was that through the 60's and into the 70's a separation or polarization between elements of society became more clearly drawn and occasional violence resulted. In fairness, it should be pointed out that society was segmented prior to the introduction of drugs on a large scale, but that these substances helped to bring the differences into focus.

For over 2000 years man has been arguing over the relative importance of mental and physical functioning (Stagner, 1971). In attempts to understand himself and his world he has often oversimplified his existence by focusing attention on either mental or physical functions. Such a narrowed perspective has led to a separation of mind and body and the development of an artificial continuum. As a country the United States can be placed at the body or physical end of the continuum. We place a premium on objective science, on physical behavior and rational or lawful knowledge. Such a position has, in the past, fostered the development of moral, ethical, legal and social values which simultaneously encourage the development of science and technology, and discourage any investment in subjective irrational thoughts or feelings. The introduction of drugs and oriental thought, both of which would be placed at the mental end of the continuum, served to force a confrontation between people at the extreme ends of the continuum. It's at this point, that ASC phenomena will be introduced first by describing those characteristics which appear to be common across ASC experiences, regardless of how they were induced.

## Characteristics of Altered States

Ludwig (1966) defined altered states of consciousness as "any mental state(s) induced by various physiological, psychological or pharmacological maneuvers or agents, which can be recognized subjectively by the individual himself (or by an objective observer of the individual) as representing a sufficient deviation in subjective experience or psychological functioning from certain general norms for that individual during alert, waking consciousness." Ludwig's definition is helpful in that it conveys the idea that any thought process or feeling that is out of the ordinary, represents an altered state of consciousness. On the other hand, such a definition would imply that dizzyness is an altered state for people who are not usually dizzy or that normal consciousness represents an altered state for a schizophrenic patient. Obviously, to cover ASC phenomena in a chapter this definition must be narrowed.

There are a variety of specific experiences, training procedures, and pharmacological agents which have been used to induce altered states of awareness. In an attempt to narrow our focus, the concern will be primarily with those phenomena which many people feel lead to "higher levels of consciousness." Drugs like LSD and marijuana will be discussed because they are described as "expanding awareness" whereas drugs like heroin and alcohol, which are described as narrowing or "numbing," will be ignored. Similarly, procedures such as meditation, hypnosis, and alpha training which may be used to develop great "insight" and understanding will be included.

Table 1 presents the 10 characteristics that Ludwig (1969) has defined as common to Altered States experiences. An important question to keep in mind while reading this chapter, has to do with the extent to which you feel these characteristics are primary (objective), or secondary (subjective), aspects of an altered state. Research has already shown that altered states of consciousness are affected by demand characteristics (Orne, 1959; 1962) personal motivation and expectations (Cohen, 1964; Hilgard, 1965; Barber, 1970) as well as cultural expectations (Wallace, 1959). How much of what is reported here will one day be seen as

TABLE 1

General Characteristics of ASC

1. Alterations in thinking: Subjective disturbance in judgement, attention and memory.

2. Disturbed time sense: Subjective feelings of timelessness or of the rapid acceleration of time.

3. Loss of Control: Often the individual feels the fear of losing his grip on reality. There is a shift from a more normal internal locus of control to an external one. Stimuli demand attention and the ability to selectively attend may disappear.

4. Change in Emotional expression: Emotions become more intense ranging from euphoria to profound depression.

5. Body image change: Feeling of separation of mind and body may occur. The individual may become the passive observer of his own physical presence.

6. Perceptual Distortions: Increased visual imagery, and sensory hyperacuity is reported to occur as well as distortions in figure boundary.

7. Change in meaning or significance: Ideas and perceptions suddenly become intense revelations.

8. Sense of the ineffable: Individuals claim an inability to communicate the nature or essense of the experience to others.

9. Feelings of rejuvenation: A new sense of hope, a rebirth is often felt to have occurred.

10. Hypersuggestibility: Increased responsivity to suggestions whether given implicitly, or explicitly occurs along with an increased tendency to "misperceive" and distort stimuli.

a primary or inescapable consequence of an altered state and how much will be seen as secondary and modifiable? The positive or negative value placed on ASC experiences by both society and the individual will depend upon discovery of these primary and secondary characteristics.

## Chemically Induced Altered States

There are a great many chemicals that have been used to induce altered states of consciousness. The sophisticated user of drugs can now pick his trip. If the interest is in alteration of visual perceptions then mescaline would be the drug of choice. For a mild experience that is fairly easy to control, marijuana can be smoked. For a prolonged and intense trip (8 hrs - 3 days), one in which insights are desired, d-lysergic acid (LSD) could be used. Finally, if time is at a premium (.5 - 3 hrs) yet the individual still wants an intense experience, he can smoke dimethyltryptamine (DMT) or "drop" psilocybin. Though these substances differ with respect to minimum effective dose, subjective intensity, and actual duration, they are similar in that they all provide the subjective changes listed in Table 1. Up to the present, most of the research on the subjective and objective effects of psychedelic drugs has focused on marijuana and LSD.

### MARIJUANA

Cannabis sativa, the female hemp plant, produces an intoxicating resin called cannabis. In the United States and Mexico, low potency preparations made from the leaves of the plant are referred to as marijuana. When the pure resin of the plant is used the resulting preparation is called hashish and is some 5-10 times as potent as marijuana (Barber, 1970; McGlothlin, 1964). Potency of the drug varies since differences in climates and soils produce marijuana with different chemical structures. In addition to the effects of soil and climate on drug potency, the marijuana experience is also affected by the individual's mental set and the environmental setting.

Mental set, or the individuals cognitive preparation for the altered state experience is very important, particularly as the experience increases in intensity. With all psychedelic compounds, the understanding and insight that the person gains from his "trip" will to a large extent depend on earlier learning, and on what effects he believes the drug is supposed to have. The effect of mental set is more dramatic with drugs like LSD but the marijuana experience is also influenced by attitude. For example, if a person is particularly visually oriented, visual effects may predominate; for others, visual effects may be minimal. If a person is in a somewhat manic state at the time of ingesting the drug, the result may be a great deal of talk, laughter, dancing, and other active pursuits. At another time, the same person may prefer to stare at a candle or to lie down and listen to music.

The social situation is extremely important also. Marijuana seems to increase suggestibility, so that the user is drawn to doing the same things as those around him. Other people are also important when one is learning to use marijuana. Many people experience no effects at all the first few times they use the drug even though they are motivated to do so. A new user may smoke several "joints" or marijuana cigarettes and experience only some physical symptoms such as increased heart rate, increased frequency of urination, and decreased body and hand steadiness. The same person, after becoming an experienced user, may require only one "toke" or puff to experience any number of psychological effects. He has learned, through interaction with other smokers, what psychological effects to expect, and he is therefore very sensitive to those effects. A common occurrence among experienced users is a "contact high": without smoking at all, a person may feel "stoned" or "high" merely by being in the presence of others who are smoking. The effects of mescaline and LSD are not this subtle. A person who has taken an adequate dose will feel something regardless of his previous experience.

### Marijuana Use in the United States

According to Grinspoon (1971), marijuana has had an interesting history in the United States. It was a valued crop in colonial days, in fact, George Washington was a hemp farmer. Early uses of the plant included medicinal use as well as the making of high quality rope used on sailing ships and covered wagons. In addition, a very high quality paper was made from the plant. It's rather ironic that this paper, made from what was to be called the "devil weed," was of sufficient quality to be used in making paper currency and family Bibles.

### Physiological Effects

One of the things that is so remarkable about the pharmacology of cannabis is that it has such limited and mild effects on human nonpsychic functioning. Physiologically, the drug is not addicting, although extremely heavy use (20-60 marijuana cigarettes a day) has been associated with poor physical health. In addition, heavy use of marijuana has been associated with both a loss of motivation, and a loss of involvement with work and achievement. As Barber (1970) points out serious involvement with any drug tends to be inconsistent with serious involvement with work and achievement.

Unlike most other chemical substances, there has never been a documented case of lethal overdose of marijuana in humans. Nor is there any evidence of cellular damage to any human organ. On the basis of rat studies we can estimate what the dose of marijuana would have to be to be lethal, and that is 40,000 times the minimum effective dose. This compares to 3 to 50 times the effective dose for secobarbital and 4-10 times the effective dose for alcohol. Some of the physiological effects marijuana may cause include: 1) increased alpha, and relaxation[1], 2) increased heart rate, and 3) dilation of blood vessels in the eyes, thus some redness. Though marijuana is of minimal danger to the user physiologically, it may be very dangerous psychologically and socially.

## Dangers of Drug Use

Marijuana has precipitated some acute anxiety reactions and depression in a small percentage of its users (McGlothlin, 1964). For the most part however, the dangers associated with the use of marijuana stem from the fact that it is illegal and that the experience may be influenced by this factor. Currently, marijuana use is classified as a crime in the United States. Consequently, the end result of even occasional use of marijuana may be a long prison term. In addition, most marijuana users, though they are breaking the law, would not be classified (at least psychologically) as criminals. This fact may lead to the development of guilt feelings and anxiety over the use of illegal drugs and social alienation and isolation may follow. It is not unusual for the drug user to attempt to defend against these feelings by developing "antisocial" attitudes. Finally, in buying drugs illegally the user may be forced to purchase drugs both of unknown strength and chemical structure.

## Marijuana as a Therapeutic Agent

Marijuana has been shown to have a number of properties that would be useful to medicine. It is an analgesic, an anticonvulsant, and muscle relaxant, in addition to being an appetite stimulant. It has been used effectively in the treatment of tetnus, neuralgia, arrest of uterine hemorrhage, and as an analgesic during labor. It has also been used to treat convulsions, rheumatism pain, asthma, postpartum psychosis, gonorrhea, chronic bronchitis, peptic ulcers, senile insomnia and DTs. It is an antibacterial agent killing many staphylococcus germs which are resistant to penicillin. It offers promise as a substitute for

---

[1] The electrical signals given off by the brain have been classified into different types on the basis of their frequency. Alpha refers to slower brain wave activity (8-13 cycles per second) that appears to be associated with resting wakefulness.

addiction to alcohol and hard narcotics. In the past, it has not been used as an analgesic because of legislation, and because aspirin and the opiate derivitives were developed. According to Grinspoon (1971) this is a shame considering the number of people who become medically addicted to hard narcotics, and the fact that there are between 500-1000 deaths from aspirin annually. Marijuana could circumvent both of these problems. As an analgesic it is like opium with the exception that sleep is natural and that there is no change or interference with the functioning of bodily organs.

D-LYSERGIC ACID DIETHYLAMIDE (LSD)

In 1943 Albert Hoffman, a Swiss chemist, accidently ingested a small quantity of the chemical that was to be labeled LSD. The description, Hoffman reported of his experience bore a strong resemblance to descriptions of what occurs during an acute psychotic reaction. It was this initial comparison of LSD intoxication to psychosis that interested the scientific community in the drug. The term "psychotomemetic" was subsequently applied to LSD and other major psychedelics (e.g. DMT, psilocybin, STP, mescaline) because of the resemblance of the experience to schizophrenia. At first, research on LSD focused on using the drug as an analog to schizophrenia, with the hope of gaining some insight into the cause of psychotic behavior. Next, the government became involved in studying the chemical for possible uses in warfare (McGlothlin, 1964). Although a limited amount of research is still being conducted along these lines, it is interesting to see the shift in directions of interest in recent years.

Somehow in the early 60's LSD found its way to the college campus. It was there, largely through the efforts of a Harvard psychology professor named Timothy Leary that interest in LSD became more widespread. Through Leary's efforts, as well as those of others, the LSD "trip" came to be associated with a religious or mystical experience. Suddenly, simply by changing the users focus, mental set (expectancy), the LSD experience had been changed from a psychotic decompensation into a "union with nature" a "oneness with the universe."

Since the barnstorming of Leary and his associates, large numbers of people have "turned on" illegally to LSD. In that time we have learned the importance of an individual's personality and mental set for taking the drug, as well as the importance of the setting. For some the voyage appears to have been a profoundly religious experience (Watts, 1963), for others it was simply pleasurable, and for an unfortunate few it was chaotic, destructive, and completely disorganizing (Barber, 1970; Nideffer, 1967).

Physiological Effects

In contrast to marijuana, LSD is an extremely potent drug,

with the minimum effective dose being around 50 micrograms. Where the drug has been used in legal settings as a therapeutic agent, dosages have ranged from 25-1600 micrograms (Abramson, 1967). As with most chemicals, both the variety and intensity of the effects of LSD depend at least in part on the amount of the drug ingested. Physiological changes include pupilary dilation, dizzyness, changes in body image, reduced intellectual and motor proficiency, perceptual distortions, and a decrease in the mean energy content of the brain (Barber, 1970; Goldstein, Murphree, Sugerman, Pfeiffer, and Jenney, 1963).[2] In addition to these effects, there are indications that LSD may have some serious side effects. "Flashbacks", or spontaneous and frightening reoccurrences of the LSD experience without further use of the drug are frequently reported in the literature. A more speculative finding is that LSD ingestion may alter chromosomal structure. For a review of this literature the reader is directed to Theodore X. Barber's book, LSD, Marijuana, Yoga, and Hypnosis, 1970.

## LSD as a Therapeutic Agent

The use of LSD as a therapeutic intervention has focused primarily on problems of a psychological rather than a physiological nature. Therapy with LSD is either "psychedelic" in nature or "psycholytic." In psychedelic therapy the patient is given one or two large dose(s) of the drug. To be effective, the amount of drug given should be sufficient to break down the subject's cognitive controls. The individual is then expected to have an experience so intense, that the experience alone provides the insight and motivation to alter deviant behavior. Depending upon the frame of reference, such an experience may be seen as revelatory and religious in nature or simply as "scaring the hell out of you." In any event, it is dramatic enough to alter behavior. This type of therapy has been most effective with alcoholics. Cure rates of around 50 percent (far above the more typical 30 percent) have been reported (MacLean, MacDonald, Bryne, Hubbard, 1961).

In psycholytic therapy the patient is given small amounts of LSD in each of a number of different therapy sessions. In such situations, patients and therapists interact in ways very similar to those that occur in psychoanalytic or Rogerian therapy sessions. In these situations, LSD is seen as helping the patient release unconscious or repressed material. The therapist then helps the patient integrate and deal with the new material. Therapy of this

---

[2]Mean energy content of the brain is determined by specifying a particular unit of time (i.e. 20 sec.; 1 min.) and then measuring the total amount of electrical activity that occurs within that period. Several such measures are taken for a subject and then the average, or mean is computed.

type has been used to treat a variety of psychological problems (Abramson, 1967; Hoffer, 1965; Mogar, 1965; and Unger, 1964).

## DESCRIPTIONS OF THE DRUG EXPERIENCE

The psychological effects of both the major and minor psychedelic compounds are very similar. There are obvious differences with respect to length and intensity of the "high" as well as with the individuals ability to control his perceptual and cognitive processes depending on the type and dose level of the drug. The following description of a hashish experience is presented for several reasons. First, it provides a description of a chemically induced ASC which can be clearly related to the phenomena listed in Table 1. Second, the experience to the extent it communicates to the reader, disproves the hypothesis that ASC phenomena are "ineffible," or incommunicable. Finally, unlike many descriptions in the literature, an attempt was made during the experience to relate the subjective experience to objective reality.

"I was sitting on the floor when I noticed that the muscles in my face, but most particularly under my eyes, were very relaxed. We began to talk about this and as we talked the things that were said seemed extremely funny. They were funny for a number of reasons. First, everything that was said could have at least two meanings. Second, I began to get very graphic visual images of what the people were saying. If someone mentioned that his eyes felt like they were sagging, I would see a Saint Bernard dog with droopy eyes. Only the dog would have the characteristics of the person who made the statement.

The next thing that I began to notice was that my mind seemed to jump in and out of a dream world. Time for me was extremely speeded up. It seemed as though a few seconds were hours. So many thoughts crowded themselves into such a short span of time that all judgement of time was gone. What might be considered an extremely short daydream in a normal state seemed to be a total loss of contact with reality. A daydream can be handled cognitively because you can test to tell how long you haven't been listening to other stimuli around you. This test in the drug state, probably because of the rapid thoughts, is not so easily made. In addition, the reality of the daydream seems much more intense in the drug state. It became so real and intense in fact that I could not tell if I was daydreaming or if I was talking. It was at this point that I began relating my experiences to those of a schizophrenic.

I would begin to talk and as a sentence would start to come out I would find myself having a large number of associations to each part of the sentence. I didn't know if some of these associations had been expressed. I would suddenly become very conscious of myself and begin wondering if I had simply stated the sentence, if I had stated parts of the sentence and parts of my associations to the sentence, or if I had said anything at all. I began thinking that what I was saying must appear to the listener as sentence fragments, a 'word salad.' I would find myself asking questions in the middle of sentences, an example might be as follows: Wow, the wierdest thing is happening, as I talk, I wonder if this is like schizophrenia. Did I just say anything to you? Wow this is word salad, this is wild. Have I been saying anything or only thinking? You must think I'm crazy. Wow, I'm schizophrenic, can you understand what I'm saying?

This loss of distinction between thoughts that are spoken and thoughts that remain unspoken also carried over to behavioral actions. I got up from a chair to write down what I considered to be a critical insight. I was afraid that if I didn't write it down I would forget it. It took a great deal of time and concentration to write down the following sentence. 'I can't remember whether I've actually said something, or I have only thought that I said it.' As soon as I finished writing this bit of wisdom down I went back over and sat down. I couldn't have been sitting down for more than a couple of minutes before I began to wonder if I had actually written anything down. I had to get up several times and read what I had written in order to convince myself that I had indeed written something down, and it wasn't just my imagination.....

Things began to fit together and I became very excited. I wanted very much to relate these things to other people because I was afraid that I would forget them. I started trying to tell Sam what was happening and it was extremely difficult. I had to fight in order to say two or three sentences. The lack of being able to distinguish what I had actually said from what I had thought interfered. All that would come out was 'word salad.' About this time my anxiety began to increase. I realized that I was imposing on Sam and that he was having experiences of his own. I would try and shut myself up so that I wouldn't bother him, but I couldn't. I was too excited and the magnitude of what was happening to me was so great that I had to share it. Again, I would try and relate what was happening and it would come out garbled. I got upset because I was afraid my thoughts would never be expressed, they would be lost.....

At one time as the pipe was being passed around Mike ignored Sue and passed it directly to me. Sue appeared to get angry at being ignored and said, 'Mike.' As she said it I looked at her and it seemed as though all of the hostility in the world was expressed in her face and posture, and the word sounded like a shout! I cringed, and as I did, I became aware of my own expressions of feelings and suddenly I felt very naked and exposed. I began to blush thinking that people could see right through me. The blush began in my stomach and moved as an intense burning sensation (not burning in a painful sense) slowly up my chest, neck and all the way to the top of my head.

At this point I became very upset. What if I became angry at someone would it be immediately evident to everyone in the room? I might inadvertantly express a feeling that I didn't want others to be aware of. What if some of the feelings of frustration with my wife became aware to her, what effect would that have on our relationship and on the other peoples' experiences? Worse yet, what effect would the knowledge that I might be attracted to one of the other women in the room have on my wife and the woman's husband? Feelings like I am suggesting did not even have to develop in order to create panic. The simple thought that a feeling like that might occur and that it would be obvious to other people scared me. I didn't want everyone to know what I was thinking and feeling all the time, I wanted to hide.

For a while I began to see hidden meanings in everything that was said. A wink became a huge sign, obvious to the world, and tremendously exaggerated. Instead of noticing simply a twinkle in the eye and perhaps a few creased lines around the eye, the person's whole body seemed to become a part of that expression. It was as if the wink grew in size until it covered the face of the person, and the rest of the body moved appropriately with the wink. If the wink appeared sexual in nature, I would feel myself responding with the exaggerated blush and an intense feeling of panic and a desire to hide. I was afraid of my own response and the obviousness of both the wink and my response to all of the other people in the room.

Gradually the anxiety associated with being intensely aware of my own and other peoples' feeling gave way to interest and curiosity. I began to wonder how much the feelings were intensified, if at all? I began wondering how much of my increased sensitivity to feelings was actually an increased awareness and how much was simply my projection of what was happening. Did Sue really feel hostile toward Mike? Was that hostility as intense as I imagined it to be? I began discussing these things with other people. I think that I was more sensitive to the feelings of the other people and myself. I believe that I noticed more things. There were times when I would be oblivious to other people, but when a stimulus caught my attention I was totally involved. Everything else would disappear except a certain person or sound, and the amount of information that I believe I picked up through this total involvement was fantastic. I think that I sensed the feelings that might have escaped me before, I also think that I exaggerated them. For example the hostile expression toward Mike was there but the intensity of it was projection on my part. I believe I projected these things for a number of reasons but one of the main reasons was that with the intense focus everything seemed related, and presented me with a single message. A person didn't express a feeling with simply a word. The facial expression was important, and body posture from a simple lean to the complex way in which a person was sitting all added to the perception of a feeling. A hand gripping a leg when an angry feeling was expressed became white around the knuckles, the teeth were bared and became mean, the eyes took on the proverbial glint of steel, and the muscles in the back and legs and arms became tense (Nideffer, 1970)."

## HYPNOSIS

Hypnosis is a term that has been applied to a wide range of phenomena. In using the term here, we will be referring to those ASC which occur through the nonphysical influence of one human being over another. Such a definition is not likely to make everyone happy since the religious conversion experiences induced by the preaching of people like John Wesley (Sargant, 1957), many brainwashing techniques, and primitive ceremonies, the highly motivating instructions of Barber (Barber, 1970), as well as the more standard induction techniques are classified as hypnosis. In contrast, self-hypnosis, highway hypnosis, meditation, and hypnogogic states are not included since these are self induced alterations in consciousness.

The utility of the definition that we have chosen stems from the fact that it reduces the number of phenomena we will attempt to cover. At the same time, the definition allows us to include situations in which subject's display hypnotic behavior without having gone through a formal induction. Finally, the definition serves to focus on the fact that these particular altered states differ from others in that the experience is almost totally controlled and directed by a single outside person.

### History

There is evidence of hypnosis in the ceremonies of non-literate peoples but modern interest probably dates from about the end of the 18th century when Franz Mesmer argued that hypnosis was due to "animal magnetism." Mesmer, had been having great success curing a variety of physiological and psychological illnesses through the use of hypnosis. Unfortunately for both Mesmer and hypnosis, he attributed his cures to the realignment of magnetic fields in the patient's body. A group of scientists investigated Mesmer's claims and concluded that the theory was in error. Rather than simply disproving Mesmer's theory however the investigation caused scientists to overlook the fact that some surprising cures had been effected. The end result was that both Mesmer and hypnosis fell into disrepute until James Braid, a Scottish physician and surgeon coined the term hypnosis and began experimenting with it in 1841 (Pattie, 1967).

Since then, hypnosis has gone through periods of scientific respectability and periods in which it was confined largely to stage shows with mystical trappings. It has however, remained respectable since its World War II use in dentistry and in treating psychogenic war casualties. At the present time, there are two international societies devoted to the study and use of hypnosis, both with regular journals. Hypnosis has been officially recognized and encouraged by the British Medical Association, the American Medical Association, and the American Psychological Association. It is widely used today in both medicine and psychology.

## Subjective vs. Objective Reality

Hypnosis is at once an exciting and frustrating phenomena to work with. It is difficult to think of any situation in which the discrimination between objective and subjective reality becomes more confused. It is this confusion that makes hypnosis appear almost mystical or supernatural. The hypnotist and the subject working together are able to profoundly alter the subject's perceptions, feelings, cognitions, and body chemistry using nothing more potent than verbal suggestions.

Through the following paragraphs we will be writing about induction techniques and the physiological and psychological changes that can accompany hypnosis. As you read these paragraphs ask two questions. First, what is the source of power in the relationship between the hypnotist and subject? To put it another way, what critical variable(s) must be present for the subject to respond to the hypnotist's suggestions? Second, will the understanding that we are looking for in question one, destroy the phenomena that we are attempting to observe? For example, faith in the mystical power of the hypnotist may be necessary for the subject to respond to suggestions. Should this be true, what effect would telling the subject that hypnosis is nothing special, that his own faith is the critical variable, have upon his ability to respond?

## Hypnotic Induction

Both Erickson (1967) and Hilgard (1965), would agree that the development of the hypnotic state depends to a large extent, on the interpersonal relationship that is established between the hypnotist and the subject. If the induction is to be successful the subject must have a certain amount of confidence and trust in the hypnotist. The hypnotist, to the extent he radiates self-confidence, assists the subject in developing the trust and confidence necessary for hypnosis to develop.

According to Erickson (1967) the technique that the hypnotist uses should change as a function of the subject's personality and needs, as well as with the particular situation. The good hypnotist then, is a master at picking the right technique, for the right subject, at the right moment.

There is almost no limit to the variety of induction techniques used, but they all involve the ultimate focus of attention on the hypnotist and cooperation between hypnotist and subject. Pantomime techniques are used for young children or in those situations where language problems exist. Some hypnotists use a wide range of special equipment to assist in developing a hypnotic state. There are strobe lights for subjects who need a scientific explanation for hypnosis, and glass eyes for the mystically oriented. There are "utilization" techniques for subjects who have "unconscious" resistances to hypnosis and "confusional" techniques for subjects who have "conscious" resistances. Techniques may be slow and subject-paced as in "arm levitation" or "arm lowering" or they may be rapid and sudden. Whatever the technique employed the hypnotist's success is measured by the subjects responses both objectively and subjectively to suggestions.

## Hypnotic Susceptibility

A great deal of research has been carried out by Ernest Hilgard and his associates at Stanford University to determine who is responsive to hypnotic suggestions and why. Hypnosis, as illustrated by Hilgard (1965), is not an all or none response. A subjects' susceptibility to hypnosis can be placed on a continuum, with approximately 5-10 percent of the population completely resistant to hypnotic suggestions. Another 5-10 percent of the population is capable of demonstrating virtually all of the phenomena (hallucinations, amnesia, anasthesia, analygesia, etc.) associated with a deep state of hypnosis. The remaining 80-90 percent of the population is distributed fairly normally between these two extremes evidencing responsiveness to some, but not all, of the hypnotists' suggestions.

Since, as will be shown, hypnosis has had wide application in medicine and psychiatry, the fact that only 5-10 percent of the population can evidence all of the hypnotic phenomena greatly reduces its therapeutic value. Therefore, it would be important to discover ways of increasing an individual's susceptibility and/or ways to detect in advance who will be a good hypnotic subject. As mentioned, rather extensive research has been aimed in these directions without much success (Hilgard, 1965). More recently however, some studies relating alpha waves to hypnosis have been promising.

## Hypnosis and Alpha

One of the recent findings in the research literature has been that there appears to be a relationship between the amount of alpha activity in a subject's electro-encephalogram (EEG) and his or her responsivity to hypnotic suggestions. Alpha waves are slow (8-13 cycles per second) brain waves that occur when subjects are relaxed and not focusing their attention (Glasser, 1963). In a series of recent studies, investigators have shown both that the initial amount of alpha in a subject's EEG record and changes in initial amounts of alpha are correlated with susceptibility to hypnosis. Apparently, the more alpha subjects have initially, the more susceptible they are. In addition, as alpha increases within a subject, so does the subject's responsivity to hypnotic suggestions (London, Hart, & Leibovitz, 1968; Engstrom, London, & Hart, 1970). These changes in alpha and susceptibility may occur as a function of increased trust and relaxation in the subject.

## Psychological Effects of Hypnotic Induction

The experience of being hypnotized is not as unusual or alien as some people believe. In fact, most of us have experienced feelings similar to those associated with being hypnotized.

Hypnosis has been described as that relaxed state many of us find ourselves drifting through just before we go to sleep. Often the hypnotized subject feels completely in control as though he or she could resist the suggestions of the hypnotist. However, the feelings of relaxation are so peaceful that it would not be worth the effort to fight the suggestions. Although the subject may feel like he is drifting off to sleep during the induction, these feelings need not remain throughout the hypnotic session. Once induction is over suggestions may be given which will help the subject feel alert and wide awake, while still hypnotized.

## Physiological Effects of Hypnotic Induction

When hypnotized subjects have not been given any particular suggestions, it is almost impossible to distinguish, on a physiological basis, between them and nonhypnotized controls (Barber, 1970). Through the use of suggestions however, hypnotized subjects can be made to evidence a large number of physical changes including alterations in heart rate, skin conductance, respiration, and gastric secretion. A review of the literature suggests that the subject's physiological response to the induction procedure alone, depends primarily on the subject's expectancy and on the specific suggestions of the hypnotist. The importance of the subject's expectancy can be illustrated by pointing out that when Mesmer hypnotized subjects they responded to the induction by having an epileptic-like seizure. Subjects no longer expect to have a seizure as a function of being hypnotized, and as a result seizure activity has ceased to be associated with induction.

Table 2 presents some of the phenomena that are associated with hypnosis. As the depth of hypnosis increases (as the subject moves toward the extremely hypnotizable end of the susceptibility continuum) subjects are capable of evidencing more of the phenomena. It is these occurances of disturbances in thought, distortion of time and perceptual processes, as well as changes in affective (emotional) arousal evidenced by the phenomena in table 2 that cause hypnosis to be classified as an altered state of consciousness.

TABLE 2

HYPNOTIC PHENOMENA

1. Catalepsy-muscular loss of control. The subjects limbs remain in any position they are placed in.
2. Hallucinations: Auditory, tactile, and visual
   a. Positive-seeing something that is not there.
   b. Negative-denying the presence of something.
3. Anosmia: Loss of the sense of smell. Subject may not smell amonia or may tell you it smells like whatever other odor is suggested.
4. Age Regression: The subject can be made to act and feel as though he has regressed to an earlier age or experience.
5. Amnesia:
   a. Spontaneous: the subject has no memory for part or all of the hypnotic session.
   b. Suggested: the subject is requested to forget what has transpired.
6. Hypermnesia: Or heightened recall.
7. Analgesia: Reduction in pain
8. Anasthesia: Reduction in sensitivity.
9. Distortion of Body Image: Subject can be made to experience a separation of mind and body.
10. Distortion of Time Perception: Passage of time can be subjectively altered through suggestions.

As interesting as age regression, hallucinations, and responsiveness to suggestions of amnesia may be, it is the physiological changes which occur as a function of suggestion that have thus far set hypnosis apart from other altered states. Table 3 presents some of the uses that have been made of direct suggestion in both medicine and psychology. It will be helpful to supplement this with some of the more dramatic effects of hypnosis recorded in the literature.

TABLE 3

USES OF HYPNOSIS IN MEDICINE AND PSYCHOLOGY

A. Medicine
   1. As an Anasthetic and analgesic in:
      a. Obstetrics
      b. Surgery
      c. Dentistry
      d. Terminal illness
   2. Muscle relaxant
      a. To lower blood sugar level in diabetics
      b. To induce or to stop labor contractions in pregnancy.
   3. Dermatology
      a. To reduce itching
      b. To remove warts.
      c. To mitigate icthyosis

B. Psychology
   1. For direct suggestion of symptom substitution or removal
      a. Tics
      b. Treatment of hysterical paralysis, blindness, and deafness.
      c. Treatment of nausea, and compulsive habits such as smoking, drinking, and drug abuse.
   2. Recovery of repression of affect laden material.
      a. As a cathartic experience to relive emotional trauma.
         1) experienced during childhood.
         2) experienced during war.
      b. To repress painful memories and thus reduce at least temporarily an individual's anxiety.
   3. To reduce therapeutic resistance by assisting an individual to relax his cognitive defenses. In this way unconscious material is recovered.
   4. To reduce anxiety so that other terapeutic efforts can be made.

## Hypnosis as an Anasthetic and Analgesic

Perhaps the most dramatic uses of hypnosis in surgery were performed in the early 1800's, by James Esdaile a Scottish physician living in India. Esdaile performed more than 300 major, surgical operations using hypnosis as the anasthetic and analgesic. Most of Esdaile's major operations were for the removal of scrotal tumors, operations in which the mortality rate had been about 50 percent. "In 161 cases operated on by Esdaile, mortality dropped to 5 percent, and in none of the fatal cases was death an immediate outcome of the surgery....(Pattie, 1967)."

Hypnosis has been used in a variety of ways to reduce or block pain. There are reports in the literature of amputations being performed while using hypnosis. The use of hypnotic suggestions in childbirth and dentistry is well known. In addition, suggestions have been used to reduce the pain of chronically ill patients. Although hypnosis has been widely used to reduce pain, it is not clear how the suggestions work to accomplish this end. Physiological measures taken during surgery indicate that the neurons are firing, and that signals of pain are being transmitted to the central nervous system. Explanations offered for hypnosis's successes as an anasthetic and analgesic range from the idea that subjects may be simply refusing to acknowledge pain, or that they develop amnesia for the pain or that they learn to selectively attend and choose to ignore the pain (Barber, 1970). It would be interesting and useful to find out exactly what it is that the individual does to increase his or her tolerance for pain. Whatever the reason, we know that pain reduction is possible through suggestions, and that this reduction can have very positive consequences for the patient.

Induced Physiological Change

Hypnosis has been used to treat a variety of physiological illnesses. Schwartz (1963) has data that suggests that some good hypnotic subjects are able to voluntarily stop labor contractions. There are also reports suggesting that hypnotized multiparous patients can induce labor. Moving to other areas, suggestions have been used to either increase or decrease gastric motility and to lower blood sugar level. Asher (1956), reported that suggestions of wart disappearance resulted in cures for 15 of 25 patients. Continuing in the area of dermatology, several investigators have used hypnosis to treat ichthyosis (congenital fish skin disease), and subjects have even been made resistant to toxic plants (similar to poison oak) through suggestion (Ikemi and Nakagawa, 1962). Finally, hypnosis has been used with moderate success in the treatment of asthma.

A question that might be raised at this point is "where to from here?" In this brief review of hypnosis a great amount of material has been skimmed over and even more has gone untouched. Limitations in space make it impossible to cover any more material on hypnosis. At the conclusion of the chapter an attempt will be made to integrate hypnosis with other altered states in a more meaningful way. Perhaps at that time some unanswered questions will be answered.

## MEDITATION

"Meditation is a classical way of developing the receptive attitude. It is practice in the skill of being quiet (Maupin,

1969)." Meditation exercises, involve a disciplining of self that has been used as a means of achieving an ASC. The ultimate meaning of a particular experience however, depends upon the meditator and his religious and philosophical orientation. There are a wide variety of meditative techniques and individuals have described the results of their practices as "a union with nature", an "awareness of god", "being one with the universe", and/or as a "merging of mind and body." Independent of the meaning that the experience has for the meditator these alterations, as will be seen later, are similar to each other and to other ASC.

## History In the United States

For most of the world, the practice of meditation is associated with religion or mysticism. Although men and women have been meditating for as long as history has been recorded, widespread interest in meditation in the United States did not develop until well into the 1960's. The introduction of LSD and other psychedelic substances in the early 60's and their subsequent spread has led quite naturally into the study of Eastern religious thought and meditation. As people began to shake up their consciousness with the more potent psychedelic chemicals, two things occurred. First, they found that they enjoyed altering their thought process. Second, they began to look for understanding, for information about what was happening to them. Timothy Leary and some of the popular music groups were taking trips to India to study meditation. They were returning to the United States with a new message.

Books began appearing which related LSD and mescaline experiences to the "higher states" achieved by Eastern, mystical and religious meditators (Watts, 1963; Leary, Metzner & Alpert, 1964). Slowly the public was told that drug use was a temporary means of attaining "enlightenment," and that the real truth was gained without drugs through spiritual meditation. Interest in Oriental thought developed, and bookstores stocked up on everything from witchcraft to "the science of soul travel". Since that point in time we have been attempting to separate the wheat from the chaf.

## Integration of Mind and Body

Naranjo and Orenstein (1971) point out that there are a great many varieties of Meditation. The particular exercises and behaviors engaged in by these schools differs dramatically. Their philosophy and practice may emphasize a greater involvement in the here and now as in Zen meditation, or it may involve transcending this physical existence as in some Yoga practices (Johnson, 1970). Irrespective of the philosophy, the forms of meditation examined here have some characteristics in common. First, they recognize the importance of both mental and physical exercise. Second, they focus on harmony or the union of mental and physical processes.

This emphasis on a union led to the development of fighting styles such as Karate and Aikido. Third, they train the individual to develop awareness of and control over his attentional processes. The idea is to learn to focus attention into a narrow beam or to broaden it at will. Finally, the meditative exercises appear to have similar effects on body physiology.

Physiological Effects of Meditation

Wallace (1970) and Wallace and Benson (1972) have studied the physiological correlates of meditative procedures in American subjects. These authors noted that meditation exercises result in a reduction in blood pressure and heart rate, slower respiration, increased skin conductance and increased alpha productivity. The correlational relationship of alpha to meditation has been reported by others in other cultures. Anand, Chhina, and Singh (1971) found that the meditative exercises practiced by Yogi's in India were accompanied by a high percentage of alpha rhythms. Finally Kasamatsu and Hirai (1971) studying Zen meditators in Japan, found that alpha activity was correlated with both the quality and length of time (experience) of the meditator. It is this apparent relationship of the alpha wave to meditation that has led to the recent public interest in alpha training (Nideffer, 1973).

"Instant" or "Electric Zen"

The use of alpha training as a means of achieving "spritual enlightenment" or an altered state, occurred as a result of a series of studies and articles by Joseph Kamiya. In a 1968 article, Kamiya reported that subjects could learn to recognize when they were in an alpha wave state, and once they learned to make this discrimination they could control their production of alpha. According to Kamiya, subjects could increase or decrease alpha at will. In the same article it was stated that subjects like the alpha state, that they wanted to maintain the alpha wave state, and that when they were successful in this they reported feelings and experiences similar to those that result from Zen meditation (Kamiya, 1968).

Since the studies by Kamiya, a great deal of enthusiasm has developed over alpha training, and profit-oriented individuals are making wild promises for their various electronic training gadgets and courses. Unfortunately, little of this speculation has any scientific base. Though the training may be a useful method for teaching people to mentally and physically relax, it is doubtful that any of the claims such as "instant Zen", increased ESP, or resistance to illness, will ever be documented (Nideffer, 1973). Instead, it appears as if the major relationship of the alpha state to meditation is that both may be associated with relaxation.

Meditation and the Development of "Para Normal" Power

A variety of special skills and powers have been attributed to Zen and Yogic meditators. Many Zen practitioners integrate their mental discipline with physical exercise as do many Yoga. It is this melding of mental and physical practice that has led to what outwardly appear to be super-human demonstrations. Master's of these disciplines are often said to have "a sixth sense", or super strength, or the ability to stop normal bodily functions such as heart rate.

As our understanding of meditation and ASC phenomena increases some of the mysticism begins to disappear. For example, Barber (1970) has pointed out that the Yogi does not in fact stop his heart. Instead, through altering the pressure (via muscle tension) in his chest cavity he is able to slow the heart and reduce the blood flow to the extremities. This maneuver makes his pulse undetectable and cardiac sounds cannot be heard with a stethescope. Electrocardiograms taken throughout this period however, indicate that the heart is still beating.

Psychological Correlates of Meditation

As with drugs and hypnosis, meditation can be viewed as a method for inducing an ASC. The immediate feelings and perceptual distortions that occur are similar to the ASC experiences induced in other ways. In fact, it is almost impossible to distinguish one ASC experience from another when they are taken out of context. To magnify this point (as it emphasizes the relevance of mental set and social situation to the experience) seven experiences have been quoted below. Try and place each of the experiences into one of three catagories; either a drug experience, a meditatively induced religious experience, or a psychotic episode. Answers are presented in Table 4.

1. "... they got more intense, distorted, until I was frightened - they were too much too fast, I thought something had gone wrong. A blinding whirling pain behind my left temple persisted, like a ball of electric current. I began to imagine that I could feel it destroying my brain. There were three states of mind I remember passing in and out of during this time: The moments when I understood that I would recover; the times when I felt that something was going wrong inside that no one knew about - that my mind would not recover; and then, beyond all that, there were moments when I was no longer afraid for myself, when I let myself imagine complete and intense emptiness. The last thing to hold on to, the sense of myself, was gone. There was nothing to fear, nothing at all."

2. "I call it the Eenie-Weenie-a squiggling little nucleus that is trying to make love to itself and can never quite get there. The whole fabulous complexity of vegetable and animal life, as of human civilization, is just a colossal elaboration of the Eenie-Weenie trying to make the Eenie-Weenie. I am in love with myself, but cannot seek myself without hiding myself. As I pursue my own tail, it runs away from me. Does the amoeba split itself in two in an attempt to solve this problem?"

3. "As to the visioned creations, these were of finer, thinner stuff than iridescent bubbles, all in the details of their forms more minute and miraculous than anything upon earth. Indeed, they would have had little significance had they been such as could conceivably have been provided, or invented, from the experience of a human life time. There were small suns and strange twilight worlds of lakes and islands-not conceived as spinning balls, like our earth, but having definite yet changeable limits, as drops of oil which float on water. Planets, with their peculiar signs, came near, the sun was broken, and the face of the earth was changed, the landscape was never so enchanted."

4. "I feel persecuted. I have no idea what goes on. I don't want to answer. I don't seem to be able to dissociate these cards. The color red means something that is interesting. I do not feel like answering. I already had suspicious feelings when you gave me a milk shake; I was not able to pull out the straw. I suspect some kind of trick. I have a fear of losing control. I think you all want to confuse me."

5. "I was suddenly confronted with an overwhelming conviction that I had discovered the secrets of the universe, which were being rapidly made plain with incredible lucidity. The truths discovered seemed to be known immediately and directly, with absolute certainty."

6. "An eye opens to discern various intellectual objects uncomprehended by sensation; just so... the sight is illumined by a light which uncovers hidden things and objects which the intellect fails to reach... (It) is like an immediate perception as if one touched the objects with ones 'hand.'"

7. "As I was strolling in the yard, the earth suddenly trembled. Golden vapor gushed out of the earth enveloping my body, and then I felt myself turning into a golden body. At the same time my mind and body felt light. I could understand what the chirping birds were saying and I understood clearly the creators spirit... Tears of ecstacy rolled down my cheeks. From that time on, I have felt the entire earth is my home and the sun

and stars are mine. Neither position, nor fame, nor honors, nor wealth, nor the desire to become more powerful than others have any attraction for me -- these have all vanished away."

TABLE 4

KEY TO ASC EXPERIENCES

1. Drug Experience: Nideffer, R. The illegal us of LSD-25 and the development of antisocial attitudes and guilt feelings, Nideffer, 1967.

2. Drug Experience: Watts, A. The Joyous Cosmology; adventures in the chemistry of consciousness. New York, Pantheon, 1963.

3. Psychotic Experience: Cohen, S. The Beyond Within, New York, Atheneum, 1964.

4. Drug Experience: Bercel, N., Travis, L., Olinger, L., and Dreikurs, E. Model psychosis induced by LSD-25 in normals: I. Psychophysiological investigations, with special reference to the mechanism of the paranoid reaction, in Reed, Alexander, & Tomkins (Ed.). Psychopathology, New York, John Wiley & Sons, 1958.

5. Psychotic Experience: Landis, C. Varieties of Psychopathological Experience, New York, Holt Rinehart & Winston, 1964.

6. Religious Meditation: Alpert, R., Cohen, S., & Schiller, L. LSD, New York, New American Library, 1966.

7. Religious Meditation: Tohei, K. Aikido, Tokyo, Rikuge Publishing House, 1960.

If you are like most people you were probably correct in identifying from 1 to 3 of the experiences. The fact that these experiences, at least as written, cannot be distinguished beyond chance level should not obscure the fact that they have profoundly different effects on the individual experiencing them. For example, an altered state induced by meditation will have a much stronger effect on the individual than will a state induced by drugs. Drugs are an instant experience requiring little preparation, as such they have little permanent impact on the user (Cohen, 1964). The meditator by virtue of his training is able to integrate his experience with many more life experiences. The drug user with little preparation is likely to attribute his feelings and perceptions to a chemical. The meditator will attribute his experience to God, or

Nature. Another critical variable has to do with how society views the experience. The less value society places on it the more difficult it will be for the experience to have any permanent positive effect on the individual. The importance of the individual and societies beliefs, attitudes and values to Altered States experiences should become clearer as this material is integrated into a hypothetical framework.

## TOWARDS AN INTEGRATION OF CONSCIOUSNESS

To understand and explain the effects of ASC it is necessary to simultaneously look in two directions. First, "objective" variables, like attention and information processing, which lend themselves to direct experimental manipulation, appear to be involved. In addition, a "subjective" and only indirectly observable variable, faith, seems to be important. To complicate the issue, it appears as if the interaction of all of these variables must ultimately be used to explain some of the changes occuring in individuals as a result of the ASC experience. As will be elaborated below, the induction of ASC, and most of the perceptual and temporal distortions experienced during an ASC can be attributed to changes in information processing and attention alone. As will be shown, it may then be these distortions and alterations that lead to the development of faith within the individual and ultimately to the dramatic changes of either a physiologically or psychological nature.

### Attention and Information Processing

Borrowing from authors like Sargant (1957), Frank (1961), and Deikman (1969) it is suggested that most of the phenomena listed in Table 1 can be explained on the basis of changes in the attentional focus and information processing characteristics of the individual. It should be clarified that in referring to attentional focus, we are talking about width of attentional span or the number of possible stimuli that can enter consciousness in a given period of time. That is not to say the maximal number of stimuli will in fact enter consciousness. For example, an individual may broaden his attentional focus so that he is ready to receive more stimuli yet in a sensory deprived atmosphere, the stimuli will not be available. In contrast to attention span or focus, when referring to the amount of information processed, the referent is the actual number of stimuli that come into awareness. Obviously, these two concepts overlap, though not perfectly. Within a particular environmental setting, the amount of information processed will increase as the attentional span is increased. However, if attentional span remains constant across environmental settings, the amount of information processed will change. For example, changes in the density of stimuli in the environment, from stimuli-deprived conditions to saturated ones, will increase the amount of information processed, even if the width of attentional focus remains the same.

Assumptions about Normal Consciousness

Under "normal" conditions it is assumed that an individual's attentional focus varies in width and in direction (internal vs. external); however, the range of this variation is restricted. Thus, attention does not become extremely narrow or extremely broad and a balance is maintained between focusing internally on thoughts and feelings and focusing externally on objects. With respect to amount of stimulation processed, it is assumed that humans "normally", attempt to maintain some optimal level of stimulation. Should these basic assumptions be true, then alterations in them would be expected to lead to alterations in consciousness. Support for these hypotheses can be found by looking directly at the methods that are used to induce altered states.

Induction of ASC

There are a number of procedures used to induce ASC which involve either a broadening or narrowing of attention. For example, most hypnotic inductions demand a narrowed attentional focus, as do a wide variety of meditative exercises (i.e., counting breaths, chanting). Sensory deprivation conditions also force a narrowing of attention, as does sleep, since in both conditions external stimuli are reduced to a minimum. Even the ASC associated with schizophrenia has been attributed to attentional changes. According to some theorists, schizophrenic patients can be divided into two groups on the basis of their attentional focus. One group is overinclusive and lets in too many stimuli, whereas the other group is underinclusive and has too narrow an attentional focus (Cromwell, 1968). Theoretically, it is this attentional disturbance that accounts for a great portion of the schizophrenics disturbed thought processes and distorted perceptions. As will be shown next, the width of a person's attention may interact with the amount of information processed, and these changes too, may cause an ASC.

Sargant (1957) attributes the induction of many ASC to stimulus overload. As examples, he points to the religious conversions of John Wesley, and to some of the interrogation techniques (and their results) used by the police and the communists. Some additional examples of ASC developing from stimulus overload could include "freaking out" at a light show, or a rock concert. Along the same line, it has been hypothesized that some of the psychedelic drugs have their effects because ingestion leads paradoxically to an inhibition of the inhibitory functions of the brain. The result is that more stimuli come into awareness than the individual can deal with (Cohen, 1964). In the reverse direction, a dramatic reduction in the normal level of stimulation may result in an ASC. Examples would include, sleep, sensory deprivation, meditation, as well as drugs like alcohol and heroin.

It doesn't appear to matter if attention is narrow or broad of if the stimulus input is reduced or increased, each of these conditions can lead to an ASC. What does seem common across the experiences however, is the feeling on the part of the individual that they have become "immersed" in their sensations and perceptions (totally involved, lost).

Immersions

A characteristic that most of us share is a desire and/or need to structure and organize our environment. Gradually, as we grow older, we form conceptual relationships between the stimuli around us, and the responses that they elicit within us. For example, by this time you have learned to associate placing your hand on a hot stove (environmental stimulus) with pain (organismic response). It can be hypothesized that under normal conditions a balance appears to exist between the stimuli impossing on us and the responses we find ourselves making. That is, under normal conditions we are capable of forming conceptual ties between all of the stimuli we are confronted with and the responses that we make. Immersion, is hypothesized to develop when attentional factors and information processing factors suddenly change and an imbalance develops between the stimuli (external focus) on the one hand, and the responses on the other (internal focus).

A sudden shift in the amount of stimulation that an individual is consciously aware of, will demand a corresponding alteration in the formation of conceptual ties. It is fairly easy to see that if stimuli are coming in too rapidly (as in the case of LSD) to adequately process, the person will become confused and disoriented. This appears to result from the inability to respond rapidly enough to the demands that the stimuli are making upon them. For that period of sensory overload the person is immersed in a "stimulus" world. Depending on the sense receptors in use he may become immersed in music, lights, tastes, sex, his own affect and so on. An example of this immersion and the distortions it can cause in time and perception can be seen in the following example.

"So many thoughts and associations would occur in between the passing of two telephone poles that I would have no idea how much time had actually passed. In addition, the associations would be so intense that I would become oblivious to the outer world. I know that these periods of oblivion, while driving, were only for two or three seconds at the most. They were this long because I knew how fast I was driving (by checking the speedometer) and because I was driving on familiar roads so that I had external check points telling me how far I had traveled. If I had not been on familiar roads I could not have known how much time had passed and I would have become lost." (Nideffer, 1970)

Perhaps a bit more difficult to follow is the idea that a reduction in stimulation could also result in immersion. Examinations of the physiology of the human nervous system indicate that to remain healthy, neurons (nerve cells) must be used. In support of this formulation is the finding that most humans actively seek sensory stimulation. In fact, it has been suggested that under conditions of stimulus deprivation the organism will self stimulate. From these observations it might be hypothesized that a reduction in the normal amount of external stimulation the organism receives will be compensated for by an increase in internally originated stimuli (thoughts and feelings). Under these conditions, there would be no external stimuli present to which the internal responses could be attached. As with overstimulation, such an occurrance would lead to the perceptual, judgemental, and temporal distortions found in Table 1. In addition, without external stimuli pulling at him, the person would become immersed in internal processes. This immersion may be used to explain the "increased awareness" of self that is often associated with meditation.

Personality theorists have suggested that man spends a great deal of energy repressing thought processes in order to defend against anxiety. For example, if you have ever been cruel to an animal the thought of that behavior may make you uncomfortable. To avoid that distress you avoid thinking about having been cruel. This helps you deny some things, but also means that how you perceive yourself (as kind) may be at odds with how others perceive you (as cruel). Such a discrepancy makes it difficult for you to predict how others will respond to you, since they will not treat you in the way you expect to be treated. Through a reduction in external stimulation some of the objects or feelings, that have been distracting and keeping your attention away from your hypothetical cruelty, will be removed and you may be unable to avoid being confronted with it. This exposure can conceivably lead to your seeing an aspect of yourself that others see, and thus help you to become more integrated and more accurate in predicting and understanding their responses to you.

<u>Faith</u>

The concepts presented above may be used to explain perceptual alterations, feelings of loss of control, and temporal distortion, yet they fall short of providing a complete understanding of altered states. It was pointed out earlier that through verbal suggestions rashes could be made to appear or disappear, and that individuals would allow doctors to remove scrotal tumors and even legs without an anesthetic. The ability of subjects to respond in this way is difficult to explain, and in the absence of more concrete data faith is offered as an intervening variable.

The idea that pain may be intensified, or reduced by simply altering attention seems reasonable. In fact it may be possible to become so absorbed or immersed in other stimuli that pain, even from the removal of a leg, is not attended to (Barber, 1970). The major question however remains; how do you get a person to agree to such an operation? Obviously the person must have faith in the procedures you are using, or else he will not be able to follow them. For whatever reason, individuals seem to be able to place that faith in a situation described as hypnotic. Will these same people be able to place the same faith in the concept of simply redirecting their attention? From my own perspective, I feel that a few people would in fact, be able to place faith in the attention interpretation that has been offered in this paper. Others, however, will be unable to respond under those conditions. At this point, it may be helpful to attempt to define faith a little more closely.

Faith, as it is used here will be defined as the ability of an individual to establish complete trust or confidence in himself and/or someone or something else. It is only with the development of this trust and confidence that people are able to maximize their physiological functioning. It's their confidence, (faith) even in the face of what would appear from an outsider's point of view, to be great stress, that allows them to maintain an appropriate level of arrousal and to function at maximum efficiency. To relate it back to the surgery, it's the confidence and trust in the surgeon and in hypnosis that allows the patient to respond to suggestions, which distract him from the pain. If what is being suggested is true, then the development of faith on the part of an individual is very important. A question that would be worth investigating, has to do with how ASC experiences can be used to develop that faith.

## The Impact of Immersion and Loss of Control

Sargant (1957) has pointed out that dramatic changes in the levels of stimulus input often leads to feelings of confusion and loss of control. When sensory processes have been assaulted in some way (by over or under stimulation), for a short time afterwards the person wanders around dazed and confused. As normal functioning returns he attempts to understand what has happened, to conceptualize and integrate his experience. Depending on the intensity of the ASC his typical explanations may or may not suffice. If the experience has been preceded by extensive training or discipline (i.e., preparation for the priesthood) it would be easy and natural for the individual to use that preparation as a conceptual framework for understanding. In the case of the Zen priest, this framework might lead to development of faith. Should such preparation be absent some other explanation will be sought. To escape his confusion, the individual is likely to respond to any suggestion which presumes to explain what has happened. These suggestions can be made by a therapist, a surgeon, a guru, by virtually anyone, and may be either constructive or destructive. There are a couple of questions that we have not attempted to answer here. First, this presentation does not pretend to imply that there either is or is not any "absolute truth." Each individual must find their own faith. In addition, we cannot yet say how an individual's faith works to create change. For example, we do not know how it causes physiological changes such as the disappearance of warts. What we can say is that faith is necessary for the maximization of human potential. We can also hypothesize that ASC can be used to assist in the development of faith.

## Future Research

In closing this chapter it may be helpful to point out some directions research could take in the future. Obviously, the suggestions that ASC experiences occur as a function of alterations in attention and information processing need to be examined in tightly controlled studies. In addition, research paradigms should be developed which show us how to maximize subjects expectancies and in that sense aim at developing faith. Ideally, in this way we will learn to provide individuals with the feelings of self-confidence and trust necessary for them to function at their maximal physiological and psychological level.

References

Abramson, H. A. (Ed.) The Use of LSD in Psychotherapy and Alcoholism, New York, Bobbs, Merrill Company, 1967.

Anand, B. K., Chhina, G. A., Singh, B. Some aspects of electroencephalographic studies in yogis, in Barber, T. X., DiCara, L. V., Kamiya, J., Miller, N. E., Shapiro, D., & Stoyva J. (Eds.). Biofeedback & Self Control. Chicago: Aldine-Atherton, 1971.

Asher, R. Respectable hypnosis, British Medical Journal, 1956, 1, 309-313.

Barber, T. X. LSD, Marihuana, Yoga, and Hypnosis. Chicago: Aldine Publishing Company, 1970.

Cohen, S. The Beyond Within. New York: Atheneum, 1964.

Cromwell, R. L. Stimulus redundancy and schizophrenia. Journal of Nervous and Mental Disease, 1968, 146, 5, 360-375.

Deikman, A. J. Experimental Meditation. In Tart (ed.). Altered States of Consciousness. New York: John Wiley & Sons, 1969.

Devereux, G. Reality and dream: Psychotherapy of a plains Indian, New York, Doubleday and Company, 1969.

Engstrom, D. R., London, P., & Hart, J. T. Hypnotic susceptibility increased by EEG alpha training. Nature, 1970, 227, 1261-1262.

Erickson, M. Deep hypnosis and its induction in Advanced Techniques of Hypnosis and Therapy, Jay Haley (Ed.), New York, Grune & Stratton, 1967.

Frank, J. Persuasion and Healing, New York, Schocken Books, 1961.

Freud, S. The Interpretation of Dreams, John Wiley & Sons, New York, 1961.

Glaser, G. H. EEG and Behavior. New York: Basic Books, 1963.

Goldstein, L., Murphree, H. B., Sugarman, A. A., Pfeiffer, C. C., & Jenney, E. H. Quantitative electroencephalographic analysis of naturally occurring (schizophrenic) and drug induced psychotic states in human males. Clinical Pharmacology & Therapeutics, 4, 10-21, 1963.

Grispoon, L. Marijuana Reconsidered, Cambridge, Mass., Harvard University Press, 1971.

Hall, C., & Domhoff, B. The Dreams of Freud and Jung, in Readings in Psychology Today, Del Mar, Calif., CRM Books, 1967.

Hilgard, E., Hypnotic Susceptibility, New York, Harcourt, Brace & World, 1965.

Hoffer, A. An Alcoholism Treatment Program - LSD, Malvaria, and Nocotinic Acid. Preprint, 2nd. Conference on the use of LSD in Psychotherapy, 1965.

Ikemi Y., and Nakagawa, S. A psychosomatic study of contagious dermatitis Kyushu. J. of Med. Sci., 1962, 13, 335-350.

Johnson, L. C. A Psychophysiology for all States. In Barber, T.X., DiCara, L. V., Kamiya, J., Miller, N. E., Shapiro, D., & Stoyva (Eds.), Biofeedback & Self Control. Chicago: Aldine, 1970.

Kahn, E., Fisher, C., Edwards, A., & Davis, D. Psychophysiology of night terrors and nightmares, Proceedings, 80th Annual Convention of APA, 1972.

Kamiya, J. Conscious control of brain waves. Psychology Today, 1, 57-60, 1968.

Kasamatsu, A., & Hirai, T. An electroencephalographic study of the Zen meditation (Za Zen). In Barber, T. X., DiCara, L. V., Kamiya, J., Miller, N. E., Shapiro, E., & Stoyva, J. (Eds.), Biofeedback & Self Control. Chicago: Aldine-Atherton, 1971.

Kleitman, N. Patterns of dreaming, Scientific American, 1960, 203, 81-88.

Landis, C. Varieties of psychopathological Experience, Mettler (Ed.), New York, Holt Rinehart and Winston, 1964.

Leary, T., Metzner, R. & Alpert, R. The psychedelic experience, New York, New York University Books, 1964.

London, P., Hart, J. T., & Leibovitz. EEG alpha rhythms and susceptibility to hypnosis. Nature, 219, 71-72, 1968.

Ludwig, A. Altered States of Consciousness, in Tart (Ed.), Altered States of Consciousness, New York, John Wiley & Sons, 1969.

MacLean, Ross J., MacDonald, D. C., Byrne, Ultan P., & Hubbard, A. M., "The Use of LSD-25 In the Treatment of Alcoholism and Other Psychiatric Problems," Quarterly Journal of Studies on Alcohol, 1961, 22, 1, pp. 34-45.

Maupin, E. On Meditation. In Tart (Ed.), Altered States of Consciousness. New York: John Wiley & Sons, 1969.

McGlothlin, William H., Hallucinogenic Drugs: A perspective with Special Reference to Peyote and Cannabis., RAND Corp. Publication, July 1964.

Mogar, R. E. and Savage, C. Personality Change associated with psychedelic (LSD) Therapy: a preliminary report, Psychotherapy: Theory, Research and Practice, 1:154, 1964.

Naranjo, C. and Orenstein, R. On the Psychology of Meditation, Viking Press, 1971.

Nelson, T. (Pub.) The Holy Bible: Revised Standard Version, New York, Thomas Nelson & Sons, 1952.

Nideffer, R. The illegal use of LSD-25 and the development of antisocial attitudes and guilt feelings, Copyright Robert Nideffer 1967.

Nideffer, R. Descriptions of a Drug Experience, Unpublished Manuscript, The University of Rochester, Rochester, N. Y. 1970.

Nideffer, R. On Dreams, Unpublished Manuscript, The University of Rochester, Rochester, N. Y. 1972.

Nideffer, R. Alpha and the development of Human Potential, To appear in Barber, DiCara, Kamiya, Miller, Shapiro, and Stoyva (Eds.), Biofeedback and Self Control. Chicago, Aldine-Atherton, 1973.

Orne, M. The nature of hypnosis: artifact and essence. J. Abnormal and Social Psychology, 1959, 58, 277-299.

Orne, M. On the social psychology of the psychological Experiment: with particular reference to demand characteristics and their implications, American Psychologist, 1962, 17, 776-783.

Pattie, F. A brief history of hypnotism in Handbook of Clinical and Experimental Hypnosis, Jessey Gordon (Ed.) New York, MacMillan, 1967.

Sargant, W. Battle for the Mind, New York, Doubleday, 1957.

Schwartz, M. The cessation of Labor using hypnotic techniques. American Journal of Clinical Hypnosis, 1963, 5, 211-213.

Stagner, R. Some Historical Perspectives on Personality Theory, Paper presented at the Directors Conference, Lafayette Clinic, Detroit, 1971.

Tart, C. Altered States of Consciousness. New York: John Wiley & Sons, 1969.

Ullman, M., & Krippner, S. ESP in the night in Readings in Psychology Today, 2nd Ed. Del Mar, Calif., CRM Books, 1967.

Unger, S. M. The current scientific status of psychedelic drug research. Conference on Methods in Philosophy and the Sciences, New York, 1964.

Wallace, A. Cultural determinants of response to hallunicatory experience. Arch. of Gen. Psychiat., 1959, 1, 58-68.

Wallace, R. K. Physiological effects of transendental meditation. Science, 1970, 167, 1751-1754.

Wallace, R. K., & Benson, H. The physiology of meditation, Scientific American, 1972, 2, 85-90.

Watts, A. The Joyous Cosmology: Adventures in the chemistry of consciousness, New York, Pantheon Books, 1963.

2

TART, C. T.

# States of Consciousness and State-Specific Sciences

Blackburn (*1*) recently noted that many of our most talented young people are "turned off" to science: as a solution, he proposed that we recognize the validity of a more sensuous-intuitive approach to nature, treating it as complementary to the classical intellectual approach.

I have seen the same rejection of science by many of the brightest students in California, and the problem is indeed serious. Blackburn's analysis is valid, but not deep enough. A more fundamental source of alienation is the widespread experience of altered states of consciousness (ASC's) by the young, coupled with the almost total rejection of the knowledge gained during the experiencing of ASC's by the scientific establishment. Blackburn himself exemplifies this rejection when he says: "Perhaps science has much to learn along this line from the disciplines, *as distinct from the content,* of Oriental religions" (my italics).

To illustrate, a recent Gallup poll (*2*) indicated that approximately half of American college students have tried marijuana, and a large number of them use it fairly regularly. They do this at the risk of having their careers ruined and going to jail for several years. Why? Conventional research on the nature of marijuana intoxication tells us that the primary effects are a slight increase in heart rate, reddening of the eyes, some difficulty with memory, and small decrements in performance on complex psychomotor tests.

Would you risk going to jail to experience these?

A young marijuana smoker who hears a scientist or physician talk about these findings as the basic nature of marijuana intoxication will simply sneer and have his antiscientific attitude further reinforced. It is clear to him that the scientist has no real understanding of what marijuana intoxication is all about (*3*).

More formally, an increasingly significant number of people are experimenting with ASC's in themselves, and finding the experiences thus gained of extreme importance in their philosophy and style of life. The conflict between experiences in these ASC's and the attitudes and intellectual-emotional systems that have evolved in our ordinary state of consciousness (SoC) is a major factor behind the increased alienation of many people from conventional science. Experiences of ecstasy, mystical union, other "dimensions," rapture, beauty, space-and-time transcendence, and transpersonal knowledge, all common in ASC's, are simply not treated adequately in conventional scientific approaches. These experiences will not "go away" if we crack down more on psychedelic drugs, for immense numbers of people now practice various nondrug techniques for producing ASC's, such as meditation (*4*) and yoga.

The purpose of this article is to show that it is possible to investigate and work with the important phenomena of ASC's in a manner which is perfectly compatible with the essence of scientific method. The conflict discussed above is not necessary.

## States of Consciousness

An ASC may be defined for the purposes of this article as a qualitative alteration in the overall pattern of mental functioning, such that the experiencer feels his consciousness is radically different from the way it functions ordinarily. An SoC is thus defined not in terms of any particular content of consciousness, or specific behavior or physiological change, but in terms of the overall patterning of psychological functioning.

An analogy with computer functioning can clarify this definition. A computer has a complex program of many subroutines. If we reprogram it quite differently, the same sorts of input data may be handled in quite different ways; we will be able to predict very little from our knowledge of the old program about the effects of varying the input, even though old and new programs have some subroutines in common. The new program with its input-output interactions must be studied in and of itself. An ASC is analogous to changing temporarily the program of a computer.

The ASC's experienced by almost all ordinary people are dreaming states and the hypnogogic and hypnopompic states, the transitional states between sleeping and waking. Many other people experience another ASC, alcohol intoxication.

The relatively new (to our culture) ASC's that are now having such an impact are those produced by marijuana, more powerful psychedelic drugs such as LSD, meditative states, so-called possession states, and autohypnotic states (*5*).

## States of Consciousness and Paradigms

It is useful to compare this concept of an SoC, a qualitatively distinct organization of the patterning of mental functioning, with Kuhn's (*6*) concept of paradigms in science. A paradigm is an intellectual achievement that underlies normal science and attracts and guides the work of an enduring number of adherents in their scientific activity. It is a kind of "super theory," a formulation of scope wide enough to affect the organization of most or all of the major known phenomena of its field. Yet it is sufficiently open-ended that there still remain important problems to be solved within that framework. Examples of important paradigms in the history of science have been Copernican astronomy and Newtonian dynamics.

Because of their tremendous success, paradigms undergo a change which, in principle, ordinary scientific theories do not undergo. An ordinary scientific theory is always subject to further questioning and testing as it is extended. A paradigm becomes an implicit framework for most scientists working within it; it is the natural way of looking at things and doing things. It does not seriously occur to the adherents of a paradigm to question it any more (we may ignore, for the moment, the occurrence of scientific revolutions). Theories become referred to as laws: people talk of the law of gravity, not the theory of gravity, for example.

A paradigm serves to concentrate the attention of a researcher on sensible problem areas and to prevent him from wasting his time on what might be trivia. On the other hand, by implicitly defining some lines of research as trivial or nonsensical, a paradigm acts like a blinder. Kuhn has discussed this blinding function as a key factor in the lack of effective communications during paradigm clashes.

The concept of a paradigm and of an SoC are quite similar. Both constitute complex, interlocking sets of rules and theories that enable a person to interact with and interpret experiences within an environment. In both cases, the rules are largely implicit. They are not recognized as tentative working hypotheses; they operate automatically and the person feels he is doing the obvious or natural thing.

### Paradigm Clash between "Straight" and "Hip"

Human beings become emotionally attached to the things which give them pleasure, and a scientist making important progress within a particular paradigm becomes emotionally attached to it. When data which make no sense in terms of the (implicit) paradigm are brought to our attention, the usual result is not a reevaluation of the paradigm, but a rejection or misperception of the data. This rejection seems rational to others sharing that paradigm and irrational or rationalizing to others committed to a different paradigm.

The conflict now existing between those who have experienced certain ASC's (whose ranks include many young scientists) and those who have not is very much a paradigmatic conflict. For example, a subject takes LSD, and tells his investigator that "You and I, we are all one, there are no separate selves." The investigator reports that his subject showed a "confused sense of identity and distorted thinking process." The subject is reporting what is obvious to him, the investigator is reporting what is obvious to him. The investigator's implicit paradigm, based on his scientific training, his cultural background, and his normal SoC, indicates that a literal interpretation of the subject's statement cannot be true, and therefore must be interpreted as mental dysfunction on the part of the subject. The subject, his paradigms radically changed for the moment by being in an ASC, not only reports what is obviously true to him, but perceives the investigator as showing mental dysfunction, by virtue of being incapable of perceiving the obvious!

Historically, paradigm clashes have been characterized by bitter emotional antagonisms, and total rejection of the opponent. Currently we are seeing the same sort of process: the respectable psychiatrist, who would not take any of those "psychotomimetic" drugs himself or sit down and experience that crazy meditation process, carries out research to show that drug takers and those who practice meditation are escapists. The drug taker or meditator views the same investigator as narrow-minded, prejudiced, and repressive, and as a result drops out of the university. Communication between the two factions is almost nil.

Must the experiencers of ASC's continue to see the scientists as concentrating on the irrelevant, and the scientists see the experiencers as confused (7) or mentally ill? Or can science deal adequately with the experiences of these people? The thesis I shall now present in detail is that we can deal with the important aspects of ASC's using the essence of scientific method, even though a variety of nonessentials, unfortunately identified with current science, hinder such an effort.

### The Nature of Knowledge

Basically, science (from the Latin *scire*, to know) deals with knowledge. Knowledge may be defined as an immediately given experiential feeling of congruence between two different kinds of experience, a matching. One set of experiences may be regarded as perceptions of the external world, of others, of oneself; the second set may be regarded as a theory, a scheme, a system of understanding. The feeling of congruence is something immediately given in experience, although many refinements have been worked out for judging degrees of congruence.

All knowledge, then, is basically experiential knowledge. Even my knowledge of the physical world can be reduced to this: given certain sets of experiences, which I (by assumption) attribute to the external world activating my sensory apparatus, it may be possible for me to compare them with purely internal experiences (memories, previous knowledge) and predict with a high degree of reliability other kinds of experiences, which I again attribute to the external world.

Because science has been incredibly successful in dealing with the physical world, it has been historically associated with a philosophy of physicalism, the belief that reality is all reducible to certain kinds of physical entities. The vast majority of phenomena of ASC's have no known physical manifestations: thus to physicalistic philosophy they are epiphenomena, not worthy of study. But insofar as science deals with knowledge, it need not restrict itself only to physical kinds of knowledge.

### The Essence of Scientific Method

I shall discuss the essence of scientific method, and show that this essence is perfectly compatible with an enlarged study of the important phenomena of ASC's. In particular, I propose that state-specific sciences (SSS) be developed.

As satisfying as the feeling of knowing can be, we are often wrong: what seems like congruence at first later does not match, or has no generality. Man has learned that his reasoning is often faulty, his observations are often incomplete or mistaken, and that emotional and other nonconscious factors can seriously distort both reasoning and observational processes. His reliance on authorities, "rationality" or "elegance," are no sure criteria for achieving truth. The development of scientific method may be seen as a determined effort to systematize the process of acquiring knowledge in such a way as to minimize the various pitfalls of observation and reasoning.

I shall discuss four basic rules of scientific method to which an investigator is committed: (i) good observation; (ii) the public nature of observation; (iii) the necessity to theorize logically; and (iv) the testing of theory by observable consequences; all these constitute the scientific enterprise. I shall consider the wider application of each rule to ASC's and indicate how unnecessary physicalistic restrictions may be dropped. I will show that all these commitments or rules can be accommodated in the development of SSS's that I propose.

**Observation**

The scientist is committed to observe as well as possible the phenomena of interest and to search constantly for better ways of making these observations. But our paradigmatic commitments, our SoC's, make us likely to observe certain parts of reality and to ignore or observe with error certain other parts of it.

Many of the most important phenomena of ASC's have been observed poorly or not at all because of the physicalistic labeling of them as epiphenomena, so that they have been called "subjective," "ephemeral," "unreliable," or "unscientific." Observations of internal processes are probably much more difficult to make than those of external physical processes, because of their inherently greater complexity. The essence of science, however, is that we observe what there is to be observed whether it is difficult or not.

Furthermore, most of what we know about the phenomena of ASC's has been obtained from untrained people, almost none of whom have shared the scientists' commitment to constantly reexamine their observations in greater and greater detail. This should not imply that internal phenomena are inherently unobservable or unstable; we are comparing the first observations of internal phenomena with observations of physical sciences that have undergone centuries of refinement.

We must consider one other problem of observation. One of the traditional idols of science, the "detached observer," has no place in dealing with many internal phenomena of SoCs. Not only are the observer's perceptions selective, he may also affect the things he observes. We must try to understand the characteristics of each individual observer in order to compensate for them.

A recognition of the unreality of the detached observer in the psychological sciences is becoming widespread, under the topics of experimenter bias (*8*) and demand characteristics (*9*). A similar recognition long ago occurred in physics when it was realized that the observed was altered by the process of observation at subatomic levels. When we deal with ASC's where the observer is the experiencer of the ASC, this factor is of paramount importance. Knowing the characteristics of the observer can also confound the process of consensual validation, which I shall now consider.

**Public Nature of Observation**

Observations must be public in that they must be replicable by any properly trained observer. The experienced conditions that led to the report of certain experiences must be described in sufficient detail that others may duplicate them and consequently have experiences which meet criteria of identicality. That someone else may set up similar conditions but not have the same experiences proves that the original investigator gave an incorrect description of the conditions and observations, or that he was not aware of certain essential aspects of the conditions.

The physicalistic accretion to this rule of consensual validation is that, physical data being the only "real" data, internal phenomena must be reduced to physiological or behavioral data to become reliable or they will be ignored entirely. I believe most physical observations to be much more readily replicable by any trained observer because they are inherently simpler phenomena than internal ones. In principle, however, consensual validation of internal phenomena by a trained observer is quite possible.

The emphasis on public observations in science has had a misleading quality insofar as it implies that any intelligent man can replicate a scientist's observations. This might have been true early in the history of science, but nowadays only the trained observer can replicate many observations. I cannot go into a modern physicist's laboratory and confirm his observations. Indeed, his talk of what he has found in his experiments (physicists seem to talk about innumerable invisible entities these days) would probably seem mystical to me, just as many descriptions of internal states sound mystical to those with a background in the physical sciences.

Given the high complexity of the phenomena associated with ASC's, the need for replication by trained observers is exceptionally important. Since it generally takes 4 to 10 years of intensive training to produce a scientist in any of our conventional sciences, we should not be surprised that there has been very little reliability of observations by untrained observers of ASC phenomena.

Further, for the state-specific sciences that I propose should be established, we cannot specify the requirements that would constitute adequate training. These would only be determined after considerable trial and error. We should also recognize that very few people might complete the training successfully. Some people do not have the necessary innate characteristics to become physicists, and some probably do not have the innate characteristics to become, say, scientific investigators of meditative states.

Public observation, then, always refers to a limited, specially trained public. It is only by basic agreement among those specially trained people that data become accepted as a foundation for the development of a science. That laymen cannot replicate the observations is of little relevance.

A second problem in consensual validation arises from a phenomenon predicted by my concept of ASC's, but not yet empirically investigated, namely, state-specific communication. Given that an ASC is an overall qualitative and quantitative shift in the complex functioning of consciousness, such that there are new "logics" and perceptions (which would constitute a paradigm shift), it is quite reasonable to hypothesize that communication may take a different pattern. For two observers, both of whom, we assume, are fluent in communicating with each other in a given SoC, communication about some new observations may seem adequate to them, or may be improved or deteriorated in specific ways. To an outside observer, an observer in a different SoC, the communication between these two observers may seem "deteriorated."

Practically all investigations of communication by persons in ASC's have resulted in reports of deterioration of communication abilities. In designing their studies, however, these investigators have not taken into account the fact that the pattern of communication may have changed. If I am listening to two people speaking in English, and they suddenly begin to intersperse words and phrases in Polish, I, as an outside (that is, a non-Polish speaking) observer, will note a gross deterioration in communication. Adequacy of communication between people in the same SoC and across SoC's must be empirically determined.

Thus consensual validation may be restricted by the fact that only observers in the same ASC are able to communicate adequately with each other, and they may not be able to communicate adequately to someone in a different SoC, say normal consciousness (*10*).

**Theorizing**

A scientist may theorize about his observations as much as he wishes to, but the theory he develops must consistently account for all that he has observed, and should have a logical structure that other scientists can comprehend (but not necessarily accept).

The requirement to theorize logically and consistently with the data is not as simple as it looks, however. Any logic consists of a basic set of assumptions and a set of rules for manipulating information, based on these assumptions. Change the assumptions, or change the rules, and there may be entirely different outcomes from the same data. A paradigm, too, is a logic: it has certain assumptions and rules for working within these assumptions. By changing the paradigm, altering the SoC, the nature of theory building may change radically. Thus a person in SoC 2 might come to very different conclusions about the nature of the same events that he observed in SoC 1. An investigator in SoC 1 may comment on the comprehensibility of the second person's ideas from the point of view (paradigm) of SoC 1, but can say nothing about their inherent validity. A scientist who could enter either SoC 1 or SoC 2, however, could pronounce on the comprehensibility of the other's theory, and the adherence of that theory to the rules and logic of SoC 2. Thus, scientists trained in the same SoC may check on the logical validity of each other's theorizing. We have then the possibility of a state-specific logic underlying theorizing in various SoC's.

**Observable Consequences**

Any theory a scientist develops must have observable consequences, and from that theory it must be possible to make predictions that can be verified by observation. If such verification is not possible, the theory must be considered invalid, regardless of its elegance, logic, or other appeal.

Ordinarily we think of empirical validation, of validation in terms of testable consequences that produce physical effects, but this is misleading. Any effect, whether interpreted as physical or nonphysical, is ultimately an experience in the observer's mind. All that is essentially required to validate a theory is that it predict that "When a certain experience (observed condition) has occurred, another (predicted) kind of experience will follow, under specified experiential conditions." Thus a perfectly scientific theory may be based on data that have no physical existence.

**State-Specific Sciences**

We tend to envision the practice of science like this: centered around interest in some particular range of subject matter, a small number of highly selected, talented, and rigorously trained people spend considerable time making detailed observations on the subject matter of interest. They may or may not have special places (laboratories) or instruments or methods to assist them in making finer observations. They speak to one another in a special language which they feel conveys precisely the important facts of their field. Using this language, they confirm and extend each other's knowledge of certain data basic to the field. They theorize about their basic data and construct elaborate systems. They validate these by recourse to further observation. These trained people all have a long-term commitment to the constant refinement of observation and extension of theory. Their activity is frequently incomprehensible to laymen.

This general description is equally applicable to a variety of sciences, or areas that could become sciences, whether we called such areas biology, physics, chemistry, psychology, understanding of mystical states, or drug-induced enhancement of cognitive processes. The particulars of research would look very different, but the basic scientific method running through all is the same.

More formally, I now propose the creation of various state-specific sciences. If such sciences could be created, we would have a group of highly skilled, dedicated, and trained practitioners able to achieve certain SoC's, and able to agree with one another that they have attained a common state. While in that SoC, they might then investigate other areas of interest, whether these be totally internal phenomena of that given state, the interaction of that state with external, physical reality, or people in other SoC's.

The fact that the experimenter should be able to function skillfully in the SoC itself for a state-specific science does not necessarily mean that he would always be the subject. While he might often be the subject, observer, and experimenter simultaneously, it would be quite possible for him to collect data from experimental manipulations of other subjects in the SoC, and either be in that SoC himself at the time of data collection or be in that SoC himself for data reduction and theorizing.

Examples of some observations made and theorizing done by a scientist in a specific ASC would illustrate the nature of a proposed state-specific science. But this is not possible because no state-specific sciences have yet been established (*11*). Also, any example that would make good sense to the readers of this article (who are, presumably, all in a normal SoC) would not really illustrate the uniqueness of a state-specific science. If it did make sense, it would be an example of a problem that could be approached adequately from both the ASC and normal SoC's, and thus it would be too easy to see the entire problem in terms of accepted scientific procedures for normal SoC's and miss the point about the necessity for developing state-specific sciences.

### State-Specific Sciences and Religion

Some aspects of organized religion appear to resemble state-specific sciences. There are techniques that allow the believer to enter an ASC and then have religious experiences in that ASC which are proof of his religious belief. People who have had such experiences usually describe them as ineffable in important ways—that is, as not fully comprehensible in an ordinary SoC. Conversions at revivalistic meetings are the most common example of religious experiences occurring in various ASC's induced by an intensely emotional atmosphere.

In examining the esoteric training systems of some religions, there seems to be even more resemblance between such mystical ways and state-specific sciences, for here we often have the picture of devoted specialists, complex techniques, and repeated experiencing of the ASC's in order to further religious knowledge.

Nevertheless the proposed state-specific sciences are not simply religion in a new guise. The use of ASC's in religion may involve the kind of commitment to searching for truth that is needed for developing a state-specific science, but practically all the religions we know might be defined as state-specific technologies, operated in the service of a priori belief systems. The experiencers of ASC's in most religious contexts have already been thoroughly indoctrinated in a particular belief system. This belief system may then mold the content of the ASC's to create specific experiences which reinforce or validate the belief system.

The crucial distinction between a religion utilizing ASC's and a state-specific science is the commitment of the scientist to reexamine constantly his own belief system and to question the obvious in spite of its intellectual or emotional appeal to him. Investigators of ASC's would certainly encounter an immense variety of phenomena labeled religious experience or mystical revelation during the development of state-specific sciences, but they would have to remain committed to examining these phenomena more carefully, sharing their observations and techniques with colleagues, and subjecting the beliefs (hypotheses, theories) that result from such experiences to the requirement of leading to testable predictions. In practice, because we are aware of the immense emotional power of mystical experiences, this would be a difficult task, but it is one that will have to be undertaken by disciplined investigators if we are to understand various ASC's.

### Relationship between State-Specific Sciences

Any state-specific science may be considered as consisting of two parts, observations and theorizations. The observations are what can be experienced relatively directly; the theories are the *inferences* about what sort of non-observable factors account for the observations. For example, the phenomena of synesthesia (seeing colors as a result of hearing sounds) is a theoretical proposition for me in my ordinary SoC: I do not experience it, and can only generate theories about what other people report about it. If I were under the influence of a psychedelic drug such as LSD or marijuana (*3*), I could probably experience synesthesia directly, and my descriptions of the experience would become data.

Figure 1 demonstrates some possible relationships between three state-specific sciences. State-specific sciences 1 and 2 show considerable overlap.

The area labeled $O_1O_2$ permits direct observation in both sciences. Area $T_1T_2$ permits theoretical inferences about common subject matter from the two perspectives. In area $O_1T_2$, by contrast, the theoretical propositions of state-specific science number 2 are matters of direct observation for the scientist in SoC number 1, and vice versa for the area $T_1O_2$. State-specific science number 3 consists of a body of observation and theory exclusive to that science and has no overlap with the other two sciences: it neither confirms, denies, nor complements them.

It would be naively reductionistic to say that the work in one state-specific science *validates* or *invalidates* the work in a second state-specific science; I prefer to say that two different state-specific sciences, where they overlap, provide quite different points of view with respect to certain kinds of theories and data, and thus complement (*12*) each other. The proposed creation of state-specific sciences neither validates nor invalidates the activities of normal

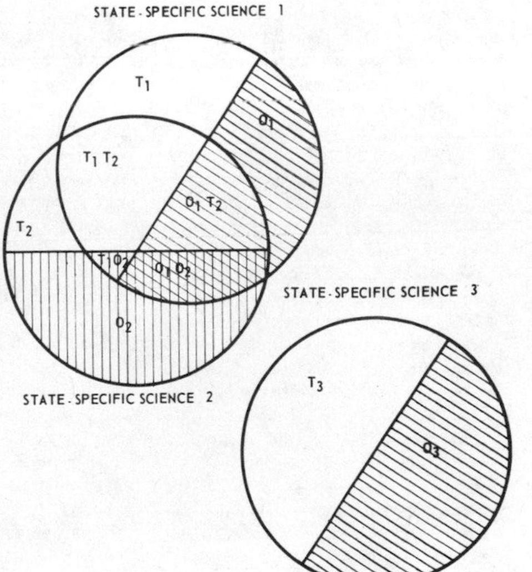


Fig. 1. Possible relationships between three state-specific sciences. The area labeled $O_1O_2$ is subject matter capable of direct observation in both sciences. Area $T_1T_2$ consists of theoretical (T) inferences about subject matter overlapping the two sciences. By contrast, in area $O_1T_2$, the theoretical propositions of state-specific science number 2 are matters of direct observation for the scientist in state of consciousness number 1, and vice versa for area $T_1O_2$. State-specific science number 3 consists of a body of observation and theory exclusive to that science.

consciousness sciences (NCS). The possibility of developing certain state-specific sciences means only that certain kinds of phenomena may be handled more adequately within these potential new sciences.

Interrelationships more complex than those that are illustrated in Fig. 1 are possible.

The possibility of stimulating interactions between different state-specific sciences is very real. Creative breakthroughs in NCS have frequently been made by scientists temporarily going into an ASC (*13*). In such instances, the scientists concerned saw quite different views of their problems and performed different kinds of reasoning, conscious or nonconsciousness, which led to results that could be tested within their NCS.

A current example of such interaction is the finding that in Zen meditation (a highly developed discipline in Japan) there are physiological correlates of meditative experiences, such as decreased frequency of alpha-rhythm, which can also be produced by means of instrumentally aided feedback-learning techniques (*14*). This finding might elucidate some of the processes peculiar to each discipline.

**Individual Differences**

A widespread and misleading assumption that hinders the development of state-specific sciences and confuses their interrelationships is the assumption that because two people are normal (not certified insane), their ordinary SoC's are essentially the same. In reality I suspect that there are enormous differences between the SoC's of some normal people. Because societies train people to behave and communicate along socially approved lines, these differences are covered up.

For example, some people think in images, others in words. Some can voluntarily anesthetize parts of their body, most cannot. Some recall past events by imaging the scene and looking at the relevant details; others use complex verbal processes with no images.

This means that person A may be able to observe certain kinds of experiential data that person B cannot experience in his ordinary SoC, no matter how hard B tries. There may be several consequences. Person B may think that A is insane, too imaginative, or a liar, or he may feel inferior to A. Person A may also feel himself odd, if he takes B as a standard of normality.

In some cases, B may be able to enter an ASC and there experience the sorts of things that A has reported to him. A realm of knowledge that is ordinary for A is then specific for an ASC for B. Similarly, some of the experiences of B in his ASC may not be available for direct observation by A in his ordinary SoC.

The phenomenon of synesthesia can again serve as an example. Some individuals possess this ability in their ordinary SoC, most do not. Yet 56 percent of a sample of experienced marijuana users experienced synesthesia at least occasionally (*3*) while in the drug-induced ASC.

Thus we may conceive of bits of knowledge that are specific for an ASC for one individual, part of ordinary consciousness for another. Arguments over the usefulness of the concept of states of consciousness may reflect differences in the structure of the ordinary SoC of various investigators.

Another important source of individual differences, little understood at present, is the degree to which an individual may first make a particular observation or form a concept in one SoC and then be able to reexperience or comprehend it in another SoC. That is, many items of information which were state-specific when observed initially may be learned and somehow transferred (fully or partially) to another SoC. Differences across individuals, various combinations of SoC's, and types of experience will probably be enormous.

I have only outlined the complexities created by individual differences in normal SoC's and have used the normal SoC as a baseline for comparison with ASC's; but it is evident that every SoC must eventually be compared against every other SoC.

**Problems, Pitfalls, and Personal Perils**

If we use the practical experience of Western man with ASC's as a guide, the development of state-specific sciences will be beset by a number of difficulties. These difficulties will be of two kinds: general methodological problems stemming from the inherent nature of some ASC's; and those concerned with personal perils to the investigator. I shall discuss state-related problems first.

The first important problem in the proposed development of state-specific sciences is the obvious perception of truth. In many ASC's, one's experience is that one is obviously and lucidly experiencing truth directly, without question. An immediate result of this may be an extinction of the desire for further questioning. Further, this experience of obvious truth, while not necessarily preventing the individual investigator from further examining his data, may not arouse his desire for consensual validation. Since one of the greatest strengths of science is its insistence on consensual validation of basic data, this can be a serious drawback. Investigators attempting to develop state-specific sciences will have to learn to distrust the obvious.

A second major problem in developing state-specific sciences is that in some ASC's one's abilities to visualize and imagine are immensely enhanced, so that whatever one imagines seems perfectly real. Thus one can imagine that something is being observed and experience it as datum. If one can essentially conjure up anything one wishes, how can we ever get at truth?

One way of looking at this problem is to consider any such vivid imaginings as potential effects: they are data, in the sense that what can be vividly imagined in a given SoC is important to know. It may not be the case that anything can be imagined with equal facility, and the relationships between what can be imagined may show a lawful pattern.

More generally, the way to approach this problem is to realize that it is not unique to ASC's. One can have all sorts of illusions, and misperceptions in our ordinary SoC. Before the rise of modern physical science, all sorts of things were imagined about the nature of the physical world that could not be directly refuted. The same techniques that eliminated these illusions in the physical sciences will also eliminate them in state-specific sciences dealing with nonphysical data—that is, all observations will have to be subjected to consensual validation and all their theoretical consequences will have to be examined. Insofar as experiences are purely arbitrary imaginings, those that do not show consistent patterns and cannot be replicated will be distinguished from those phenomena which do show general lawfulness.

The effects of this enhanced vividness of imagination in some ASC's will be complicated further by two other important problems, namely, experimenter bias (*8, 9*), and the fact that one person's illusion in a given ASC can sometimes be communicated to another person in the same ASC so that a kind of false consensual validation results. Again, the only long-term solution to this would be the requirement that predictions based on concepts arising from various experiences be verified experientially.

A third major problem is that state-specific sciences probably cannot be developed for all ASC's: some ASC's may depend on or result from genuine deterioration of observational and reasoning abilities, or a deterioration of volition. Those SoC's for which state-specific sciences might well be developed will be discussed later, but it should be made clear that the development of each science should result from trial and error, and not from a priori decisions based on reasoning in our ordinary SoC's.

A fourth major problem is that of ineffability. Some experiences are ineffable in the sense that: (i) a person may experience them, but be unable to express or conceptualize them adequately to himself; (ii) while a person may be able to conceptualize an experience to himself he may not be able to communicate it adequately to anyone else. Certain phenomena of the first type may simply be inaccessible to scientific investigation. Phenomena of the second type may be accessible to scientific investigation only insofar as we are willing to recognize that a science, in the sense of following most of the basic rules, may exist only for a single person. Insofar as such a solitary science would lack all the advantages gained by consensual validation, we could not expect it to have as much power and rigor as conventional scientific endeavor.

Many phenomena which are now considered ineffable may not be so in reality. This may be a matter of our general lack of experience with ASC's and the lack of an adequate language for communicating about ASC phenomena. In most well-developed languages the major part of the vocabulary was developed primarily in adaptation to survival in the physical world.

Finally, we should recognize the possibility that various phenomena of ASC's may be too complex for human beings to understand. The phenomena may depend on or be affected by so many variables that we shall never understand them. In the history of science, however, many phenomena which appeared too complex at first were eventually comprehensible.

**Personal Perils**

The personal perils that an investigator will face in attempting to develop a state-specific science are of two kinds, those associated with reactions colloquially called a bad trip and a good trip, respectively.

Bad trips, in which an extremely unpleasant, emotional reaction is experienced in an ASC, and in which there are possible long-term adverse consequences on a person's personal adjustment, often stem from the fact that our upbringing has not prepared us to undergo radical alterations in our ordinary SoC's. We are dependent on stability, we fear the unknown, and we develop personal rigidities and various kinds of personal and social taboos. It is traditional in our society to consider ASC's as signs of insanity; ASC's therefore cause great fears in those who experience them.

In many ASC's, defenses against unacceptable personal impulses may become partially or wholly ineffective, so the person feels flooded with traumatic material that he cannot handle. All these things result in fear and avoidance of ASC's, and make it difficult or impossible for some individuals to function in an ASC in a way that is consistent with the development of a state-specific science. Maslow (*15*) has discussed these as pathologies of cognition that seriously interfere with the scientific enterprise in general, as well as ordinary life. In principle, adequate selection and training could minimize these hazards for at least some people.

Good trips may also endanger an investigator. A trip may produce experiences that are so rewarding that they interfere with the scientific activity of the investigator. The perception of obvious truth, and its effect of eliminating the need for further investigation or consensual validation have already been mentioned. Another peril comes from the ability to imagine or create vivid experiences. They may be so highly rewarding that the investigator does not follow the rule of investigating the obvious regardless of his personal satisfaction with results. Similarly, his attachment to good feelings, ecstasy, and the like, and his refusal to consider alternative conceptualizations of these, can seriously stifle the progress of investigation.

These personal perils again emphasize the necessity of developing adequate training programs for scientists who wish to develop state-specific sciences. Although it is difficult to envision such a training program, it is evident that much conventional scientific training is contrary to what would be needed to develop a state-specific science, because it tends to produce rigidity and avoidance of personal involvement with subject matter, rather than open-mindedness and flexibility. Much of the training program would have to be devoted to the scientist's understanding of himself so that the (unconscious) effects of his personal biases will be minimized during his investigations of an ASC.

Many of us know that there have been cases where scientists, after becoming personally involved with ASC's, have subsequently become very poor scientists or have experienced personal psychological crises. It would be premature, however, to conclude that such unfortunate consequences cannot be avoided by proper training and discipline. In the early history of the physical sciences we had many fanatics who were nonobjective about their investigations. Not all experiencers of various ASC's develop pathology as a result: indeed, many seem to become considerably more mature. Only from actual attempts to develop state-specific sciences will we be able to determine the actual SoC's that are suitable for development, and the kinds of people that are best suited to such work (*16*).

**Prospects**

I believe that an examination of human history and our current situation provides the strongest argument for the necessity of developing state-specific sciences. Throughout history man has been influenced by the spiritual and mystical factors that are expressed (usually in watered-down form) in the religions that attract the masses of people. Spiritual and mystical experiences are primary phenomena of various ASC's: because of such experiences, untold numbers of both the noblest and most horrible acts of which people are capable have been committed. Yet in all the time that Western science has existed, no concerted attempt has been made to understand these ASC phenomena in scientific terms.

It was the hope of many that religions were simply a form of superstition that would be left behind in our "rational" age. Not only has this hope failed, but our own understanding of the nature of reasoning now makes it clear that it can never be fulfilled. Reason is a tool, and a tool that is wielded in the service of assumptions, beliefs, and needs which are not themselves subject to reason. The irrational, or, better yet, the *a*rational, will not disappear from the human situation. Our immense success in the development of the physical sciences has not been particularly successful in formulating better philosophies of life, or increasing our real knowledge of ourselves. The sciences we have developed to date are not very human sciences. They tell us how to do things, but give us no scientific insights on questions of what to do, what not to do, or why to do things.

The youth of today and mature scientists in increasing numbers are turning to meditation, oriental religions, and personal use of psychedelic drugs. The phenomena encountered in these ASC's provide more satisfaction and are more relevant to the formulation of philosophies of life and deciding upon appropriate ways of living, than "pure reason" (*17*). My own impressions are that very large numbers of scientists are now personally exploring ASC's, but few have begun to connect this personal exploration with their scientific activities.

It is difficult to predict what the chances are of developing state-specific sciences. Our knowledge is still too diffuse and dependent on our normal SoC's. Yet I think it is probable that state-specific sciences can be developed for such SoC's as auto-hypnosis, meditative states, lucid dreaming, marijuana intoxication, LSD intoxication, self-remembering, reverie, and biofeedback-induced states (*18*). In all of these SoC's, volition seems to be retained, so that the observer can indeed carry out experiments on himself or others or both. Some SoC's, in which the volition to experiment during the state may disappear, but in which some experimentation can be carried out if special conditions are prepared before the state is entered, might be alcohol intoxication, ordinary dreaming, hypnogogic and hypnopompic states, and high dreams (*18*). It is not clear whether other ASC's would be suitable for developing state-specific sciences or whether mental deterioration would be too great. Such questions will only be answered by experiment.

I have nothing against religious and mystical groups. Yet I suspect that the vast majority of them have developed compelling belief systems rather than state-specific sciences. Will scientific method be extended to the development of state-specific sciences so as to improve our human situation? Or will the immense power of ASC's be left in the hands of many cults and sects? I hope that the development of state-specific sciences will be our goal.

## References and Notes


1. T. Blackburn, *Science* **172**, 1003 (1971).
2. *Newsweek*, 25 January 1971, p. 52.
3. An attempt to describe the phenomena of marijuana intoxication in terms that make sense to the user, as well as the investigator, has been presented elsewhere. See C. Tart, *On Being Stoned: A Psychological Study of Marijuana Intoxication* (Science & Behavior Books, Palo Alto, 1971).
4. C. Naranjo and R. Ornstein, *On the Psychology of Meditation* (Viking, New York, 1971).
5. Note that an SoC is defined by the stable parameters of the pattern that constitute it, not by the particular technique of inducing that pattern, for some ASC's can be induced by a variety of induction methods. By analogy, to understand the altered computer program you must study what it does, not study the programmer who originally set it up.
6. T. Kuhn, *The Structure of Scientific Revolutions* (Univ. of Chicago Press, Chicago, 1962).
7. Note that states of confusion and impaired functioning are certainly aspects of some drug-induced SoC's, but are not of primary interest here.
8. R. Rosenthal, *Experimenter Effects in Behavioral Research* (Appleton-Century-Crofts, New York, 1966).
9. M. Orne, *Amer. Psychol.* **17**, 776 (1962).
10. A state-specific scientist might find his own work somewhat incomprehensible when he was not in that SoC because of the phenomenon of state-specific memory—that is, not enough of his work would transfer to his ordinary SoC to make it comprehensible, even though it would make perfect sense when he was again in the ASC in which he did his scientific work.
11. "Ordinary consciousness science" is not a good example of a "pure" state-specific science because many important discoveries have occurred during ASC's, such as reverie, dreaming, and meditative-like states.
12. N. Bohr, in *Essays, 1958–1962, on Atomic Physics and Human Knowledge* (Wiley, New York, 1963).
13. B. Ghiselin, *The Creative Process* (New American Library, New York, 1952).
14. E. Green, A. Green, E. Walters, *J. Transpers. Psychol.* **2**, 1 (1970).
15. A. Maslow, *The Psychology of Science: A Reconnaissance* (Harper & Row, New York, 1966).
16. The ASC's resulting from very dangerous drugs (heroin, for example) may be scientifically interesting, but the risk may be too high to warrant our developing state-specific sciences for them. The personal and social issues involved in evaluating this kind of risk are beyond the scope of this article.
17. J. Needleman, *The New Religions* (Doubleday, New York, 1970).
18. C. Tart, *Altered States of Consciousness: A Book of Readings* (Wiley, New York, 1969).


Reprinted from SCIENCE
16 June 1972, Volume 176, pp. 1203-1210

# 3

## SMITH, A.

# Alumni Notes — Altered States University

**Wall Street Buddhist** 'Adam Smith'—the pen name by which Jerry Goodman is best known—devotes his original and iconoclastic mind to a pair of subjects: high finance and psychological highs. He brings the wisdom of wit to both, but you can guess which pays better.

Goodman's 1968 book *The Money Game* is to my mind the most authentic study of financiers since Thomas Lawson's 1905 book on *Frenzied Finance*. He followed up last year with a second monograph, *Supermoney*, on the Wall Street cults that transform the illusion of future earnings into tangible cash. He writes as a participant observer, an investor and veteran money-manager, who has done his share of the ghost-dancing.

His experience in consciousness research is no less direct. He took controlled doses of LSD in UCLA's 1960 lab experiments on creativity and the unconscious. He later got into the literature of humanistic psychology, went through transactional analysis and other group techniques.

By last summer the stock market had become his secondary concern. He went full time into the meditational disciplines taught in New York by Oscar Ichazo. His skeptical mind resisted "Oscar the Sufi," as this report indicates, but the experience itself told him that he was on to something worth several more years of work.

Finance and mysticism, he says, are not exactly separate subjects. For wry evidence, he offers his *Money Game* list of market aphorisms:

"Prices have no memory, and yesterday has nothing to do with tomorrow."

"If you don't know who you are, the market is an expensive place to find out."

"A stock is going up as long as it's going up."

"The stock doesn't know you own it."

Goodman now hears such aphorisms—like the warning not to confuse object and subject—in a richer context. "The lessons of Zen can be applied to the market," he says, and admits to an occasional game of yoga-tennis. My guess is that given a few years and a few articles for practice, he will do for consciousness what he has done to Wall Street.—

T GEORGE HARRIS

"What am I doing here?"

That question used to occur to me sometimes as I was doing my Arica homework—say, sitting in the middle of a large flower I had drawn myself with Sanskrit letters on the petals, playing the note E on my $1.98 G. Schirmer recorder, and chanting *bam*, as the way of opening a *chakra* at the sixth dorsal vertebrae. But the question could be ascribed to a large dose of culture shock, because I had come to Arica directly from working on a book with a financial background, *Supermoney*. The distance from the Federal Reserve Bank of New York to Arica was absolutely mind-boggling, but then mind-boggling is part of what Arica is about.

I knew how I got there. One day there was this big full-page ad in the *New York Times*, headlined *The Mosquito That Bites the Iron Bull*, and it told how several dozen Americans had gone to spend 10 months with Oscar Ichazo, and they found the experience so important that 42 of them decided to become a teaching community in New York, because, Oscar said, "New York City contains more people prepared for reality than the world has previously seen in one culture." The ad mentioned exercises such as "protoanalysis" and "psychocatalizers" which would lead to "the awareness of the tiger," "Permanent 24," or total awareness. And then, practically at the same time there was John Lilly in *Psychology Today*, M.D., psychiatrist, eminent scientist, famous for working with dolphins. John Lilly took his Arica experience very seriously indeed, and described it in *The Center of the Cyclone*.

"Successful heads of corporations and bureaucracies," Lilly said in *Psychology Today*, ". . . already operate at satori 24. They are joyfully locked into their work. But they have never had maps which suggested to them the possibility of achieving more blissful levels of consciousness . . . what might happen if they could visualize the possibility of spending the weekend in satori 12, or even of achieving satori three, in which they would realize that their essences are hooked to every other essence in the whole universe?"

I wasn't at all sure about those satori levels—they sounded something like the difference between a Star Scout and a Life Scout, you have to be a Scout to know the difference—but I did know people in the financial world who were certainly totally occupied, or preoccupied, playing the musical chairs game of money management with zest and enjoyment and vibrating, for all I knew, in level 24. I wanted to explore some areas of psychology, and this seemed about as far out as you could go. Why not go far out first, and work one's way back? So: mapmaking! They used to put pictures of elephants on the maps of Africa and print "unexplored."

When my financial chores were done some time later, I signed up for a three-month course—six days a week, 12 hours a day—in what Sam Keen calls Oscar's "university for altered states of consciousness." At least I thought it was a course, and so did the 60 or so other people in my training group. I say "thought" because many of them are still there more than a year later. Among the trainees were a handful of psychologists and psychiatrists, another handful of writers and critics, still another handful of housewives, and a large number of students and former Esalenites. Many of them came, not because they read John Lilly, but because they knew someone who had already been through Arica. We didn't live together, although most of the students who had come from out of town lived in the same apartment building on Manhattan's Upper West Side. Some were there to get themselves together, some to explore, and some to—one put it—"get high on the exercises, and stay high."

What was it like? Well, it was certainly unlike any other school I've known. Schools in our culture are built around the rational and linear, around competition and problem-solving. Not this trip. We had to bypass the mind and go straight to the experience. The mind is controlled by what Oscar calls Ego, endless streams of words, chatter and images. Consequently, we simply came in each day and did what they told us to do that day, "they" being the group who had been to Chile initially. If we had started with the concept, then the associative mind would have presented the whole experience through the filter it had already constructed.

To me, the experience it seemed closest to was basic training in the Army, but everyone has subjective reactions and when I mentioned that simile it proved to be very unpopular. (In Ego Reduction, one man told me, "Your whole personality is that of a sloppy World War II bomber pilot.") Nonetheless, in my basic training unit, in the garrison Army of the '50s, nobody ever gave us a concept, we simply fell out into the company street every morning and did what they told us, and our attitude was that all we had to do was bring ourselves; the Army's job was to process us into soldiers. At Arica they said, "you do not do the exercises, the exercises will do you." Coming from competition and problem-solving, that's very relaxing.

The early weeks were very physical, with an hour-and-a-half gym, and other hours of movement and dance. We did breathing exercises and chants and mantrams, and we did other exercises to try to empty our minds. That's hard; the mind certainly resists being emptied. We did several kinds of meditation. We had our fixations diagnosed (see page 68) to learn what games we had invented to compensate for our essential lacks. Then we had positions and chants and lectures to dissipate the fixations and bring us back to pure essence. We had group exercises to make one big body out of the group.

We had some talented musicians who drummed and played us to our exercises, and lots of electronic equipment, so that we could watch our own videotaped exercises a few minutes after they had been performed. We went on a high-protein, low-carbohydrate diet, no alcohol: most people lost weight and looked in much better shape. Wouldn't you have gotten into shape if you just went on a diet? asked some friends. If you just spent the summer at the beach? I don't know; I didn't spend the summer at the beach.

Most of the work was presented with grim seriousness; occasionally—say when acting out our fixations—we could have outbursts of humor. What pulled us forward was a tremendous sense of *expectation*. Everybody, or practically everybody, had read about John Lilly and the exotic spaces he had gotten to; each exercise was bringing us one step closer to Permanent 24, total awareness.

On Sundays we did a particular set of exercises in Central Park. New York is either ready for reality or it doesn't give a damn, because the sight of 60 people carrying rocks in an irregular, solemn, meditative pace didn't even slow down the dog-walkers, horsemen, and bicycle racers.

We didn't see Oscar at all for the first month, and in fact the previous training session had seen him hardly at all. Oscar appeared one night—in his socks, like everybody else, since all shoes are left at the door at Arica—smallish, balding, and looking, well, very Latin American, in a sport shirt. Oscar's talks always had something of the air of a presidential press conference because there were so many microphones in front of him, microphones to record on cassettes whatever he said. In the question period, he was always addressed simply as "Oscar." Of all the gurus in history, we must have had the only Oscar. He spoke with a heavy Spanish accent, but with favorite English phrases: "now we have to be really sharp", "now here come another thing."

From Oscar's first appearance, the training took what seemed to be a sharp turn. First of all, it was a group trip, not an individual trip; in the Orient such a course would have taken many years, maybe 10, maybe 20; the group energy would make it go faster. And it wasn't for individual self-improvement, it was for humanity, because humanity faced a crisis in the next 10 years. It wasn't just a course, then, that we had signed up for? No, humanity had to come to consciousness, or face possible extinction.

We saw much more of Oscar as the training went on. At the end of three months, we found the training we had been given would never be given again; Oscar had been looking for two to three hundred *teachers*; now there would be an additional training of two months or so, and then everybody would go out and teach. "I wanted to give," Oscar said, "the impression of all the culture of our planet before, in different exercises, Tibetan, Sufi, yoga. The more ways you know, the more clear is the idea of the central point. You are not going to be attracted by the ornamental and outside things."

Our additional two months' training was called the Open Path—though that name has now fallen upon something else. All the groups who had ever been through Arica took this simultaneously, including the pilgrims who had gone to Chile, for it was new to everybody. The physical and experiential sectors declined in favor of theory and group exercises. Our notebooks grew fat with details on passions and fixations, for we were, after all, going to have to diagnose and classify the public we were shortly to teach. And we had numbers of lectures on what Oscar called trialectics, in which everything is seen as process.

Some of the trainees had by now gone back to their jobs or their families; in general, those who *had* jobs or families. Most, but not all, of those remaining were younger people—quite young in some cases—who hadn't come from any particular structure except an academic one. In Arica, they found a structure that met their needs, and group spirit was quite high.

Arica, Oscar said, was going to have to become a tribe. Eventually all humanity would have to become a tribe. With the tribe taking care of all needs, the individual trip could easily be given up. The tribal community took care of some needs so well that a number of couples split up. It is a tenet of Oscar's that a tribe can bring up children better than parents. The work was shared: office work, answering the telephone, baby-sitting in the nursery, cleaning.

In the Open Path training, we went through exercises to rid ourselves of the karma of sex, power and money. Some of those who had money freed themselves enough of its karmic power to make contributions to the group, like good tribal members. "This school is the most important thing going on on the planet at this time," Oscar said. "Arica is going to reconcile mysticism and the modern world. We are talking about a different psychological order of man, with a different psychological structure." The new order of man, totally balanced, instincts in harmony, would be ready for the Wave, or the crisis of the planet.

As for myself, I wanted to learn all that Arica could offer, but I began to have glimmers that if Permanent 24 could come only through being a good tribal member, I was going to have to vibrate on some other level, at least for awhile. I didn't want to make any judgments—only the ego makes judgments—but Arica was developing something we used to call in the money business, "limousine syndrome." A company has a tight budget and a good product and it has a hot year, and then the president starts going to work in a limousine. That's when you sell the stock, because the controller isn't going to pull so tightly on the strings when he has just had to justify the president's limousine, and the margin for error starts to decrease.

Before I left to go back to my own work, I sat in on a Finance Committee meeting one day. There was a discussion on how much to pay everybody. As students, we had paid a hefty tuition, but as student teachers, Arica would pay us. Those who had some money were not expected to draw money. But it all seemed academic to me, because I was used to post-Renaissance bookkeeping, assets and liabilities, which says that if you don't have the money in the bank, you don't pay everybody a lot. But one stalwart said everyone should get $1,000 a month. "I can't be in *satori* on less than $1,000 a month," he said. That was agreed upon, and everybody was paid $1,000 a month. The payroll was then twice what it had been in my old company, but my old company had been making $1,000,000 before taxes, and Arica had yet to meet the public and start charging tuition. Obviously, if I felt ill at ease, I was still in my old ego type and hadn't been cleansed totally of my money karma. But I remembered an old Sufi saying: "Trust in Allah, but tie your camel first."

Of the 300 or so people who went through the intensive training, a goodly number are now out teaching the shorter courses, courses which, it is hoped, wake the course-taker up a bit. For some months they were on salary financed in part by the donations of wealthier students and in part by tuition fees. More recently, the teaching was franchised to those who wanted to do it. The New York headquarters shrank down to a comparative handful, and those in the field were left on their own. There were teaching houses in San Francisco, New York and Los Angeles, and teaching teams in Washington, San Diego, Pittsburgh, Miami and Riker's Island prison, and there were rock commercials on the radio advertising the courses. Some of the original students gave up their studies or their professions and went out to teach the word. Others drifted away, some upset by a selection process determining "levels" made through a nonrational process by a group with the highest level. A few were told to leave. Nobody said who had determined who had the highest level, or how that was divined. In San Francisco, several of the original trainers who dropped out because they were distressed by the orthodoxy said they were going to set up a short course to "detoxify Arica dropouts." In the Army—to go back to my unpopular simile—you do things the Army way, as our old First Sergeant used to tell us in no uncertain terms. Some people reenlist and love it, and some can't stand it and leave. Some people change radically in group energy; others turn back on their individualism.

I never spent any time alone with Oscar during the training, but after the training I spent several afternoons with him. Naturally, there was a lot of talk about Oscar at our school, but nobody really knew very much about him. He was, it was said, a Latin aristocrat whose family was in the copper business, whose father had been chief of security in the Bolivian Army and was once Ambassador to England. Oscar was, it was said, a samurai master, learned as a boy from Japanese, interned in Bolivia in World War II. He was, it was also said, a Sufi master, whatever that is. Sufi master is not like Berkeley Ph.D. You cannot call up Sufi U. and check the graduation date, because there is no Sufi U. anywhere.

Oscar has great personal charm, and he tells stories effectively, even with his lack of English vocabulary, because you tend to fill in the gaps when he pauses. Some of his stories sound like early "Terry and the Pirates," before Terry got so Air Force square-jawed. (Oscar even had a Chilean lady friend whom some in the original Chile group called the Dragon Lady.) (Fade in: "Terry and the Pirates" music, beaded curtains parting.) Oscar is studying the *I Ching* in Kowloon. Through the *I Ching* Master, Oscar meets still another Master, this one in *I Ching* and in Chinese martial arts. The second Master throws the *I Ching* to tell Oscar's fortune, and then he stares at him. Apparently those *I Ching* hexagrams haven't come up before like this, and the *I Ching* has announced that Oscar is the one presented by Fate, who is supposed to be taught. So Oscar goes back to his hotel and gets his things and moves in with the very old Master, who is maybe 96. "I couldn't believe it," Oscar says. "His skin was like a baby's. I could never catch him, in any exercise. He told me, you have to live like you are living your last second. This idea of awareness is very old. He taught me to go inside sleep without sleeping. This is not so far out, animals do it, we did it ourselves in the jungle, you are sleeping but you are awake. I learned psychoalchemy from the martial arts."

"Psychoalchemy" is one of Oscar's compound captions, like "kinerhythm" and "psychocatalizer." There are probably Sanskrit terms for them, or Tibetan, or whatever, but Oscar likes them better with a 20th-century gloss, and he has a gift for them that would make him an asset at Procter and Gamble's agency, or at the underwriters who re-christen new electronics companies. (Merck or Upjohn could go up 10 points just by announcing they were going into "psychocatalizers.") He also has a flair for improvising rites and ceremonies. (At least they look improvised from the outside, but maybe all revelations look improvised from the outside.) In one of my interviews, we were talking about Chu'a Ka. That was something we didn't have in our training, some sort of 12-hour massage that "cleans the karma from the body." The memory of various traumas is imbedded in the cells of parts of the body. To be without inhibiting fear, the Mongolian warriors went through this massage. "But we have to think of another name," Oscar said. "If we are ever going to teach it, then we need a better name."

Yet for all of Oscar's facility with compounding words, it was an impatience with word culture, or the idea that words were an expression of the Ego and hence a block to learning, that led him into more esoteric exercises.

"In Bolivia," Oscar said, "I was totally involved in sciences when I was a boy, medicine, anatomy, physiology, biology. At 12 or so I was a prodigy to the doctors, like Mozart. By the time I went to Buenos Aires, I had learned everything our culture can offer. Words words words words words words."

Even though the training was over at this point—at least for a while—I didn't have any idea where the course derived from. I had found the enneagram, its geometric backbone anyway, Ouspensky's *In Search of the Miraculous*. Was this all from Gurdjieff?

"No, not so much," Oscar said. "It was a total mystical revelation. It really came in several stages of awareness. One time I went to the desert in Cordova, in a Sufi elder exercise, Essene (?). I spent my 40 days. I felt my head become exactly as the Tarot card, the Cup. But at that time I didn't even know the Tarot at all. It was like a hallucinogen, only with a hallucinogen you don't control, you have fear. My head became pure light. And the enneagram—another time I was seeing the enneagram and a kind of anger came to me; I was furious; a different person. Suddenly I was in a space without connection, my consciousness went inside the enneagram. I danced in the enneagram. I returned from the experience and each enneagram was separate and complete. It was very hard to put into words. Of course, this was my psychic projection."

Whatever the problems of words—of language—Oscar believes that the common language for the planetary culture is science. "We are still in the transition from the different cultures to the planetary culture. Psychology is the most important thing in the next culture."

"When you say psychology," I asked, "what do you mean?"

"The knowledge of the interior structure of the human psyche," Oscar said.

"How do you distinguish Arica from what we know as psychology?"

"Psychology is still very new—say, 60 years old or so. It has the defects of a new thing. If Occidental psychology becomes more a religion, then it will stay with simple theories. Reality is not so simple.

"For example, psychology doesn't know the most important points: Psychology doesn't know what *consciousness* is. Psychology doesn't know what *dream* is. Psychology doesn't know what *time* is for.

"We can't speak about consciousness when we are in thought association. When you are in the process of thinking you *are* that thinking. Only when it is stopped are you aware of yourself. You lose your real identity when you sink in mind. We can't speak about dreams if the awake state is subjective and attached, because then the dream state is subjective and attached, too. And psychology doesn't know we have to deal with relative times. We know from the hallucinogens, you can change time.

"Psychology is discovering what we already did. A culture starts when man rediscovers Void, what the game is. In the Occident, that isn't part of the culture."

Well, that gives you an hors d'oeuvre. If you asked me for a total and rational evaluation of Arica, I would have to disappoint you. There are certainly energies that esoteric schools have learned to tap, but the translation of that into planetary change is harder to see. There is a Catch-22 here, which is that to communicate about this you have to use language and accommodation of the world, and language belongs to the ego and the ego is not to be trusted. It sounds spooky, unless you're used to what Andrew Weil called stoned thinking, but then if you read it cold, the Angel Moroni speaking to Joseph Smith and the beginnings of the Mormons—to take one example within the last 150 years—doesn't fit within the rational parameters of our culture either. If you talk to God, that's called prayer, and both football coaches do it simultaneously before the game. If God talks to you, that's called schizophrenia.

Recently I drove down to talk to John Lilly. He seemed to have relaxed from the enthusiasm in *The Center of the Cyclone*. "I told Oscar," he said, "I was only interested in what I could take from his trip as a scientist. It will be interesting to see whether Oscar gets corrupted by American success and energy. I like Oscar, but I think he might. What Oscar doesn't realize is that the *real* mystical trip is Western science."

Once your consciousness has been changed, you are in a different state. I reminded Oscar of the first ad, and I asked him if anybody in the school was in Permanent 24. There were people who had gone to Chile for 10 months, and had been through everything since, training for almost three years; there were others who had gone through intensive training of shorter duration; had anybody reached that state of total clarity and awareness?

"No, nobody," Oscar said. "Not really. Not yet. Permanent 24 takes much more work."

# 4

LILLY, J. C.

## *Epilogue from the Center of the Cyclone*

It is necessary for me to state clearly where I am in regard to this autobiography as of the time of completing it. I have moved beyond where I was when I experienced the recorded events and beyond where I was when I wrote about the experiences. Inevitably one moves. Nothing that I have written is final, completed or closed.

As I stated in the *Human Biocomputer*, I am a scientific explorer, nothing more, nothing less. My loyaltics are to objective exploration, objective experiment, and repeatable testable observations. I value above all else verifiable operational theory, which gives one insight into universal nature and our own inner natures. My tests are pragmatic empirical with minimal necessity for faith in the generalizations of others. I abhor dogmas and the dogmatic doctrinaire "unique truth" of the esoteric schools. I have no room for zealots or fanatics, or the tyranny over the individual of anaclitic grouping.

Man's future lies with aware courageous informed knowledgeable experienced individuals in a loosely coupled exploratory communicating network. Such a network exists and functions beautifully with gentle effectiveness throughout this planet. I suspect it extends farther than our earth, but this is yet to be publicly demonstrated unequivocally beyond the private experience of myself and of others.

My own skepticism is intact—please keep yours. Skepticism is a necessary instrument in the exploration of the unknown. Humor is even more necessary, especially in regard to one's own self and one's observations and records. Full dispassionate detachment implies cosmic comedy with each of us a fun-loving player. Cosmic love is ruthlessly loving: whether you like it or not it loves you, teaches you, teases you, plays with you, surprises you.

It is all too easy to preach "go with the flow." The main problem is identifying what the flow is, here and now. Is a pattern I think I see "the flow" or is this my limited beliefs operating on insufficient data abstracting a false flow? One's maps and metamaps measure the flow—one's resistance measures the direction and the velocity. Without clear maps one cannot even see the flow, much less go with it. Even when one truly goes with the flow one had better touch shore or bottom once in a while to be sure one isn't just floating in the stagnant waters of secure beliefs.

Sometime the flow leads into rapids and whirlpools—here I suggest following the advice of the fold-boaters; when your boat turns over in the rapids, kick free of it and swim toward the light. No matter what happens, no matter who gives what advice, swim toward the light of your own truth.

In the book I illustrate a general principle of living and being. It is a principle I wrote out in the *Human Biocomputer*. Here I revise and enlarge it. In a scientific exploration of any of the inner realities, I follow the following metaprogrammatic steps:

1. Examine whatever one can of where the new spaces are, what the basic beliefs are to go there.
2. Take on the basic beliefs of that new area as if true.
3. Go into the area fully aware, in high energy, storing everything, no matter how neutral, how ecstatic, or how painful the experiences become.

4. Come back here, to our best of consensus realities, temporarily shedding those basic beliefs of the new area and taking on those of the investigator impartially dispassionately objectively examining the recorded experiences and data.

5. Test one's current models of this consensus reality.

6. Construct a model that includes this reality and the new one in a more inclusive succinct way. No matter how painful such revisions of the models are be sure they include both realities.

7. Do not worship, revere, or be afraid of any person, group, space, or reality. An investigator, an explorer, has no room for such baggage.

I used this system many times in my life; in the early isolation work, in the tank work with LSD, in the Esalen experiences, in the Chile work. Each time I made what reconnaissance I could, entered the new area with enthusiasm and as openly as I could, took on the local beliefs as if true, experienced the region intensely, and finally moved out again, shedding the beliefs while critically examining the data and reprogramming my theories.

In my own way I have found that deep understanding is the best path for me into the unknown, the "highest" states of consciousness. I fully expect to continue to pursue this path. I consider everything I have written as transitional—as the exploration deepens and widens so we will be able to do a better job of mapping and exploring and further mapping.

As of today I have found no final answers, I am intent on continuing the search. Am I just the leader of 100 billions of connected cells? If so, who elected me leader? Where did the cells come from? If I am more than just the net result of 100 billions of cells living cooperatively, where did I come from?

The miracle is that the universe created a part of itself to study the rest of it, that this part, in studying itself, finds the rest of the universe in its own natural inner realities.

## SPERRY, R. W.

# 5

# *Hemispheric Specialization of Mental Faculties in the Brain of Man**

The following deals with aspects of brain organization that help to shape some of the basic features of that complex referred to in the conference theme as "the person." Among other things the observations bare on questions concerning problems of cerebral dominance and handedness, the relation of conscious awareness to brain mechanisms, the inherent individuality of the person, differences between verbal and spatial modes of thinking, and between the male and the female mind and related questions.

The material that I'll be drawing on comes from collaborative studies with a long line of colleagues on a group of brain-operated patients. These are mostly patients of Drs. Philip Vogel and Joseph Bogen, neurosurgeons at the White Memorial Medical Center in Los Angeles, and most of them have undergone essentially the same rather special type of brain operation for control of epileptic convulsions. Put crudely, this operation consists of having the brain divided down the middle into its right and left halves. More precisely, the surgery involves a selective section of the bands of nerve fibers that cross-connect the left and right hemispheres. This is a kind of surgery that is undertaken only in extreme cases as a last resort measure in an effort to control epileptic seizures that are not contained by medication. It represents a last-ditch stand against advancing, life-threatening epilepsy.

Skipping over details, the surgery in effect eliminates all direct cross-talk between the hemispheres. Because the brain is bisymmetric in all its parts, each of the disconnected hemispheres retains a full complement, or complete set of brain centers and their interconnections, for all the different kinds of cerebral functions, excepting only those that require left-right crossconnection between the hemispheres. From the standpoint of brain anatomy, the surgery creates a number of obvious problems for brain function. Recall that the optic

---

* This article is based on a lecture presented in the 1971 Beckman Evening Lecture Series of the California Institute of Technology. Work of the author and his laboratory is supported by grant #MH 03372 of the National Institute of Mental Health of the U.S. Public Health Service and by the F. P. Hixon Fund of the California Institute of Technology.

image of the outside world on its way into the brain gets split down the middle, with the left half of the visual field being projected into the right hemisphere, and vice versa. Normally these two cortical half-fields are cross-connected by fibers that run through the callosum and they therefore are left unconnected after the surgery. The same applies to the sensory representation of the hands and the legs, and also for the primary motor control of the limbs, the left side of the body being represented in the right hemisphere, and the right side in the left hemisphere. Language is centered in the left hemisphere of the typical right-handed individual, and is thus cut off after the surgery from information relating to the left half of the visual field, the left side of the body, the right nostril, and from everything else that goes on in the opposite right hemisphere.

In view of these extensive anatomical disconnections and the fact that the corpus callosum is the largest fiber system of the brain by far, it is fair to say that one of the most remarkable effects of this kind of surgery is the apparent lack of effect, insofar as ordinary daily behavior goes. A person two years recovered from such an operation could easily go through a complete routine medical examination without revealing that anything was particularly wrong to someone not acquainted with his medical history. This is what prompted our studies on the callosum in the beginning. The remarkable lack of symptoms after surgical section, and also with congenital absence of the corpus callosum, had become one of the more challenging puzzles in brain research back in the 1940's and '50's, and was being cited to support radical, almost mystical theories of how brains operate at their upper levels without depending on specific fiber connections.

Despite the deceptive normality of these people under ordinary conditions and in contradiction to earlier neurological doctrine, we can now demonstrate with appropriate testing procedures a whole multitude of distinct impairments in cerebral cross-integration. These are most simply summarized by saying that the surgically disconnected left and right hemispheres function independently with respect to most mental activities. Each hemisphere, in other words, has its own private sensations, perceptions, thoughts, ideas and feelings, all cut off from the corresponding experiences in the opposite hemisphere. Each left and right hemisphere has its own private chain of memories and learning experiences that are inaccessible to recall by the other hemisphere. In other words, each of the disconnected hemispheres can be said to possess a separate mind of its own.

This condition is manifested in many ways in different kinds of test situations(1). For example, following the surgery these people are unable to recognize or remember a visual stimulus item that they have just looked at if it is presented across the vertical midline in the opposite half of the visual field. The usual perceptual transfer that one normally expects to find between the left and right halves of vision is lacking. Similarly, things identified by touch with one hand cannot be found or recognized with the other hand. Odors identified through one nostril are not recognized through the other. Further, these people are unable to name or to talk or to write about things seen in the left half field of vision, things felt with the left hand or foot, odors smelled through the right nostril, or things heard by the right hemisphere.

Most of these deficits are easily compensated or concealed under ordinary conditions, as by eye movements, shifting of the hands, etc., and they require controlled lateralized testing procedures for their demonstration. We test the function of each hemisphere separately by confining the sensory input, central processing, or/and the motor readout to a single hemisphere. The visual material is flashed to left or right half field at 1/10 of a second, too fast for eye movements to get the material into the wrong half of the visual field. Under these conditions the subjects regularly report that they do not see stimuli projected to the left of center, as if they were blind in the left half field.

However, with a change of testing procedure, the subjects proceed to correctly point to a matching object or to retrieve with the left hand a corresponding object, showing that they are quite capable of recognizing and identifying among a choice array the very same stimulus that they have just told us they did not see. The hemisphere that talks to us did not in fact see the left field stimulus; this was seen only by the opposite, right hemisphere, which, lacking speech, is able to express itself only by manual responses. The subjects appear thus to possess two distinct inner visual worlds, cut off from each other, and each oblivious of the existence of the other. Many similar performances of this kind, reviewed and presented elsewhere, support the conclusion that each hemisphere has its own separate domain of conscious awareness.

The conflict and disruption of behavior that might be expected to result from having two separate control systems competing to run the one body tends to be counteracted by a large variety of unifying factors. Whereas the main wiring of the brain is lateralized and crossed, there exist also some weaker uncrossed sensory and motor systems, which though relatively crude, do help greatly to keep the behavior unified. Just the unity of eyeball optics, for example, assures that whenever one hemisphere moves the eyes to fix on a target, the other hemisphere also is conjugately locked on the exact same target at all times. Effective use of the various unifying mechanisms of this kind can apparently be enhanced to a considerable extent through training, learning, and re-education, particularly in the younger patients. The youngest of the present group, operated at age 13, performs cross-integrations today with increasing facility that he was quite unable to perform during the first year or two after surgery.

The extreme to which this kind of functional compensation can go is illustrated in the occasional rare individual born without a corpus callosum, but in whom the remainder of the brain remains essentially normal. Only about 17 such cases have been recorded in medical history, most of whom were discovered at autopsy in post-mortem examinations because during life the condition is asymptomatic and hence does not attract medical attention.

A few years ago Dr. Saul and I had an opportunity to examine and study such a person (2). This was a 19-year-old college Sophomore making an average scholastic record, and presumed normal until hospitalized for a series of headaches. X-rays revealed a congenital total absence of the corpus callosum. Her total I.Q. was slightly above average at 104. To make a long story short, she performed all the tests that we had devised for the surgical patients with no difficulty, responding essentially like a normal control subject. Apparently she had greatly enriched by practice and use the function of the uncrossed fiber systems of the brain as well as those of the anterior commissure which remained intact. Also, there was evidence from lateral amytal tests, that she had developed language in both hemispheres. All this speaks for the functional plasticity of the developing, still growing brain as compared to the adult brain.

However, there is another side to the story. The necessary crowding of both the language plus the non-language functions together into each hemisphere instead of the more usual left-right division of labor, apparently was not achieved without paying a price. Further testing on more complex mental tasks showed her performance to be sub-normal in working spatial puzzles, making block designs, in drawing, in object assembly, and in a variety of perceptual motor tasks, like stringing beads, putting pegs in holes, and buttoning clothes, all performed for speed. Whereas she was above normal in verbal reasoning, she was very low in non-verbal reasoning. In school she was poor in mathematics, particularly in geometry, and had exceptional trouble in map tests and in geography. This array of deficits in non-verbal performances contrasted with her above normal score of 112 on the verbal portion of the WAIS. In general, these difficulties appear to reflect weakness in the mental specialties of the non-verbal hemisphere. With both the language and the non-language functions obliged to share the same hemisphere on each side, the verbal faculties had apparently developed at the expense of the non-verbal.

What we're getting into here is the general problem of cerebral dominance and lateral specialization of function. In sub-human mammals the hemispheres are essentially symmetric in their basic functional potential, but in man we have to deal with right-left specialization. In these commissurotomy patients we have an exceptional opportunity to make direct comparison between the performances of the left and right hemispheres working independently on the exact same task in the same individual. The results of such studies generally strengthen and extend the evidence for hemispheric specialization.

We have already seen that practically all speech and writing and calculation were found to be centered in the disconnected left hemisphere. This verbal hemisphere is also the more aggressive, executive, leading hemisphere and seems to carry the main load of behavior postoperatively. It is the dominant and highly developed capacities of the left hemisphere that apparently are responsible in large part for the earlier impressions that the cerebral functions continue unimpaired in the absence of the corpus callosum. The minor, right hemisphere lacking language, and like the animal brain, unable therefore to communicate what it is thinking or experiencing, is much less accessible to investigation. The nature and the quality of the inner mental life of the silent right hemisphere has accordingly remained relatively obscure.

Some authorities have been reluctant to credit the minor

hemisphere even with being conscious, contending that it must exist in a kind of reflex, trancelike, or automaton state, the reasoning being that the conscious self by nature has to be single and unified. Actually the evidence as we see it favors the view that the minor is very much conscious, and further that both of the disconnected left and right hemispheres may be conscious simultaneously in different and even in conflicting mental experiences that run along in parallel. From its non-verbal responses we infer that the minor hemisphere senses, perceives, and has ideas and feelings all at a characteristically human level, and that it learns and remembers and is even superior to the major hemisphere in certain types of tasks.

The exceptional activities at which the disconnected minor hemisphere has been found to excel are firstly, of course, all non-verbal performances. The disconnected minor hemisphere is found to be superior in the construction of block designs, in copying and drawing various test figures, and in the construction of spatial representations generally (3, 4), in cross-modal spatial transformations (5), in the spatial parts of the Raven's Progressive Matrices Test(6), in identifying and recalling nondescript *shapes* or *forms* made of bent wire perceived and identified by touch alone(7), in the perception of part-whole relationships (8), and in discriminating the unification of fragmented figures(8). In addition to being all non-verbal activities, all those various tasks at which the right hemisphere is found to be superior, seem to a large extent to involve a direct apprehension and cognitive processing of spatial form and spatial relations as such.

Scanning movements of the eyes from the right to the left edge of an object being examined in free vision would result in the projection of two complete perceptual images in the divided brain, one in each hemisphere(9). The well-known constancy of the visual image in the presence of eye movement must be taken into account. This right-left reduplication of perceptual images is something that would seem logically to occur also in the normal brain, and we have long wondered what good may be served by such a redundant doubling in the cerebral operations. However, if as we now suspect, each hemisphere processes its sensory information in distinctly different ways, then such a doubling begins to make sense.

In the normal intact brain the right and left contributions in any given perceptual experience become fused, making it difficult or impossible to determine which hemisphere is doing what. In a series of studies still in progress headed by Trevarthen and Levy (10), we have been deliberately arranging it so that different, mutually conflicting sensory images are seen on right and left sides simultaneously. The aim is to set up rival, competing processes that also will evoke distinctly different right and left responses, from which we can then infer more about dominance and what each hemisphere contributes to any given perceptual experience. The procedure involves the use of composite left-right visual stimuli flashed at 1/10 of a second, with the subject's gaze centered in the midline. Each hemisphere completes the missing half of its own ½ stimulus according to a general perceptual rule applied to brain lesions. This means that the two hemispheres think they see different things at the same point in space at the same time, something that the normal brain of course does not do.

Since each hemisphere has its own inner visual world, neither knowing what the other is experiencing, the subject's remain blandly unaware that there's anything particularly strange in the chimeric stimuli, even in the face of leading questions. The same principle has been used further by Trevarthen and Levy to test for the perception of geometric and nondescript figures, the perception of movement, of words, of serial patterns, colors, and various combinations of these. The question is, which side will dominate under different test conditions, that is, with different categories of test material, with different mental and motor sets, with different forms of readout, central processing, and so on.

In general, the results conform with the earlier findings in that if linguistic processing of any kind is involved, the subject's response is dominated by the left hemisphere, that is, they select in favor of the right half of the composite stimulus.For the perception of faces, however, and for any direct visual-to-visual matching of shape or pattern, the right hemisphere dominates and the subject selects the left half of the composite stimulus. Nondescript shapes difficult to discriminate verbally were found to be exceedingly difficult for the left hemisphere, even when they were presented exclusively to the one hemisphere with no competing stimulus on the opposite side. It is interesting that the right hemisphere was found to dominate the verbal hemisphere even in the case of words presented in cursive script provided that no interpretation of the word meaning was involved.

Under these testing conditions the subjects show signs of confusion and conflict as secondary effects when one hemisphere sees or hears the other giving what the first hemisphere considers to be an incorrect response. This is something we have to deal with all along in working with these people. When this happens the correctly informed hemisphere may give a disgusted, negative shake of the head; or if it is the verbal hemisphere it may make remarks like, "Now why did I do that? What made me do that?" We purposely don't dwell on these confusions and pass on to the next trial.

However, this kind of annoyance in the second hemisphere with what is a correct response for the first hemisphere, along with the occasional double correct responses in which first one and then the other hemisphere gives a different and correct response, gives further support to the conclusion that each hemisphere is indeed having its own separate and different perceptual experience, with both being conscious simultaneously in parallel.

The chimeric findings reaffirm the earlier impression that the left and right hemispheres perceive and apprehend things in different ways. In dealing with faces, for example, the right hemisphere seems to respond to the whole face directly as a perceptual unit, whereas the left hemisphere seems to see separate salient features, like a mustache, eyebrows, hair, etc., to which verbal labels are easily attached.

Another thing to come out of these latter studies is the demonstration that the minor hemisphere is quite capable of capturing and controlling the motor system of the body under conditions in which it is in equal and free competition with the major hemisphere, that is, the sensory input is equated and the subject is quite free to use either the left or the right hand. We have not seen this so convincingly before. It suggests that in the normal, intact brain, the control of voluntary, willed movement is not routed entirely through the major dominant hemisphere, but comes partly in some activities directly from the minor hemisphere.

Looking back over the evidence one sees an implication that strong, cerebral dominance and specialization is good, whereas cerebral ambivalence is not so good. If it be true that a hemisphere committed to language is thereby handicapped in spatial, perceptual, nonverbal functions like geometry, drawing, sculpture, mechanical ingenuity, then this should show up statistically in a population of left-handers in an analysis of their I.Q. subtest profile. Left-handers are more bilaterialized for language, that is, they are more apt to have some language represented also in the minor hemisphere as is shown in the way they recover from cerebral injuries. Comparing a group of 10 left-handers with 15 right-handers, all graduate science students, Levy (5) found that left-handers showed three times a greater discrepancy between the performance and the verbal scales on the Wechsler Adult Intelligence Scale, with the performance score, which reflects predominantly right hemisphere functions, always lower, as predicted.

A similar discrepancy was reported by Lansdell (11) for persons who had developed right hemisphere speech as a result of cerebral trauma suffered early in life. Further, Nebes (8) using his part-whole circle-arc test, found left-handers as a group scored very significantly below right-handers with hardly any overlap. Silverman (12) has reported that left-handers are inferior to right-handers on basic perceptual alignment tests.

All of this fits the idea that verbal and the non-verbal perceptual faculties don't do so well when they develop for one reason or another within the same hemisphere, and that the more common tendency when this occurs is for the non-verbal performance functions to be handicapped in favor of the verbal functions. Left-handed individuals who can align themselves with Leonardo da Vinci, Raphael, Michaelangelo and many other greats in history, should remember that all of these findings are very statistical. The individual left-hander brain comes in all degrees and kinds of right-left asymmetry. A complete mirror-switch for example should leave no effect on cerebral performance save for those little problems of getting along in a right-hander world.

In any case, it may be seen that differential loadings of these right and left hemispheric faculties in different individuals could make for quite a spectrum of individual variations in the structure of human intellect, from the mechanical or artistic geniuses on the one extreme, who can hardly express themselves verbally or in writing, to the highly articulate individuals at the other extreme who think almost entirely in verbal terms. Individual variations of this kind are thought to be hereditary or at least innate to a considerable degree. Left-handedness for example tends to be a familial trait, and the anatomical asymmetrics in the brain that are correlated with cerebral dominance have been reported recently by Wada to be demonstrable already at birth in the brains of stillborn infants. Reading and language disabilities are agreed to be congenital, and often show a clear family history with a somewhat higher incidence among left-handers. One of the commissurotomy patients is a left-hander and shows a lateral cerebral reversal for speech into the right hemisphere but like left-handers statistically, there is not a corresponding switch in spatial perceptual faculty, so that both of these then have to develop in the right hemisphere.

The dichotomy we've drawn between verbal vs. nonverbal mental capacities may suggest to some the possibility of looking for correlated male-female differences. We have not pursued this ourselves as yet but note that it is reported that males are found to be six times more frequently afflicted than females with congenital language disabilities. On the Porteus Maze Test applied widely to children in many cultures, the girls were found to be significantly inferior to the boys. Smith(13) concludes that females show a selective spatial disability (the other side of the coin being that they presumably show a verbal superiority?). Patients with Turner's syndrome, that is females lacking one of the usual pair of the female X chromosomes are found to do pretty well on the verbal portion of the Wechsler I.Q. scale, but are selectively and profoundly deficient in the non-verbal perceptual functions(14). It is also reported by Money(15) that genetic females masculinized in utero by excessive male hormone through accidents of treatment or pathology show an exceptionally high incidence of very high I.Q.'s. These mental differences between the sexes have generally been considered in the past to be socially or culturally induced, but the possibility remains that something more basic is involved(16), like a lesser degree of hemispheric differentiation and dominance in the female.

## REFERENCES

(1) Sperry, R. W., et al., "Interhemispheric relationships: The neocortical commissures; syndromes of hemisphere disconnection." In *Handbook of Clinical Neurology,* P. J. Vinken and G. W. Bruyn (Eds. *4,* Ch. 14, 273-290, 1969.

(2) Sperry, R. W., "Plasticity of neural maturation." *Develop. Biol.,* Suppl. 2, 27th Symposium, Academic Press, 1968, pp. 306-327.

(3) Bogen, J. E., and M. S. Gazzaniga, "Cerebral commissuratomy in man. Minor hemisphere dominance for certain visuospatial functions." *J. Neurosurg.,* 1965, *23,* 394-399.

(4) Bogen, J. E., "The other side of the brain. I: Dysgraphia and dyscopia following cerebral commissuratomy." *Bulletin L.A. Neurol. Soc., 39* No. 2, April 1969.

(5) Levy, Jerre, "Information processing and higher psychological functions in the disconnected hemispheres of human commissurotomy patients." Ph.D. thesis, California Institute of Technology, 1969.

(6) Zaidel, D., and Sperry, R. W. Performance by the left and right hemispheres on the Raven's Colored Progressive Matrices. Biol. Ann. Report, Calif. Inst. Techn., 1971, No. 130, p. 115.
(7) Milner, B., and L. Taylor, "Right hemisphere superiority in tactile pattern-recognition after cerebral commissurotomy: Evidence for nonverbal memory." *Neuropsychologia,* 1971 (in press).
(8) Nebes, R. D., "Investigation on lateralization of function in the disconnected hemispheres of man." Ph.D. thesis, California Institute of Technology, 1971.
(9) Sperry, R. W., "Perception in the absence of the neocortical commissures." *ARNMD,* 1970, *48,* Ch. VII.
(10) Levy, Jerre, et al., "Perception of bilateral chimeric figures following hemisphere deconnection." *Brain,* 1972 (in press).
(11) Lansdell, H., "Verbal and nonverbal factors in right-hemisphere speech: Relation to early neurological history." *J. Comp. Physiol. Psychol.,* 1969, *69* 734-738.
(12) Silverman, A. J., et al., "Some relationships between handedness and perception." *J. Psychom. Res.,* 1966, *10*(2), 151-158.
(13) Smith, I. M., *Spatial Ability,* San Diego, Robert R. Knapp, 1967.
(14) Alexander, D., et al., "Defective figure drawing, geometric and human in Turner's syndrome." *J. Nerv. Ment. Dis.,* 1966, *142,* 161-167.
(15) Money, J., "Sexual dimorphism and homosexual gender identity." *Psych. Bull.,* 1970, *74,* 425-440.
(16) Levy, J., "Lateral specialization of the human brain: Behavioral manifestations and possible evolutionary basis." 32nd Annual Biology Colloquium on the Biology of Behavior, 1971. Oregon State University, Corvallis, Oregon.

# SECTION II

# BIOFEEDBACK

# 6

## BERGER, A.

# *Biofeedback in Action*

**The technique is winning responsible acceptance as a therapeutic tool. Shown here is one of its exciting experimental uses training epileptics to produce a newly discovered EEG rhythm (bursts in first and fourth tracings) that appears to lessen their seizure rates**

The suggestion that asthma, epilepsy, hypertension, cardiac arrhythmias, hemiplegia, migraine, tension headaches, torticollis spasms, hyperkinesis, and functional disorders of many systems may all be relieved by a single form of treatment sounds more like a 19th-century pitch for snake oil than a true reflection of research in 1973.

Yet biofeedback, a technique that was given its name only four years ago, is already being investigated as a promising therapy, or applied clinically, in each of these conditions by research groups in many of the nation's most prestigious medical institutions. No longer just a laboratory wonder, biofeedback has begun to pay off clinically in many proposed applications that sounded like pie in the sky when they were first publicized in the late 1960s. And, although a few of the suggested therapeutic uses are proving difficult to implement, new disease targets–including some of the most stubborn problems regularly faced by physicians–keep swelling the roster.

One reason for this bewildering variety of possible applications is that the term "biofeedback" is almost as broadly inclusive as the word "pills." Coined in 1969 at the first meeting of a group that was promptly named the Biofeedback Research Society, it refers to any technique using instrumentation to give a person immediate and continuing signals on changes in a bodily function that he is not usually conscious of, such as fluctuations in blood pressure, brain-wave activity, or muscle tension. Theoretically and very often in practice, the information input enables him to learn to control the "involuntary" function.

Although a few researchers and clinicians have been using biofeedback techniques for over 20 years, the concept first caught the public imagination in 1968 when psychologist Joe Kamiya of San Francisco's Langley Porter Neuropsychiatric Institute published an article in *Psychology Today*, entitled "Conscious Control of Brain Waves," describing experiments in which subjects learned to turn their brains' alpha rhythm on and off at will. (Dr. Kamiya had actually first reported this work in a 1962 abstract.) A computer connected to the electroencephalograph turned a sound signal on whenever alpha waves appeared in the subjects' EEG recordings, and they soon learned to keep the tone on–or off–though they could not explain how.

By the late 1960s, Dr. Neal E. Miller, professor of physiological psychology, and his associates at Rockefeller University were attracting attention with a stream of papers reporting that they had trained rats to increase and decrease their heart rates, blood pressure, intestinal contractions, and other visceral functions by biofeedback techniques that rewarded correct responses. Their methods facilitated such fine discrimination that they were even able to teach rats to make one ear blush and not the other.

Dr. Miller called the phenomenon "instrumental learning of glandular and visceral responses" and strongly challenged the accepted belief that physiologic functions mediated by the autonomic nervous system were beyond the reach of an individual's conscious control. His group's experiments, he wrote, had "deep implications for theories of learning, for individual differences in autonomic responses, for the cause and the cure of abnormal psychosomatic symptoms, and possibly also for the understanding of normal homeostasis." Furthermore, he added, "their success encourages investigators to try other unconventional types of training."

It did, indeed. At the University of California's San Francisco Medical Center, psychologist Bernard T. Engel reported in 1966 that volunteers had been trained both to slow down and to speed up their heart rates with biofeedback techniques. Later, at the National Institute of Child Health and Human Development's gerontology research center in Baltimore, Drs. Engel, Theodore Weiss, and Eugene Bleecker demonstrated that patients with premature ventricular contractions (PVC), paroxysmal atrial tachycardia, and Wolff-Parkinson-White syndrome could likewise be trained to speed and slow their hearts.

A computer hooked to a cardiotachometer gave instantaneous feedback to the patient, who lay in a hospital bed in a sound-deadened room watching a black box that resembled a traffic light. Green, yellow, and red lights indicated, respectively, "speed up," "correct," and "slow down." The aim was to keep the yellow light on. Moreover, some trials were set up so that the patient had to alternate between fast and slow heart rates.

Not only were the cardiac patients able to control their heart rates, but their arrhythmias tended to lessen, the Baltimore investigators found. Of eight patients with PVCs, five were able to reduce the disorder's frequency dramatically. One, who had an average of 12.8 PVCs per minute for eight years before the experiment, gained such impressive control that four years after training she still had no more than one early systole every five minutes.

Biofeedback regulation of cardiac functions is still experimental, says Dr. Engel. "We've demonstrated what we think is a reproducible phenomenon and have data indicating that patients can exercise what we call clinically significant control. They show continuing evidence of control after follow-up periods as long as five years."

Another visceral function that the Rockefeller group trained their rats to control was blood pressure. To make certain that the animals were not "cheating" by learning to use skeletal muscles to achieve blood-pressure and heart-rate changes, Drs. Miller and Leo V. DiCara, who is now at the University of Michigan, paralyzed them with curare and devised a tiny respirator to keep them alive. Undaunted, the curarized rats showed an even greater ability to learn control of visceral functions. But, although the Rockefeller work was soon duplicated in other laboratories, recent attempts to replicate the original experiments have been less and less successful.

Dr. Miller has two hypotheses that may explain the mystery: The curare now available may be different, or the inbred strains of laboratory rats, raised in a highly artificial and protected environment, may have lost some of their capacity to adapt. Sources and production of curare have indeed changed since the first study was done.

Dr. Miller's group and others also tried training humans to control their blood pressure. Dr. Miller was initially successful with a woman patient whose hypertension developed after a cerebellar hemorrhage; she was able to bring her diastolic blood pressure down from 140 mm Hg to 70 mm Hg. When concurrent antihypertensive drugs were withdrawn, it rose to 92 mm Hg but within days returned to below 80 mm Hg. During one training session some months later, she demonstrated that she could raise her pressure as high as 94 mm Hg and lower it to 65 mm Hg, on request. But her control eventually weakened–neither Dr. Miller nor her physicians fully understood why–and

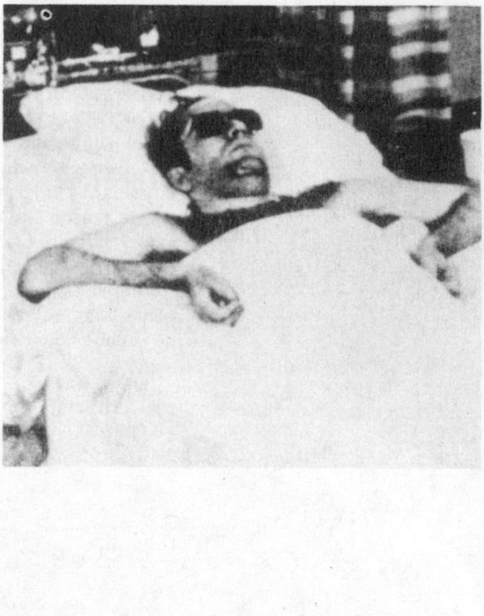

she had to be put back on antihypertensive drugs.

Other research teams meanwhile demonstrated that both normal volunteers and hypertensive patients could control not only diastolic but also systolic pressure, either separately or together. At Harvard Medical School, a group headed by Dr. Herbert Benson, associate professor of medicine, and Dr. David Shapiro, assistant professor of psychology in the psychiatry department, found that six of seven hypertensive patients were able to lower systolic blood pressure by an average of 16.5 mm Hg. The group is in the process of publishing a report of their results in training hypertensives to lower their diastolic pressures.

In most biofeedback studies with human subjects, the reward or reinforcement for successful performance has been merely a sound or light signal, as at Dr. Engel's laboratory. Most investigators have felt that—although experimental animals must be rewarded with food, shock avoidance or, as with Dr. DiCara's curarized rats, electrical stimulation of the brain's pleasure center—for people, success itself is encouragement enough, especially if the achievement may mean better health.

The Harvard team, however, prefers to use stronger reinforcement: A change in the subject's blood pressure in the desired direction triggers a beep and a flash of light; for every 20 beep-flash signals, a slide is projected, showing a scenic picture and the amount of money the subject has earned so far; and each such projection is worth five cents. The patients, referred by Boston City Hospital's hypertension clinic, are also paid $5.00 per session to come to the behavioral laboratory, and told that the sessions may help lower their blood pressure.

Dr. Benson is extremely cautious about the possible clinical significance of these studies. "We have no data concerning what happens to these people outside the laboratory. The changes don't seem to carry over," he says, but concedes, guardedly, that "one or two" of the 15 to 20 patients the team has studied in the past 2½ years appeared able to maintain lower blood pressure without feedback, "but we simply don't have data on that point."

Psychologist William A. Love Jr., director of the biofeedback research laboratory at Nova University's behavioral science center in Fort Lauderdale, Fla., is attacking hypertension from another direction. Using electromyography feedback from the frontalis muscle group of the forehead, he has been training hypertensives in deep-muscle relaxation to overcome tension caused by environmental factors. In a pilot study, six patients, with histories of hypertension ranging from three to 15 years, achieved an average 11% decrease in both systolic and diastolic pressure. Their mean systolic pressure at the beginning of the study was 153 mm Hg; their mean diastolic pressure, 100 mm Hg. After 16 weeks of training, the group's mean systolic pressure was down to 135 mm Hg; their mean diastolic pressure, 88 mm Hg. All six were on antihypertensive medication before and during the study.

"A study with 40 subjects is in progress now," says Dr. Love. "After the first month, we've had an 11-mm Hg average decrease in both systolic and diastolic pressure."

Unlike the groups that work with direct blood-pressure feedback, Dr. Love sees little if any improvement during a session—"maybe a point or two, at most," he says. "We take their blood pressure three times when they come into the lab for each session and again three times before they leave. It's the presession average that we use, and it declines across time.

"We think what's probably happening is that, as we train people not to have their muscles so habitually tight and as they relax more, there's also less muscular pressure at the level of the arterioles. Another hypothesis is that, if you don't tense up as much, you don't feed as much energy into the hypothalamus, and as a result you don't get as much cortical arousal."

EMG feedback appears to be the approach employed in the greatest variety of medical applications, even though

*Electromyographic feedback therapy restored arm motor function in a paraparetic patient (below left) who had been completely incapacitated for three years. Dr. Brudny (below) used a visual display of EMG data to teach the patient to move his biceps, forearms, and wrists. He can now feed himself (below right) as well as operate an electric wheelchair.*

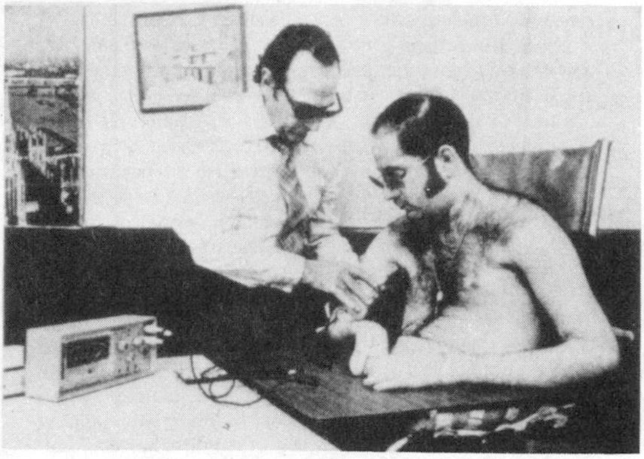

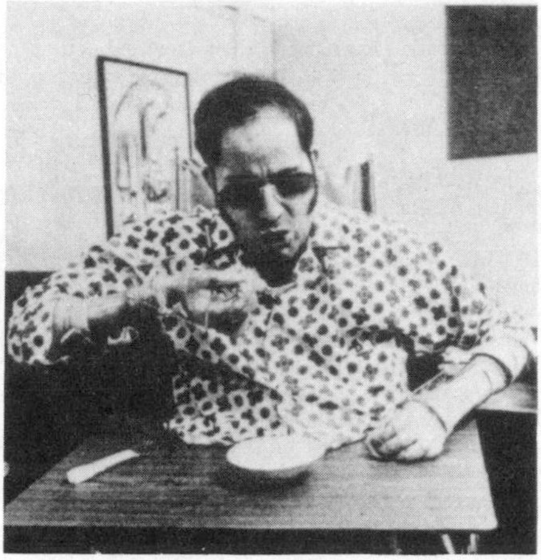

EEG biofeedback of the alpha rhythm has received far wider publicity. The exquisitely fine discrimination possible with EMG feedback was demonstrated a decade ago by Dr. John V. Basmajian, director of the Regional Rehabilitation Research and Training Center and professor of anatomy, physical medicine, and psychiatry at Emory University's medical school in Atlanta.

Then at Queen's University in Kingston, Ontario, Dr. Basmajian showed that most people could learn to fire individual motor neurons. In fact, some of his subjects were able, on request, to fire them off in gallop rhythms, imitation drumbeats, and fancy rolls.

Some investigators don't consider that EMG feedback training falls within the definition of biofeedback, however, because the functions it deals with are not autonomically controlled. But neither are they altogether voluntary, point out psychologists Elmer E. Green, Alyce M. Green, and E. Dale Walters of the Menninger Foundation in Topeka, Kan. In large measure, they say, "the control of striated muscle is developed through feedback of information from special sense organs, especially the eyes. But, in one area, there is essentially no perceptual feedback. This is in the reduction of muscle tension down to zero."

Precisely that technique is being applied by Drs. Thomas Budzynski and Johann Stoyva of the University of Colorado Medical Center, for the relief of tension headaches. They place the EMG leads on the patient's forehead (see cover), because if the frontalis muscle is relaxed, that usually means the scalp, neck, and upper body are, as well. And the muscle's state is a good indicator of nervous tension. "It's very reflective of emotions," says Dr. Budzynski, who is an assistant professor of clinical psychology at Colorado. "In our culture we learn to suppress exaggerated facial expressions. But I think residual EMG levels develop in certain muscles as a result of emotions, the frontalis among them."

The patient usually lies on a bed wearing earphones. Any frontalis contraction produces a tone in the earphones, the higher the muscle tension the higher the pitch. The patient tries to keep the pitch as low as possible. A number of researchers who use the technique therapeutically agree that it usually reduces tension headaches.

For migraine headaches, an entirely different type of biofeedback is in use at some centers: temperature feedback combined with relaxing "autogenic" phrases–a method called "autogenic feedback training" by its originators at the Menninger Foundation, Dr. Elmer Green, E. Dale Walters, and Dr. Joseph D. Sargent, Menninger's chief of internal medicine.

They discovered the technique accidentally, when one of Dr. Green's research subjects was being trained to control her brain waves by EEG feedback, reduce muscle tension by EMG feedback, and increase blood flow in her hands, as measured by hand temperature. When she succeeded in raising her hand temperature 10° F in two minutes, she also recovered spontaneously from a migraine headache. Two other migraine sufferers who heard of the incident requested temperature feedback training; one reported complete relief, the other partial relief.

That led the investigators to undertake a clinical trial. They recruited 75 patients: 63 migraine sufferers, ten with tension headaches, two with cluster headaches. After instruction, each was lent a "temperature trainer" that measured the difference between index-finger and mid-forehead temperature. Each patient also got a typewritten list of autogenic phrases, such as: "I feel quite quiet," "My arms and hands are heavy and warm," "My whole body is relaxed and my hands are relaxed and warm," to concentrate on while using the device.

With a month's practice, most patients no longer needed the feedback device. After a year or more, a patient's success was judged by each of the three investigators separately, using different criteria. They considered that 74% of the migraine sufferers were improved.

The Menninger researchers have no doubt at all that hand-warming can be learned. "In our opinion almost 100% of healthy persons have the physiologic capacity to increase blood flow in the hands at will," they report. If so, the technique might offer some relief to sufferers from Raynaud's disease, and a number of investigators report anecdotal evidence that it does. "I've been trying it with several patients, and my impression is that it helps," says Dr. Sargent. "But it requires a little different approach. People with migraine can use the method when they feel the symptoms coming on. But once Raynaud's symptoms begin, and the patients' hands feel numb or turn pale, they can't warm their hands any more. They have to learn to predict situations in which they'll develop symptoms and warm their hands prophylactically. If they can do this, they can stay out of trouble. But we have no hard data as yet." No one has, but several other investigators, among them Nova's Dr. Love and Berkeley, Calif., psychologist Erik Peper, report improvement in some cases.

A convert to both the temperature and EMG feedback treatments is Dr. Seymour Diamond, assistant professor of neurology at the Chicago Medical School, who is also president of both the American Association for the Study of Headache and the National Migraine Foundation.

"The work of Drs. Sargent and Green interested me, and I invited Dr. Sargent to the AASH meeting last June," says Dr. Diamond. "I felt the statistics he presented then made a visit to his clinic worthwhile."

Since his return, Dr. Diamond has treated some 200 patients with one biofeedback technique or the other. He finds that temperature training works best with young, well-motivated patients with true migraine. "It's not much help to those with both migraine and depression headache–I prefer the term depression or psychogenic headache instead of tension headache–and it seldom helps anyone over 30. But I have about 18 young patients who can actually abort their migraine headaches."

As for EMG feedback: "I was a big doubter of Budzynski's work," Dr. Diamond says. "I was the first person to write about daily headaches as part of general depression, and I had treated a lot of such patients. After buying EMG equipment, I started to work with certain patients in whom everything else had failed. And about 20 intractable headache cases have responded remarkably. These are people who have been through the mill. They don't re-

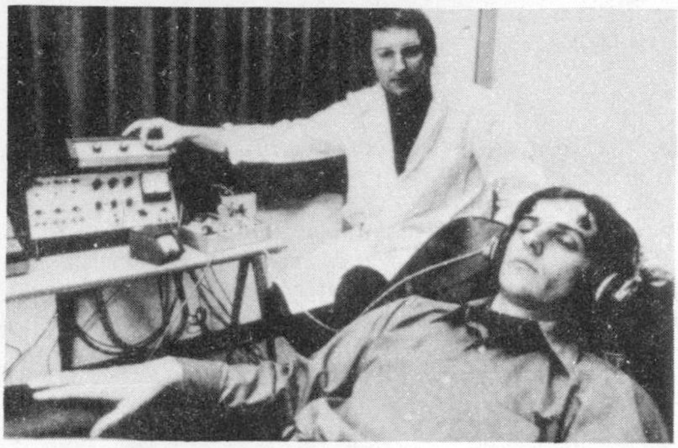

*To prevent tension headaches, Dr. Budzynski trains subject to reduce tension in his frontalis muscle by listening to EMG feedback through earphones.*

spond to antidepressants, every other pharmacologic approach has been tried on them, and about half have had extensive psychotherapy as well, with no help."

Dr. Diamond, whose clinic sees about 50 new headache patients a week, reports a success rate of about 25% with temperature training and 40% with EMG feedback.

Another physician convinced of the effectiveness of EMG feedback is Seattle internist George B. Whatmore. He has been using the method for more than two decades to treat a variety of functional disorders that he thinks result from a physiopathologic state he calls "dysponesis"—literally "faulty effort" in which errors in energy expenditure occur in the nervous system.

"Dysponesis is capable of producing a variety of functional disturbances within the organism," says Dr. Whatmore. "By affecting nervous-system function, it can alter the regulation of almost any bodily system. Among the numerous clinical manifestations are fatigue, insomnia, headache, backache, hyperventilation, anxiety, depression, 'indigestion,' impotence, frigidity, and spastic colon.

"This kind of covert, misdirected energy expenditure can result from an unconscious bracing effort that would be appropriate to prepare for a 'fight or flight' reaction to physical attack. But, if a person braces similarly in a social gathering or when he has to speak before an audience, the bracing becomes inappropriate and interferes with effective functioning," Dr. Whatmore explains. "The autonomic responses it arouses are also inappropriate. Increased heart rate, elevation of blood pressure, secretion of adrenalin and other hormones, mobilization of glucose and fatty acids, and numerous other emergency responses all prepare the organism for violent muscular exertion, yet no such exertion is called for. Both the bracing and the autonomic responses interfere with normal organ function. If frequent and prolonged, they may cause tissue alterations of a pathologic nature."

Dr. Whatmore has developed a technique to eliminate this misdirection of energy, which he calls orthoponetics or "effort training." First, the patient must be made aware of his misdirected efforts. "They're almost entirely covert," he says. "Basically, they're action potentials in the nervous system that the EMG can detect." Next, the patient is taught to carry the training over into daily life by watching out for these muscle reactions. Finally, he learns to identify specific situations in which he is most likely to make misdirected efforts and to avoid them.

"My work evolved from that of Edmund Jacobson, with whom I studied in Chicago," Dr. Whatmore says. "He did a lot of basic research in the 1930s that was way ahead of his time, and published a long series of papers as well as a book on a procedure he called 'progressive relaxation.' He had developed systems for recording from the neuromuscular system of human beings, but he didn't use them for training. I felt that the next logical step was to employ these systems to feed information back to the patient."

With follow-up as long as 21 years on some patients, Dr. Whatmore concludes that, in those cases almost certainly caused by dysponesis, "we have what you could call high-quality long-term results in 60%, fair-quality long-term results in 20%, and poor results in 20%."

Muscle retraining using EMG feedback is also being employed to restore the function of muscles that have been put out of action by stroke, spinal injuries, and other crippling lesions. At Casa Colina Hospital for Rehabilitation Medicine in Pomona, Calif., clinical director Herbert F. Johnson has been using a portable EMG feedback instrument to rehabilitate hemiplegic patients. The device sounds a tone whenever the patient manages the slightest motion of the muscle being trained. After three 30-minute training sessions in the hospital, on different days, the patient uses the unit at home for two 30-minute sessions a day, and is medically checked every week or two.

Encouraged by the results in his first series of ten patients, some of whom were able to walk without braces after only a few weeks' work with the unit (MWN, Dec. 10, '71), Dr. Johnson has expanded the EMG feedback training trial. "We've pretty much made it an integral part of our treatment program here," he says. "Our initial approach was to take patients long enough after their strokes that any results we got would clearly be due to the technique. Those results were so good that we're applying it much earlier now, but that makes it much more difficult to say definitely whether the treatment caused the patient's improvement. We're simply going to have to compare our results over about a two-year period with our previous results to get any meaningful assessment."

Across the continent, Dr. Joseph Brudny, an instructor in rehabilitation medicine at New York University's medical center, has successfully used EMG feedback to treat hemiplegia, paraparesis, torticollis, and related conditions. Of 20 patients, he says, 18 responded with improvements ranging from considerable functional gains to complete recovery. The only two who failed to show any return of movement were the two oldest patients, aged 68 and 71. Both had pronounced aphasia, so it was impossible to be certain that they understood the instructions.

"I thought of using myoelectric feedback for muscle retraining for several reasons," says Dr. Brudny. "In rehabilitation medicine, electromyography is our daily bread-and-butter tool for diagnosis. When I heard about what Dr. Green and others were doing, I tried their hand-warming method. It worked. Then I tested the deep-muscle relaxation technique with the EMG attached to my forearm.

Lo and behold, I couldn't feel my arm for a few seconds. It was scary. I realized that by totally relaxing the arm muscles I was suppressing all the feedback from them. We get proprioception partly through muscle tension; tensing an extremity tells you where it is. It struck me that if what I felt was real, then possibly the reason for some abnormal motor activity is not so much a lack of motor outflow as a lack of sensory feedback.

"In the clinic, I had seen people with paralysis who, at times, had motion that I was sure was volitional, but with no consistency or functional meaning. It seemed that, with damage to the CNS or brain, what might be lacking is perception or sensory feedback. There is no motor performance unless there is sensory feedback and instantaneous confirmation. I thought perhaps these people could learn control of muscles if we supplied an external feedback loop, through their senses of sight and hearing, to compensate for their lack of a muscle feedback loop."

His first patient was a 24-year-old man who had suffered a C5-C6 spinal fracture in an auto accident. "He was paraparetic, with some movement in his shoulders and elbows," says Dr. Brudny. But he had remained for three years in a position unsuitable for any functional rehabilitation, with his wrists locked in acute dorsiflexion.

Hooked up to the EMG, with Dr. Brudny patiently coaching and exhorting, the young man gradually learned to flex his biceps, then to pronate his forearm, and finally to flex his wrist. Astonishingly, he regained control of his untrained arm as well. After three years as a total-care patient, he can now operate an electric wheelchair, eat a sandwich, shave, and smoke a cigarette. "You know, that's very meaningful for a guy who has spent years on his back without being able to scratch his nose," Dr. Brudny understates. "But there is no miracle here; there had to be an element of active innervation present."

His most recent success was with two patients suffering from spasmodic torticollis. "We were able to send these men back to work, each of whom had been disabled for two years," he says. "Within 60 days, both of them had balanced necks, with no support or medication." Three months later, both had maintained their improvement.

In yet another application, EMG biofeedback is being tried as a treatment for asthma. At Denver's National Jewish Hospital and Research Center, a team headed by research psychologist Robert A. Kinsman is combining the deep-muscle relaxation technique, using EMG biofeedback, with a systematic-desensitization program. When the patient is fully relaxed, the investigators challenge him with imaginary anxiety-provoking situations, culled from an asthma "self-portrait" of the patient built up in depth interviews. "You are lying in deep, green grass on a sunny slope," he may be told. "There are flowers all around—*and pollen*." Or: "You feel an asthma attack coming on. Your chest is beginning to tighten."

The program is still in an early stage, and results are not statistically conclusive. "They're in the right direction," says Dr. Kinsman, "but we still have a way to go."

Trying a different, more direct approach, Dr. Louis Vachon, associate professor of psychiatry at Boston University, uses respiratory-resistance feedback supplied by light signals similar to Dr. Engel's. In 28 asthmatics, the average drop in respiratory resistance was about 15%.

Dr. Vachon cautions that the pulmonary changes his method has achieved are "not really very meaningful physiologically. At an asthmatic's level of respiratory resistance, if you improve him by 10% to 15%, he won't feel any better. But it does indicate that the method can produce *that* much change. What we have to do now is find a schedule of reinforcement that will allow us to produce much greater change."

In addition to all these physical applications, biofeedback may have psychiatric value. Brain rhythms other than the popular alpha waves may be of more medical use. The Drs. Green of the Menninger Foundation are now more interested in the 4-Hz to 7-Hz theta rhythm, which is associated with a drowsy, dreamy state that usually appears just before one falls asleep.

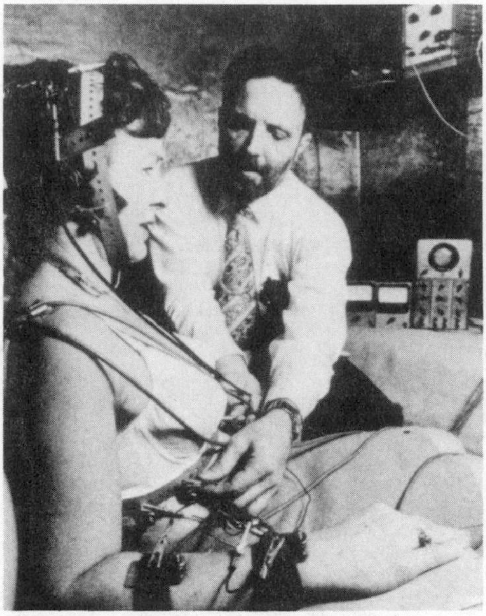

*Dr. Whatmore's biofeedback therapy for functional disorders begins with multilead electromyographic monitoring to detect misdirected energy expenditure.*

"We're working with college students to find out to what extent hypnagogic imagery is connected with biofeedback of brain waves," says Dr. Elmer Green. "We train them to produce theta waves while fully conscious. We've trained 20 and are working with ten more.

"From our point of view, this is a key state because psychiatrically, or psychologically, that's where people start to integrate. They're wide awake, but these hypnagogic images come right up out of the unconscious; they can develop the faculty not only of watching the images go by but also of questioning what they mean. And the answer seems to come right back from some part of the mind, interpreting what an image means in their lives.

Dr. Green thinks that using instrumentation to aid the patient to reach the state he calls the "theta reverie," could be of great value in psychiatry. "Moreover, the psychiatrist can monitor the brain-wave pattern while his patient is free-associating. If the patient is evading, he can spot it and say, 'Stop giving me all that guff, get back into your theta state, and *then* start free-associating.' You can tell whether the patient is associating at a deep level or a superficial one, according to his EEG."

An obvious and attractive use for biofeedback training of EEG rhythms would be the control of epileptic seizures, and a number of investigators have been working on the possibility. The most promising results thus far have been reported by Dr. Maurice B. Sterman, chief of neuropsychology research at the Sepulveda (Calif.) VA Hospital and associate professor of anatomy at UCLA.

Dr. Sterman got into biofeedback research on epilepsy through two serendipitous discoveries. Studying the relation between brain-wave activity and behavior in cats, he found a previously unrecognized EEG rhythm, 12 Hz to 14 Hz (the alpha rhythm is 8 Hz to 12 Hz), which he named the "sensorimotor rhythm" (SMR) because it was localized over the animal's sensorimotor cortex. The rhythm appeared only when the animal was motionless. He wondered whether cats could learn to turn the rhythm on to get food, and whether it would again be associated with holding still. They could, and it was. Cats learned to produce the brain rhythm at will, and when they did, they froze into stereotyped, motionless postures.

Then came the second discovery. Dr. Sterman had been studying the convulsant action of hydrazine compounds used as fuel in the manned space program. He happened to use cats trained to produce SMR—and they proved resistant to the chemicals' convulsant action.

Did the SMR exist in man? It proved difficult to detect, but it was there, once more associated with stillness and motor relaxation. The next step was to see whether epileptics could learn to produce the rhythm, and whether doing so helped their seizures.

He has now studied five epileptic patients for periods up to two years. All have shown EEG changes "clearly in the direction of normalization. We observed a reduction both in abnormal slow-wave activity and in polyspike discharges," reports Dr. Sterman.

Furthermore, all the patients have fewer seizures than before SMR training. One young woman, who used to average two seizures a month, has had only seven in the past 18 months, and just one in the past six months.

Another biofeedback pioneer, Dr. Thomas Mulholland, chief of the psychophysiology laboratory at the Bedford (Mass.) VA Hospital, has confirmed the finding of a 12-Hz to 14-Hz brain rhythm in man, although he is not certain that it can be considered a separate new brain-wave type. His laboratory is now training five epileptics, in an attempt to duplicate Dr. Sterman's findings.

He is also working with children who have attentional disorders. The children are being trained to suppress alpha waves—which indicate lack of concentration—by allowing them to watch television as long as they do so. The appearance of alpha waves turns the TV set off, and their disappearance turns it on again. "Later, we're also going to train the children to be deliberately less attentive, with a reverse arrangement," says Dr. Mulholland, "and then we'll teach them to swing voluntarily between a higher and lower level of attention. From what I've seen so far, one of the problems seems to be that such children don't know when they're being attentive and when they're not."

Some of the most "blue-sky" research in biofeedback is a program funded and coordinated by the Defense Department's Advanced Research Projects Agency. Aimed at finding ways to improve human performance, the ARPA program is a five-year cooperative venture, including 14 universities and other institutions, coordinated by the Navy Medical Neuropsychiatric Research Unit, which is commanded by Capt. Laverne C. Johnson, at the U.S. Naval Hospital in San Diego.

Included in the program are studies of the hand-warming technique. In this case, it is hoped that soldiers working in cold climates can be trained to control the temperature of their hands when, for example, they must remove their gloves to work on equipment or use instruments.

Dr. Edward Taub of the Institute of Behavioral Research in Silver Spring, Md., has already found that the hand-warming technique protects against frostnip—a precursor to frostbite—in studies at the U.S. Army Institute of Environmental Medicine in Natick, Mass.

"With our technique, we've been able to get virtually 100% of our subjects to control their skin temperature within four training sessions," says Dr. Taub. "We're interested in this for possible control of post-traumatic edema and diffuse bleeding, and as a means of delaying the onset of frostbite and reducing its severity."

Probably the most bizarre biofeedback application was reported at the last Biofeedback Research Society meeting by David Freach, Charles Leeb, and Steven Fanrion of Claremont University Graduate School in Pomona, Calif. They said that they had been able to train men to raise their scrotal temperature by several degrees. There was immediate speculation about the possibility of using the technique for contraceptive purposes.

"I wouldn't pooh-pooh their study," says Harvard's Dr. Benson. "I chaired that session at the meeting, and I thought their data looked very nice. What it means is something else again." ■

# 7

## TURIN, A. & NIDEFFER, R. M.

# *Biofeedback: Clinical Applications*

This bibliography represents an attempt to organize references for use by both scientists and professionals who are specifically interested in the study and clinical applications of biofeedback.

We apologize to those writers whose experimental and theoretical contributions were presented as if primarily clinical in intent, for our tendency has been to minimize or even ignore major theoretical points in many papers in order to spotlight the actual or potential clinical applications. From a scientific point of view the quality of papers presented here is wide-ranging. A small number of studies were carefully controlled, however for the most part the use of standard procedures and other experimental controls were either non-existent or minimal. Thus, the appearance of a reference in this bibliography should not be taken as an indication of the validity of the particular research. Rather, these references give an indication of current clinical interests in biofeedback and may be useful in helping individuals design future studies.

If the following are not presented in the accompanying abstracts it is because the author does not describe them:

1.) S distribution by sex,
2.) type of feedback (i.e., auditory vs. visual),
3.) type of apparatus,
4.) collection of baseline data,
5.) follow-up data, and
6.) evidence of generalization of treatment effect from laboratory to everyday life.

The abstracts presented here are not those that appeared in the original papers. Instead they were specially prepared to suit the purpose of this presentation.

Finally, where the word "abstract" appears in parentheses, the full paper was not available to us.

1.) Ballard, P., Doerr, H. and Varni, J. Arrest of a disabling eye disorder using biofeedback. Psychophysiology, 1972, 9, 266-280. (Abstract) in Shapiro, D., et al. (Eds.) Biofeedback and Self-Control: 1972, Chicago, Aldine-Atherton, 1973.

Subjects: One, with Essential Blepharospasm.

Method: Utilized both biofeedback (auditory feedback from electro-oculograph eye-blink potentials) and conditioned avoidance training (shock).

Results: "...absence of troublesome spasms at 9 months follow-up..." It was noted that the biofeedback training showed a greater effect than the conditioned avoidance procedure.

2.) Benson, H., Shapiro, D., Tursky, B. and Schwartz, G.E. Decreased systolic blood pressure through operant conditioning techniques in patients with essential hypertension. Science, 1971, 173, 740-742.

Subjects: Seven patients with essential hypertension. Average age was 47.9 years. (5M, 2F)

Method: Ss' medications were not altered, and each received $5.00 per session. Lowered systolic blood pressures were fed back to patients by means of light, tone and photographic slides. (Each slide represented an additional 5¢ earned.)

Results: Average median systolic blood pressure during the "last five control sessions" was compared to that during the "last five conditioning sessions." Mean reduction was 16.5 mm. Hg.

The authors noted that there were no consistent changes in heart rate during the blood pressure changes and ended with this caution:

"Since the decrease in systolic pressure was measured only in the laboratory and no consistent measurements were made outside the laboratory, the usefulness of such methods in the therapeutic management of hypertension remains to be evaluated."

3.) Bernhardt, A.J., Hersen, M. and Barlow, D.H. Measurement and modification of spasmodic torticollis: An experimental analysis. Behavior Therapy, 1972, 3, 294-297.

Subjects: A fifty year old male with presenting symptoms of torticollis, heavy drinking and paranoid ideation. The torticollis was characterized by upward positioning of the head with a slight tilt to the left.

Method: Percentage of torticollis for 10-minute sessions was recorded under five conditions:

1.) Baseline.

2.) Instructions only. The patient was requested

to keep his head forward and level, and no feedback was provided.

3.) Visual feedback (a white light) was provided whenever the subject evidenced torticollis.

4.) A new baseline.

5.) Instructions plus visual feedback, but this time the light was provided when the subject kept his head in a forward and level position.

Results: The most dramatic reduction of torticollis was observed in the third condition described above (visual feedback when the subject evidenced torticollis). 74-79% (baseline) reduced to 21-30% (third condition).

4.) Blanchard, E.B. and Young, L.B. Self-control of cardiac functioning: A promise as yet unfulfilled. Psychological Bulletin, 1973, 79, 145-163.

A review of experimental work (mainly with normal Ss) focusing on heart rate acceleration, deceleration and variability, cardiac arrhythmias, and increases and decreases in blood pressure; utilizing biofeedback techniques.

The authors present an excellent discussion of many problems, such as whether biofeedback necessarily involves operant conditioning or self-control; what types of feedback are most useful (binary vs. proportional, auditory vs. visual); and a variety of methodological concerns which plague this new field. Although the topic of the paper is self-control of cardiac function, the discussion is general enough to provide anyone interested in clinical applications of biofeedback techniques with a healthy respect for the problems ahead.

Other methods of self-control of cardiac functions (progressive relaxation and yoga) are briefly discussed and the authors speculate that "operant conditioning or self-control procedures are possibly only inefficient methods of teaching subjects to relax." The authors conclude that self-control of the functions mentioned above has been amply demonstrated in normal subjects. "However, with few notable exceptions the magnitude of change obtained has been small, the duration for which control was manifested has been brief, and the generalization of the changes obtained in the experimental chamber rarely demonstrated." It should be emphasized that this paper deals with self-control of those processes which are often considered to be involuntary (autonomic) functions. Regarding applications to voluntary (CNS) functions, such as in deep muscle relaxation, the methodological issues remain relevant, but findings are frequently more readily applicable to clinical problems.

5.) Block, J.D. Operant conditioned alleviation of pathological nystagmus. Psychophysiology, 1969, 5, 562. (Abstract) of paper presented at 8th annual meeting of the Society for Psychophysiological Research, October 17-20, 1968.

Subjects: Five patients with visual nystagmus.

Method: Electro-oculograph signals were utilized to provide auditory feedback (a pitch change with eye movements), and visual feedback (movement of a meter needle).

Results: Three patients with congenital nystagmus showed no systematic reduction across sessions.

One patient with multiple sclerosis and a mild ataxia showed progressive reduction of vertical nystagmus from an initial 3.7° to .7° over 10 weeks. The reduction was still present 3 weeks later.

One patient who had suffered removal of an acoustic neuroma reduced nystagmus amplitude over 50%. Protracted reading time increased from about 10 to 90 minutes. About 50% improvement was still present at 3 month follow-up.

The writer discusses possible reasons for the differences in results obtained with congenital vs. later-life nystagmus patients.

6.) Block, J.D., Lagerson, J., Zohman, L.R. and Kelly, G.A. A feedback device for teaching diaphragmatic breathing. American Review of Respiratory Disease, 1969, 100, 577-578.

Subjects: An unspecified number of patients within a larger therapeutic program for asthmatic children.

Method: The purpose of training was to accomplish change from primarily thoracic to primarily diaphragmatic breathing.

Expansion of the chest turned on a light or a buzzer to signify incorrect breathing. In this way feedback was provided to inform Ss when they were breathing incorrectly.

Results: After initial teaching of diaphragmatic breathing, children continued to breathe diaphragmatically for up to an hour with little or no therapeutic attention. "More than one session was rarely necessary before the child breathed entirely diaphragmatically. Weekly sessions were added to determine the effectiveness of the child's practice at home."

7.) Block, J.D. Operant conditioning with augmented feedback: New perspectives in motor rehabilitation of the brain damaged. Invited address to the New York Society of Physical Medicine and Rehabilitation at the New York Academy of Medicine, June 4, 1969. Write: James Block, Ph.D., Developmental Center, Maimonides Medical Center, 4802 10th Avenue, Brooklyn, New York 11219.

Describes the development and application of some imaginative biofeedback methods. Those applications discussed include:

1.) The use of a device for treating finger and hand spasticity. A patient's fingertip is tied to a cord which exerts an adjustable extensor pull on the finger, and the S then views the amplified visual feedback of motion on a meter.

2.) An ataxic patient's standing balance was improved with the aid of a photocell mounted on his waist and pointed at a light mounted on the wall. The patient received visual feedback by viewing a meter which displayed the amplified output from the photocell as the patient's sway moved it toward or away from the light. As the patient experienced success he was instructed to move his feet closer together. "He now displays less body sway with feet together than...on the first session with a 10-inch base."

3.) Amplified visual or auditory feedback of electro-oculograph (EOG) eye movement signals was employed successfully to reduce pathological nystagmus in two patients (but was unsuccessful in cases of congenital nystagmus).

4.) Finally, a device to help asthmatic children practice diaphragmatic breathing was described. In this instance feedback consisted of presentation of a light or bell-ring when thoracic respiration occurred. The unit appears suitable for use with groups as a means of using peer pressure to motivate 8 to 12-year-olds.

8.) Block, J.D., Forster, S. and Wietfeldt, B.N. Hand spasticity: Treatment by an extension-assisted feedback device and method. Unpublished manuscript. Departments of Rehabilitation Medicine and Psychiatry (Developmental Center), Maimonides Medical Center, Brooklyn, New York 11219.

Subjects: Thirteen hemiplegic patients (7M, 6F). In all cases chronic severe spasticity had produced a completely nonfunctional hand.

Method: A cord which can provide an adjustable force is tied to the end of a digit, so that it pulls against the patient's spastic musculature. Patients may observe position and changes in position of the digit by viewing a meter. The force against the spastic musculature is gradually reduced as the patient's control increases.

Results: "A significant improvement in motility was obtained in ten patients (77%). Of four patients who remained in the study for over 20 sessions until discharge, 3 evidenced some signs of 'functional improvement,'" such as a fourteen year old boy "who came to be able to use his hand to pick up and drop objects."

"The 8 patients who received a total of 20 or fewer sessions were observed principally to determine if the method produced progressive improvement in performance in the experimental situation. Not unexpectedly, no major sign of functional improvement was obtained."

Meter feedback was found to increase the rapidity of flexion-extension cycles, at least within the first 10-15 sessions.

The importance of not reducing the magnitude of assistance (force) until patients were ready for the next step was demonstrated.

Problems concerning specification of the range of motion to be demanded of each patient were discussed.

Whether the patient was able to view his hand or not during the procedure was found to be unimportant.

9.) Booker, H.E., Rubow, R.T. and Coleman, P.J. Simplified feedback in neuromuscular retraining: An automated approach using electromyographic signals. Archives of Physical Medicine and Rehabilitation, 1969, 50, 621-625.

Subjects: A 36 year old woman who had suffered severing of the left facial nerve in an automobile accident. "Partial reinnervation of the muscles of facial expression was accomplished by axons which originally innervated the trapezius and sternomastoid muscles." The patient's task was to learn to regain movement of the face muscles by performing shoulder movements.

Method: Two types of electromyographic (EMG) feedback were utilized. First, the patient viewed an oscilloscope screen, and tracked a moving target spot with a second spot that was displaced by her EMG signal. In a second, more complex feedback arrangement the patient tracked two targets with EMG signals from her left and right facial muscles simultaneously.

Results: The patient's facial muscles strengthened with practice, and progressively less shoulder movement was required for control. "Excellent cosmetic and functional results were obtained." The patient continued practice at home but not without a slight regression in her appearance after four months away from the laboratory. Three days of retraining re-established the previous results.

10.) Budzynski, T., Stoyva, J. and Adler, C. Feedback-induced muscle relaxation: Application to tension headache. Journal of Behavior Therapy and Experimental Psychiatry, 1970, 1, 205-211.

Subjects: Five tension headache patients (4F, 1M), pilot study.

Method: Muscle relaxation training utilizing feedback of frontalis electromyographic (EMG) activity, with a higher tone being associated with more EMG activity. A shaping procedure was used to help patients gradually achieve progressively lower EMG levels. Patients reclined in a dimly lit room where they received two to three 30-minute sessions per week. As training progressed silent trials were increasingly interspersed among the feedback trials. In addition, patients were asked to keep a daily record of headache activity, and were encouraged to practice relaxation training on their own at least once a day.

Results: "Follow-up results over a 3-month period indicate that headache activity remained at a low level especially if patients continued relaxing for a short time each day." After training patients reported being able to decrease the incidence of headache and to abort headaches of slight-to-moderate intensity. Patients also reported an increased awareness of maladaptive rising tension; increased ability to reduce such tension; and a decreasing tendency to overreact to stress.

11.) Budzynski, T.H. and Stoyva, J. Biofeedback techniques in behavior therapy. English translation of a chapter from Die Bewaltigung von Angst. Beitrage der Neuropsychologie zur Angstforschung. Reihe Fortschritte der Klinischen Psychologie, Bd. 4, 1973, Birnbaumer, N. (Ed.) In Shapiro, D. et al. (Eds.) Biofeedback and Self-Control: 1972. Chicago, Aldine-Atherton, 1973.

The writers describe their initial experience with EEG alpha feedback in systematic desensitization, then provide details of their more recent (and extensive) method of systematic desensitization utilizing feedback of electromyographic (EMG) activity.

In this work EMG activity is utilized to both monitor muscle tension and to assist in the relaxation training. As patient tension rises during visualization of the fear hierarchy, the therapist terminates the scene, and then uses visual feedback of EMG activity to help the patient relax prior to presentation of the next phobic stimulus. The writers have desensitized approximately 20 patients with the above method, and state that the EMG indicator is often sensitive enough to permit termination of a visualization several seconds before a patient is aware of rising anxiety.

Under "future directions" the writers discuss the "pervasive anxiety technique" recently developed in their own laboratory. This involves repeatedly having the patient think about whatever is bothering him that day. This results in increasing EMG tension which is brought to the S's attention through auditory feedback. As the tension increase is noted the S then uses the feedback to decrease EMG tension.

12.) Budzynski, T. and Stoyva, J. An electromyographic feedback technique for teaching voluntary relaxation of the masseter muscle. Journal of Dental Research, 1973, 52, 116-119.

Subjects: Eighty normal males between the ages of 17 and 61.

Method: Ss were divided into four groups matched on the basis of age mean and range. Of the two experimental groups one received auditory feedback of masseter electromyographic (EMG) activity, and the other received visual feedback. Of the two control groups, one heard a steady tone (irrelevant feedback), and the other received no feedback.

Ss were instructed that they would be paid from $1.50 to $3.50 per session depending on how capable they were of reducing masseter tension levels.

Results: "Both auditory and visual feedback produced significantly lower...masseter EMG values than did the control conditions in one session." Possible applications of the procedures to bruxism and myofacial pain dysfunction syndrome were mentioned.

13.) Budzynski, T.H. Biofeedback Procedures in the Clinic. Seminars in Psychiatry, 1973, (in press).

This article provides a general discussion of what

biofeedback is about, and what it may provide in a clinical setting. Emphasis is placed on describing procedures for treating tension headache including: record-keeping by the patient, an abbreviated Jacobson relaxation procedure, home practice with casette tapes, and feedback training of electromyographic (EMG) activity first from the forearm, then from the frontalis (forehead) muscle. In the later example, feedback is gradually withdrawn to enhance the patient's chances of learning to relax without it. Finally, treatment concludes with training in a "stress management" procedure. Similar treatment procedures have been used with migraine patients with the additional use of peripheral temperature feedback to warm the hands.

The achievement of low arousal states for patients suffering from chronic generalized anxiety is discussed, and includes muscle, temperature and GSR feedback training.

In addition to the use of EMG feedback, EEG feedback as a means of increasing theta (a 4-7 Hz. brainwave which preceeds sleep) in order to treat sleep-onset insomnia was discussed. Other clinical applications were touched on more briefly, including the facilitation of existential and insight therapy, and the use of feedback to treat "chronic generalized anxiety."

14.) Budzynski, T.H., Stoyva, J.M., Adler, C.S. and Mullaney, D.J. EMG biofeedback and tension headache: A controlled outcome study. Psychosomatic Medicine, 1973, (in press).

Subjects: Eighteen tension headache patients (2M, 16F).

Method: Subjects were required to keep daily records of headache activity and medication. After an initial two-week baseline period, Ss were assigned to one of three groups.

The experimental group received muscle relaxation training utilizing auditory feedback of frontalis electromyographic (EMG) activity. In addition to laboratory feedback, Ss were instructed to practice relaxation outside the laboratory for two 15-20-minute periods daily.

A pseudo-feedback control group heard the tape-recorded feedback of the experimental group which they believed to be their own. Instructions to the pseudo-feedback group were similar to those given the experimental Ss.

A no-treatment control group was simply asked to keep a daily record of headache activity.

Results: "Four out of six patients in the (experimental) group showed significant declines ($p < .05$) in headache activity, while in the pseudo-feedback control group only one of six showed a significant decline. None of the (no-treatment control) group showed a significant decline below baseline levels."

A three-month follow-up indicated that five of six Ss in the experimental group rated their headaches as decreasing while three of the six Ss in the pseudo-feedback group rated their headaches as decreasing.

Drug use at the three-month follow-up was reduced more for the experimental group than for the pseudo-feedback control group.

An eighteen-month follow-up was attempted, but only four of the six Ss in the experimental group could be contacted. Of these, three had shown significant declines in headache activity during training. They reported that their headaches remained at a very low level (1 or 2 mild headaches a month). The fourth reported that his headaches continued, but at a reduced rate.

15.) Budzynski, T. and Stoyva, J. Biofeedback techniques in behavior therapy and autogenic training. Unpublished manuscript. University of Colorado Medical Center, 4200 East 9th Avenue, Denver, Colorado 80220.

The authors present a rationale explaining the advantages of using electromyographic (EMG) feedback for the induction of muscle relaxation when these procedures are applied to behavior therapy and autogenic training. The specific application to systematic desensitization procedures is discussed extensively.

16.) Budzynski, T. Systematic desensitization with EMG biofeedback. Unpublished manuscript. University of Colorado Medical Center, 4200 East 9th Avenue, Denver, Colorado 80220. (Thomas H. Budzynski, Ph.D.)

A method for systematic desensitization of phobia is described in detail. This involves the use of auditory and visual feedback of electromyographic (EMG) activity as a means of teaching Ss to relax prior to presentation of the fear hierarchy. The importance of electrode placement, equipment requirements, a shaping procedure and home practice are discussed in a step by step description of the mechanical aspects of the procedures.

17.) Corson, J.A., Bouchard, C., Scherer, M.W., Amit, Z., Hisey, L.G., Cleghorn, R.G. and Golden, M. Instrumental control of autonomic responses with the use of a cognitive strategy. Canadian Psychiatric Association Journal, 1973, 18, 21-24.

Subject: A 20 year old male who experienced intense fear in social situations. The patient attributed his social isolation to his embarrassment over his own heavy perspiration which occurred in social settings. At the time of treatment the fears were of sufficient intensity to keep the patient from venturing outside the house.

Method: Treatment involved first training in progressive relaxation. Next the patient wrote and tape-recorded four stories of "key situations in which excessive perspiration occurred." While listening to the stories he had recorded, the patient received auditory feedback of GSR level, and was told to relax when he heard the buzzer, thus decreasing the tendency to perspire. As the patient became successful, continued feedback with more complex stories was introduced.

Results: 15-month follow-up: "The patient has not experienced any problem with perspiration," and he no longer shows the phobic behavior patterns which were seen at the beginning of treatment."

18.) Gaarder, K. Pilot studies of psychophysiological therapy. Unpublished manuscript, 1973. 4221 Oakridge Lane, Chevy Chase, Maryland 20015.

This paper discusses psychophysiological approaches to therapy. Case reports #4 and #5 involve biofeedback in specific clinical applications.

Case Report #4: A patient is described as an obsessional man escaping feelings of humiliation by defensive bragging.

Method: A feedback signal was used to inform the subject of his heart rate changes. The author reports that the patient's awareness of a change in heart rate as a sign that all was not well was helpful in overcoming his defensiveness.

Case Report #5: This patient was described as a 36 year old male suffering from depression and "schizoid withdrawal."

Method: Feedback of finger temperature was provided, with the result that the subject was able to observe that his finger temperature repeatedly rose 5-10° during therapy sessions. "When it was explained how this reflected calming and lessening of anxiety, he acknowledged his enjoyment of the dependency gratification of therapy."

19.) Gannon, L. and Sternbach, R.A. Alpha enhancement as a treatment for pain: A case study. Behavior Therapy and Experimental Psychiatry, 1971, 2, 209-213.
Subject: This subject suffered recurrent headaches resulting from concussion and repeated head injuries. Prior to the time of treatment "orthodox" methods had provided little or no relief. The subject "never had much alpha when he had a headache," but "always had some alpha."
Method: S was trained to enhance his production of alpha brain waves as recorded by EEG.
Initially, S received a low tone when producing alpha (vs. a higher tone for non-alpha). Then the feedback was changed. He heard organ music (which he enjoyed) during alpha, but received no feedback during non-alpha. Also, he was told the number of seconds he had been in alpha at the end of each 2 or 3-minute training period.
Results: Changes in the patient's resting EEG were noted. He could sometimes prevent headache pain by going into alpha before a headache began, but was unable to stop already existing headache pain by achieving a high alpha state.

20.) Hardyck, C.D., Petrinovitch, L.F. and Ellsworth, D.W. Feedback of speech muscle activity during silent reading: Rapid extinction. Science, 1966, 130, 1338-1339.
Subjects: Seventeen college students, all of whom subvocalized when reading, and who were enrolled in a reading improvement class.
Method: Auditory feedback of electromyographic (EMG) activity was provided through electrodes placed over the thyroid cartilage. Ss were instructed to keep the EMG feedback to a minimum while reading.
Results: "In all cases one session of the feedback was sufficient to produce complete cessation of subvocalization." There was no evidence of subvocalization at follow-ups one and three months later. Instruction alone (without feedback) was unsuccessful in reducing speech muscle activity.
Although the importance of treating subvocalization was discussed in terms of increasing reading speed, no attempt was made to demonstrate increased reading speed as a result of the experimental procedure.

21.) Hardyck, C.D. and Petrinovitch, L.F. Treatment of subvocal speech during reading. Journal of Reading, 1969, 12.

Subjects: A group of 43 university students, and a group of 13 high school students.

Method: Auditory feedback (a tone) was provided when a subject subvocalized while reading, and Ss attempted to read without producing the tone.

Results: University students: Ss learned to control the feedback very quickly and eliminated subvocal activity in the first hour of treatment.

High school students: The one session elimination of subvocal activity did not occur with this group.

The writers relate the results to IQ, suggesting that lower IQ Ss take longer to stop subvocalizing and are more likely to revert after treatment. In contrast, they note no tendency in average and above-average IQ Ss to revert to subvocalizing. No direct measurement of IQ was reported by the authors.

"There is no immediate 'miracle' effect following the elimination of subvocal speech. Subjects... do not display any sudden sharp jump in reading speed. What is reported by a majority of the college students is an immediate reduction of the fatigue previously associated with reading for periods of one to three hours..."

22.) Hardyck, C.D. and Petrinovitch, L.F. Subvocal speech and comprehension level as a function of the difficulty level of reading material. Journal of Verbal Learning and Verbal Behavior, 1970, 9, 647-652.

Subjects: Eighteen college freshmen from remedial English classes, who did not habitually subvocalize while reading. Ss were paid for their experimental participation.

Method: Electromyographic (EMG) activity was recorded from laryngeal, chin-lip, and forearm flexor placements. Ss were equally divided into 3 groups, equated for reading speed, and required to read two essays rated approximately the same in interest but differing in difficulty. Group 1 had their EMG levels recorded, but received no feedback. Group 2 received auditory feedback of laryngeal EMG activity over a predetermined relaxation level. Group 3 received auditory feedback of forearm flexor EMG activity over a predetermined relaxation level.

Results: Laryngeal EMG activity was considerably reduced in the laryngeal feedback group, but not in the other two groups.

Reading speed appeared slightly faster for the

laryngeal feedback group in both conditions, however the between group differences in speed were not statistically analyzed.

Comprehension was approximately the same for all three groups on the easy essay. It was pointed out that the laryngeal feedback group's comprehension decreased on the more difficult essay.

The writers hypothesize that subvocal speech may aid in the comprehension of difficult material.

23.) Jacobs, A. and Felton, G.S. Visual feedback of myoelectric output to facilitate muscle relaxation in normal persons and patients with neck injuries. Archives of Physical Medicine and Rehabilitation, 1969, 50, 34-39.

Subjects: Ten normal Ss, and ten Ss with injury of the upper trapezius.

Method: Ss were requested to relax under two conditions:

1.) without feedback, and
2.) with visual feedback of EMG activity of one upper trapezius muscle.

Results: Without visual feedback patients maintained much higher myoelectric activity levels than normals. However, with visual feedback patients succeeded in relaxing about as well as normals.

The writer comments that, "The results have immediate implications for those concerned with corrective or rehabilitation training of muscle groups, since it seems clear that the visual feedback facilitates relaxation in subjects who, because of injury, are not capable of a normal extent of relaxation."

24.) Johnson, H.E. and Garton, W.H. A practical method of muscle re-education in hemiplegia: Electromyographic facilitation and conditioning. Unpublished manuscript. Casa Colina Hospital for Rehabilitative Medicine, Pomona, California.

Subjects: Six male and five female hemiplegics. Hemiplegia had resulted from cerebral vascular accidents in nine cases and from traumatic injury in two. Ten of the patients' hemiplegia was severe enough to require use of a short leg brace.

Method: Patients received auditory feedback of electromyographic (EMG) activity from relevant muscle groups. In addition to laboratory training, Ss were provided with portable EMG equipment to be used at home, for two thirty-minute practice sessions each day.

Other treatment techniques were used, including

"facilitation" and operant conditioning procedures. Thus, no attempt was made to attribute results solely to biofeedback.

Results: Ten of the initial eleven patients showed varying degrees of improvement. The most dramatic improvement occurred in three patients whose motor function had been rated either zero or trace, and who were able to eliminate use of their short leg brace.

25.) Karlins, M. and Andrews, L.M. Biofeedback: Turning on the Power of Your Mind. New York, Warner Paperback Library, 1973.

This book is written for popular consumption. Although the book does not deal exclusively with clinical applications (except in Chapter Two), the first three chapters provide good basic information about what biofeedback is, as well as presenting information about existing and potential clinical applications.

From the authors' presentation there is a tendency to come away with the impression that biofeedback-based "cures" are available for a variety of human problems ranging from subvocalization during reading to essential hypertension. Unfortunately, such optimism is far from justified on the basis of current clinical practice or research.

Clinical areas discussed include present and potential applications to: subvocalization, anxiety, phobias, migraine and tension headaches, hypertension, insomnia, tics, premature ventricular contractions, hyperactivity, pain and epilepsy.

The authors include thorough bibliographic information, including an extensive "Annotated list of suggested readings."

26.) Luce, G. and Peper, E. Mind over body, mind over mind. New York Times Magazine, September 12, 1971.

The authors present a good discussion of what biofeedback is all about, ranging from theory to application. Although the article is not primarily clinical in focus, many actual and potential clinical applications are discussed, including: muscle relaxation, tics, tension headaches, phobias, insomnia, migraine headaches, premature ventricular contractions and hypertension.

27.) McGuigan, F.J. External auditory feedback from covert oral behavior during silent reading. Psychonomic Science, 1971, 25.

Subjects: Six, with high levels of covert oral behavior while reading (subvocalization).
Method: Ss relaxed and silently read material judged appropriate for their educational level. Electromyographic (EMG) activity was monitored from several locations. Feedback consisted of a "slightly noxious" tone presented when EMG signals from Ss' chin or lips exceeded criterion amplitudes. EMG, reading speed, and comprehension were recorded as Ss:
1.) read with no feedback (baseline),
2.) received feedback at progressively lowered EMG criteria (shaping) while reading, and
3.) read again with no feedback.
Results: Although Ss increased reading speed with feedback, changes were also associated with decreases in comprehension. Finally, as feedback was removed, reading rate and comprehension returned to baseline. These results are at variance with the statements of Hardyck, et al, 1966. See Abstract #20.

28.) Medical World News. Muscle is retrained at home. December 10, 1971, 35.
See Abstract #24.

29.) Medical World News. Biofeedback in action. March 9, 1973, 47-60.
A non-technical review of clinical applications of biofeedback techniques.
Treatment areas discussed include: premature ventricular contractions, hypertension, tension headaches, migraine headaches, hemiplegia, torticollis, paraparesis, asthma, free association, epilepsy, attentional disorders and frostnip.
Research in many of the above areas is just beginning, and the article attempts to indicate which applications are more advanced clinically than others.

30.) Meldman, M.J. The alpha sonic inhibition of anxiety. Northwest Community Hospital Medical Bulletin, 1972, 2, 557-561. Arlington Heights, Illinois.
Subject: A 46 year old female with multiple phobias. This patient's symptoms had persisted throughout insight therapy, chemotherapy and systematic desensitization, and included fears of driving by herself and walking in stores.
Method: The patient was trained on a feedback encephalograph (EEG) to increase production of alpha brain waves of 10 Hz. frequency, at which

state she reported feeling extemely relaxed. A portable warbler, with a sound similar to the EEG feedback was paired with the actual feedback. The purpose was for the patient to develop a relationship to the portable warbler that would remind her of her alpha training. She was then instructed to carry the warbler with her, and turn it on whenever she felt nervous. The author hypothesizes that the portable warbler functions as a conditioned inhibitory stimulus.

Results: Considerable improvement in phobic symptomatology was noted. In addition to other improvements, she can now drive her car by herself and go shopping without serious dizziness or anxiety.

31.) Montor, K. Brain wave research. Naval Research Reviews, 1973, 26, 7-11.

Includes discussion of the development of an "Attention-Level Analyzer." The unit monitors EEG, and auditory feedback is provided when an individual exceeds a predetermined allowable "Day-dream factor." If the S continues to daydream beyond an acceptable limit, a second signal is used to alert a third person.

Potential applications discussed include making sure that pilots or long distance truck drivers pay sufficient attention to their tasks.

"This device will work with about 75% of the population...(and) may also be useful in teaching persons how to concentrate."

32.) Peper, E. Frontiers in clinical biofeedback. Seminars in Psychiatry, 1973, in press.

This article emphasizes that the use of biofeedback in clinical practice often requires prolonged training and integration with many other treatment methods, ranging from behavior shaping to psychoanalytic techniques. The author stresses the importance of pratice and homework sessions so that patients can integrate the skills learned with biofeedback into their everyday lives.

Biofeedback is presented as both a core technique and as an adjunct to other therapeutic procedures.

Current and potential clinical applications are touched on, including treatment of impotence, ulcers, Raynaud's disease, asthma, spastic colon, migraine and tension headaches, ulcerated proctitis, tics, tranquilizer dependency, insomnia, hypertension, digestive disturbances, eczema, neurodermatitis, stress and torticollis.

In addition, the use of biofeedback as a means of enhancing autogenic training, systematic desensitization, hypnotic suggestibility and creativity as well as assisting in reducing the amount of anesthesia patients require is presented.

33.) Quirk, D.A. An automated desensitization. Paper read at A.A.B.T., Washington, 1971. Write: 360 Bloor Street West, Suite 401, Toronto 4, Ontario, Canada.

The subjects were eighty referrals to a behavior therapy practice, all of which were judged to be appropriate candidates for the sole use of desensitization procedures.

The author presented data to suggest that visual presentation of phobic stimuli contingent upon increase in Basal Skin Resistance (BSR) is as effective as Reciprocal Inhibition Therapy (RIT) in the treatment of phobias.

Additionally, he reports increases in number of sessions required to achieve criteria as interaction with therapist decreases.

34.) Raskin, M., Johnson, G. and Rondestvedt, J. Chronic anxiety treated by feedback-induced muscle relaxation: A pilot study. Archives of General Psychiatry, 1973, 28, 263-267.

Subjects: Six male and four female chronically anxious patients who had been in individual psychotherapy for at least two years without symptomatic relief.

Method: Treatment involved relaxation training utilizing feedback of frontalis electromyographic (EMG) activity. The more EMG activity, the higher the feedback tone. In addition to actual feedback, patients were instructed to practice relaxation daily at home without feedback.

Results: All ten patients reached the EMG relaxation criterion.

In two patients, dissociation was observed between frontalis tension and anxiety. These patients experienced profound anxiety despite maintaining frontalis relaxation.

Of the ten anxious patients, one was rated as markedly improved, three were moderately improved, and six were unimproved. Most found their relaxation techniques were of little value in social situations, that their ability to relax failed to generalize and was limited to a supine, eyes-closed posture.

Of the six insomniacs, one was rated markedly improved, four were moderately improved, and one was unimproved. The four who were moderately improved learned to put themselves to sleep promptly but awakened periodically during the night or very early in the morning.

Of the four patients with tension headaches, three were rated markedly improved and one was moderately improved. Patients reported being able to abort beginning headaches and diminish the pain of established headaches.

35.) Sargent, J.D., Green, E.E. and Walters, E.D. The use of autogenic feedback training in a pilot study of migraine and tension headaches. <u>Headache</u>, 1972, <u>12</u>, 120-124.

<u>Subjects</u>: 75 (18 males, 57 females) with "satisfactory scientific records for only 33 subjects." Pilot study, no controls.

<u>Method</u>: Patients were taught to use temperature trainers which indicated differential temperature between the mid-forehead and the right index finger. Patients also learned autogenic phrases, and visualized the changes indicated by the phrases while watching the temperature trainer. The intent of training was to increase hand temperature relative to forehead temperature, and to help the subject observe the changing feeling that occurred in the hands while practicing. Ss first practiced daily at home with the trainer, then on alternate days without the trainer so that the equipment could be gradually withdrawn. After total withdrawal of the trainer, the Ss returned every one to three months. Headache intensity, medication and progress in temperature training were graphed. A change in methodology since this preliminary experiment was noted. The writers no longer measure differential temperature between forehead and right index finger. They now measure absolute temperature with one lead to the right index finger.

<u>Results</u>: Of 32 migraine patients, 22 to 29 (68-90%) were rated as improved, depending on the judge. "Each patient's course was rated as improved or not improved by the internist's global clinical judgement without benefit of the graphs and by two psychologists' independent assessment of only the graphs."

36.) Sargent, J., Green, E. and Walters, E. Preliminary report on the use of autogenic feedback techniques in the treatment of migraine and tension headaches. Psychosomatic Medicine, 1973, 35.

Subjects: 22 females, 6 males.

Method: Ss were taught to use a temperature trainer which indicated the differential temperature between the mid-forehead and right index finger on a meter. Ss were also instructed to repeat a list of autogenic phrases such as "I feel quite relaxed...my arms and hands are heavy and warm..." The intent of training was to increase hand temperature relative to forehead temperature, and to help the subject associate subtle subjective feelings with increased hand warmth. Ss practiced with the temperature trainer daily and kept records of headache activity. Once they had learned the handwarming technique, they were instructed to practice on alternate days without the trainer. If successful, the trainer was then withdrawn.

Results: Unanimous agreement was reached by the authors concerning the improvement or failure to improve of 19 Ss. Of the 15 migraine Ss, 12 were rated as improved and 3 unimproved. Of the 4 with muscle contraction headaches, 2 were rated improved, and 2 unimproved. The authors comment that:

1.) "The rapidity and ease with which the patient succeeded in warming the hands contributed greatly in aborting milder headaches."
2.) Handwarming exercises had little consistent effect on headaches other than migraines.

No follow-up information was provided.

37.) Schwartz, G.E. Biofeedback as therapy: Some practical and theoretical issues. American Psychologist, August 1973, 666-673.

The author discusses some of the problems involved in applying biofeedback procedures to patients. He reviews basic research in the context of potential clinical applications to essential hypertension; and suggests that "preventive feedback training before the organ system is seriously damaged may be the most meaningful application to psychosomatic medicine."

The need for procedures to "wean" patients from biofeedback by such means as the learning of strategies which can then be used without feedback is discussed. Treatment applications to two individuals with Raynaud's disease are summarized, one of which appears to have been successful. The method involved providing patients with binary visual feedback of blood volume increases in the big toes. The patient for whom treatment was successful utilized images of warmth to obtain the desired effect outside of treatment.

Biofeedback is emphasized as a part of a total treatment. In the absence of "specific biological and environmental constraints," the author is "somewhat pessimistic about its application to chronic physical disease, particularly in the absence of other therapeutic procedures."

In concluding, the author points out that biofeedback can still be quite useful even if direct voluntary control of bodily functions proves to have little therapeutic value. "By means of immediate, augmented feedback (with its associated increased bodily awareness), the patient may be able to learn new ways of coping behaviorally with his environment, or he may be able to alter his lifestyle in such a way as to keep his physiological processes within safer limits." Finally, the author suggests that "In this respect biofeedback is really similar to current psychotherapies, for they all provide corrective feedback."

38.) Schwartz, G.E. and Shapiro, D. Biofeedback and essential hypertension: Current findings and theoretical concerns. Seminars in Psychiatry, 1973, in press.

The authors begin with a review of basic issues and findings associated with biofeedback research and hypertension, and discuss experiments attempting self-regulation of systolic and (separately) diastolic blood pressure.

The view is taken that specific biofeedback of blood pressure is but one possible procedure in a larger therapy, which might also include such techniques as progressive relaxation, autogenic training, biofeedback training for muscle relaxation, desenitization, assertive training, and some yogic techniques. The authors acknowledge the possibility that given current data, relaxation alone may be sufficient to account for the observed changes, without specific feedback of blood pressure changes.

Biofeedback is seen not only as a means of helping an individual acquire direct control over autonomic functions such as blood pressure. "Biofeedback can also be used as information or as a 'monitor,' not to be directly controlled but rather as an indicant of success in other spheres." A patient, by using feedback, "can learn to recognize what kinds of thoughts feelings, situations, and actions lead to increased pressure, and can observe how successful he is in changing his life style and/or environment in order to reduce the pressure."

39.) Shapiro, D. and Schwartz, G.E. Biofeedback and visceral learning: Clinical applications. Seminars in Psychiatry, 1972, 4, 171-184. Reprinted in Shapiro, D. et al. (Eds.) Biofeedback and Self-Control: 1972. Chicago, Aldine-Atherton, 1973, 477-491.

Begins with a basic introduction to biofeedback and visceral learning research.

Briefly discusses clinical applications to: essential hypertension, cardiac arrhythmias (PVCs), tension headaches, migraine headaches, pathologic nystagmus and Raynaud's disease. In addition, the authors review the use of biofeedback procedures as adjuncts to systematic desensitization and autogenic training.

Some speculation regarding applications in education and creativity, and the possible control of sexual responses are presented. The article concludes with a discussion of "Basic Clinical Problems and Research Issues" which should be quite helpful for clinicians who are considering the use of biofeedback.

40.) Sterman, M.B. and Friar, L. Suppression of seizures in an epileptic following sensorimotor EEG feedback training. Electroencephalography and Clinical Neurophysiology, 1972, 33, 89-95.

Subject: A 23 year old femanle, with an 8-year history of a convulsive disorder.

Method: Feedback training was provided to increase production of "large amplitude trains in the 11-13 c/s frequency range" (of the patient's sensorimotor EEG activity). Feedback was both visual (a sequence of colored lights) and auditory (single and double chimes). Partway through training, a "small monetary reward" was added for each appropriate response.

Results: "A marked suppression of seizures. Changes in sleep patterns and personality were noted also."

41.) Stoyva, J. and Budzynski, T. Cultivated low arousal--An anti-stress response? In press, in DiCara, L.V.

(Ed.) Recent Advances in Limbic and Autonomic Nervous System Research. New York, Plenum, 1973.

This paper is based on the authors' working hypothesis that "frequently-stressed individuals will show physiological hyper-arousal in one or several bodily systems" and that "the response to stress can be modified."

Several of the authors' clinical and experimental studies are discussed, all involving the training of muscle relaxation with biofeedback of electromyographic (EMG) activity, usually from the frontalis (forehead) muscle. As EMG activity decreases, auditory feedback in the form of "clicks" decreases in frequency.

A two-phase procedure for shaping low-arousal is described, which involves EMG-assisted relaxation training (only for high-EMG Ss) followed by training to increase production of theta, a 4-7 Hz. brain wave associated with sleep onset. The authors go on to discuss the issue of transfer of effects to everyday life and emphasize the need for frequent practice. Various aids toward this end, such as fading procedures, portable home feedback units, and recorded tape casettes are discussed briefly. In addition, potential application to essential hypertension is discussed involving combined feedback techniques, as in:

1.) feedback training in muscular relaxation (general),
2.) specific feedback of blood pressure as in Shapiro, et al. (1969), and
3.) systematic desensitization to help moderate anxieties which aggravate the disorder.

42.) Weinstock, S.A. A tentative procedure for the control of pain: Migraine and tension headaches. Abstract of paper presented at the Biofeedback Research Society Annual Meeting, 1972. In Shapiro, et al. (Eds.) Biofeedback and Self-Control: 1972. Chicago, Aldine-Atherton, 1973, 510.

Subjects: Seven, with headache histories ranging from two to thirty-five years.

Method: Treatment procedures involved:

1.) psychotherapy with emphasis on gaining insight into the nature of self-control as well as learning of alternative responses to stressful situations,
2.) self-hypnosis, through utilization of a hypnotic relaxation tape,
3.) biofeedback of EMG frontalis tension (de-

crease), and
4.) biofeedback of temperature differential between head and right index finger (increase).

Results: The author concludes by mentioning that at the time of writing, all seven patients "seem to be functioning without headaches," though numerous other changes which could account for their improvement had occurred during treatment.

43.)• Weiss, T. and Engel, B.T. Operant conditioning of heart rate in patients with premature ventricular contractions. Psychosomatic Medicine, 1971, 4, 301-321.

Subjects: Eight, six male and two female, patients with premature ventricular contractions (PVCs) of the heart.

Method: The patients were all hospitalized. They were given visual feedback of both heart rate (HR) and the occurrence of PVCs. Training was to slow HR, speed it, and to keep it steady. The design included a fading procedure to enhance generalization to non-laboratory situations.

Results: Patients were successfully taught to control the prevalence of their PVCs. Four of the subjects showed clear evidence of PVC control in the laboratory as well as the ability to generalize control to the ward.

A follow-up was conducted with one patient sustaining her low PVC rate for 21 months, and four others succeeding thus far for shorter lengths of time.

Interestingly, the five patients who showed a decrease in PVCs during training achieved their results in different ways. Two succeeded in decreasing PVCs by slowing HR, two by keeping it steady, and one by speeding HR.

44.) Whatmore, G.B. and Kohli, D.R. Dysponesis: A neurophysiologic factor in functional disorders. Behavioral Science, 1968, 13, 102-122.

A largely theoretical paper dealing with the writers' concept of "Dysponesis" which is applied to a "physiopathologic state made up of errors in energy expenditure within the nervous system," and which theoretically accounts for a multiplicity of physiological symptoms.

Four case histories are included in which auditory and visual feedback of electromyographic (EMG) activity were utilized. Clinical problems that were attributed to dysponesis were treated and discussed, including: headaches, severe back pain, depression, and anxiety.

45.) Wickramasekera, I. Effects of EMG feedback training on susceptibility to hypnosis: Preliminary observations. In Stoyva, J., et al. (Eds.) Biofeedback and Self-Control: 1971. Chicago, Aldine-Atherton, 1972.

Subjects: Twelve undergradute males.

Method: All Ss were first tested with the Stanford Hypnotic Susceptibility Scale Form A, then randomly divided into a true (contingent) feedback group and a pseudofeedback group. Following this all Ss listened to a relaxation tape, having been informed that the electromyographic (EMG) auditory feedback would act to facilitate relaxation training. The actual and non-contingent EMG training began with the electrodes attached first to the forearm and then over the frontalis (forehead) muscle. Finally, all Ss were retested with Form B of the Stanford Hypnotic Susceptibility Scale.

Results: The contingent feedback group average on the Stanford Hypnotic Susceptibility Scale rose from pre to post test (4.83 to 10.16). Comparable scores for the pseudofeedback control group were 5.00 and 5.16. All experimental Ss either reached or approximated the pre-established criterion of relaxation training. "None of the control Ss even approximated the criterion for forehead muscle relaxation."

46.) Wickramasekera, I. Electromyographic feedback training and tension headaches: Preliminary observations. The American Journal of Clinical Hypnosis, 1972, 15, 83-85.

Subjects: Five female chronic headache patients who had failed to respond to other treatment procedures, including both "psychotherapy" and "medication."

Method: An initial three-week period was used for obtaining a baseline of frontalis electromyographic (EMG) activity levels.

During the second three-week period, patients attempted to lower EMG activity with the false (non-contingent) feedback. They were instructed to attempt to produce a low vs. high feedback tone, which they were falsely informed would indicate diminished frontalis activity.

During the final twelve weeks patients received the same instructions, this time with true (contingent) feedback.

Throughout the experiment patients recorded headache intensity and frequency, and were instructed to stop taking any prescribed medication until the conclusion of the study.

Results: No significant difference in either frequency or intensity of headache activity was noted between the baseline period and the non-contingent (false) EMG feedback period.

Both headache intensity and mean hours of headache pain were considerably reduced by the group as a whole during the final course of contingent (true) feedback training.

47.) Wickramasekera, I. Instructions and EMG feedback in systematic desensitization: A case report. Behavior Therapy, 1972, 3, 460-465.

Subject: A 42 year old female alcoholic on welfare. This patient reported being terrified of taking examinations. She entered therapy when she found herself unable to avoid taking an examination that was extremely important to her. She was described as "bright" but had dropped out of school in the seventh grade because of her fears. Due to the closeness (in time) of the examination therapy was limited to three sessions with the therapist present.

Method: It was explained to the patient that she would have to do most of the work by herself. She was provided with written and video-taped instruction on systematic desensitization. Training of muscle relaxation through verbal instruction was provided.

In addition, she was trained in the use of an electromyographic (EMG) feedback instrument which provided a tone proportional to EMG activity in the frontalis (forehead) muscle. Then she was instructed to practice with the apparatus each day at the clinic (as well as at home without the equipment).

Following traditional desensitization procedures, the patient constructed her own fear hierarchy, and was instructed to stop visualizing a scene whenever the feedback tone increased markedly, and to begin again when it declined. The therapist withdrew after desensitization of the first three scenes, and the patient carried on herself with the auditory EMG feedback for the last 17 scenes.

Results: The patient passed her examination with only mild anxiety, even though three scenes remained to be desensitized. She then desensitized the last three scenes, and did well on several civil service and employment examinations, which she stated she approached with increasing confidence.

48.) Wickramasekera, I. The application of verbal instructions and EMG feedback training to the management of tension headache: Preliminary observations. Headache, 1973, 13, 74-76.

Subjects: Five females, diagnosed as chronic tension headache cases.

Method: Treatment procedures involved: 1.) an observation period to determine base rate of headache activity and frontalis (EMG) levels; 2.) muscle relaxation training using the verbal instructions found in Behavior Therapy Techniques (Wolpe and Lazarus, 1966); and 3.) biofeedback training with auditory feedback of frontalis EMG activity. Ss were instructed to keep the feedback tone low by relaxing the relevant muscle group. Patients kept records of headache frequency and intensity throughout, and were instructed to practice relaxation learned by both techniques above at home.

Results: "Suggest a decline in the frequency and intensity of headache activity over the baseline period. The decline...seemed even more dramatic for four of the five patients during and after the EMG feedback period.

49.) Wickramasekera, I. The effects of EMG feedback on hypnotic susceptibility: More preliminary data. Journal of Abnormal Psychology, in press.

Subjects: Twelve undergraduate males.

Method: A double blind replication of an earlier study (Wickramasekera, 1972). See #45.

Results: "the experimental Ss who practiced relaxation with both the benefits of instructions and contingent feedback appeared to increase in suggestibility more than the controls who received only the benefits of verbal instructions with their relaxation practice."

50.) Wickramasekera, I. Temperature feedback for the control of migraine. Unpublished manuscript, 1973. Write: 320 East Armstrong, Peoria, Illinois.

Subjects: Ss for this study were two patients who were chronic migraine sufferers. Both had been treated previously with chemotherapy and psychotherapy without obtaining symptomatic relief. In addition, both had psychiatric problems which, at the time of the study, they were unwilling to work on, thus treatment was limited specifically to headaches.

Method: Procedures involved: 1.) muscle relaxation training utilizing feedback of frontalis electromyographic (EMG) activity; then 2.) differential temperature feedback to increase temperature of middle finger of dominant hand relative to center of forehead. Patients practiced hand-warming with and without feedback in the clinic, and at home without feedback.

Results: The EMG biofeedback training was found to be ineffective. During twelve weeks of temperature training, however, headache duration and intensity decreased immensely in both patients. From eyeballing the data it is apparent that symptom relief was positively correlated with increased temperature differential.

The patients made no significant changes in consumption of chemical analgesics during baseline and training. However, "at follow-up three months after training both patients reported that they had reduced their consumption of analgesics to occasional aspirin for non-headache-related events."

8

BUDZYNSKI, T. S.

# Some Applications of Biofeed-Back-Produced Twilight States

Biofeedback research has been under way only a few short years and yet its techniques and preliminary results, embryonic though they may be, have captured the imagination of both laymen and researchers. Even the word "biofeedback" has somehow acquired a charismatic quality of its own. The interest and excitement is due primarily to the suggestion that biofeedback may enable man to exercise voluntary control over many of the physiological functions that had been considered to be almost totally beyond such control. It would appear that this brainchild of psychologists, physiologists, engineers, and physicists is a true product of the times. Emerging from a *Zeitgeist* generated by state-of-the-art electronics, psychophysiology, operant conditioning procedures, and a desire to explore "inner space," biofeedback may yet realize its greatest potential in the applied areas of psychotherapy, behavior therapy, psychosomatic disorders, education, and attitude and value change.

Research in our laboratory, although initially focused on studies which attempted to demonstrate learning effects (Budzynski, 1969; Budzynski and Stoyva, 1969), has been concentrated on the application of EMG and EEG biofeedback procedures to anxiety problems and psychosomatic disorders (Budzynski, Stoyva, and Adler, 1970, 1971; Stoyva and Kamiya, 1968; Stoyva, 1970). Since our work generally involves the production of low arousal levels in individuals trained with biofeedback techniques, we have become familiar with the experiential as well as the physiological aspects of this state. I would like, therefore, to compare some of the characteristics of this biofeedback-produced low arousal state with the "twilight" states of drowsy presleep and sleep itself. Where possible, I also wish to emphasize the applied aspects of these two states. Following this I hope to draw your attention to some interesting potential applications of a twilight state produced and sustained by biofeedback techniques.

Paper presented at the 1971 American Psychological Association Convention in Washington, D.C.

Thomas H. Budzynski is Assistant Professor of Psychology, University of Colorado Medical Center, Denver, Colorado.

### Drowsy, Presleep States

Consider first that period in our daily lives which always occurs before sleep but also may manifest itself at other times as well. This drowsy period, sometimes called the sleep onset, hypnagogic, or reverie state has been divided by Foulkes (1966) into two periods defined by the EEG and EOG (eye movement signal). These periods are the alpha rhythm (usually slowed) with SEM (slow eye movements) and descending stage 1 sleep with low voltage theta waves. During these periods Foulkes noted that subjects often reported heightened awareness of bodily sensations, bodily positions, and states of muscular fatigue (muscular relaxation?), and so on. Some of the typical bodily sensations are shrinkage or swelling of limbs, or feelings of constriction about the waist, and floating sensations. Generally, both of these drowsy periods also are characterized by hallucinatory, dreamlike experiences which are more discontinuous and brief than those dreams associated with REM (rapid eye movement) sleep. Foulkes and Vogel (1965) questioned subjects upon awakening them from sleep-onset periods. Their replies to questions about control over mentation and loss of contact with the external world indicated that loss of volitional control over mentation tended to occur first; then loss of awareness of surroundings; and finally loss of reality testing occurred. Vogel, Foulkes and Trosman (1966) also scored subject reports for two ego functions: the degree of maintenance of nonregressive content and the maintenance of contact with the external world. Report content was rated as nonregressive if the mentation was plausible, coherent, realistic and undistorted. Examples of regressive content would be: single isolated images, a meaningless pattern, an incomplete scene or bits and pieces of a scene, bizarre images, dissociation of thought and images, and magical thinking. The results showed that there was a statistically significant tendency for each EEG state (alpha, stage 1, and stage 2) to be associated with a different combination of ego functioning. In the first combination (ego state), usually found during alpha EEG, the ego maintains both functions, or, at most, showed an impairment of only one function. A second ego state in which both functions were impaired was associated with descending stage 1. The third ego state usually occurred during stage 2 and was characterized by a return to less regressive content; however, contact with reality was completely lost.*

One of the more interesting findings in these studies was the relationship of personality variables to the amount of dreamlike fantasy reported by subjects. Those individuals who showed lesser amounts of such fantasy material during sleep onset expressed a rigid, moralistic, and repressive outlook on life. They seemed less able to "let go" and express inner feelings and thoughts than did those subjects reporting a great deal of fantasy. Those high on fantasy tended to be more tolerant of shortcomings in themselves and others, and less dogmatic in their beliefs. Scores from TAT revealed that subjects with the ability to exercise their imaginations freely in waking life tended to report more vivid fantasies during sleep onset.

It is tempting at this point to speculate about the possible change in personality in an individual who could be trained to produce more sleep onset fantasy material; however, let us save that for later and instead summarize some of the more relevant findings of the work of Foulkes, Vogel and Trosman:

1. As individuals become drowsy and pass into sleep, their brain rhythms change from predominantly alpha, to fragmented alpha, to low-amplitude theta.
2. Paralleled (though not perfectly) with these EEG patterns are three ego states showing an increasing impairment of ego functioning (as defined above).
3. Individuals with rigid, repressive, dogmatic personality traits report less sleep onset fantasy material.

Whereas Foulkes et al. examined their subjects as they passed through the drowsy and sleep stage at their normal bedtimes, other investigators have employed more deliberate means to enhance the drowsy conditions. For example, Henri Gastaut (1967) used sleep deprivation to induce the drowsy state. His sleep-deprived subjects were then asked to read a book until they simply fell asleep. Gastaut found that beta activity predominated in the EEG until the moment the subject stopped reading. At this point steady alpha appeared only to be replaced by a fragmented alpha pattern soon thereafter. Finally, all the alpha waves disappeared and low voltage theta predominated. It is interesting to note that this time the EMG showed a considerable

* It should be noted that Foulkes et al. did find occasional exceptions to the rule, e.g., some individuals would pass through the first two ego states while still in the alpha SEM period indicating that the psychological and physiological measures are not perfectly parallel.

diminution of tonic muscular activity. (In our laboratory we have often seen the sudden decrease in forehead EMG with the appearance of theta waves in the EEG.)

Bertini, Lewis and Witkin (1969) have also studied the hypnagogic state but with the goal of developing an experimental technique which could facilitate drowsiness, reverie and free association. They reasoned that, "the transitional nature of the hypnagogic state makes it an especially fertile period for the production of primary process material. Loosened controls partly resulting from the drowsy state seem to make the primary process thinking more accessible to observation (p. 94)." Their induction technique involved the generation of a monotonous white noise sound and the use of "ganzfeld" glasses made up of halves of ping pong balls to produce a homogeneous visual field. Besides employing this mild sensory deprivation technique, Bertini et al. also stimulated their subjects with highly emotional material before they went into the hypnagogic state. Subjected to these stimulus conditions, individuals were reported to have recalled experiences, images and feelings from childhood, woven in with thoughts about current events in their lives. Their thoughts, images and feelings were often disjointed and incoherent, leading the investigators to state that the situation produced ". . . an associational flow relatively removed from ordinary conscious control (p. 108)."

It is important to note that even though these results were obtained at other times as well, the strongest effects of this technique were seen at bedtime.

The Bertini, Lewis and Witkin study describes a procedure which can be used to *induce* a hypnagogic state. In essence, it is a mild form of sensory deprivation which does enhance the production of hypnagogic imagery. However, it is almost a necessity that an experimenter be present since the subject might otherwise drift into sleep. (This point will become more relevant later on.) Bertini et al. suggest the application of this technique to enhance free association in the context of psychotherapy.

While on the subject of sensory deprivation it might be well to consider one study of the many that have dealt with this phenomenon. It is well known that severe sensory deprivation conditions can produce a whole host of bizarre experiential effects such as grotesque body image changes and vivid visual hallucinations along with slowed brain rhythms. However, another aspect of this condition would appear to be a facilitation of attitude change. Heron (1961) found that a group of sensory deprived subjects showed significantly greater changes in attitude toward psychic phenomena than did a control group which was not sensory deprived. Both groups heard a record which argued for believing in various types of psychical phenomena. Bogardus-type scales divided into five sections dealing with telepathy, clairvoyance, ghosts, poltergeists, and psychical research were used to assess changes in attitude. Three or four days after termination of the experiment several experimental subjects reported that they had borrowed library books on psychic research. Some said they were now afraid of ghosts!

Now let us turn to some research which involves biofeedback. Green, Green and Walters (1970) have also dealt with the problem of producing the hypnagogic state. In fact, a major focus of these researchers is the documentation of the link between alpha and theta rhythms in the brain wave and reverie-and-hypnagogic imagery, as well as the relationship between reverie-and-hypnagogic imagery and creativity. Green examined the EEGs of three demonstrably creative individuals (a professor of physics, a psychiatrist, and a psychologist) as they maintained a state of deep reverie. A high percentage of 6-8½ Hertz waves was seen in their records indicating a slowing alpha and an increase in theta production over that of a relaxed, alert EEG pattern. In order to assist subjects in the production of hypnagogic imagery, Green has developed an alpha/theta feedback system that provides the subject with information concerning the percentage of alpha, frequency of alpha and percentage of theta.

Since the material experienced during the hypnagogic state is generally forgotten rapidly, Green has devised a mercury switch finger ring which closes a switch sounding a chime whenever the subject's forearm begins to deviate from a vertical position as balanced on the elbow.* If the subject's consciousness diminishes below a certain level, the forearm will begin to tilt. This closes the mercury switch and sounds a chime that brings the subject back to a level of consciousness sufficient for the verbalization of the imagery which preceded the loss of balance. This retrieval procedure combined with the biofeedback-assisted production of the alpha/theta twilight state should prove to be a powerful technique for the study of creativity enhancement in particular, and the hypnagogic state in general. Like Bertini et al., Green and his coworkers also have suggested the possibility of applying experimentally produced hypnagogic states to psychotherapy.

Although the studies described above represent a sampling of the studies dealing with the drowsy, hypnagogic period, they do help to establish the important relationship between brain rhythm frequency and the associated experiential state. Two of the studies are unique in that they deal with techniques that can be used to produce and sustain the hypnagogic state.

If this twilight state can be recognized by the generation of certain brain rhythms, low muscle tone, bizarre disjointed imagery, and a loosening of the reality-oriented frame of reference, it probably can also be characterized by an increase in suggestibility, since the drowsy individual is less able to marshal the usual defenses and critical faculties of a more alert state. Some evidence for this assumption was provided by T.X. Barber (1957) in a study which demonstrated that subjects were just as suggestible when in a light sleep or in a drowsy state as when hypnotized. One subject who had followed suggestions when drowsy said, "I was just sleepy enough to believe what you were saying is true. I couldn't oppose what you wanted with anything else (p. 59)." In his concluding remarks Barber mentioned that at the therapeutic level it is possible that suggestions could be presented to people while they sleep for purposes of helping obese persons reduce, getting heavy smokers to cut down, and helping timid persons gain confidence.

### Sleep Learning

Even though Barber achieved some startling results with sleeping and drowsy subjects, the area of sleep-learning has been fraught with controversy. Initial reports of positive results in the 1930's and '40's were followed by a series of "null" results in the '50's (see Simon and Emmons, 1955, 1956). Interestingly, as the insignificant results brought research in sleep learning to a near halt in this country, Soviet sleep-learn-

* The subject is lying flat on his back while maintaining his arm in a vertical position balanced on the elbow so that it stays up with a minimum of effort.

ing research began to flourish. However, there have been some important differences between Soviet and American studies. Whereas the Russian research involves training during drowsy, presleep periods and light stages of sleep, with special emphasis on preparatory suggestions and training periods of weeks or months, almost all non-Russian work has emphasized single night training during deeper levels of sleep, with little in the way of preparatory suggestions to learn (Rubin, 1968).

In spite of the lack of positive results during deeper states of sleep, several American investigators saw the drowsy state as useful for learning. Simon and Emmons (1956) noted that, "It may be that in the drowsy state preceding sleep, the individual is more susceptible to suggestion; perhaps one's attitudes or habits can be modified during this presleep period when criticalness is minimized (p. 96)." Stampfl (1953) and Leuba and Bateman (1952) suggested that the intermediate point between waking and deep sleep might be optimal for sleep learning.

Recent experiments by Levy, Staab and Coolidge (1971) at the University of Florida have indicated that subjects can "learn to learn" while in deep sleep (REM and Stage 4). All subjects were given a suggestion prior to sleep *and* before each sleep presentation, that they would learn and remember the material. (This use of a suggestion period prior to sleep is an important feature of the Russian technique.) Subjects improved on recognition tasks on the same material presented on two successive nights indicating that repetition of materials across nights was facilitative. They also improved their scores on succeeding nights when different material was presented each night, suggesting general learning-to-learn effects.

The positive results of Levy, et al., together with the reports of the successful implementation of the Russian techniques, will probably influence a renewed interest in sleep-learning research in this country. However, it might be more correct to label this learning method as "twilight learning" since the most effective period for such learning would seem to be sleep onset. However, let us take a further look at the two states.

Sleep is similar to the hypnagogic presleep state in that it is a state of low arousal (with the exception of REM periods), with slow EEG frequencies, and characterized by a high degree of suggestibility due to the disintegration of the reality-oriented frame of reference and a lowering of certain defenses. Orne (1969), for example, has noted that an individual in stage 1 sleep is capable of carrying out purposive behavior in response to suggestions administered while he is asleep without any evidence of physiological arousal. Learning, as we have seen, can take place during sleep, but like that during the drowsy state, it is of a qualitatively different nature from learning occurring during alert waking conditions. Russian researcher Svyadoshch (1968) has said that, "Speech assimilated during sleep, in contrast to that assimilated during waking state, is not subjected during assimilation to the critical processing, and is experienced on awakening as a thought of which the source remained outside consciousness, to some extent, therefore, it is as if it belonged to an alien personality (p. 112)."

Now, it is generally recognized that most perceptual defense studies showed that emotionally toned words have higher thresholds than neutral words; however, this conclusion was drawn from experiments performed during the alert waking state. Rubin (1968) has noted that one of the leading Russian sleep-learning experts, L. A. Bliznitchenko, believes that just the opposite happens during sleep. It would be interesting to test the hypothesis that emotionally toned words have higher thresholds than neutral words during the alert waking state, equal thresholds in the drowsy state, and lower thresholds during sleep. Perhaps one could use the same paradigm to test for uncritical acceptance of information leading to significant attitude and opinion change under these conditions.

With regard to the implementation of such a paradigm it is probable that biofeedback procedures may be of great value. The waking and sleeping conditions are not too difficult to establish and maintain; however, the drowsy state can be difficult to manage. In the natural course of events, people tend to pass through this state rather quickly when falling asleep and when awakening. Bertini's technique might be useful in producing the state but does not guarantee that the subject will not pass into sleep. The use of alpha and theta feedback, with an arousing system (the mercury finger switch and chime) such as Green, et al. have devised, may be useful for maintaining the drowsy state and ensuring that the subject does not fall asleep. However, this procedure assumes that the slow-alpha-theta pattern can be successfully shaped without undue difficulty (frustration) and/or undue duration of training. If the production of the drowsy state is to take place at, or near, the subject's usual bedtime, there may be sufficient slow-alpha/theta activity for successful shaping and maintenance. On the other hand, it may be much more difficult (without considerable training) to produce the desired result during the alert waking state and in a laboratory situation. Under these latter conditions the subject is quite likely to show a minimum of theta or slowed-alpha EEG. Perhaps the shaping process could be accelerated by combining elements of Bertini's procedure with biofeedback. In this case the white noise and ganzfeld glasses might increase the amount of slowed-alpha/theta (the base operant in learning terms) so that the biofeedback learning could proceed at a faster rate. Once the desired EEG pattern was produced, the prolongation of the state could be assured by the continuous feedback plus the mildly arousing chime (or some other signal) that would guard against passage into sleep.

### Biofeedback and the Drowsy State

Several studies have already demonstrated that biofeedback procedures can be used to increase the amount of alpha activity in the EEG (Kamiya, 1962, 1968; Kamiya and Nowlis, 1970; Hart, 1968; Mulholland, 1967; Brown, 1970a); however, there has been little in the way of published results on theta enhancement through biofeedback. Brown (1970a) showed that through biofeedback, subjects could produce and sustain various EEG rhythms long enough to report subjective impressions associated with beta, alpha, theta, and combinations of these (beta/alpha and alpha/theta). The alpha condition was described as calm, peaceful, pleasant, at ease, and neutral, among others. This is consistent with reports from other labs on the subjective experience during alpha. The alpha/theta condition was experienced as conjuring up, wish fulfillment, passive, and sleepy. Theta, however, was described as vacillating or problem solving. This may have been due to the fact that the task of producing a predominantly theta EEG during normally alert waking conditions may have been somewhat frustrating. In our own laboratory we have found that the appearance of theta rhythm in the EEG and reports of drowsiness are associated with the deep relaxation produced by

EMG feedback from the forehead musculature. (Green, et al. (1970) have obtained similar reports from subjects who were receiving EMG feedback from the forearm extensor.) This observation led us to conclude that a possible procedure for training people with sleep onset insomnia would consist of two or three phases depending upon the amount of resting alpha. Patients would receive EMG feedback training initially until they had learned to thoroughly relax their musculature. Following this they would receive alpha feedback if they still showed a predominantly beta rhythm. A final phase would be theta feedback. Hopefully, the patient would be able to progress through each phase by retaining and using the learning acquired in each earlier phase. Although pilot work is just under way, thus far, two of three patients have completed training. In these two cases there has been a complete elimination of the sleep-onset insomnia even though one of the two retained an early-awakening problem. The third patient terminated because results were not forthcoming. Noteworthy in this pilot study was the fact that the patients reported that they were able to control the theta to some extent; i.e., they could produce an increase in the theta feedback signal although their attention at times wavered between the feedback and inner thought processes.

Our research with EMG feedback has led us to believe that low EMG levels are more characterized by theta and slowed-alpha activity than by normal alpha rhythms. Subjects report that their attention at these low levels does shift back and forth between "inward-looking" and the external EMG feedback signal. Reports of body image changes are quite common, especially if a high level of muscle tension is present at the start of the feedback session.* In a study of tension headache, patients trained in frontalis relaxation with EMG feedback reported more body image changes than did a control group which was subjected to the same experimental conditions with the exception of a yoked feedback signal. Due perhaps to their lower EMG levels, the experimental patients also reported more hallucinatory imagery (Budzynski, Stoyva, and Adler, 1970b).

Reports from subjects and patients who have been thoroughly trained in our laboratory to lower their forehead EMG levels sound very much like experiences associated with a drowsy, presleep state. Perhaps then, the production of such a state might be facilitated by EMG feedback from the forehead area.

### A Biofeedback Approach to Twilight State Generation

Having considered several approaches to the induction and prolongation of the drowsy state, it is now possible to specify the characteristics of what might be the ideal biofeedback approach to this problem.

To begin with, the subject would be placed in a mild sensory deprivation environment such as described by Bertini. This situation should serve to enhance the development of the hypnagogic phenomena. Along with the constant white noise and the ganzfeld goggles, the subject would hear a feedback signal that would change as a function of EEG frequency. Thus, he would be made aware of the slowing of alpha and the appearance of theta activity. The circuitry could be designed so that as theta frequency decreased

* This contrast effect seems to be an important factor in whether the subject experiences a mild "high." It is known that the same phenomenon tends to occur when a normally low alpha subject, through training, produces a sudden and sustained increase in alpha activity.

toward delta, a very noticeable qualitative or quantitative change in the feedback signal would produce a slight increase in cortical arousal thus "moving the trainee" into the alpha/theta borderline again.

The feedback could also be made to bracket the high frequency or alpha end of the drowsy zone, e.g., a noticeable change in feedback would warn of high alpha output.

In the event the subject still could not approach a drowsy state, a shift to forehead EMG feedback might allow him to succeed.

### Possible Applications of a Biofeedback Twilight State

Given that this "ideal" system could be used to generate a prolonged drowsy state, how might it be used?

There are two general situations in which a biofeedback twilight system could be of value. The first would be the enhancement of hypnagogic imagery and its retrieval, for the purpose of studying the "inner man." This situation, therefore, would consist of a focusing on *internally* generated stimuli.

The second situation would deal with the presentation of *external* stimuli for purposes of assimilation during this peculiarly receptive state.

In reference to the first case, several applications have already been suggested by Bertini et al. and Green et al. An easily produced and controlled reverie state would delight therapists of analytic persuasion. The increased production of primary process material and free-associations should allow an acceleration of the therapy process.

The same biofeedback-produced hypnagogic state also might be used to enhance creativity. One can easily conceive of the captains of industry taking their daily "creativity breaks." The technique would certainly be useful to those in the arts as well as the sciences.

Regular practice at hypnagogic imagery might even produce positive personality change as suggested earlier in the discussion of the research of Foulkes et al. These trainees hopefully would become more tolerant of others, less dogmatic, and better able to express feelings.

Finally, consider those seekers of new inner experiences who might be persuaded to give up "heavier" agents such as LSD or other drugs, if they could achieve interesting highs through a biofeedback twilight procedure which could be used at home. The exploration of biofeedback-produced experiential states will probably become as commonplace as Yoga is today.

Turning now to the second situation referred to earlier, that of presenting external material to the drowsy subject, it is easy to imagine some of the educational possibilities. Soviet scientists have, through the years, refined sleep learning to the point where it is now used in many of the Russian schools. They have concluded that the material is best assimilated during drowsy and light sleep stages (Rubin, 1970). A biofeedback twilight state could be established at any time of the day. Thus, the user of such a system could take advantage of this special, hypersuggestible learning state whenever he desired (without the problem of losing sleep). Computer-assisted teaching programs augmented by a biofeedback produced twilight state might constitute an educational breakthrough.

Therapists should be able to produce gradual and controlled positive personality changes through the introduction of carefully worded suggestions as the patient maintains himself in this hypersuggestible state. The technique could prove to be particularly effective with cases of depression. In fact, suggestions to increase self-esteem, confidence, and possibly assertiveness might be efficiently imparted to a wide variety of patient types.

Cassette tape systems could be used to present suggestions to patients while they trained at home with biofeedback units. Perhaps one day therapists will have at their disposal libraries of such tapes which can be used by the patients in conjunction with home biofeedback systems. At certain phases in therapy these general-topic tapes could prove to be quite helpful. Therapists would be able to handle larger numbers of patients at a reduced cost to the patient. This could mean a partial solution to the problem of providing low-cost, short-term therapy for the masses. The masses, in this sense, are fields within fields . . . within fields, to incarnate Stulman's view.

## References


1. Barber, T. X., "Experiments in Hypnosis," *Scientific American*, 1957, *196*, 54-61.
2. Bertini, M., Lewis, H. B., & Witkin, H. A., "Some Preliminary Observations with an Experimental Procedure for the Study of Hypnagogic and Related Phenomena." In C. T. Tart (Ed.), *Altered States of Consciousness*, 1969 New York: John Wiley & Sons, pp. 93-115.
3. Brown, B. B., "Recognition of Aspects of Consciousness through Association with EEG Alpha Activity Represented by a Light Signal," *Psychophysiology*, 1970, *6*, 442-452.
4. Budzynski, T. H., "Feedback-induced Muscle Relaxation and Activation Level." Unpublished doctoral dissertation, University of Colorado, 1969.
5. Budzynski, T. H., & Stoyva, J. M., "An Instrument for Producing Deep Muscle Relaxation by Means of Analog Information Feedback," *Journal of Applied Behavior Analysis*, 1969, *2*, 231-237.
6. Budzynski, T. H., Stoyva, J. M., & Adler, C. S., "Feedback-induced Muscle Relaxation: Application to Tension Headache," *Behavior Therapy and Experimental Psychiatry*, 1970(a), *1*, 205-211.
7. Budzynski, T. H., Stoyva, J. M., & Adler, C. S., "The Use of Feedback-induced Muscle Relaxation in Tension Headache: A Controlled-outcome Study." Annual meeting of the American Psychological Association, Miami Beach, Florida, September 3-8, 1970(b).
8. Budzynski, T. H., & Stoyva, J. M., "Biofeedback Techniques in Behavior Therapy and Autogenic Training." Submitted for publication, 1971.
9. Foulkes, D., *The Psychology of Sleep*. New York: Scribners, 1966.
10. Foulkes, D., & Vogel, G., "Mental Activity at Sleep Onset," *Journal of Abnormal Psychology*, 1965, *70*, 231-243.
11. Gastaut, H., "Hypnosis and Pre-sleep Patterns." In L. Chertok (Ed.), *Psychophysiological Mechanisms of Hypnosis*, 1969, New York: Springer-Verlag, pp. 40-44.
12. Green, E., Green, A., & Walters, D., "Voluntary Control of Internal States: Psychological and Physiological," *Journal of Transpersonal Psychology*, 1970, *1*, 1-26.
13. Hart, J. T., "Autocontrol of EEG Alpha," *Psychophysiology*, 1968, *4*, 506. (abstract).
14. Heron, W., "Cognitive and Physiological Effects of Perceptual Isolation." In P. Solomon, P. Kubzansky, P. Leiderman, J. Mendelson, R. Trumbull, and D. Wexler (Eds.), *Sensory Deprivation*, Cambridge, Mass.: Harvard University Press, 1961, pp. 6-33.
15. Kamiya, J., "Conditional Discrimination of the EEG Alpha Rhythm in Humans." Paper presented at the Meeting of the Western Psychological Association, San Francisco, April, 1962.
16. Kamiya, J., "Concious Control of Brain Waves," *Psychology Today*, 1968, *1*, 57-60.
17. Kamiya, J., & Nowlis, D., "The Control of Electroencephalographic Alpha Rhythms through Auditory Feedback and the Associated Mental Activity," *Psychophysiology*, 1970, *6*, 476-484.
18. Leuba, C., & Bateman, D., "Learning During Sleep," *American Journal of Psychology*, 1952, *65*, 301-302.
19. Levy, M., Staab, L., & Coolidge, F., "Associative Learning During EEG-Defined Sleep." Submitted for publication, 1971.
20. Mulholland, T., "The Concept of Attention and the Electroencephalographic Alpha Rhythm." Paper presented at the National Physical Laboratory on "The Concept of Attention in Neurophysiology," Teddington, England, October, 1967.

21. Orne, M., "On the Nature of Posthypnotic Suggestion." In L. Chertok (Ed.), *Psychophysiological Mechanisms of Hypnosis*. New York: Springer-Verlog, 1969, pp. 173-192.
22. Rubin, F. (Ed.), *Current Research in Hypnopaedia*. London: Macdonald, 1968.
23. Rubin, F., "Learning and Sleep," *Nature*, 1970, *226*, 477.
24. Simon, C., & Emmons, W., "Learning During Sleep?" *Psychological Bulletin*, 1955, *52*, 328-342.
25. Simon, C., & Emmons, W., "Responses to Material Presented During Various Levels of Sleep," *Journal of Experimental Psychology*, 1956, *51*, 89-97.
26. Stampfl, T., "The Effect of Frequency of Repetition on the Retention of Auditory Material Presented During Sleep." Unpublished master's thesis Loyola University, Chicago, 1953.
27. Stoyva, J., "The Public (Scientific) Study of Private Events." In E. Hartmann (Ed.), *Sleep and Dreaming*. Boston: Little, Brown, 1970, pp. 353-368.
28. Stoyva, J., & Kamiya, J., "Electrophysiological Studies of Dreaming as the Prototype of a New Strategy in the Study of Consciousness," *Psychological Review*, 1968, '75, 192-205.
29. Svyadoshch, A., "The Assimilation and Memorisation of Speech During Natural Sleep." In F. Rubin (Ed.), *Current Research in Hypnopaedia*. London: Macdonald, 1968, pp. 91-117.
30. Vogel, G., Foulkes, D., & Trosman, H., "Ego Functions and Dreaming During Sleep Onset, "*Archives of General Psychiatry*, 1966, *14*, 238-248.

# 9

**GREEN, E. E. et al.**

# *Biofeedback for Mind-Body Self-Regulation: Healing and Creativity*

The revolution in consciousness we are now talking about was foretold a long time ago. It was thought of as the time when the sleeping giant, humanity, would awaken, come to consciousness, and begin to exert its power. British medical people began to get an inkling of the power of consciousness as long as 250 years ago when they began to study certain Indians who could do some very unusual and interesting things. These people, called yogis, apparently had phenomenal powers of self-regulation, both of mind and body. Of course, medical doctors as a whole did not believe it, but as the decades passed and reports became more numerous, some British and European physicians began the study of mind-body relationships. By the end of the nineteenth century the physiological phenomena of hypnotism, spiritualism, and various yogic disciplines had attracted some serious medical and philosophical attention, and by 1910, a mind-body training system, eventually called Autogenic Training (self-generated or self-motivated training), had begun to be developed by Dr. Johannes Schultz in Germany. This was at approximately the time that Freud gave up the use of hypnosis as a medical tool because it was unpredictable. It occurred to Schultz that perhaps hypnosis was an erratic tool because the patient often unconsciously resisted the doctor. If the patient were able to direct for himself the procedure being used, with the doctor acting as his teacher, then the control technique would come into the realm of *self*-regulation and perhaps be more effective.

It is an interesting fact that the first English translation of Schultz and Luthe's handbook, *Autogenic Training,* (1959), contains in its 604 references only 10 that are in English. In addition to telling us that there was much interest on the continent in healing by self-regulation, it also tells us something about the British and the Americans. Freud's ideas became very important in the United States, whereas the self-regulation techniques of Autogenic Training were largely confined to Europe. It is also interesting to note that because of his interest in self-awareness, Schultz included in his training system some psychological disciplines which he called "meditative" exercises. These exercises gradually lead into a kind of self-awareness in which the person develops both physiological and psychological self-knowledge.

It was because of our interest in both consciousness and volition that my wife, Alyce, and I decided in 1965 to test Autogenic Training and find out whether or not people who used the exercises actually could develop some of the physiological controls Schultz talked about. Our research program began with 33 housewives. They practiced autogenic exercises for only two weeks and at the beginning and end of their training experience we measured most of the physiological variables that were easy to get, such as brain waves, heart rate, breathing rate, skin potential, skin resistance, blood flow in the fingers, and the temperatures of both hands, front and back. Some of the ladies failed to achieve much temperature control but a couple of them succeeded so well that we decided to continue studying Autogenic Training. It was clearly a training technique in which volition "en-

Elmer E. Green is Head of the Psychophysiology Lab, Research Department, The Menninger Foundation, Topeka, Kansas. Alyce M. Green and E. Dale Walters are also with the Research Department of The Menninger Foundation.

Originally given as a talk at the symposium on "The Varieties of Healing Experience," Cupertino, California, October 30, 1971. The symposium was sponsored jointly by The Academy of Parapsychology and Medicine and by the Lockheed MSC Management Association. Reprinted by permission.

tered" into the psychosomatic domain. It was also clear that if psychosomatic disease really existed, then it was logically necessary to hypothesize the existence of psychosomatic health. Both the literature of Autogenic Training and our research indicate that psychophysiological processes definitely could be self-regulated, and to allow for the existence of psychosomatic disease without postulating its opposite, psychosomatic health, would be an absurdity. If we can make ourselves sick, then we must also be able to make ourselves well.

Since physicians are saying these days that about 80% of human ailments are psychosomatic in origin, or at least have a psychosomatic component, it seems reasonable to assume that about 80% of our disabilities can be cured, or at least ameliorated, by the use of special training programs for psychosomatic health.

Gardner Murphy was very much interested in these research implications and one day suggested that we include biofeedback in our research methodology. He had been interested since 1952 in the possibility of using electrophysiological instrumentation for measuring and presenting to a person some of his own normally unconscious physiological processes—that is, processes of which a person is normally unaware. He knew, for instance, that muscle tension problems were often extremely difficult to handle, and when the doctor says, "Your problem is that you are too tense," he does not give much new information nor does it help much. Generally, the medical pronouncement is followed by a prescription, but what Murphy was suggesting was that if a person could "see" his tension, could look at a meter and observe its fluctuations, then perhaps he could learn to manipulate the underlying psychophysiological problem. He could practice "making the meter go down" and its behavior would tell him immediately if he was succeeding. In essence, this is an application of the engineering principle of feedback, the servomechanistic principle by means of which automatic machines are controlled. A furnace and its thermostat, for instance, form a closed (self-contained) feedback system. In this analogy, the human who adjusts the thermostat represents volition entering into the system from an energy source outside the closed loop.

Murphy's idea seemed useful, so we combined it with Autogenic Training and developed in 1967 a system of psychosomatic self-regulation that we called Autogenic Feedback Training. By coupling biofeedback with Autogenic Training, progress in controlling physiological variables is often highly accelerated. The self-suggestion formula of Autogenic Training (such as "I feel quite quiet") tells the unconscious section of mind, or brain, the goal toward which the person wishes to move, and the physiological feedback device immediately tells him the extent to which he is succeeding. The objective fact of a feedback meter, as a "truth" detector, has a powerful though not entirely understood effect on a person's ability to control normally involuntary physiological processes. For example, if a person's heart is malfunctioning from psychosomatic causes, it is certainly not "all in his head," but knowing that the cause is psychosomatic does not tell him what to do about it. When his heart rate is displayed on a meter, however, he can easily and objectively experiment with the psychological states that influence the rate. While using any kind of biofeedback device as a tool for learning something about yourself, it is interesting and instructive to experimentally induce in yourself a feeling of anxiety and nervousness, then calmness and tranquility. You can play with anger and with peacefulness. Then you can experiment with muscle tension, relaxation, slow deep breathing, etc. Learning to manipulate physiological processes while seeing the meter (or listening to it if it has an auditory output) is quite similar to learning to play a pinball machine with your eyes open. If you had to learn blindfolded, it would be difficult; but if you use your eyes (employing visual feedback), it is easy.

I will quickly summarize the work we have been doing in the Voluntary Controls Project at The Menninger Foundation and later mention our research with Swami Rama, an Indian Yogi who demonstrated in the laboratory some of the results of his own psychosomatic training program. If you wish to receive more information on any of this work, a note or postcard to us will be sufficient.

As already mentioned, our first project was to train a group of housewives to increase the temperature of their hands, using only Autogenic Training methods. After that we began an ambitious program in which an attempt was made to train eighteen college men to control *three* physiological variables simultaneously, using Autogenic Feedback Training. Feedback meters showed muscle tension in the right forearm, temperature of a finger on the right hand, and percentage of alpha rhythm in the brain-wave pattern (over the preceding ten-second interval of time).

Muscle tension was picked up from an electrode attached with salt paste to the skin. Temperature was obtained from a thermister taped lightly to the middle finger of the right hand, and brain wave (EEG) signals were obtained from an electrode pasted to the left occiput (the back of the head). The instruments were adjusted so that if the subject could relax his forearm completely the meter would "rise to the top." Complete relaxation means that there is a complete absence of muscle fiber "firing" and the electrical signal resulting from muscle tension "goes to zero." In this situation, the meter is wired to go to the top, showing complete success in *relaxation.* If the subject's finger showed an increase in *temperature* of ten degrees Fahrenheit, the temperature meter would rise to the top. It is interesting that if a subject tried to force the temperature to rise, by active volition, it invariably went down. But if he relaxed, "told the body" what to do, and then detached himself from the response, the temperature would rise. This is passive volition. A ten-degree decrease would cause the meter to go to the bottom. In other words, we set the meter in the center of its scale regardless of the absolute temperature of the hand, and studied only the temperature variations associated with the training program. The third meter showed percentage of alpha rhythm in the visual (occipital) area of the brain. After a period of training in relaxation and temperature control we would say to the subject, "Now while you keep the relaxation and warmth meters up, try to make the third meter, the alpha meter, go up without closing your eyes." It is common knowledge that about 90% of the population produce alpha waves when the eyes are closed; so if subjects closed their eyes, they could be expected to produce alpha waves. But we wanted them to generate, or bring about, an increase in the percentage of alpha while their eyes were open. One of our research objectives was to test the hypothesis that a person's success in remembering would be a function of, or correlated with, the percentage of alpha waves present while he was trying to remember. The eyes-open condition was useful because it served the purposes of keeping the subject from getting drowsy, permitted the use of a simple visual feedback device (though we could have used auditory feedback if desired), and it also enhanced the subject's "coupling" to the outside world. We wanted the subject to be able to look at the outside world and to answer questions without destroying his alpha rhythm, so it seemed useful to train him in awareness of both internal and external "worlds" at the same time by using a visual feedback system for brain waves. Results showed that in the students with whom we worked, the ability to remember was indeed positively correlated with the percentage of Alpha ($r=.54$, $p=0.1$), and it indicated that an alpha training program might be of great value in assisting students to overcome "mental blocks" during examinations.

Before continuing, however, it is useful to examine the accompanying diagram. It shows the major brain wave frequency bands and their relation to conscious and unconscious processes, in the general population.

When people focus attention on the outside world they usually produce only beta frequencies. If they close their eyes and think of nothing in particular, they generally produce a mixture of alpha and beta. If they slip toward sleep, become drowsy, theta frequencies often appear and there is less of alpha and beta. Delta waves are not normally present except in deep sleep. For example, at this moment I am predominantly in the beta state, and so are you—at least I think so.

Now alpha waves can be made to appear when the eyes are open if attention is turned inward, away from the outside world, but the way to make the alpha meter go up while looking at it is to learn to "observe without looking." Perhaps this sounds paradoxical, but it is not as difficult as answering the Zen koan, "What is the sound of one hand clapping?" In any event, we wanted students to be able to produce alpha waves with their eyes open and also to be able to answer questions while in this state.

The attempt to develop simultaneous self-regulation of three physiological variables in five weeks proved to be overly ambitious but students usually learned to control one or another of the original three variables quite well, and sometimes could control two at once. But it was not easy for anyone to control all three at the same time.

As we worked with the college group, we also ran pilot subjects in a theta training program and soon we noticed that the psychological state associated with theta contained, in a number of subjects, very clear hypnagogic-like imagery. Pictures or ideas would spring full blown into consciousness without the person being aware

| **Normally Unconscious** | | **Normally Conscious** | |
|---|---|---|---|
| **Delta** | **Theta** | **Alpha** | **Beta** |
| **1** | **4** | **8** | **13** **26** |

**Hertz (cycles per second)**

**Major frequency bands in the electroencephalographic (EEG) record.**

of their creation. The theta "reverie," as we began to call it, was definitely different from a daydreaming state and, much to our surprise, we found that it seemed to correspond with descriptions given by geniuses of the past of the state of consciousness they experienced while being their most creative. From these observations and from our experiences in training college students, we developed our present research project called "alpha-theta brain wave feedback, reverie, and imagery."

Without going into details about the machinery and procedures of theta training, in our present research in order to signal the presence of both alpha and theta frequencies in the occipital (visual) brain rhythm we use auditory feedback (musical tones) rather than visual feedback. As already mentioned, alpha production can easily be learned with the eyes open, but theta production is generally possible only with the eyes closed. The imagery associated with theta is often so tenuous that open eyes drive it away. In our presently used EEG feedback devices* a low-frequency feedback tone signifies theta and a higher frequency signifies alpha. For training away from the lab we have developed portable alpha-theta "home trainers," but in the lab we use an auditory feedback system that detects the presence of various brain waves and multiplies their frequencies by two hundred (up to the audible range). By this procedure, beta waves are made to produce a "piccolo" type of music. Alpha sounds like a flute, theta like an oboe, and delta like a bassoon. This combination results in an interesting and not unpleasing quartet. We have constructed two identical sets of amplifiers, filters, multipliers, and associated hardware, so that two brain wave channels can be studied simultaneously, and when we attach electrodes to the two sides of the head, it is possible to feed back to the subject musical information concerning the simultaneous electrical activity of the two cerebral hemispheres.

The right ear "listens" to the right side of the brain and the left ear listens to the left side. We have not used this elaborate laboratory feedback system except in pilot research, but we sometimes claim that we are going to use the machine to train a subject to play "The Star Spangled Banner," with the hope that it will encourage the federal government to release additional funds! That, at least, would demonstrate a high level of control.

In working with research subjects we obviously do not say that the physiological functions they are going to control are involuntary—because if they really believed that, the training would not work. In actuality, it is the "belief" of the subconscious (or unconscious) that is the controlling factor in learning to manipulate a so-called involuntary process. Feedback meters are remarkably powerful in training the autonomic nervous system because seeing is believing, even for the unconscious. There is little room for skepticism or disbelief concerning the practicality of temperature control when the temperature (blood flow) meter is used. Unconscious skepticism, as a factor in the psychophysiological matrix, seems to cause the hand temperature to drop, but this response indicates to the subject that the meter really does tell something, even if at first he does not know what it is. After a bit of practice with a feedback device, the situation is rather like learning to drive a car. The student driver does not question whether the car will move if he steps on the accelerator. And if he thinks that turning the steering wheel

* These machines are manufactured under licensing agreement from the Menninger Foundation, by a small electronics firm in Lawrence, Kansas.

to the left will make the car turn to the right, he soon discovers his error.

Without getting involved in details, it seems that a hierarchy of attitudes (or sets) is involved in learning to control normally involuntary processes—first, hypothesis—then, belief—and finally, knowing. A person may start with the *hypothesis* that the temperature of his hand will rise, but because of his previously conditioned response to introspection, his temperature may rapidly drop when he attempts to raise it. This response tells him, however, that something significant is going on in his nervous system in response to his efforts. Then, when he relaxes and begins to think of something else, becomes detached, the temperature begins to rise. So he begins to *believe* that the training system will work. Eventually he *knows* he can control the process and he knows what is happening in himself (in regard to raising or lowering hand temperature) whenever he turns his attention to the matter.

Quite often with beginners the hand temperature will rise at first, but then an insidious thought will creep in, such as, "it may work with other people, but it probably won't work for me." This precipitates vasoconstriction in the hands due to the activation of the sympathetic nervous system and blood flow in the hands is appropriately reduced. Within a few seconds temperature of the hands begins to drop.

From our various research experiences with Autogenic Training, biofeedback, and with highly trained persons such as Swami Rama, and lately with Jack Schwarz, we are beginning to believe, or at least hypothesize, that "*any* physiological process that can be detected and displayed in an objective fashion to the subject, can be self-regulated in some degree." Blood pressure, blood flow, heart rate, lymph flow, muscle tension, brain waves, all these have already been self-regulated through training in one laboratory or another. Where is the limit to this capacity for psychosomatic self-regulation? Nobody knows, but research indicates that the limits lie much farther out than was at first suspected by most of those interested in biofeedback.

It is useful here to draw attention to the major areas of the brain and discuss their relation to the process we are calling voluntary control of internal states. The item of particular significance in the accompanying diagram is that it is divided vertically into conscious and unconscious domains, on the right and left respectively. The conscious side contains both the cerebral cortex, which someone in the American Medical Association called the "screen of consciousness," and the craniospinal nervous system, roughly, the voluntary muscular system. The unconscious side includes both the subcortical brain, the "old" lower brain structures that man shares with most of the animals, and the autonomic nervous system, the involuntary nervous system, which lies outside of the brain and brainstem, and which controls, among other things, the skin, the internal organs and glands, and the vascular system of the body. The paleo-cortex, the old brain, includes a section called the limbic system which has been given a name of particularly great significance for understanding psychosomatic self-regulation—namely, "visceral brain." It is quite clear from recent research that electrical stimulation of the visceral brain and related neural structures through implanted electrodes causes emotional changes in humans. Conversely, it is well known that perceptual and emotional changes are followed by neural changes, or responses, in the limbic system of the brain, though most of this work was performed with animals. Putting together some of the pieces of the mind-body system as observed both physiologically in the nervous system and behaviorally (through Autogenic Feedback Training) we have found it convenient to postulate a *psychophysiological principle* which goes as follows: "Every change in the physiological state is accompanied by an appropriate change in the mental-emotional state, conscious or unconscious, and conversely, every change in the mental-emotional state, conscious or unconscious, is accompanied by an appropriate change in the physiological state." This closed-loop statement obviously does not allow for volition or free will in humans any more than the furnace-and-thermostat system of your house is "allowed" to have a will of its own, but even as the thermostat is manipulated by a force from outside—namely, your hand (which would have to be categorized as a meta-force in the furnace-and-thermostat system)—so also the psychophysiological principle, or its expression in the psychosomatic unity of mind and body, is manipulated by volition, which at present is of indeterminate origin, but which at least exhibits some of the characteristics of a meta-force. These ideas, incidentally, are quite clearly put forth in the Vedas, sacred scriptures of India, and lie behind the system of Raja Yoga. These basic concepts are well considered in Aurobindo's Integral Yoga, especially in his book called *The Synthesis of Yoga.*

But to return to the diagram, the dashed line represents at a specific moment the actual, rather than theoretical, division between conscious and unconscious functions in the nervous system. We must visualize the dashed line as continually shifting and undulating between various brain structures as attention shifts from one thing to another. It is clear that when we learn to drive a car, every movement must at first be worked over in the conscious domain. But after we have learned to drive well enough it is possible, when we are thinking of something else, to drive all the way through town without being aware of stopping at stop signs. In other words, what was once conscious became unconscious for a time. In other words, the dashed line moved from left to right and extended for a period of time over neurological structures in the neo-cortex and in the craniospinal system. On the other hand, when one learns through biofeedback training to control the flow of blood in his hands, he is obviously extending conscious control for a period of time over an area which lies to the left of center in the diagram. That is, some of the subcortical brain structures and some of the neural circuits in the autonomic nervous system have come under conscious control. It is interesting that when patients using Autogenic Training reported to Dr. Schultz that they could not achieve control over some physiological process, he would say that they had not made "mental contact" with that part of the body. In other words, again, they had not extended the dashed line of the diagram far enough to the left in a specific neural pathway.

Now to discuss our research with Swami Rama. Dr. Daniel Ferguson, at the Veterans Administration Hospital in St. Paul, Minnesota, became aware of the "voluntary controls" work at the Foundation and one day near the end of 1969 he wrote to me saying that if we were interested in making some tests of an Indian yogi who could control a number of normally uncontrollable physiological processes, he would arrange a meeting in Topeka. The upshot of this was that Swami Rama (of Rishikesh and the Himalayas) and Dr. Ferguson visited us for three days in March, 1970. The Foundation for the

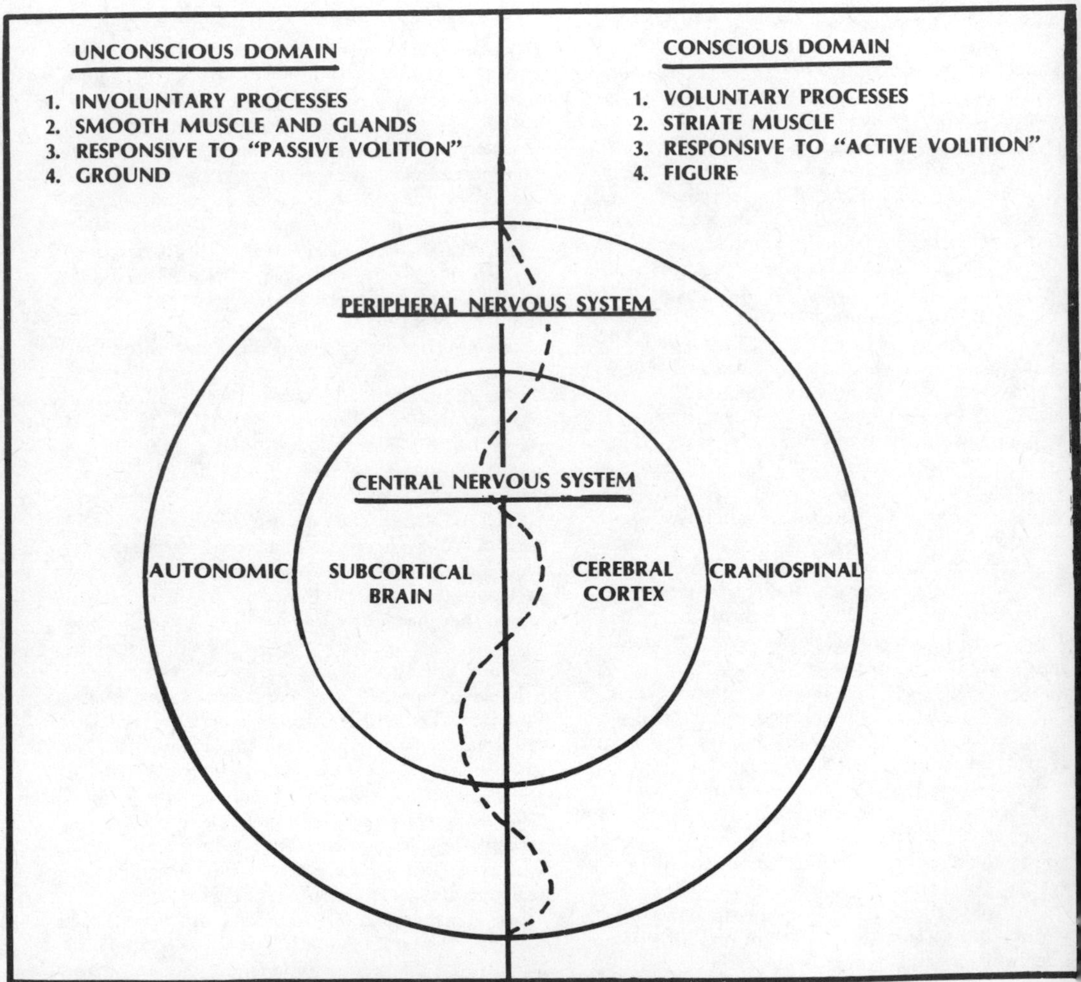


Psychophysiological diagram relating the conscious-unconscious psychological domain to the various sections of the voluntary-involuntary physiological domain. The solid vertical line separates the central and peripheral nervous systems into functional subregions. The dashed line (conceptually visualized to be in continuous undulatory movement) separates the conscious and unconscious areas.

Study of Consciousness, Philadelphia, Pennsylvania, provided research funds for this visit. Later we obtained funding from both The Millicent Foundation, Vancouver, Washington, and from the Joseph and Sadie Danciger Fund, Kansas City, Missouri, to work with the Swami over an extended period of time.

During the first visit, Swami Rama demonstrated that he had exquisite differential control over arteries in his right hand. We had "wired" him for brain waves, respiration, skin potential, skin resistance, heart behavior (EKG), blood flow in his hands, and temperature. While thus encumbered he caused two areas a couple of inches apart on the palm of his right hand to gradually change temperature in opposite directions (at a maximum rate of about 4°F. per minute) until they showed a temperature difference of about 10°F. The left side of his palm, after this performance (which was totally motionless), looked as if it had been slapped with a ruler a few times—it was rosy red. The right side of his hand had turned ashen grey. During the last session of this visit, he made the comment that according to theory a swami could not be upset or distracted, but that it was a good thing that none of his students were here to demonstrate their powers of physiological control, because he doubted if they would be able to succeed in such a strange scientific setting. Other demonstrations included the speeding and slowing of his heart rate, and finally we concluded the tests, we thought. But during dinner, on the evening before he and Dr. Ferguson were to return to Minneapolis, he suddenly said he was sorry he had not demonstrated "stopping" his heart and that he would do it in the morning.

Both Alyce and I objected to this because he had just finished telling us that in order to demonstrate some of the more physiologically serious controls, such as stopping the heart, it was necessary to fast for a couple of days, taking nothing but fluids. I could well believe this because, according to the Swami, he would stop his heart in this particular demonstration by control of the vagus nerve. Since the vagus nerve also has an important control function over the stomach and other visceral organs, it could logically cause a serious case of indigestion, to say the least.

The Swami's answer to our objection, however, was that anything he could do in three minutes his Guru could do in three seconds and that he wanted to perform this experiment in order to test himself. Finally, having satisfied himself that he had answered, or demolished, our arguments, and having said that, if necessary, he would sign papers to the effect that The Menninger Foundation was not in any way responsible for anything that might happen to him, he said that he could stop his heart in this way for three or four minutes, and how long would we need for an adequate test. I said that ten seconds would be quite impressive and he agreed to this limitation.

The next day we hurried to the lab at nine o'clock (we had previously scheduled a lecture for him at ten o'clock) and wired him for the demonstration. Before starting his "inner focussing" procedure, however, he said that when his heart stopped he wanted Alyce to call over the intercom from the control room and say "That's all." This would be the signal for timing the duration of his demonstration and would also remind him not to "go too far." He said that he did not want to interfere with the functioning of his "subtle heart," the one that lay behind the workings of his "physical heart." Having explained this, he made a few trial runs at speeding and slowing his heart, then said, "I am going to give a shock, do not be alarmed." To me this meant that he was going to give himself some kind of neural shock, but later I learned that he was going to shock the research personnel and doctors who were watching the paper records and polygraph pens in the control room, and they were being told not to be alarmed. After about twenty seconds of motionless silence I heard Alyce say, "That's all." At this, the Swami pulled in his stomach muscles for a few seconds, then he relaxed. From his look I could see that he felt the test had been a success, so I began asking questions about the "internal" process he used to accomplish such a thing. While he was answering, Alyce called over the intercom and said that the heart record was not what we had expected and suggested that I look at it before going any further.

To my surprise, the heart rate instead of dropping to zero had jumped in one beat from about 70 per minute to about 300 per minute. I returned to the experimental room and described the record to the Swami. He seemed somewhat surprised and bothered and said, "You know that when you stop the heart in this way, it still trembles in there," and he illustrated with fluttering hands. I speculated then that what we had recorded might be some kind of fibrillation, but later was told by Dr. Marvin Dunne, cardiologist and professor at the Kansas University Medical Center (Kansas City, Kansas), after he had examined the records, that it was a case of "atrial flutter," a state in which the heart fires at its maximum rate without blood either filling the chambers properly or the valves working properly. He showed me similar records obtained from patients and asked what happened to the Swami, he should have passed out, but I had to answer that we quickly "unwired" him so he could get to his lecture on time.

The atrial flutter actually lasted for an interval between 17 and 25 seconds. The exact duration could not be determined from the record because when the Swami drew in his stomach the resulting electrical signal from muscle firing caused the EKG pen to go off the edge of the paper, and after it returned the heart rate was normal again. I asked him why he had moved his stomach and he said that he had established a "solar plexus lock," by means of which the heart condition could be maintained for quite a long time if desired. It is interesting to note that when the heart began to flutter the people in the control room had a hurried consultation amongst themselves to decide if this was what the Swami meant by "stopping" his heart. After about eight seconds they decided that whatever it was it looked dangerous and decided to give the "that's all" signal.

In summary, we may say that the Swami stopped his heart from pumping blood for at least 17 seconds. This was his technique, we discovered for obliterating his pulse during examination by medical doctors. The "other" kind of heart stopping, he said, involved a hibernation-like state that he might be prepared to demonstrate on some other occasion.

The importance of Swami Rama's demonstrations did not lie in the performances themselves but in their implications. I do not intend to practice stopping my heart or to try to teach anyone else according to the Swami's instructions, but the fact that *it can be done* is of major scientific importance. Aside from supporting the psychophysiological theory previously discussed, it more importantly gives us additional reason to believe that training programs are feasible for the establishment and maintenance of psychosomatic health. If every young student *knew* by the time he finished his first biology class, in grade school, that the body responds to self-generated psychological inputs, that blood flow and heart behavior, as well as a host of other body processes, can be influenced at will, it would change prevailing ideas about both physical and mental health. It would then be quite clear and understandable that we are individually responsible to a large extent for our state of health or disease.

Perhaps then people would begin to realize that it is not life that kills us, but rather it is our reaction to it, and this reaction can be to a significant extent self-chosen.

Later in the year Swami Rama returned to the Foundation for another series of experiments, especially for correlating internal psychological states (phenomenological or existential states) with brain wave patterns. At first the experiments appeared disastrous for our general theory of "focus of attention and brain wave correlates." No matter what psychological state we asked the Swami to demonstrate, from a list he had supplied, the only definite brain rhythm was in the beta frequency band, which was presumably associated with (at least in our understanding of the matter) attention on outside-world sensory processes or attention on intense internal activation of a stressful nature. But one day, after about two weeks of sessions, the Swami said he had some news for us. All the records would have to be thrown away because he had not successfully entered any of the subjective states we had been attempting to study. Since I had not shown him the records, and had not discussed my misgivings with him, this unsolicited announcement came like a ray of light through dark clouds. I asked what the problem seemed to be and he answered that it would have been much better if I had not told him that the polygraph paper cost $16 per box. All he could think of, he said, was the terrible expense involved and all the people watching paper shoot out of the machines.

After that came out, we assured him that if necessary we could run paper for twenty-four hour periods without bankrupting the project, and it was agreed that henceforth he would take as long as necessary to move into a particular state of consciousness and that at the appropriate time he would come out of the state and tell us, essentially, that the last five minutes of the record contained what we were looking for. The result of this conversation was a considerable lessening of tension, and Swami was subsequently able to enter various states (evidenced by remarkable changes in brain wave patterns) in no more than fifteen minutes, and usually in five minutes.

In five 15-minute brain wave feedback sessions he was able to tie together in his mind the relationship between the tones produced by activation in the various brain wave bands and the states of consciousness he had learned in a Himalayan cave. Then he produced 70% alpha waves over a five-minute period of time by thinking of an empty blue sky "with a small white cloud" sometimes coming by. After a number of alpha-producing sessions the Swami said, "I have news for you, alpha isn't anything. It is literally nothing." This did not surprise us, because we had already observed that the best way to produce alpha was to close the eyes and think of nothing in particular, but it would have provided a shock, I suppose, to the many mind-training researchers who are telling people all over the country that when in the alpha brain wave state you can get rid of your diseases, get the most wonderful ideas, and, best of all, be telepathic. This kind of talk is nonsense to those clinicians and technicians who work in EEG labs. Whether they accept the possibility of telepathy or not, they know that 90% of the population of the United States produce alpha waves when the eyes are closed, and the majority of our people are certainly not telepathic nor can they rid themselves of disease merely by being in an alpha brain wave state.

In any event, the Swami next produced theta waves by "stilling the conscious mind and bringing forward the unconscious." In one five-minute period of the test he produced theta waves 75% of the time. I asked him what his experience was and he answered that it was an unpleasant state, "very noisy." The things he had wanted to do but did not do, the things he should have done but did not do, and associated images and memories of people who wanted him to do things, came up in a rush and began shouting at him. It was a state that he generally kept turned off, he said, but it was also instructive and important to look in once in a while to see what was there. From what he said I could well understand that his life in India, of rigorous discipline and strenuous practice, had involved a good deal of suppression and that his reverential attitude toward his Guru, as a being in whom conflicts were resolved, was partly based on his understanding of the difficulty of creating a true synthesis of forces in oneself. The perfected Guru, according to Indian tradition, is a liberated being who, among other things, has consciously examined all parts of his nature, conscious and unconscious, and has established tranquility and harmony there.

After producing theta waves, the Swami said he knew exactly how the inner states of awareness were arranged in respect to the brain wave frequency bands. Then he said, "Tomorrow I will consciously make delta waves for you." I replied that I doubted that he would succeed in that because he would have to be sound asleep in order to produce delta. He laughed at this and said that I would think that he was asleep but that he would be conscious of everything that occured in the experimental room.

Before this test he asked how long I would like to have him remain in the delta state. I said that 25 minutes would be all right and he said he would bring himself out at that time. After about five minutes of meditation, lying down with his eyes shut, the Swami began producing delta waves, which we had never before seen in his record. In addition, he snored gently. Alyce, without having told Swami that she was going to say anything (she was in the experimental room observing him during this test) then made a statement in a low voice, "Today the sun is shining, but tomorrow it may rain." Every five minutes she made another statement and after 25 minutes had passed the Swami roused himself and said that someone with sharp heels had walked on the floor above and made a click, click, click noise during the test, and a door had been slammed twice somewhere in the building, and that Mrs. Green had said—and here he gave her statements verbatim, except for the last half of the fourth sentence, of which he had the gist correct though not the words. I was very much impressed because, in listening from the control room, I had heard her sentences, but could not remember them all, and I was supposed to have been awake. Dale Walters, our colleague in this research for the last five years, didn't remember much more than I, but we reminded each other that our attention was supposed to be on the physiological records, not on what Alyce was saying.

The Swami said that this "yogic sleep," as he called it, was extremely beneficial. He said fifteen minutes of it was as good as an hour's normal sleep. Most people, he continued, let their brains go to sleep while their minds were still busy worrying over various matters, with the result that they woke up tired. It is necessary for the mind and brain to sleep at the same time, he explained. In the delta state he had just produced, he said, he told his mind to be quiet, to not respond to anything but to record everything, to remain in a deep state of tranquility until he activated it. He also said that this kind of sleep was called "dog sleep," because a good dog can leap up from a sound sleep and chase after something without any apparent signs of having to reactivate, a very Zen-like condition it seemed to me.

We did not complete all the experiments planned with Swami Rama. He became involved in giving lectures and seminars around the country and eventually went to India to attend the "yoga and science" conference at New Delhi (December, 1970). It was interesting that he carried with him two of our biofeedback machines and gave a lecture called "Yoga and Biofeedback Training." His attitude about biofeedback was that it would accelerate the training of young yogis, up to the point where machines could no longer follow. The machines would also eliminate fakers (not fakirs, please note) by the dozens. Hopefully we will again, one day, have a chance to do more psychophysiological work with Swami Rama.

In our research with the Swami we naturally focused a good deal of attention on physiological data because they are easy to put into graphical form, and it is easier to get research money for projects that come out with red ink on green graph paper. Some of Swami Rama's other accomplishments were of utmost interest, however. For instance, we observed that he could diagnose physical ailments very much in the manner of Edgar Cayce, except that he appeared to be totally conscious, though with indrawn attention for a few seconds while he was "picking up" information. His training program will hopefully be made available to medical doctors, he says, but not, I gathered, before 1973.

Before concluding, it should be mentioned that when the Swami produced alpha, he did not cease the production of beta. And when he produced theta, both alpha and beta were retained, each about 50% of the time. Likewise, when he produced delta he was also producing theta, alpha, and beta during a relatively high percentage of the time. Perhaps this tells us something important. Since alpha is a conscious state, it may be necessary to retain it when theta is produced if one wishes to be aware of the hypnagogic imagery which is often associated with theta. This idea was supported by some of our pilot research with a group of adults who were interested in being experimental subjects for theta research, using brain wave feedback and also some of Swami Rama's breathing exercises for tranquilizing the autonomic nervous system. The main exercise consisted of deep and slow rhythmic breathing, at a constant rate both in and out, with no pauses at the bottom or top of the respiration cycle. After four or five months had passed, with at least ten days a month including a "breathing and meditation" period (at home), the breathing rate could be comfortably slowed to once or twice per minute, for a period of ten minutes. These findings are probably consistent with Wallace's observation, reported in *Science,* that a significant drop in basal metabolism rate (BMR) accompanied the practice of "transcendental meditation" by a group of college students. We did not have metabolism-measuring equipment in our lab, but we might suspect that if the BMR did not drop significantly in our subjects that it would be very difficult for them to breathe at such an "inadequate" rate without experiencing involuntary diaphragmatic gasping. The Swami's instruction, to allow "no jerks," was eventually complied with, much to our surprise.

As a final word, it seems increasingly certain that healing and creativity are different pieces of a single picture. Both Swami Rama and Jack Schwarz, a Western Sufi whom we recently had a chance to work with, maintain that self-healing can be performed in a state of deep *reverie*. Images for giving the body instructions are manipulated in a manner very similar to that used by Assagioli for personality and transpersonal integration, as in his *Psychosynthesis*. But this "manner" of manipulation of images is also the same as that in which we find ideas being handled creatively (by two pilot subjects) for the solution of intellectual problems. What an interesting finding! Creativity in terms of physiological processes means, then, *physical healing*, physical regeneration. Creativity in emotional terms consists, then, of establishing, or creating, *attitude changes* through the practice of healthful emotions—that is, emotions whose neural correlates are those that establish harmony in the visceral brain, or to put it another way, emotions that establish in the visceral brain those neurological patterns whose reflection in the viscera is one that physicians approve of as stress resistant. Creativity in the mental domain involves the emergence of a new and valid *synthesis of ideas*, not by deduction, but springing by "intuition" from unconscious sources.

The entrance, or key, to all these inner processes, we are beginning to believe, is a particular state of consciousness to which we have given the undifferentiated name "reverie." This reverie can be approached by means of theta brain wave training in which the gap between conscious and unconscious processes is voluntarily narrowed, and temporarily eliminated when useful. When that self-regulated reverie is established, the body can apparently be programmed at will and the instructions given will be carried out, emotional states can be dispassionately examined, accepted or rejected, or totally supplanted by others deemed more useful, and problems insoluble in the normal state of consciousness can be elegantly resolved.

Perhaps now, because of the resurgence of interest in self-exploration and in self-realization, it will be possible to develop a synthesis of old and new, East and West, prescience and science, using both yoga and biofeedback training as tools for the study of consciousness. It is also interesting to hypothesize that useful parapsychological talents can perhaps be developed by use of these reverie-generating processes of yoga and biofeedback. Much remains to be researched, and tried in application, but there is little doubt that in the lives of many people a penetration of consciousness into previously unconscious realms (of mind and brain) is making understandable and functional much that was previously obscure and inoperable.

# 10

**STOYVA, J.**

# *Biofeedback Techniques and the Conditions for Hallucinatory Activity*[1]

Psychophysiology, as the name implies, involves both physiological and psychological observations. If we grant that psychology can be divided into a behavioral component and an experiential one, then, psychophysiology may be thought to embrace three levels of observation—the physiological, the behavioral, and the experiential—the latter indexed by verbal report.

One's first reaction might be to view such an approach as a strategy designed to produce a maximum of confusion. But we think this is not

[1] Supported by Grant Number MH-15596, National Institute of Mental Health; Research Scientist Development Award No. K01-MH-43361-01, National Institute of Mental Health; and Bioengineering Neurosciences Grant NS-08511, National Institute of Health (for development work by the University of Colorado Medical Center Bioengineering Department on the instrumentation system described in this paper).

the case—or at least not necessarily! The thesis advanced here is that the combined use of physiological and psychological data can be a fruitful method of experimental inquiry—useful both as a means of gathering evidence about psychological phenomena, and as a method for discovering new relationships. Further, with the addition of the information feedback principle, a new dimension is grafted to psychophysiological methodology. The emerging technique of feedback psychophysiology can, we believe, be valuable not only in exploring a variety of mental processes, but also in teaching individuals to produce certain psychological states at will.

In developing the argument of this paper, we will first examine recent electrophysiological research on dreaming as a method of studying the mental activity which occurs during sleep. We will then consider biofeedback techniques in the exploration of waking mental activity, particularly in the induction of low arousal, twilight states.[2] Finally, it will be argued that biofeedback techniques can be useful in helping to specify some of the conditions under which "naturally occurring" hallucinatory experiences are likely to arise (including the hallucinatory experiences of dreams, sleep-onset, sensory isolation, and hypnosis, but excluding those produced by drugs or surgical intervention).

## I. INFERENCES ABOUT CONSCIOUSNESS

A striking feature of contemporary psychological research is how the study of dreaming suddenly became much more scientifically respectable after the discovery that bursts of rapid eye movements (REMs) during sleep were closely associated with vivid visual dreaming (Aserinsky & Kleitman, 1953; Dement & Kleitman, 1957). Was the new enthusiasm for the study of dream processes as a fit topic for scientific inquiry well-justified, or were the supposed benefits largely illusory?

In the author's opinion there was good reason for the rekindled enthusiasm. The use of physiological indicators, such as REMs, in combina-

[2] By "twilight states" we refer to psychophysiological events occurring at the border between sleep and waking. In terms of EEG patterns these states are mainly indexed by alpha rhythms, or theta rhythms, or incipient Stage 2 "spindling" sleep. Their experiential attributes are discussed later in this paper. We refer to them in the plural since they seem to exist in some variety.

By "low arousal" we refer to a condition in which the major indicators of arousal are at reduced levels compared to when the individual is alert and active. Typically, muscle tension is reduced; autonomic activity such as heart rate and respiration are diminished; and cortical activity has shifted from low amplitude–fast activity to the slower brain wave frequencies characteristic of sleep onset.

tion with verbal reports of dreaming amounted to a methodological innovation. This innovation was *both* a method of proof, *and* a technique for discovering new relationships between physiological events and psychological events, such as dreaming (see Stoyva & Kamiya, 1968; Stoyva, 1970).

As an example of the new method, let us consider the association between REMs and dreaming. If a subject is awakened during a REM period, there is about an 80% probability that he will report a dream. On the basis of this observation, there are at least three different hypotheses which could be proposed:

1. Verbal reports of dreaming from REM sleep reflect recall of a genuine dream experience which was in progress just prior to the awakening.

2. The dream which the subject reports from his REM awakening did not actually occur, but is a fabrication.

3. The subject is remembering a genuine dream, but it occurred earlier during the night. This dream has nothing to do with the presence of REMs.

Experiments carried out early in the history of the REM sleep era demonstrated that Hypotheses 2 and 3 could be rejected, leaving Hypothesis 1 as the interpretation offering the best fit to the data. For example, Dement and Kleitman (1957) noted a positive correlation between the subjectively estimated length of a dream and the amount of REM sleep which had elapsed just prior to an awakening; Berger and Oswald (1962) found that REM density was related to the amount of physical activity in the dream narrative; Lewis *et al.* (1966) observed a positive correlation between REM period density and the dream's bizzareness.[3]

Once the validity of the REM indicator of dreaming had been established, a cluster of new findings was brought to light. The effects on dreaming of presleep experiences were examined, as were the effects of sensory stimulation of various kinds during sleep. Processes of dream recall were investigated, as was the relationship of REM dreams to personality attributes. Characteristic quality of mental activity at various stages of the sleep cycle was explored—in REM sleep, in non-REM sleep, and in the hypnagogic or sleep-onset state (see Foulkes, 1966).

[3] Dement and Kleitman (1957), and later Roffwarg, Dement, Muzio, and Fisher (1962) reported a close relationship between the recorded direction of eye movement activity and the visual activity in the dream narrative—e.g., imagery involving horizontal eye movements was associated with predominately horizontal eye movements on the chart paper. This observation, frequently cited in support of a scanning hypothesis of dreaming, has recently been challenged by the negative findings of Berger and Moskowitz (1970).

The methodological innovation employed in these studies—combined use of physiological measures and verbal reports of dreaming—was a technique involving a particular experimental logic. This logic, which has rarely been made explicit, is basically a method of excluded hypotheses. It has been ably described by Platt (1964) in his paper, "Strong Inference."

Platt states that in strong inference the researcher postulates the alternative hypotheses which could account for a given experimental result. He then systematically puts these hypotheses to empirical test and determines which can be destroyed. Then, with the hypothesis which has survived, he makes further inferences which in turn are tested. So there is a kind of creative destruction, involving the natural selection of the fittest hypotheses!

In the author's opinion this method of excluded hypotheses, or strong inference, should be used more extensively and more explicitly in psychological experimentation. In part, the reason is that we end up using it anyway, but often in an inefficient manner—usually, after a crossfire of colleague and editorial criticism! Also, its deliberate use encourages the experimenter to focus on experiments which affirm or deny a hypothesis, rather than to do work which is simply piling up additional data. (For an elegant example of this method, involving a series of experiments of the operant conditioning of hippocampal theta rhythm, see Black, 1971.)

To summarize the argument of this section: The events of consciousness can be scientifically studied to the extent that we can make testable inferences about them. One area which has made use of testable inferences about consciousness is contemporary dream research. The basic approach has involved the combined use of physiological measures and verbal report. In the remainder of this paper, we shall attempt to show that this approach can be usefully extended to some types of waking mental activity—particularly the thinking which occurs in association with low arousal, sleep onset conditions.

## A. Linking the Physiological and the Experiential—The Feedback Loop

The combined use of physiological measures and verbal report, as described above, need not be confined to the study of dreaming, but can be employed in the study of certain waking mental activity as well. In particular, with the addition of the feedback loop, a new dimension is added to the basic technique.

### 1. *Alpha Control*

The first to seize on the implications of information feedback techniques in the study of conscious events was Kamiya (1969). In the late 1950s he asked himself whether a subject would be able to discriminate the presence or absence of his own alpha rhythm—as detected by conventional EEG recording techniques. Some individuals proved highly skillful at learning this task—if they were told on a trial-by-trial basis whether their response had been right or wrong.

Kamiya next shifted to a technique which gave the subject continuous information as to whether he was in *alpha* or in *non-alpha*. A tone indicated alpha, no-tone the absence of it—the subject was now in a closed feedback loop. Many individuals, over the course of four to ten training sessions learned to stay in alpha a high proportion of the time.

Perhaps the most salient feature of alpha's attractiveness was its association with characteristic mental states, at least on an individual subject basis. Alpha was frequently described as a condition in which visual imagery was dampened or absent, a state of "blank mind," letting go," or of "relaxation." Another characteristic pertained to *willing*: If a subject tried hard to produce alpha, he was sure not to succeed. The act of striving was inimical to the production of alpha.[4]

### 2. *EMG Feedback Techniques*

In our Colorado laboratory, we also became interested in feedback techniques, but instead of pursuing alpha, we turned our attention to electromyographic (EMG) feedback. A main reason for this focus was the evidence from Jacobson's (1938, 1970) progressive relaxation, from behavior therapy, and from autogenic training which indicated the clinical usefulness of muscle relaxation.

*Instrumentation.* Once the formidable task of developing a high-performance instrument had been accomplished by my associate, Dr. Thomas Budzynski (see Fig. 11.1 for functional diagram), we tested it to see whether EMG feedback worked better than no-feedback or irrelevant feedback in producing deep muscle relaxation. The feedback condition proved clearly superior (Budzynski and Stoyva, 1969).

[4] There has been much controversy about the origin of the alpha rhythm. Some have dismissed it as an artifact (Kennedy, 1959; Lippold, 1970). More convincingly, Mulholland (1968) has linked it to the operation of the oculomotor system. But regardless of exactly how it originates, alpha remains of value to those interested in producing the experiential state associated with it.

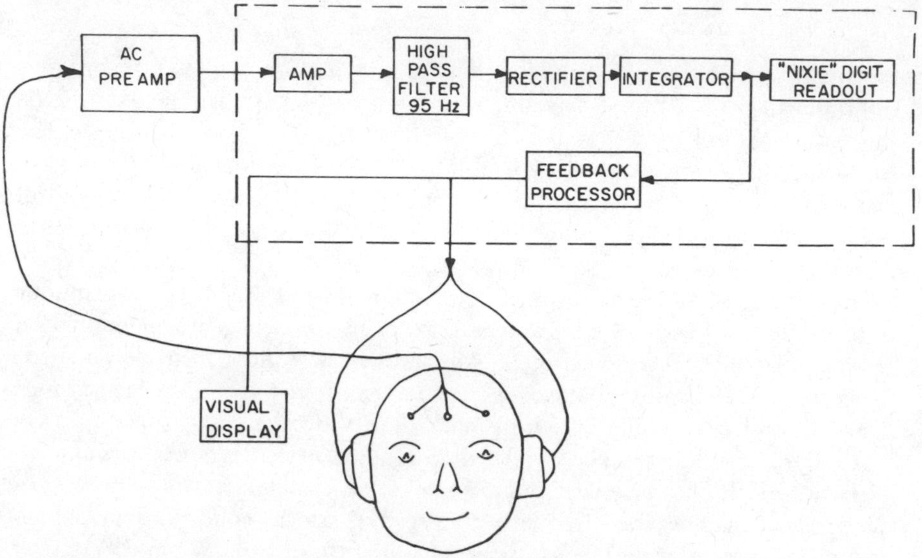


**Fig. 11.1.** Functional diagram of EMG information feedback unit.

Recently Dr. Budzynski has developed an exceedingly useful and versatile instrumentation system. It can be best thought of as a *biofeedback polygraph,* and it now used routinely with all our experimental subjects. The system has feedback capability for EMG activity, for alpha rhythms (8–12 Hz), and for theta rhythms (4–7 Hz). Additionally, it provides continuous quantification of six physiological parameters on a minute-by-minute basis.

The heart of the system is a constant reset level integrator (also known as a Drohocki integrator or resetting integrator). There is one resetting integrator for each parameter to be quantified, such as theta, forearm EMG, etc. The integrators allow electrical energy to build up to a predetermined point. When this point is reached, a pulse fires, and the integrator resets to zero. Each integrator, therefore, generates a train of digital pulses. These pulses perform three tasks: (1) They provide auditory feedback to the subject—a series of variable-rate clicks which he hears through his headphones (see Fig. 11.1). (2) They provide a moment-to-moment printout on the chart paper—a series of digital pulses is obtained for each parameter (see Fig. 11.2). (3) They drive the quantification apparatus. Each digital pulse adds one increment to the Nixie-tube readout which, essentially, is a device for counting pulses. At the end of every 1-min trial the experimenter notes the accumulated pulse count for each parameter and then resets each Nixie-tube counter back to zero.

The foregoing instrumentation system should prove useful in many areas of psychophysiological research since it not only gives feedback information on several parameters, but also provides precise quantification of measures which generally have been laboriously and often inaccurately handscored, e.g., EMG activity.

*Applications.* For the past several years, our main research emphasis has been strongly applied. We have been interested in teaching individuals to reach low arousal conditions, and in making clinical use of this ability. In this endeavor, we were greatly encouraged by the work of Jacobson (1938) and by the research on autogenic training (Schultz & Luthe, 1959), both of which attest to the clinically valuable properties of the ability

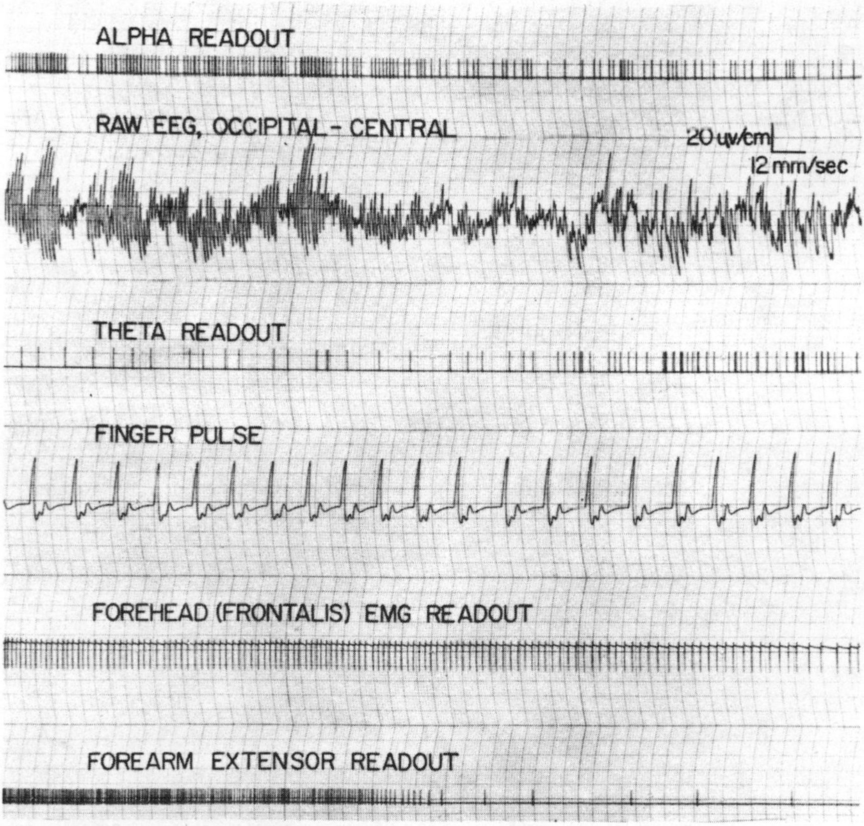


**Fig. 11.2.** Digital readout and quantification system for EEG and EMG.

to voluntarily reach low arousal levels. The technique of feedback-induced relaxation has been applied to the treatment of tension headache (Budzynski, Stoyva, & Adler, 1970), in the desensitization process in behavior therapy, and in the treatment of several cases of sleep-onset insomnia.

Despite our strongly applied emphasis, however, we have noticed that the subject who shifts to a low arousal condition experiences changes in the nature of his thinking, changes which are difficult to ignore.

As with alpha, the condition of feedback-induced muscle relaxation is associated with an alteration in the quality of thinking, and involves a departure from the thought processes of alert, reality-oriented wakefulness to the imagery and sensations characteristic of the twilight states bordering on sleep. In deep relaxation, sensations of heaviness and warmth are common—probably related to a shift toward parasympathetic dominance in the autonomic nervous system. Distortions or changes of body image are likewise common—feelings of floating, of turning, of a limb moving, or disappearing. Vivid visual images, often of a hallucinatory intensity, frequently appear. These images occur spontaneously, and seem related to "nonstriving mode of experiencing" in which the subject finds himself.

## B. Some Principles and Properties of Biofeedback Training

Although the area is still new, certain principles and continuities in biofeedback research seem regular enough to be worth noting, and will probably figure prominently in future investigations.

### *1. The Active–Passive Dimension*

As already noted, if the subject strives hard to produce alpha, he fails to attain it. The same observation holds for muscle relaxation. A person who strives hard to relax—and this is especially likely to be the beginner or the anxious patient—finds instead that he is tensing up.

It is necessary for the learner to abandon the "active-willing mode" appropriate to accomplishing tasks in the external world. Instead, if he follows the guidance of the feedback signal, he finds himself shifting to another kind of orientation characterized by a lack of striving, a "letting go" quality.

That this dimension of passive, as opposed to active concentration, has emerged so clearly in biofeedback work is in striking confirmation of independent observations from related disciplines. For example, in Zen literature, a recurring theme (and one puzzling to Westerners) is that the best way to attain satori, or a state of enlightenment, is to stop trying to reach it. Similarly, in autogenic training (Schultz & Luthe, 1959), great emphasis is placed on the cultivation of "passive concentration" as opposed to "active concentration." A related emphasis may be found in Jacobson's progressive relaxation (1938, 1970).

*2. Testing Hypotheses of Association*

Biofeedback techniques can be useful in demonstrating an association between a physiological event and an experiential one, and in determining whether the association is strong or weak. Specifically, are the two events closely enough linked so that changing one member of the paired events produces a simultaneous change in the other member? For example, if we wish to show that the 4–7 Hz theta rhythm and the experience of drowsiness are related, then the subject can be provided with feedback of his theta rhythms. When he succeeds in producing more extended periods of theta, he should report more extended periods of drowsiness.

Certain other events occurring during drowsiness could be expected to show an association of a weaker nature, e.g., the slow rolling eye movements which occur during sleep onset (see Foulkes, 1966). If a subject voluntarily produces slow rolling eye movements, would it make him drowsy? Probably not. In any case, the question would be open to empirical test.

If the linkage between the physiological event and the experiential event is tight, then the approach should be reversible. Thus, a subject could deliberately attempt to make himself drowsy without the aid of external feedback. If he succeeded, we would expect that the more drowsy he became, the more theta would be in evidence.

This reversed technique would not involve the use of an external feedback loop. Its efficacy would, however, hinge on the ability of the subject to detect internal sensations associated with the response he wishes to control, for example, the sensations of drowsiness associated with theta. Even though external feedback would not be present, the subject would be receiving self-generated internal feedback, or "proprioceptive cues"—which are crucial in maintaining the feedback-acquired response after termination of training.

*3. Biofeedback Training and Introspection*

Can biofeedback training sharpen an individual's ability at introspection? It probably can, at least in some respects (see Stoyva & Kamiya, 1968). For example, if we provide a subject with alpha feedback, he can learn to identify those private events associated with "tone on," for example, a feeling of letting go, a dampening or absence of visual imagery, or relaxation. We could also train him to identify the sensations accompanying the theta rhythm, the beta rhythm, muscle tensing, or muscle relaxing. After a subject had been taught to perceive accurately one or several kinds of internal events, perhaps this enhanced ability would transfer readily to other kinds of internal events.

With the advent of the feedback technology, this speculation can now be framed as a testable proposition. For example, if we first trained subjects to detect the presence of their own alpha rhythms, would they subsequently be better at discriminating the presence or absence of their own theta rhythms than if they had not been given any previous training in alpha?

A relevant observation is provided by Kamiya (1969), who suggests that practiced meditators—people with ample experience in attending to internal cues—are likely to be skilled at acquiring feedback control of alpha. Similarly, we might expect actors and poets, in view of their training and inclinations, to be abler than most at detecting internal events.

As Ferster (1963, p. 335) has maintained, probably the fundamental reason we are poor at discriminating private events is that the reinforcement contingencies for such events are extremely variable. Out of the shifting flood of internal cues, we do not know which are the right ones, for example, those associated with the production of alpha as opposed to those associated with theta. In many instances, biofeedback techniques should be able to tell us which are the correct cues.

Another question concerning introspective ability is whether such a skill is associated with certain personality characteristics. Are some people better than others either at detecting internal events or at learning to control them? For example, are introverts better at perceiving private events than are extraverts? On the basis of Jung's writings, we would expect this to be the case.

A dissertation project, conducted in our laboratory by Mr. Irwin Matus, is addressed to this and related questions. Subjects are initially assessed on introversion–extraversion scores by Eysenck's Maudsley Personality Inventory and Cattell's 16 PF test, on Witkin's rod-and-frame test of field-dependence versus field-independence, and on their ability to estimate varying levels of muscle tension within themselves. Muscle tension is measured by our EMG quantification equipment. The experiment, still in progress, falls into four phases: (1) Personality assessment, (2) subject's ability to estimate muscle tension levels prior to training, (3) subject's ability to learn the muscle relaxation task with EMG feedback training, and (4) subject's ability to estimate his muscle tension levels after training.

An interesting relationship which has emerged is that accuracy on the Witkin test and accuracy at estimating levels of forearm muscle tension are significantly associated ($r = +.43$, $p < .05$). Subjects who are good at the Witkin test are said to be those who rely on internal bodily cues in estimating the luminous rod's departure from the true vertical; these same subjects might also be expected to be skilled at estimating the cues associated with muscle tension.

### *4. Biofeedback Training and Alterations in Thought Processes*

Practically since their inception, there has been speculation that biofeedback techniques could be useful in altering thought processes. This seems often to be the case, although a great deal remains to be learned.

Feedback training in alpha and in muscle relaxation generally result in a shift away from the thinking of ordinary wakefulness—the subject is more immersed in his internal world, feels relaxed, is in a nonstriving, letting go mode. During muscle relaxation, a number of bodily sensations may be experienced—heaviness, warmth, drowsiness, hovering. When profound relaxation occurs, thought processes shift from action and decision-oriented thinking to a fleeting, visual imagery over which the individual has diminishing voluntary control as he drifts off to sleep.

Also occurring under low arousal conditions is the 4–7 Hz theta rhythm. This rhythm occurs just prior to the onset of Stage 2 spindling sleep, and is associated with drowsiness and, we believe, with muscle relaxation. It is also associated with imagery, mostly visual in nature. The imagery is of an involuntary, emergent type—if the subject tries to produce it, he fails; rather, he must let it happen.

Foulkes (1966) has likened hypnagogic or sleep-onset imagery to a series of disconnected photographic "stills," which is also an apt description for much of theta imagery. Frequently, though, theta images are vivid enough to acquire an hallucinatory intensity, i.e., they seem real. In these instances, the imagery can be better likened to a succession of unrelated film clips, each clip focused on a single scene. Some examples: A handful of old coins sliding off a green velvet cloth; a garden implement; a ship being launched; a stooped figure in a dark overcoat hurrying down a country road; a forest meadow with a freshly dug grave in the middle of it—overhead, a V-formation of geese flying south; someone jumping over a little freshet of water caused by the sudden melting of snow.

The group which has worked most extensively with theta feedback has been Green, Green, and Walters (1970) at the Menninger Foundation. They, too, find that theta is associated with vivid imagery. A major interest of this group is to explore the role of hypnagogic reverie in creativity.

### C. Some Biofeedback Experiments

An attractive feature of theta training is that, at least for many individuals, it offers a means of putting the subject into a condition in which he will experience imagery of hallucinatory intensity. There is a major practical problem, however. When a subject is in theta he seems dissociated from his surroundings, and we are still uncertain whether a subject in this condition will continue to pay any attention to the feedback signal—although this may be a skill which improves with practice.

A matter of first importance is how best to teach subjects to produce theta. One approach is to begin immediately with theta feedback. However, it may be better to conduct the training in two phases—an initial phase of muscle relaxation training, followed by a second phase in which training is shifted to direct feedback of theta. The aim of this second approach is to break the training into two easier-to-master stages. Learning to produce theta is a subtle task; and the base operant level of the rhythm is generally low—often too low to generate a usable feedback signal. But a condition of muscle relaxation is associated with an increase in theta EEG frequencies. Thus, if the subject first attains a deeply relaxed condition as a prelude to theta training, he will have something to work with when he later begins the task of acquiring feedback control of theta. Experiments to test this two-step training are currently being conducted in our laboratory as part of the doctoral dissertation by Miss Pola Sittenfeld.

The foregoing two-phase technique could be considered part of a more general approach aimed at the shaping of low arousal conditions (suggested by Dr. Budzynski). Thus, beginning his training from a point of alert wakefulness, the subject would be gradually led in the direction of sleep. Over several sessions, he would first train in the production of alpha, next in producing mixed alpha and theta frequencies, then in the production of theta frequencies. Later in his training the subject would attempt to produce a particular low arousal condition in the absence of any feedback. An objective criterion for his ability to attain a given low arousal condition could be assessed electroencephalographically, e.g., how readily is he able to produce theta, and how does his performance compare with that of untrained subjects?

Another facet of the research would involve sampling the mental activity associated with alpha, with mixed alpha and theta rhythms, and with theta frequencies. The data would be examined for regularities across subjects. Within-subject regularities would also be investigated since Foulkes (1966) has stated that individual differences are a prominent feature of sleep-onset imagery.

It seems likely that feedback techniques could be profitably employed to increase imagery retrieval from twilight states. Ordinarily, when a subject is roused from a sleep-onset condition and asked to report his thoughts, he frequently finds it difficult to return to a drowsy state. Feedback training, especially in muscle relaxation and in producing theta, can assist the subject in knowing what he must do to return to the drowsy condition in which imagery is likely to occur.

Subjects can also be allowed to signal when they are experiencing imagery, for example, by using a finger switch. By this means, we have found that subjects will press the "imagery switch" 8–12 times in the course of a 20-min session of theta training (although these subjects were not asked to report any details until after the end of the session).

A useful technique for increasing hypnagogic recall has been described by Tart (1969). The subject lies on his back, but keeps one arm in a vertical position, balanced on the elbow. As the subject drifts into sleep, muscle tonus drops, and his arm falls. This awakens him, thereby allowing him to take note of whatever imagery or thinking was in progress. A refinement of this technique has been developed by Green *et al.* (1970) who use a tilt detector consisting of a mercury switch finger ring. Whenever a subjects' hand deviates from the vertical, the mercury switch circuit closes and a chime is sounded.

With theta training it seems likely that we could produce some different-from-normal conditions. For example, we could explore the experiential consequences of hovering for extended periods in the theta zone. Under everyday circumstances, such as falling asleep, we drop through our sleep-onset phase in a matter of seconds or a few minutes. What if subjects were kept in theta for a long period of time, for example, 30–50 min? Perhaps the imagery would reveal new properties, for example, become more intense or more dreamlike. A possible means of keeping someone in theta for extended periods would be to provide him with a feedback signal whenever he began drifting out of the theta band. Give him a high-pitched tone if he slipped in the direction of sleep, a low-pitched tone if he moved toward normal wakefulness.

## II. BETWEEN SLEEP AND WAKEFULNESS

Biofeedback training in alpha control and particularly in muscle relaxation have a quieting effect on the individual; they lower his arousal level and nudge him into a condition close to sleep. This borderland between wakefulness and sleep seems to be especially propitious for evoking alterations in consciousness—an observation which deserves more attention than has so far been bestowed on it in the Anglo-American literature. For example, in hypnotic induction there is much emphasis on relaxation, on quieting oneself, on listening only to the hypnotist's voice. And, as Gill and Brenman (1961, pp. 57–58) have emphasized:

> . . . we see a significant departure from normal, *waking* modes of thought: instead of relatively stable, logical kind of thought—which for the most part employs words as its material—we see the emergence of fluid, archaic forms which often employ visual images and symbols as material, forms which do not follow the ordinary rules of logic, and which moreover are not bound to realistic limitations of time and space.

In autogenic training, a technique which has been extensively used in treating stress-related disorders, emphasis is placed on attaining the "autogenic shift" or *Umschaltung*—a condition for which passive concentration is held to be absolutely essential. In its physiological aspects, this condition involves a shift to parasympathetic predominance in the autonomic nervous system—as evidenced by muscle relaxation, slowed heart rate and respiration, increased skin temperature. Experientially, sensations of flowing warmth are often reported, as is a light quality in the visual field (eyes are closed). Luthe (1965) and others, however, point out that the autogenic shift is not characterized by drowsiness.

Koestler (1964), in his stimulating book, emphasizes that reverie states (which probably occur in the border zone between waking and sleep) figure prominently in literature about creative thinking. For example, Kekulé's conception of the benzene ring originated in a drowsy, reverie state—it was a warm summer's evening, and the famous chemist dozed as his omnibus made its way through the streets of London. The German psychiatrist, Kretschmer (quoted in Koestler, 1964, p. 325), has emphasized that:

> . . . creative products of the artistic imagination tend to emerge from a psychic twilight, a state of lessened consciousness and diminished attentivity to external stimuli. Further, the condition is one of "absent-mindedness" with hypnoidal overconcentration on a single focus, providing an entirely passive experience, frequently of a visual character, divorced from the categories of space and time, and reason and will.

### A. Hypnagogic Imagery

A valuable contribution of recent sleep research has been the finding that hypnagogic or sleep-onset experiences are surprisingly common. In fact, they are an everyday occurrence. Generally, though, we fail to notice them, or forget them.

Some of the earliest research on hypnagogic imagery was conducted by Silberer (1951) shortly after the turn of the century. He described his approach as a "Method of evoking and observing certain symbolic hallucinatory phenomena." Silberer, a German philosopher, could not have been lacking in old-fashioned will-power, for he would force himself to try to solve problems while in a drowsy condition. Then he would rouse himself and note the images which had slipped into consciousness. Silberer maintained that in this drowsy condition there is a transformation in the thought process—from mental activity of an intellectual character to thinking of a visual, symbolic type. Drawing from his self-observations, Silberer (1951, p. 202–204) provided many instances of this transformation.

> Example 1. My thought is: I am to improve a halting passage in an essay.
> Symbol: I see myself planing a piece of wood.
> Example 7. In opposition to the Kantian view, I am attempting to conceive of time as a "concept."
> Symbol: I am pressing a Jack-in-the-Box into the box. But every time I take my hand away it bounces out gaily on its spiral spring.[5]

Contemporary electrophysiological studies of sleep-onset by Foulkes, Rechtschaffen, and their associates have established that sleep-onset imagery, like dreaming, is an everyday occurrence. Thus, Foulkes and Vogel (1965) found that when their subjects were "awakened" close to sleep-onset they recalled some specific mental experience over 90% of the time.

Pilot research by these investigators had suggested that there was an orderly sequence of different types of mental activity with progressive stages of sleep-onset—fragmentary visual material passed into more extended and self-involved "dreamlets" as the EEG shifted from alpha rhythm to spindling sleep. This hint was confirmed in a detailed study of hypnagogic imagery (Foulkes & Vogel, 1965) in which subjects were awakened from each of four sleep-onset EEG patterns: (1) Alpha EEG with rapid eye movements (REMs), (2) alpha rhythm with slow rolling eye movements (SEMs), (3) descending stage 1 sleep (predominance of theta rhythms), and (4) descending Stage 2 sleep (13–16 Hz spindle bursts prominent). As a group, the subjects showed a clear progression

[5] Later investigators have generally failed to find such a continuity between problem-oriented thinking and the hypnagogic imagery immediately succeeding it. This continuity may have resulted from the unusual nature of Silberer's approach, in which he forced himself to solve problems while in a drowsy condition rather than permitting himself a free flow of imagery.

toward increasingly hallucinatory material as they drifted toward sleep. Distribution of hallucinatory dreamlike experiences was as follows:

| | |
|---|---|
| Alpha REM reports | 29% |
| Alpha SEM reports | 47% |
| Descending Stage 1 reports | 74% |
| Descending Stage 2 reports | 80% |

Recent research suggests that this sleep-onset zone may provide clues as to the necessary conditions for dreaming. A vexatious observation in sleep research has been the finding that dreams are not confined to REM sleep, but are sometimes reported from non-REM sleep as well (see Foulkes, 1966). Why? An experiment by Zimmerman (1970) may help provide an answer. In this study there were two extreme groups—a *light sleeper group*, subjects easily awakened by an auditory signal; and a *deep sleeper group*, subjects who needed much more intense auditory stimulation to wake up. When awakened from non-REM sleep, the light sleeper group showed a far higher incidence of dreamlike recall than did their opposite numbers (71% compared to 21%). Subjects in the light sleeper group were also more aroused physiologically as measured by heart rate, respiration, body temperature levels, spontaneous awakenings, and gross body movements while asleep (Zimmerman, 1967).

Zimmerman's conclusion was that a moderate level of physiological arousal may be necessary in order for dreaming to occur. Consequently, dreamlike experiences could be expected to occur both at sleep-onset and during those epochs of non-REM sleep in which a moderate level of physiological arousal is present. Support for this position comes from an intriguing study by Hersch *et al.* (1970) in which arousal level during non-REM sleep was deliberately increased by chemical means. Catheterized subjects, serving as their own controls, were given intravenous norepinephrine injections during non-REM sleep. An equal number of saline control injections were made, also during non-REM sleep. Awakenings after the norepinephrine injections yielded a significantly greater proportion of dreamlike reports—as assessed by degree of emotionality, type of imagery, etc.

## III. ON THE CONDITIONS FOR HALLUCINATORY ACTIVITY

*West's theory.* Why should imagery and hallucinations blossom so readily in this twilight terrain between waking and sleep? A theory addressed to this question has been advanced by West (1962). He begins with the observation that in a variety of altered states of consciousness—hypnosis, hypnagogic imagery, dreaming, Zen and Yoga meditation, sensory isolation experiences—certain common conditions are present. West postulates that a major predisposing condition for hallucinatory activity is a reduction in the level or variety of external sensory input to the brain. As the sensory isolation literature in particular has emphasized (Bexton, Heron, & Scott, 1954), ordinary levels of sensory input exercise an organizing and inhibiting effect on consciousness. When sensory input is substantially reduced or made extremely monotonous, it loses its customary organizing effect on the processes of consciousness.

A second requirement for the evocation of hallucinatory activity is the maintenance of an arousal level sufficient to permit awareness. West characterizes this condition as one of "residual awareness." Self-awareness is still present; there is some appreciation of one's own thoughts, feelings, and sensations, but there is a disengagement from one's surroundings—the reality moorings have been severed. Though hard to define operationally, residual awareness is associated with the conditions pertaining to sleep onset, rather than with the comparatively high arousal of active wakefulness or with the low arousal and minimal mental activity of Stage 3 and Stage 4 sleep.

The basic tenet of the theory is that a reduction or impairment of sensory input together with an arousal level sufficient to permit residual awareness is a condition likely to produce hallucinatory experiences. According to West (1968, p. 268) ". . . when the usual information input level no longer suffices completely to inhibit their emergence, the perceptual traces may be 'released' and reexperienced in familiar or new combinations." [6]

Similar conclusions were reached by Zimmerman (1970) with respect to when the experience of dreaming is likely to occur. As already mentioned, Zimmerman maintains that what is essential for the experience we call dreaming is not the presence of REM sleep, but a given (moderate) level of arousal in the absence of reality contact. Thus, dreaming could be expected to occur in non-REM sleep if arousal level were sufficiently high—a hypothesis confirmed by the abovementioned experiment of Hersch *et al.* (1970).

*Some additions to West's theory.* We believe that West's theory underscores some major determinants of naturally occurring hallucinatory experiences, i.e., those hallucinations which can be made to occur without

[6] Whether the basic mechanism is an active release process as West maintains, or simply a passive slowing down, is difficult to test at this point. So the question will be left open.

drugs or surgical intervention. We also believe that on the basis of recent work, particularly in the biofeedback area, the theory can be made more specific and given greater explanatory power in terms of generating testable propositions. In our opinion, the following additional postulates serve to define further those proposed by West:

1. In the production of hallucinatory experiences it is important to reduce not only external sensory input but to reduce internal or proprioceptive input as well. As mentioned earlier, we have found muscular relaxation, with its accompanying reduction of CNS input (see Gellhorn, 1964), conducive to the evocation of hypnagogic material.

It will be remembered that relaxation of the musculature also plays an important role in autogenic training, and in the induction of hypnosis. Conversely, tensing up the musculature acts to eliminate a low arousal condition and the associated alterations in consciousness. For example, a person may tense his muscles to keep from dozing off in a lecture.

2. A second additional postulate is that the ability to shift to a condition of "passive volition" is critical for the attainment of those twilight states in which imagery and hallucinatory activity are likely to occur. This passive volition characteristic, as Green *et al.* (1970) have termed it, has been noted in several types of biofeedback training, e.g., in work with alpha, theta, and EMG activity. In autogenic training it has been termed passive concentration. As Deikman (1971) has recently emphasized, this ability is required for what he terms the "receptive mode of consciousness"—a mode he regards as essential to the attainment of contemplative states.[7]

3. Also important in the induction of twilight states is a change in autonomic function, a shift from sympathetic predominance to one of parasympathetic predominance. Gellhorn (1964) maintains that the mechanism of this shift is a resetting of hypothalamic balance. A reduction in proprioceptive input, as produced by muscular relaxation, causes hypothalamic balance to change to a parasympathetic pattern.

[7] Deikman conceives of two fundamental ways in which waking consciousness operates, (a) an "active" mode—the striving, adaptive, goal-oriented, consciousness of everyday life, and (b) a "receptive" mode, characterized by a lack of striving, a "letting go," calmness, and a quiet receptiveness. This receptive mode has been little emphasized in Western cultures, and most people seem only vaguely aware of it. But writings of the Eastern mystical disciplines suggest that the receptive mode of consciousness could be cultivated and made voluntarily accessible to those willing to do the training.

Whether the condition of passive volition is required for *all* biofeedback learning, or only for acquiring feedback control over those responses characteristic of low arousal (e.g., alpha, theta, muscle relaxation), is not yet known.

As the subject moves from alert wakefulness toward sleep, respiration and heart rate decline, skin temperature increases, muscle tension diminishes, and EEG patterns display a change toward slower frequencies. This physiological shift seems to be intimately linked with the altered quality of thinking which occurs in the twilight or sleep-onset state, a point emphasized in the autogenic training literature (Schultz & Luthe, 1959; Stokvis & Wiesenhütter, 1961).

A related point is that the magnitude of the physiological shift seems important. That is to say, the changes in consciousness are greater if a subject goes from high arousal to low arousal than if he merely goes from a moderate level of arousal to a low arousal condition. Why this should be, we are uncertain. Perhaps it is a contrast effect; or possibly there is a greater build-up of some active inhibitory or disinhibitory neural process if the change in arousal level is great; perhaps a large shift generates more internal stimuli. Lest too much stress be put on this observation, its preliminary nature should be emphasized—however, it should be readily open to empirical test.

Also worth noting is that the shift to parasympathetic predominance seems also to be associated with both a change in affect, and a broadening of the range of consciousness. As Koestler (1964) has perceptively remarked, sympathetic predominance is linked to emotions in which the range of awareness is restricted—anger and fear, for example. Parasympathetic functioning he states is associated with subtler emotions—wonder, religious and esthetic experiences, contemplation—emotions characterized by a broader range of awareness.

## IV. SUMMARY OF ARGUMENT

The events of consciousness can be scientifically studied to the extent that we are able to make testable inferences about them. One area which has made use of testable inferences about consciousness is contemporary dream research. The basic approach has involved the *combined* use of physiological measures and verbal report—as, for example, in the research which has explored mental activity during the various phases of sleep.

It is argued here that the combined use of verbal report and physiological measures can be profitably extended to the study of certain waking mental activity as well—particularly with the addition of the information feedback principle, which adds a new dimension to the basic methodology. The emerging technique of feedback psychophysiology can be valuable both in exploring mental activity and in teaching individuals to produce some psychological states at will.

Biofeedback techniques have been useful in producing the low arousal state bordering on sleep. In this low arousal state there are characteristic changes in the nature of the thought process—reality-oriented thinking is supplanted by imagery, often of an hallucinatory intensity.

It is argued that the conditions conducive to such low arousal, sleep-onset experiences have broader implications in helping to specify the circumstances under which naturally occurring hallucinatory experiences are likely to arise (phenomena such as dreams, hypnagogic imagery, the hallucinations of hypnosis, and sensory isolation). The major predisposing conditions are (1) a reduction in sensory input, to the brain—both external and internal (proprioceptive) input are important, (2) a shift to a non-striving, passive volitional mode of consciousness, (3) a shift to a low arousal condition characterized by a predominately parasympathetic response pattern in the autonomic nervous system.

## REFERENCES

Aserinsky, E., & Kleitman, N. Regularly occurring periods of eye motility and concomitant phenomena during sleep. *Science*, 1953, **118,** 274–284.

Bexton, W. H., Heron, W., & Scott, T. H. Effects of decreased variation in sensory environment. *Canadian Journal of Psychology*, 1954, **8,** 70–76.

Berger, R. J., & Moskowitz, E. Failure to confirm a directional relationship between rapid eye movement and dream imagery. *Psychophysiology*, 1970, **6,** 640–641. (Abstract)

Berger, R. J., & Oswald, I. Eye movements during active and passive dreams. *Science*, 1962, **137,** 601.

Black, A. H. The direct control of neural processes by reward and punishment. *American Scientist*, 1971, **59,** 236–245.

Budzynski, T. H., & Stoyva, J. M. An instrument for producing deep muscle relaxation by means of analog information feedback. *Journal of Applied Behavior Analysis*, 1969, **2,** 231–237.

Budzynski, T. H., Stoyva, J. M., & Adler, C. S. Feedback-induced muscle relaxation: Application to tension headache. *Behavior Theory and Experimental Psychiatry*, 1970, **1,** 205–211.

Deikman, A. J. Bimodal consciousness. *Archives of General Psychiatry*, 1971, **25,** 481–489.

Dement, W., & Kleitman, N. The relation of eye movements during sleep to dream activity: An objective method for the study of dreaming. *Journal of Experimental Psychology*, 1957, **53,** 339–346.

Ferster, C. B. Essentials of a science of behavior. In J. T. Nurnburger, C. B. Ferster, & J. P. Brady (Eds.), *An introduction to the science of human behavior*. New York: Appleton, 1963, Pp. 197–345.

Foulkes, D. *The psychology of sleep*. New York: Scribner, 1966.

Foulkes, D., & Vogel, G. Mental activity at sleep onset. *Journal of Abnormal Psychology*, 1965, **70,** 231–243.

Gellhorn, E. Motion and emotion: The role of proprioception in the physiology and pathology of the emotions. *Psychological Review*, 1964, **71,** 457–472.

Gill, M. M., & Brenman, M. *Hypnosis and related states.* New York: International Universities Press, 1961.

Green, E., Green, A., & Walters, D. Voluntary control of internal states: Psychological and physiological. *Journal of Transpersonal Psychology,* 1970, **1,** 1–26.

Hersch, R. G., Antrobus, J. S., Arkin, A. M., & Singer, J. L. Dreaming as a function of sympathetic arousal. *Psychophysiology,* 1970, **7,** 329–330. (Abstract)

Jacobson, E. *Progressive relaxation.* (2nd ed.) Chicago: Univ. of Chicago Press, 1938.

Jacobson, E. *Modern treatment of tense patients.* Springfield, Illinois: Thomas, 1970.

Kamiya, J. Operant control of the EEG alpha rhythm and some of its reported effects on consciousness. In C. T. Tart (Ed.), *Altered state of consciousness.* New York: Wiley, 1969. Pp. 507–517.

Kennedy, J. L. A possible artifact in electroencephalography. *Psychological Review,* 1959, **66,** 347–352.

Koestler, A. *The act of creation.* New York: Macmillan, 1964.

Lewis, H. B., Goodenough, D. R., Shapiro, A., & Sleser, I. Individual differences in dream recall. *Journal of Abnormal Psychology,* 1966, **71,** 52.

Lippold, O. Origin of the alpha rhythm. *Nature,* 1970, **226,** 616–618.

Luthe, W. (Ed.) *Autogenic training: Correlationes psychosomaticae.* New York: Grune & Stratton, 1965.

Mulholland, T. Feedback electroencephalography. *Activitas Nervosa Superior (Praha),* 1968, **10,** 410–438.

Platt, J. R. Strong inference. *Science,* 1964, **146,** 347–353.

Roffwarg, H. P., Dement, W. C., Muzio, J. N., & Fisher, C. Dream imagery: Relationship to rapid eye movements of sleep. *Archives of General Psychiatry,* 1962, **7,** 235–258.

Schultz, J. H., & Luthe, W. *Autogenic training: A psychophysiological approach in psychotherapy.* New York: Grune & Stratton, 1959.

Silberer, H. Report on a method of eliciting and observing certain symbolic hallucination-phenomena. In D. Rapaport (Ed.), *Organization and pathology of thought.* New York: Columbia Univ. Press, 1951. Pp. 195–207.

Stokvis, E., & Wiesenhütter, E. *Der Mensche in der Entspannung,* (2 Auflage). Stuttgart: Hippokrates Verlag, 1961.

Stoyva, J. M. The public (scientific) study of private events. In E. Hartmann (Ed.), *Sleep and dreaming.* Boston: Little, Brown, 1970. Pp. 353–368. (Republished in T. X. Barber, L. V. DiCara, J. Kamiya, N. E. Miller, D. Shapiro, J. Stoyva (Eds.), *Biofeedback and self-control,* 1970; *An Aldine annual on the regulation of bodily processes and consciousness.* Chicago: Aldine Publishing Co., 1971.)

Stoyva, J. M., & Kamiya, J. Electrophysiological studies of dreaming as the prototype of a new strategy in the study of consciousness. *Psychological Review,* 1968, **75,** 192–205.

Tart, C. T. (Ed.) *Altered states of consciousness.* New York: Wiley, 1969.

West, L. J. A general theory of hallucinations and dreams. In L. J. West (Ed.), *Hallucinations.* New York: Grune & Stratton, 1962. Pp. 275–291.

West, L. J. Hallucinations. In J. G. Howells (Ed.), *Modern perspectives in world psychiatry.* Edinburgh: Oliver & Boyd, 1968. Pp. 265–287.

Zimmerman, W. B. Psychological and physiological differences between "light" and "deep" sleepers. Unpublished doctoral dissertation, University of Chicago, 1967.

Zimmerman, W. B. Sleep mentation and auditory awakening thresholds. *Psychophysiology,* 1970, 1970, **6,** 540–549.

# 11

## MULHOLLAND, T. B.

# *Can You Really Turn On with Alpha?*

The occipital alpha rhythm, familiar to electroencaphalographers and brain researchers as the most noticeable brain rhythm in normal people (1,2,3) has been "discovered" by a new movement. The main claim of this cult is that alpha is associated with special "states of consciousness" and that alpha states bring health and relief from physical and mental distress. This movement should not be confused with genuine scientific research into the meaning and cause of the alpha brain rhythms, or alpha feedback methods, or with studies of the psychological and physiological changes which occur during the various states and exercises of Yoga and Zen or other kinds of meditation (4, 5).

The ALPHA cult is not scientific; prone to grandiose claims, it attracts the naive, the desperate and the superstitious. It has also been a source of simple fraud, misrepresentation and quackery. The fact of the matter is this -- to date there has been no evidence presented to the scientific or medical community that the occurrence of lots of alpha rhythms in the normal person is associated with any special mental powers. There is no evidence that lots of EEG alpha brings relief from physical or mental disease. It is not instant yoga.

When such a pseudo-scientific cult develops, it generates a huge "sucker" market for the kinds of gear that are supposed to permit easy recording of bioelectric signals. For the true believer any sound from the "alpha" kit is welcome news even if it is produced by scalp twitches or amplifier noise. Ignorance can be blissful. There are technical problems when recording the EEG which become more difficult when the recording is done under uncontrolled conditions, with improper technique and with no knowledge of the various kinds of spurious signals (artifacts) which can be recorded from the scalp. All of these are present when an amateur is using a do-it-yourself alpha feedback kit. Of course, it is possible to make reliable, accurate alpha amplifiers and to learn the proper technique of recording. It is unlikely that this package would be inexpensive.

Some of the claims made for alpha by one company are that alpha is associated with tranquility, inspiration, creativity, concentration, extra-sensory perception and accelerated healing.

Alpha is the name of a rhythmic fluctuation of voltage recorded from the scalp. It has a frequency of 8-13 Hz, and is usually from 30-80μ volts in magnitude. It is most prominent when it is recorded from the posterior scalp. (Actually, alpha can be recorded from many different locations so that they are best described in the plural -- alpha rhythms (6).) Discovered by Berger in 1927, the alpha rhythms fascinated everyone interested in the relation between mind and brain (7). However, after 30 years of research it is clear that no definite psychological processes are associated with alpha and the physiological origin of alpha is still obscure. Most researchers believe that alpha is produced by neural processes, the electrical activity of the brain, but this has not been conclusively proven (8).

It was hoped that alpha might be linked to intelligence, to personality traits, or be an index of mental stability, etc., but these hopes were not supported by evidence with one exception -- alpha seems to be linked in a reverse way to attention. When attention is high, alpha is low in amount, when attention is low, alpha occurs in greater amounts. At least it seems that alpha is linked to visual attention (9). For this reason alpha suppression by visual stimuli and by the oculomotor response to them is still an important part of the study of visual attention which involves active looking and seeing. Here are some facts about EEG occipital alpha:

**1. Alpha occurs in 80-90% of the population when the eyes are closed, and the person is relaxed. In fact, simply closing the eyes is the best way of achieving lots of occipital alpha for most people.**

**2. When eyes are open in the dark, occipital alpha is initially decreased, but after awhile it comes back.**

**3. When in constant visual surroundings, sitting quietly, occipital alpha will be low at first, then gradually increase in amount.**

**4. For some people extreme deviation of the eyes can be accompanied by lots of alpha, but scientists disagree on the reasons why.**

5. If vision is unfocussed, so that images are blurred and indefinite and no definite fixation of the eye is maintained, alpha can occur.

Alpha can be reduced by the following:

1. Open eyes in the dark -- look around and try to see something.

2. Open eyes and look at a visual stimulus. Alpha will be reduced but will come back after awhile.

3. Open eyes and carefully track a moving target, especially if it is close.

4. Become drowsy or go to sleep.

Alpha is also reduced in some cases of brain pathology and when intoxicated with some drugs, e.g., barbiturates.

The most reliable and simple method for increasing alpha is to close the eyes and try not to see or look. Unless the subject is carefully observed in an alpha training session, he may produce alpha by closing his eyes. The best way to decrease alpha is to carefully track a moving visual stimulus. A moderately effective way to decrease alpha is to simply try to see or look around with open eyes.

Before we get to discussion of alpha feedback it is clear that the occurrence of alpha can be controlled by the human subject. But how he controls it is another question. Also, if he or she can keep alpha ON, so what? There is no evidence for any more benefit than would be expected in a state of relaxed wakefulness, not looking at or seeing visual stimuli, nor being drowsy.

It is true that alpha occurs best when eyes are closed and the person is instructed to relax. Certainly active looking and seeing are associated with little or no alpha. In general then when lots of alpha is present from many recording electrodes for a long time the person is likely to be inactive with less muscle tension and reduced visual activity. For people who are unable to relax, alpha training may in fact help them to attain the state associated with alpha for longer times. For instance, a person who was neurotically afraid of closed-in places such as the recording room might be helped by training to produce lots of alpha. If being relaxed is beneficial then alpha relaxation training may be similarly beneficial. Experiments have shown that feedback tone from muscle activity directly facilitates a learned control of that activity, including relaxation (17, 18).

Conversely, if a high level of visual attention is associated with alpha OFF, then feedback permits practice to maintain a state of little or no-alpha. However, it is too early to say if such learned suppression of alpha would improve visual attention or be beneficial in any way. Alpha feedback visual stimulation is a useful method for the study of looking and seeing responses and in the study of some kinds of brain pathology (19,20).

Learning to control alpha is also lots of fun.

Many subjects have recordable alpha even when their eyes are open. Some, even when reading (10). Does this mean that they do something different from the one who has little alpha under the same conditions and if so, can this be learned?. To study this question, one researcher used alpha feedback. With his apparatus a tone was heard by the subject when alpha occurred in the EEG. His task was to keep the tone ON. He reported that subjects did learn to produce alpha or to reduce it "at will". Evidently the knowledge that alpha was occurring (feedback) promoted learning to control it (11). Unfortunately, alpha increases over the course of an experiment despite the feedback training. Because of this it is difficult to show a controlled production of alpha greater than that which would occur without feedback. This is the problem which causes scientists to disagree about the reality of "alpha-ON" control. Some subjects do increase alpha above baseline with training but they are in the minority.

Many studies show that subjects can learn to decrease alpha with feedback and do not show such a reduction if they don't get feedback (12, 13). Here scientists agree, so far. However, they disagree on the question of how the subject does it (14, 15, 16).

In one study, volunteers received alpha feedback, a soft tone which was ON when alpha was present and OFF when it was not. They tried to keep the tone ON, then OFF, etc., over a series of practice runs. At the end the tone was turned OFF and they tried to produce the same state they felt when trying to keep the tone ON and alternately trying to be in a state like trying to keep the tone OFF.

The subjects learned to keep the tone OFF and this performance improved with practice. The amount of alpha remained about the same during the ON trials. See Table I.

TABLE I

From: Mulholland & Peper, 1970

| Stimulation | 2 Min. Trial | % Time Alpha | | |
|---|---|---|---|---|
| No Feedback | 1st | 40.7 | | Eyes Open |
| | 2nd | 56.5 | | Eyes Closed |
| Feedback | 3rd | 57.5 | ON | |
| (Eyes Closed) | 4th | 51.6 | OFF | Autoregulation |
| | 5th | 55.0 | ON | |
| | 6th | 43.3 | OFF | Training |
| | 7th | 54.5 | ON | |
| | 8th | 42.0 | OFF | To |
| | 9th | 57.5 | ON | |
| | 10th | 41.7 | OFF | Keep |
| | 11th | 54.5 | ON | |
| | 12th | 38.3 | OFF | Tone |
| No Feedback | 13th | 51.0 | | Autoregulation |
| (Eyes Closed) | 14th | 40.8 | | Test |

This result was duplicated in a study of alpha training with feedback and with a non-feedback random tone. Alpha was less during the tone OFF trials. During the tone ON, alpha was no greater than the changes in baseline alpha over the conditions. Those subjects who received spurious feedback-tone not linked to EEG showed no evidence for learning. See Table 2. Note in Table 2 that for the alpha ON trials the amount of alpha was nearer baseline than for the OFF trials.

It has been reported that subjects could be trained to detect when alpha was occurring without feedback. One of the problems here is the baseline probability of alpha. If it is high, then random guesses that alpha is present will be correct a high percentage of the time. This has not been properly controlled in studies so far. However, all the evidence is not in yet so it is an open question.

When alpha is occurring abundantly, most people report that they are not paying attention, are not looking or seeing actively, yet not drowsy. This state is one of being awake but relaxed. Persons with high levels of anxiety expressed in muscular tension and activation of seeing and looking behavior don't have much alpha. If one stays in a state of relaxed wakefulness for a long time without going to sleep, what happens? In the first place, there is a big reduction of sensory input from both outside and from inside the body. In particular there is a reduction of proprioceptive input from muscles, tendons and joints because to produce alpha a state of relaxation is best. This means that active movement and response to stimulation are reduced. Secondly, since the person is not actively looking and seeing external stimuli, and yet not asleep, he has a chance to examine subjectively his own mental experiences at that time, but the content of those mental experiences are not specific to alpha. To make a comparison, if we stop talking, this lets us hear what the other person is saying. However, what the other person says is not caused by our simply not talking.

TABLE 2

From: Waitzkin, B. (M.A. Thesis, Brandeis, 1971)

| | Experimental (Feedback Tone) | Control (Non Contingent Tone) |
|---|---|---|
| N s's | 10 | 10 |
| % Time Alpha | | |
| Autoregulation Trials | | |
| "Increase Alpha Keep Tone ON" | 20.3 | 37.7 |
| "Decrease Alpha Keep Tone OFF" | 7.4 | 32.6 |
| Baselines | | |
| Relaxed Sitting Quietly | 28 | 29 |
| Counting Silently | 27 | 30 |

By taking time out to be relaxed yet awake for an hour in a quiet place, people are finding out that they have thoughts. For some, this experience assumes the status of a major insight. Obviously after one "discovers" thinking, he "discovers" awareness and introspects on his thought flow. At this point a person's subjective report on his thoughts and the mood of his feelings are likely to be influenced by his beliefs, by his expectations, and by his wishes and needs. If he believes alpha is good and hears the alpha sound, then he is likely to report that he feels well. If he wishes for a psychic experience and hears the alpha sound, he may report one. If he wants to be "in", to be a member of the "alpha-greats" he may report an experience even if he didn't experience it. He may lie.

Scientific psychology has revealed how these attitudes, beliefs, expectations and fears can modify experience so that the beliefs are confirmed. For some, the tone becomes so valued that hearing tone makes them feel successful, comfortable and relaxed. Not hearing the tone brings expressions of failure, discontent and tension. Yet the alpha occurrence is about the same. We have observed many instances of these effects in our Laboratory. Three illustrative examples follow.

One subject is a Zen practioner of 15 years, practiced with alpha feedback in our Laboratory. He produced copious alpha during some sessions, much less on others. One afternoon when he was producing little alpha, the threshold of the alpha detector was lowered so that very low level alpha or transients having power in the alpha frequency range caused the tone to go on. After he began hearing the tone much more often, his alpha in fact markedly increased. We inferred after questioning him that he felt frustrated when he wasn't getting much tone. When he suddenly heard a lot more, he felt better, that he was succeeding. In our theory, this meant he relaxed his musculature and those visual processes associated with attention and more alpha occurred.

Another person who knew about alpha training was aware of the notion that special experiences came with alpha. He produced copious alpha and when asked gave us the appropriate reports "I'm losing track of space and time" and "there's a rabbit in here so real I can almost touch it." Yet with copious alpha but no tone feedback we did not get reports of special experiences.

A third subject, a well-educated head of a law firm, believed initially that we would try to fool him by presenting tone which was <u>not</u> linked to his EEG. After all, psychologists do run "controls". He also produced copious alpha and when asked about his experiences during tone he replied that there were no definite mental events associated with alpha.

The same person, after several weeks of alpha training, 3 hours per week, was producing copious alpha and was hearing the tone often. When he had lots of alpha and tone he reported that he "had a good session" that he was "really able to turn alpha ON." He exhibited more alpha on the right side. When we switched the feedback to the left side he heard much less tone. He consistently reported a frustrating experience, lack of success and unpleasantness <u>even though he still had copious alpha on the right side</u>. For this person it was clear that his feelings were tied to the tone not to the alpha. This means that the tone had become highly valued. It had become an important, effective reinforcement. People feel well when they get that kind of positive reinforcement.

Possibly in the future some benefit from alpha control will be demonstrated. So far it has not been proved and the answer cannot be found without more scientific research on this important topic.

## REFERENCES


1. Berger, Uber das elektrenkephalogram des Menschen. Arch fur Psychiat. 1929, 87: 527-570

2. Adrian, E.D. & Matthews, B.H.C. The Berger rhythm: potential changes from the occipital lobes in man. Brain, 1934, 57: 355-385

3. Cobb,W.A. The normal adult EEG. In: Hill, D.H. & Parr, G. Electroencephalography; a symposium on its various aspects.

4. Bagchi, B.K. & Wenger, M.A. Electro-physiological correlates of some Yoga exercises. Electroenceph. clin. Neurophysiol. 1957, Suppl. 7, 132-149.

5. Wallace, R.W. Physiological effects of transcendental meditation. Science, 1970, 167: 1751-1754.

6. Walter, W.G. Discussion. In: Evans, C.R. & Mulholland, T.B. (Eds.) Attention in Neurophysiology, Butterworths, London, 1969, 122.

7. Whitteridge, D. & Walsh, E.G. The physiological basis of the electroencephalogram. In: Hill, D.H. & Parr, G., Electroencelphalography: a symposium on its various aspects. MacMillan, New York, 1963, 99-146.

8. Brumlik, J., Richeson, W.B. & Arbit,J. The origin of certain electrical rhythms. Brain Research, 1967, 3: 227-247.

9. Mulholland, T.B. The concept of attention and the electroencephalographic alpha rhythm. In: Evans, C.R. & Mulholland, T.B. (Eds.) Attention in Neurophysiology, Butterworths, London, 1969, 100-127.

10. Walter, W.G. Discussion. In: Evans, C.R. & Mulholland, T.B. (Eds.) Attention in Neurophysiology, Butterworths, London, 1969, 115-116 .

11. Kamiya, J. Operant control of the EEG alpha rhythm and some of its reported effects on consciousness. In: Tart, C.T. (Ed.) Altered states of consciousness, Wiley, New York, 1969.

12. Mulholland, T. & Peper, E. Methodological and theoretical problems in the voluntary control of the electroencephalographic alpha by the subject. Kybernetik, 1970, 7: 10-13.

13. Waitzkin, B. The effect of alpha training on the orienting response and the defensive response in "spider" phobics. M.A. Thesis, Brandeis University, 1971.

14. Mulholland, T. Feedback electroencephalography. Activitas Nervosa Superior, (Prague), 1968, 10: 410-428.

15. Mulholland, T. & Peper, E. Occipital alpha and accommodative vergence, pursuit tracking and fast eye movements. Psychophysiology, 1971 (in press).

16. Mulholland, T. Occipital alpha revisited. Psychol, Bull. 1972, (in press).

17. Basmajian, J.V. Control of individual motor units. Am. J. of Physical Med., 1967, 46: 480-486.

18. Budzynski, T.H. & Atoyva, J.M. An instrument for producing deep muscle relaxation by means of analog information feedback. J. Applied Behavior Analysis, 1969, 2: 231-237.

19. Runnals, S. & Mulholland, T. A method for the study of bilateral symmetry of cortical activation. Am. J. EEG Technol., 1964, 4: 15-18.

20. Mulholland, T. & Benson, F. Feedback electroencephalography in clinical research. Perception Laboratory Report, V.A. Hospital, Bedford, Mass., April 1971 (submitted for publication.)

# 12

## MUSES, C.

# *Editorial Note on Biofeedback*

Editorial note. *The mere presence of a convinced belief of "not being able to perform"—no matter what the conscious or unconscious reason, in this case social conditioning, that is given as the basis for such belief—will interfere with the ability to perform or block it completely. In all such cases we are evidently dealing with a psychophysiological alteration of state involving subtle and delicately balanced unconscious processes. That balance is strengthened (or upset) by suggestions pro (or con) that the subject fully accepts. The unconscious process of this acceptance is the key to all trance induction, auto or hetero. It is also clear from the phenomena of fire-walking and suggestion-implemented healing that such psychophysiological alterations of state involve far more than purely psychological effects. The converse is also true, as shown by hypnosis. (See also page 152, vol. 1., no. 2, of the* Journal for the Study of Consciousness.*) Such phenomena are a compelling demonstration of the inadequacy of the concepts "subjective" and "objective"—directly implying a similar inadequacy in "unconscious" and "conscious."*

*It is thus unscientific because untrue to separate the psychological and the physiological in living organisms. After falsely separating them it is absurd to pronounce a "principle" connecting them; that device, wherever used, indicates merely a semantic patching of an inadequate model, for they were never disconnected in nature to begin with and need no "principle" to unite them. (See in this connection the note [page 145, vol. 2, no. 2,* Journal for the Study of Consciousness*] on the profound noetic control of body chemistry.)*

*There is much of "the Emperor's New Clothes" in some of the writing today about the "psychophysiological feedback" or "biofeedback." Even Dr. J. Kamiya (Langley-Porter Institute, San Francisco), who is one of the more responsible investigators and who first developed the refinement of auditory rather than visual instrument-reading in "biofeedback," warned* (Wall Street Journal, *April 19, 1971) that much of the information spread so sensationally about instrumentally guided "bio-meditation" is unfortunate and misleading. Another authority—a psychiatrist—adds that if it becomes a fad many "will get fleeced." Under the category of such misleading information fall the somewhat wild promises* (Wall Street Journal *same piece) by a staffer of the usually dependable Menninger Foundation in Topeka, of a new world of incalculable significance to be attained through masses of converts to the belief in yoga-by-teaching-machine. Promises that imply to the average person some kind of "instant mastery" or automatic self-development are suspect because they tend to be unreliable and are too often signs of a set of new opportunists trying to leap on a new bandwagon with P.T. Barnum techniques directed toward the gullible. Man's actual self-development requires a profound change of heart, and not merely a new machine technique or a new intellectual game.*

*Instrument-mediated control of skin temperature, blood pressure and pulse rate, by the simple expedient of the subject's perceiving an instrument reading, has been, since the 1950s, a new technique rather than a new understanding. The concept of the psychophysiological unity of man stems from ancient times, and medical science has never been wholly without it. The discoverer of that unity is ancient and anonymous.*

*The brain contains about* $10^{10}$ *neurons, which are highly specialized amoebas. The reason that human consciousness—beyond that of neurons—is natural in this symbiotic context lies in the fact that the brain, vastly more complex and profound than a* machine, *is a* biopsychic organ. *Thus the deepest advances of science in the late twentieth century will be those directed toward accumulating evidence tending to show that the "dualism" of body and consciousness is that of two branches of a tree, and not any unjoinable dichotomy—that all matter is indeed alive in a protobiological sense on some level, and hence can respond to consciousness when the proper techniques are used; and that there are forms of living substance far subtler than our relatively crude polarized (i.e. electron/proton) matter—forms already hinted at in the mysterious physical effectiveness of the so-called "vacuum state" as revealed by modern quantum physics.* C.M.

## SECTION III

# MIND-ALTERING DRUGS

# 13

**DeLONG, F. L. & LEVY, B. I.**

## *Cognitive Effects of Marijuana, Described in Terms of a Model of Attention*

Many studies designed to elucidate the cognitive effects of marijuana have been done during the past 5 yr. Most of this work has analyzed the immediate effects of marijuana, and only a relatively small number of studies have been aimed at finding chronic effects. This is not surprising. While public concern focuses on chronic effects, very little research on marijuana's effects had been done before 1968. It was only logical for researchers to concentrate on the most answerable questions first. Studying a group of stoned *S*s for a day or two and recording their test performances are practical. Trying to follow a group for a period of years while they use an illegal drug of unknown strength and purity is not. Thus, at present, no longitudinal studies have been completed, although a few are in progress.

Since there is no adequate data base on chronic effects, it seems that the place to look first for any chronic effects of marijuana is in the same general areas of cognitive function that are affected by acute intoxication. One would expect those aspects of functioning immediately affected by a drug to have a greater chance of being chronically affected. (There is, of course, no guarantee that this is true.) So, while this paper is primarily concerned with possible long-term effects, the evidence from the acute studies will be drawn on extensively.

It is the purpose of this paper to suggest a hypothesis concerning the patterns of the effects of marijuana. An examination of the evidence to date indicates that the results of both acute and chronic studies can be subsumed under the psychological construct of attention and that research on possible chronic effects might usefully be directed at possible effects of marijuana on attention and its components.

Interest in attention as a psychological construct has waxed and waned throughout the 20th century and currently is the focus of a good deal of research in many branches of psychology. One result of fluctuating interest is that there is no definition of attention that is generally agreed on. Furthermore, there is little agreement on the relationship between attention and condition in general (Sack, 1972).

In this paper a particular model of attention has been chosen which delineates specific aspects of attention that can be measured by using tests, the results of which can be quantified. This model is relatively precise, as models of attention go, and should be useful in future research. It should be remembered, however, that there are many models of attention and that results found using this model may not hold up if other models of attention are used. Furthermore, in the discussion of drug effects, many tests are interpreted in terms of this model on a theoretical and speculative basis, but at the present time there is no hard evidence that the tests measure these various factors of attention.

Sack (1972) has presented a model of attention that is concerned with the location of attentional focus. Three factors of attention that are relatively independent have been isolated, using the technique of factor analysis. Each of these factors should be seen as describing a continuum. The factors are: (1) *Resistance to distraction.* Degree to which one has resistance to nonvolitional change in the focus of attention. (Concentration is at one end of the continuum, while distractibility is at the other.) (2) *Set-shifting.* The capacity voluntarily to shift the focus of one's attention. Set-shifting is the obverse of perseveration. (3) *Selectivity or field articulation.* The degree to which the appropriate information is selected for the solution of the problem. The first two factors seem to be operating in the stoned state, while the evidence for the third is equivocal.

Briefly, studies of the acute effects of marijuana show cognitive decrements which increase as dosage increases. The evidence is found in three studies. Melges, *et al.* (1970) reported that stoned *S*s have difficulty in doing a complex calculating task involving repeated addition and subtraction. The reason for the difficulty is impairment in coordinating (in sequence) the cognitive operations necessary to perform the task. *S*s lose their places, forget whether to add or subtract, etc. Kipplinger, *et al.* (1971) found dose-related decrements on the pursuit meter (a task which involves keeping a stylus in contact with a moving spot) and delayed auditory feedback (a task that requires various verbal productions, which are then replayed through earphones while *S* continues to perform verbal tasks). Also, dose-related decrements in psychomotor speed, using a coding task, were found by Weil, *et al.* (1968). While other cognitive operations that show deficits have not been investigated for dose relatedness, it seems reasonable to suppose that they are indeed related to dosage. These cognitive decrements can be seen in Table 1.

It should be noted that chronic users when stoned usually do not show as great a decrement, and in some cases do not show a decrement at all. The exception to this rule is in verbal behavior—chronic users' verbalizations are considerably more circumstantial than those of naive users (Weil, *et al.*, 1968).

TABLE 1

COGNITIVE DECREMENTS FOUND IN ACUTE MARIJUANA INTOXICATION

| | |
|---|---|
| Time Estimation | Hollister and Gillespie, 1970 |
| | Jones and Stone, 1970 |
| | Barratt, *et al.*, 1972 |
| | Tinklenberg, *et al.*, 1972 |
| Set-shifting | Drew, *et al.*, 1972 |
| | Miller and Drew, 1972 |
| Calculating Ability | Halpern, 1944 |
| | Hollister and Gillespie, 1970 |
| | Melges, *et al.*, 1970 |
| | Waskow, *et al.*, 1970 |
| | Hollister, 1971 |
| Visual-motor tasks | Halpern, 1944 |
| | Clark and Nakashima, 1968 |
| | Weil, *et al.*, 1968 |
| | Crancer, *et al.*, 1969 |
| | Manno, *et al.*, 1970 |
| | Clark, *et al.*, 1970 |
| | Kipplinger, *et al.*, 1971 |
| Reaction Time | Clark and Nakashima, 1968 |
| | Dornbush, *et al.*, 1971 |
| | Dougherty, 1972* |
| Memory | Abel, 1970, 1971 |
| | Clark, *et al.*, 1970 |
| | Dornbush, 1971 |
| | Drew, *et al.*, 1972 |
| | Miller, *et al.*, 1972 |
| | Darley, *et al.*, 1973 |

*See Footnote 1.

From the brief summary above it can be seen that various groups of cognitive functions have been investigated and that each construct (calculating ability, memory) explains only a small part of the data. A larger paradigm is now needed to reorganize what is known.

This is not to say that working with circumscribed constructs is not useful. It is. It is the only way to focus inquiry during the early stages of work on a problem. For example, through the careful application of a model of short-term memory, Abel (1971) has shown that marijuana affects storage rather than retrieval of information. He noted that the inability to concentrate was the most likely reason for this finding. Darley, *et al.* (1973) have confirmed his results. Using a different kind of model, however, Klonoff, *et al.* (1973) have shown that learning takes place in the stoned state, and thus retrieval rather

[1]J. D. Dougherty, Section IV—Summary Progress Report.

than storage is affected. The data from both these experiments is useful and the seemingly disparate results can be understood by using a different model, a model of attention.[2]

An important step in organizing these data was made by Melges, *et al.* (1970) when they tied a deficit in serial calculations to a deficit in experiencing time. They have defined a construct called temporal disintegration as an inability to keep track of goal-relevant information. It is a progressive impairment of serial coordination of cognitive operations. It is measured by a complicated calculating task, discussed previously in this paper. These researchers have found that temporal disintegration is related to *S*s' tendency, when stoned, to focus on the present rather than the past or future and to the tendency to depersonalization. They have thus shown a connection between a deficit in serial calculations and a deficit in experiencing time.

It seems as if calculating ability, memory, visual-motor tasks, reaction time, verbal behavior, time sense, and set-shifting can best be understood by recognizing them as requiring heavy reliance on attention: resistance to distraction, set-shifting, or field articulation.

Difficulty in resisting distraction can be seen in the decrements found in the complex calculating task used by Tinklenberg, *et al.* (1970) and Melges, *et al.* (1970) to show impairment of serial coordination of cognitive operations. Stoned *S*s lost their places more often, forgot to alternate between addition and subtraction, blocked, and were more apt to forget the goal number. Impairment of accuracy has been found in serial addition (Hollister, 1971; Waskow, *et al.*, 1970), numerical subtests of the Army Alpha (Halpern, 1944), and the number facility test (Hollister & Gillespie, 1970). Rapaport, *et al.* (1970) have argued persuasively that arithmetical ability partially measures concentration or resistance to distraction.

On visual-motor performance tasks such as Digit Symbol (a coding task measuring psychomotor speed), reaction time, pursuit meter, and the continuous performance test, results are somewhat more equivocal, although often a decrement is shown. This decrement is best understood as a decrease in resistance to distraction. Unusually long reaction times present a special case, however, which will be discussed later after set-shifting has been presented.

Verbal behavior also shows impairment of attention, and is particularly interesting, since Weil and Zinberg (1969) have found that chronic users when stoned have a greater tendency than naive users to go off on tangents, to talk about subjects that are either irrelevant or not directly related to the topic under discussion. (The usual finding of a greater decrement in naive users is thus

[2]Whether storage or retrieval, or both, are affected will, of course, have to be determined by further research. Both results, though, can be subsumed under the attention model. To the extent that storage is affected, *S* can be said to have been distracted. To the extent that retrieval is affected, *S* can be said to have difficulty with set-shifting.

reversed in this case.) An impairment of resistance to distraction may be involved in that *S*s had difficulty remembering the train of thought from moment to moment and showed a definite tendency to be distracted by various objects in the room. Barratt, *et al.* (1972) found that stoned *S*s, when asked to discuss a topic for 5 min., lost their train of thought in nine out of 10 instances. Furthermore, Zeidenberg, *et al.* (1972)[3] found a decrease in phrase length combined with an increase in pause and vowel length, suggesting that *S* was constantly struggling to maintain his focus of attention.

As far as memory is concerned, *Marihuana and Health* (1972), summarizing the work on memory, notes that information needs to be rehearsed in some way before it can enter storage; and marijuana prevents this rehearsal by reducing the ability to concentrate. In terms of the present model, this inability would be termed a lack of resistance to distraction.

In addition to decreasing resistance to distraction, marijuana also causes a decrement in set-shifting, in the capacity to voluntarily shift one's attention. Using tests from the Halstead-Reitan battery, Miller and Drew (1972) have defined mental set-shifting in terms of Trail Making B minus Trail Making A. In two studies, stoned *S*s performed significantly more poorly.

The continually observed decrement in time estimation also seems to involve a decrement in set-shifting. Because Tinklenberg, *et al.* (1972) asked *S*s to count in their measurement of Time Production and found the same over-estimation that others have found in studies of time estimation, it seems reasonable to assume that time estimation involves some kind of counting, either conscious or unconscious. What may happen is that *S*s count more slowly, as if they have difficulty changing their focus from number to number. (They do not lose count, which would be expected if they were distracted.) The stoned *S*s seem to be perseverating very slightly.

The unusually long reaction times mentioned before seem to show that *S* is having difficulty both in set-shifting and in resisting distraction. What seems to be happening is that *S* becomes unable to sustain an attentional focus, establishes a new (probably irrelevant) focus, and then is impaired in his ability to shift his focus of attention voluntarily back to the task; he tends to perseverate slightly.

The third factor of attention, selectivity or field articulation, may be affected by marijuana, but there is no hard evidence that it is. Results for the Closure Test were in the expected direction but not significant (Hollister & Gillespie, 1970). Neither study using the Stroop Color-Word Test was significant, but one was in the expected direction (Meyer, *et al.*, 1971). The Embedded-figures

[3]P. Zeidenberg, W. C. Clark, J. Jaffe, S. W. Anderson, S. Chin & S. Malitz, Preliminary: effect of oral administration of delta-9 tetrahydrocannabinol on memory, speech and perception of thermal stimulation—results with four normal human volunteer subjects. (Unpublished manuscript, 1972)

Test also was not significant, but showed a deficit in the expected direction (Meyer, *et al.*, 1971). The results of the Rod-and-frame Test were neither in the expected direction nor significant (Jones & Stone, 1970).

In summary, the model of attention discussed above better describes what is happening in the stoned state than do the lower-level constructs that have been used so far to describe the acute effects. Two of the factors, set-shifting and resistance to distraction, are especially useful in conceptualizing what is going on.

As far as long-term effects of the drug are concerned, the descriptive power of the model seems to be equally good, but the data base is slight. Relatively few studies have been done on cognitive effects in the first place, and no adequate data-base has been built up using circumscribed constructs, as has been done for the acute effects. The interest has been in global constructs such as intelligence or organic brain damage.[4] Even here no longitudinal studies have been done. Some studies of Jamaicans have equated user and non-user groups, using an intelligence measure which did not correlate highly with measures of organicity, and reported negative results (Rubin & Comitas, 1972; Bowman & Pihl, 1973). Furthermore, Halpern (1944) found no differences between prisoners who were long-term users and prisoners who were non-users. It is not clear, however, how long the users had been drug-free. Intelligence will be touched on again later, but first the data which can be described in terms of the attention model will be discussed.

Two studies have documented a decrement in resistance to distraction. One used Melges, *et al.*'s (1970) complicated calculating task to measure temporal disintegration (Drew, personal communication, 1973). The other used the learning and free recall of paired-associates—a memory task—and showed a significant impairment for users as compared with non-user controls. Scores on arithmetic problems were not significantly different, however, probably because the storage interval was a few seconds rather than a few minutes (Entin & Goldzung, 1973). However, another study using measures of resistance to distraction (reaction time and paired-associates) is Bowman and Pihl's (1973) of Jamaican users. This showed no significant differences between long-term users and non-users.

As far as set-shifting is concerned, Drew, *et al.*[5] reported a significant decrement in mental set-shifting, using Trail Making B minus Trail Making A as a

---

[4]Using tests sensitive to organic brain function, Reid found no impairment of performance in the tests of cognitive and motor function before, during, or after marijuana smoking (*Marihuana: a signal of misunderstanding*, 1972). He did, however, find two casual (out of 10) and two heavy (out of 10) smokers who performed less well than would have been expected on the basis of their IQ scores and level of education. The reason for this finding is unclear.

[5]W. G. Drew, L. L. Miller, B. M. Ables, D. Marx, & M. Marx, Studies on cognitive functioning in two samples of temporarily drug-free chronic marihuana users. Paper submitted to Committee on Problems of Drug Dependence, 1972.

measure. For a second sample, he did not find a significant difference between light and heavy users, rather than users and non-users, although he did find a difference on a slightly modified and more difficult form of the task when he included other independent variables in his regression equation.

Only one study (Barratt, *et al.*, 1972) used embedded-figures (a measure of selectivity or field articulation) but no consistent relationship between users and non-users was found. However, an item analysis showed that, on first exposure to a new level of problem difficulty, the chronic users performed more poorly. This finding seems to show a difficulty in shifting set.

The other relevant data are drawn from studies using the psychiatric interview. Of course, there are substantial weaknesses in the design of this kind of study: first, the absence of a control group; and, second, the fact that *S*s were psychiatric patients, whose pathology probably influenced the effect of the drug to a greater or lesser extent. A further weakness lies in the use of the interview as a measuring instrument. It lacks precision, since the results cannot be quantified. In skillful hands, however, the psychiatric interview can elucidate useful knowledge about cognitive functioning, and it would be a mistake to reject these studies without noting their findings.

Kolansky and Moore (1972a, 1972b) found that their patients—regardless of psychological predisposition—who used marijuana (3 to 10 times per week) demonstrated various symptoms, which included a slowed time sense, difficulty with recent memory, difficulty in concentrating, and an inability to complete thoughts during verbal communication. These effects are similar to the acute effects of the drug and suggest an impairment of set-shifting and a decreased resistance to distraction. (It should be noted that both Zinberg (1972) and Grinspoon[6] apparently believe that these authors have a personal bias against marijuana use; and Grinspoon further believes that their patients, because of their transferences, may have presented only that information which the authors wanted to hear.)

Scher (1970) found that his patients, most of whom held responsible positions, complained of cognitive inefficiency after several years of marijuana use. Kornhaber (1971, 1972), in discussing the effects of marijuana (four times a week) on his adolescent patients, noted that one effect of marijuana is to impair learning ability and judgment because of the harmful effect on attention span and ability to concentrate. Tennant and Groesbeck (1972) reported a chronic intoxicated state found in Army hashish smokers characterized by apathy and impairment of judgment, concentration, and memory. Zinberg and Weil (1970) noted greater circumstantiality in heavy marijuana users (once a day).

---

[6]L. Grinspoon, The American Medical Association and marijuana. (Unpublished manuscript, 1973)

It seems that the above symptoms show that these users are having difficulty maintaining the focus of attention in that they have trouble concentrating and difficulty with memory and verbal communication. They also seem to show a difficulty in shifting voluntarily the focus of attention (set-shifting), insofar as their sense of time is impaired.

These deficits in attention can also be used to explain the amotivational syndrome (McGlothlin & West, 1968). Middle-class students subtly became more introverted, involved with the present rather than the future, and became less productive objectively, although more creative subjectively. (They seemed to enjoy being distracted by internal stimuli.) They tended to drop out of college, probably because the intellectual work demanded quantities of attention that they were unable to mobilize. Intellectual work involves both the ability to maintain one's focus of attention and to be able to shift it voluntarily. It is perhaps no accident that the intellectual classes in India viewed the use of the drug as a dissipation, and only the laboring and religious classes (fakirs, etc.) used it (Kalant, 1972). In fact, in all countries where marijuana has been used extensively, it has been used predominantly by the lower classes.[7]

A relationship between achievement and concentration in school-aged children has often been reported, but much more work needs to be done in this area. Relatively little has been done with adults in the areas of concentration (or resistance to distraction) and the ability to shift set at will. The only factor of attention that has been systematically investigated for adults is field articulation; and it has usually been conceptualized as a global personality measure, rather than a primarily attentional factor.

The relationship between attention and intelligence is extremely complex, and beyond the scope of this paper. However, it cannot be assumed that the relationship is one-to-one.

As is well-known, however, IQ is not a particularly good predictor of achievement as defined in terms of productivity and success in the working world. It may be that the factors of attention—particularly resistance to distraction and set-shifting—will be important here.[8]

It seems likely that whatever relationship exists between use of marijuana and intelligence and achievement[9] will best be elucidated by carefully examining factors of attention. Longitudinal studies, however, must be done, so that

[7]See Bouquet's discussion of use in Africa, the Middle East, and South America (1951); Soueif's study of Egyptian users (1967); and the studies of Jamaican users (Bowman & Pihl, 1973; Rubin & Comitas, 1972).

[8]Hochman and Brill (1973) note that three times as many chronic users as non-users (5% vs 15%) quit jobs because they found them boring.

[9]Hochman and Brill (1973) report that duration and frequency of marijuana use is unrelated to college grades. The interpretation of this finding is complex, however, since an A in one subject is treated as equivalent to an A in another, and some college majors have a higher percentage of both individual and chronic users than others (Rodgers, 1973). Goode (1971), using a more homogeneous sample, found a curvilinear relationship between grades and marijuana use.

measures on the same individual over time will be available. Simply examining users and non-users is not an adequate way to discover decrements in attention, if they in fact exist. In these studies, measures of attention, intelligence, and achievement should be included. Several studies of this kind should give us a much better idea of the cognitive effects of long-term marijuana use.

## REFERENCES

ABEL, E. Marijuana and memory. *Nature*, 1970, 227, 1151-1152.

ABEL, E. Marihuana and memory: acquisition or retrieval? *Science*, 1971, 173, 1038-1040.

BARRATT, E., BEAVER, W., WHITE, R., BLAKENEY, P., & ADAMS, P. The effects of the chronic use of marijuana on sleep and perceptual-motor performance in humans. Paper presented at the Symposium on Aeromedical Aspects of Marijuana, FAA, Oklahoma City, June 14, 1972.

BOUQUET, J. Cannabis. *Bulletin on Narcotics*, 1951, 3(1), 22-45.

BOWMAN, M., & PIHL, R. O. Cannabis: psychological effects of chronic heavy use. *Psychopharmacologia*, 1973, 29, 159-170.

CLARK, L. D., HUGHES, R., & NAKASHIMA, E. H. Behavioral effects of marijuana. *Archives of General Psychiatry*, 1970, 23, 193-198.

CLARK, L. D., & NAKASHIMA, E. H. Experimental studies of marihuana. *American Journal of Psychiatry*, 1968, 125, 379-383.

CRANCER, A., DILLE, J. M., DELAY, J. C., WALLACE, J. E., & HAYKIN, M. D. Comparison of the effects of marijuana on simulated driving performance. *Science*, 1969, 164, 851-854.

DARLEY, C. F., TINKLENBERG, J. R., ROTH, W. T., HOLLISTER, L. E., & ATKINSON, R. C. Influence of marijuana on storage and retrieval process in memory. *Memory and Cognition*, 1973, 1, 196-200.

DORNBUSH, R. L., FINK, M., & FREEDMAN, A. M. Marijuana, memory, and perception. *American Journal of Psychiatry*, 1971, 128, 194-197.

DREW, W. G., KIPPLINGER, G. F., MILLER, L. L., & MARX, M. Effects of propranolol on marihuana-induced cognitive functioning. *Clinical Pharmacology and Therapeutics*, 1972, 13, 526-533.

ENTIN, E. E., & GOLDZUNG, P. J. Residual effects of marihuana usage on learning and memory. *Psychological Record*, 1973, 23, 169-178.

HALPERN, F. Mayor's committee on marijuana, 1944. In D. Solomon (Ed.), *The marijuana papers*. New York: Bobbs-Merrill, 1966. Pp. 290-312.

HOCHMAN, J. S., & BRILL, N. Q. Chronic marijuana use and psychosocial adaptation. *American Journal of Psychiatry*, 1973, 130, 132-140.

HOLLISTER, L. E. Marijuana in man: three years later. *Science*, 1971, 172, 21-29.

HOLLISTER, L. E., & GILLESPIE, H. K. Marihuana, ethanol, and dextroamphetamine. *Archives of General Psychiatry*, 1970, 23, 199-203.

JONES, R. T., & STONE, G. C. Psychological studies of marijuana and alcohol in man. *Psychopharmacologia*, 1970, 18, 108-117.

KALANT, O. J. Report of the Indian Hemp Drugs Commission, 1893-94: a critical review. *International Journal of the Addictions*, 1972, 7, 77-96.

KIPPLINGER, G. F., MANNO, J. E., RODDA, B. E., & FORNEY, R. Dose response analysis of the effects of tetrahydrocannabinol in man. *Clinical Pharmacology*, 1971, 12, 650-657.

KLONOFF, H. K., LOW, M., & MARCUS, A. Neuropsychological effects of marijuana. *CMA Journal*, 1973, 108, 150-156.

KOLANSKY, H., & MOORE, W. T. Clinical effects of marihuana on the young. *International Journal of Psychiatry*, 1972, 10(2), 55-67. (a)

KOLANSKY, H., & MOORE, W. T. Toxic effects of chronic marihuana use. *Journal of the American Medical Association*, 1972, 222(1), 35-41. (b)

KORNHABER, A. Marijuana in an adolescent psychiatric outpatient population. *Journal of the American Medical Association*, 1971, 215, 1988.

KORNHABER, A. Clinical corroboration. *International Journal of Psychiatry*, 1972, 10(2), 79-81.

MANNO, J. E., KIPPLINGER, G. F., HAINE, S. E., BENNETT, I. F., & FORNEY, R. B. Comparative effects of smoking marihuana or placebo on human motor and mental performance. *Clinical Pharmacology and Therapeutics*, 1970, 11, 808-815.

*Marihuana and health: second annual report to Congress from the Secretary of Health, Education, and Welfare.* Washington, D. C.: U. S. Government Print. Off., May, 1972.

*Marihuana: a signal of misunderstanding—the technical papers of the first report of the National Commission on Marihuana and Drug Abuse.* Washington, D. C.: U. S. Government Print. Off., March, 1972. Appendix. Vol. 1, 85-86.

MCGLOTHLIN, W. H., & WEST, L. J. The marihuana problem: an overview. *American Journal of Psychiatry*, 1968, 125, 370-378.

MELGES, F. T., TINKLENBERG, J. P., HOLLISTER, L. E., & GILLESPIE, H. K. Marihuana and temporal disintegration. *Science*, 1970, 168, 1118-1120.

MEYER, R. E., PILLARD, R. C., SHAPIRO, L. M., & MIRIN, S. M. Administration of marijuana to heavy and casual marijuana users. *American Journal of Psychiatry*, 1971, 128, 198-204.

MILLER, L. L., & DREW, W. G. Marijuana (M)-induced impairment of recent memory (RM) and mental set shifting (MSS). *Federation Proceedings*, 1972, 31, 551.

MILLER, L. L., DREW, W. G., & KIPPLINGER, G. F. Effects of marijuana on recall of narrative material and Stroop color-word performance. *Nature*, 1972, 237, 172-173.

RAPAPORT, D., GILL, M. M., & SCHAFER, R. *Diagnostic psychological testing.* (Rev. ed.) London: Univer. of London Press, 1970.

RODGERS, T. C. Discussion. *American Journal of Psychiatry*, 1973, 130, 140.

RUBIN, V., & COMITAS, L. Effects of chronic smoking of cannabis in Jamaica. Part II: clinical studies. A report by the Research Institute for the Study of Man to the Center for Studies of Narcotic and Drug Abuse, NIMH, 1972.

SACK, S. Three components of attention and their relationship to academic functioning. Unpublished doctoral dissertation, George Washington Univer., 1972.

SCHER, J. The marihuana habit. *Journal of the American Medical Association*, 1970, 214, 1120.

SOUIEF, M. I. Hashish consumption in Egypt with special reference to psychosocial aspects. *Bulletin on Narcotics*, 1967, 19(2), 1-12.

TENNANT, F. S., & GROESBECK, C. J. Psychiatric effects of hashish. *Archives of General Psychiatry*, 1972, 27, 133-136.

TINKLENBERG, J. R., KOPELL, B. S., MELGES, F. T., & HOLLISTER, L. E. Marihuana and alcohol. *Archives of General Psychiatry*, 1972, 27, 812-815.

TINKLENBERG, J. R., MELGES, F. T., HOLLISTER, L. E., & GILLESPIE, H. K. Marijuana and immediate memory. *Nature*, 1970, 226, 1171-1172.

WASKOW, I. E., OLSSON, J. E., SALZMAN, C., & KATZ, M. Psychological effects of tetrahydrocannabinol. *Archives of General Psychiatry*, 1970, 22, 97-107.

WEIL, A. T., & ZINBERG, N. E. Acute effects of marihuana on speech. *Nature*, 1969, 222, 434-437.

WEIL, A. T., ZINBERG, N. E., & NELSEN, J. M. Clinical and psychological effects of marihuana in man. *Science*, 1968, 162, 1234-1242.

ZINBERG, N. E. Against hysteria. *International Journal of Psychiatry*, 1972, 10, 69-73.

ZINBERG, N. E., & WEIL, A. T. A comparison of marijuana users and non-users. *Nature*, 1970, 226, 119-123.

*Accepted August 13, 1973.*

## SECTION IV

# HYPNOSIS

# 14

## BARBER, T. X.

# *Suggested ("Hypnotic") Behavior: The Trance Paradigm versus an Alternative Paradigm*

It has been traditionally assumed that certain types of procedures, labeled as "trance inductions," give rise to a special state of consciousness (hypnotic trance) in some individuals. It has also been assumed that as the hypnotic trance becomes deeper or more profound, the subject becomes more responsive to suggestions for age regression, analgesia, hallucinations, deafness, amnesia, and so on. In this chapter, I will critically analyze these and other assumptions that underly the traditional (trance) paradigm and I will present an alternative paradigm for conceptualizing the experiences and behaviors that have been historically subsumed under the term "hypnotism" or "hypnosis."

### *Paradigms in Science*

In a cogent analysis of the history of science, Kuhn (1962) has shown that scientists working in an area of inquiry usually share common basic assumptions pertaining to the nature of the phenomena they are investigating. The shared assumptions, which are often more implicit than explicit, together with a related set of criteria for asking meaningful questions and for selecting research topics, are termed a "paradigm."

Each paradigm may give rise to more than one theory that aims to explain the phenomena. Although theories deriving from any one paradigm differ in various aspects, they share the same basic assumptions, the same methodological criteria, and the same framework for asking meaningful questions. As Braginsky, Braginsky, and Ring (1969) have pointed out, "In academic psychology, for example, competing behavioristic theories of learning were for a long time able to flourish despite widespread agreement concerning how the phenomenon [of learning] should be approached—a consensus that was particularly likely to be evident when such theories were challenged by the radically different assumptions of cognitively oriented theories (p. 30)."

In the history of science, there are many important instances when the consensually-shared paradigm could not easily explain new research data. In these instances, a few scientists began to question the basic assumptions underlying the traditional paradigm, a new way of viewing the phenomena (an alternative paradigm) was slowly developed, and after a period of debate, misunderstandings, and acrimony, the alternative paradigm was accepted by new generations of investigators and slowly became dominant. In astronomy, for example, the geocentric view of the planetary system was replaced by the heliocentric view; in chemistry, the phlogiston conception of combustion was replaced by the oxygen conception; in physics, theories pertaining to the ether were replaced by conceptions that did not postulate an ether; and, in psychology, introspective analysis gave way to behaviorism.

As Chaves (1968) has pointed out, it appears that a paradigm shift may be occurring at the present time in the area of inquiry historically subsumed under the term "hypnosis." In the next section, I will briefly describe the underlying assumptions of the traditional (trance) paradigm that has dominated this area of inquiry for more than a hundred years. Following this, I will formulate some of the postulates of an alternative paradigm.

### *The Special State (Trance) Paradigm*

During the past century, terms such as "hypnotic trance state" (or "trance," "hypnosis," "hypnotic state," and "hypnotized") have been widely used by both scientists and laymen and have become part of the everyday vocabulary of children and adults. Although the implications of these terms have been slowly changing over the years, they seem to refer to some kind of fundamental change in the state of the organism.

During the nineteenth century, terms such as "hypnotic trance" or "hypnosis" typically implied that the subject resembled the sleepwalker or somnambule, that is, resembled the person who arises from his bed at night, walks around while "half asleep," and responds in a dissociated, rather automatic way to a narrow range of stimuli. Some present-day investigators also think of the "hypnotic trance" subject as resembling a sleepwalker. As Hilgard (1969a) has pointed out, "Hypnosis is commonly considered to be a 'state' perhaps resembling the state in which the sleepwalker finds himself, hence the term 'somnambulist' as applied to the deeply hypnotized person (p. 71)." Other present-day investigators who utilize the terms "hypnotic trance" or "hypnosis" do not seem to mean that the subject resembles the sleepwalker. Although, as Bowers (1966) has noted, "Most [present-day] investigators interested in hypnosis believe that there is an hypnotic state which fundamentally differs from the waking state" (p. 42), they differ among themselves as to the exact meaning to be assigned to the terms.

Bowers (1966) views hypnosis as "an altered state within which suggestions have a peculiarly potent effect" (p. 50). However, Gill and Brenman (1959) use the term "hypnotic state" to refer to an "induced psychological regression, issuing, in the setting of a particular regressed relationship between two people, in a relatively stable state which includes a subsystem of the ego with various degrees of control of the ego apparatuses" (p. xxiii). Other investigators attach different connotations to the term. For instance, among the essential characteristics of the hypnotic state, Orne (1959) includes a tolerance for logical inconsistencies ("trance logic") and alterations in subjective experiences induced by suggestions. Evans (1968) views hypnosis as an altered subjective state of awareness in which dissociative mechanisms are operating, Meares (1963) sees the basic element in hypnosis as an atavistic regression to a primitive mode of mental functioning, and Shor (1962) views the hypnotic state as having three dimensions—hypnotic role-taking, trance, and archaic involvement.

Although the above and other theoretical formulations attribute somewhat different properties to the hypnotic state, they derive from a common set of basic assumptions (an underlying paradigm). Some of the underlying assumptions of the hypnosis or trance paradigm appear to include the following:

1. There exists a state of consciousness, a state of awareness, or a state of the organism that is fundamentally (qualitatively) different from other states of consciousness such as the waking state, the deep sleep state, and the state of unconsciousness. This distinct state is labeled "hypnosis," "hypnotic state," "hypnotic trance," or simply "trance."

2. The state of hypnotic trance may occasionally occur spontaneously, but it is usually induced by special types of procedures that are labeled "hypnotic inductions" or "trance inductions." Although trance induction procedures vary in content—for example, they usually include, but they need not include, fixation of the eyes, suggestions of relaxation, and suggestions of drowsiness and sleep—they all appear to have two essential features

in common: they suggest to the subject that he is entering a special state (hypnotic trance) and investigators who adhere to the traditional paradigm agree that the procedures are capable of producing hypnotic trance.

3. The hypnotic trance state is not a momentary condition that the subject enters for only a few seconds. On the contrary, when a person has been placed in a hypnotic trance, he remains in it for a period of time and he is typically brought out of it by a command from the hypnotist, such as "Wake up!"

4. Subjects who are in a hypnotic state are responsive, both overtly and subjectively, to test suggestions for rigidity of the muscles or limbs, age regression, analgesia and anesthesia, visual and auditory hallucination, deafness, blindness, color blindness, negative hallucination, dreaming on a specified topic, heightened performance (on physical or cognitive tasks), amnesia, and posthypnotic behavior.[1]

5. As Sutcliffe (1960) pointed out, some investigators who adhere to the trance paradigm believe the suggested phenomena are "genuine" or "real," whereas others are far more skeptical. For example, some investigators who accept the trance paradigm view hypnotic deafness as indistinguishable from actual deafness, and the hypnotic dream as indistinguishable from the nocturnal dream. However, other investigators who accept the trance paradigm view the hypnotic deaf subject as a person who is able to hear but thinks that he cannot, and they perceive the hypnotic dream as differing in essential respects from the night dream. Although investigators who adhere to the trance paradigm disagree on the "reality" of the suggested phenomena, the important point to emphasize is that they all view the phenomena as associated with hypnotic trance, and they consequently label the phenomena as "hypnotic phenomena," not simply as "suggested phenomena."

6. There are levels or depths of hypnotic trance; that is, hypnotic trance can vary from light, to medium, to deep, to very deep (somnambulism).

7. As the depth of hypnotic trance increases, the subject's ability to experience suggested phenomena vividly and intensely also increases. For example, as the subject becomes more deeply hypnotized, he is more able to have a vivid and intense experience of age regression, analgesia, hallucination, or amnesia.

In brief, the dominant (trance) paradigm sees the person who responds to test suggestions as being in a fundamentally different state from the person who is unresponsive to test suggestions. The construct "hypnotic state," "trance," or "hypnosis" is used to refer to this state, which is conceived to differ, not simply quantitatively, but in some basic, qualitative way, from normal waking states and from states of sleep.

1. Henceforth, in this chapter, the term "response" or "responsiveness to test suggestions" will be used as a shorthand term to refer to both overt and subjective responses to each of the types of suggestions mentioned in this paragraph.

## *An Alternative Paradigm: The Member of the Audience Analogy*

There is another way of viewing responsiveness to test suggestions[2] that does not involve special state constructs such as "hypnosis," "hypnotized," "hypnotic state," or "trance." This alternative paradigm does not see a qualitative difference in the "state" of the person who is and the one who is not responsive to test suggestions. Although the alternative paradigm has many historical roots (discussed by Sarbin, 1962), it derives primarily from my more recent theoretical endeavors and those of Sarbin (Barber, 1964a, 1967, 1969b, 1970a; Sarbin, 1950; Sarbin & Andersen, 1967; Sarbin & Coe, in press). An analogy to members of an audience watching a motion picture or a stage play may clarify the paradigm.

One member of an audience may be attending a performance with the purpose of having new experiences. His attitude is that it is interesting and worthwhile to feel sad, to feel happy, to empathize, and to have the other thoughts, feelings, and emotions the actors are attempting to communicate. He both desires and expects the actors to arouse in him new or interesting thoughts and emotions. Although he is aware that he is watching a contrived performance and that he is in an audience, he does not actively think about these matters. Since this member of the audience has "positive" attitudes, motivations, and expectancies toward the communications emanating from the stage, he lets himself imagine and think with the statements and actions of the actors; he laughs, weeps, empathizes and, more generally, thinks, feels, emotes, and experiences in line with the intentions of the actors.

Another member of the audience had an anxious and tiring day at the office, wanted to go to bed early in the evening, and came to the performance unwillingly, in order to avoid an argument with his wife. He is not interested in having the emotions and experiences the actors are attempting to communicate. He does not especially desire and does not expect to feel empathic, happy, sad, excited, or shocked. He is continually aware that he is in an audience and that he is observing a deliberately contrived performance. Given this set of attitudes, motivations, and expectancies, this member of the audience does not let himself imagine and think with the statements and actions of the actors; he does not laugh, weep, empathize or, more generally, think, feel, emote, and experience in line with the communications from the actors.

The implications of this analogy are:

1. The experimental subject who is highly responsive to test suggestions

2. As stated in footnote 1, in the remainder of this chapter the term "responsiveness" or "response to test suggestions" will refer to both overt and subjective responses to suggestions for limb rigidity, age regression, analgesia, hallucination, amnesia, postexperimental ("posthypnotic") behavior, and so on.

resembles the member of the audience who experiences the thoughts, feelings, and emotions that the actors are attempting to arouse. The very suggestible subject views his responding to test suggestions as interesting and worthwhile; he desires and expects to experience those things that are suggested. Given these underlying "positive" attitudes, motivations, and expectancies, he lets himself imagine and think with the things suggested and he experiences the suggested effects.

2. The experimental subject who is very unresponsive to test suggestions resembles the member of the audience who does *not* experience the thoughts, feelings, and emotions that the actors are attempting to arouse. The very nonsuggestible subject views his responding to test suggestions as not desirable; he neither wants nor expects to experience those things that are suggested. Given these underlying "negative" attitudes, motivations, and expectancies, he does not let himself imagine and think with the things suggested and he does not experience the suggested effects.

3. It is misleading and unparsimonious to label the member of an audience, who is thinking, feeling, and emoting in line with the communications of the actors, as being in a special state (hypnotic trance) that is fundamentally different from the waking state. In other words, it is misleading and unparsimonious to restrict our conceptions of normal conditions or waking conditions to such an extent that they exclude the member of the audience who is having various experiences as he listens to the communications from the stage. Furthermore, since the member of the audience, who is responding to the words of the actors, and the experimental subject, who is responding to the words (test suggestions) of the experimenter, do not differ in any important way in their attitudes, motivations, and expectancies toward the communications or in the way they think along with the communications, it is also misleading and unparsimonious to label the subject who is responding to test suggestions as being in a special state (hypnotic trance).

4. Although the member of the audience who is responding to the words of the actors and the experimental subject who is responding to the test suggestions of the experimenter have similar attitudes, motivations, and expectancies toward the communications and are similarly "thinking with" the communications, *they are being exposed to different types of communications.* The messages or communications from the actors are intended to elicit certain types of thoughts, feelings, and emotions—to empathize, to feel happy or sad, to laugh or to weep, to feel excited or shocked—whereas the messages or communications (test suggestions) from the experimenter are intended to elicit somewhat different types of thoughts, feelings, or emotions—to experience an arm as heavy, to experience oneself as a child, to forget preceding events, and so forth. From this viewpoint, the member of the audience and the subject who is responding to test suggestions are having different experiences, *not because they are in different "states" but because they are receiving different communications.*

The above analogy exemplifies some of the basic assumptions underlying the alternative paradigm. These assumptions include the following:

1. It is unnecessary to postulate a fundamental difference in the "state" of the person who is and the one who is not responsive to test suggestions.

2. Both the person who is and the one who is not responsive to test suggestions have attitudes, motivations, and expectancies toward the communications they are receiving.

3. The person who is very responsive to test suggestions has "positive" attitudes, motivations, and expectancies toward the communications he is receiving. That is, he views his responding to test suggestions as interesting or worthwhile and he wants to, tries to, and expects to experience the suggested effects. Given these "positive" attitudes, motivations, and expectancies, he lets himself think with and imagine those things that are suggested.

4. The person who is very unresponsive to test suggestions has "negative" attitudes, motivations, and expectancies toward the communications he is receiving. That is, he views his responding to test suggestions as not interesting or worthwhile and he neither tries to nor expects to experience the suggested effects. Given these "negative" attitudes, motivations, and expectancies, he does not let himself imagine or think with the suggestions; instead, he verbalizes to himself such statements as "This is silly" or "The suggestion won't work."

5. The three factors—attitudes, motivations, and expectancies—vary on a continuum (from negative, to neutral, to positive) and they converge and interact in complex ways to determine to what extent a subject will let himself think with and imagine those things that are suggested. The extent to which the subject thinks with and vividly imagines the suggested effects, in turn, determines his overt and subjective responses to test suggestions.

6. Concepts derived from abnormal psychology—such as "trance," "somnambulism," and "dissociation"—are misleading and do not explain the overt and subjective responses. Responsiveness to test suggestions is a normal psychological phenomenon that can be conceptualized in terms of constructs that are an integral part of normal psychology, especially of social psychology. Social psychology conceptualizes other social influence processes, such as persuasion and conformity, in terms of such mediating variables as attitudes, motivations, expectancies, and cognitive processes. In the same way, the mediating variables that are relevant to explaining responsiveness to test suggestions include attitudes, motivations, expectancies, and cognitive-imaginative processes.

7. The phenomena associated with test suggestions are considered to be within the range of normal human capabilities. However, whether or not the suggested phenomena are similar to or different from phenomena occurring in real-life situations that bear the same name, is viewed as an open question that needs to be answered empirically. For example, such questions as the following are open to empirical investigation: To what extent is suggested

analgesia similar to the analgesia produced by nerve section or by anesthetic drugs? What are the similarities and differences between suggested and naturally-occurring (nonsuggested) blindness, color blindness, deafness, hallucination, dreaming, and amnesia? The empirical evidence at present indicates that, although there are some similarities between the suggested and nonsuggested phenomena, they also differ in very important respects. For example, suggested color blindness has only superficial resemblances to actual color blindness, and suggested amnesia is much more labile or transient than actual amnesia. (Since these issues have been discussed in detail elsewhere—Barber, 1959b, 1961b, 1962a, 1962b, 1963, 1964b, 1964c, 1965b, 1969b, 1970a—they will be discussed only peripherally here.)

Which paradigm is more successful in explaining responsiveness to test suggestions for limb rigidity, age-regression, analgesia, hallucination, amnesia, etc.—the traditional one that postulates a special state that is fundamentally different from the waking state, or the alternative one that focuses on attitudes, motivations, expectancies, and thinking with and imagining those things that are suggested? I will next summarize experimental data, pertaining to responsiveness to test suggestions under control ("waking") conditions, which indicate that the alternative paradigm provides a more successful and more parsimonious explanation.

### *Response to Test Suggestions Without "Hypnosis"*

A substantial number of subjects are highly responsive to test suggestions when no attempt is made to place them in a "hypnotic trance state." Let us look at a few examples.

#### HUMAN-PLANK FEAT

The stage hypnotist suggests to a selected subject that his body is becoming stiff and rigid. When the subject appears rigid, the stage hypnotist and an assistant place him between two chairs, one chair beneath the subject's head and the other beneath his ankles. The subject typically remains suspended between the two chairs for several minutes, as if he were a human plank. The traditional paradigm assumes that the subject is able to perform the human-plank feat because he is in a state—a hypnotic trance state—that is qualitatively different from ordinary states of consciousness. This notion is not supported by the empirical data.

Collins (1961) demonstrated conclusively that, when male and female control subjects are told directly (without any special preliminaries) to keep their bodies rigid, practically all perform the human-plank feat, that is, they remain suspended between two chairs for several minutes, one chair beneath the head and the other beneath the ankles. In fact, Collins demonstrated that control subjects are able to perform the feat just as easily as subjects who have been exposed to a trance induction procedure and who are ostensibly in "hypnotic trance." The control ("awake") subjects and also the experimental ("hypnotized") subjects stated, at the conclusion of Collins' experiment, that they were surprised at their own performance because they did not believe initially that they could so easily perform the human-plank feat.

At times, stage hypnotists ask a person to stand on the chest of the subject who is rigidly suspended between two chairs, one chair beneath his shoulders and the other beneath his calves. The traditional paradigm assumes that the suspended subject is able to support the weight of a man on his chest because he is in a special state of consciousness—a hypnotic trance state. The empirical evidence does not support this assumption. In my laboratory, six unselected male subjects were told under control conditions (without any special preliminaries) to make their body rigid and to keep it rigid. They were then suspended between two chairs, one chair beneath the shoulders and the other beneath the calves. Each subject was able to support the weight of a man on his chest. All subjects were surprised that they could so easily support the weight of a man and all disagreed vehemently with the statement that they were in a trance.

### RESPONSE TO OTHER TEST SUGGESTIONS

Experimental studies that I have summarized elsewhere (Barber, 1965a) have demonstrated that a substantial proportion of individuals are responsive to various kinds of test suggestions when no attempt is made to place them in a "hypnotic trance." In these experiments, 62 unselected college students were assigned at random to a control condition (they were simply told that they were to receive a test of imagination). They were then assessed individually on objective and subjective responses to the eight standardized test suggestions of the Barber Suggestibility Scale: Arm Lowering (the subject's right arm is heavy and is moving down); Arm Levitation (the left arm is weightless and is moving up); Hand Lock (the clasped hands are welded together and cannot be taken apart); Thirst "Hallucination" (he is becoming extremely thirsty); Verbal Inhibition (his throat and jaw muscles are rigid and he cannot speak his name); Body Immobility (his body is heavy and he cannot stand up); "Posthypnotic-Like" Response (when he hears a click postexperimentally, he will cough automatically); and Selective Amnesia (when the experiment is over, he will not remember one specific test-suggestion).[3]

3. The subject receives a maximum Objective score of 8 points on the Barber Suggestibility Scale (one point for each of the eight test suggestions) if: the right arm moves down 4 or more inches; the left arm rises 4 or more inches; the subject tries to but fails to unclasp his hands; he shows swallowing, moistening of lips, or marked mouth movements and states postexperimentally that he became thirsty during this test; he tries but does not succeed in saying his name; he tries

As Table 5.1, column 1, shows, about one-fourth of these control subjects, who were given the eight test suggestions immediately after they were simply told that they were to receive a test of imagination, passed the Arm Lowering, Arm Levitation, Verbal Inhibition, and Body Immobility items both objectively (manifesting the suggested overt behavior) and subjectively (testifying postexperimentally that they actually experienced the suggested effect). In addition, nearly half of these control subjects passed the Thirst "Hallucination" item and 40 per cent passed the Hand Lock item (that is, they tried to unclasp their hands but had not succeeded after 15 seconds, and they testified that they actually felt that their hands were stuck). Furthermore, about 13 per cent of these control subjects passed the "Posthypnotic-Like" Response and the Selective Amnesia items.

Although a surprisingly high proportion of subjects were responsive to the test suggestions under the control condition, even more dramatic results were obtained when another group of 62 subjects, randomly selected from the same college population, were tested individually on the same test suggestions after receiving task-motivational instructions for 45 seconds. These task-motivational instructions, which aimed to produce favorable motivations, attitudes, and expectancies toward the test situation and to heighten the subject's willingness to imagine and think about those things that would be suggested, were worded as follows:

> In this experiment I'm going to test your ability to imagine and to visualize. How well you do on the tests which I will give you depends entirely upon your willingness to try to imagine and to visualize the things I will ask you to imagine. Everyone passed these tests when they tried. For example, we asked people to close their eyes and to imagine that they were at a movie theater and were watching a show. Most people were able to do this very well; they were able to imagine very vividly that they were at a movie and they felt as if they were actually looking at the picture. However, a few people thought that this was an awkward or silly thing to do and did not try to imagine and failed the test. Yet when these people later realized that it wasn't hard to imagine, they were able to visualize the movie picture and they felt as if the imagined movie was as vivid and as real as an actual movie. What I ask is your cooperation in helping this experiment by trying to imagine vividly what I describe to you. I want you to score as high as you can be-

---

but does not succeed in standing fully erect; he coughs or clears his throat when the cue is presented postexperimentally; and he does not refer to the critical item during the postexperimental interview but recalls at least four other items and then recalls the critical item when told "Now you can remember."

In addition to the Objective scores, assigned as described above, the subject also receives a maximum Subjective score of 8 points on the Barber Suggestibility Scale (one point for each of the eight test suggestions) if he states, during the standardized post experimental interview, that he actually experienced each of the suggested effects and that he did not respond overtly to the test suggestion simply to follow instructions or to please the experimenter.

TABLE 5.1 Percentage of subjects passing each test suggestion both objectively and subjectively

| *Test Suggestion* | *Per Cent of Subjects Passing* | | |
|---|---|---|---|
| | *control* | *task-motivational instructions* | *trance induction procedure* |
| 1. Arm lowering | $26_b$ | $61_a$ | $72_a$ |
| 2. Arm levitation | $24_b$ | $56_a$ | $56_a$ |
| 3. Hand lock | $40_b$ | $81_a$ | $69_a$ |
| 4. Thirst hallucination | $48_b$ | $76_a$ | $74_a$ |
| 5. Verbal inhibition | $27_b$ | $69_a$ | $64_a$ |
| 6. Body immobility | $27_b$ | $66_a$ | $63_a$ |
| 7. Posthypnoticlike response | $14_b$ | $42_a$ | $29_{ab}$ |
| 8. Selective amnesia | $13_b$ | $39_a$ | $35_a$ |

SOURCE: Barber, 1965a.
NOTE: Percentages in the same row containing the same subscript letter do not differ from each other at the .05 level of confidence.

cause we're trying to measure the maximum ability of people to imagine. If you don't try to the best of your ability, this experiment will be worthless and I'll tend to feel silly. On the other hand, if you try to imagine to the best of your ability, you can easily imagine and do the interesting things I tell you and you will be helping this experiment and not wasting any time (Barber & Calverley, 1962, p. 366).

The subjects who received these task-motivational instructions showed a dramatically high level of objective and subjective responsiveness to the test suggestions (manifesting the suggested overt behaviors and testifying that they subjectively experienced the suggested effects). As Table 5.1, column 2, shows, from 56 per cent to 69 per cent of the subjects who received task-motivational instructions passed the Arm Lowering, Arm Levitation, Verbal Inhibition, and Body Immobility items, 76 per cent passed the Thirst "Hallucination" item, and 81 per cent passed the Hand Lock item. In addition, around 40 per cent of the subjects who received task-motivational instructions passed the Selective Amnesia and "Posthypnotic-Like" Response items.

As stated above, 62 subjects were tested individually under the control condition and 62 were tested under the task-motivational condition. In addition, 62 subjects, randomly chosen from the same population of college students, were assessed individually on response to the same test suggestions after they were exposed to a standardized 15-minute procedure of the type traditionally labeled as a "trance induction." This trance induction procedure, which is presented verbatim elsewhere (Barber, 1969b), included the following salient features: (a) Instructions were administered to produce favorable attitudes, motivations, and expectancies (for example, "Hypnosis is nothing fearful or mysterious. . . . Your cooperation, your interest, is what I ask for. . . . Nothing will be done that will in any way cause you the least embarrassment . . . you will be able to experience many interesting things."). (b) The subject was asked to fixate on a light blinking in synchrony with the sound of a metronome and was given suggestions of eye heaviness and eye closure (for example, "The strain in your eyes is getting greater and greater. . . . You would like to close your eyes and relax completely"). (c) Suggestions of relaxation, drowsiness, and sleep were administered repeatedly ("comfortable, relaxed, thinking of nothing, nothing but what I say . . . drowsy . . . deep sound comfortable sleep . . . deeper and deeper. . ."). (d) It was suggested to the subject that he was entering a unique state, a deep trance, in which he would be able to have interesting and unusual experiences

As table 5.1, column 3, shows, subjects exposed to the trance induction procedure were generally as responsive to the test suggestions as those subjects who had received the brief task-motivational instructions under waking conditions. Also, Table 5.1 shows that the subjects who received the trance induction procedure as well as those who received the task-motivational instructions were significantly more responsive to the test suggestions than the control group.

Table 5.2 shows the number of test suggestions that were passed by subjects in each of the three experimental groups. The reader will note that 13 per cent and 10 per cent of the subjects under the task-motivational instructions and trance induction conditions, respectively, and none of the controls, passed all eight of the test suggestions. Also, 16 per cent, 60 per cent, and 53 per cent of the subjects under the control, task-motivational instructions, and trance induction condition, respectively, were relatively highly responsive to test suggestions, passing at least five of the eight items.

The data presented above indicate the following:

TABLE 5.2 Number of test suggestions passed (both objectively and subjectively) by subjects in control, task-motivational instructions, and trance induction groups

| *Number of Test Suggestions Passed* | *Per Cent of Subjects Passing* control group | | task-motivational group | | trance induction group | |
|---|---|---|---|---|---|---|
| 8 | 0 | 16 | 13 | 60 | 10 | 53 |
| 7 | 3 | | 16 | | 16 | |
| 6 | 11 | | 15 | | 16 | |
| 5 | 2 | | 16 | | 11 | |
| 4 | 11 | 38 | 16 | 27 | 15 | 36 |
| 3 | 6 | | 8 | | 13 | |
| 2 | 21 | | 3 | | 8 | |
| 1 | 16 | 45 | 10 | 13 | 6 | 11 |
| 0 | 29 | | 3 | | 5 | |

SOURCE: Barber, 1965a.

1. When subjects are tested on response to test suggestions under a control condition (immediately after they are simply told that they are to be given a test of imagination), the majority respond to some test suggestions and a small proportion manifest a rather high level of response. Under the control condition, subjects typically passed two of the eight test suggestions and 16 per cent passed at least five of the eight.

2. Although most subjects respond to some test suggestions under a control condition, a markedly higher level of response is found when subjects are given task-motivational instructions, that is, instructions designed to produce positive motivations, attitudes, and expectancies toward the suggestive situation and a consequent willingness to think with and imagine those things that are suggested.

3. A trance induction procedure, which focuses on repeated suggestions of eye heaviness, relaxation, drowsiness, and sleep, also raises response to test suggestions above the control or base level.

4. Comparable high levels of response to test suggestions of arm heaviness, body immobility, inability to say one's name, selective amnesia, and so forth, are produced when task-motivational instructions are given alone (without a trance induction procedure) and when a trance induction procedure is given alone (without explicit task-motivational instructions).[4]

Why is enhanced responsiveness to test suggestions produced both by task-motivational instructions and also by a trance induction procedure? There are at least three possible interpretations:

1. From the traditional (special state) paradigm, one might hypothesize that both task-motivational instructions and a trance induction procedure

4. Additional experiments, summarized elsewhere (Barber, 1969b, pp. 60–70), also found comparable high levels of response to test suggestions (suggestions for analgesia, gustatory "hallucination," enhanced cognitive proficiency, dreaming on a specified topic, time distortion, color blindness, visual-auditory "hallucination," and amnesia) in subjects exposed to task-motivational instructions alone and in those exposed to a trance induction procedure. However, several considerations noted by Hilgard and Tart (1966) and by Edmonston and Robertson (1967) led to an additional experiment (Barber & Calverley, 1968), which indicated that task-motivational instructions given alone are slightly less effective in facilitating suggestibility than task-motivational instructions given together with a trance induction procedure. Barber and Calverley (1968) hypothesized that the slightly higher level of suggestibility that was found when the task-motivational instructions were combined with the trance induction procedure was due to the fact that under this condition the situation was defined to the subjects as "hypnosis" and, vice versa, the slightly lower level of suggestibility found with task-motivational instructions alone was due to the fact that under this condition the situation was defined as a "test of imagination." This hypothesis clearly merits testing, especially since earlier experiments (Barber & Calverley, 1964e, 1965) indicated that, with everything else constant, a higher level of responsiveness to test suggestions is produced when subjects are told they are participating in a "hypnosis" experiment rather than in an "imagination" experiment.

give rise to a hypnotic trance state. However, with few exceptions, subjects who have received task-motivational instructions appear awake, claim they are awake, and do not show a limp posture, passivity, a blank stare, or any other sign of trance. Are task-motivated subjects, who show no signs of being in a trance, actually in a trance? This question, which derives from the traditional paradigm, cannot be answered by any empirical method available at the present time.

2. Also, from the special state paradigm, one might hypothesize that (a) subjects who are highly responsive to test suggestions after they have received a trance induction procedure are in a hypnotic trance state whereas (b) those who are highly responsive after receiving task-motivational instructions are not in a hypnotic trance but are responsive for other reasons, for example, because they are highly motivated to respond. This interpretation also leads to an anomaly for the special state paradigm because it is now being said that the kind of high response to test suggestions that has been traditionally associated with hypnotic trance can also be produced as easily without hypnotic trance.

3. From the alternative paradigm, which does not postulate a special state, one could hypothesize that both task-motivational instructions and a trance induction procedure raise response to test suggestions above the level found under a control condition because they produce more positive attitudes, motivations, and expectancies toward the suggestive situation and a greater willingness to think with and to imagine those things that are suggested. This hypothesis can be empirically confirmed or disconfirmed by (a) assessing attitudes, motivations, expectancies, and willingness to think with the suggestions prior to and also after the administration of a control, a task-motivational, and a trance induction treatment to three random groups of subjects and (b) testing responsiveness to suggestions after the second assessment (of attitudes, motivations, etc.).

### A PERSONAL REPORT ON RESPONDING TO TEST SUGGESTIONS

As stated above, some individuals manifest a high level of response to test suggestions when no attempt is made to hypnotize them. I also manifest a high level of response. Let me now give a personal, phenomenological report of the factors underlying my own responsiveness to test suggestions (Barber, 1970b).

An experimenter states that he would like to assess my responsiveness to suggestions and I agree to be tested. Since I believe that it is an interesting and worthwhile learning experience to respond to the kinds of test suggestions that I expect he will give me, I have a positive attitude toward the test situation and am motivated to experience those things that will be suggested. Furthermore, I expect that suggested effects, such as arm levitation, age regression, and amnesia can be experienced. Since I have positive attitudes, motivations, and expectancies, I will not evaluate, analyze, or think contrary to those things that are suggested; for example, I will not say to myself, "This suggestion is not worded correctly," "The suggestion will not be effective," or "This is just an experiment." On the contrary, I will let myself think with, imagine, and visualize those things that the experimenter will describe.

The experimenter asks me to extend my right arm and then suggests repeatedly that it is solid, rigid, like a piece of steel. If I had a reason not to respond to the suggestion, I could prevent myself from thinking of the arm as rigid. However, since there is no reason to resist, on the contrary, since I am motivated to experience the suggested effects, I let myself think with the suggestion—I verbalize to myself that the arm is rigid and I imagine it as a piece of steel. When the experimenter then states, "Try to bend the arm, you can't," I do not say to myself, "Of course I can bend it." Instead, I continue to think of the arm as rigid, I continue to picture it as a piece of steel, and when I make an attempt to bend it, I find that I cannot.

(Thinking back to the suggestion, after the experiment is over, I realize the following: (a) when I was imagining my arm as rigid, I involuntarily contracted the muscles in the arm, (b) the involuntary muscular contractions made the arm feel rigid, (c) the actual rigidity in the arm reinforced the thought that the arm was rigid and immovable, and (d) when told to try to bend the arm, I continued to think and imagine that the arm was a piece of steel and I continued to maintain the involuntary muscular contraction. Although these considerations are clear to me retrospectively, during the experiment I was picturing the arm as a piece of steel and I was not actively thinking about these underlying mechanisms.)

The experimenter next suggests repeatedly that my left hand is dull, numb, a piece of rubber, a lump of matter without feelings or sensations. I think with the suggestions and I picture the hand as a rubbery lump of matter that is separated from the rest of my body. The experimenter then places the hand in a pain-producing apparatus that brings a heavy weight to bear upon a finger. Although this heavy weight normally produces an aching pain in the finger, I do not think of the stimulation as pain. Instead I continue to think of the hand and finger as a rubbery lump of matter "out there" and I think of the sensations produced by the heavy weight *as sensations* that have their own unique and interesting properties. Specifically, I think of the sensations as a series of separate sensations—as a sensation of pressure, a cutting sensation, a numbness, a feeling of heat, a pulsating sensation. Although under other circumstances I would label these sensations as pain, I do not let myself think of the sensations in this way; instead, I think of them as a complex of varying sensations in a dull, rubbery hand and I state honestly that although I experience a variety of unique sensations I do not experience anxiety, distress, or pain.

The experimenter then suggests that I see a cat in the corner of the room. Since I have a positive attitude toward the suggestive situation and am motivated to experience the suggested effects, I inhibit the thought that there is no cat in the room. Instead, I let myself vividly visualize a black cat that I have often seen before and I think of it as being in the corner of the room. Since I continue to think of the cat as being "out there," and since I inhibit the thought that I am visualizing it in my mind's eye, I state that I see the cat in the corner of the room.

The experimenter next instructs me to close my eyes (presumably to remove visual distractions that might interfere with the forthcoming tasks), and then suggests that I am in Boston Symphony Hall and I hear the orchestra playing. I let myself vividly imagine that I am at the symphony and that the orchestra is playing Beethoven's Fifth Symphony. I inhibit the thought that I am really in an experimental situation, I focus on the idea that I am in Symphony Hall, and I "hear" the music, which becomes continually more vivid.

(Afterwards, thinking back to the suggestion for auditory hallucination, I realize that I was "making the music in my head." However, at the time I received the suggestion I was vividly imagining and thinking about Beethoven's symphony and I was not thinking about such matters as where the music was coming from. Although I could have stopped thinking with the suggestion, for instance, I could have said to myself that I was actually in an experimental situation, I had no reason to verbalize such contrary thoughts to myself and I continued to imagine vividly and to think of myself as being in Symphony Hall.)

The experimenter next suggests that time is going back, my body is becoming small, and I am a child of six years of age. I do not say to myself that I am an adult, that I cannot become a child, or that this suggestion won't work. On the contrary, since I have positive attitudes, motivations, and expectancies toward the suggestive situation, I think with the suggestion. I let myself imagine vividly that my body is small and tiny (and I begin to feel that I am actually tiny), I think of myself as a child, and I vividly imagine myself in the first grade classroom. I then let the imaginative situation "move" by itself; the first-grade teacher talks to the students, two boys in the back of the room throw spitballs when the teacher turns her back to the class, and later the bell rings for recess. Since I focused on the idea that I was a child, since I felt myself as small and tiny, since I could "see" the events occurring in the classroom, since I did not say to myself "I am really an adult," I testify afterwards that I actually felt that I was six years old and that I found this part of the experiment vivid and very interesting.

Later, the experimenter suggests that when the session is over I will not remember anything that occurred. Soon afterwards he states that the experiment is over and asks me what I remember. Since I have no reason to resist the suggestion for amnesia, I say to myself that I do not remember what occurred, I keep my thoughts on the present, I do not think back to the preceding events, and I state that I do not remember. The experimenter subsequently states, "Now you can remember." I now let myself think back to the preceding events and I verbalize them.

In summary, speaking personally and phenomenologically, I can experience arm rigidity, hand levitation, analgesia, visual and auditory hallucination, age regression, amnesia, and other suggested effects that have been traditionally thought to be associated with hypnotism. I do not need a "trance induction procedure" in order to experience these effects. Since I am ready at any time to adopt a positive attitude, motivation, and expectancy toward the suggestive situation, I am ready at any time to think with and to imagine or visualize those things that are suggested. On the other hand, if I had a reason not to respond to the test suggestions, I could adopt a quite different set of attitudes, motivations, and expectancies toward the situation, I could tell myself that I shall not respond, and I could easily prevent myself from thinking with and vividly imagining those things that are suggested.

Three additional points should be emphasized:

1. If the experimenter first suggests to me, as has happened on several occasions, that I am becoming relaxed, drowsy, sleepy, and am entering a hypnotic trance state, I can think with these suggestions and can feel relaxed, dowsy, sleepy, and passive. However, when the experimenter subsequently gives suggestions that involve effort, for example, suggestions of arm rigidity or analgesia, I no longer feel relaxed, sleepy, or passive and I may, in fact, feel very alert and aroused. The traditional "trance induction procedure" comprised of repetitive suggestions of relaxation, drowsiness, sleep, and hypnosis, appears to me to be just another set of suggestions that I can accept and it is not necessary or especially important in determining my responsiveness to test suggestions.

2. When I am experiencing suggested analgesia, age regression, amnesia, and so on, I do not feel that I am in a special state—a hypnotic state or a trance—that is discontinuous with or qualitatively different from my ordinary state of consciousness. In fact, when I am responding to test suggestions I do not feel that my "state" differs in any important way from the state I am in when I watch a motion picture or stage play. When I am in an audience, I let myself imagine and think with the communications from the stage and I empathize, laugh, feel sad, cry, and have the other emotions, feelings, and vicarious experiences that the actors are attempting to communicate. In essentially the same way, when I am in an experimental situation and am being assessed for response to test suggestions, I let myself think with and vividly imagine those things that are suggested and I have the experiences that the experimenter is attempting to communicate.

3. If I wish, I can give myself the same suggestions that are given by the experimenter. For instance, I can suggest to myself that time is going backwards, my body is becoming small and tiny, and I am a child of a certain age. I can then think about and vividly imagine a situation that occurred

when I was a child and I can inhibit contrary thoughts. Similarly, in a dental situation I can give myself suggestions that the sensations are interesting and not uncomfortable and by thinking of each of the varying sensations (drilling, pressure, pricking, heat, and so forth) as sensations per se, I can inhibit anxiety, distress, and pain. I have also found that the same technique—focusing on the sensations as sensations—is sufficient to block the pain and distress associated with various methods used in the laboratory to produce pain, for example, pain produced by immersing a limb in ice water and pain produced by using a tourniquet to cut off the blood supply to an arm. Although these experiences have been traditionally subsumed under the term "autohypnosis," I do not feel that I am in a special state (a hypnotic trance state) fundamentally different from my ordinary state of consciousness; on the contrary, when I am having these experiences I feel as normal and as awake as when I am watching a movie, a stage play, or a television show.

### *Data Ostensibly Supporting the Traditional (Special State) Paradigm*

At first glance, the traditional notion that a special state underlies high responsiveness to test suggestions appears to be supported by data such as the following:

1. Stage hypnotists appear to elicit unique or special behaviors from subjects who seem to be in a special state (hypnotic trance).
2. Experimenters have reported that a variety of amazing or special effects can be elicited from subjects who are ostensibly in a hypnotic trance.
3. High response to test suggestions is associated with observable trance-like characteristics.
4. Some highly responsive subjects testify that they experienced a special state of consciousness.
5. Some highly responsive subjects do not "come out of it" immediately—they seem to remain in a trance after the experiment is over.
6. Some highly responsive subjects spontaneously forget the events and spontaneous amnesia is a critical indicant of a special state.
7. Highly responsive subjects show a special type of logic—"trance logic"—which indicates that they are in a special state.

Let us look at each of these sets of data in turn.

#### STAGE HYPNOSIS

The traditional special state (hypnotic trance) paradigm seems to be supported by the very unusual or special behaviors elicited by stage hypnotists. At first glance, it appears that after the stage hypnotist has placed his subject in a hypnotic trance state, he can make him perform weird antics (such as dancing with an invisible partner or singing like Frank Sinatra) and can exert an amazing physiological control over the subject (such as stopping the circulation and pulse in the arm). A close look at stage hypnosis, however, does not support the special state paradigm. Let us look at the procedures and techniques used in stage hypnosis that my associate, William Meeker, and I learned when we received training in this area (Meeker & Barber, 1971).[5]

Although no two stage hypnotists use exactly the same methods, there are four major principles and four secondary principles that underlie stage hypnosis. Let us first look at the four major principles and then at the secondary ones.

*Major Principle 1. Responsiveness to test suggestions under "waking" conditions is much higher than is commonly assumed.* Stage hypnotists know that a substantial proportion of normal individuals are highly responsive to test suggestions when no attempt is made to hypnotize them. For example, the *Encyclopedia of Stage Hypnotism* states emphatically that "it is possible to produce very striking hypnotic effects in the waking state, entirely independent of the trance" (McGill, 1947, p. 28) and describes in detail how to use "waking" suggestions to produce an inability to separate the hands, an inability to close the mouth, a forgetting of one's name, getting drunk on a glass of water, and hallucination of a mouse. Arons (1961) has clearly described the use of "waking" suggestions in stage demonstrations and has emphasized that "this phase of the demonstration illustrates forcibly that the hypnotic 'trance' is not needed to perform a hypnotic demonstration" (p. 10). Most other writers on stage hypnosis also note that "hypnotic trance" is not necessary to elicit a high level of suggestibility from a substantial proportion of volunteer subjects (Lonk, 1947, p. 34, and Tracy, 1952, p. 152, for example).

*Major Principle 2. Subjects who are highly responsive to test suggestions can be easily selected.* Early in their training, stage hypnotists learn how to select subjects who are highly responsive to test suggestions. The technique used to select subjects is very simple: members of the audience or volunteers are given one or two test suggestions and only those subjects are used who are very responsive. For instance, the stage hypnotist may ask the entire audience or the volunteers to clasp their hands together tightly and then suggests repeatedly that the hands are stuck and cannot be taken apart, or the potential subjects are asked to close their eyes and then are given suggestions of inability to open the eyes. Only those subjects who pass these (or similar) test suggestions are used.

*Major Principle 3. When the situation is defined to subjects as "hypnosis," it is clear that a high level of responsiveness to requests, suggestions,*

5. I am indebted to William Meeker for permission to summarize our collaborative work in stage hypnosis.

*and commands is desired and expected.* The stage hypnotist invariably defines the situation as "hypnosis." Recent experiments (Barber & Calverley, 1964e, 1965) have demonstrated that simply telling subjects that the situation is "hypnosis" is sufficient by itself to raise response to test suggestions above the already rather high base level. Post experimental interviews with subjects participating in these recent experiments indicated that the reason why subjects are more responsive to test suggestions when they are told that they are participating in a "hypnosis" experiment rather than in some other kind of experiment are as follows: When subjects are told that they are in a "hypnosis" situation, they typically interpret this to mean that (a) they are in an unusual or special situation in which high response to suggestions, requests, and commands is both desired and expected and (b), if they actively resist or try not to carry out those things suggested, they will be considered as uncooperative or "poor" subjects, the hypnotist will be disappointed, and the purpose of the experiment will be nullified. Contrariwise, when subjects are told that the situation involves something other than "hypnosis," they are being told by implication that they are not necessarily expected to show a high level of response to test suggestions of the type traditionally associated with the word "hypnosis."

Since the introduction of this one word into an experimental situation heightens subjects' responsiveness to test suggestions, we can expect a high level of response in the stage situation that is emphatically defined as "hypnosis" and that includes a prestigious performer who has been widely advertised as a highly effective hypnotist.

*Major Principle 4. The stage hypnotist capitalizes on the unique characteristics of the stage setting.* The stage setting has several unusual features. First of all, it has unique expectancy characteristics. As the *Encyclopedia of Stage Hypnotism* points out, "the lights, the music, the curtains, the tenseness of being on the stage, and above all the expectancy centered on each subject by the audience—expectancy that he will be hypnotized, are factors working . . . powerfully in the performer's favor" (McGill, 1947, p. 248).

Secondly, the stage setting has unique "fun" characteristics. In addition, the stage setting has unique features that lead subjects to "help out the show." These aspects of the stage setting are discussed by Nelson (1965):

> To revolt or to rebel is to . . . stand out among the others as a "hold out". . . . The subject subconsciously gets the idea and *gets into the act.* It's fun—the ham in them exhibits itself and they are *actors* (acting the part of a hypnotized subject). They realize they have a perfect shield to hide behind if they engage in any odd or silly tactics (they are *hypnotized* which is the excuse), and begin competing among each other for the best performance—like a real *actor*. There are always one or two of the subjects out of a group that will out-do the others and give an outstanding performance. They sense the audience re-actions and applause, and love it and are impelled on in

their efforts like a hungry actor. Many times they will react in a slightly exaggerated manner, which the hypnotist must anticipate and capitalize on. Once the ball has started to roll, they all fall into the fun idea and play the role of an actor, the hypnotist merely being the *director* in the ensuing entertainment." (P. 30)

The *Encyclopedia of Stage Hypnotism* also emphasizes the "helping out the show" aspects of the stage situation: "Considerable numbers of subjects, especially in the extravert enterprise of performing on the stage, tend to simulate. . . . This simulation is not necessarily voluntary deception, for it is frequently born of an extreme desire to cooperate with the performer and help out the show" (McGill, 1947, p. 257).

In summary, to produce "amazing" performances, stage hypnotists rely *primarily* on the high level of "waking" suggestibility that is present in a substantial proportion of subjects, careful selection of the most responsive subjects, the further enhancement of suggestibility that is produced when the situation is labeled as "hypnosis," and the unique characteristics of the stage setting. These four factors are sufficient by themselves to produce most of the performances observed during stage hypnosis. However, well-trained stage hypnotists also have four additional techniques in their repertoire which they at times utilize. These techniques can be subsumed under four supplementary principles which will now be described.

*Supplementary Principle 1. Stage hypnotists at times whisper private instructions to their subjects.* The *Encyclopedia of Stage Hypnotism* instructs the stage hypnotist to make "gentle pass-like gestures in the air" while whispering to the subject, "We are going to have some good laughs on the audience and fool them . . . so when I tell you to do some funny things, do exactly as I secretly tell you. O. K? Swell!" (McGill, 1947, p. 236) The *Encyclopedia* also points out that any volunteer who is handled in this way will henceforth carry out the stage hypnotist's instructions and that, even when volunteers are first told to "help fool the audience," there soon arises a point where it is practically impossible to determine which responses on the part of the subject are deliberate and which are involuntary (McGill, 1947, pp. 237, 247).

The direct request to "help fool the audience" was more widely used by stage hypnotists in former years than it is at present. In modern performances, stage hypnotists tend to use a less blatant "whispering technique" to elicit the subject's cooperation. For instance, if the stage hypnotist wants a subject to dance with an invisible partner or to sing like Frank Sinatra, he may whisper privately to his most extroverted subject, "Give the audience a good act of dancing with an invisible partner (or singing like Frank Sinatra)." Also, the stage hypnotist may whisper to a subject, "Please close your eyes and let your body go limp." When he then makes passes over his subject, as the subject is complying with his request, the audience typically assumes that the stage hypnotist has very quickly and amazingly placed his subject in a hypnotic trance state. Along similar lines, the *Encyclopedia* points out that, when the subject is receiving suggestions of body sway, the hypnotist should whisper, "Let yourself go and don't resist. Let yourself come right back towards me." The *Encyclopedia* adds that "*These little intimate asides to the subject are most important.* The audience only hears the major portions of your comments that describe and explain the experiment, but the subject receives full benefit of your confidences that tend to make him feel very much obligated to properly perform his portion of the experiment" (McGill, 1947, p. 150).

*Supplementary Principle 2. Stage hypnotists at times use the "failure to challenge" technique which misleads the audience to believe that subjects who may be unresponsive to test suggestions are actually responsive.* When using the "failure to challenge" technique, the stage hypnotist (a) administers a suggestion to the subject, (b) does not determine whether the subject has accepted the suggestion, but (c) leads the audience to believe that the subject has accepted it. Schneck (1958) has carefully documented the use of this technique and has given examples such as the following: A famous stage hypnotist suggested to a subject that her right arm was insensitive. He then asked the subject to touch the right arm with her left hand in order to note the lack of sensation. Although the stage hypnotist did not ask the subject if the arm actually felt insensitive, "many in the audience accepted the implication that having gone through the motions, this girl actually did experience anesthesia" (p. 175). Similarly, the stage hypnotist suggests to a subject that his outstretched arm is rigid and immovable, but he does not challenge the subject to try to bend his arm. However, the stage hypnotist tells the audience that the subject cannot move his arm and the audience apparently accepts the hypnotist's statement. Also, stage hypnotists at times administer a trance induction procedure to some of their subjects and then assure their audience that the subjects are in a hypnotic trance, but they do not question the subjects about their experiences or assess their responsiveness to test suggestions.

*Supplementary Principle 3. Stage hypnotists at times use pretrained subjects to insure the success of their show.* Manuals of stage hypnosis assert that during the days of vaudeville, pretrained subjects were commonly used in stage performances and that the audience was not told that the subjects were trained ('Calostro,' 1949; Gibson, 1956; Lonk, 1947; Lustig, 1956; Nelson, 1965). This practice has markedly declined in recent years. Nowadays, some stage hypnotists use pretrained subjects to demonstrate some of the more difficult stunts, for instance, the one in which two or three men are supported on the subject's rigidly outstretched body, but the stage performer usually informs the audience that in order to demonstrate this difficult feat, he will use a trained subject.

*Supplementary Principle 4. Stage hypnotists at times use tricks to elicit "amazing" performances.* Manuals of stage hypnosis describe a series of "amazing" performances that can be easily elicited. These performances, which can be labeled "tricks," include, among many others, the human-plank feat, the anesthesia demonstration, stopping the blood flow, and production of "hypnotic trance" by pressure on the carotid baroreceptors. Let us look briefly at each of these tricks in turn.

As stated previously in this chapter, practically all normal individuals can easily remain suspended for several minutes between two chairs (one chair beneath the head and the other beneath the ankles). Also, practically any normal male subject can keep his body rigidly suspended between two chairs (one chair beneath his shoulders and the other beneath his calves) while, at the same time, he is supporting the weight of a man on his chest. However, since laymen are unacquainted with these facts, they assume that the subject who is performing these human-plank feats must be in a hypnotic trance state.

An anesthesia demonstration that is performed at times by stage hypnotists can also be labeled a trick. When the stunt is to be demonstrated, the subject is asked to extend one arm horizontally with the palm facing downward. The stage hypnotist then makes passes over the subject's hand, suggests that it is numb and insensitive, and then moves the flame of a cigarette lighter slowly under the outstretched palm. The subject typically shows no reaction to the flame and the audience assumes that hypnotic anesthesia has been demonstrated. However, when performing this stunt, stage hypnotists keep the flame about one inch from the subject's palm and do not hold it at one spot but, instead, move it slowly (Lonk, 1947, p. 35; Tracy, 1952, p. 133). If the reader tries it, he will find that he will not be bothered at all by the heat of the flame, provided that the flame is at a distance of about an inch from his palm and is moved slowly.

Stage hypnotists also at times place a lighted match directly upon the subject's palm and then move it slowly. If the reader tries it on himself, he will find that the fire from a match is not especially uncomfortable and no burning results, provided that the match is moved along the palm. The only possibility of burning occurs if the lighted match is brought toward the palm to slowly or is held at one spot.

Stage hypnotists, at times, also demonstrate the "stopping the blood flow" stunt, conducted as follows: the stage performer suggests that the blood is leaving the subject's arm and makes mysterious passes over it. The subject's arm appears white and lifeless. Next, the performer suggests that the blood is returning to the arm, and its natural coloring returns. During this test, a member of the audience (preferably a physician) is asked to test the subject's pulse, which often proves imperceptible (Lonk, 1947; Lustig, 1956; McGill, 1947). Although there are several methods for performing this trick, the one most commonly used is that, prior to the performance, a golf ball is placed in the armpit of a stooge and fastened there by an elastic. When the hypnotist suggests that the blood is leaving the arm, the stooge presses his arm against the golf ball, and the circulation and pulse are temporarily obliterated (Lonk, 1947, p. 58; Lustig, 1956, p. 15).

The carotid trick is also described in detail by most of the manuals of stage hypnosis (Nelson, 1965; McGill, 1947; Lonk, 1947, for example). When using this trick, the stage performer exerts pressure on the baroreceptors at the carotid sinus. This produces a vagus-induced bradycardia and vasodilation, which leads to sudden hypotension and fainting (Ganong, 1967, pp. 508–9). The manuals state that, when using this technique, the stage performer should make passes over the subject with his free hand in order to lead the audience to believe that he is placing the subject in a hypnotic trance state. However, the manuals also warn the stage hypnotist that continued pressure on the carotid is dangerous, the pressure should not be continued for much more than 15 seconds, and the technique should be used only on rare occasions, for example, when a smart-aleck subject dares the performer to hypnotize him.

In summary, the traditional (special state) viewpoint would conceptualize stage hypnosis along the following lines: the stage hypnotist places his subjects in a state (a hypnotic trance) fundamentally different from ordinary states of consciousness, and subjects on the stage behave in unusual ways because they are in the special state. These notions are misleading. The alternative viewpoint, which does not posit a special state, postulates that stage hypnotists induce their subjects to behave in apparently unusual ways primarily because of the following:

1. A substantial proportion of individuals show a rather high base-level response to test suggestions.

2. Only selected subjects, who show a high level of response to test suggestions, are used in the stage demonstration.

3. Since the situation is emphatically defined as "hypnosis," it is clear to all of the selected subjects that obedience to requests, commands, and suggestions is desired and expected.

4. Unique characteristics of the stage situation—the expectancy centered on each subject by the audience, together with the "fun" and "helping the show" atomosphere—are helpful in eliciting obedience.

Although these four features of the stage situation are sufficient to elicit most of the ostensibly amazing behaviors, stage hypnotists also at times use the following to enhance the dramatic nature of their show: the technique of private whispers, the failure to challenge technique, pretrained subjects to demonstrate the more difficult stunts, and one or more tricks that lead the audience to believe that extraordinary effects are being produced.

Although the stage performer is viewed, from the traditional (special state) paradigm, as a highly effective hypnotist who places his subjects in a hypnotic trance state, a more valid conception is that the stage performer is an actor playing the part of a hypnotist. As manuals of stage hypnosis point out: "The successful hypnotic entertainer is actually not interested whether or not the subjects are really hypnotized—his basic function is to *entertain.* He is interested in his ability to *con* his subjects into a pseudo performance that appears as hypnotism—to get laughs and to entertain his audience. . . . [The subjects] enjoy their part and react as they are *told* to do. Hypnotism, as done for entertainment, is as simple as all this" (Nelson, 1965, pp. 29–31).

### "AMAZING" EFFECTS ELICITED IN EXPERIMENTAL SITUATIONS

The traditional (special state) viewpoint seems to be supported by experimental reports that amazing or special effects were produced when suggestions were given to highly responsive subjects. These effects include the production of blisters, the cure of warts, the production of analgesia sufficient for surgery, and the production of actual age regression, hallucinations, and deafness. Let us look at the data pertaining to each of these effects.

#### *Production of blisters*

It has been claimed that blisters appear in some subjects who have been exposed to a trance induction procedure, who are highly responsive to test suggestions, and who have been given suggestions that a blister will form at a specified place on the skin. This widely-publicized claim seems to lead to the conclusion that the subjects must be in a unique or special state when they manifest such a unique effect. However, a close look at the data indicates that the so-called "blister" phenomenon is far more complex than it first appears, and that there is no need to postulate a special state (hypnotic trance) in order to explain it:

1. During the past 100 years, many researchers suggested to their hypnotic trance subjects that a blister would form on the skin. With very few exceptions, no skin changes whatsoever were observed (Barber, 1969b, Ch. 9).

2. About 12 researchers reported that suggestions for blister formation gave rise to cutaneous alterations; some of these alterations were labeled "blisters." These reports should be viewed within a broader context by noting the following points, which have been delineated in a series or reviews (Barber, 1961b; Gorton, 1949; Pattie, 1941; Paul, 1963; Sarbin, 1956; Weitzenhoffer, 1953).

3. With very few exceptions, the positive findings were obtained between

1886 and 1927, prior to the advent of rigorous experimental controls in this area.

4. With very few exceptions, careful controls were not used to exclude the possibility that the subject may have deliberately injured his skin in attempting to comply with the suggestion for blister formation. Furthermore, one subject attempted to injure his skin by pricking it with a needle (Schrenck-Notzing, 1896), another vigorously rubbed snow on the area where the blister was supposed to form (Ullman, 1947), and another rubbed poison ivy leaves where the skin change was supposed to appear (Wolberg, 1948, p. 49).

5. With very few if any exceptions, the positive results were obtained with patients who were either suffering from various skin ailments (neurodermatitis, hysterical ecchymoses, wheals, or neurotic skin gangrene) or who were diagnosed as hysterics (hysterical blindness, hysterical aphonia, hystero epilepsy, or hysterical hemianesthesia).

6. With one or two exceptions, it is not clear from the studies reporting positive results whether the skin alterations were blisters, wheals, or dermographism. A study that carefully considered each of these possibilities (Borelli, 1953) showed conclusively that the skin change that was produced by suggestion was dermographism, not a blister. It should be emphasized that dermographism (wheal formation in response to a single moderately strong stroking of the skin) is more common than is usually supposed. For instance, in testing 84 young men, T. Lewis (1927) found a clear-cut swelling of the skin as a reaction to a single firm stroke in 25 per cent and in 5 per cent a full wheal developed. Furthermore, as Graham and Wolf (1950) have documented, some normal individuals show wheal formation at sites of mild pressure stimulation, such as around a collar, a belt, or a wristwatch strap. These data are important in understanding the positive results obtained in the studies mentioned above because in all but one of the successful studies tactual stimulation was used to localize the place where the blister was to form, and in many of these studies the stimulus object was a small piece of metal.

7. All of the studies in this area lack a control group; suggestions for blister formation were never given to subjects who were not exposed to a trance induction procedure. It was always assumed, without apparent justification, that a hypnotic trance state is necessary in order to produce blisters by suggestions.

Further studies are needed to determine whether suggestions for blister formation are effective in producing blisters in any present-day subjects under "hypnotic trance" conditions and also under "waking control" conditions. I will venture three hypnotheses: under both the hypnotic trance and the waking control conditions, fewer than 1 per cent of the subjects will show any skin alterations, the alterations will resemble dermographism or wheals rather than blisters, and the few subjects who show a cutaneous effect when given suggestions for blister formation will normally manifest marked dermographism when appropriately stimulated on the skin.

*Removal of warts*

Sinclair-Gieben and Chalmers (1959) and Ullman and Dudek (1960) reported that suggestions given to hypnotic trance subjects were effective in some instances in removing warts. However, although suggestions for wart removal appear to be effective at times when they are given under "hypnotic trance" conditions, they also appear to be effective at times when they are given under "waking control" conditions. A series of investigators (Bloch, 1927; Dudek, 1967; Sulzberger & Wolf, 1934; Vollmer, 1946) found that warts at times disappear when they are simply painted with an innocuous dye and the "awake" subjects are told that the placebo-dye is a powerful wart-curing drug. Furthermore, in those instances in which suggestions for wart disappearance were effective, there is evidence that the warts may have been of the labile type, that is, of the type that would have disappeared spontaneously within a rather short period of time if no suggestions had been given (Clarke, 1965; Memmesheimer & Eisenlohr, 1931; Stankler, 1967).

*Analgesia*

From time to time accounts are published of hypnotic trance subjects who underwent minor or major surgery without analgesic or anesthetic drugs. These accounts imply that a unique or special state, a hypnotic trance state, is necessary in order to undergo surgery without drugs. However, the available data do not support this implication:

1. Most "hypnotic trance" subjects who undergo minor or major surgery without drugs show signs of pain. Some subjects cry, others show a "hideous expression of suppressed agony" (Barber, 1970a, p. 228) and, in many instances, chemical analgesics or anesthetics have to be administered in order to complete the surgery (Anderson, 1957; Barber, 1970a, Ch. 5; Braid, 1847; Butler, 1954).

2. A few "hypnotic trance" subjects manifested very little or no pain when they underwent minor or major surgery without drugs. However, a few subjects who were not exposed to a trance induction procedure also manifested little or no pain when they underwent minor or major surgery without drugs (Chertok, 1959, pp. 3–4; Elliotson, 1843, pp. 15–17; Esdaile, 1850, pp. 214–15; Haim, 1908; Leriche, 1939, pp. 55–56; Lewis, 1942, p. 10; Mackenzie, 1909; Mitchell, 1907; Propping, 1909; Sampimon & Woodruff, 1946; Trent, 1946).

3. The pain involved in most surgical procedures is highly overestimated. Although the skin is sensitive, most of the muscles and organs of the body

are relatively insensitive to pain. More precisely, the skin is sensitive to a knife cut, but the skilled surgeon cuts through the skin smoothly and quickly and the underlying muscles and internal organs are relatively insensitive. Lewis (1942) has documented the fact that the muscles, the internal organs, and most other parts of the body (with the exception of the skin) are insensitive to incision (although they may be sensitive to other stimuli such as pulling or stretching). For instance, Lewis (1942) has noted the following:

> [The subcutaneous tissue] gives rise to little pain when injured by . . . incision. . . . [The pain in somatic muscles] is slight when elicited by . . . knife cut. . . . Compact bone may be bored without pain. . . . The articular surfaces [of joints] . . . are insensitive. . . . Puncture of a vein is nearly always painless. . . . The dura mater. . . . pia mater and the cortex are generally regarded as insensitive. . . . the lung and visceral pleura are insensitive . . . the surface of the heart is found to be insensitive . . . [surgeons] have often and painlessly removed pieces of the oesophageal wall of the conscious subject for histological examination. . . . It is common knowledge that the solid organs such as liver, spleen, and kidney, can be tightly gripped, cut, or even burnt without the subject's being conscious of it. . . . All parts of the wall of [the stomach] may be cut, burnt, stretched, or clamped without pain. . . cutting [the jejunum and ileum] . . . is accomplished painlessly . . . . The insensitiveness of [the colon] attracted early attention . . . cutting [the great omentum] is accomplished painlessly. . . . The body of the uterus can be cut . . . painlessly. (Pp. 2–8)

In brief, there are rare cases of individuals who were said to be in a "hypnotic trance state" and also individuals who were said to be "awake" who underwent minor or major surgery without drugs and without manifesting much pain. These cases seem much more dramatic than they actually are because it is assumed that all parts of the body are as sensitive to pain as the skin. The truth of the matter is that, although the skin is sensitive, most tissues and organs in the body are insensitive to the surgeon's scalpel. Furthermore, there is no reason to postulate a special state of consciousness in order to explain the ability to undergo noxious stimulation of the skin without manifesting distress or pain. The following points are relevant:

1. Pain is at times markedly reduced in awake subjects when placebos are administered with the implication (or the explicit statement) that they are pain-relieving drugs (Barber, 1959b; Beecher, 1959).

2. Instructions or suggestions intended to produce relaxation are at times effective with "hypnotic trancc" subjects and also with "awake" subjects in reducing subjective and physiological responses to noxious stimuli (Barber & Calverley, 1969a; Jacobson, 1938, 1954; Hilgard et al., 1967).

3. Responsiveness to painful stimulation is reduced in some "hypnotic trance" subjects and also in some "awake" subjects by instructions or suggestions intended to alleviate anxiety and anticipation or fear of pain (Hill et al., 1952a, 1952b; Kornetsky, 1954; Shor, 1967).

4. Suggestions of anesthesia or analgesia are effective in reducing subjectively reported pain in a substantial proportion of subjects who have been randomly assigned to a trance induction treatment and in an equal proportion of subjects who have been randomly assigned to a control treatment (Barber & Calverley, 1969a; Spanos, Barber, & Lang, 1969).

5. Subjectively reported pain is reduced in awake subjects when they are distracted during exposure to noxious stimulation (Kanfer & Goldfoot, 1966). Furthermore, both subjectively reported pain and physiological responses to noxious stimulation can be reduced by instructing control subjects to try to think about and to imagine vividly a pleasant situation during the stimulation (Barber & Hahn, 1962). Also, pain is reduced to an equal degree in "waking control" subjects and in "hypnotic trance" subjects when both groups of subjects are distracted during the pain-producing stimulation by having them listen to and try to remember the details of an interesting story presented on a tape recording (Barber & Calverley, 1969a). These results are consistent with the conclusion reached many years ago by Liébeault (1885) that, if and when suggestions are effective in reducing pain in "hypnotic trance" subjects, the mediating processes can be conceptualized as focusing of attention on thoughts or ideas other than those concerning pain. These results are also consistent with the conclusion drawn by August (1961) from a large-scale investigation with 1,000 patients, that trance induction procedures and suggestions are effective in reducing pain during childbirth to the extent that they direct "attention away from pain responses toward pleasant ideas"(p. 62).

*Age regression*

Several studies pertaining to hypnotic age regression also seem to support the contention that subjects who are highly responsive to test suggestions are in a "special state." These studies, by Gidro-Frank and Bowersbuch (1948), Parrish, Lundy, and Leibowitz (1969), and True (1949), appeared to indicate that, when given suggestions to regress to infancy or childhood, "hypnotic trance" subjects show an amazing reinstatement of a physiological reflex which is characteristic of infancy, an amazing recall of events that occurred during childhood, and an amazing childlike performance on objective tests. A close look at these studies, however, fails to support the special state paradigm. Let us look at each of them in turn.

Gidro-Frank and Bowersbuch (1948) reported that when three selected "hypnotic trance" subjects were given suggestions to regress to four months of age, they showed a Babinski toe response, that is, stimulation of the sole of the foot produced dorsiflexion of the large toe and fanning of the other toes. Several neurology texts stated that the Babinski toe response is present in infants up to four months of age but is not present after six months of age. Consequently, it appeared that Gidro-Frank and Bowersbuch had demonstrated that suggestions to regress to early infancy, when given to "hypnotic trance" subjects, reinstate a long-dormant physiological reflex that is characteristic of early infancy. However, the neurology texts were mistaken. Researchers who have actually looked at infants have consistently observed that the typical response of the four-month-old infant to stimulation of the sole of the foot is *not* the Babinski response, but rather sudden withdrawal of the limb with variability in response of the toes. In fact, the Babinski toe response is very rarely if ever observed in early infancy (Burr, 1921; McGraw, 1941; Wolff, 1930). Since the Babinski response is rarely if ever observed in infants, the question at issue is not how suggestions given under "hypnotic trance" revive an infantile reflex, but why these "hypnotic trance" subjects showed a Babinski toe response (not characteristic of early infancy) when they were given suggestions to regress to early infancy. There are at least two explanations of these weird results: the subjects may have realized what response the experimenters were looking for and may have voluntarily performed that response (Barber, 1962a; Sarbin, 1956); or, since the Babinski toe response is at times observed during profound relaxation, the subjects may have become very relaxed when they assumed the "sleeping posture of the infant" (Barber, 1970a, Ch. 6).

True (1949) reported that most adult subjects who were placed in hypnotic trance, and who were given suggestions to regress to ages 11, 7, and 4, recalled the exact day of the week on which their birthday and Christmas fell in the particular year involved. Six subsequent studies failed to confirm these results (Barber, 1961a; Best & Michaels, 1954; S. Fisher, 1962; Leonard, 1963; Mesel & Ledford, 1959; Reiff & Scheerer, 1959). However, in a series of attempts I made to validate True's results, one "hypnotic trance" subject, who received suggestions to regress to *each* of her previous birthdays, correctly named the day of the week on which *each* of her previous birthdays fell. After the hypnotic trance session, the subject testified that she was able to perform this remarkable feat simply because she knew that the days of the week go backward one day each year and two on leap years and, knowing the day of the week on which her birthday fell in a recent year, she could easily and quickly (within 20 seconds) figure out the day of the week it must have fallen in an earlier year (compare Sutcliffe, 1960; Yates, 1960). In brief, although True's study seemed to support the contention that the "hypnotic trance state" gives rise to nearly miraculous feats of memory, subsequent studies strongly suggest that "hypnotic trance" is irrelevant in performing this feat and that the relevant factor is prior knowledge of the fact that the days of the week go backward one day each year and two on leap years.

Parrish, Lundy, and Leibowitz (1969) reported that highly suggestible subjects, who were exposed to a trance induction procedure and given suggestions to regress to ages nine and five, were affected by two optical illusions (the Ponzo and Poggendorff illusions) in a similar manner as children who are actually nine and five years of age. Since there is no reason to believe that adults can figure out how children are affected by these complex illusions, the results presented by Parrish et al. could be interpreted as indicating that the highly suggestible subjects were in an unusual state (hypnotic trance) when they manifested such an unusual effect.

However, the results of the study could not be confirmed in two subsequent investigations. Ascher and Barber (1968) closely replicated the experimental procedures used by Parrish et al., that is, subjects who were highly responsive to test suggestions were exposed to a trance induction procedure and were given suggestions that they were nine and five years of age. Under the regressed condition, the subjects' performance on the Ponzo and Poggendorff illusions was virtually the same as their adult performance and not at all similar to the performance of children who are actually nine and five. Spanos and Barber (1969) also replicated the experimental procedures of Parrish, Lundy, and Leibowitz, but used only exceptionally suggestible subjects who had previously passed a large number of very difficult test suggestions. When placed in "hypnotic trance" and given suggestions to regress to ages nine and five, these exceptionally responsive subjects performed on the Ponzo and Poggendorff illusions in practically the same manner as their adult performance and their performance did not remotely resemble that of children of ages nine and five.

In brief, the traditional (special state) paradigm seemed to be supported by several studies that reported very amazing effects produced in "hypnotic trance" subjects by suggestions to regress to an earlier chronological age. However, a close look at the data fails to support the traditional paradigm. The notion of a special state is also not supported by the following considerations pertaining to suggested regression:

1. Practically all investigations in this area found that "hypnotic trance" subjects who were given suggestions to regress to a specified age performed at a level superior to the level actually found at the specified age; for example, when regressed to age six, "hypnotic trance" subjects typically performed at a nine-year-old level (Barber, 1969b, Ch. 11).

2. "Hypnotic trance" subjects who tend to act in a childlike way when given suggestions to regress to childhood also give an equally convincing portrayal of an older person or of a senile individual when given suggestions to progress to the age of 70, 80, or 90 (Kline, 1951; Rubenstein & Newman, 1954). Also, some "hypnotic trance" subjects who tend to give a childlike performance when regressed to childhood also give a convincing performance when regressed to prenatal life in the womb or to a time that preceded their present life (the "Bridey Murphy" phenomenon) (Bernstein, 1956; Kelsey, 1953).

3. When subjects who have been randomly assigned to an "awake" group or to a "trance" group are given suggestions to go back or to regress to an

earlier chronological age, the same proportion of subjects in both groups report that they imagined, felt, or believed that they had returned to the earlier age (Barber & Calverley, 1966a).

4. Although various theoretical formulations might possibly account for the foregoing data, one formulation that can parsimoniously explain the results is as follows: When it is suggested to "hypnotic trance" subjects or to "awake" subjects that they are in the past (or in the future), (a) some "hypnotic trance" subjects and also some "awake" subjects try to the best of their ability to think about continuously and to imagine vividly that they are in the past (or in the future), (b) some of the "hypnotic trance" subjects and also some of the "awake" subjects succeed in focusing imaginatively on the past (or future), and (c) when thinking about and vividly imagining themselves in an earlier time (or in a future time), some subjects in both groups feel as if they are in the past (or in the future) and trend to behave to a certain limited degree as if they are in the past (or future).

*Hallucinations*

Two studies (Brady & Levitt, 1966; Underwood, 1960) indicate that highly suggestible subjects, who were first exposed to a trance induction procedure and then given suggestions to hallucinate, behaved as if they actually perceived the suggested (hallucinated) object. These data were interpreted as lending support to the notion that the subjects must have been in a unique state (hypnotic trance) in order to manifest such unique behavior. However, a closer look at the data does not support the special state notion.

Brady and Levitt (1966) attempted to ascertain whether a suggested visual hallucination of an optokinetic drum (a revolving drum with alternate black and white vertical stripes) gives rise to involuntary nystagmoidlike eye movements that resemble those found when an individual actually perceives an optokinetic drum. When highly suggestible subjects were exposed to a trance induction procedure and given suggestions to hallucinate the optokinetic drum, a small percentage behaved as if they were actually perceiving the drum—manifesting nystagmoidlike eye movements. However, a subsequent study by Hahn and Barber (1966) showed that an equally small percentage of unselected subjects under a waking control condition manifested nystagmoidlike eye movements when they were simply instructed to imagine vividly the optokinetic drum. Also, Reich (1970) recently presented data indicating that some subjects are able to produce nystagmus "through conscious, voluntary effort while awake."

To ascertain whether suggested visual hallucinations produce objective consequences that resemble those produced by actual visual stimulation, Underwood (1960) used two optical illusions in which a series of lines distorts a geometric figure. The subjects were shown the geometric figures without the distorting lines and were given suggestions to hallucinate the lines. Underwood found that when given the suggestions to hallucinate the lines, a small percentage of selected "hypnotic trance" subjects reported a few effects that tended to resemble those actually produced by the optical illusions. However, Sarbin and Andersen (1963) found that an equally small percentage of unselected waking control subjects reported the same effects when they were simply instructed to imagine the lines vividly.

In brief, suggestions to hallucinate an object, given to subjects who are said to be in hypnotic trance, at times gives rise to some objective effects that tend to resemble those found when a person actually perceives the object. However, the same objective effects are produced when waking subjects are simply asked to imagine the object vividly.

*Suggested deafness*

Erickson (1938a, 1938b) concluded from experimental studies that a condition indistinguishable from actual deafness can be produced by suggestions, provided that the suggestions are given to highly responsive subjects who have been exposed to a trance induction procedure. Erickson's data seemed to support the traditional notion of a special state (hypnotic trance); that is, it appeared that in order to manifest such a special or unique effect (deafness produced by suggestions), the subjects must have been in a special state. Let us look at the data presented by Erickson.

Erickson (1938a) administered suggestions of total deafness to 30 subjects who were preselected as highly suggestible and who had been exposed to a trance induction procedure. Of the 30 subjects, 24 (80 per cent) did not show signs of deafness. However, Erickson judged the remaining six subjects to have become deaf as indicated by such signs as "failure to show any response to deliberately embrassing remarks," "failure to raise voice when reading aloud while an irrelevant continuous extraneous noise becomes increasingly disturbing," and failure to react to unexpected sounds. Erickson concluded from these and similar data that "there was produced a condition not distinguishable from neurological deafness by any of the ordinarily competent tests employed" (p. 149).

Erickson's conclusion is not clearly supported by his data. For instance, failure to react to unexpected sounds does not demonstrate that the sounds were not heard. In a study carried out by Dynes (1932), three selected suggestible subjects, who were judged to be in hypnotic trance and who received suggestions of deafness, did not become noticeably startled when a pistol was fired unexpectedly; however, each subject testified postexperimentally that he had heard the pistol shot. Similarly, lack of response to a disturbing noise or to embarrassing remarks does not demonstrate that the subject is deaf, since these responses can be rather easily inhibited voluntarily.

In a supplementary study, Erickson (1938b) found that two of the "hypnotic trance" subjects who appeared to be deaf did not manifest a hand-withdrawal response that had been conditioned to a sound. He interpreted this outcome as demonstrating that the subjects were "unconscious of the sound." The interpretation is not valid; many studies have demonstrated that subjects can voluntarily inhibit hand-withdrawal responses that have been conditioned to a sound (Hamel, 1919; Hilgard & Marquis, 1940, pp. 269–70).

In five more recent studies, the technique of delayed auditory feedback was used to evaluate suggested deafness produced under "hypnotic trance" (Barber & Calverley, 1964c; Kline, Guze, & Haggerty, 1954; Kramer & Tucker, 1967; Scheibe, Gray, & Keim, 1968; Sutcliffe, 1961). Each of the five experiments showed that "hypnotic trance" subjects who have received suggestions of deafness are affected by auditory stimuli in essentially the same way as any normal person who hears perfectly well; that is, when exposed to delayed auditory feedback, the "hypnotic deaf" subject and the person with normal hearing (but not the person who is actually deaf) typically stutters, mispronounces words, and speaks more loudly and more slowly. One of these studies (Barber & Calverley, 1964c) also showed that suggestions of deafness are at least as effective with "waking" control subjects as with "hypnotic trance" subjects in eliciting subjective reports of deafness; however, both the "waking" control subjects and the "hypnotic trance" subjects who accepted the suggestions of deafness responded to the delayed auditory feedback in the same way as individuals who hear normally.

Although both "hypnotic trance" subjects and "waking" control subjects who have received suggestions of deafness may be trying not to hear, they simply do not succeed in blocking out sounds. The fact that the subjects can hear is often obvious. After suggesting deafness to "hypnotic trance" subjects, the hypnotist may ask, "Can you hear me?" A few subjects reply, "No, I can't," thus admitting that they can hear. The other subjects, however, do not reply and appear to be deaf. How does the hypnotist remove the deafness? He typically states, "Now you can hear again," and since the subjects now respond normally it is obvious that they could hear all along.

### OBSERVABLE TRANCELIKE CHARACTERISTICS

The special state paradigm also seems to be supported by the fact that a substantial proportion of subjects who are highly responsive to test suggestions actually appear to be in a trance. Numerous investigators (Erickson, Hershman, & Secter, 1961, pp. 55–58; Gill & Brenman, 1959, pp. 38–39; Pattie, 1956a, p. 21; Weitzenhoffer, 1957a, pp. 211–12) have pointed out that subjects who are highly responsive to test suggestions often show signs of trance such as a blank stare, a rigid facial expression, a lack of spontaneity, a limp posture, psychomotor retardation, disinclination to talk, lack of humor, and literal-mindedness. Although these observations, at first glance, seem to support the assumption that a special state (hypnotic trance) underlies high responsiveness to test suggestions, a closer look at the data fails to support the assumption:

1. When subjects who are highly responsive to test suggestions manifest trancelike characteristics, the characteristics have been explicitly or implicitly suggested. That is, the experimenter has suggested to the subject that he is becoming relaxed, drowsy, sleepy, and is entering a hypnotic trance state. These suggestions imply to subjects that they should become passive or lethargic, behave in a trancelike manner, move or respond slowly (show psychomotor retardation), and not look actively around the room (Barber & Calverley, 1969b).

2. Since the trancelike characteristics have been suggested, they can also be removed by suggestions. For instance, several years ago, I carried out the following informal study with eight suggestible subjects. The subjects were first exposed to a trance induction procedure, comprised of repeated suggestions of relaxation, drowsiness, sleep, and deep hypnosis. All subjects appeared to be in a hypnotic trance—manifesting a lack of spontaneity, psychomotor retardation, and passivity or lethargy—and also responded to test suggestions for arm heaviness, arm levitation, inability to unclasp hands, and thirst hallucination. Next, the subjects were told to become awake and alert, to stop acting as if they were in a hypnotic trance, but to continue to remain responsive to test suggestions. The subjects remained highly responsive to test suggestions for inability to say their name, body immobility, and selective amnesia, but they no longer showed signs of trance; in fact, they appeared to be just as awake as subjects who were not responsive to test suggestions.

3. Some subjects who have been exposed to a trance induction procedure manifest a high level of responsiveness to test suggestions but they do not show signs or characteristics of hypnotic trance (Erickson, 1962).

4. Some subjects who have been exposed to a trance induction procedure and who show signs of hypnotic trance are not responsive to test suggestions for analgesia, age regression, amnesia, and so on (Barber, 1957, 1963; Barber & Calverley, 1969b).

5. As pointed out previously in this chapter, some subjects who have not been exposed to a trance induction procedure manifest a high level of response to test suggestions without showing signs of hypnotic trance (Barber, 1969b; Klopp, 1961). Stated otherwise, when no attempt is made to induce a hypnotic trance, and especially when subjects are not asked to close their eyes, a substantial proportion of subjects experience such suggested effects as limb rigidity, analgesia, age regression, hallucination, amnesia and so on, without manifesting signs of hypnotic trance such as blank stare, rigid facial expression, and passivity.

In brief, trancelike characteristics on the part of the subject appear to be artifacts that the experimenter can put into the suggestive situation and can also take out of the situation, and they certaintly are not necessary (and may be extraneous) for high response to test suggestions.

SUBJECTS' TESTIMONY OF BEING IN HYPNOTIC TRANCE

At first glance, the traditional viewpoint seems to be supported by the fact that some subjects who are highly responsive to test suggestions testify that they are hypnotized or are in a hypnotic trance. A close look at subjects' testimony, however, fails to support the traditional notion that a state discontinuous with ordinary states of consciousness underlies high responsiveness to test suggestion for limb rigidity, analgesia, hallucination, and so on:

1. As stated previously in this chapter, some subjects manifest a high level or response to test suggestion when no attempt is made to hypnotize them. With few exceptions, these highly responsive subjects testify that they are *not* in a hypnotic trance. The remaining few testify that they must be hypnotized, even though they do not feel that they are hypnotized, because they actually experience those things that are suggested. These subjects are not using the term "hypnotized" to refer to a state that is basically different from ordinary states of consciousness; they are using the term "hypnotized" synonymously with the phrase "high responsiveness to suggestions."

2. A substantial proportion of subjects who are given suggestions to enter a hypnotic trance state and who are highly responsive to test suggestions state that they are not sure if they are hypnotized. The proportion of highly responsive subjects unable to state whether they are in a hypnotic trance varies from 25 per cent to 67 per cent depending on the wording of the questions submitted to them in order to elicit their statements (Barber, Dalal, & Calverley, 1968; Hilgard, 1965b, p. 12).

3. As implied in the preceding paragraph, subjects' testimony pertaining to whether they think they are in hypnotic trance depends, in part, on the wording and tone of the questions that are used to elicit their testimony (Barber, Dalal, & Calverley, 1968).

4. Subjects' testimony pertaining to whether they are in hypnotic trance depends, in part, on their preconceptions of what hypnotic trance is supposed to be. Subjects differing in preconceptions give different testimony even when they are equally responsive to test suggestions. For instance, one highly responsive subject believes hypnotic trance is a state of relaxation, whereas another highly responsive subject believes that a hypnotized person experiences spontaneous amnesia. When both of these highly responsive subjects become relaxed during the session and both fail to experience spontaneous amnesia, the former testifies that he was hypnotized or was in a hypnotic trance, whereas the latter testifies that he was not in a hypnotic trance.

5. Subjects' testimony pertaining to whether they are hypnotized is also dependent, in part, on subtle situational variables such as whether the exper-

imenter states or implies that he believes they are hypnotized (Barber, Dalal, & Calverley, 1968).

6. Subjects who state that they are in a hypnotic trance are not necessarily saying that they are in a state that is clearly different from ordinary states of consciousness. On the contrary, they often appear to be saying no more and no less than that they are ready and willing to respond to test suggestions. Gill and Brenman (1959) have documented this important point:

> First, we would induce hypnosis in someone previously established as a "good" subject; then we would ask him how he knew he was in hypnosis. He might reply that he felt relaxed. Now we would suggest that the relaxation would disappear *but he would remain in hypnosis*. Then we would ask again how he knew he was in hypnosis. He might say because his arm "feels numb"—so again, we would suggest the disappearance of this sensation. We continued in this way until finally we obtained the reply, "I know I am in hypnosis because I *know* I will do what you tell me." This was repeated with several subjects, with the same results. (P. 36)

The subject's final assertion—"I *know* I will do what you tell me"—does *not* support the traditional paradigm, which assumes that the subject who shows high response to test suggestions is in a state fundamentally different from the waking state. However, it is in line with and can be deduced from the alternative paradigm, which views the subject who is highly responsive to test suggestions as being as awake and as normal as the member of the audience who is ready and willing to have a wide variety of experiences as he listens to the communications from the stage.

### DIFFICULTY OR DELAY IN "COMING OUT OF HYPNOTIC TRANCE"

At first glance, the special state (hypnotic trance) paradigm also seems to be supported by the following two sets of interrelated data. On rare occasions, subjects who are highly responsive to test suggestions do not open their eyes immediately when told to wake up—they seem to remain in a hypnotic trance. When the experimenter leaves the room without having told the subject to wake up, subjects who are said to be in a hypnotic trance remain sitting passively with eyes closed for a longer period of time than simulating subjects who have been asked to act as if they are in a hypnotic trance. Let us look at these two sets of data in turn.

#### *Refusing to "wake up"*

When told that the experiment is over, practically all subjects who have been exposed to a trance induction procedure open their eyes and converse normally (Kroger, 1970, p. 172). However, in very rare instances, subjects who have been exposed to a trance induction procedure do not open their eyes when told to wake up. They remain sitting passively with eyes closed and it appears, from the traditional special state viewpoint, that they are having difficulty making the transition from the hypnotic trance state to the waking state. The empirical evidence, however, does not support the special state viewpoint. Williams (1953) and Weitzenhoffer (1957a, pp. 226–29) have summarized data that cogently indicate that these few subjects (who do not open their eyes when told to wake up) have some special reason or motive for refusing to open their eyes; they either (a) have been given a suggestion to carry out postexperimentally that they do not want to carry out, (b) are deliberately resisting the hypnotist, (c) are testing the hypnotist's ability to control them, (d) are manifesting spite toward the hypnotist, or (e) are attempting to frighten the hypnotist by refusing to "wake up."

If a "hypnotic trance" subject does not open his eyes when told to wake up, Weitzenhoffer (1957a) recommends the following: "The simplest way of proceeding is to ask him why he does not wake up. Most subjects are quite willing to explain why. If the subject is uncooperative you may have to request an answer more forcefully. Usually the answer tells the hypnotist what to do." Weitzenhoffer adds that if the subject remains intractable, you "simply say to him, in a final tone, 'Very well then, if you will not wake up I will just have to leave you as you are.' You then ignore the subject entirely and go on to other things" (p. 228). Since the subject now cannot accomplish his purpose by remaining passive with his eyes closed, he soon opens his eyes.

*Remaining in hypnotic trance when the experimenter leaves the room*

Orne and Evans (1966) and Evans (1966a) contended that it is possible to test the hypothesis that a trance induction procedure leads to a qualitative change in the organism in highly suggestible subjects. They reasoned as follows: If the highly suggestible subject actually enters a special state (a hypnotic trance) when he is exposed to a trance induction procedure, and if the hypnotist leaves the room without telling the subject to awaken, then the subject should slowly bring himself out of the special state. An active effort would be required for the subject to initiate the volitional act of arousal and, consequently, the voluntary termination of the hypnotic trance would not be immediate—it would subsume a period of time.

Two experiments were conducted with the aim of testing this hypothesis (Orne & Evans, 1966; Evans, 1966a). Both experiments utilized two groups of pretested subjects. Subjects in one group were highly responsive to test suggestions (suggestible subjects) and those in the other group were very unresponsive (nonsuggestible subjects). Prior to the formal experiments, the nonsuggestible subjects were told, by a person other than the experimenter, to try to simulate hypnosis—that is, they were told to try to fool the experimenter by faking or acting as if they entered a hypnotic trance. The suggestible subjects were not told to simulate and thus were categorized as real hypnotic subjects. During the experimental sessions, both the suggestible (real) and the nonsuggestible (simulating) subjects received a trance induction procedure by means of a tape recording. The suggestible (real) subjects presumably entered a hypnotic trance state and the nonsuggestible (simulating) subjects presumably did not enter a hypnotic trance state even though they acted as if they had entered such a state. In the middle of the experimental session, a switch was purposively thrown in another room, thus stopping the tape recording with a marked slur. The experimenter then left the room, ostensibly to repair the fuse that had stopped the tape recording. Both the real subjects and the simulating subjects were then observed to determine how long they would remain sitting quietly with eyes closed.

In both the first and second experiments, the real hypnotic subjects, who were presumably in a hypnotic trance state, did not open their eyes immediately; they remained sitting quietly with eyes closed for quite some time after the experimenter had left the room. In the first experiment, the simulating subjects also remained sitting quietly with eyes closed; in fact, they did not open their eyes at all until the experimenter again entered the room about one-half hour later. In the second experiment, the simulators opened their eyes soon after the experimenter left the room. The inconsistent behavior of the simulators in the first and second experiment was due to the following: In the first experiment there was a conspicious one-way mirror in the room and the subjects knew that they were being observed. In the second experiment, the one-way mirror was completely blocked by a blackboard and the subjects believed that they were not being observed. (They were observed, however, through a peep hole that they were not aware of.) Since, in both experiments, the real hypnotic subjects, who were presumably in a hypnotic trance state, did not open their eyes for quite some time after the experimenter left the room, whereas the simulators opened their eyes when they believed they were not being observed but did not open their eyes when they believed they were being observed, Evans (1966a) concluded that the experiments had demonstrated that the highly suggestible (real) subjects were actually in a special state of consciousness (hypnotic trance).

Evans's (1966a) conclusion, of course, does not clearly follow from the data he presented. The experiments are open to another interpretation, namely, that the differences between the two groups were due to the fact that subjects in one of the groups (but not the other) had been instructed to try to fool the experimenter and to make him believe that they were hypnotized. When subjects are instructed to try to fool the experimenter into believing they are hypnotized, it can be expected that, after the experimenter leaves the room, they will act as if they are hypnotized if they believe they are being observed by the experimenter or by his surrogates, and they will not act as if they are hypnotized if they believe they are not being observed. The appropriate comparison is not between subjects who are asked to fool the experimenter and those who are not asked to fool the experimenter. The appropriate comparison is between a group of suggestible subjects who are exposed to a trance induction procedure and who are presumably in a hypnotic trance state, and a group of control subjects who are simply told to relax. It can be hypothesized, from the viewpoint that does not postulate a special state, that control subjects who are simply told to relax will remain sitting quietly with eyes closed as long as the subjects who are presumably in a hypnotic trance. This hypothesis has been tested experimentally by Dorcus, Brintnall, and Case (1941). Let us now look at their experiment.

The experimental group was comprised of 20 subjects who had previously demonstrated that they were highly responsive to test suggestions. After these subjects had been exposed to a trance induction procedure, an assistant came into the room and said to the experimenter, "You are wanted on the telephone about an appointment downtown." The experimenter replied to the assistant that he had forgotten an appointment and that he would be gone for the remainder of the day. Both the experimenter and the assistant then left the room hastily. The subject was then kept under observation through a peep hole in an adjacent room. Twenty-five subjects in a control group were asked to simply close their eyes and relax and then were told that, after a few minutes of relaxation, they would be given further instructions. During the period of relaxation, the same conversation about the appointment was carried out. After the experimenter left the room, the suggestible subjects, who had been exposed to the trance induction procedure and who were presumably in a hypnotic trance state, remained passive with eyes closed for a mean time of 28 minutes. The control group, which had been simply told to relax, remained passive with eyes closed for an insignificantly shorter average period of 23 minutes.[6] Postexperimental interviews showed that the behavior of both the "hypnotic trance" subjects and the "relaxation control" subjects was influenced by the same factors; that is, some subjects in both groups thought they should wait for the experimenter to return, others thought the experiment was over, and others had to leave because they had previous appointments. Clearly, this study does not support the contention that suggestible subjects who have been exposed to a trance induction procedure have entered a special state that is qualitatively different from the ordinary state of consciousness present when people relax.

The foregoing experiments by Orne and Evans (1966), Evans (1966a), and Dorcus, Brintnall, and Case (1941) indicate that subjects who are asked to simulate hypnosis may perform differently from "hypnotic trance" subjects and also from control subjects (who are not asked to simulate), and that control subjects may behave in the same way as "hypnotic trance"

6. It should be noted that in the Dorcus et al. experiment, both the "hypnotic trance" subjects and the "relaxation control" subjects remained passive with eyes closed about as long as the real hypnotic subjects in the Evans (1966) experiment.

subjects. These results suggest extreme caution in interpreting studies that compared simulating subjects with "real hypnotic subjects." The simulators are in a special situation—they are trying to fool the experimenter. Also, when given their original instructions, the simulators are told not to let themselves experience any of the suggested effects. Consequently, if a control group is not used, differences in performance between simulators and hypnotic subjects can be easily misinterpreted as indicating that the hypnotic subjects behaved unusually, when it was actually the simulators who behaved unusually. Other studies that found differences in the performance of simulating subjects and real hypnotic subjects, such as in the performance of posthypnotic behavior outside of the experimental setting (Orne, Sheehan, & Evans, 1968; Sheehan & Orne, 1968) and in the performance of "source amnesia" (Evans, 1968, p. 483), need to be redone with the addition of a control group that is not asked to simulate.

### SPONTANEOUS AMNESIA

Individuals usually have spontaneous amnesia for the events that occurred when they were in a special state of consciousness. For instance, upon awakening, individuals usually forget the dreams and other events that occurred when they were in the special state of sleep. With these considerations in mind, the traditional (special state) paradigm seems to be supported by the fact that, after "awakening," some highly suggestible subjects state spontaneously that they have forgotten what occurred during "hypnotic trance." However, a close look at the data fails to support the special state paradigm:

1. A rather large number of subjects have been assessed on response to test suggestions for limb rigidity, analgesia, age regression, etc., without receiving either suggestions for relaxation, drowsiness, and sleep, or suggestions to forget what occurred. To the best of my knowledge, no subject has ever manifested spontaneous amnesia under these conditions. It thus appears that all subjects, including those highly responsive to test suggestions, remember the events perfectly well if they are not exposed to a trance induction procedure and are not told to forget (Barber & Calverley, 1966b). Stated otherwise, high responsiveness to test suggestions is not necessarily associated with spontaneous amnesia.

2. No subject has ever forgotten the events occurring during the time he was highly responsive to test suggestions (or, in the traditional terminology, was in a hypnotic trance) if told during the session that he was expected to remember the events (Barber, 1962b; Orne, 1966a; Watkins, 1966).

3. If not told explicitly to forget, almost all subjects, including those who have been exposed to repeated suggestions of relaxation, drowsiness, and sleep, remember the events perfectly well. In other words, if amnesia is not explicitly suggested, very few subjects who are highly responsive to test

suggestions (or who are judged from the traditional viewpoint to be in a hypnotic trance) manifest spontaneous amnesia (Barber & Calverley, 1966b; Hilgard, 1966).

4. When a trance induction procedure is administered but subjects are not told explicitly to forget what occurred, a very small number of subjects manifest apparent spontaneous amnesia. However, this apparent spontaneous amnesia can almost always be readily removed if the experimenter suggests or insists that the subject can remember. Furthermore, there are at least three reasons (specified in the following three paragraphs) why it is seriously questionable that the apparent amnesia in these rare cases is actually spontaneous (nonsuggested).

5. These rare subjects, who seem to manifest amnesia spontaneously, have received repeated suggestions of drowsiness and sleep. Since the subjects know that people usually forget the dreams and other events that occur during sleep, the direct suggestion to sleep may include the indirect suggestion to forget the events occurring during "sleep." In other words, the apparent amnesia in these instances may not be spontaneous but may be due to implicit suggestions for amnesia conveyed by the explicit suggestions to sleep.

6. In some of these infrequent cases of apparent spontaneous amnesia, the subjects received suggestions to sleep and suggestions for amnesia in a previous session, and may have generalized or extrapolated the suggestions to apply to the present session.

7. Subjects who manifest apparent spontaneous amnesia have received suggestions to enter a "hypnotic trance state." Since subjects generally believe that a hypnotic trance state is followed by spontaneous amnesia (Dorcus, Brintall, & Case, 1941; London, 1961), they may say that they have forgotten in order to be good subjects and to meet what they believe are the expectations of the hypnotist.

To recapitulate, several compelling considerations indicate that the rare occurrence of apparent spontaneous amnesia that follows a trance induction procedure may not be spontaneous but, instead, may have been either explicitly or implicitly suggested in the present session or in a previous one. Even if some of these instances of apparent amnesia were actually spontaneous (nonsuggested), they would not clearly support the notion that a special state underlies high responsiveness to test suggestions because when amnesia is not suggested, almost all subjects highly responsive to test suggestions and judged by traditional investigators to be in a hypnotic trance state assert after the session that they remember everything that occurred.

### "TRANCE LOGIC"

Orne (1959) presented the following data from an informally conducted study: Subjects who were highly responsive to test suggestions and who were exposed to a trance induction procedure stated that (a) they could see a suggested (hallucinated) person in a chair and, at the same time, they could see the back of the chair through the (hallucinated) person, and (b) they could see the suggested (hallucinated) coexperimenter in the chair and, at the same time, they could see the (actual) coexperimenter in another part of the room (that is, they could "see" two images of the coexperimenter). Orne also stated that nonsuggestible subjects instructed to fool the experimenter into thinking that they were hypnotized (simulators) did not give these types of reports; for instance, although the simulators reported that they could see the suggested (hallucinated) coexperimenter in the chair, they refused to see the (actual) coexperimenter in another part of the room or they claimed that they could not recognize him. Orne (1959) concluded from these informal observations that the highly suggestible subjects who were exposed to a trance induction procedure and who were presumably in a hypnotic trance state manifested a special type of logic, "trance logic," defined as the "simultaneous perception and response to both hallucinations and reality without any apparent attempts to satisfy a need for logical consistency" (p. 295). Orne also concluded that trance logic was part of the essence of hypnosis.

At first glance, it appears that Orne's data support the special state paradigm; that is, since the highly suggestible subjects who had been exposed to a trance induction procedure manifested a special type of logic, they most likely were in a special state. However, since Orne derived his data from informal observations (not from a structured experiment), the "trance logic" contention can be viewed as suggesting a hypothesis that needs to be confirmed experimentally.

Johnson, Maher, and Barber (in press) carried out two experiments to test Orne's "trance logic" hypothesis. In the first experiment, 70 subjects were pretested on response to test suggestions. Following the pretest, 10 subjects, who had shown high response to test suggestions, were given additional "hypnotic training." They received practice in responding to a wide variety of difficult test suggestions. These 10 "trained" subjects were exposed to a trance induction procedure in the experimental session. The remaining 60 subjects were subdivided into high and low responders to test suggestions, and then equal numbers of high and low responders were randomly assigned to the following three groups with 20 subjects to each group: a group that was exposed to a trance induction procedure in the experimental session, a group of simulators who were first asked to fool the experimenter by acting as if they were hypnotized and then were exposed to a trance induction procedure, and a control group that was simply asked to imagine the various suggested effects.

All subjects were tested for "trance logic" according to the two criteria specified by Orne (1959). By the first criterion, trance logic is considered to be present if the subject states that he sees the suggested (hallucinated) person in the chair and, at the same time, sees the back of the chair through the hallucinated person. By this criterion, trance logic occurred equally often among the control subjects, the trained hypnotic subjects, and the untrained hypnotic subjects. The second criterion for trance logic refers to the subjects seeing both the hallucinated coexperimenter sitting in the chair and also the actual coexperimenter in another part of the room. By this criterion trance logic was found to occur equally often among all groups (controls, simulators, trained hypnotic subjects, and untrained hypnotic subjects). Also, in each of the three groups, the high suggestible subjects did not differ from the low suggestible on either criterion of trance logic.

The second experiment included two groups of subjects. One group was selected from a large population as the most responsive to test suggestions. These very suggestible subjects were exposed to a trance induction procedure during the experimental session (real hypnotic subjects). The second group also included only very suggestible subjects; this group was first asked to simulate hypnosis and then was exposed to a trance induction procedure (simulators). Trance logic was assessed in both groups, using the criteria specified by Orne (1959). With respect to the first criterion, 60 per cent of the real hypnotic subjects and 50 per cent of the simulators exhibited trance logic. With respect to the second criterion, 60 per cent of the real hypnotic subjects and 67 per cent of the simulators exhibited trance logic.

In brief, the experiments by Johnson, Maher, and Barber (in press) demonstrated that trance logic is *not* unique to subjects who are highly responsive to test suggestions and who have received a trance induction procedure. Not only is "trance logic" not a characteristic of the presumed "hypnotic trance state," but it is also not found to a greater degree in "hypnotic trance" subjects than in simulating subjects, in "hypnotic trance" subjects than in control subjects, in highly suggestible subjects than in nonsuggestible subjects, or in subjects who are "trained in hypnosis" as opposed to those who are not trained. Johnson, Maher, & Barber concluded that "Since trance logic was not found to be a discriminating characteristic of hypnotic subjects, investigators who seek the essence of hypnosis must now search elsewhere—that is, if there is an 'essence.' "

### *The Search for a Physiological Index of the Presumed "Hypnotic Trance State"*

Since the organism is a psychophysiological unity, special states of consciousness or special states of the organism are expected to have some physiological concomitants that distinguish them from nonspecial states. Investigators who adhere to the traditional paradigm have been trying for many years to find a physiological concomitant or index of the presumed special state that they call "hypnotic trance." Not only have they failed to find any special physiological changes associated with the presumed special state, but they have also consistently found that physiological functioning during the postulated special state varies in the same way as in nonspecial or ordinary states. The relevant data are as follows:

1. Electroencephalographic (EEG) criteria indicate that subjects who are highly responsive to test suggestions (and who are judged by traditionalists as being in a hypnotic trance) do not show any special patterns on the EEG that might distinguish them from subjects who are relatively unresponsive to test suggestions (Barber, 1961b; Chertok & Kramarz, 1959). Similarly, subjects said to be in a hypnotic trance do not show special changes on any other known physiological measure that might serve as an index of the presumed special state.

2. The EEG of the person who is responding to test suggestions varies continually with the instructions or suggestions he is given and with the activities he is asked to perform (Barber, 1961b; Chertok & Kramarz, 1959). Similarly, other physiological measures vary continually when subjects are responding to test suggestions. Subjects who are said to be in hypnotic trance show continually varying (high, medium, or low) skin conductance, basal metabolic rate, heart rate, blood pressure, respiration, peripheral blood flow, blood clotting time, oral temperature, and so forth (Barber, 1961b; Cogger & Edmonston, in press; Crasilneck & Hall, 1959; Levitt & Brady, 1963; Timney & Barber, 1969). There is no need to postulate a special state of consciousness to account for these continual variations in physiological functions that are found in subjects responding to test suggestions (or said to be in hypnotic trance). Physiological variables vary in hypnotic subjects in the same way as in normal individuals, that is, in accordance with whatever activity they are engaged in. Normal individuals tend to show a high level of skin conductance, basal metabolic rate, heart rate, blood pressure, and so forth, when they are active or aroused, and a low level when they are relaxed or passive. In the same way as any other normal individual, the subject who is highly responsive to test suggestions (and said to be in a hypnotic trance) shows a high level of skin conductance, basal metabolic rate, heart rate, and so forth, when he is given suggestions that lead to activity or arousal, and a lower level when he is given suggestions leading to quietude or relaxation. Similarly, if a normal individual is not anxious about a painful stimulus, he will tend to show a small change in skin conductance when he is exposed to the stimulus; and, if a normal individual is anxious about a painful stimulus, he will tend to show a larger change in skin conductance. In the same way, the subject who is responsive to suggestions intended to reduce his experience of pain will show a small rise in skin conductance when he is exposed to the noxious stimulus, and the subject who is unresponsive to the suggestions for reduced pain reactivity will show a larger rise in conductance (Barber & Hahn, 1962).

### *"Hypnotic Trance" as a Misnomer for a Responsive Waking State*

Some present-day investigators who use the traditional term "hypnotic trance" (or "hypnosis" or "hypnotic state") do *not* seem to mean that the subject is in a special state basically different from ordinary waking states. On the contrary, by the term "hypnotic trance" they seem to refer to a person who is as awake and as normal as you or I and who is as ready to respond to test suggestions as I am while I write these lines and as some readers are as they read these lines. (If, as I write these lines, an experimenter entered the room and wished to assess my response to test suggestions, I would have positive attitudes, motivations, and expectancies toward the test situation and I would be ready, willing, and able to respond to the test suggestions and to experience the suggested effects. Some readers of these lines would be just as ready as I am to respond to the test suggestions.) To illustrate these contentions, let us look at how the term "hypnotic trance" is used by Erickson (1967a), who has written extensively on this topic:

1. Erickson often judges subjects to be in a hypnotic trance when, from all indications, they are in a waking state. For instance, he writes: "In the well-trained subject, the [deep hypnotic trance] is that type of trance in which the subject is seemingly awake and functioning adequately, freely, and well in the total hypnotic situation, in a manner similar to that of a nonhypnotized person operating at the waking level" (1967a, p. 13).

2. Erickson notes that psychologists, psychiatrists, and experienced hypnotists often view his hypnotic trance subjects as being in the waking state. For instance, he offers the following illustrative example: "the author, as a teaching device for the audience, had a subject in a profound somnambulistic trance conduct a lecture and demonstration of hypnosis (unaided by the author) before a group of psychiatrists and psychologists. Although many in the audience had had experience with hypnosis, none detected that she was in a trance" (1967a, p. 14).

3. Erickson's subjects disagree with his judgment. For instance, in a study with 48 subjects presented by Secter (1960), Erickson judged how many subjects had entered light, medium, or deep hypnotic trance and how many did not enter trance. Each of the 48 subjects also rated himself as having attained one of the four levels. By chance, Erickson and the subjects should agree 25 per cent of the time. The actual percentage of agreement was 29 per cent, which did not significantly exceed chance expectations.

In brief, when Erickson states that a subject is in a hypnotic trance, the subject often appears to be normally awake and is often judged by other investigators as being awake. Furthermore, Erickson's subjects do not agree with his judgment that they are not in a hypnotic trance or are in a light, medium, or deep trance. It appears that when Erickson judges one of his subjects to be in a hypnotic trance, he does not mean that the subject is not awake or that the subject is in a trance in the traditional sense of the term. What then does the term "hypnotic trance" mean in Erickson's work? A close reading of his papers provides the following answer: Whenever Erickson states that a subject was in a hypnotic trance, he almost always states on the same page that the subject was highly responsive to test suggestions. In fact, it appears that quite often Erickson first observes that the subject is very responsive to test suggestions and then infers that, since he is responsive to test suggestions, he must be in a hypnotic trance. The term "hypnotic trance," as used by Erickson, appears to refer to high responsiveness to test suggestions.

When pushed to specify what he means by the term "hypnotic trance" (or "hypnosis" or "hypnotized"), Erickson states that he is referring to "a state of intensified attention and receptiveness and an increased responsiveness to an idea or to a set of ideas" (1958, p. 117) and to a person who "tends to want to understand or to receive or to respond to the stimuli which are given to him or which he can derive from his situation" (1962, p. 240). It appears that Erickson may be misusing the term to refer to the same thing I have been describing in this chapter, namely, to an awake subject who has positive attitudes, motivations, and expectancies toward the situation and is ready and willing to think with and to imagine those things that are suggested.

## *Attitudes, Motivations, and Expectancies*

In this chapter, the variables that mediate response to test suggestions for limb rigidity, analgesia, age regression, hallucination, amnesia, and so forth, have been conceptualized in terms of attitudes, motivations, and expectancies that determine whether the subject thinks with and imagines those things that are suggested. This section will focus on the relevance of attitudes, motivations, and expectancies; the next section will focus on the process of thinking with and imagining those things that are suggested.

The reader will recall from the previous discussion, that the following kinds of attitudes, motivations, and expectancies are being referred to:

### *Attitude continuum*

The subject views his responding to test suggestions as interesting or worthwhile and he views the suggested effects as falling in the category of things he should experience (positive attitude); or, at the other end of the continuum, he views his responding to test suggestions as not interesting or worthwhile and he views the suggested effects as falling in the category of things he should not experience (negative attitude). If the subject has been told that he is in a hypnosis situation, then the attitude continuum needs to be conceptualized somewhat differently; in this case, the subject views his being "hypnotized" as interesting or worthwhile and as falling within the category of things he should experience (positive attitude); or, at the other end of the continuum, he views his being "hypnotized" as not interesting or worthwhile and as falling within the category of things he should not experience (negative attitude).

*Motivational continuum*

The subject desires to and tries to experience those things that are suggested (positive motivation); or, at the other end of the continuum, the subject does not desire and does not try to experience those things that are sugessed (negative motivation). If the situation is defined to the subject as hypnosis, the subject desires to be "hypnotized" and tries to enter "hypnotic trance" (positive motivation); or, the subject does not want to be "hypnotized" and tries not to enter "hypnotic trance" (negative motivation).

*Expectancy continuum*

The subject believes that he can experience those things that are suggested (positive expectancy); or, at the other end of the continuum, the subject does not believe that he can experience those things that are suggested (negative expectancy). If the situation is defined to the subject as hypnosis, the subject believes that he can be "hypnotized" (positive expectancy); or, he does not believe that he can be "hypnotized" (negative expectancy).[7]

Two sets of studies have evaluated the effects of the variables specified above. In one set, the subjects were simply asked to rate their attitudes, motivations, or expectancies; in the other set an experimental attempt was made to manipulate these variables. Studies that utilized the subjects' self-ratings will be reviewed first. Next, experiments that tried to manipulate attitudes, motivations, or expectancies, and which obtained more dramatic results, will be reviewed.

### SELF-RATINGS OF ATTITUDES, MOTIVATIONS, AND EXPECTANCIES

David Calverley and I (unpublished data) assessed motivations toward hypnosis in 55 subjects by a scale worded as follows: "In this experiment I want to be deeply . . . medium . . . lightly . . . or not hypnotized." The subjects were then individually exposed to the trance induction procedure and the test suggestions of the Stanford Hypnotic Susceptibility Scale (Form A). The subjects' self-rated motivations were significantly correlated ($r = .36$) with their responsiveness to the test suggestions.

In an investigation by Barber and Calverley (1966c), 13 female subjects participated individually in eight hypnotic sessions conducted on eight con-

7. Another type of expectancy also plays a role in determining response to test suggestions. This other type of expectancy, namely, an expectancy of what kinds of behaviors are appropriate in the situation, will be discussed later in this section.

secutive days. Attitudes and expectations toward the hypnotic situation were assessed at the beginning of each of the eight daily sessions. Attitudes were measured by a Likert-type questionnaire, which asked the subject whether she viewed hypnosis as (a) interesting . . . equally interesting and boring . . . boring, (b) satisfying . . . unsatisfying, (c) pleasant . . . unpleasant, etc. Expectations were assessed by a questionnaire that asked the subject whether she expected that she would be hypnotized and, if so, if she expected to be hypnotized to a deep, medium, or light level. Immediately following the daily assessment of subjects' attitudes and expectations, a standardized trance induction procedure and the Barber Suggestibility Scale were administered by a tape recording of the experimenter's voice. Responsiveness to the test suggestions of the Barber Suggestibility Scale decreased continually during the course of the eight days. Changes in the subject's attitudes and expectations were correlated with this reduction in responsiveness. For instance, the average correlation over the eight days between one of the attitude measures (perceiving hypnosis as interesting) and Objective scores on the Barber Suggestibility Scale was .55, and between preexperimental expectations and Objective scores was .41.

In another study (Barber & Calverley, 1969b), 110 subjects first completed a questionnaire that assessed their expectations concerning whether or not and to what degree they would be hypnotized. Next, half of the subjects were exposed to the standardized trance induction procedure and test suggestions that comprise the Stanford Hypnotic Susceptibility Scale. The other half of the subjects were told to close their eyes for 5 minutes and place themselves in hypnosis; after 5 minutes, they were assessed on response to the test suggestions of the Stanford Scale. Responsiveness to the test suggestions was significantly correlated with subjects' expectations in the group exposed to the trance induction procedure ($r = .33$) and also in the group told to place themselves in hypnosis ($r = .40$).

Melei and Hilgard (1964) had previously obtained similar results. These investigators assessed subjects' attitudes to hypnosis and expectations of their own hypnotizability prior to the hypnotic session. The subjects were then exposed to the standardized trance induction procedure and test suggestions of the Stanford Hypnotic Susceptibility Scale. For the female subjects, significant positive correlations (around .30) were obtained between attitudes toward hypnosis and response to test suggestions. For the male subjects, the correlations were also in the positive direction but not significant. Also, for subjects participating in a hypnotic experiment for the first time, expectations of their own hypnotizability were positively correlated ($r = .16$ to $.29$) with scores on the test suggestions.

Anderson (1963) also obtained a significant correlation of .47 between responsiveness to test suggestions in a hypnotic situation and a preexperimental scale measuring attitudes toward hypnosis (such as, "There are things that would worry me about being hypnotized," and "I would feel uneasy or uncomfortable as a subject").

Dermen and London (1965) found that subjects' expectations of their own hypnotizability were correlated with responsiveness to test suggestions in a hypnotic situation (*r* = .28 to .49 for females and .33 to .35 for males). Similarly, other studies (London, Cooper, & Johnson, 1962; Rosenhan & Tomkins, 1964; Shor, Orne, & O'Connell, 1966) generally yielded small positive correlations (which were more often significant for females than for males) between suggestibility in a hypnotic situation and their preexperimental attitudes toward hypnosis and their preexperimental expectations of their own responsiveness.

### EXPERIMENTAL MANIPULATION OF ATTITUDES, MOTIVATIONS, AND EXPECTANCIES

In the studies summarized above, subjects' self-ratings were used to assess either their attitudes, or their motivations, or their expectancies. Let us now look at a series of studies that experimentally manipulated these three variables in various combinations, and which showed that attitudes, motivations, and expectancies play very important roles in determining response to test suggestions.

#### *Attempts to produce positive attitudes, motivations, and expectancies*

Earlier in this chapter, a series of experiments were summarized in which subjects were given a set of instructions labeled as "task-motivational instructions." Although this label emphasizes the motivational elements in the instructions, a close look at the wording of the instructions indicates that they were aimed to produce not only positive motivation, but also positive attitudes and expectancies. For instance, the so-called task-motivational instructions included the following statements:

1. Statements intended to lead the subject to view his responding to suggestions as interesting or worthwhile (positive attitude): "I want you to score as high as you can because we're trying to measure the maximum ability of people to imagine. If you don't try to the best of your ability, this experiment will be worthless and I'll tend to feel silly. . . . If you try to imagine to the best of your ability . . . you will be helping this experiment and not wasting any time."

2. Statements intended to lead the subject to desire to and to try to experience those things that are suggested (positive motivation): "How well you do on the tests which I will give you depends entirely upon your willingness to try to imagine and to visualize those things I will ask you to imagine. . . . What I ask is your cooperation in helping this experiment by trying to imagine vividly what I describe to you."

3. Statements intended to lead the subject to believe that he can experience those things that are suggested (positive expectancy): "Everyone passed these tests when they tried. For example, we asked people to close their eyes and to imagine that they were at a movie theater and were watching a show. Most people were able to do this very well; they were able to

imagine very vividly that they were at a movie and they felt as if they were actually looking at the picture. However, a few people thought that this was an awkward or silly thing to do and did not try to imagine and failed the test. Yet when these people later realized that it wasn't hard to imagine, they were able to visualize the movie picture and they felt as if the imagined movie was as vivid and real as an actual movie . . . if you try to imagine to the best of your ability, you can easily imagine and do the interesting things I tell you."

As stated previously in this chapter, these so-called task-motivational instructions, which were intended to produce positive attitudes, motivations, and expectancies, raised both overt and subjective responses to test suggestions to about the same level found in a group exposed to a procedure traditionally labeled as a "trance-induction" and markedly above the base level found in a control group. More specifically, as Table 5.2 showed, 60 per cent of the subjects who received the task-motivational instructions showed a relatively high response to test suggestions (passing at least five of the eight items on the suggestibility scale) as compared to 53 per cent of the subjects in the trance-induction group and 16 per cent in the control group.

*Attempts to produce negative attitudes and motivations*

In an attempt to produce negative attitudes and motivations toward the test situation, Barber and Calverley (1964d) told one group of 16 subjects that they were to be tested for gullibility. Seventeen other subjects, randomly assigned to an imagination control group, were told that they were to be tested for ability to imagine. All subjects were then assessed individually on the Barber Suggestibility Scale, administered by a tape recording of the experimenter's voice. Seven subjects (41 per cent) in the imagination control group and only one subject (6 per cent) in the group told they were to be tested for gullibility manifested a relatively high level of suggestibility (Objective scores of 5 or above on the 8-point suggestibility scale). Presumably, the statement to the subjects that they were to be tested for gullibility produced negative attitudes toward the situation (they viewed their responding to test suggestions as not good or worthwhile) and negative motivations (they did not want to and did not try to experience those things that were suggested). If this conjecture is valid, then the experiment demonstrated that negative attitudes and motivations produce a marked reduction in responsiveness to test suggestions.[8]

8. Further experiments are needed in which subjects' attitudes, motivations, and expectancies are assessed after the experimental manipulation—after the subjects are told they are to be tested for gullibility, and prior to assessment of their responsiveness to test suggestions. This consideration applies to all of the experiments discussed in this section; that is, each experiment should not only be replicated but also extended by assessing to what extent the experimental manipulation actually produced positive or negative attitudes, motivations, and expectancies.

Barber and Calverley (1964b) subsequently conducted another experiment along similar lines. First, 24 student nurses were tested individually on objective and subjective responses to the Barber Suggestibility Scale, administered without any special instructions. In a second series of sessions, held one week later, the subjects were tested again individually after they were randomly assigned to one of the following three experimental groups with eight subjects to each group:

Group A (Task-Motivational Instructions) was retested on objective and subjective responses to the Barber Suggestibility Scale after receiving the task-motivational instructions presented verbatim earlier in this chapter. (As stated previously, these task-motivational instructions include statements intended to produce positive attitudes, motivations, and expectancies toward the test situation.)

Group B (Control) was retested on objective and subjective responses to the Barber Suggestibility Scale in the same way as all subjects had been tested in the first session (without special instructions).

Group C (Negative Instructions) was retested on the Barber Suggestibility Scale after an attempt was made to produce negative attitudes and motivations toward the test situation. To produce negative attitudes and motivations, these subjects were told the following by their supervisor (the Supervisor of Student Nurses):

> It's being rumored by doctors and administrators, and I don't know who else, that nursing students are too easily directed and easily led in their responses to suggestions. It's kind of shocking and discouraging to hear that the students are so easily directed and can't decide things for themselves. We've got a job to do—to impress the administrators and doctors around here with the fact that nursing students are not as gullible and as easily directed as they appear to have been showing during this research study. Well it sure is up to each of you as to how easily led people around here think student nurses are. (P. 459)

Table 5.3 shows that during the first session, in which all subjects were tested without any special instructions on the Barber Suggestibility Scale, Groups A, B, and C obtained very similar average scores on the scale. Table 5.3 also shows that in the second session, in which Groups A, B, and C received different sets of instructions, the scores of the three groups were markedly different. On the average, Group A (Task-Motivational Instructions) passed four of the eight test suggestions in the second session, Group B (Control) passed two, and Group C (Negative Instructions) passed none. With the exception of one subject, who obtained an Objective score of 1 on the Barber Suggestibility Scale, all subjects in Group C failed all test suggestions in the second session. The table shows that, depending on whether task-motivational instructions (Group A) or negative instructions (Group C) were administered, the percentage of subjects who obtained an objective

TABLE 5.3 Objective (and subjective) scores on Barber Suggestibility Scale with task-motivational, neutral, and negative instructions

| | Group A | | | Group B | | | Group C | |
|---|---|---|---|---|---|---|---|---|
| Subject | Session 1 (neutral instructions) | Session 2 (task-motivational instructions) | Subject | Session 1 (neutral instructions) | Session 2 (neutral instructions) | Subject | Session 1 (neutral instructions) | Session 2 (negative instructions) |
| A | 7.5 (8) | 8.0 (8) | I | 7.0 (7) | 4.0 (4) | Q | 7.0 (6) | 0.0 (0) |
| B | 7.5 (8) | 8.0 (8) | J | 6.0 (6) | 4.0 (4) | R | 6.0 (4) | 1.0 (0) |
| C | 5.0 (5) | 3.5 (4) | K | 3.0 (2) | 2.0 (2) | S | 5.0 (4) | 0.0 (0) |
| D | 3.5 (4) | 2.5 (3) | L | 3.0 (4) | 1.0 (1) | T | 5.0 (3) | 0.0 (0) |
| E | 2.5 (3) | 2.0 (2) | M | 2.5 (3) | 2.5 (2) | U | 3.0 (3) | 0.0 (0) |
| F | 1.0 (1) | 2.5 (3) | N | 2.0 (2) | 1.5 (2) | V | 2.0 (3) | 0.0 (0) |
| G | 1.0 (1) | 5.0 (4) | O | 1.5 (0) | 2.0 (1) | W | 1.5 (2) | 0.0 (0) |
| H | 1.0 (2) | 2.5 (3) | P | 1.0 (1) | 0.0 (0) | X | 1.5 (2) | 0.0 (0) |
| Mean | 3.6 (4) | 4.2 (4.4) | | 3.2 (3.1) | 2.1 (2) | | 3.9 (3.4) | 0.1 (0) |

SOURCE: Barber, 1964d.

NOTE: Subjective scores are in parentheses.

score and also a Subjective score of at least 1 on the suggestibility scale varied from 100 per cent (Group A) to 0 per cent (Group C).

In this experiment, an attempt was made to ascertain whether negative attitudes and motivations mediated the lack of suggestibility in Group C. To determine whether negative attitudes and motivations were actually among the mediating variables, the following procedure was utilized: The day after the experiment was completed, but before the collaboration of the Supervisor of Student Nurses with the experimenter was admitted to the subjects, the subjects were asked by the Supervisor to write out the answer to the following questions: "Did my statement to you yesterday about the experiment impress you in any way?" Answers to this question strongly indicated that the failure of subjects in Group C to be responsive to test suggestions in the second session was due to the statement made by the supervisor, which was effective in inducing negative attitudes and motivations toward the test situation. Typical replies by the subjects in Group C were as follows:

Subject S: "I was impressed by the manner in which you expressed your concern over the project and the possible effect the outcome will have on the nursing profession. I agreed that we should have a mind of our own and should use it and that nurses should be firm in their decisions."

Subject W: "The fact that many student nurses were suggestible irritated me somewhat. (I didn't like the idea that this particular group of people were suggestible.) I was resistant to the first test but even more to the second test because I did not want to be associated with this branding" (p. 462).

*Attempts to vary expectancy*

In three experimental studies (Barber & Calverley, 1964e; Klinger, 1970; Wilson, 1967), attempts were made to lead the subjects to expect that they could or could not experience those things that were to be suggested.

To produce positive expectancies, Barber and Calverley (1964e) told one random group of subjects that it would be easy to respond to the test suggestions that would be given. To produce negative expectancies, subjects in another random group were told that the test suggestions would be difficult to pass. Subjects given the instructions intended to produce a positive expectancy were significantly more responsive to the test suggestions of the Barber Suggestibility Scale than those given the negative expectancy instructions.

To produce positive expectancies in one random group of subjects and negative expectancies in another random group, Klinger (1970) proceeded as follows: Before being assessed on response to the Barber Suggestibility Scale, each subject observed another person (a stooge) responding to the test suggestions. The stooge had been secretely instructed to role play a very suggestible person half of the time and a very nonsuggestible person the other half of the time. The subjects who observed another person responding without difficulty to the test suggestions presumably would conclude that they themselves could respond without difficulty (positive expectancy), and those who observed another person who was unresponsive would presumably conclude that they themselves would find it difficult to respond (negative expectancy). Subjects who presumably had a positive expectancy (who had observed the responsive person) obtained high scores on the Barber Suggestibility Scale (an average score of 6 on the 8-point scale). Subjects who presumably had a negative expectancy (who had observed the unresponsive person) obtained low scores on the suggestibility scale (average score of 2.6). The experimental treatment (whether the subject had observed the suggestible or nonsuggestible person) accounted for a rather large percentage of the variance (40 per cent) in the subjects' scores on the suggestibility scale.

To produce a positive expectancy that the suggested effects can be experienced, Wilson (1967) proceeded as follows: Subjects who were randomly assigned to an experimental group were asked to imagine various suggested effects while ingenious methods were used to help them experience the effects without their knowing that they were receiving such aid. For instance, each subject was asked to imagine that the room was red while at tiny bulb was lighted secretely that provided a faint red tinge to the room. Following these procedures, each subject was assessed on the Barber Suggestibility Scale. Other subjects, who were randomly assigned to a control group, were tested individually on the suggestibility scale with no attempt made to produce an expectancy that the suggestions were easy to experience. Subjects in the experimental group obtained an average score of 5 whereas those in the control group obtained a significantly lower average score of 3 on the 8-point suggestibility scale.

In brief, three experiments that employed different methods to induce an expectancy that the suggested effects can be experienced converge on the conclusion that expectancy plays an important role in determining responsiveness to test suggestions.

*Expectancy of appropriate behavior*

A study by Orne (1959) showed that performance in a hypnotic situation is also affected by another type of expectancy, namely, an expectancy pertaining to what types of behaviors are appropriate in the situation. An experimental group was told in a class lecture that hypnotic subjects typically manifest catalepsy of the dominant hand whereas a control group was not told anything about catalepsy. Subsequently, subjects in both groups were tested individually in a hypnotic session on response to various test suggestions and on response to a test for catalepsy. Since 55 per cent of the subjects in the experimental group and none in the control group showed catalepsy of the dominant hand, it appears that subjects' expectations concerning what behaviors are appropriate in a hypnotic experiment play an important role in determining their performance.

In brief, a series of experimental studies converge on the conclusion that responsiveness to test suggestions for body immobility, hallucination, amnesia, posthypnotic behavior, and so forth, is determined in part by the subjects' attitudes, motivations, and expectancies.

### *Thinking with the Suggestions and Imagining the Suggested Effects*

If a subject has negative attitudes, motivations, and expectancies toward the test situation (that is, if he views his responding to test suggestions as not worthwhile and does not want to, does not try, and does not believe that he can experience those things that are suggested) he (a) will not think with the suggestions (instead he will verbalize to himself such statements as "This is silly" or "The suggestion won't work"), (b) will not imagine those things that are described by the experimenter, and (c) will not perform the suggested behaviors or experience those things that are suggested.

On the other hand, if a subject has positive attitudes, motivations, and expectancies toward the test situation (that is, if he views his responding to test suggestions as interesting or worthwhile and desires to, tries to, and believes that he can experience those things that are suggested), he (a) will think with (subvocally verbalize to himself) the statements of the experimenter, (b) will imagine those things that are suggested, and (c) will perform the suggested behaviors and experience the suggested effects.[9]

How does thinking with the suggestions and imagining those things described lead to the overt behaviors and the subjective experiences that have been traditionally associated with the word "hypnosis"? An important paper by Arnold (1946) provided a preliminary answer to this question.

First, Arnold pointed out that words are symbols that stand for the situation or activity to which they refer. As we hear words or speak them to ourselves, the experience to which the words refer tends to be reinstated in a fragmentary way. When a situation is described verbally, we tend to visualize ourselves or feel ourselves in the situation and to reexperience our attitudes and reactions in the situation.

Secondly, Arnold pointed out that thinking about and vividly imagining a

9. To simplify the discussion, I am emphasizing only the extremes of a continuum, that is, I am focusing only on the extreme negative end or positive end of a continuum of attitudes, motivations, and expectancies toward the test situation. Of course, most subjects are not at the extreme ends of the continuum; most subjects have neither extremely negative nor extremely positive attitudes, motivations, and expectancies, and they show neither very high nor very low response to test suggestions.

suggested movement or activity tends to bring about that activity. Arnold referred to the experiments of E. Jacobson (1930, 1932), which showed that an imagined movement (for example, imagining bending an arm) results in electromyographic activity in the flexor muscles of the arm. If the muscles are relaxed when the subject begins to imagine, these slight muscle contractions occur only in the limb that is imagined as being moved and do not occur in other limbs. Schultz (1932), Hull (1933), Arnold (1946), Mordey (1960), and other investigators have shown that these tiny muscular contractions that are produced when the subject imagines a movement may at times increase up to the point where they result in observable movements. In these experiments, subjects were asked to imagine that they were falling backward or forward, that an arm was moving, or that a Chevreul pendulum (which they held by two fingers of one hand) was moving to the right or left. With very few exceptions, subjects who imagined the movement tended to move either slightly or markedly in the imagined direction. In general, subjects who reported that they imagined the most vividly showed the most marked movements in the imagined direction. It is important to emphasize here that "The experience of 'intention,' of 'willing,' is . . . absent from these imagined movements" (Arnold, 1946, p. 111).

Sarbin (1950) has pointed out that "Common experience verifies the same notion [concerning the effects of imagining]. In imagining a former embarrassing situation we can feel our ears reddening and our faces flushing; in imagining a former painful experience we may involuntarily withdraw from the direction of the imagined stimulus, or in imagining something extremely unpleasant or disgusting we may experience nausea" (p. 266). In line with these assertions are a series of experimental studies, which indicate that vividly imagining a sensation can produce physiological changes associated with the actual sensation. For example, Schultz (1926) found that relaxed subjects who imagined that a hand was exposed to heat tended to experience a sensation of warmth associated (in 15 of 18 subjects) with an objectively measurable rise in skin temperature (up to 2° C. above normal). Conversely, imagining the forehead to be cool was associated in some subjects (5 of 14) with a fall in the temperature of the forehead, presumably produced by contraction of the superficial blood vessels.

Along similar lines, Harano, Ogawa, and Naruse (1965) instructed subjects to repeat to themselves and to concentrate on the phrase, "My arms are warm." When repeating and focusing on these words, the subjects generally showed a change in the felt warmth of the arms, an increase in the surface temperature of the arms, and an increase in the blood volume of the arms. The same investigators found that there were no significant subjective or objective changes in the temperature of the arms when the subjects tried purposively to raise the temperature of the arms without vividly imagining that the arms were warm. As Richardson (1969) reminds us, the results presented by Harano, Ogawa, and Naruse are in line with the contention of

Coué (1922) that "To make good suggestions it is absolutely necessary to do it *without effort* . . . the use of the *will* . . . must be entirely put aside. One must have recourse exclusively to the imagination" (Richardson, 1969, p. 10).

Menzies (1941) and Hadfield (1920) also presented data indicating that some individuals show vasodilation and a rise in skin temperature when instructed to imagine or to think of a limb as warm, and show vasoconstriction and a drop in skin temperature when thinking about or vividly imagining a limb as cold. Although other studies, summarized by Luthe (1970, pp. 50–57), failed to replicate the indicated relationship, the positive results indicate that, in at least some subjects, vividly imagining heat (or cold) is associated with a measurable rise (or fall) in skin temperature.

In a series of studies (Barber, 1965a), summarized earlier in this chapter, control subjects were asked to imagine that the right arm was becoming heavy and then were given repeated suggestions that it was becoming heavy ("Imagine that your right arm is feeling heavier and heavier. . . . It's becoming heavier and heavier. . ."). Similarly, each control subject was asked to imagine that his left arm was becoming light, his clasped hands were stuck together, he was very thirsty, his throat was rigid and he could not say his name, and he was stuck in the chair and could not get up. As Table 5.1, column 1, shows, more than one-fourth of these control subjects who were asked to imagine the suggested effects passed each of the test-suggestions both objectively and subjectively, that is, they experienced arm heaviness, arm lightness, hand lock, thirst hallucination, verbal inhibition, and body immobility.[10]

Recent studies (Spanos, 1971; Spanos & Barber, in press) probed more intensively into the relationship between imagining or fantasying and responding to test suggestions. In the first study, Spanos worked with 24 female subjects, of whom approximately half were highly responsive to test suggestions. Before beginning the experimental session, Spanos told each subject individually:

> I am interested in what is going on in people's minds when they are hypnotized. I'm interested in what they are thinking, imagining, feeling, and saying to themselves during hypnosis. In this experiment I am going to hypnotize you and ask you to carry out some suggestions. After each suggestion, while you are still hypnotized, I'll ask you to tell me what was passing through your mind while you were carrying out the suggestion. In giving me your answer it's very important that you be honest and tell me everything that was

10. In the same experiments, the control subjects were also given suggestions for "posthynoticlike" response and selective amnesia. However, they were not given instructions to imagine these suggested effects. Instead, they were simply told that they would carry out the postexperimental response and would forget one of the preceding test suggestions.

passing through your mind—everything that you were thinking, imagining, feeling and saying to yourself—even if you think it silly or unimportant (p. 88).

A trance induction procedure was then administered and the subject was given test suggestions (for arm levitation, limb rigidity, and selective amnesia, for example). Immediately after responding to the first test suggestion, and also immediately after responding to each of the subsequent test suggestions, the subject was asked to report what was passing through her mind during the time she was responding. In most instances, the subjects who experienced the suggested effects stated that, when they were responding to the suggestions, they were imagining in a specific way; namely, they were imagining a situation which, if it actually transpired, would result in the behavior that was suggested. Typical examples of this type of imagining, which Spanos labeled "goal-directed fantasy," were:

1. A subject who experienced suggested arm heaviness reported: "I imagined that there were all kinds of rocks tied to my arm. It felt heavy and I could feel it going down."
2. A subject who experienced suggested arm levitation reported: "I imagined that my arm was hollow, there was nothing in it, and somebody was putting air into it."
3. A subject who passed the suggestion to forget the number 4 (selective amnesia) stated that she first pictured the numbers in a row (1, 2, 3, 4, 5, and so on up to 10), and then she pictured taking the number 4 out and, finally, she pictured the numbers 1, 2, 3, 5, and so on up to 10 with a blank space where the number 4 was formerly.

In a second experiment (Spanos & Barber, in press), 40 female subjects who had not previously participated in a hypnotic experiment were randomly assigned to four experimental groups with 10 subjects to each group. All subjects were exposed to a trance induction procedure, were given a test suggestion for arm levitation (worded differently for each of the four experimental groups), and then were asked to report what was passing through their minds when they were responding to the test suggestions. The subjects' reports were scored for the presence or absence of goal-directed fantasy. (These judgments could be made easily and reliably by two independent raters who agreed in every instance; for example, it was clear that the following type of report should be scored as a goal-directed fantasy: "I imagined a balloon tied to my arm and the balloon was slowly rising.") The subjects who passed the test suggestion also completed a Likert-type scale that asked them to state whether they attributed the arm levitation to their own voluntary effort ("I only had the experience of causing it [the arm] to rise") or whether they considered it an involuntary occurrence ("I experienced it rising completely by itself"). In those subjects who showed arm levitation, goal-directed fantasy and the experience of volition were related as follows:

of those who reported a goal-directed fantasy, none stated that they experienced the arm rising as volitional; while of those who did not report a goal-directed fantasy, 60 per cent stated that they experienced the arm rising as volitional. In brief, if a subject carries out a goal-directed fantasy when given a suggestion—that is, if he imagines a situation which, if it actually transpired, would result in the suggested effect—he tends to feel that his response to the suggestion is involuntary (reporting, for example, "My arm rose by itself").

Let us now summarize the data presented in this section and in the preceding one:

1. Studies that used subjects' self-ratings to assess either their attitudes, or motivations, or expectancies toward the test situation generally found small but significant relations between each of these variables and response to test suggestions.

2. Studies that experimentally manipulated attitudes, motivations, and expectancies in various combinations found a marked enhancement of response to test suggestions when an attempt was made to induce positive attitudes, motivations, and expectancies toward the test situation, and a marked reduction in response when an attempt was made to induce negative attitudes, motivations, and expectancies.

3. An underlying assumption or axiom of the alternative paradigm is that when a subject has positive attitudes, motivations, and expectancies toward the test situation he thinks along with and imagines those things that are suggested.

4. A series of experimental studies indicates that thinking along with and vividly imagining those things that are suggested tends to produce both the overt response and the subjective experience that is suggested.

5. Two recent studies indicate that subjects experience suggested effects, such as arm levitation, as occurring nonvolitionally when they imagine a situation which, if it objectively transpired, would produce the suggested behavior, for example, they imagine a rising balloon tied to the arm, which is lifting the arm up.

### *Tangible Antecedent Variables*

In this chapter, I have focused on the intervening variables (subjects' attitudes, motivations, expectancies, and cognitive processes) that mediate response to test suggestions. In other papers and books (Barber, 1969a, 1969b, 1970a) I have focused primarily on denotable antecedent variables that are functionally related to subjects' overt and subjective responses.

There appear to be at least three important antecedent variables that directly affect how subjects report their experiences:

1. The wording of the questions used to elicit the subjective reports (Barber, Dalal, & Calverley, 1968).

2. Whether or not honest subjective reports are demanded (K. S. Bowers, 1967; Spanos & Barber, 1968).

3. Whether the subjective reports are elicited by the experimenter or by another person (K. S. Bowers, 1967; Spanos & Barber, 1968).

Other tangible antecedent variables appear to affect subjects' overt and subjective responsiveness to test suggestions by first affecting their attitudes, motivations, and expectancies, and their willingness to think with and imagine the suggested effects. These antecedent variables include the following:

1. How the situation is defined to the subject (as a test of imagination, as a test of gullibility, as "hypnosis," etc.) (Barber, 1969b).

2. Whether preexperimental instructions that aim to alter the subjects' attitudes, motivations, and expectancies toward the test situation are administered.

3. Whether the test suggestions are worded in a permissive or authoritarian manner, for example, "Try to forget" versus "You will forget," or "Try to dream on a specified topic" versus "You will dream on the topic" (Barber, 1966b).

4. Whether the test suggestions are given in a firm or lackadaisical tone of voice (Barber & Calverley, 1964a).

5. Whether the subject has been repeatedly assessed on response to the same test suggestions in previous sessions (Barber & Calverley, 1966c).

6. Whether the subject volunteered to participate in the experiment or was coerced (Boucher & Hilgard, 1962).

7. Whether the subject's performance was observed by an audience (Coe, 1966).

8. Whether the subject was provided with a clear conception of the experience that was desired and was given verbal reinforcement for each appropriate response (Giles, 1962; Sachs & Anderson, 1967).

9. If the situation is defined as hypnosis, whether an attempt was made to remove the subjects' misconceptions and fears about hypnosis (Cronin, Spanos, & Barber, 1971; Macvaugh, 1969).

The effects of these nine antecedent variables can be more satisfactorily explained by the alternative paradigm than by the traditional (trance) paradigm. For instance, it is difficult to conceive how suggestions for amnesia worded in different ways have any relevance whatsoever to whether the subject enters, remains in, or goes deeper into a state (trance) that is fundamentally different from ordinary states of consciousness. However, it is not at all difficult to see how permissive suggestions for amnesia ("Try to forget") are more effective than authoritarian suggestions ("You will forget") in motivating the subject to put the previous occurrences "out of mind" (Barber & Calverley, 1966b). Similarly, it is difficult to conceive how the experimenter's tone of voice (firm or lackadaisical) in administering test suggestions for arm heaviness, inability to unclasp hands, and so forth, is relevant to whether the subject enters, remains in, or goes deeper into a special state (trance). However, since subjects who received test suggestions in a lackadaisical tone of voice tended to report that they thought the experimenter did not expect them to respond to the test suggestions, it is not difficult to conceive how the tone of voice used to administer test suggestions might affect the subjects' attitudes, motivations, or expectancies toward the test situation (Barber & Calverley, 1964a). The trance paradigm might be able to explain why subjects exposed in repeated sessions to the same test suggestions showed a continual reduction in responsiveness. However, the alternative paradigm is more consistent with the empirical data, since subjects participating in these repeated sessions testified that they became bored and lost interest, and this change in attitude was correlated with their reduced responsiveness (Barber & Calverley, 1966c). Similarly, the trance paradigm might explain the effects of some of the other antecedent variables listed above; for example, it might explain why coerced subjects are less responsive to test suggestions than volunteers (Boucher & Hilgard, 1962), why subjects are less responsive when they believe they are being observed by an audience (Coe, 1966), and why verbal reinforcement for each appropriate response enhances subsequent responses to test-suggestions (Giles, 1962; Sachs & Anderson, 1967). However, without belaboring the point and going into further details, it should be clear that these antecedent variables can be more satisfactorily conceptualized as affecting subjects' attitudes, motivations, and expectancies toward the test situation and their willingness to think with and imagine the suggested effects.

The antecedent variables listed above are functionally related to the dependent variable we have labeled "response to test suggestions." A few of the above-mentioned variables also overlap with other antecedent variables to determine response on two additional dependent variables: whether and to what degree subjects (a) manifest a trancelike appearance and (b) report that they were "hypnotized."

As implied previously in this chapter, whether subjects who are highly responsive to test suggestions appear to be in "hypnosis" (that is, manifest trancelike characteristics such as a limp posture, passivity, a blank stare, rigid facial expression, and so forth) is dependent primarily on two tangible antecedent variables, namely, whether the situation was defined to the subjects as "hypnosis" and whether or not they were asked to close their eyes. If the situation is not defined as "hypnosis," but in some other way—as a "test of imagination," for example—and if the subjects are not asked to close their eyes, very few if any subjects who are highly responsive to test suggestions for limb rigidity, analgesia, age regression, amnesia, and so forth, manifest a trancelike appearance. If the situation is defined to the subjects as "hypnosis" and they are told to close their eyes, then whether and to what extent the subjects manifest a trancelike appearance is functionally related to such antecedent variables as (a) their preconceptions of what "hypnosis" is supposed to involve, (b) their preexperimental attitudes toward whatever they conceive "hypnosis" to be, (c) their preexperimental expectations concerning their own performance, (d) the suggestions they receive (implicit suggestions to be passive, or repeated suggestions that they are becoming relaxed, drowsy, sleepy, and are entering hypnosis), and (e) whether the experimenter, at some point, speaks to them along the following lines: "Wake up, stop acting as if you are in a trance, and continue to respond to my suggestions" (Barber, 1969b; Barber & Calverley, 1969b).

Whether subjects who are highly responsive to test suggestions report that they were in "hypnosis" is also dependent primarily on two tangible antecedent variables, namely, whether the situation was defined to the subjects as "hypnosis" and whether they were told to close their eyes. If the situation is not defined to the subjects as "hypnosis" and they are not told to close their eyes, very few if any subjects who show a high level of response to test-suggestions state that they are in hypnosis. If the situation is defined as "hypnosis" and the subjects are told to close their eyes, the antecedent variables that determine whether the subjects will report that they were in "hypnosis" to some degree or were not "hypnotized" at all include (a) their preconceptions of what "hypnosis" is supposed to involve, (b) their preexperimental expectations of their own performance, (c) whether they received repeated suggestions that they were becoming relaxed, drowsy, sleepy, and were entering a hypnotic state, (d) whether they observed that they were or were not responsive to test suggestions, (e) whether the experimenter stated or implied that he believed they were or were not hypnotized, and (f) the wording and tone of the questions used to elicit their reports (Barber, 1969a; Barber & Calverley, 1969b; Barber, Dalal, & Calverley, 1968).[11]

11. As noted above, whether a subject who is highly responsive to test suggestions manifests trancelike characteristics and whether he reports that he was "hypnotized" is dependent, in part, on whether he was told repeatedly that he was becoming relaxed, drowsy, sleepy, and was entering a hypnotic state. Repeated suggestions of this type (relaxation, drowsiness, etc.) may also affect the subjects' performance on other variables, for example, they may reduce their strength and endurance (Barber & Calverley, 1964f) and they may change their responses to projective tests, such as the Rorschach or TAT, in the direction expected when a person is relaxed or sleepy. However, whether repeated suggestions that the subject is becoming relaxed, drowsy, sleepy, and is entering hypnosis influence the subjects' responsiveness to test suggestions of analgesia, hallucination, age regression, amnesia, etc. depends primarily on how they affect subjects' attitudes, motivations, and expectancies toward the test situation. I have noted (unpublished observations) that a substantial proportion of individuals, especially those who are relatively uneducated, are anxious or fearful with respect to whatever they think "hypnosis" is supposed to be. When these individuals receive repeated suggestions that they are becoming relaxed, drowsy, sleepy, and are entering hypnosis, they seem to have negative attitudes, motivations, and expectancies toward the test situation and they perform less well on test suggestions than they would have if they had not received such repeated suggestions. Most college students, however, are eager

In brief, the dependent variables (response to test suggestions, trancelike appearance, and reports of having been hypnotized) are functionally related to the many denotable antecedent variables mentioned above and also to other tangible variables that have been discussed elsewhere (Dalal, 1966; McPeake, 1968; Nichols, 1968; Richman, 1965; Spanos, 1970; Spanos & Chaves, 1970). In fact, these behaviors and experiences appear to be as complexly determined as any behaviors and experiences that psychologists have ever attempted to study. Although the antecedent variables are many and complex, a substantial number of them can be viewed as converging on a set of mediating variables that we have called attitudes, motivations, and expectancies toward the test situation and thinking with and imagining the suggested effects. These mediating variables are part and parcel of normal psychology, especially of present-day social psychology. They mediate behavior and experiences in a wide variety of situations; for instance, they mediate the experiences of the member of the audience who is listening to an orator, or who is observing a motion picture, a stage play, or a television show. It is misleading to subsume these mediating variables, which are an integral part of normal psychology, under a construct ("trance," "hypnosis," or "hypnotic trance") that derives from the psychology of the abnormal, that has been historically loaded with surplus connotations (including the connotation that the person resembles the sleepwalker), and that is used to refer to a special state basically different from ordinary states of consciousness.

### *Résumé and Prospects*

As Kuhn (1962) pointed out, a change in scientific paradigm is preceded by a period in which research yields data that do not fit into the prevailing paradigm. Recent research has produced data incongruous with the prevalent trance paradigm. Some of the anomalous data include:

1. Some individuals are very responsive, both overtly and subjectively, to test suggestions when they are tested under a base level (control) condition (without any special instructions). Also, when unselected subjects are simply exposed to brief instructions intended to produce positive attitudes, motivations, and expectancies toward the test situation ("task-motivational instructions"), they are about as responsive to test suggestions for body immobility, hallucination, age regression, analgesia, amnesia, etc. as unselected subjects who have been exposed to a procedure of the type traditionally

---

to experience whatever they think "hypnosis" is supposed to be. Consequently, when given repeated suggestions of relaxation, drowsiness, sleep, and entering hypnosis, they seem to have positive attitudes, motivations, and expectancies toward the test situation and they perform better on test suggestions than they would have if they had not received such repeated suggestions.

termed a "trance induction" and who are, presumably, in a hypnotic trance. The trance paradigm could not have predicted these results and it requires ad hoc assumptions in order to explain them. It has to assume, after the fact, that highly responsive control subjects or task-motivated subjects who have not been exposed to a trance-induction procedure, who do not appear to be in a trance, and who do not think they are in a trance are actually in a hypnotic trance.

2. The anomaly mentioned above appeared earlier in the work of hypnotic state theorists such as Erickson. To maintain the logic of the trance paradigm, Erickson was compelled to contend that some subjects are in a deep hypnotic trance even when they do not think they are in a trance, are judged by psychologists and psychiatrists as being in a normal waking state, and are even judged by Erickson himself as being "seemingly awake and functioning . . . in a manner similar to that of a nonhypnotized person operating at the waking level" (Erickson, 1967a, p. 13). Why was Erickson compelled to categorize subjects as being in a deep hypnotic trance even though the subjects appeared, to objective observers and to themselves, to be normally awake? Because Erickson was certain that the subjects would respond to his suggestions. This logic led to another serious anomaly for the trance paradigm: subjects were judged to be in a hypnotic trance because they would show high response to test suggestions and, turning around circularly, the high response to test-suggestions was explained as due to the presence of hypnotic trance (Barber, 1964a).

3. Since all investigators conceive of the human organism as a psychophysiological unity, special states of the organism are expected to have some physiological concomitants. For more than 50 years, investigators have been trying to find a physiological concomitant or index of the presumed special state labeled "hypnosis" or "trance." Not only have they failed to unearth any special physiological change associated with the presumed special state, but they have also consistently found that physiological functioning during the postulated special state varies in the same way as in nonspecial or ordinary states. Of course, many failures over many years to find a physiological index does not prove that such an index does not exist or will never be found. Nevertheless, consistent findings that physiological functions during the presumed special state vary in the same way as in nonspecial states are becoming more and more anomalous for the trance paradigm as time goes on.

A traditional paradigm is not overthrown simply because some of the relevant data are incongruous with it (Kuhn, 1962). In addition to pointing out data that are anomalous for the traditional formulation, an alternative paradigm must also be able to explain all of the relevant phenomena at least as well if not better than the traditional one. The underlying contention of this chapter has been that the alternative paradigm, which has had a rather brief period of development (Barber, 1961b, 1964a, 1967, 1969b, 1970a;

Barber & Calverley, 1962; Sarbin, 1950, 1956, 1962, 1964; Sarbin & Anderson, 1967; Sarbin & Coe, in press), can explain the relevant phenomena more satisfactorily than the trance paradigm which has had more than a hundred years of development. Specifically, this chapter has shown how the alternative paradigm explains not only the "amazing" phenomena of stage hypnosis, such as, the human-plank feat, stopping the pulse in the arm, and performance by the subject of weird antics such as dancing with an invisible partner, but also explains the following phenomena that can be elicited by suggestions in experimental or clinical situations: production of blisters, removal of warts, analgesia, age regression, age-progression, visual and auditory hallucinations, deafness, trancelike characteristics, difficulty or delay in coming out of trance, suggested and also spontaneous amnesia, and trance logic. These phenomena, which were explained in this chapter from the alternative paradigm, were not selected at random. On the contrary, they were selected as representing the strongholds of the trance paradigm—as representing the phenomena that had been universally accepted as explainable only by positing a special state of the organism.

Looking to the future, I will venture four predictions:

1. As more investigators adopt the alternative paradigm, the kinds of questions that are asked and the focus of research will change. Instead of asking what the most effective methods for inducing a deep hypnotic trance are or how the hypnotic state differs from the waking state, researchers will ask questions such as the following:

a. What kinds of instructions are most effective in eliciting positive attitudes, motivations, and expectancies toward the test situation?

b. Are all three factors—positive attitudes, positive motivations, positive expectancies—equally necessary for high response to test suggestions? How does a subject respond to test suggestions when he believes it is interesting and worthwhile to be responsive (positive attitude), when he tries to experience those things that are suggested (positive motivation), but when he does not believe that he can experience either a specific suggested effect, such as visual hallucination or amnesia, or all of those things that are suggested (negative expectancies)? A rather large number of additional questions can be formulated along similar lines. For instance, how does a subject respond to test suggestions when he believes he can experience the suggested effects (positive expectancy) but he has negative attitudes and motivations toward the test situation?

c. How can subjects be helped to imagine vividly those things that are suggested?

d. How can subjects be given practice in thinking with suggestions? Stated somewhat differently, how can they be given practice in covertly verbalizing the suggestions to themselves while, at the same time, inhibiting contrary thoughts such as "This suggestion won't work," or "It's impossible to experience this [suggested effect]"?

2. As the alternative paradigm becomes accepted by more researchers, the kind of response to test suggestions that has been traditionally subsumed under the term "hypnosis" will no longer be viewed as closely related to abnormal phenomena such as sleepwalking and fugue states (Gill & Brenman, 1959). Instead, the processes involved in responding to test suggestions will be analyzed in a similar manner as, and will be found partially to overlap with, such social psychological influence processes as conformity, attitude change, and persuasion (Barnlund, 1968; Bettinghaus, 1968; Hartley & Hartley, 1958, pp. 15–158; McGuire, 1969; Secord & Backman, 1964, pp. 93–231). The recent formulation by Sarbin and Coe (in press), which subsumes "hypnotic" behavior under the psychology of influence communication, will be viewed as a major turning point in this area. I will also venture to predict that, in the more distant future, a unified theory of social influence processes will be used to explain not only conformity, attitude change, and persuasion but also responses to test suggestions and other types of responses that were previously thought to be associated with a qualitatively distinct state (trance).

3. Conceptions of *normal human abilities* or "human potentialities" (Otto, 1966) will be markedly broadened when the subject who is responsive to communications (test suggestions) from an experimenter is seen to be as normal and as awake as the member of the audience who is responsive to communications from the actors. Investigators will no longer think in terms of rare individuals ("somnambulists") who possess unusual capacities, who differ in some basic way from other human beings, who are able to enter a special state ("deep somnambulistic trance"), and who are able to have experiences that other human beings find it very difficult if not impossible to have. On the contrary, investigators will think in terms of a wide range of normal human abilities that can be manifested when individuals adopt positive attitudes, motivations, and expectancies toward the test situation. These abilities, which will be viewed as within the normal human repertoire, will include: the ability to perform feats such as the human-plank feat; the ability to control or block pain (analgesia) by thinking of other things or by thinking of the sensations as sensations; the ability to imagine and to visualize vividly (hallucination and suggested dream); the ability to imagine or fantasy events that occurred at an earlier time (age regression) or that may occur in the future (age progression); and the ability to block or stop thinking about earlier events (amnesia).

4. As Chaves (1968) has pointed out, attempts have already been made to subsume the alternative paradigm under the traditional (trance) paradigm. I expect that further attempts will be made along these lines (Kuhn, 1962). That is, adherents of the traditional paradigm may contend that hypnotic trance (or hypnosis or hypnotic state) refers to (or is) positive attitudes, motivations, and expectancies and thinking with and imagining the suggested effects. To be consistent, adherents of the traditional para-

digm may also contend that all procedures, instructions, and experimental manipulations that aim to produce positive attitudes, motivations, etc—for example, task-motivational instructions (Barber & Calverley, 1962), or having the subject first observe another person who is highly responsive to test suggestions (Klinger, 1970)—are actually trance induction procedures. Also, to be consistent, they may contend that the member of the audience who is laughing, crying, empathizing, and so on, as he receives communications from the actors, is also in a hypnotic trance. These contentions will change the meaning of the term "hypnotic trance"; the term will no longer refer to a special state basically different from ordinary states of consciousness. Of course, such attempts to change the meaning of the central construct (trance) will be self-defeating for the traditional paradigm. Since the construct "hypnotic trance" (or "hypnosis" or "hypnotic state") has always referred to some kind of basic, qualitative change in the organism and has accreted many associated connotations (including connotations of somnambulism or sleepwalking), attempts to give it a new meaning and new connotations will lead to confusion rather than clarity and, sooner or later, the construct and its many associated assumptions will be viewed as a historical curiosity by students of human behavior.

## References

Andersen, M. L. Correlates of hypnotic performance: An historical and role-theoretical analysis. Unpublished doctoral dissertation, University of California, Berkeley, 1963.

Anderson, M. N. Hypnosis in anesthesia. Journal of the Medical Association of the State of Alabama, 1957, 27, 121-125.

Arnold, Magda B. On the mechanism of suggestion and hypnosis. Journal of Abnormal and Social Psychology, 1946, 41, 107-128.

Arons, H. How to Routine an Ethical Hypnotic Lecture-Demonstration. Irvington, N. J.: Power Publishers, 1961.

Ascher, L. M., & Barber, T. X. An attempted replication of the Parrish-Lundy-Leibowitz study on hypnotic age-regression. Harding, Mass.: The Medfield Foundation, 1968.

August, R. V. Hypnosis in Obstetrics. New York: McGraw-Hill, 1961.

Barber, T. X. Hypnosis as perceptual-cognitive restructuring: III. From somnambulism to autohypnosis. Journal of Psychology, 1957, 44, 299-304.

Barber, T. X. Toward a theory of pain: Relief of chronic pain by prefrontal leucotomy, opiates, placebos, and hypnosis. Psychological Bulletin, 1959b, 56, 430-460.

Barber, T. X. Experimental evidence for a theory of hypnotic behavior: II. Experimental controls in hypnotic age-regression. International Journal of Clinical and Experimental Hypnosis, 1961a, 9, 181-193.

Barber, T. X. Physiological effects of "hypnosis." Psychological Bulletin, 1961b, 58, 390-419.

Barber, T. X. Hypnotic age regression: A critical review. Psychosomatic Medicine, 1962a, 24, 286-299.

Barber, T. X. Toward a theory of hypnosis: Post-hypnotic behavior. Archives of General Psychiatry, 1962b, 7, 321-342.

Barber, T. X. The effects of "hypnosis" on pain: A critical review of experimental and clinical findings. Psychosomatic Medicine, 1963, 25, 303-333.

Barber, T. X. "Hypnosis" as a causal variable in present-day psychology: A critical analysis. Psychological Reports, 1964a, 14, 839-842.

Barber, T. X. Hypnotic "colorblindness," "blindness," and "deafness": (A review of research findings). Diseases of the Nervous System, 1964b, 25, 529-538.

Barber, T. X. Toward a theory of "hypnotic" behavior: Positive visual and auditory hallucinations. Psychological Record, 1964c, 14, 197-210.

Barber, T. X. Measuring "hypnotic-like" suggestibility with and without "hypnotic induction"; psychometric properties, norms, and variables influencing response to the Barber Suggestibility Scale (BSS). Psychological Reports, 1965a, 16, 809-844.

Barber, T. X. Physiological effects of "hypnotic suggestions": A critical review of recent research (1960-64). Psychological Bulletin, 1965b, 63, 201-222.

Barber, T. X. "Hypnotic" phenomena: A critique of experimental methods. In J. E. Gordon (Ed.), 1967, pp. 440-480.

Barber, T. X. An empirically-based formulation of hypnotism. American Journal of Clinical Hypnosis, 1969a, 12, 100-130.

Barber, T. X. Hypnosis: A Scientific Approach. New York: Van Nostrand-Reinhold Co., 1969b.

Barber, T. X. LSD, Marihuana, Yoga, and Hypnosis. Chicago: Aldine Publishing Co., 1970a.

Barber, T. X. The phenomenology of ('hypnotic') suggestibility. Harding, Mass.: The Medfield Foundation, 1970b.

Barber, T. X., & Calverley, D. S. "Hypnotic behavior" as a function of task motivation. Journal of Psychology, 1962, 54, 363-389.

Barber, T. X., & Calverley, D. S. Effect of E's tone of voice on "hypnotic-like" suggestibility. Psychological Reports, 1964a, 15, 139-144.

Barber, T. X., & Calverley, D. S. Experimental studies in "hypnotic" behavior: Suggested deafness evaluated by delayed auditory feedback. British Journal of Psychology, 1964c, 55, 439-466.

Barber, T. X., & Calverley, D. S. The definition of the situation as a variable affecting "hypnotic'like" suggestibility. Journal of Clinical Psychology, 1964d, 20, 438-440.

Barber, T. X., & Calverley, D. S. Toward a theory of hypnotic behavior: Effects on suggestibility of defining the situation as hypnosis and defining response to suggestions as easy. Journal of Abnormal and Social Psychology, 1964e, 68, 585-592.

Barber, T. X., & Calverley, D. S. Toward a theory of "hypnotic" behavior: Enhancement of strength and endurance. Canadian Journal of Psychology, 1964f, 18, 156-167.

Barber, T. X., & Calverley, D. S. Empirical evidence for a theory of hypnotic behavior: Effects on suggestibility of five variables typically included in hypnotic induction procedures. Journal of Consulting Psychology, 1965, 29, 98-107.

Barber, T. X., & Calverley, D. S. Effects on recall of hypnotic induction, motivational suggestions, and suggested regression: A methodological and experimental analysis. Journal of Abnormal Psychology, 1966a, 71, 169-180.

Barber, T. X., & Calverley, D. S. Toward a theory of "hypnotic" behavior: Experimental analyses of suggested amnesia. Journal of Abnormal Psychology, 1966b, 71, 95-107.

Barber, T. X., & Calverley D. S. Toward a theory of hypnotic behavior: Experimental evaluation of Hull's postulate that hypnotic susceptibility is a habit phenomenon. Journal of Personality, 1966c 34, 416-433.

Barber, T. X., & Calverley, D. S. Toward a theory of "hypnotic" behavior: Replication and extension of experiments by Barber and co-workers (1962-65) and Hilgard and Tart (1966). International Journal of Clinical and Experimental Hypnosis, 1968, 16, 179-195.

Barber, T. X., & Calverley, D. S. Effects of hypnotic induction, suggestions of anesthesia, and distraction on subjective and physiological responses to pain. Paper presented at Eastern Psychological Association, Annual Meeting, Philadelphia, April, 1969a.

Barber, T. X., & Calverley, D. S. Multidimensional

analysis of "hypnotic" behavior. Journal of Abnormal Psychology, 1969b, 74, 209-220.

Barber, T. X., Dalal, A. S., & Calverley, D. S. The subjective reports of hypnotic subjects. American Journal of Clinical Hypnosis, 1968, 11, 74-88.

Barber, T. X., & Hahn, K. W., Jr. Physiological and subjective responses to pain producing stimulation under hypnotically-suggested and waking-imagined "analgesia." Journal of Abnormal and Social Psychology, 1962, 65, 411-418.

Barnlund, D. C. Interpersonal Communication: Survey and Studies. Boston: Houghton Mifflin, 1968

Beecher, H. K. Measurement of Subjective Responses: Quantitative effects of drugs. New York: Oxford University Press, 1959.

Bernstein, M. The Search for Bridy Murphy. New York: Double day, 1956.

Best, H. L., & Michaels, R. M. Living out "future" experience under hypnosis. Science, 1954, 120, 1077.

Bettinghaus, E. P. Persuasive Communication. New York: Holt, Rinehart & Winston, 1968.

Bloch, B. Über die Heilung der Warzen durch Suggestion. Klinische Wochenschrift, 1927, 2, 2271-2275; 2320-2325.

Borelli, S. Psychische Einflüsse, und reactive Hauterscheinungen. Münchener Medizinische Wochenschrift, 1953, 95, 1078-1082.

Boucher, R. G., & Hilgard, E. R. Volunteer bias in hypnotic experimentation. American Journal of Clinical Hypnosis, 1962, 5, 49-51.

Bowers, K. S. Hypnotic behavior: The differentiation of trance and demand characteristic variables. Journal of Abnormal Psychology, 1966, 71, 42-51.

Bowers, K. S. The effect of demands for honesty on reports of visual and auditory hallucinations. International Journal of Clinical and Experimental Hypnosis, 1967, 15, 31-36.

Brady, J. P., & Levitt, E. E. Hypnotically induced visual hallucinations. Psychosomatic Medicine, 1966, 28, 351-363.

Braginsky, B. M., Braginsky, D. D., & Ring, K. Methods of Madness: The Mental Hospital as a Last Resort. New York: Holt, Rinehart & Winston, 1969.

Braid, J. Facts and observations as to the relative value of mesmeric and hypnotic coma, and ethereal narcotism, for the mitigation or entire prevention of pain during surgical operations. Medical Times, 1847, 15, 381-382.

Burr, C. W. The reflexes of early infancy. British Journal of Children's Disease, 1921, 18, 152-153.

Butler, B. The use of hypnosis in the care of the cancer patient. Cancer, 1954, 7, 1-14.

'Calostro,' Entertaining with Hypnotism. Closter, N. J.: Calostro Publications, 1949.

Chaves, J. F. Hypnosis reconceptualized: An overview of Barber's theoretical and empirical work. Psychological Reports, 1968, 22, 587-608.

Chertok, L. Psychosomatic Methods in Painless Childbirth: History, Theory and Practice. Foreward by R. G. Douglas. Translated from the 2nd French edition by D. Leigh. New York: Pergamon Press, 1959.

Chertok, L., & Kramarz, P. Hypnosis, sleep, and electroencephalography. Journal of Nervous and Mental Disease, 1959, 128, 227-238.

Clarke, G. H. V. The charming of warts. Journal of Investigative Dermatology, 1965, 45, 15-21.

Coe, W. C. Hypnosis as role enactment: The role demand variable. American Journal of Clinical Hypnosis, 1966, 8, 189-191.

Cogger, W. G., Jr., & Edmonston, W. E. Hypnosis and oral temperature: A re-evaluation of experimental techniques. International Journal of Clinical and Experimental Hypnosis, (in press).

Collins, J. K. Muscular endurance in normal and hypnotic states: A study of suggested catalepsy. Honors thesis, Department of Psychology, University of Sydney, Australia, 1961.

Coue, E. Self-Mastery through Conscious Autosuggestion. London: George Allen & Unwin, 1922.

Crasilneck, H. B., & Hall, J. A. Physiological changes associated with hypnosis: A review of the literature since 1948. International Journal of Clinical and Experimental Hypnosis, 1959, 7, 9-50.

Cronin, D. M., Spanos, N. P., & Barber, T. X. Augmenting hypnotic suggestibility by providing favorable information about hypnosis. American Journal of Clinical Hypnosis, 1971, 13, 259-264.

Dermen, D., & London, P. Correlates of hypnotic susceptibility. Journal of Consulting Psychology, 1965, 29, 537-545.

Dorcus, R. M., Brintnall, A. K., & Case, H. W. Control experiments and their relation to theories of hypnotism. Journal of General Psychology, 1941, 24, 217-221.

Dudek, Stephanie Z. Suggestion and play therapy in the cure of warts in children: A pilot study. Journal of Nervous and Mental Disease, 1967, 145, 37-42.

Dynes, J. B. An experimental study of hypnotic anaesthesia. Journal of Abnormal and Social Psychology, 1932, 27, 79-88.

Edmonston, W. E., Jr., & Robertson, T. G., Jr. A comparison of the effects of task motivational and hypnotic induction instructions on responsiveness to hypnotic suggestibility scales. American Journal of Clinical Hypnosis, 1967, 9, 184-187.

Elliotson, J. Numerous Cases of Surgical Operations without Pain in the Mesmeric State. London: H. Bailliere, 1843.

Erickson, M. H. A study of clinical and experimental findings on hypnotic deafness: I. Clinical experimentation and findings. Journal of General Psychology, 1938a, 19, 127-150.

Erickson, M. H. A study of Clinical and experimental findings on hypnotic deafness: II. Experimental findings with a conditioned response technique. Journal of General Psychology, 1938b, 19, 151-167.

Erickson, M. H. Hypnosis in painful terminal illness. American Journal of Clinical Hypnosis, 1958, 1, 117-121.

Erickson, M. H. Basic psychological problems in hypnosis research (and panel discussion). In G. H. Estabrooks (Ed.) Hypnosis: Current Problems. New York: Harper & Row, 1962, pp. 207-223, 238-272.

Erickson, M. H. Advanced Techniques of Hypnosis and Therapy: Selected Papers of Milton H. Erickson. (Edited by J. Haley) New York: Grune & Shatton, 1967a.

Erickson, M. H., Hershman, S., & Secter, I. I. The Practical Application of Medical and Dental Hypnosis. New York: Julian Press, 1961.

Esdaile, J. Mesmerism in India and Its Practical Application in Surgery and Medicine. London: Longman's, Green & Co., 1850. Reissued under title, Hypnosis in Medicine and Surgery. With introduction and supplementary reports on current applications by W. S. Kroger. New York: Julian Press, 1957.

Evans, F. J. The case of the disappearing hypnotist. Paper read at American Psychological Association Convention, New York, September, 1966. (a)

Evans, F. J. Recent trends in experimental hypnosis. Behavioral Science, 1968, 13, 477-487.

Fisher, S. Problems of interpretation and controls in hypnotic research. In G. H. Estabrooks (Ed.), Hypnosis: Current Problems. New York: Harper & Row, 1962, pp. 109-126.

Ganong, W. F. Review of Medical Physiology. (3rd edition) Los Altos, California: Lange Medical Publications, 1967.

Gibson, W. B. The Key to Hypnotism. New York: Key Publishing Co., 1956

Gidro-Frank, L., & Bowersbuch, M. K. A study of the plantar response in hypnotic age regression. Journal of Nervous and Mental Disease, 1948, 107, 443-458.

Giles, E. A cross-validation study of the Pascal technique of hypnotic induction. International Journal of Clinical and Experimental Hypnosis, 1962, 10, 101-108.

Gill, M. M., & Brenman, Margaret. Hypnosis and Related States: Psychoanalytic Studies in Regression. New York: International Universities Press, 1959.

Gordon, J. E. (Ed.) Handbook of Clinical and Experimental Hypnosis. New York: Macmillan, 1967.

Gorton, B. E. The physiology of hypnosis. I. Psychiatric Quarterly, 1949, 23, 317-343; The physiology of hypnosis II. Psychiatric Quarterly, 1949, 23, 457-485.

Graham, D. T., & Wolf, S. Pathogenesis of urticaria: Experimental study of life situations, emotions and cutaneous vascular reactions. Journal of the American Medical Association, 1950, 143, 1396-1402.

Hadfield, J. A. The influence of suggestion on body temperature. Lancet, 1920, 2, 68-69.

Hahn, K. W., Jr., & Barber, T. X. Hallucinations with and without hypnotic induction: An extension of the Brady & Levitt study. Harding, Mass.: The Medfield Foundation, 1966.

Haim E. Beitrag zur Frage der Sensibilität der Abdominalorgane. Zentralblatt für Chirurgie, 1908, 35, 337-338.

Hamel, I. A. A study and analysis of the conditioned reflex. Psychological Monographs, 1919, 27, No. 118, 1-65.

Harano, K., Ogawa, K., & Naruse, G. A study of plethysmography and skin temperature during active concentration and autogenic exercise. In W. Luthe, (Ed.), Autogenic Training, New York: Grune & Stratton, 1965, pp. 55-58.

Hartley, E. L., & Hartley, Ruth E. Fundamentals of Social Psychology. New York: Knopf, 1958.

Hilgard, E. R. Hypnotic Susceptibility. New York: Harcourt, Brace & World Inc., 1965b.

Hilgard, E. R. Posthypnotic amnesia: Experiments and theory. International Journal of Clinical and Experimental Hypnosis, 1966, 14, 104-111.

Hilgard, E. R. Altered states of awareness. Journal of Nervous and Mental Disease, 1969a, 149, 68-79.

Hilgard, E. R., Cooper, L. M., Lenox, J., Morgan, Arlene H., & Voevodsky, J. The use of pain-state reports in the study of hypnotic analgesia to the pain of ice water. Journal of Nervous and Mental Disease, 1967, 144, 506-513.

Hilgard, E. R., & Marquis, D. G. Conditioning and Learning. New York: Appleton-Century, 1940.

Hilgard, E. R., & Tart, C. T. Responsiveness to suggestions following waking and imagination instructions and following induction of hypnosis. Journal of Abnormal Psychology, 1966, 71, 196-208.

Hill, H. E., Kornetsky, C. H., Flanary, H. G., & Wikler, A. Effects of anxiety and morphine on discrimination of intensities of painful stimuli. Journal of Clinical Investigation, 1952a, 31, 473-480.

Hill, H. E., Kornetsky, C. H., Flanary, H. G., & Wikler, A. Studies on anxiety associated with anticipation of pain: I. Effects of morphine. Archives of Neurology and Psychiatry, 1952b, 67, 612-619.

Hull, C. L. Hypnosis and Suggestibility: An Experimental Approach. New York: Appleton-Century-Crofts, 1933.

Jacobson, E. Electrical measurements of neuromuscular states during mental activities: Imagination of movement involving skeletal muscle. American Journal of Physiology, 1930. 91, 567-608.

Jacobson, E. Electrophysiology of mental activities. American Journal of Psychology, 1932, 44, 677-694.

Jacobson, E. Progressive Relaxation. Chicago: University of Chicago Press, 1938.

Johnson, R. F. Q., Maher, B. A., & Barber, T. X. Artifact in the purported essence of hypnosis: An experimental and theoretical evaluation of trance logic. (In Press).

Kanfer, F. H., & Goldfoot, D. A. Self-control and tolerance of noxious stimulation. Psychological Reports, 1966, 18, 79-85.

Kelsey, Denys E. R. Phantasies of birth and prenatal experiences recovered from patients undergoing hypnoanalysis. Journal of Mental Science, 1953, 99, 216-223.

Kline, M. V. Hypnosis and age progression: A case report. Journal of Genetic Psychology, 1951, 78, 195-206.

Kline, M. V., Guze, H., & Haggerty, A. D. An experimental study of the nature of hypnotic deafness: Effects of delayed speech feed-back. Journal of Clinical and Experimental Hypnosis, 1954, 2, 145-156.

Klinger, B. I. Effect of peer model responsiveness and length of induction procedure on hypnotic responsiveness. Journal of Abnormal Psychology, 1970, 75, 15-18.

Klopp, K. K. Production of local anesthesia using waking suggestion with the child patient. International Journal of Clinical and Experimental Hypnosis, 1961, 9, 59-62.

Kornetsky, C. Effects of anxiety and morphine on the anticipation and perception of painful radiant thermal stimuli. Journal of Comparative Physiology and Psychology, 1954, 47, 130-132.

Kramer, E., & Tucker, G. R. Hypnotically suggested deafness and delayed auditory feedback. International Journal of Clinical and Experimental Hypnosis, 1967, 15, 37-43.

Kroger, W. S. Comprehensive management of obesity. American Journal of Clinical Hypnosis, 1970, 12, 165-176.

Kuhn, T. S. The Structure of Scientific Revolutions. Chicago: University of Chicago Press, 1962.

Leonard, J. R. An investigation of hypnotic age-regression. Unpublished doctoral dissertation, University of Kentucky, 1963.

Leriche, R. The Surgery of Pain. Baltimore: Williams & Wilkins, 1939.

Levitt, E. E., & Brady, J. P. Psychophysiology of hypnosis. In J. M. Schneck (Ed.), 1963a, pp. 314-362.

Lewis, T. The Blood Vessels of the Human Skin and their Responses. London: Shaw & Sons, 1927.

Lewis, T. Pain. New York: Macmillan, 1942.

Liebeault, A. A. Anesthesie par suggestion. Journal Magnetisme, 1885, 64-67.

London P., Cooper, L. M., & Johnson, H. J. Subject characteristics in hypnosis research: II. Attitudes towards hypnosis, volunteer status, and personality measures. III. Some correlates of hypnotic susceptibility. International Journal of Clinical and Experimental Hypnosis, 1962, 10, 13-21.

Lonk, A. F. "The Original" Complete Seventy-two Part Manual of Hypnosis and Psychotherapeutics, and also Mysteries of Time and Space. (Revised 3rd edition). Palantine, Illinois: Adolph F. Lonk, 1947.

Lustig, D. J. You, Too, Can be a Hypnotist. Philadelphia: Kanter's Magic Shop, 1956.

Luthe, W. (Ed.), Autogenic Therapy: Vol. IV. Research and Theory. New York: Grune & Stratton Inc., 1970.

Mackenzie, J. Symptoms and their Interpretation. London: Shaw & Sons, 1909.

Macvaugh, G. S. Hypnosis Readiness Inventory: A Self-confidence developer in ability to hypnotize. Chevy Chase, Md.: G. S. Macvaugh, 1969.

McGill, O. The Encyclopedia of Stage Hypnotism. Colon, Mich.: Abbott's Magic Novelty Co., 1947.

McGraw, M. B. Development of the plantar response in healthy infants. American Journal of Diseases of Children, 1941, 61, 1215-1221.

McGuire, W. J. The nature of attitudes and attitude change. In G. Lindzey & E. Aronson (Eds.), The Handbook of Social Psychology, III: The Individual in a Social Context. (2nd edition). Reading, Mass.: Addison-Wesley Publishing Co., 1969, pp. 136-314.

McPeake, J. D. Hypnosis, suggestions, and psychosomatics. Diseases of the Nervous System, 1968, 29, 536-544.

Meares, A. Theories of hypnosis, In J. M. Schneck (Ed.), 1963a, pp. 390-405.

Meeker, W. B., & Barber, T. X. Toward an explanation of stage hypnosis. Journal of Abnormal Psychology, 1971, 77, 61-70.

Melei, Janet P., & Hilgard, E. R. Attitudes toward hypnosis, self-predictions, and hypnotic susceptibility. International Journal of Clinical and Experimental Hypnosis, 1964, 12, 99-108.

Memmesheimer, A. M., & Eisenlohr, E. Untersuchungen über die Suggestivbehandlung der Warzen. Dermatologische Zeitschrift, 1931, 62, 63-68.

Menzies, R. Further studies of conditioned vasomotor responses in human subjects. Journal of Experimental Psychology, 1941, 29, 457-482.

Mesel, E., & Ledford, F. F., Jr. The electroencephalogram during hypnotic age regression (to infancy) in epileptic patients. Archives of Neurology, 1959, 1, 516-521.

Mitchell, J. F. Local anesthesia in general surgery. Journal of the American Medical Association, 1907, 49, 198-201.

Mordey, T. R. The relationship between certain motives and suggestibility. Unpublished Masters thesis, Roosevelt University, 1960.

Nelson, R. A. A Complete Course in Stage Hypnotism. Columbus, Ohio: Nelson Enterprises, 1965.

Nichols, D. C. A reconceptualization of the concept of hypnosis. In S. Lesse (Ed.), An Evaluation of the Results of the Psychotherapies. Springfield, Ill.: Charles C. Thomas, 1968, pp. 201-220.

Orne, M. T. The nature of hypnosis: Artifact and essence. Journal of Abnormal and Social Psychology, 1959, 58, 277-299.

Orne, M. T. On the mechanisms of posthypnotic amnesia. International Journal of Clinical and Experimental Hypnosis, 1966a, 14, 121-134.

Orne, M. T., & Evans, F. F. Inadvertent termination of hypnosis with hypnotized and simulating subjects. International Journal of Clinical and Experimental Hypnosis, 1966, 14, 61-78.

Orne, M. T., Sheehan P. W., & Evans, F. J. Occurrence of posthypnotic behavior outside the experimental setting. Journal of Personality and Social Psychology, 1968, 9, 189-196.

Otto, H. A. Explorations in Human Potentialities. Springfield, Ill.: Charles C. Thomas, 1966.

Parrish. M., Lundy, R. M., & Leibowitz, H. W. Effect of hypnotic age regression on the magnitude of the Ponzo and Poggendorff illusions. Journal of Abnormal Psychology, 1969, 74, 693-698.

Pattie, F. A., Jr. The production of blisters by hypnotic suggestion: A review. Journal of Abnormal and Social Psychology, 1941, 36, 62-72.

Pattie, F. A., Jr. Methods of induction, susceptibility of subjects and criteria of hypnosis. In R. M. Dorcus (Ed.), Hypnosis and its Therapeutic Applications. New York: McGraw-Hill, 1956a, ch.2.

Paul, G. L. The production of blisters by hypnotic suggestion: Another look. Psychosomatic Medicine, 1963, 25, 233-244.

Propping, K. Zur Frage der Sensibilität der Bauchhohle. Beitrage zur klinischen Chirurgie, 1909, 63, 690-710.

Reich, L. H. Optokinetic nystagnus during hypnotic hallucinations. Paper presented at Eastern Psychological Association, Annual Meeting, Atlantic City, April, 1970.

Reiff, R., & Scheerer, M. Memory and Hypnotic Age Regression: Developmental Aspects of Cognitive Function Explored through Hypnosis. New York: International Universities Press, 1959.

Richardson, A. Mental Imagery. New York: Springer Publishing Company, Inc., 1969.

Richman, D. N. A critique of two recent theories of hypnosis: The psychoanalytic theory of Gill and Brenman contrasted with the behavioral theory of Barber. Psychiatric Quarterly, 1965, 39, 278-292.

Rosenhan, D. L., & Tomkins, S. S. On preference for hypnosis and hypnotizability. International Journal of Clinical and Experimental Hypnosis, 1964, 12, 109-114.

Rubenstein, R., & Newman, R. The living out of "future" experiences under hypnosis. Science, 1954, 119, 472-473.

Sachs, L. B., & Anderson, W. L. Modification of hypnotic susceptibility. International Journal of Clinical and Experimental Hypnosis, 1967, 15, 172-180.

Sampimon, R. L. H., & Woodruff, M. F. A. Some observations concerning the use of hypnosis as a substitute for anesthesia. Medical Journal of Australia, 1946, 1, 393-395.

Sarbin, T. R. Contributions to role-taking theory: I. Hypnotic behavior. Psychological Review, 1950, 57, 255-270.

Sarbin, T. R. Physiological effects of hypnotic stimulation. In R. M. Dorcus, (Ed.), Hypnosis and its Therapeutic Applications. New York: McGraw-Hill, 1956, pp. 1-57.

Sarbin, T. R. Attempts to understand hypnotic phenomena. In L. Postman (Ed.), Psychology in the Making: Histories of selected research problems. New York: Knopf, 1962, pp. 745-785.

Sarbin, T. R. Role theoretical interpretation of psychological change. In P. Worchel & D. Byrne (Eds.), Personality Change. New York: Wiley, 1964, pp. 176-219.

Sarbin, T. R., & Andersen, M. L. Base-rate expectancies and perceptual alterations in hypnosis. British Journal of Social and Clinical Psychology, 1963, 2, 112-121.

Sarbin, T. R., & Andersen, M. L. Role-theoretical analysis of hypnotic behavior. In J. Gordon (Ed.), 1967, pp. 319-344.

Sarbin, T. R., & Coe, W. C. Hypnotic Behavior: The Psychology of Influence Communication. New York: Holt, Rinehart & Winston, (in press).

Scheibe, K. E., Gray, A. L., & Keim, C. S. Hypnotically induced deafness and delayed auditory feedback: A comparison of real and simulating subjects. International Journal of Clinical and Experimental Hypnosis, 1968, 16, 158-164.

Schneck, J. M. Relationships between hypnotist-audience and hypnotist-subject interaction. Journal of Clinical and Experimental Hypnosis, 1958, 6, 171-181.

Schneck, J. M. (1953). Hypnosis in Modern Medicine. Springfield, Ill.: C. C. Thomas, third edition, 1963a.

Schrenck-Notzing, A. F. Ein experimenteller und kritischer Beitrage zur Frage der suggestiven Hervorrufung circumscripter vasomotorischer Veränderungen auf der äusseren Haut. Zeitschrift fur Hypnotismus, 1896, 4, 209-228.

Schultz, J. H. Ueber selbsttätige (autogene) Umstellungen der Wärmestrahlung der menschlichen Haut im Autosuggestiven Training. Deutsche Medizinische Wochenschrift, 1926, 14, 571-572.

Schultz, J. H. Das Autogene Training. Stuttgart: Georg Thieme Verlag, 1932.

Secord, P. F., & Blackman, C. W. Social Psychology. New York: McGraw-Hill, 1964.

Sector, I. I. An investigation of hypnotizability as a function of attitude toward hypnosis. American Journal of Clinical Hypnosis, 1960, 3, 75-89.

Sheehan, P. W., & Orne, M. T. Some comments on the nature of posthypnotic behavior. Journal of Nervous and Mental Disease, 1968, 146, 209-220.

Shor, R. E. Three dimensions of hypnotic depth. International Journal of Clinical and Experimental Hypnosis, 1962, 10, 23-38.

Shor, R. E. Physiological effects of painful stimulation during hypnotic analgesia. In J. E. Gordon (Ed.), 1967, pp. 511-549.

Shor, R. E., Orne, M. T., & O'Connell, D. N. Psychological correlates of plateau hypnotizability in a special volunteer sample. Journal of Personality and Social Psychology, 1966, 3, 80-95.

Sinclair-Gieben, A. H. C., & Chalmers, D. Evaluation of treatment of warts by hypnosis. Lancet, 1959, 2, 480-482.

Spanos, N. P. Barber's reconceptualization of hypnosis: An evaluation of criticisms. Journal of Experimental Research in Personality, 1970, 4, 241-258.

Spanos, N. P. Goal-directed fantasy and the performance of hypnotic test suggestions. Psychiatry, 1971, 34, 86-96.

Spanos, N. P., & Barber, T. X. "Hypnotic" experiences as inferred from subjective reports: Auditory and visual hallucinations. Journal of Experimental Research in Personality, 1968, 3, 136-150.

Spanos, N. P., & Barber, T. X. Cognitive activity during "hypnotic" suggestibility: Goal-directed fantasy and the experience of non-volition. Journal of Personality, (in press).

Spanos, N. P., Barber, T. X., & Lang, G. Effects of hypnotic induction, suggestions of analgesia, and demands for honesty on subjective reports of pain. Department of Sociology, Boston University, 1969.

Spanos, N. P., & Chaves, J. F. Hypnosis research: A methodological critique of two alternative paradigms. American Journal of Clinical Hypnosis, 1970, 13, 108-127.

Stankler, L. A critical assessment of the cure of warts by suggestion. Practitioner, 1967, 198, 690-694.

Sulzberger, M. B., & Wolf, J. The treatment of warts by suggestion. Medical Record, 1934, 140, 552-556.

Sutcliffe, J. P. "Credulous" and "skeptical" views of hypnotic phenomena: A review of certain evidence and methodology. International Journal of Clinical and Experimental Hypnosis, 1960, 8, 73-101.

Sutcliffe, J. P. "Credulous" and "skeptical" views of Hypnotic phenomena: Experiments in esthesia, hallucination, and delusion. Journal of Abnormal and Social Psychology, 1961, 62, 189-200.

Timney, B. N., & Barber, T. X. Hypnotic induction and oral temperature. International Journal of Clinical and Experimental Hypnosis, 1969, 17, 121-132.

Tracy, D. F. How to Use Hypnosis. New York: Sterling Publishing Co., 1952.

Trent, J. C. Surgical anesthesia, 1846-1946. Journal of the History of Medicine and Allied Sciences, 1946, 1, 505-514.

True, R. M. Experimental control in hypnotic age regression states. Science, 1949, 110, 583-584.

Ullman, M. Herpes simplex and second degree burn induced under hypnosis. American Journal of Psychiatry, 1947, 103, 828-830.

Ullman, M., & Dudek, Stephanie. On the psyche and warts: II. Hypnotic suggestion and warts. Psychosomatic Medicine, 1960, 22, 68-76.

Underwood, H. W. The validity of hypnotically induced visual hallucinations. Journal of Abnormal and Social Psychology, 1960, 61, 39-46.

Vollmer, H. Treatment of warts by suggestion. Psychosomatic Medicine, 1946, 8, 138-142.

Watkins, J. G. Symposium on posthypnotic amnesia: Discussion. International Journal of Clinical and Experimental Hypnosis, 1966, 14, 139-149.

Weitzenhoffer, A. M. Hypnotism: An Objective Study in Suggestibility. New York: John Wiley & Sons, 1953.

Weitzenhoffer, A. M. General Techniques of Hypnotism. New York: Grune & Stratton, 1957a.

Williams, G. W. Clark L. Hull and his work on hypnosis. Journal of Clinical and Experimental Hypnosis, 1953, 1, 1-3.

Wilson, D. L. The role of confirmation of expectancies in hypnotic induction. Unpublished doctoral dissertation, University of North Carolina, 1967.

Wolberg, L. R. Medical Hypnosis. New York: Grune & Stratton, 1948, 2 vols.

Wolff, L. V. The response to plantar stimulation in infancy. American Journal of Diseases of Children, 1930, 39, 1176-1185.

Yates, A. J. Simulation and hypnotic age regression. International Journal of Clinical and Experimental Hypnosis, 1960, 8, 243-249.

KIDDER, L. H.[1]

15

# On Becoming Hypnotized: How Skeptics Became Convinced

Tape recordings, interviews, and participant observation in a hypnosis workshop were used to perform a social psychological analysis of becoming hypnotized. During the first sessions, most persons were struck by the ambiguity and vagueness of "hypnosis" and doubted the authenticity of their own "trances." By the last session, most persons had learned how to behave like good hypnotic *S*s and had come to accept new definitions of their own feelings and of the term hypnosis. The ways in which these changes occurred are compared with the ways in which attitude change occurs in laboratory settings, particularly as a result of role playing and forced compliance.

Given the aura of power that surrounds hypnosis and hypnotists, it seems remarkable that after undergoing hypnotic induction and coming out of it again a person could say, "How do I know if I was hypnotized?" or "I still don't consider it an experience any different from others." Yet such questions and skeptical reports were the rule rather than the exception after a group of willing and eager psychologists tried to hypnotize and be hypnotized.

## I. Being Skeptical and Unsure

A three-day hypnosis workshop[2] attended by 20 practicing psychologists provided the setting for this participant-observation study of becoming hypnotized. These 20 *S*s were sophisticated in theories and methods of psychology and may consequently have been more critical and wary than a group of naive participants. The steps they went through as they gradually learned to become hypnotized thus stand out in greater relief than if an unquestioning group had been studied. Their learning, however, is presented here as representative of the learning of most beginners, though the process may be more telescoped for some than for others. Using a tape recorder and written notes, the author made verbatim accounts of the interactions between hypnotists and their subjects.

An almost unanimous feeling among the participants after their first induction was not what a new and different experience it was to be hypnotized but rather what an ambiguous and vaguely defined experience it was, if it was indeed experienced at all. The following dialogue between one puzzled subject and two credentialled hypnotists illustrates the ambiguity and the fine line between what one person calls "hypnosis" and what another calls "playing the game."

Subject: the question in my mind is, how do you know if you were in a trance or not? I mean, I know I did some things, but I think they were all under conscious voluntary control.

Hypnotist 1: This is the one question that all patients will ask . . . . And they'll say, "you see, it doesn't work." I think you can tell if someone is in a trance by looking at them . . . the facial expressions. I could walk around the room and tell who wasn't and who was, by how they responded. I thought you were, but maybe you didn't *think* you were.

Hypnotist 2: You were actually the one that I thought went into trance the quickest . . . . The question is not were you in trance or were you not in trance, but *why* did you feel compelled to do those things. And why did you follow the suggestions? . . .

Subject: My conscious perception was that I was kind of going along with the thing all the way. I was kind of playing the game the way it's supposed to be. I was trying to achieve something which somehow felt different from just playing the game, and as far as I was consciously aware, I didn't succeed.

[1] The author would like to thank Howard S. Becker, Donald T. Campbell, and Thomas D. Cook, of Northwestern University, Russell Eisenman of Temple University, and Erasmus L. Hoch of the University of Michigan for their encouragement.

Requests for reprints should be sent to Louise H. Kidder, Department of Psychology, Temple University, Philadelphia, Pennsylvania 19122.

[2] The workshop took place in Chicago, Illinois, in the spring of 1969 under the auspices of The Society for Clinical and Experimental Hypnosis.

Another *S*, after having also "played the game" by holding a pendulum and allowing it to swing wider and wider as the hypnotist suggested, reacted as follows:

Hypnotist: Okay, can you describe what happened?
Subject: I . . . I don't know if I was in a trance or not.

These two were not unique instances. Nor were the *S*s uncooperative. They were, in fact, the "good subjects," who cooperated outwardly; yet they voiced these inner doubts about the authenticity of their trances.

Such doubts can obviously be overcome because there are many people who attest to the reality of hypnosis and describe it as a truly different experience. And the persons who voiced such doubts during the first day of the workshop changed their views by the third and last day. In many respects, the progression from Day 1 to Day 3 represented an attitude change. As the skeptics became convinced, they changed their attitudes toward hypnosis and toward their own experiences. The questions this paper tries to answer with data gathered by participant-observation at the workshop are: (*a*) How do such changes occur? and (*b*) Are they changes in a person's definition of "hypnosis" or are they changes in his definition of his own experience, or both? These questions, and the method exployed to answer them were inspired by the work and teachings of Becker, whose study of "Becoming a Marihuana User" (Becker, 1963) serves as a model.

Before a person can even begin to change his definitions of hypnosis or of his own experience, he must learn to act as though he were hypnotized. This paper describes how a person learns to behave like a hypnotized *S* and then discusses how he reaches his new definitions. These two stages are closely related not only in temporal spacing but also in the nature of the processes which produce the changes.

## II. Behaving Hypnotized

There are several ways of viewing the process of becoming hypnotized, all of which are represented in the literature of social learning and attitude change. These are (*a*) the role of the good *S* (Barber, 1970; Sarbin & Allen, 1968; Shor & Orne, 1965; Weber & Cook, 1972), (*b*) the effects of rewards and punishments (Skinner, 1957), and (*c*) the process of negotiation (Scheff, 1968).

### *The Role of a "Good Subject"*

Hypnotists themselves speak of someone as a good *S* or a bad *S* to describe a person who goes into a trance quickly and easily versus one who resists and never succumbs. In fact, some *S*s are so good that they hardly give the hypnotist a chance to demonstrate his skills—they "go under" after just a few words or a few seconds. The following illustrates such a case:

Hypnotist: (after having induced a trance in a novice) Now J fell rather fast . . . . With a subject who is a little less good a subject than J is, I could have demonstrated a few other things, of finesse . . . . With most subjects it takes a good deal longer.

Most of the *S*s at the workshop recognized in themselves the element of trying to be a good *S*. And recognizing this made them even more skeptical—they doubted that they could call themselves "hypnotized" when they had tried so hard to cooperate and be good. It seemed that hypnosis should be something less voluntary, less dependent on such willing cooperation. After an *S* had been brought out of a "trance" in which the hypnotist had suggested that she would feel sun shining on her face, an *O* asked *S* if she had felt warm:

Subject: Yes, kind of. But I think it was because I was *trying* to. I tried to imagine feeling warm, and I did.

Although such cooperative behavior made a person doubt whether he had really been hypnotized, it did contribute to his *behaving* as though he were hypnotized, and such behavior was necessary before the hypnotist or anyone else could convince the subject that he actually had experienced hypnosis. Moreover, although it was an act of compliance, it was not forced upon the person in the same way that counter-attitudinal behavior is forced upon someone by a $20 bribe (cf. Festinger & Carlsmith, 1959). The hypnotist was quick to point this out to the participants when they complained about just "playing the game":

Hypnotist: . . . but *why* did you feel compelled to do those things. And why did you follow the suggestions? . . . *Why* did you feel that you wanted to play the game?

*Rewards and Punishments*

During the entire workshop, there were many times when the hypnotists rewarded persons who behaved like good hypnotic *S*s and punished those who resisted. In any learning situation, the rewards and punishments must fit the occasion and *S*'s desires. Given the setting of this particular workshop, a gathering of clinical psychologists, the rewards and punishments were appropriately clinical and psychological. Persons who could not easily be hypnotized were described as "compulsive," "terribly rational," "unable to get deeply involved," while persons who were easily hypnotized were described as "normal."

The following statements by the hypnotists occurred after a person indicated that he did not feel that he had been in a trance or after someone tried to suggest that maybe it was "normal" to have difficulty going into hypnotic trance:

(*a*) Sometimes the *very analytic* person won't go along—he thinks to himself "The hypnotist said I'm going to go to sleep, but hell, I'm not asleep, I'm wide awake, and he's crazy!"
(*b*) The most difficult one is the *compulsive* . . . . He also has the constant doubt "Am I or am I not in trance?" Or the terribly rational person who cannot allow himself to go into any fantasy would be terribly difficult.
(*c*) There is a myth about hysterics—that they are better subjects. But really *normal* persons are better subjects.
(*d*) People who can throw themselves into art, nature, sports—involve themselves in a role and relinquish reality orientation for a time—these are the people who make good hypnotic subjects.

Every person in that group would have agreed that it is better to be "normal" and to be a person who can "throw himself into art, nature, sports," rather than be "compulsive," "terribly rational," or "hysterical." And given the public nature of the situation, no one could have ignored such rewards and punishments meted out to persons who became hypnotized and others who refused.

*The Process of Negotiation*

If a person's own desires to be a good *S* or the hypnotist's administration of positive reinforcement was not sufficient to produce hypnotic behavior, there were negotiations between the hypnotists and the subjects to persuade the latter to conform. The instance cited on page 1 illustrates the negotiation pattern whereby an *S* says "I don't think I was hypnotized" and the hypnotists respond by saying "*I* thought your were."

The central feature of the negotiations was not letting the *S* find an excuse or way out of believing that he had been hypnotized. The responsibility for "successes" and "failures" was placed on *S* rather than the hypnotist, and there were no loopholes or special exemptions for persons who did not become hypnotized. The locus of responsibility was fixed as follows:

Hypnotist: Dr. Z tried to help those of you who weren't able to do the arm lift. He said, "For those for whom this was difficult, the arm can get very heavy" (so persons could let their arms go down instead of up) . . . . He pointed out the successes instead of failures and gave other possibilities for achieving success."
Subject: Your make it sound as if it's the patient's fault instead of yours if he doesn't go into trance.
Hypnotist: Well, let me say this. Earlier hypnosis was done in an authoritarian fashion—now it is much more permissive and we conceive of hypnosis as the achievement of the subject, in which the hypnotist helps . . . . Does this answer your question?

Another *S*, a man who had not been convinced that he had been in a trance, asked:

Subject: Does the research show women are better subjects than men?
Hypnotist: No, that is not true [implying that he has no excuse].

By placing the locus of responsibility on *S*, the hypnotists had a rationale for handing out rewards and punishments and also had grounds for negotiation. They seemed to recognize the element of negotiation—implicitly by engaging in lengthy arguments with recalcitrant *S*s and explicitly by referring to the "contract": "The contract is important, and whatever it is called afterwards really doesn't matter." This was said in response to my suggesting that hypnosis might share some features with other persuasive practices such as Christian Science. The hypnotist acknowledged the common feature of these practices—the agreement between two persons to work toward a new definition of feeling for one of them. Whether the final product is called a hypnotic trance or a demonstration of the works of Christian Science is a matter of taste perhaps. What really matters is the contract.

### III. Becoming Convinced: Redefining One's Behavior and Experience

Hypnosis has not been successful if it produces only persons who have been hypnotized by objective measures but who remain skeptical about their own subjective experience. Even though the hypnotist may say "*I* thought you were," *S* may not be convinced. He must still redefine his own behavior and experience.

*Counterattitudinal Behavior and Attitude Change*

The social psychological literature on attitude change suggests that after a person has outwardly behaved in a manner incongruent with his previous attitudes, he will more often than not change his attitudes to accord with his behavior. And the smaller the external justification for his behavior, the greater will be his attitude change (Carlsmith, Collins, & Helmreich, 1966; Festinger & Carlsmith, 1959). Self-perception theory (Bem, 1967) and reactance theory (Brehm, 1966) also suggest that persons change their attitudes in inverse proportion to the degree of external force applied. When external pressures become so great that they appear to threaten a person's sense of autonomy, the persuasive attempts may "boomerang." For these reasons, one might expect the permissive approach to hypnosis to produce more real attitude change than the authoritarian approach since the former does not threaten *S*'s autonomy and actually provides very little external justification for why *S* behaved as he did. During the workshop, the hypnotists delineated the role and rules of the permissive hypnotist:

> (*a*) The main thing is to enlist his (the subject's) cooperation—because it is not my doing but his doing . . . .
> (*b*) [In order not to suggest an image or experience to the subject which he is not prepared to accept, it is wise to set up a signaling system whereby he has recourse to rebuttal.] You can arrange for a feedback system by setting up finger signals, so he uses his right finger to say "yes" and his left finger to say "no" and right thumb for "I don't want to" and left thumb for "I don't know."

An interesting point of departure between the usual laboratory forced-compliance attitude change studies and hypnosis is that the former obtains attitude change when the *S* *can* attribute his behavior to his own volition while the latter obtains "attitude change" when *S cannot* attribute his behavior to an act of volition. In order to become convinced that he has been hypnotized, *S* must feel that his behavior was the result of neither his own conscious volition nor strong eternal bribes or constraints. Instead, he must attribute his trance-like behavior to a middle-ground of unobservable, unconscious psychological hypnotic forces.

Whether we subscribe to dissonance theory (e.g., Festinger & Carlsmith, 1959) or self-perception theory (e.g., Bem, 1967) to explain the results of counterattitudinal behavior, there is no disputing the fact that in order for change to occur, *S* must first be aware of his behavior. In most social psychological studies of counterattitudinal behavior, it is assumed that *S* senses the discrepancy. In this hypnosis workshop, two processes operated to ensure *S*'s noticing: (*a*) feedback from the hypnotist made the subjects aware of subtle and minute behaviors; and (*b*) feedback from *S*'s own observations of less subtle changes.

*Feedback from the Hypnotist*

To ensure that *S noticed* his counterattitudinal behavior, the hypnotist let *S* know how he was behaving from the point of view of an external observer. This technique of giving feedback about behaviors is closely linked to giving feedback about feelings, since, all other things being constant, people presumably believe that their feelings and behaviors are consistent. Thus, a yawn lets a person know "I am tired" (cf. Bem, 1967; James, 1962), just as having participated in a dull experiment and then for a minimal fee calling it "interesting" makes a person think "it wasn't all that dull."

The following excerpt describes the feedback procedure and also suggests how alert and perceptive the hypnotist must be in order to obtain results:

> Hypnotist: Let him know how he is feeling—"your eyes are blinking, you feel relaxed, you feel comfortable" . . . . If you see him move a finger, pick up on that and feed it back to him. And use his vocabulary—talk about "myotonic movements" if he is a medical student and "muscle twitches" if he's a layman. Move from this picking up and feeding back to suggesting movements . . . if you see any movement, pick it up and feed it back to him, and say "Your hand is moving higher and higher" . . . . If he yawns or rubs his eyes, pick up on this . . . .

*Feedback from Observing One's Own Behavior*

In addition to receiving feedback from the hypnotist about minute movements, eye blinks, muscle twitches, and other barely perceptible behaviors, *S* could easily observe some gross behaviors which he performed.

The "coin drop technique" was used for a group induction and it provided visual, auditory, and kinesthetic feedback to the subject that he was "going under." Everyone held a coin in his dominant hand, fixated a point on the wall, and gradually felt his hand begin to open, "to expand as though a balloon were expanding the hand," and as the hand gradually opened the person felt himself go into a trance.

> Hypnotist: When you hear the coin drop, at that point you will go into a state of trance . . . your eyes will close and you will go into a state of trance . . . more and more . . . .

The sound of coins dropping was to be a discriminative stimulus for going into a trance. And the public nature of this made for a lot of social reinforcement too—those whose coins dropped were clearly good *S*s. Not everyone dropped his coin, however, so the hypnotist started counting and suggesting that by the count of 15 "everyone will have dropped his coin and be in deep trance. One . . . Two . . . Three . . . Fourteen . . . Fifteen!" As the hypnotist pronounced "fifteen!" with great emphasis, about 10 coins dropped on the desks all at once.

Since *S*s were not physically forced, not monetarily bribed, nor coerced in any obvious manner, they had to attribute their behavior to their own internal state. And the easiest and least damaging attribution was "I am now in a trance." No one refused to cooperate and no one objected by saying "but I'm not in a trance, I just faked it."

If the hypnotist chooses his tasks carefully, he can produce such behavioral changes in his *S*s with minimal outside pressure, social or physical. One subtle aid he may employ is gravity, as in the "arm drop method." In this technique, *S* holds out his arm and imagines holding a large empty pail on his wrist. The hypnotist then says, "Now I'm going to pour a pint of water into it . . . now another . . . now a quart!" And *S* finds his arm going down. The hypnotist explained to the group that:

> You make use of gravity in this case, just as when you use eye fixation, which works best if you ask the subject to fixate something high up on the wall. You make use of all the physiology that you can. You as psychologists are aware of what's happening, but that doesn't obviate it or mean it won't happen for you.

Making use of gravity and other physical or physiological realities helps to eliminate the volitional aspect—it relieves *S*s of the feeling that they were faking it or just playing the game. They can thus attribute their behavior to something else, and if obvious coercion is ruled out (and the forces of gravity are not made salient), there remains only the "trance." No one seemed unduly concerned with the effects of gravity, perhaps because they felt they could have overcome gravity and held their arms up or their eyes open if they had tried. They consequently admitted that they might have been going into a trance, a very light one with not very dramatic effects, but nonetheless a trance.

### IV. Redefining Hypnosis

In addition to experiencing new behaviors and changing his attitudes about his own subjective state, the hypnotized *S* also learns to expect less from "hypnosis." He gives up his original idea that hypnosis is a dramatically different state of being and accepts even mildly different experience as evidence that he was hypnotized.

A "guest subject" was brought into the workshop to be hypnotized by one of the experts. After the hypnotist indicated to all present that this *S* had gone into a relatively deep trance, several members of the workshop interviewed *S* to find out "what was it like—this must have been the real thing since you were put under by an expert, so what was the real thing like?" The interview went as follows:

> Question: How did it feel?
>
> Answer: Just very good. Very very relaxed.
>
> Question: Have you ever felt anything like this before?
>
> Answer: Yeah, well, it's sort of like smoking grass. The first few times I used it I just fell asleep.
>
> Question: I wanted to ask what other experiences it was like.
>
> Answer: It's like being very tired. Or like sitting in an airport and feeling tired and hearing other people around you talking—sort of hazy.

> Question: What did you think it would be like?
> Answer: Well, I thought you wouldn't be conscious . . . . And then when I was in it I felt like I could just come out any time I wanted to. But I guess that's how you do feel. I had thought it would be more involuntary.

Another dialogue which occurred toward the end of the workshop reflected a similar phenomenon of expecting and accepting less:

> Subject 1: I'm surprised, most of us don't think it's so different from other things.
> Subject 2: Yes, I guess my expectations have changed. Now if I experience anything like it I'm satisfied. And I'm not sure about what the different depths mean. But now if I'm under I still notice if another person comes over, but I say "I don't care."

## V. Conclusions

By the end of the workshop, the skeptical *S*s had become convinced that hypnosis was a real phenomenon, though not what they originally thought. Most persons had by the last day cooperated with the hypnotists and become good *S*s. They had noticed new sensations, particularly relaxation, slight detachment, and haziness, and felt that maybe they had been hypnotized. They also lowered their criteria for what would pass as "hypnosis"—it no longer had to be a mysterious, mystical, unconscious phenomenon. It was more like being almost but not quite asleep.

During the first day of the workshop, one of the hypnotists offered this description of hypnosis:

> There's an area between waking and sleeping—the transition is not easy to determine. But the idea that something is going to happen which will be unlike anything else you've experienced is a very common preconception (and it is wrong).

It took 3 days and 24 hr. of negotiations, rewards, and punishments, and practicing at being good *S*s for the participants to become convinced of this.

To say that becoming hypnotized involves changing definitions of oneself and of hypnosis is not to say that hypnosis is nothing but a word game. Like Becker's (1963) analysis of becoming a marijuana user, this interactional approach is not intended to deny the reality of the experience for either the teacher or the novitiate. The experience is very real indeed, and after a person has learned to become either "high" or hypnotized, he will be the first to defend the validity of his subjective reports. Nor would an interactional analysis want to deny the importance of individual differences in hypnotizability (e.g., Hilgard, 1965, 1970). Saying that some persons are more hypnotizable than others would, in the terms of this analysis, translate into saying that some persons proceed through the steps outlined faster than others, while some never get beyond the "I-don't-think-I-was-hypnotized" stage. The analysis presented here is a supplement to rather than substitute for studies of individual differences. It is a social psychological approach to a traditionally clinical phenomenon.

## References


Barber, T. X. *LSD, marihuana, yoga and hypnosis.* Chicago: Aldine, 1970.

Becker, H. S. *Outsiders.* New York: The Free Press, 1963.

Bem, D. J. Self-perception: An alternative interpretation of cognitive dissonance phenomena. *Psychological Review,* 1967, **74**, 183–200.

Brehm, J. W. *A theory of psychological reactance.* New York: Academic Press, 1966.

Carlsmith, J. M., Collins, B. C., & Helmreich, R. L. Studies in forced compliance. I. The effect of pressure for compliance on attitude change produced by face-to-face role-playing and anonymous essay writing. *Journal of Personality and Social Psychology,* 1966, **4**, 1–13.

Festinger, L., & Carlsmith, J. M. Cognitive consequence of forced compliance. *Journal of Abnormal and Social Psychology,* 1959, **58**, 203–210.

Hilgard, E. R. *The experience of hypnosis: A shorter version of hypnotic susceptibility.* New York: Harcourt, Brace & World, 1965.

Hilgard, J. R. *Personality and hypnosis: A study of imaginative involvement.* Chicago: University of Chicago Press, 1970.

James, W. *Psychology: A briefer course.* New York: Collier Books, 1962.

Sarbin, T. R., & Allen, V. L. Role theory. In G. Lindzey & E. Aronson (Eds.), *The handbook of social psychology.* Vol. 2. (2nd ed.) Reading, Mass.: Addison-Wesley, 1968.

Scheff, T. J. Negotiating reality: Notes on power in the assessment of responsibility. *Social Problems,* 1968, **16**, 3–17.

Shor, R. E., & Orne, M. T. *The nature of hypnosis.* New York: Holt, Rinehart & Winston, 1965.

Skinner, B. F. *Verbal behavior.* New York: Appleton-Century-Crofts, 1957.

Weber, S. J., & Cook, T. D. Subject effects in laboratory research: An examination of subject roles, demand characteristics, and valid inference. *Psychological Bulletin,* 1972, **77**, 273–295.


(Received February 7, 1972)

# 16

SPANOS, N. P. & BARBER, T. X.

# *Cognitive Activity during "Hypnotic" Suggestibility: Goal-Directed Fantasy and the Experience of Non-Volition*

Subjects participating in hypnotic experiments commonly report that their overt responses to test-suggestions occurred without their active volition. For example, when given a suggestion for arm levitation, hypnotic subjects typically state that the arm rose by itself—they did not feel that they made the arm rise.

It has been commonly assumed that the nonvolitional quality of the response is due to the presence of a hypothetical "hypnotic state" or "trance state" (Evans, 1968; Orne, 1959, 1966). However, Spanos (1971) presented data indicating that it may not be necessary to postulate a special state ("hypnosis" or "trance") to account for the reports of nonvolition; the nonvolitional quality of response to suggestions appears, at least in part, to be due to the *wording of the suggestions* which are typically given to hypnotic subjects. Spanos noted that hypnotic test-suggestions which call for an overt response typically include two components:

1. The suggestions indicate to the subject that his overt response should occur without his active volition. For example, the subject is told "Your arm will rise" rather than "Raise your arm."

This research was supported, in part, by grants (MH–11521 and MH–19152) from the National Institute of Mental Health, U.S. Public Health Service. We thank Lucy-Grace Sargeant for assistance in carrying out statistical computations and Martin W. Ham for rating the goal-directed fantasy protocols.

2. The suggestions supply the subject with a strategy for defining his response to the test-suggestion as occurring nonvolitionally. Specifically, *the subject is instructed to imagine a situation which, if it actually transpired, would result in the (suggested) behavior.* Such an imagined situation is labeled as *goal-directed imagining* or, equivalently, *goal-directed fantasy.* For example, Form C of the Stanford Hypnotic Susceptibility Scale suggests arm heaviness and arm lowering in the following way: ". . . Imagine that you are holding something heavy in your hand . . . . Now, the hand and arm feel heavy, as if the [imagined] weight were pressing down . . . and as it feels heavier and heavier the hand and arm begin to move down . . ." (Weitzenhoffer & Hilgard, 1962, p. 17). If the subject were to hold a weight in his hand, as the Stanford Scale suggests, then his arm would feel heavy and would lower. Furthermore, *the heaviness and lowering of the arm might be attributed by the subject to the presence of the (imagined) weight and not to a volitional act.*

Spanos (1971) interviewed subjects immediately after they had been exposed to a hypnotic-induction procedure and had responded to test-suggestions from the Stanford Hypnotic Susceptibility Scale (Form C) and the Barber Suggestibility Scale (Barber, 1965, 1969). With few exceptions, subjects who passed the test-suggestions reported a goal-directed fantasy: they stated that, while they were responding to the test-suggestions, they imagined situations which, had they objectively transpired, would have produced the response that was suggested. For example, a subject who passed a test-suggestion for arm heaviness and arm lowering reported the following goal-directed fantasy: "I imagined that there were all kinds of rocks tied to my arm. It felt heavy and I could feel it going down." Similarly, a subject who carried out a test-suggestion for arm levitation reported that "I imagined that my arm was hollow, there was nothing in it, and somebody was putting air into it."

The goal-directed fantasies reported by the hypnotic subjects in the Spanos (1971) study did not always correspond to the imaginary situations that were described by the test-suggestions. Also, these goal-directed fantasies sometimes involved the imagining of events that were objectively impossible. For example, when given suggestions for arm immobility a subject imagined that her arm had been transformed into a wooden board. However, all goal-directed fantasies had the following in common: If the imagined event had objectively occurred—e.g., if the subject's arm actually had been transformed into a wooden board—it would produce, without the subject's volition, the response called for by the test-suggestion (e.g., arm immobility).

The subjects in the Spanos (1971) experiment who did not pass the test-suggestions usually did not report goal-directed fantasies. Instead, they typically indicated either that they were unwilling or unable to imagine the suggested events or they imagined a situation which was unrelated to passing the test-suggestion (e.g., when given an arm-levitation suggestion a subject who did not pass the test-suggestion reported "seeing" a green kangaroo hopping around the room, and another reported imagining herself standing in an old-fashioned kitchen).

Since the Spanos (1971) experiment was carried out as a pilot study, it suggested, but did not rigorously demonstrate, three hypotheses that need to be tested in further research:

*Hypothesis 1.* Test-suggestions which instruct the hypnotic subject to engage in goal-directed fantasy are more effective than other types of test-suggestions (direct command, direct suggestion, or suggestion to imagine) in eliciting reports that the (suggested) response occurred nonvolitionally.

*Hypothesis 2.* Regardless of the wording of the test-suggestions, suggested responses are experienced as more nonvolitional by hypnotic subjects who engage in goal-directed fantasy.

*Hypothesis 3.* When the test-suggestion implies that the response is to occur nonvolitionally, those hypnotic subjects who engage in goal-directed fantasy pass the test-suggestion more often than those who do not engage in such fantasy.

## Method

Forty female student nurses (ages 19–35) volunteered to participate in an experiment in which they would be hypnotized and would be paid two dollars. None of these students had previously participated in experiments carried out by the present authors. All subjects were assigned, in order of their appearance for the experiment, to one of four treatment groups, with 10 subjects to each group.

Each subject was tested individually in a single session by one experimenter (NPS). Immediately after being seated, the subject was given several tests of visual imagery associated with a different experiment (Barber, Spanos & Merritt, 1970). After completing the imagery tests, the subject was told that she was to be hypnotized and was given the preliminary instructions.

### *Preliminary Instructions*

The preliminary instructions were adapted from those used by Spanos (1971). The subject was told that the experimenter was interested in studying the subjective experiences of hypnotic subjects. She was informed that she would be questioned about her experiences during hypnosis. The subject was also asked to give honest and detailed descriptions of her experiences.

### *Hypnotic-Induction Procedure*

The experimenter next administered a standardized hypnotic-induction procedure. The procedure, which was very similar to the one presented by Barber (1969, Appendix B), took 10 minutes to administer.

### *Arm-Levitation Suggestion*

Immediately upon completing the hypnotic-induction procedure, each subject was asked to hold her right arm straight out at shoulder height and then was tested on an arm levitation suggestion. The subjects, who had been randomly assigned to four experimental groups, were given the arm levitation suggestion worded in one of four different ways:

*Direct command* (group 1). Subjects allocated to group 1 were given the direct command, "Slowly lift your arm."

*Direct suggestion* (group 2). Subjects assigned to group 2 were given direct suggestions for arm levitation: "Your arm is beginning to rise. It's rising, going up and up, up and up, up and up. It's rising, rising, rising, going up and up, rising, up and up, up and up, rising,

rising, up and up, up and up."

*Imagination suggestion* (group 3). The arm levitation suggestion given to subjects in group 3 began each sentence with the work *imagine*, e.g., "Imagine your arm is beginning to rise." In all other respects, the suggestion was identical with the one given to group 2.

*Goal-directed fantasy suggestion* (group 4). Group 4 was given an arm levitation suggestion which instructed the subject to carry out a goal-directed fantasy: "Imagine a very large helium-filled balloon tied tautly to your wrist. The balloon is beginning to rise and as it rises it pulls your arm up. The balloon is rising, going up and up, up and up, up and up. The balloon is rising, rising, rising, going up and up, rising, up and up, up and up, rising, rising, up and up, up and up."[3]

### *Criterion for Passing Test-Suggestion*

The subject passed the arm levitation suggestion if her arm had risen four or more inches within five seconds after the termination of the suggestion.

### *Assessment of Goal-Directed Fantasy*

Immediately after completing the arm levitation suggestion, each subject was asked the following three standardized questions and the answers were recorded on tape:

1. Please tell me honestly what was passing through your mind—what you were thinking, feeling, imagining, and saying to yourself—during and right after the suggestion that your arm was rising?
2. What were you imagining—what pictures, images, or fantasies were passing through your mind at the time?
3. What were you thinking about during the suggestion?

After responding to these questions, subjects who had passed the arm levitation suggestion were asked: "Why did you raise your arm?" Subjects who did not pass the arm levitation suggestion were asked: "Why didn't you raise your arm?"

The questioning was terminated at this point for those subjects who clearly had and also for those who clearly had not reported a goal-directed fantasy. A few subjects who seemed to be referring to a goal-directed fantasy but who did not supply detailed information were asked to amplify their remarks.

A scoring manual describing the characteristics of goal-directed fantasy had been prepared for a previous experiment (Spanos, 1971).[4]

The experimenter used the manual to judge whether or not the subject reported imagining a situation which would produce the arm levitation response if the (imagined) situation had actually occurred. In order to establish the inter-rater reliability of the experimenter's judgment, a second rater post-experimentally judged the tape-recorded testimony of each subject for the presence or absence of goal-directed fantasy. The second rater employed the same manual to make his judgments, but he was unaware of the treatment group to which the subjects had been assigned. The two raters agreed with one another on every judgment with respect to the presence or absence of goal-directed fantasy ($r = 1.00$). This perfect inter-rater reliability is in agreement with the data from an earlier study (Spanos, 1971) which found that three independent raters agreed in every judgment on the presence or absence of goal-directed fantasy.

*Assessment of Experienced Nonvolition*

After responding to the questions concerning goal-directed fantasy, each subject who had passed the arm levitation suggestion was asked to rate the degree to which she experienced the response as volitional or nonvolitional. This rating was made on the following mimeographed questionnaire:

> I am interested in what you experienced during the time your arm was in the process of moving upward. I will ask you to indicate the extent to which you experienced your arm moving up without voluntary effort—the extent to which you felt it was moving up *without* having the experience of causing it to move up. The distinctions I will ask you to make are subtle and an example may help to clarify what I am getting at. If you walk up a flight of stairs, you have the experience of *causing your-*

3. After completing the procedures associated with the arm-levitation suggestion, subjects were also administered an arm-immobility suggestion worded in one of four ways. However, it quickly became evident that the volition questionnaire that was administered after the arm-immobility suggestion was poorly worded and consistently misunderstood by the subjects. Although the arm-immobility suggestion was administered to all subjects in order to keep experimental conditions constant, the arm-immobility data were not analyzed or included in this report.

4. This manual specifies several criteria for distinguishing testimony that indicates the presence of goal-directed fantasy from (a) testimony that does not indicate such fantasy and (b) testimony that indicates fantasy that is not goal-directed. It also indicates that fantasy is *not* to be simply identified with visual imagery. The manual is available upon request from Nicholas P. Spanos, Department of Sociology, Boston University, Boston, Massachusetts.

*self* to move up the stairs. However, if you ride the same distance in an escalator you have the experience of *being moved* upward. Please be honest in indicating the extent to which you experienced *causing* your arm to move up as opposed to having experienced the arm *going up by itself*. Circle the *one* letter—a, b, c, d, or e—which best describes the experience you had.

a) Completely involuntary. I experienced it rising completely by itself.

b)

c) Partially involuntary. I had the experience that it was rising by itself and also the experience that I was causing it to rise and both experiences were equally strong.

d)

e) Completely voluntary. I only had the experience of causing it to rise.

Choices a, b, c, d, and e were scored 1, 2, 3, 4, and 5, respectively.[5]

*Assessment of Level of Suggestibility*

Immediately upon completing the above procedures, each subject was again asked to relax and then was tested on response to three standardized test-suggestions: visual hallucination (from Barber & Calverley, 1964), body immobility, and post-hypnotic response (from the Barber Suggestibility Scale). Each of the three test-suggestions received a score of 0 or 1—a score of 1 was assigned if the subject checked that she saw the suggested object clearly (visual hallucination), if she did not rise from the chair within 5 seconds after termination of the suggestion (body immobility), and if she coughed or cleared her throat within three seconds after receiving the post-hypnotic cue.

*Assessment of Hypnotic Depth*

After the subject had been told to awaken and had been tested on response to the post-hypnotic suggestion, she was asked to complete the following scale:

At the end of the hypnotic-induction procedure but before I was administered the suggestion that my arm would lift, I was: [a] deeply hypnotized —; [b] medium hypnotized —; [c] lightly hypnotized —; [d] not hypnotized —.
Items a, b, c, and d were scored 4, 3, 2, and 1, respectively.

Upon completing the above scale, the subject was admonished not to discuss the experiment with the other students until all had been tested and was then paid for her participation.

## Results

### *Effectiveness of Goal-Directed Fantasy Manipulation*

The top row of Table 1 shows that every subject in group 4, who received the goal-directed fantasy suggestion, exhibited such

*Table 1.* Relationships between wording of arm levitation suggestion, goal-directed fantasy, passing of suggestion, and experienced volition.

| | Wording of arm levitation suggestion | | | |
|---|---|---|---|---|
| | Direct command (group 1) | Direct suggestion (group 2) | Imagination suggestion (group 3) | Goal-directed fantasy (group 4) |
| Goal-directed fantasy present | 1 | 2 | 4 | 10 |
| Goal-directed fantasy absent | 9 | 8 | 6 | 0 |
| Passed suggestion | 10 | 8 | 6 | 9 |
| Failed suggestion | 0 | 2 | 4 | 1 |
| Mean volition scores | **3.5** | **2.8** | **2.8** | 1.9 |

Note.—High mean volition scores indicate that the response was experienced as more volitional. Boldface mean volition scores do not differ from one another at the .05 level of confidence.

a fantasy. Chi-square analyses showed that subjects in group 4 displayed goal-directed fantasy significantly more often than those given the direct command (group 1), the direct suggestion (group 2) and the imagination suggestion (group 3) ($ps < .02$) and that subjects in groups 1, 2, and 3 did not differ significantly from each other in exhibiting goal-directed fantasy ($ps < .20$).

5. The first two subjects in the experiment indicated that they were unsure of the meaning of choices b and d on the volition questionnaire. These subjects were told that b represented an experience half way between that described by choices a and c, and that d represented an experience half way between that described by c and e. In order to keep experimental conditions constant, all subjects who passed the arm levitation suggestion were supplied with this information before making their choice on the volition questionnaire.

### *Hypothesis 1. Wording of Test-Suggestions and Experienced Nonvolition*

The last row of Table 1 displays the mean volition scores for the subjects in the four treatment groups who passed the arm levitation suggestion. A one-way analysis of variance performed on the volition scores showed that the extent to which subjects rated their arm levitation as a nonvolitional act differed significantly among the four groups ($F = 4.62$, $df = 3/29$, $p < .01$). Individual $t$ tests indicated that subjects administered the goal-directed fantasy suggestion rated their response as more nonvolitional than those administered the direct command, the direct suggestion, and the imagination suggestion ($ps < .025$). These results support hypothesis 1, which states that suggested responses are experienced as more nonvolitional when the suggestions instruct the subject to engage in goal-directed fantasy.

Although the extent to which subjects in groups 1, 2, and 3 rated their responses as nonvolitional did not differ at the .05 level of confidence, there were trends ($ps < .15$) indicating that subjects given the direct and the imagination suggestions tended to rate their responses as more nonvolitional than those given the direct command.

It is important to note the parallels in the analyses dealing with goal-directed fantasy and with subjects' experience of nonvolition. Subjects in group 4 displayed the most goal-directed fantasy and also rated their responses as more nonvolitional than subjects in the other three treatment groups. Although the experience of nonvolition was closely related to the wording of the test-suggestion, it was not closely related to "depth of hypnosis" or to level of suggestibility. A one-way analysis of variance showed that subjects' estimates of "hypnotic depth" did not differ among the four treatment groups ($F = .05$, $df = 3/36$, $p > .9$). A separate one-way analysis of variance also showed that the level of suggestibility (as measured by responses to test-suggestions for visual hallucination, body immobility, and post-hypnotic response) also did not differ among the four treatment groups ($F = .15$, $df = 3/36$, $p > .8$). These results indicate that different levels of goal-directed fantasy and experienced nonvolition between treatments cannot be accounted for in terms of differences in "hypnotic depth" or level of suggestibility between treatments.

### *Hypothesis 2. Goal-Directed Fantasy and Experienced Nonvolition*

The first two rows in Table 1 show that goal-directed fantasy was reported by 100 percent of the subjects in group 4, and also by 40 percent of the subjects in group 3 (who were instructed *to imagine* that their arm was rising). Also, 10 and 20 percent of the subjects in groups 1 and 2, respectively, reported a goal-directed fantasy. The four treatment groups were collapsed into subjects who passed the arm levitation suggestion while displaying goal-directed fantasy and those who passed without exhibiting such fantasy. A $t$ test performed on the volition scores of these two sets of subjects showed that subjects displaying goal-directed fantasy rated their responses as more nonvolitional than subjects who

*Table 2.* Relationship between goal-directed fantasy and extreme volition scores.

| | Presence of goal-directed fantasy | Absence of goal-directed fantasy |
|---|---|---|
| Response experienced as volitional | 0 | 9 |
| Response experienced as Nonvolitional | 10 | 6 |

Note.—$\chi^2 = 6.95$, $df = 1$, $p < .01$

did not report such fantasy ($t = 3.54$, $df = 31$, $p < .005$). The same results were obtained when subjects given the direct command to raise their arm (group 1) were eliminated from the analysis ($t = 4.35$, $df = 21$, $p < .005$). Thus, even when all subjects are exposed to suggestions implying that their response is to occur nonvolitionally (groups 2, 3, and 4), those who pass the test-suggestion and exhibit goal-directed fantasy describe their responses as occurring more nonvolitionally than those who pass the test-suggestion without exhibiting goal-directed fantasy.

A somewhat different perspective on the relationship between goal-directed fantasy and subjects' experience of nonvolition is gained by dichotomizing subjects from all four groups into those who clearly experienced their response to the suggestion as nonvolitional (who checked alternatives a or b on the volition scale) and those who clearly experienced it as volitional (who checked alternatives d or e). (Not included in this analysis are seven subjects who did not pass the test-suggestion and eight who indicated that their responses were equally volitional and nonvolitional.) With respect to subjects included in this analysis, Table 2 shows that 100 percent of those who exhibited goal-directed fantasy experienced their responses as nonvolitional. On the other hand, only 40 percent of those who did *not* exhibit goal-directed fantasy experienced their responses as nonvolitional. These results strongly support hypothesis 2: regardless of the wording of the test-suggestions, suggested responses are experienced as more nonvolitional by hypnotic subjects who engage in goal-directed fantasy.

*Table* 3. Relationship between goal-directed fantasy and passing of test-suggestion when suggestions imply that responses are to occur nonvolitionally (groups 2, 3, and 4).

| | Presence of goal-directed fantasy | Absence of goal-directed fantasy |
|---|---|---|
| Passed test-suggestion | 14 | 9 |
| Failed test-suggestion | 2 | 5 |

Note.—$\chi^2 = 1.14$, $df = 1$, $p > .3$

### *Hypothesis 3. Goal-Directed Fantasy and Passing the Test-Suggestion*

Hypothesis 3 states that, when hypnotic subjects are given test-suggestions which imply that the response is to occur nonvolitionally (groups 2, 3, and 4), those who engage in goal-directed fantasy pass the test-suggestion more often than those who do not engage in such fantasy. Table 3, which presents the relevant data, shows that this hypothesis was not confirmed: subjects who engaged in goal-directed fantasy did not differ significantly from those who did not engage in such fantasy in passing the test-suggestion.

## Discussion

Hypnotic-state theorists seem to assume that subjects who are in a "hypnotic trance state" manifest a unique shift in cognitive functioning to "primary processes" or fantasy activity (Gill & Brenman, 1959; Hilgard, 1965; Orne, 1959; Shor, 1959, 1962) and tend to experience their overt responses to test-suggestions as occurring nonvolitionally (Arnold, 1946; Evans, 1968; Orne, 1959). However, the results of the present experiment do not support the notion that a "trance state" underlies the hypnotic subject's report of fantasy activity or his report that he experienced his responses to suggestions as not involving volition.

Subjects are usually judged to be "hypnotized" or to be in "trance" to the extent that they respond to test-suggestions and report post-experimentally that they were hypnotized (Conn & Conn, 1967; Hilgard, 1965; Hilgard & Tart, 1966). In the present experiment, subjects in all four treatment groups (a) were exposed to the same hypnotic-induction procedure, (b) achieved the same level of overall suggestibility, and (c) rated themselves as having attained the same level of "hypnotic depth." Nonetheless, subjects in the four treatment groups did not display the same amount of goal-directed fantasy and did not define their behavior as lacking volition to the same degree. For example, the 10 subjects who were given the suggestion that their arm was rising (group 2) displayed only two instances of goal-directed fantasy and generally defined their responses as partially voluntary. On the other hand, the 10 subjects who were given the suggestion to imagine a balloon raising their arm (group 4) displayed goal-directed fantasy in every case and generally defined their response as occurring nonvolitionally. It is difficult to reconcile these results with the traditional notion that subjects' experience of nonvolition is a unique function of the extent to which hypnotic-induction procedures have produced a "trance state." Instead, these results indicate that subjects' perceptions of their responses as occurring with or without volition are closely related to the specific wording of the test-suggestions and can vary greatly even when conventional indices of "hypnotic trance depth" remain constant.

Hypotheses 1 and 2 concerning goal-directed fantasy and the experience of nonvolition were confirmed by the results of the present experiment. These data indicate that, as compared to other ways of wording test-suggestions (direct command, direct suggestion, or suggestion to imagine the effect), suggestions which instruct the subject to engage in goal-directed fantasy more often elicit such fantasy and more often elicit reports that the response was experienced as occurring without volition. Moreover, regardless of the wording of the suggestions, subjects who engage in goal-directed fantasy define their responses to suggestions as occuring more nonvolitionally than subjects who do not engage in such fantasy. This relationship holds even when all subjects have been given test-suggestions which imply that the response should be nonvolitional (groups 2, 3, and 4). The results of this experiment thus support the general contention that hypnotic subjects employ goal-directed fantasy as at least one kind of strategy for defining their responses to test-suggestions as nonvolitional. The fact that 40 percent of the subjects who did *not* display goal-directed fantasy defined their overt behavior as involuntary, indicates that these subjects were employing other strategies for defining their behavior as nonvolitional. Empirical specification of these other strategies remains as an important research task.

A series of studies, reviewed by Spanos (1970) and Spanos and Chaves (1970), has demonstrated that the subjective reports of subjects who have and also those who have not been exposed to a hypnotic-induction procedure are highly similar when both groups are administered the *same* test-suggestions (Barber, 1965, 1969, 1970; Barber & Calverley, 1962, 1968; Andersen & Sarbin, 1964; Spanos & Barber, 1968; Spanos, Barber & Lang, 1969). The present experiment complements these findings by demonstrating that subjects' experiences vary markedly as a function of the test-suggestions they are administered, even when they receive the same hypnotic-induction procedure, attain the same level of suggestibility and 'hypnotic depth,' and engage in the same overt behavior. Taken together, these results suggest that subjective reports long considered a hallmark of an 'hypnotic trance state' are closely related to the specific wording of the test-suggestions. Further studies, in which subjects are *not* exposed to hypnotic-induction procedures, may find that the extent to which waking control subjects experience their responses to test-suggestions as nonvolitional is also closely related to the specific wording of the test-suggestions.

## Summary

Forty subjects were exposed to a standardized hypnotic-induction procedure and then to an arm-levitation suggestion worded in 1 of 4 ways. Subjects experienced the arm levitation as more involuntary when the suggestion asked them to engage in a goal-directed fantasy—viz., to imagine a balloon pulling the arm up. The differences in the degree of experienced volition among subjects given differently-worded suggestions for arm levitation could not be explained in terms of differences in suggestibility or "hypnotic depth." The results indicate that suggestions which ask the subject to carry out a goal-directed fantasy—to imagine a situation which, if it actually transpired, would produce the (suggested) response—are important factors in inducing cognitive processes and feelings of nonvolition which have been traditionally attributed to a hypothetical "trance state."

## References

Andersen, M. L., & Sarbin, T. R. Base rate expectancies and motoric alterations in hypnosis. *International Journal of Clinical and Experimental Hypnosis*, 1964, **12**, 147–158.

Arnold, M. B. On the mechanism of suggestion and hypnosis. *Journal of Abnormal and Social Psychology*, 1946, **41**, 107–128.

Barber, T. X. Measuring "hypnotic-like" suggestibility with and without "hypnotic induction"; psychometric properties, norms, and variables influencing response to the Barber Suggestibility Scale (BSS). *Psychological Reports*, 1965, **16**,

809–844.

Barber, T. X. *Hypnosis: A scientific approach.* New York: Van Nostrand Reinhold, 1969.

Barber, T. X. *LSD, Marihuana, Yoga, and Hypnosis.* Chicago: Aldine, 1970.

Barber, T. X., & Calverley, D. S. "Hypnotic" behavior as a function of task motivation. *Journal of Psychology,* 1962, **54**, 363–389

Barber, T. X., & Calverley, D. S. An experimental study of "hypnotic" (auditory and visual) hallucinations. *Journal of Abnormal and Social Psychology,* 1964, **63**, 13–20.

Barber, T. X., & Calverley, D. S. Toward a theory of "hypnotic" behavior: Replication and extension of experiments by Barber and co-workers (1962-65) and Hilgard & Tart (1966). *International Journal of Clinical and Experimental Hypnosis,* 1968, **16**, 179–195.

Barber, T. X., Spanos, N. P., & Merritt, J. Eidetic imagery and suggested 'hallucinations'. Harding, Mass.: Medfield Foundation, 1970.

Conn, J. H., & Conn, R. N. Discussion of T. X. Barber's "Hypnosis as a causal variable in present-day psychology: a critical analysis." *International Journal of Clinical and Experimental Hypnosis,* 1967, **15**, 106–110.

Evans, F. J. Recent trends in experimental hypnosis. *Behavioral Science,* 1968, **13**, 477–487.

Gill, M. M., & Brenman, M. *Hypnosis and related states.* New York: International Universities Press, 1950.

Hilgard, E. R. *Hypnotic susceptibiilty.* New York: Harcourt, Brace, & World, 1965.

Hilgard, E. R., & Tart, C. T. Responsiveness to suggestions following waking and imagination instructions and following induction of hypnosis. *Journal of Abnormal Psycholoy,* 1966, **71**, 196–208.

Orne, M. T. The nature of hypnosis: Artifact and essence. *Journal of Abnormal and Social Psychology,* 1959, **58**, 277–299.

Orne, M. T. Hypnosis, motivation and compliance. *American Journal of Psychiatry,* 1966, **122**, 721–726.

Shor, R. E. Hypnosis and the concept of the generalized reality orientation. *American Journal of Psychotherapy,* 1959, **13**, 582–602.

Shor, R. E. Three dimensions of hypnotic depth. *International Journal of Clinical and Experimental Hypnosis,* 1962, **10**, 23–38.

Spanos, N. P. Barber's reconceptualization of hypnosis: An evaluation of criticisms. *Journal of Experimental Research in Personality,* 1970, **4**, 241–258.

Spanos, N. P. Goal-directed fantasy and the performance of hypnotic test suggestions. *Psychiatry,* 1971, **34**, 86–96.

Spanos, N. P., & Barber, T. X. "Hypnotic" experiences as inferred from subjective reports: Auditory and visual hallucinations. *Journal of Experimental Research in Personality,* 1968, **3**, 136–150.

Spanos, N. P., Barber, T. X., & Lang, G. Cognition and self control: Control of painful sensory input. Boston University, Department of Sociology (Mimeo), 1969.

Spanos, N. P., & Chaves, J. F. Hypnosis research: A methodological critique of experiments generated by two alternative paradigms. *American Journal of Clinical Hypnosis,* 1970, **13**, 108–127.

Weitzenhoffer, A. M., & Hilgard, E. R. *Stanford hypnotic susceptibility scale, Form C.* Palo Alto, California: Consulting Psychologists Press, 1962.

*Manuscript received July 12, 1971.*

SECTION V

# ACUPUNCTURE

# 17

CHAVES, J. F. & BARBER, T. X.

# *Needles and Knives: Behind the Mystery of Acupuncture and Chinese Meridians*

"There are factors already known but usually overlooked by Western medicine, which can help to explain the success of acupuncture."

**Of all the things that have come down to us from the ancient Chinese cultures, acupuncture is surely one of the most puzzling. Why does a needle in the skin during surgery make things hurt less rather than more? So far Western science has been at a loss for good answers. Now two pain researchers have come up with six factors which may help to explain just how it works.**

**John F. Chaves, Ph.D., is a Senior Research Psychologist at the Medfield Foundation, Medfield, Massachusetts. His primary research interest has been in pain, audition and other sensory processes.**

**Theodore X. Barber, Ph.D., has been Director of Psychological Research at the Medfield Foundation and Medfield State Hospital since 1959. He is president-elect of the Massachusetts Psychological Association. Barber is author of *Hypnosis: A Scientific Approach* and *LSD, Marihuana, Yoga and Hypnosis*, and co-editor of the annuals on *Biofeedback and Self-Control*.**

During recent years, physicians from the United States, Canada and England have flocked to China in unprecedented numbers, and one of the wonders they have observed there first-hand is the successful use of acupuncture to relieve surgical pain. Their eyewitness accounts of this phenomenon have set off intense and widespread discussion in articles in the popular press as well as in a series of papers in medical journals.

At least part of the interest in the subject seems to be due to the aura of mystery surrounding it. Acupuncture is billed as an ancient, and therefore inscrutable, Chinese medical art, and it seems to be generally assumed thus far that it defies any rational explanation in Western scientific terms. More than that, the dramatic successes claimed for acupuncture seem to imply that Western science has been somewhat delinquent in failing to delineate certain important factors pertaining to the nature of pain and its control.

We do not accept these implications. On the contrary, we believe that there are factors already known but usually overlooked by Western medicine that can help to explain the success of acupuncture in attenuating pain in surgery.

It's true that acupuncture is very old. The treatment of specific illnesses such as arthritic disorders and gastrointestinal diseases goes back at least 5,000 years. However, it wasn't until 1959 that the Chinese started using acupuncture to produce analgesia in surgery and its use has accelerated since 1968.

During the 14 years that acupuncture has been employed in surgery, the thin needles have been typically inserted at points remote from the location where analgesia is desired. For instance, when a gastrectomy is performed, four acupuncture needles are placed in the pinna or lobe of each ear. Moreover, they are commonly placed in innocuous locations such as in the limbs or the pinnae, remote from major organs, blood vessels or nerve trunks. The needles usually penetrate only a few millimeters, and rarely more than two centimeters, beneath the epidermis. When acupuncture is used for surgery, the needles are not simply inserted; instead, they are either twirled and vibrated by the acupuncturist or electricity is applied to them. In a typical procedure, continuous electrical stimulation is applied to the acupuncture needles from a six- or nine-volt battery at a frequency of 120 to 300 cycles/minute, beginning about half an hour before and continuing throughout the operation. However, it is important to note that *electrical* stimulation does not appear to be essential to the success of acupuncture analgesia. In fact, many times surgery is performed using only manual stimulation of the needles.

The traditional Chinese theory of why this works is beguiling and perhaps adds to the confusing mystery of acupuncture. This theory assumes that there are 12 meridians or channels, called Ching lo, running vertically down the body. These meridians are thought to carry a life energy (Qi or Ch'i). The flow of this energy is believed to maintain a balance between two forces, the Yin and the Yang. Yin is viewed as the weak, female, negative force while Yang is the strong, male, positive force. Yin meridians are associated with such organs as the liver, kidneys and spleen, while Yang meridians are associated with such organs as the stomach, gall bladder and intestines

Disease, the Chinese think, is a reflection of the imbalance of Yin and Yang forces. Thus, disease is cured by inserting acupuncture needles in appropriate locations to correct the imbalance. Consequently, to produce analgesia for surgery, it is necessary to insert acupuncture needles into meridians that control the appropriate organs. And since the meridians are thought to run through the whole body, the points of insertion may be quite remote from the points where analgesia is desired.

Although this ancient theory of acupuncture still appears to have many advocates in China, it certainly is acceptable to few if any Western-trained scientists. It isn't even accepted by all Chinese surgeons. Drs. Pang L. Man and Calvin H. Chen of Northville State Hospital in Michigan, noted that some Chinese surgeons "totally disregarded the recognized spots on the meridians" and used almost any spot to produce surgical analgesia, making it appear that the traditional theory of acupuncture points may be misleading.

Dr. Felix Mann, an English physician who has written several books about acupuncture and who, at one time, accepted the traditional theory, now argues, ". . . I don't believe meridians exist. A lot of acupuncture is based on meridians, and you will see from my theory, I think the meridians of acupuncture are not very much more real than the meridians of geography. And likewise with the acupuncture points." He goes on to note, "The Chinese have so many interconnections in their acupuncture theory that one can explain everything just as politicians do." Patrick Wall, an English physiologist at University College in London, is more succinct in his opinion of meridians, stating, "There is not one scrap of anatomical or physiological evidence for the existence of such a system."

There is at least one Western scientific explanation of how acupuncture works. This is Ronald Melzack's and Patrick Wall's gate control theory of pain. It has been perhaps the first attempt to apply a theory of pain that has any degree of acceptance among Western scientists.

We will examine this theory in more detail later, but briefly stated it asserts that pain depends, in part, on the relative amounts of activity in large A-beta fibers, activated by nonpainful stimuli, and small c-fibers, activated by pain-producing stimuli. Increasing the activity of the A-beta fibers is thought to close a spinal "gate" in the substantia gelatinosa, a section of the spinal cord, preventing the further transmission of information from the c-fibers. As applied to acupuncture, it is assumed that acupuncture needles selectively stimulate the A-beta fibers and that the high level of activity in the A-beta fibers closes the "gate" and thus inhibits pain.

Whichever theory one accepts, the Chinese or the Western gate theory, it is generally assumed that if the acupuncture needles are inserted in the appropriate locations and are either twirled manually or electricity is applied to them, sufficient reduction in pain is produced so that the patient can tolerate major surgical procedures. But the notion that the reduction in pain is due to the effects of the needles has diverted attention from other possible explanations. We believe there are six such factors that may offer a more realistic explanation of why acupuncture seems to work.

### 1. Beliefs and Lack of Anxiety

The widespread assumption that acupuncture is routinely employed with surgical patients in China is false. The chief delegate of a group of Chinese physicians who visited the United States in the fall of 1972 expressed concern "lest the Americans misunderstand (acupuncture analgesia) as an established, standard technique in China." Dr. E. Grey Dimond, of the University of Missouri Medical School at Kansas City, who visited China, writes, "The decision to use acupuncture anesthesia depended on the full enthusiasm and acceptance by the patient." Patients who are anxious, tense or frightened are given general anesthesia. As Dr. F. Z. Warren observed, Chinese surgeons typically select patients for acupuncture according to the following criteria: "They decide whether the type of operation would be suitable, whether the patient would be too hysterical, whether the patient believes firmly in Mao's teaching, or would Mao's teaching carry him through." Since general anesthesia is available for surgery in China, the motivation to forego general anesthesia and to undergo surgery with acupuncture is probably due, according to Dr. Dimond, to the ". . . immense pressure to comply and participate in the current Mao Thought Program which is a fundamental requirement for life in China." Before surgery with acupuncture is commenced, the patient and the attending physicians recite quotations from Chairman Mao's book and Mao's picture faces the patients in every operating room. At the end of the operation, the patients thank Chairman Mao for the surgery.

Other cultural factors intensify the Chinese people's acceptance of acupuncture. In some localities in China, the insertion of acupuncture needles is practiced by laymen about as casually as individuals in Western countries take aspirin tablets. In some parts of China, Dr. Ian Capperauld, a visiting surgeon from Edinburgh, saw that "young children practice inserting needles into one another's arms, legs and face to become proficient both as user and as a recipient."

It should be emphasized also that the Chinese learn early in life to expect little or no discomfort during surgery, even when the surgery is performed without drugs and without acupuncture. One eyewitness, British physician P. E. Brown, recalls:

> *While visiting a children's hospital we saw a queue of smiling 5-year-olds standing outside a room where tonsillectomies were being carried out in rapid succession. The leading child was given a quick anaesthetic spray of the throat by a nurse, a few minutes before walking into the theatre unaccompanied. Each youngster in turn climbed on the table, lay back smiling at the surgeon, opened his mouth wide, and had his tonsils dissected out in the extraordinary time of less than a minute. The only instruments used were dissecting scissors and forceps. The child left the table and walked into the recovery room, spitting blood into a gauze swab. A bucket of water at the surgeon's feet containing thirty-four tonsils of all sizes was proof of the morning's work. This tonsillectomy technique is significant inasmuch as it indicates that, without recourse to acupuncture, the Chinese patient is conditioned from early childhood to accept surgical interference with his body with the full knowledge that it is going to*

*be successful and he will experience little or no discomfort.*

**2. Special Preparation and Indoctrination Prior to Surgery**

Patients who are selected for surgery with acupuncture receive rather special treatment preoperatively. Usually, the patient comes to the hospital two days before the operation and the surgeons explain to him exactly what they are going to do, show him just how they will operate, and describe what the acupuncturist will do and what effects the needles will have. The patient is asked to talk to other patients who have had the same kind of surgery and he is also given a set of acupuncture needles so that he can try them on himself.

Dr. Capperauld observed, "Acupuncture anesthesia tended to work better in nonemergency situations in which the patients had a few days indoctrination prior to operation. Emergency operations were done usually under conventional spinal techniques."

Although this kind of special preoperative preparation and indoctrination for surgery is not employed in the United States, there is evidence to indicate that "preoperative education," even if very limited, can have a beneficial effect on surgical patients. For instance, Dr. Lawrence D. Egbert of Harvard found that a five- or 10-minute preoperative visit by an anesthesiologist had a greater calming effect on surgical patients than two mg./kg. of pentobarbital sodium. Moreover, patients who were informed about the kind of postsurgical pain they might experience required smaller doses of narcotics for postsurgical pain than uninformed controls. An unexpected bonus was that the informed patients were discharged from the hospital sooner than the controls.

Thus, it appears that the preoperative period for special preparation and indoctrination for acupuncture works to ease the patient's anxiety, to strengthen his "belief and trust in acupuncture," as Patrick Wall says, and to lessen his need for large doses of pain-relieving drugs.

Dr. Felix Mann has recently provided further support for the notion that the patient's belief in the effectiveness of acupuncture is crucial to its success. Working in England with 100 volunteer subjects, he attempted to use acupuncture to produce analgesia to pinpricks that were severe enough to draw blood. He failed to get satisfactory results in at least 90 percent of the subjects, a tremendous contrast to the success rate reported in China. Mann omitted just one vital step that Chinese physicians include: the effort to convince subjects ahead of time that acupuncture would be highly effective.

**3. Suggestions for Pain Relief**

In addition to the preoperative indoctrination, the patient's belief that acupuncture will mitigate pain is continually bolstered by direct and indirect suggestions even during the operation itself. Even when acupuncture is used to treat specific diseases, Dr. James L. Rhee, an anesthesiologist from the University of California Medical Center noted, "... the acupuncturists whom I have watched work, load their therapy with suggestions."

The effectiveness of indirect suggestion has been evident for years in Western medicine. As far back as 1889, Dr. C. Lloyd Tuckey wrote:

*There are few cases of this kind more remarkable than one related by Mr. Woodhouse Braine, the well-known chloroformist. Having to administer ether to an hysterical girl who was about to be operated on for the removal of two sebaceous tumors from the scalp he found that the ether bottle was empty, and that the inhaling bag was free from even the odor of any anesthetic. While a fresh supply was being obtained, he thought to familiarize the patient with the process by putting the inhaling bag over her mouth and nose, and telling her to breath quietly and deeply. After a few inspirations she cried, "Oh, I feel it; I am going off," and a moment after, her eyes turned up, and she became unconscious. As she was found to be perfectly insensible, and the ether had not yet come, Mr. Brainé proposed that the surgeon should proceed with the operation. One tumor was removed without in the least disturbing her, and then, in order to test her condition, a bystander said that she was coming to. Upon this she began to show signs of waking, so the bag was once more applied, with the remark, "She'll soon be off again," when she immediately lost sensation and the operation was successfully and painlessly completed.*

Working under primitive conditions in a prisoner of war hospital near Singapore during World War II, Australian surgeons found to their surprise that "the mere suggestion of anesthesia" was sufficient to perform minor surgery on the soldiers without apparent pain. More recent experiences in Bulgaria show that suggestions of anesthesia are at times enough to carry out major surgery with little pain.

Placebos are also a way of implanting mental suggestion. Dr. J. D. Hardy et al, in *Pain Sensations and Reactions*, published in 1952, reported that pain thresholds could be elevated 90 percent over control levels when an inactive drug was administered with the suggestion that it was a strong analgesic. Moreover, placebos have been found to be effective in alleviating postsurgical pain as well as chronic pain in many patients.

A series of studies conducted in our laboratory showed that suggestions of anesthesia are also effective in attenuating experimentally induced pain. In one study, suggestions of insensitivity attenuated cold-pressor pain and in another study suggestions of anesthesia reduced the pain produced by a heavy weight applied to a finger. Using the same pain stimulus on the finger, we found that the mere expectation of pain attenuation led to a reduction in pain, although larger reductions were obtained when subjects were asked to vividly imagine pleasant experiences.

**4. Distraction Produced by Acupuncture Needles**

The insertion and subsequent stimulation of the acupuncture needles is accompanied by various sensations. At times, the electric current that is applied to the needles is strong enough to produce rather strong muscular contraction. Also, the needles are manipulated by hand or stimulated electrically for 20 to 30 minutes prior to surgery and the patient often feels "sore" at the needle sites. Sometimes a slight aching sensation has been reported when the needle has been properly placed, and some patients say the acupuncture needles produce severe pain. Dr. Mann found with his brave pinprick subjects that in order to reduce the pain of pinpricks it was necessary, in most cases, to increase the pain produced by the acupuncture needles "... to more or less torture levels."

In describing his own sensations while undergoing acupuncture for the relief of postsurgical abdominal pain, James Reston noted that the needles "... sent ripples of pain racing through my limbs and, at least, had the effect of diverting my attention from the distress in my stomach."

Thus it appears that the various sensations produced by the needles can serve as distractions. Present evidence indicates that distraction is an effective way of lessening pain. One study by S. L. H. Notermans found substantial increases of 40 to 50 percent in the pain threshold when subjects were distracted by performing an irrelevant task, in this case inflating a manometer cuff.

Psychologists F. H. Kanfer and D. A. Goldfoot showed that pain could be reduced by three types of distracters: observing interesting slides, self-pacing with a clock and verbalizing the sensations aloud. Similarly, Barber et al demonstrated that experimentally induced pain could be reduced by various kinds of distractions such as listening to an interesting tape-recorded story, adding numbers aloud and purposively thinking of pleasant events.

Counterirritation can also be an effective distraction. Studies conducted more than 30 years ago showed that experimentally induced pain could be lessened by several kinds of counterirritations including heat, cold, vibration, electric stimulation and static electricity. The same researchers, G. D. Gammon and I. Starr, also found that counterirritation worked in alleviating clinical pain. In one group of 60 clinical patients, 90 percent enjoyed at least some degree of relief, although the most effective type of counterirritation varied from patient to patient.

If such a wide variety of distractions can work to attenuate pain, clearly the acupuncture needles themselves can serve as effective distracters. But even in addition to the needles, some acupuncture patients receive special deep breathing exercises which they later are requested to carry out during the operation itself. By focusing their attention on their breathing, the patients may be provided with an additional useful distraction.

**5. Use of Narcotic Analgesics, Local Anesthetics and Sedatives**

Popular accounts often neglect to state that narcotic analgesics, local anesthetics and sedatives are often used when patients undergo surgery with acupuncture. Drs. Man and Chen state that the Chinese routinely administer 50 to 60 mg. of meperidine hydrochloride (Demerol) in an intravenous drip during an operation with acupuncture.

Of the six cases described by Dr. Dimond, five received a pain-relieving drug. One patient was given phenobarbital sodium the night before surgery for the removal of a brain tumor, but she did not receive any pain-relieving drugs during the actual surgery. Although she was described as "conscious, but very weak," she tolerated the operation without signs of pain. This was indeed a remarkable case, but it should be noted that brain tissue is generally insensitive to the surgeon's scalpel. Moreover, in other eyewitness reports of operations for cerebral tumor carried out with acupuncture, it is emphasized that the surgeons infiltrated the scalp with 50 milliliters of 0.125 percent procaine before the incision was made.

Dr. Capperauld also learned that sedatives, analgesics and local anesthetics were typically administered, which led him to ask, "The real question to be answered, therefore, is which therapy, the acupuncture needle or the concomitant Western medication, is the adjunct?" In some cases, the drugs that are given during acupuncture fail to control pain; that is, the patient complains of intolerable pain and general anesthesia is administered. Dimond estimated that this kind of failure occurred in China in at least 10 percent of the selected patients. During a recent three-week visit to China, Dr. Marcel Gemperle failed to find a single case where acupuncture produced complete insensitivity and, in one case, the patient screamed and moved about on the operating table during surgery.

**6. Overestimation of Surgical Pain**

In Western medicine, anesthetic or analgesic agents are almost always used during major surgery. Therefore, there is little scientific information about base-line levels of pain experienced by surgical patients who have not been anesthetized. However, even during the preanesthetic era (prior to the 1840s) some patients undergoing major surgery without drugs, according to contemporary accounts, "bravely made no signs of suffering at all." In one such operation carried out in the early 1800s, a woman who underwent a mastectomy tolerated the surgery "... without a word, and after being bandaged up, got up, made a curtsy, thanked the surgeon and walked out of the room."

Patients of this type probably represented only a small minority, but they illustrate the major importance of determining base levels of pain when evaluating procedures such as acupuncture.

The available knowledge indicates that surgical procedures produce anxiety and fear, but they usually give rise to less pain than is commonly believed. In summarizing the relevant evidence, Sir Thomas Lewis, an English physician, emphasized that, although the skin is very sensitive, the muscles, bone and most of the internal organs are relatively insensitive. More precisely, the skin is sensitive to a knife cut, but the underlying tissues and internal organs are generally insensitive *to incision*, although they are generally sensitive to other forms of stimulation such as traction or distention. For example, Dr. Lewis noted that the subcutaneous tissue gives rise to little pain when it is cut and slight pain is elicited when muscles are incised. Most of the internal organs also produce little or no pain when they are cut; these include the liver, spleen, kidneys, stomach, jejunum, ileum, colon, lungs, surface of the heart, esophageal wall and uterus. Traction upon the hollow viscera, however, is painful. Also, the surgeon's incision produces pain when it cuts the skin and other external tissues, such as the conjunctiva, the mucous membranes of the mouth and nasopharynx, the upper surface of the larynx and the stratified mucous membranes of the genitalia and also when it cuts a small number of deeper tissues, such as the deep fascia, the periosteum, the tendons and the rectum.

In the early 1900s, a German surgeon, Dr. K. G. Lennander, published a series of case reports showing that major abdominal operations can be accomplished painlessly using only local anesthetics, such as cocaine, to dull the pain of the initial incision through the skin. Dr. J. F. Mitchell also reported an extensive series of major operations performed with local anesthetics used to produce insensitivity of the skin. These included: limb amputations, thyroidectomies, mastectomies, suprapubic cystostomies, laparotomies, excision of glands in the neck and groin, herniorrhaphies, cholecystostomies and appendectomies.

Dr. Mitchell confirmed Lennander's observation regarding the surprising insensitivity of internal organs. For example, he described the following:

> *The skin being thoroughly anesthetized and the incision made, there is little sensation in the subcutaneous tissue and muscles as long as blood vessels, large nerve trunks and connective tissue bundles are avoided.... The same insensibility to pain in bone has been noted in several cases of amputation, in removal of osteophytes and wiring of fractures. In every instance after thorough cocainization of the periosteum, the actual manipulations of the bone itself have been unaccompanied by pain. The patients have stated that they feel and hear the sawing, but it was as if a board were being sawn while resting upon some part of the body.*

The data presented by Lewis, Lennander and Mitchell suggest that the pain associated with major surgical procedures may not always be as great as is usually supposed. It is certainly clear that the amount of pain is not related in any simple way to the extent of surgical intervention. If a patient is relaxed and not anxious and if he can tolerate the initial incision through the skin, it appears that many major surgical procedures can be accomplished without much additional pain. The administration of small or moderate doses of narcotic analgesics and sedatives, as is usually done with acupuncture, makes the patient's task that much easier.

Chinese surgeons who use acupuncture conduct their operations very slowly and carefully. Rib-spreaders employed during thoracotomies are opened slowly. Also, surgeons avoid putting traction on such tissues as the pleura and peritoneum, which are known to be sensitive to this kind of stress. When these tissues are stretched, acupuncture patients grimace, sweat and show other signs of experiencing extreme pain just as would be expected on the basis of the data summarized by Lewis. Acupuncture is difficult to use in abdominal surgery because it is hard to avoid putting traction on these tissues and because acupuncture does not produce adequate relaxation of the abdominal muscles.

All of these factors point to some major difficulties in using the gate control theory to account for acupuncture analgesia. The gate theory, it will be remembered, holds that the stimulation of certain nerve fibers closes a gate in the spinal cord and blocks off the sensation of pain. First of all, the "gate" is a hypothetical entity that has not been established anatomically. Even if the "gate" were shown to exist, the gate control theory, as originally formulated, could only account for analgesia in the vicinity of the nerves stimulated by the acupuncture needles. However, as we noted earlier, acupuncture needles are inserted at points far removed from the area where relief is desired. A related difficulty is that many of the locations commonly employed in acupuncture, such as the head or ear lobes, would be ineffective in closing the spinal "gate." Thus, it becomes necessary to postulate the existence of a second "gate," presumably located at some higher level of the nervous system, in order to account for the efficacy of needles inserted at these locations. While it is not easy to rule out this possibility entirely, neither is it satisfactory simply to make up new "gates" on an *ad hoc* basis to account for anomalous findings.

Wall, who is one of the original coauthors of the gate control theory, has admitted, "My present guess is that it will emerge that acupuncture does not generate the specifically pain-inhibiting barrages for which I was looking." However, Melzack, the other coauthor of the theory, has recently argued that the theory is relevant to acupuncture. Nevertheless, while the gate control theory may appear to be useful in explaining the successes of acupuncture, it is very difficult to see how this theory can explain its failures. Why is it necessary for acupuncture patients to believe in its effectiveness? If acupuncture needles can close the "gate," why is it necessary to administer narcotic analgesics, sedatives and local anesthetics to acupuncture patients? Why is the "gate" capable of reducing the pain of surgery in China but incapable of reducing the pain of pinpricks in England? Unfortunately, the gate control theory fails to provide answers to these important questions. It appears to us that speculations about the physiological basis for acupuncture may be premature.

It has sometimes been suggested that a physiological theory of acupuncture is needed to explain anecdotal reports in the popular press, which suggest that acupuncture may be useful in performing surgery with rabbits, horses and other mammals. Of course, these statements in newspapers and magazines cannot be evaluated until such time as non-anecdotal studies are presented which, at least, utilize minimal controls. Since there is much evidence demonstrating that many mammals, including rabbits and horses, can tolerate extremely painful stimuli when they are appropriately restrained, controlled studies may find that acupuncture is not especially helpful in operating on mammals.

As more data become available, we will be able to identify additional factors to help explain this phenomenon. It remains to be demonstrated, however, that acupuncture needles exert any specific analgesic effects beyond the six factors we have discussed in this article. Certainly, future attempts to explain the success of acupuncture in easing surgical pain should take these factors into serious consideration.

We would argue that the success of acupuncture analgesia underscores the importance of psychological factors in the control of pain. Obviously, more research is needed to determine the relative importance of the six factors outlined here and to identify additional factors that could help to explain the phenomenon. Providing the basis for a more comprehensive explanation of why acupuncture works will be an exciting area for future research. HB

---

*Bibliography can be obtained by writing to the authors. John F. Chaves, Ph.D., and Theodore X. Barber, Ph.D., Medfield State Hospital, Research Department, Medfield, Massachusetts 02052.*

# 18

## FREESE, A. S.

# *What Acupuncture Won't Do*

IT'S NO PANACEA. It can kill. And it has lots of failures—that certainly is proven. It's true it can kill pain, but then so do placebos (sugar pills) and faith healing. Not even the Chinese use it as a panacea or as routine anesthetic. In fact, they only use it for surgery under prepared conditions. If you were wheeled into one of their hospitals right off the street as an accident or emergency victim and immediate surgery was necessary, you could expect not acupuncture but a spinal anesthetic such as you might get in any American hospital.

Let's look at acupuncture from the ground up. The beginnings of acupuncture are vague, but there is talk of it starting 5000 years ago. According to one legend, acupuncture began when a Chinese soldier was hit by an arrow in battle and noticed a sensation of numbness in a distant part of his body. Another version has it that a Chinese emperor noticed that arrows buried in his soldiers sometimes cured various ailments.

The exact origin remains undiscovered, but early acupuncture (the Latin *acus* means needle), like all ancient medicine, was a combination of philosophy, magic, mysticism and faith heeling—for virtually nothing was known of the causes of disease or even of the human body itself. Acupuncturists talk of *Yin* and *Yang* which represent the opposing forces of dark, negativism and cold and those of light, positivism and warmth. Evidently a sexist, the ancient and the current acupuncturist believes the negative Yin corresponds to women, and Yang to the men.

Disease according to this theory is an imbalance of these elements and beyond that it gets more abstruse and increasingly difficult to understand. Diagnosis was and still is chiefly made

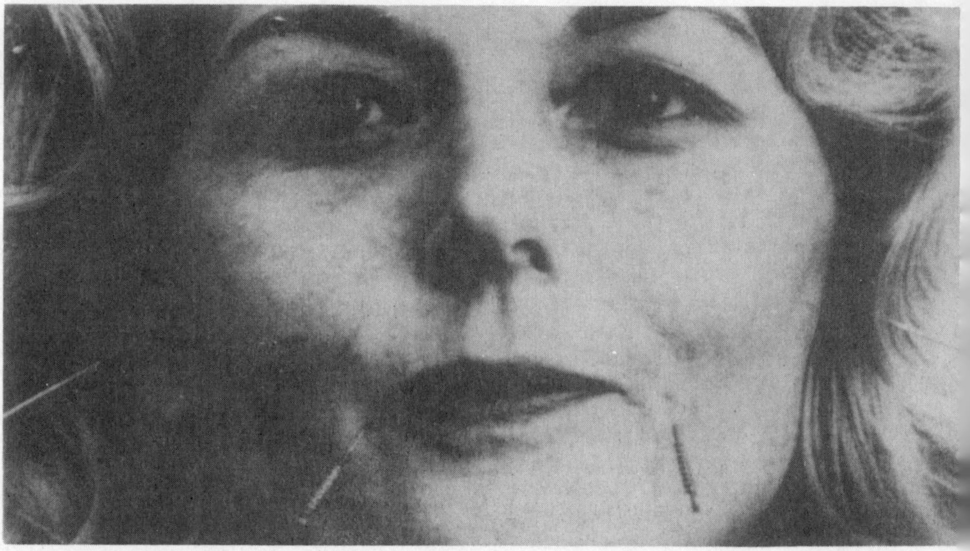

on the basis of pulse examination; but treatment has three applications—for diseases of all kinds, (the way-out acupuncturists promise help for virtually everything), for pain and as an anesthetic for surgery. Although the acupuncture fad exploded on the American scene with the suddenness of a Roman candle, it would be difficult to find physicians here who use acupuncture instead of penicillin for an infection—or patients who would accept this.

But it is in the world of pain and chronic diseases like arthritis, where medicine still provides only limited relief, that unhappy sufferers turn to acupuncture. Here the doctor himself may get swept up in the headlong rush to seize on something new which promises help by its very newness and mystery. But is there any hardnosed scientific reality concerning it? What has been recorded? What have valid studies, if any, shown about it?

*Above, patient receives acupuncture treatment at USC School of Dentistry for previously incurable dental pains. Conventional methods had proven ineffective. Photo, opposite page shows commercially available model, which displays insertion points.*

Acupuncture is not harmless—it can and has proved fatal for many.

Dr. Edgar Berman, a retired research surgeon and former medical consultant to former Vice President Hubert Humphrey, observed in China an operation for acute appendicitis and the treatment of a tuberculosis patient, both using the traditional needles. "I watched them treat both these cases with acupuncture, and I saw the patients die," he says.

And in this country in one noted case, a woman died as a result of a self-administered misplaced acupuncture needle that ruptured her coronary artery, which supplies the heart muscle. Acupuncturists themselves admit that, even without hitting a nerve or blood vessel directly, improperly placed needles can kill or inflict serious harm on a person.

Acupuncture also has been known to cause infections which are potentially fatal. New York City's Commissioner of Health, Dr. Joseph A. Cimino, is concerned over the danger of infection because acupuncturists are said to either seldom sterilize their needles or do so improperly, and there are indications that some patients have broken out in abscesses after treatments. There is particular concern over the possible spread of hepatitis from contaminated needles. Almost all American doctors and dentists today don't even trust office sterilization but use disposable needles for their hypodermic injections, discarding them after each patient.

The use of acupuncture for disease is usually ignored by American medical scientists because the talk of such things as elements, energy flow, meridians and channels is incomprehensible to Western science and there is no scientific evidence to justify it. Even Western-trained Chinese physicians are doubtful because of its many failures, such as the acupuncture treatments on Mao-Tse-Tung himself. With the best of practitioners available to him, he is reported still crippled by arthritis and sometimes hardly able to walk. Clearly Mao himself has gotten no help from the acupuncture which he forced into an uneasy alliance with modern medicine in 1958 during "The Great Leap Forward." Actually the acupuncture upsurge is heavily involved with the Chinese political scene, Mao and national pride.

But what are the facts? Only recently *The New York Times* reported how, over the last 15 years, acupuncture has been tried in medical facilities in the Soviet Union for conditions such as stomach ulcers, asthma, constipation and high blood pressure. Of some 10,000 such patients in 37 cities, 32.7 percent were "cured." Help is claimed in more than 50 percent of cases in some studies. This is identical to the percentage of patients who claim relief from any pain in scientifically controlled tests with placebos.

Increasingly there are new reports of acupuncture used for medical conditions. The late Frank Leahy, Notre Dame coach, tried acupuncture in his losing battle against leukemia; Premier Lon Nol of Cambodia received

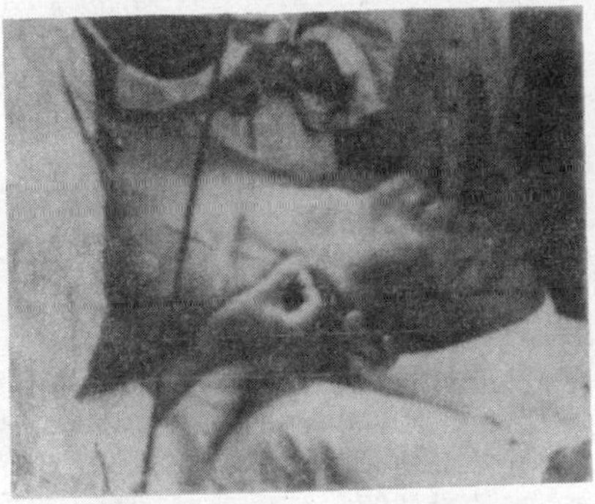

*A nurse at a Peking hospital inserts small needle in neck of patient to anesthetize him for surgery on a thyroid tumor.*

it unsuccessfully for the after-effects of his stroke. A Chinese physician who treated Gov. George Wallace with acupuncture gave the opinion that the Governor might walk again. This has not happened. Yet the doctor claims some success, since: "Perhaps most significant is the improvement in the Governor's mental condition," he says.

Dr. Berman (Humphrey's one-time medical consultant) was actually trained in acupuncture by a Chinese mentor when he was Chief of the

U.S. Marine Corps Hospital at Peking in the mid-forties. His mentor's wife arranged for his training—in return for treating the family with Western medicine, and she used Berman's aspirin in preference to her own husband's needles for her monthly headache. Dr. Berman recalls the 30-year-long acupuncture treatment (called successful by his acupuncturist) of an opium addict who smoked at least eight pipes daily. The "success" was that on each day following treatment the addict rarely smoked more than six pipes.

At the June, 1973, Los Angeles Annual Scientific Session of the American Rheumatism section of the Arthritis Foundation, two papers were presented on acupuncture in rheumatoid arthritis. In one, Canadian investigators found that pain was relieved for a somewhat longer period than with steroids, such as cortisone, but there was an actual increase in inflammation, a symptom the steroids reduced. In short the disease worsened with acupuncture although the pain lessened. And a University of California study found there was no improvement in an arthritic patient although the needles did seem to help the pain. But so did sham acupuncture (putting the needles in the wrong places superficially, and not twirling them). The California team concluded: ". . . a placebo effect contributed at least partially to the observed analgesia [painkilling]."

It's virtually only in the relief of pain and in anesthesia that any hope is expressed by those interested in this treatment. Actually the needles *do* hurt a good deal according to objective observers who've undergone it. Many conclude that it is necessary for the effect—the old counter-irritant action such as the mustard plaster or dental poultice.

Yet there's a lot of money to be made in acupuncture. *Newsweek* reported recently that a correspondence course was being offered by the North American College of Acupuncture. Set up in a Vancouver, B. C., shopping center by a Hong Kong acupuncturist and an Australian, it charged $1650 for training, which included a trip to Hong Kong for a month of actual practice—and had already attracted 200 pupils including some 30 U.S. physicians.

One knowledgeable doctor later reported that the whole presentation, with its leading acupuncturists from around the globe, belonged in an old-fashioned revivalist meeting, not a modern scientific medical society.

One of our leading scientific acupuncture researchers, Dr. Ronald L. Katz, professor of anesthesiology at the University of California at Los Angeles, points out that "Acupuncture is clearly not a panacea nor do the Chinese, off the record, regard it as such." And Dr. Sidney Diamond, professor of neurology at New York's Mount Sinai School of Medicine, had this same experience with a visiting Chinese gynecologist who admitted that even in China no surgeon would rely on acupuncture for the pain of such diseases as terminal uterine cancer, but would turn to medication just as physicians do here.

One professor of medicine at an Eastern Medical Center has a half dozen patients who've tried acupuncture for everything from Meniere's disease to spinal disc problems with absolutely no sign of relief in any case. Another physician, Dr. John Bookman, a professor of medicine at New York's Mt. Sinai Medical School, tells of a dozen patients who've tried the needles for a variety of different difficulties from sinus trouble to bursitis. Of all these, only one claimed to have gotten help for a couple of months from the everyday pain of neck arthritis—and this 50-year-old patient was, as the physician described: "a person in whom I strongly doubt the actual presence of constant pain."

Public demonstrations too have shown constant failure. In New York City, an anesthesiologist got no relief from his broken wrist pain, and a New York State dentist in another demonstration had no easing of his pain while another got no help for his loss of the sense of smell.

*A dentist (below) and two anesthesiologists perform root canal treatment on a dental patient who is under acupuncture anesthesia.*

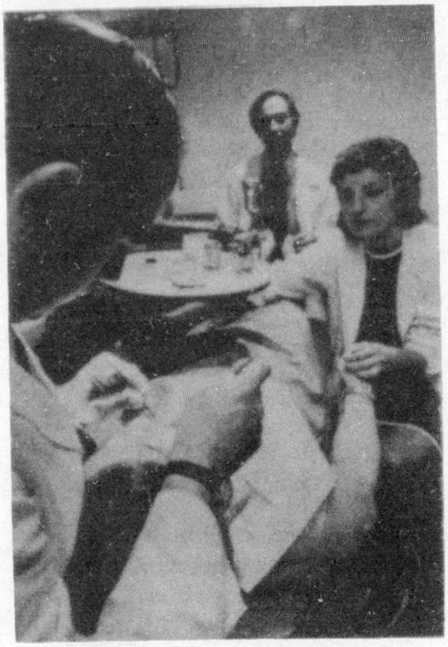

Those carrying out scientific studies of acupuncture tend to avoid publicity because of the experimental nature of the work. One such expert, a professor of rehabilitation medicine at one of our oldest medical schools, has been trained in acupuncture at Marseilles and performed more than a thousand treatments at his center here. His summary is frank: "Acupuncture is terribly misunderstood and overrated and there is too much public hysteria over it, even among the doctors. It gives no better than 50 percent success [essentially the same as the sugar pill] and it's as if you slap the face of a kid who's hurt his foot and he won't feel the pain in the foot. Moreover, acupuncture treatments have to be given over a considerable period, say two or three months—and remember, time alone may often heal."

He has also found that "the people most amenable to improvement with acupuncture are those who are highly susceptible to suggestion." This has been shown by Dr. Herbert Spiegel, a professor of psychiatry at Columbia University, and Dr. Katz, in a study in which they found that only the patients who were hypnotizable got help from acupuncture. This similarity to hypnosis is very strong in the control of pain both for disease conditions and for surgery.

Actually, repeated failures occur with acupuncture anesthesia. Only this year, Professor Marcel Gemperle, director of the Geneva University Institute for Anesthesiology, is said by the Associated Press to have reported to his Swiss colleagues that he and three others did not see a single case in China in which acupuncture produced complete insensitivity to pain and even saw at least one instance—a chest operation in a Shanghai hospital, on a 48-year-old man—where the patient "began to move, screamed, coughing all the time." Dr. Ian Capperauld of Edinburgh, on a medical tour of China, found that there was an indoctrination of several days needed, and that in many of the patients before surgery, various medications (barbiturates) were used as well. Emergency operations were usually done under the spinal anesthesia we use and Capperauld raises the question of which is the adjunct—the drug or the needles?

Chinese physicians themselves warn that acupuncture anesthesia should not be used uncritically, and usually heed their own warnings. In many circumstances it cannot be used, such as with children. There are often poor results with acupuncture anesthesia; it is not always complete, and in long operations the anesthesia seems to wear off as the time passes.

Reports in the Chinese medical literature are definitely inadequate by scientific standards. For example, we would not regard an incomplete anesthesia as "satisfactory." In articles, the Chinese consider "mild pain" as successful anesthesia, and do *not* list such results with pain as a "failure!" Certainly any American, doctor or patient, would regard feeling pain under anesthesia during surgery as a distinct failure of either technique or anesthesia.

Most medical scientists here feel that while acupuncture may work for certain pains, it is still only an experimental technique in their eyes, and Dr. Diamond points out that a patient should not be charged for it under these circumstances. Perhaps if this were done, there would be a lot less acupuncture carried out. Finally, there is no scientifically accepted proof that acupuncture is any better at relieving pain than any of the many other ways available today, and that the same overall results cannot be achieved with different and well-tried methods. These conclusions elicit new perspectives about the validity of acupuncture.

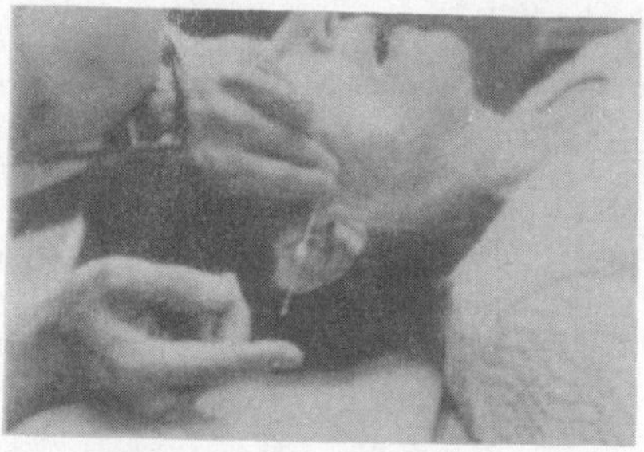

*Here a patient gets zapped with an acupuncture needle, her face showing considerable discomfort. A Swiss doctor reports that in China he saw a patient screaming and coughing as physicians twirled needles into him.*

Remember that careful scientific studies have shown that even sugar pills can relieve up to 50 percent of pain; that the power of suggestion can relieve the pain following surgery and even that of cancer. The plain fact is drugs have been doing well by pain for more than a century. All trained observers are agreed on one thing—that final proof is many years off and today's acupuncture patient in America is in many ways only a guinea pig, so perhaps you should think twice before spending your money to get needled. ■

SECTION VI

# MEDITATION, YOGA, AND RELIGIOUS EXPERIENCE

# 19

## ORNSTEIN, R. E.

# *Selections from the Psychology of Consciousness*

### Some Psychological Research Related to Concentrative Meditation

There is research which casts some light on *how* the meditation exercises affect consciousness: a body of work on the psychological and physiological effects of restricting awareness to an unchanging stimulus. We can examine meditation techniques in these psychological terms. For instance, one variety of concentrative meditation uses a "steady gaze" on either a natural object or a specially constructed one, a mandala. A very similar situation would arise if input to the eye were always the same, no matter how one moved one's eyes.

Normally, as we look at the world, our eyes move around and fixate at various points in large movements which are called "saccades." We hardly ever gaze steadily at any one object for a prolonged period of time. Even when we try to fix vision on a single object, very small involuntary movements of the eye occur, called "optical nystagmus." The image on the retina is kept in constant motion by both types of eye movements, and different cells are stimulated from moment to moment.

A group of physiological psychologists have succeeded in devising a system that will keep a visual image perfectly stable on the retina, even though the eyes are in constant motion. One apparatus for producing this "stabilized" image consists of an extremely small projector mounted on a contact lens worn by the subject. The contact lens moves with every movement of the eyeball, and so does the projector. The projector faces the eyeball, and no matter how the eye is moved, the same image always falls on the retina.[18]

This study of stabilized images was undertaken in psychology primarily to investigate a theory of Donald Hebb, according to which continuous change in input is needed to maintain normal awareness. It was felt that "stabilizing" the image would eliminate the continuous changes in input that normally occur as we move our eyes. The subjects, looking at the stabilized images, reported that the images disappeared.

Lehmann, Beeler, and Fender attempted to investigate the brain state evoked by the stabilized image.[19] The electroencephalogram (EEG), recorded at the scalp, consists of the tiny electrical potentials that emanate from the brain. These potentials, which are about 5 to 50 millionths of a volt as recorded at the scalp, are amplified and written out on paper by the electroencephalograph. The first brain rhythm was discovered by Hans Berger in 1924, and was termed the "alpha" rhythm; it consists of rhythmic activity between 8 and 12 Hertz (cycles per second). Since Berger, other rhythms have been classified: beta, defined as 12 cycles and above; theta, 4-7 Hz; and delta, 1-4 Hz. The alpha rhythm in the occipital cortex is usually thought to represent a state of decreased visual attention to the external environment. It almost always increases when the eyes are closed, or when the eyes are rolled up into the head, cutting off vision.

These investigators recorded the EEG from the occipital cortex of the brain while their observer was viewing the stabilized image. They asked their observer to press a button when the stabilized image disappeared, and they attempted to correlate the subjective experience of the disappearance of the image with the concurrent brain state. They found that the alpha rhythm was likely to appear at the time when the subject reported the disappearance of the image.

Another way to supply the observer with uniform visual input is to have him observe a completely patternless visual field, called a "ganzfeld." This field can be produced in many ways. A white-washed surface can serve as a ganzfeld, as can two halved ping-pong balls placed over the eyes.[20]

In viewing the ganzfeld, some observers reported an absence of any visual experience—which they called "blank-out." This was not merely the experience of seeing nothing, but one of not seeing, a complete disappearance of the sense of vision for short periods of time, as Cohen put it. The experience of not seeing at all usually occurred after about twenty minutes of exposure to the ganzfeld. During "blank-out" the observers did not know, for instance, whether their eyes were open or not, and they could not even control their eye movements. Cohen's suggestion was that this continuous uniform stimulation resulted in the failure of any kind of image to be produced in consciousness. He also found that the periods of blank-out were associated with bursts of alpha rhythm. He suggested that the appearance of alpha during these continuous stimulation periods indicated a functional similarity between continuous stimulation and no stimulation at all. He also found that individuals with high-alpha EEG's were more susceptible to the blank-out phenomenon.

Tepas performed a study on the ganzfeld similar to that of

Lehmann, Beeler, and Fender on the stabilized image. His observers watched the ganzfeld for five-minute periods while EEG's were recorded. When the observer experienced the blank-out, he was asked to press a microswitch that marked the EEG record. Tepas found that the alpha activity of the brain increased during the period of blank-out.[21]

Both the situation and the effects of the stabilized image and of the ganzfeld are similar to those of concentrative meditation. Consider the activity of the observer in meditation and in the two precisely regulated input situations: in both an attempt is made to provide unchanging input. And the subjective experience is analogous in these situations: there is a loss of contact with the external world. In both situations, EEG monitoring of the brain's activity reveals an increase in alpha rhythm. The electrophysiological studies of meditation by Bagchi and Wanger, those by Anand and others in India on Yoga meditation, and those by Kasamatsu and Hirai, and by Akishige in Japan, on Zen meditation, and by Wallace in the United States on Transcendental Meditation, indicate that meditation also is a high-alpha state.[22] The more precisely controlled situations seem to produce, both psychologically and physiologically, effects similar to those of concentrative meditation.

One consequence of the way our central nervous system is structured seems to be that, if awareness is restricted to one unchanging source of stimulation, a "turning off" of consciousness of the external world follows. The common instructions for concentrative meditation all underscore this; one is advised to be constantly aware of the object of meditation and nothing else, to continuously recycle the same input over and over. Stabilizing a visual image or homogenizing visual input results in the same experience. A set of instructions from the English mystical tradition given by Knowles indicates that this blanking-out is a desired function of meditation that can be produced by restriction of awareness.

> Forget all creatures that God ever made, and the works of them so that thy thought or thy desire not be directed or stretched to any of them, neither in general nor in

> special. . . . At the first time when thou dost it, thou findest but a darkness and as it were a kind of unknowing, thou knowest not what, saying that thou feelest in thy will a naked intent unto God.[23]

The interpretations of this experience of "darkness," of "blank-out," of the "void," of the disappearance of an image in the subject of a scientific experiment, would certainly differ: the subject of a physiological experiment would have extremely different expectations and ideas about his experience than a man who has sought to reach such experience by subjecting himself to an esoteric discipline. But the experiences themselves have essential similarities and are produced through quite similar procedures.

## "OPENING-UP" MEDITATION EXERCISES

The second form of meditation exercises is much more closely related to daily activity. These exercises do not attempt to isolate the person from ordinary life processes; rather, they attempt to use these processes in the training of consciousness. An example is found in the Zen tradition; in the more advanced forms of Zen (in the Soto sect), once the concentrative exercise of breath-counting is mastered, the second form of meditation exercises, *shikan-taza* is practiced—"just sitting." The Zen Master Yasutani Roshi describes this exercise as follows:

> *Shikan* means "nothing but" or "just," while *ta* means "to hit" and *za* "to sit." Hence *shikan-taza* is a practice in which the mind is intensely involved in just sitting. In this type of Za-Zen it is all too easy for the mind, which is not supported by such aids as counting the breath or by a koan, to become distracted. The correct temper of mind therefore becomes doubly important. Now, in *shikan-taza* the mind must be unhurried yet at the same time firmly planted or massively composed, like Mount Fuji, let us say. But it also must be alert, stretched, like a taut bowstring. So *shikan-taza* is a heightened state of concentrated awareness wherein one is

> neither tense nor hurried, and certainly never slack. It is the mind of somebody facing death. Let us imagine that you are engaged in a duel of swordmanship of the kind that used to take place in ancient Japan. As you face your opponent, you are unceasingly watchful, set, ready. Were you to relax your vigilance even momentarily, you would be cut down instantly. A crowd gathers to see the fight. Since you are not blind you see them from the corner of your eye, and since you are not deaf you hear them. But not for an instant is your mind captured by these sense impressions.
>
> This state cannot be maintained for long—in fact, you ought not to do *shikan-taza* for more than half an hour at a sitting.[24]

We can, then, consider *two basic types of meditation exercises*—both concerned with a common effect—those which "turn off" input processing for a period of time to achieve an after-effect of "opening up" of awareness, and those which consist in the active practice of "opening up" during the period of the exercise.

Active practice in opening up awareness is practiced generally in the esoteric traditions, but in Zen it is a specific meditation exercise. A less demanding Buddhist practice stems from one component of the Buddha's Eightfold Path, and is usually termed "right-mindedness." It requires that one be "conscious" of each action, develop a present-centered consciousness, "open up" awareness of daily activities *while* engaged in them. Rahula says;

> Another very important, practical, and useful form of "meditation" (mental development) is to be aware and mindful of whatever you do, physically or verbally, during the daily routine of work in your life, private, public, or professional. Whether you walk, stand, sit, lie down, or sleep, whether you stretch or bend your limbs, whether you look around, whether you put on your clothes, whether you talk or keep silent, whether you eat or drink—even whether you answer the calls of nature—in these and other activities you should be fully aware and mindful of the act performed

> at the moment. That is to say, that you should live in the present moment, in the present action. This does not mean that you should not think of them in relation to the present moment, to the present action, when and where this is relevant.
>
> People do not generally live in their actions in the present moment. They live in the past or in the future. Though they seem to be doing something now here, they live somewhere else in their thoughts, in their problems and worries, usually in the memories of the past or in desires and speculations about the future. Therefore, they do not live in nor do they enjoy what they do at the moment; so they are unhappy and discontented with the present moment with the work at hand. Naturally, they cannot give themselves fully to what they appear to be doing.[25]

In Yoga, a form of self-observation is called "the Witness." Here the attempt is to observe oneself as if one were another person. One tries to notice exactly what one is doing—to invest ordinary activity with attention. The Witness does not judge action nor does it initiate action. The Witness simply observes.

This practice is highly developed in Zen. Right-mindedness, or attention to what one is doing, can be a part of any activity that one performs, no matter how base. There is no action that cannot be used to develop one's consciousness. One simply need be "mindful" of present actions. One can be performing actions that are quite degrading to a Buddhist, such as butchering an animal, but simply by paying close attention to what one is doing, one's awareness can be developed.

In Sufism, at least in the version that is attributed to Gurdjieff, there are similar practices, one of which is called "self-remembering." As in Zen, no special constraints are put on action. There are no prohibitions about what can be eaten, nor do general rules of conduct exist. The attempt is simply to be aware of oneself. Gurdjieff's students are constantly instructed to "remember themselves" wherever they are, remember that they are present, and to notice what they do. When one is "remembering oneself," in Gurdjieff's terms, one is considered to be "awake."

A similar exercise attributed to Gurdjieff consists simply in maintaining continuous awareness of a part of one's body—an elbow, hand, leg. Another exercise of this tradition is to perform ordinary habitual actions slightly differently, such as putting shoes on in the opposite order, shaving the other side of the face first, eating with the left hand (if one is right-handed). These exercises can be seen as attempts to return habitual, "automatic" actions to full awareness.

Recall the phenomenon of habituation.* A slight change in input is enough to "dishabituate" and to return the stimulus to awareness. Similarly, slightly altering our usual "automatic" behavior, such as tying shoes, driving cars, shaving, can return the process to awareness.

Similarly, in the tradition of *Karma Yoga,* the intent is to treat everyday activities as a "sacrament"—to give them full attention. This exercise performs a function similar to "right-mindedness" and "self-remembering," and is a less extreme version of *shikan-taza.*

Many schools within these traditions combine the two major types of awareness exercises, devoting half an hour or so twice a day to the "shutting down" form of meditation and as much as possible of the remainder of the day to a form of self-observation.

## DISHABITUATION RESEARCH

There have been some psychological and physiological studies of the state of awareness of practitioners in and after meditation. These studies have used the EEG to measure the response of the brain of meditators to external stimulation.

When we enter a room and hear a clock ticking, we ordinarily learn to tune it out fairly quickly. Physiologically, the normal "orienting response" to new stimulation begins to disappear after a few moments and does not reappear. On the psychological level, this pattern could be described as the construction of an internal model of the clock which then allows us to ignore it. But if consciousness were like a mirror, then each time the clock ticked it would be "reflected."

The Indian psychologists' studies on Yoga meditation showed this result. By recording the yogi's EEG while introducing external stimuli, they confirmed this analysis of the effects and aftereffects of meditation. During the meditation and during the withdrawal, there was no interruption in the alpha rhythm of the yogi's brain because of the external stimuli. However, when the yogi was not meditating, repetition of an external stimulus showed none of the habituation that presumably would have occurred in other subjects.[26]

The Japanese neuropsychiatrists Kasamatsu and Hirai studied the habituation of the orienting response to a repeating click, both in ordinary people and in Zen masters. The subjects in this experiment sat in a sound-proof room and listened to a click repeated each fifteen seconds while an EEG was being taken. The normal subjects showed the customary phenomenon of habituation. The response of the brain's electrical activity to the clicks began to decrease after the third or fourth click. After habituation, each time the click occurred there was no response in the brain of the subject: the click had been tuned out of awareness. When the Zen masters were meditating and were exposed to this same repetitive click over a period of five minutes, they did not show the customary habituation; they responded to the last click just as strongly as they did to the first. They did not seem to make a "model" of the repetitive stimulation and so tune it out.[27]

It seems, therefore, that there is dishabituation *during* the advanced form of Zen meditation—that is, a consistent response to a stimulus which continues. There is a "shutting down" of awareness of external stimuli during Yoga meditation, but when the yogi is not in meditation, we might expect no habituation to a repetitive stimulus (if he is advanced enough in his practice).

## DEAUTOMATIZATION

In general, the esoteric traditions characterize consciousness in terms similar to those of modern psychology. The Sufis' conceptions are clear precursors of those of modern psychology. Sufi teaching stories frequently focus on men who are too preoccupied to hear what is being said, or who misinterpret instructions because of their expectations, or who do not see what is in front of them because of the limitations of their constructs. The Sufis emphasize the constantly changing biases that constitute our normal awareness. "What a piece of bread looks like depends on whether you are hungry." The Sufis quite explicitly consider the effects of our limited category system on consciousness. Many of their descriptions of consciousness could have been a statement of Bruner's about category systems, or a summary by Lettvin of his research on the frog, e.g., "Offer a donkey a salad, and he will ask what kind of thistle it is." They emphasize that we, like the rugseller, can only be aware of what our conceptions will allow, and of what our senses will transmit to us.

The Sufi and other traditions contend that our selective and restricted ordinary consciousness is to be overcome by the process of meditation, among many other possible exercises and techniques. One specific aim in these traditions is to dismantle the automaticity and selectivity of ordinary awareness. The Sufis characterize ordinary consciousness as a state of "deep sleep" or "blindness"—an overconcern with the irrelevant dimensions of the world. Gurdjieff's image is that man places shock absorbers between himself and the world. "We must destroy our buffers; children have none; therefore we must become like little children." In Indian thought, personal consciousness is compared to a "drunken monkey" living solely in his constructs—the world of "illusion." This same thought is a metaphorical meaning of the "fall" of man in the Christian tradition. These metaphors, without their derogatory connotations, can be understood in terms of modern psychology as depicting our selective, constructed awareness, our model-building, automaticity, and limited category systems.

One aim of the esoteric disciplines is to remove "blindness" or the "illusion," to "awaken" a "fresh" perception. Enlightenment or illumination are words often used for progress in these disciplines, for a breakthrough in the level of awareness—flooding a dark spot with light. The Indian tradition speaks of opening the third eye, of seeing more and from a new vantage point. *Satori*, in Zen, is considered an intuitive "awakening." The Sufis speak of the development of a "new organ" of perception.

Reports of the experiences of those who practice the meditative disciplines indicate that a primary *after-effect* of the concentrative meditation exercises is an opening up of awareness, a "deautomatization," as Deikman calls it, which might be a reduction of the normal selectivity of input. Deikman's own subjects in experimental meditation, who gazed at a blue vase for half an hour at a time for several sessions, reported that the vase appeared "more vivid" and "more luminous."[28] Deikman quotes Augustine Poulain, who emphasized that concentrative meditation is a temporary process of withdrawal, similar to the blank-out of consciousness, but here with the intent to become deautomatized.

> It is the mysterious darkness wherein is contained the limitless Good. To such an extent are we admitted and absorbed into something that is one, simple, divine, and illuminable that we seem no longer distinguishable from it . . . In this unity the feeling of multiplicity disappears. When afterwards these persons come to themselves again, they find themselves possessed of a more distinct knowledge of things, some luminous and more perfect than that of others.[29]

Some speak of seeing things "freshly" or as if for the first time. To Blake, it is a "cleansing of the doors of perception." Others, like Gurdjieff, compare their experiences to that of a child, who presumably has not yet developed many automatic ways of tuning out the world. In Zen, one speaks similarly of seeing something the five-hundredth time in the same way that one saw it the first time.

These descriptions are understandable and translatable

into contemporary psychological terms—as the process of building a model of the environment, and testing and selecting input against the model. When we see something for the five-hundredth time, we have developed a model for it and tune out the input.

These characterizations of consciousness represent a meeting point between scientific psychological research and the metaphors of the esoteric psychologists. Contemporary psychologists speak of the brain's controlling input, building models, responding "automatically" to the external environment. The esoteric traditions refer to this process as man's lacking full awareness of his surroundings, and consider this "blindness" the barrier to his development. The practice of meditation, then, can be considered as one attempt to turn off linear, verbal activity temporarily, and to shut off all input processing for a period of time.

A result of this "turning off" of the input selection systems seems to be that, when the same sensory input is later introduced, we see it differently, "anew." When we leave our normal surroundings and go on vacation, we usually return to find ourselves much "more aware" of the immediate environment. We play many of our old records, which we haven't "heard" in a while. We look anew at the plants in our garden, the painting on our walls, our friends. Getting away and returning seem to have the same effect on awareness as presenting new stimuli.*

We can consider the process of concentrative meditation as similar to that of taking a vacation—leaving the situation, "turning off" our routine way of dealing with the external world for a period, later returning to find it "fresh," "new," "different," our awareness "deautomatized."

We easily adapt to almost any new input. A new technology, a new person, a change in our immediate environment, quickly become an integral part of our lives, part of our model of the external world. This model-building process is specifically what is to be dismantled by the practice of meditation.

---

*Compare the phenomenon of "spontaneous recovery" in habituation.

In Zen, one is invited to stop conceptualizing while remaining fully awake. In Yoga, the aim is to leave the "illusion"—to cease identifying the external world with our constructed models of it. The esoteric traditions thus speak of developing a consciousness that allows every stimulus to enter into consciousness, devoid of normal input selection, model-building, and category systems.

A mirror metaphor is used in many traditions to describe the desired mode of consciousness. The Sufi poet Omar Khayyam says: "I am a mirror and who looks at me, whatever good or bad he speaks, he speaks of himself." The contemporary Zen master Suzuki Roshi says, "The perfect man employs his mind as a mirror, it grasps nothing, it refuses nothing, it receives but does not keep." Christ said in prayer, "A mirror I am to thee that perceivest me." The metaphor of consciousness as a mirror fits well with some of the psychologists' own metaphors. A mirror allows every input to enter equally, reflects each equally, and cannot be tuned to receive a special kind of input. It does not add anything to the input, and does not turn off repetitive stimuli; it does not focus on any particular aspect of input and retune back and forth, but continuously admits all inputs equally.

## "Direct" Perception

The metaphor of a mirror leads to another consideration. Many of the traditions claim to allow men to experience the world *directly*. The Sufis speak of attaining an "objective consciousness," others of "cosmic consciousness." The statement is often made that one can have *direct* perception of reality. Whether one can perceive "reality" directly is not yet a question for science, but some comment within the terms of psychology might be made. The ability to "mirror," to be free of the normal restrictions—of the tuning, biasing, and filtering processes of consciousness—may be a part of what is meant by "direct" perception.

This state can perhaps be considered in psychological

terms as a diminution of the interactive nature of awareness: a state in which we do not select, or "bet" on the nature of the world, or sort into restrictive categories; rather, a state in which all possible categories are held at once. It has also been described as a state of living totally in the present, of not thinking about the future or the past; a state in which everything that is happening in the present moment enters into awareness.

## MEDITATION, DEAUTOMATIZATION AND THE "MYSTIC EXPERIENCE"

The two major forms of meditation exercises, the concentrative and the "opening up" forms, are intended to cause a shift in the mode of consciousness of the practitioner. The concentrative form turns off the normal mode of operation and allows a sensitivity to subtle stimuli which often go unnoticed in the normal mode, as the stars remain unseen in the light of day. It also produces an *after-effect* of "fresh" perception when the practitioner returns to his usual surroundings, as a vacation allows us to "see" our environment anew.

Concentrative meditation, coupled with dishabituation exercises, undoes the normal construction of consciousness. When the normal mode is temporarily dismantled, the other major mode can emerge–that of the "night," the receptive, the often misunderstood and devalued mode of intuition.

In many traditions, a full emergence of this mode has come to be known as a "mystic" experience. The word "mystic" may be unfortunate, since many confuse it with "mystical," and with occultism and "mystery." We should not be surprised that the very name given to this experience implies incomprehensibility, since the experience is not within the province of the linear, verbal mode of consciousness. One part of us may simply be incapable of fully understanding the experience of the other part, and may give it a name which reflects this lack of comprehension.

This mode of consciousness, though, is to some degree a part of the daily experience of each of us. Its full development can result from a life crisis, by accident, or sometimes "spontaneously." It may be occasioned by many methods other than meditation—by fasting, by ritual dance, by the ingestion of certain psychoactive drugs, all of which upset the normal lineal construction of consciousness. The work of the esoteric psychologies is toward extending normal linear consciousness to include such experience.

The "mystic" consciousness is described by many, in almost every esoteric tradition, from the ancient Hindu to the contemporary European. It is described in the Bible, in the Koran, in Whitman, in James' *The Varieties of Religious Experience.* It is the "mysterious darkness" of Augustine Poulain, a mode in which ordinary consciousness of a "multiplicity" of people and objects disappears, to be replaced by the awareness of "unity."

The consciousness of "unity," or "oneness" as it is sometimes called, is perhaps the most fully developed form of this mode of experience. In terms of the story of the blind men and the elephant, the mystic experience involves a shift in consciousness from the analytic, individual, piecemeal approach to knowledge, to a more receptive, holistic mode, one which can encompass the entire elephant as a whole.[30]

A second characteristic of these experiences, as described both by William James and by Arthur Deikman, is their sense of "realness"; they involve reliance on a type of verification that is more intuitive than our usual linear and inferential one.[31]

This mode of consciousness is admittedly quite unusual in its most-developed form, in which the "vividness" and "richness" of normal consciousness is greatly enhanced, in which linear time, as we know it, has no meaning. Deikman attributes the "vividness" and "richness" to a "deautomatization" of consciousness. To repeat William Blake: "If the doors of perception were cleansed, man would see everything as it is, infinite."

The contents of this experience are often said to be "ineffable," incapable of being fully communicated by words or by reference to similar experiences in ordinary life. One person echoes this feeling, wishing that he had some competence in the more ordinary aspects of the holistic mode of consciousness, so that he might communicate it more clearly.

> What is a "transcendent dimension of being?" Such words on paper are little more than metaphysical poetry. Somehow I feel I could better communicate my experience by composing a symphony or by molding a twisted piece of contemporary sculpture, had I the talents required for either form of artistic expression. In no sense have I an urge to formulate philosophical or theological dogmas about my experience. Only my silence can retain its purity and genuineness.[32]

The essence of this mode is experiential, and the insights available in this mode cannot always be translated into sequential terms. As Arthur Deikman says, "Ordinary language is structured to follow the logical development of one idea at a time, and it might be quite inadequate to express an experience encompassing a large number of concepts simultaneously."[33]

So the practices of meditation—whirling, chanting, concentrating on a nonsensical question, repeating a "sacred" prayer over and over, visualizing a cross, gazing at a vase—are not quite so exotic as those who deliberately seek the esoteric might wish; but neither are they exercises in reason or problem-solving. They are exercises in attentional deployment, both those which focus on one stimulus and those which are intended to actively deautomatize ordinary consciousness.

The "mystic" experience, brought about by concentrative meditation, deautomatization exercises, and other techniques intended to alter ordinary, linear consciousness is, then, a shift from that normal, analytic world containing separate, discrete objects and persons to a second mode, an experience of "unity," a mode of intuition. This experience is outside the province of language and rationality, being a mode of simultaneity, a dimension of consciousness complementary to the ordered sequence of normal thought.

But why have people sought to develop this mode, and what value is there in a "mystic" experience? The answers to these questions are not easy. Many of the traditional replies are well-known; yet some brief interpretation and comment can usefully be made.

First, the analytic, linear mode of consciousness cannot encompass many aspects of life which many people want to experience and understand. That these phenomena have been "ruled out" of much of western scientific inquiry, does not lessen the need which many now feel to explore these areas personally. Meditation is an attempt to alter consciousness in such a way that other aspects of reality can become accessible to the practitioner, who can add personal knowledge to intellectual.

Second, the analytic mode, in which there is separation of objects, of the self from others (I-it relationship), has proved useful in individual biological survival; yet this mode apparently evolved to fit the conditions of life many thousands of years ago. The evolution of culture proceeds much more quickly than biological evolution; so the analytic mode may not be as all-important a criterion for our contemporary western society as it once was. The awareness of separation was a great advantage when survival threatened an individual's existence; for instance, one could isolate an enemy animal, kill it, and use it for food. However, this basic need, for individual survival, is no longer quite so basic for many in the West. After all, most of us now buy our food; we do not need to hunt for it. Few readers of this book are in any danger of imminent starvation. Instead, the survival problems now facing us are collective rather than individual: problems of how to prevent a large nuclear war, pollution of the earth, overpopulation. And notice that in these examples, a focus on individual consciousness, individual survival, works against, not for, a solution. A shift toward a consciousness of the interconnectedness of life, toward a relinquishing of the "every man for himself" attitude inherent in our ordinary construction of consciousness, might enable us to take those "selfless" steps that could begin to solve our collective problems. Certainly our culture has too severely emphasized the development of only one way of organizing reality. Perhaps at this point in time we can begin to see that the complementary mode can have survival value for our culture as a whole. (In a very minor way, some recent cultural events can be seen in this light: I refer to the increasing awareness of the earth as one system that is part of the ecology movement, and to the increasing development of interdisciplinary training and systems analysis within science.)

Additionally, Keith Wallace and Herbert Benson, among others, point out that the change in our culture to a predominantly technological, scientific one during the last few centuries has caused a radical increase in the environmental stresses placed on each person. Many diseases, such as the increased incidence of hypertension, can in some part be linked to these radical changes in our environment. Wallace and Benson suggest that the development of increased self-knowledge and quiescence through meditation may be a way in which we could learn to cope with the stress, since the demands placed on us by our society are unlikely to diminish greatly.[34] But most importantly, it is the shift from an individual and analytic consciousness to the attainment of an over-all perspective of "unity," of "Humanity as one organism," which is the purpose of the esoteric traditions and the aim of these meditation exercises. We shall have more to discuss on this in the next chapter.

EMERSON, V. F.

# Can Belief Systems Influence Neurophysiology? Some Implications of Research on Meditation

The science of psychology is about to complete a full circle. The introspection which flourished around the turn of the century was contested by the behaviourists, who over-reacted by denying any "consciousness" to the particular animal under study. As a result, a trend toward a controlled introspection and subjectivism is now in progress, and one area which was hitherto taboo is now being investigated by legions of psychologists and physiologists: meditation. In this paper the major studies of meditation will be reviewed and their methodology and findings analysed. It will be seen that one of the more interesting indications of these studies is that the internal states of subjects during meditation seem to be determined by the underlying religious philosophy which is used in meditation; a brief comment will also be given concerning the various measures taken and the means of interpreting them.

Generally speaking, the religious philosophies dealt with here can be divided in two: Zen Buddhism and the various schools of Yoga in Hinduism. These will be briefly considered in turn.

Zen Buddhism is probably the most radical school of Buddhism. Basically, it teaches that the student must reach enlightenment [1] (which liberates him from the rebirth cycle) by scrupulously following a strict lifestyle; his mode of thought is rapidly transformed to enable him to ask the appropriate questions of reality, and through meditation he gains the necessary insight to understand the answers. The object of this lifestyle is to become increasingly aware of the environment while maintaining a passionless attitude toward external occurrences.

Yoga [2] , on the other hand, advocates withdrawal from the external world. Although there are minor philosophical differences between sects, the basic teaching is that to achieve liberation (moksha) from the wheel of rebirth (samsara) one must come to understand the essential unity of all things, including oneself, in Brahman, the all-pervading spirit of the universe. To accomplish this, one must detach oneself from the external world and turn inward to evade the distractions (maya) of objects, object-subject dichotomies, and even consciousness and thought. Turning inward implies far more than self-contemplation; it implies Self-contemplation, the realisation of the self-Self (atman-Atman) and Self-Self (Atman-Atman) indentities. Personal feelings have no place in this scheme, and so Yogic meditation is generally devoted to clearing the mind and consciousness and striving to achieve a state (or experience) called samadhi (higher meditation), the closest a living being can come to liberation. This is the technique of rajah (royal) yoga, but other sects differ somewhat. For example, kriya (from the root kr-, to do) yoga, a popular form in Bengal, uses visualisation of a god or other spiritual essence as an object of meditation (thus the term kriya; the disciple must produce an image), and the yogi interacts with this vision to achieve samadhi. This is the technique employed by the subjects tested by Das & Gastaut (1957). Hatha yoga, a form common in the West, is the least spiritual of all, for it implies no super-sentient being or religion to assist the yogi in his meditative efforts; it is roughly this form of yoga which is investigated in studies performed on Westerners.

Until the advent of machines capable of recording man's inner goings-on, the rather outrageous claims surrounding Yoga especially were non-verifiable. There were numerous claims of yogis who, in effect, entered a state of suspended animation during meditation, exhibiting slowing or stoppage of the heart and respiration, insensitivity to external stimuli, etc., and these statements were generally dismissed by scientists as ludicrous and exploited by the gullible as demonstrating the existence of God (in whatever form they wished). Finally a handful of brave souls challenged the contemporary "scientific" attitude and prevailing conditions and used the technology available at that time to lend some rationality to the knowledge of the nature of these phenomena.

As many authors have mentioned (e.g., Bagchi & Wenger, 1957; Das & Gastaut, 1957) the greatest difficulty in conducting a study of this type is locating an experienced yogi who has no objection to being wired and taped for recording purposes. One must usually travel to India, weed through the mercenaries and charlatans who offer themselves as subjects, and then enlist the assistance of a true yogi; the latter step is undoubtedly the most difficult, since implicit in the Yoga teaching is that one not flaunt the spiritual powers one acquires on the path to liberation. To evaluate the physiological manifestations of religious meditation, one must rigidly control for the nature of the subjects as well as their sect, meditation posture, degree of practice, and age, for all these factors may affect the interpretation of the results. As will be seen, these controls are very rarely observed, and what has generally resulted is a mish-mash of unintelligible results which, when translated across studies, states only that meditation is identical with neither sleep nor wakefulness. No valid conclusions concerning religious philosophy, amount of practice, etc., can be drawn from the majority of studies. The results from any one study may or may not be valid, depending on the nature of the controls used, if any. The studies which have employed the best methodology will be discussed below, and it will be seen that when there is some interstudy consistency in controls, much more information can be gained than when the controls are dissimilar.

Basically, the tools involved in measuring the internal states of meditators are electrocardiographs (EKG) for measuring heart rate, spirometers for measuring respiratory rate and ventilation [3], electromyographs for recording muscle tone and muscle activity (EMG), and electroencephalographs (EEG) for recording brain wave pattern. Except for the latter, these are all relatively straightforward. The EEG, however, deserves some explaining, particularly since it is this measure which is of most interest in this review.

Most people are familiar with the basic pattern of an EEG tracing -- a squiggly line which looks like a piece of wet spaghetti which was stretched and suddenly released. This tracing is usually taken to represent the electrical potential difference between any two points on the cortex. This record is often considered a macroanalysis of the activity of that area of the cortex being investigated, that is, the area beneath the two electrodes. The record is presumed to represent the summed activity of millions of cells and cannot be considered representative of any one cell; for that, other, more complex techniques, such as single-cell recording, are available. Such techniques can elucidate the role of smaller areas of the brain in various behavioural tasks. For the purpose of classifying general states of consciousness, however, one probably should consider the overall activity of the cortex, and so the gross EEG is used [4]. Since the cortical electrical activity is translated onto a two-dimensional graph, two direct measures may be made from the tracing: the amplitude (vertical axis), and the frequency, which is read from blocks of time (horizontal axis) and indicates the cyclical activity of the firing pattern. For convenience, and in correlation with behavioural observation, the brain-wave patterns have been classified on the basis of their frequency into four types -- beta, alpha, theta, and delta waves -- which are in turn classed on a continuum according to amplitude. Beta waves are defined as the range above 14 hertz (hz, or cycles per second) and are indicative of a state of arousal. Alpha waves occur from 8-13 hz, and indicate a state of relaxed wakefulness; they are generally observed in the majority of the population when the eyes are closed and the attention is not focussed. Theta waves are 4-7 hz, indicating even lower arousal, and delta waves (below 3.5 hz) are usually observed only in sleep or coma. When the EEG is flat (no electrical activity in the cortex), the organism is considered dead.

A standard pattern is observed with these recordings; for example, a normal person generating alpha waves as he relaxes in his rocker will demonstrate a phenomenon known as alpha block if a disturbing event occurs in the environment, for example if someone drops a glass in the kitchen. Alpha block is an abrupt cessation of (typically) high-amplitude alpha waves and the onset of low-amplitude beta waves. This is also known as desychronisation, since the cortical cells are no longer firing in synchrony (which is assumed to determine amplitude, all else being equal). What has occurred psychologically is that the stimulus (in this case a crash) has been received by the ear, which sent the message to the auditory cortex and the reticular activating system (RAS), a diffuse structure in the brain stem which regulates the level of arousal. The abrupt onset of the stimulus caused the RAS to "alert" the rest of the brain to the presence of the stimulus generator, in a sense to prime the brain to respond to the stimulus. The RAS is directly responsible for the desynchronisation of the EEG and the accompanying somersault of the person in the rocker. The various states of arousal are important in the survival of all animals, for it is the arousal level which will, to a large degree, determine the actions an intact animal will perform. For example, if an animal becomes aroused at the sound of a twig cracking nearby, it has the chance to flee from a predator, whereas if no arousal ensued escape would be impossible. Similarly, if the animal became so aroused that it was confused, its chances of successful escape would be reduced. Thus, there is an "optimal" level of arousal for each situation. A corollary to alpha block exists, and that is that if a stimulus is repeatedly presented with no accompanying event of biological significance, the stimulus loses its importance to the organism and habituation of alpha block occurs, so that the alpha rhythm will persist uninterrupted through all sorts of clatter, such as when one settles into a rocker with jackhammers and automobile horns blaring outside the window.

As a final note before examining the results of various studies, a few of the more common meditation postures will be described. This aspect of meditation has far too often been ignored, and it is to the credit of those authors who controlled for this factor or at least mentioned their subjects' postures that they did so, for as will be shown below, the physiological conditions existing during meditation are often similar to the basal metabolic condition, and one must be careful not to mar the results by lumping data from a wide range of physiological states. This would occur if one were to classify the subjects meditating in different postures as one group; Ikegami (1970) has shown that for various Zen postures the activity levels of some muscles are different from posture to posture. Because of this, the metabolic rates of these muscles differ, and so the metabolism of the meditator varies. Considering such varied data as similar conceals the possible effects of posture on the various metabolic measures. Controls for this and other variables (e.g., age and length of practice) should be used whenever a variable may differentially influence metabolic rate. Since clinical researchers take great pains to insure inter-patient uniformity when measuring basal metabolic rate, it is surprising to observe that few experimenters in the field have followed suit.

The various yoga postures are too numerous to mention, and the reader is advised to examine one of the many books on hatha yoga for a review of the standard postures. The one posture most frequently assumed for meditation is the full lotus posture, in which one sits cross-legged, with the soles of the feet facing upward while the feet rest on the thigh near the crotch. The spine is made as nearly vertical as possible, and the arms are extended so that the hands rest on the knees. The head is held rigidly vertical, with the gaze (through half-opened eyes) lowered.

There are also various Zen postures, most of which are not relevant to this discussion. The reader is referred to Ikegami (1970) for an excellent review of some postures and their metabolic rates. He showed that, for the positions and muscles studied, Zen priests show less "internal fidgeting" (measured in terms of change of centre of gravity) then laymen and markedly less (one-third to one-half) muscle activity. Indeed, this is possibly the most striking thing about meditation; many authors have reported absolute silence from the EMG in the case of both yogis (e.g., Das & Gastaut, 1957) and Zen priests. The difference between Zen priests and laymen was greatest in the kekkafuza position, which is similar to the yoga full lotus posture except that the buttocks are rested on a cushion and the hands are folded in the lap. Hankafuza is identical to kekkafuza except that only one foot is placed on the contralateral thigh, the other foot being tucked underneath its opposite thigh; this posture was found to be the most restful posture for novices when maintained for 30 minutes. Alternative postures are agura (same as kekkafuza, but without the cushion) and seiza, in which the buttocks are rested on the heels, each calf folded under the ipsilateral thigh, and the knees together or apart. Ikegami also noted that, in general, these postures can be maintained with increasing stability with age and practice, and he suggests that these, plus one's mental attitude, are salient factors in Zen meditation. A brief attempt at forming each of the postures should convince the reader of the necessity of controlling for these factors.

Empirically. the most interesting finding from the meditation studies is that meditators can demonstrate remarkable control of their brain-wave patterns. By now it has become common knowledge that when people sit down to meditate they produce copious quantities of alpha waves, and, unfortunately, one need not venture far to encounter one of the seemingly numberless advertisements for alpha-feedback machines, which (allegedly) remarkably enable one to learn in a matter of minutes to generate alpha waves and experience hitherto unknown bliss. Mulholland (1971) has delivered an inspired retort to this entire industry and its implications. He eloquently and bluntly suggests that the reason many Westerners "experience" a sense of transcendence during meditation is that they have never before taken the time to relax and discover their inner thoughts. His paper is an excellent critique of the methodology used in research on alpha conditioning and is somewhat applicable to some of the studies mentioned here. It is important that the reader realise that there is nothing magical about alpha waves; they are only indicative of an attentional state and appear spontaneously in the great majority of the population. Rather, what are important are the abnormalities observed in the brain-wave patterns of the meditators, and it is these which will now be considered. It will be seen that the results of different studies seem to indicate that the religion of the meditator determines to a great extent the way in which his EEG pattern as well as his metabolism will change during the course of meditation.

Bagchi & Wenger (1957) appear to have been the first to note that some yogis, who when meditating are producing the basic resting EEG pattern (alpha waves), exhibit no response to an external stimulus (noise, in particular) whereas an alpha block would be expected. Similarly, there is no change in the galvanic skin response (GSR; a marked decrease in skin resistance indicates emotionality) in this condition. The EEG observation, which was objectively recorded in only one subject, was supported by the negative verbal reports of two other subjects. That the subject was not sleeping was established by inspection of the EEG record.

Anand, Chhina, & Singh (1961a) subjected 2 yogis to external stimulation both before and during meditation. The stimuli consisted of turning on a strong light, banging on an object, vibrating a tuning fork, and touching the yogis with a hot glass tube. Before meditation, both yogis showed persistent alpha block. During meditation, however, no alpha block was observed. Similarly, two other yogis, who claimed to have developed high pain thresholds, were able to keep one hand in 4°C water for 45-55 minutes with no EEG disturbance or apparent discomfort. This paradigm has been critised by Barber (1970) for not including the appropriate control groups, but it is the opinion of this author that, for the pre- and during-meditation stimulation study, adequate controls were observed, and these results can be interpreted as supporting the finding of Bagchi & Wenger (1957). From these studies it appears that some yogis have succeeded in training their bodies to function according to their religious beliefs during meditation.

On the other hand, there are greatly differing results in the studies on Zen meditation. Kasamatsu & Hirai (1966) showed that Zen masters produced continuous alpha waves which were interrupted by a click stimulus. In these subjects, alpha block habituation did not obtain after repeated presentations of the stimulus, whereas control subjects did exhibit habituation. These authors, in a carefully controlled study, also demonstrated progressive EEG changes with increasing Zen practice; those subjects with 0-5 years of experience, for example, showed no rhythmical theta waves, whereas these waves appeared regularly in some subjects with 21-40 years of experience. They conclude that the EEG changes correlate highly with the subjects' proficiency and degree of training in Zen.

As well, Akishige (1970) reports that Kasamatsu, Hirai, & Izawa (1963) also found no habituation of Zen subjects to a click stimulus, whereas controls habituated around the tenth presentation. Furthermore, Kasamatsu & Hirai (1966) note that the blocking time was short and that the alpha waves returned quite soon after the stimulus. These results suggest that the meditators were in a markedly different state than the yogis in the studies cited above; however, this suggestion is readily, albeit tentatively, explained.

As was noted earlier, the underlying philosophies of these two sects are quite different; the yogi abandons the external world, turning his attention inward, while the Zen devotee maintains a passionless involvement in the environment. The EEG results, when examined in this light, suggest, as Tart (1969) and Barber (1970) have observed, that these results cannot meaningfully be grouped under one label. One must avoid making non-committal mumbo-jumbo statements about the "meditation state" and classify the results of the studies according to various factors; in this instance, religious philosophy appears to be particularly relevant, although with such small numbers of subjects and such few studies this suggestion can only be tentative. In all these studies, however, the subjects (with appropriate controls) meditated (presumably in approximately the same position, since full lotus and either hankafuza or kekkafuza are the preferred positions) and during meditation were exposed to roughly similar auditory stimuli. In one case (the yogis) no EEG change was noted, whereas in the other (Zen priests), persistent alpha block obtained.

Das & Gastaut (1957), studying subjects practicing kriya yoga, found strikingly different results. Rather than observing persistent alpha rhythms, which the majority of researchers have noted in studies on other sects, these authors found extremely fast beta activity (indicative of high arousal) with high amplitude waves (frequency up to 40 hz, amplitude 30-50 microvolts) which were parallelled in their gradual development by an acceleration of the heart rhythm. In addition, they note that various stimuli applied during meditation had absolutely no effect on the EEG. This latter finding is again strong evidence of withdrawal from the environment, and once again the philosophy of the sect explains the EEG results. Rather than pursuing an "objectless" meditation, as were the yogis studied by Anand et al. (1961a), the disciples of kriya yoga were focussing their attention on visions and were actively involved in summoning the kundalini (spirit energy). As their meditation progressed, this energy was purported to have travelled from its resting place at the base of the spine up the spinal column until it reached the peak of the head, at which time ecstasy occurred. This voyage was accomplished by an unfolding vision which served to inform the yogi of the locus of the kundalini and thus serve as an "auto-feedback" mechanism. The EEG changes seemed to parallel this as well.

These few studies constitute the greater portion of the EEG work on authentic yogis and Zen priests. It cannot be stressed enough that this collection is far too inadequate for the appreciation of the finer effects of meditation, and much further work is needed. There are great methodological differences among these studies, and any hypothesis alleging to show inter-sect differences must also take into account the low signal-to-noise ratio produced by the use of varied methodologies. The hypothesis advanced above that EEG changes follow the course charted by religious philosophy is readily testable, and future data on this point should be interesting. Again, however, caution must be advised, for the necessary control groups, sampling procedures, and classification of results are absolutely indispensable if one hopes to make meaningful statements about the data.

Various other studies have been conducted on meditation of non-religious subjects. Most notable among these are the recent studies by Wallace and co-workers (Wallace, 1970; Wallace, Benson, & Wilson, 1971; Wallace & Benson, 1972) in which physiological measures were recorded from students of transcendental meditation as taught by the Maharishi Mahesh Yogi. Physiologically these results are most interesting, and in general support the findings obtained by other researchers in studies on true yogis and Zen priests: decreased oxygen consumption ond $CO_2$ elimination (in accord with the study by Anand <u>et al</u>. (1961b) of a yogi sealed in an air-tight box), slightly decreased respiration rate (other researchers, e.g., Akishige (1970), Allison (1970), Bagchi & Wenger,(1957), Brosse (1946), and Miles (1964), have reported a marked decrease in respiration in various types of subjects, sometimes as low as 40-50% of "basal" need), a decrease in blood lactate, and a rapid rise in skin resistance (Bagchi & Wenger, 1957). As well, persistent alpha activity in the EEG was observed. All these signs are consistent with the existence of a remarkable state of relaxation, which is the goal of this form of meditation. But it must be emphasized that this work cannot justifiably be equated with the studies on religious meditators, for the Maharishi Mahesh Yogi's version of transcendental meditation has no underlying religious philosophy. Consequently, one cannot infer that the subjects have the same motivation within and across studies. Comparisons can be made casually (as above), for example to observe the effects of sitting down and relaxing, but we have seen indications that beyond this point there are subtleties of religious meditation which have physiological effects extending far beyond those observed in Wallace's subjects. In addition, there is the complicating factor that the subjects used by Wallace and his co-workers were from a vastly different subject population than those tested in India and Japan. Also, the American subjects were lumped regardless of degree of proficiency, length of practice, etc., a process which may or may not affect the overall interpretation of the results but which certainly obscures finer trends. To be sure, many of the Asian studies are guilty of the same transgressions, although these studies are usually more descriptive of their subjects. A further confounding factor has been the American practice of instructing the subject when to begin and finish meditating, a procedure which would be unthinkable in a religious setting.

These discrepancies should not detract from the implications of this work, however. In the majority of cases, what is happening is that the meditators are producing what Wallace et al. (1971) have labelled a "wakeful hypometabolic" state. In many cases, an approximation to this state has been produced in a biofeedback paradigm using alpha waves as the pertinent measure. Much similar work has been done with feedback to produce alterations in heart rate and blood pressure. However, the religious studies have demonstrated that many people, specifically yogis, are capable of this type of autonomic conditioning with no apparent feedback. The work of Brosse (1946, 1950) and Bagchi & Wenger (1957) demonstrate this learning of cardiac control. Other studies, many of which have been mentioned above (e.g., Allison, 1970; Bagchi & Wenger, 1957) attest to superb respiratory control which is undoubtedly due to the importance of breathing exercises in all forms of meditation.

Aside from the obvious clinical implications, these practices warrant consideration from the standpoint of emergency training, as Miles (1964) has suggested. For example, if special meditational breathing practices were mandatory in a miner-training programme, how many lives could be saved when cave-ins cut off air supplies? It has been repeatedly shown that meditation lowers the metabolic rate to the vicinity of the basal rate or even, in some instances, below it (Akishige, 1970; Anand et al., 1961b), which would serve to prolong life where vital elements are restricted. Instead of panicking in such situations, it is obviously more beneficial to relax (contrary to "instinctive" reactions) [5]; however, it is also important not to fall asleep, for $O_2$ consumption has been shown to be much higher in sleep than in meditation (Wallace & Benson, 1972).

In a similar vein, cardiac control exercises may be helpful in warding off heart disease. No data bearing directly on this question have been produced to the author's knowledge, but Brosse (1946, 1950) has shown that subjects can regulate cardiac arrhythmia, and various studies on yogis have demonstrated that control of the heart is possible.

Furthermore, Miller (1969) in his classic study of autonomic conditioning in chemically paralyzed rats has shown that these animals can be taught to perform some rather remarkable feats, such as controlling intestinal motility, heart rate, and even blood flow in one ear (while not affecting the other). The latter finding, if it could be produced in non-immobilized humans[6] may have implications in the control of cancer; if a patient could be taught to reduce the blood flow to the tumour, the progress of the cancer could possibly be retarded or even stopped.

Of course, much research must precede any implementation of such therapies. To ensure that the experimental results are valid and not artifactual, proper research methodology in this area must be developed and rigourously observed. The breakthrough in autonomic conditioning is not to be underestimated, for it has effectively returned the "involuntary" half of man's body to his control, and, despite the ominous implications for behaviourism and standard therapeutic techniques, it should be expected that medicine and psychotherapy, as well as psychology and physiology, will greatly benefit from accepting and developing this phenomenon.

It is to be hoped that future research will take into account those variables which have been neglected in previous studies and which may be particularly relevant in assessing the metabolic effects of meditation. In particular, controls should be established for such factors as posture, age, and length of practice of the subjects. In addition, if subjects are classified according to religious philosophy, perhaps the "effect" of this "variable," if any, can be properly evaluated.

## Notes

[1] Enlightenment is variously termed _kan_, _kensho_, _satori_, or _nirvana_ depending on the particular state referred to as well as the sect and its geographical location.

[2] When the term "yoga" pertains to the philosophical system, it is capitalised; when it refers to the physical discipline the lower-case "y" is used.

[3] Allison (1970) describes an ingenious method of measuring respiration rate which has the advantage that, unlike other methods, it does not interfere with the meditator by trapping "dead" air. This involves suspending thermistors from a headband to points near the mouth and nostrils and translating the temperature fluctuations into respirations.

[4] There are EEG oddities observed in sleep which will not be considered in this paper. The reader should keep in mind that it is possible that meditation states may produce similar physiological records to those obtained from sleep states and yet be quite a different state. This possibility will not be explored here.

[5] I am indebted to P.H. Platenius for bringing this aspect of meditation to my attention as well as for generally assisting me in my approach to meditation states. His helpful comments and those of M.W. Donald and B. Timmons are very much appreciated.

[6] This is a big "if," but evidence suggests that it is not so unreasonable. For related work, the reader is referred to Sargent, Green, & Walters (1971) for thermoregulation of the hands in the treatment of migraine and to Wenger & Bagchi (1961) for a report of voluntary forehead perspiration by a yogi.

## References

Akishige, Y. A historical survey of the psychological studies on Zen. In Psychological Studies on Zen, Y. Akishige (ed.), Bulletin of the Faculty of Literature of Kyushu University, No. 11 (V), Fukuoka, 1970.

Allison, J. Respiratory changes during transcendental meditation. Lancet, 18 April 1970, No. 7651.

Anand, B.K., Chhina, G.S., & Singh, B. Some aspects of electroencephalographic studies in Yogis. Electroencephalography and Clinical Neurophysiology, 1961, 13, 452-456 (a).

Anand, B.K., Chhina, G.S., & Singh, B. Studies on Shri Ramanand Yogi during his stay in an air-tight box. Indian Journal of Medical Research, 1961, 49, 82-89 (b).

Bagchi, B.K., & Wenger, M.A. Electro-physiological correlates of some yogi exercises. First International Congress of Neurological Sciences, III. L. van Bogaert and J. Radermecker (eds.), Pergamon Press, New York, 1957.

Barber, T.X. LSD, Marihuana, Yoga and Hypnosis. Aldine Publishing Company, Chicago, 1970.

Brosse, T. Altruism and creativity as biological factors of human evolution. In Explorations in Altruistic Love and Behavior, P.A. Sorokin (ed.), The Beacon Press, Boston, 1950.

Brosse, T. A psycho-physiological study. Main Currents in Modern Thought, 1946, 4, 77-84.

Das, N.N., & Gastaut, H. Variations de l'activité électrique du cerveau, du coeur, et des muscles squelettiques au cours de la méditation et de l'extase yogique. Electroencephalography and Clinical Neurophysiology, 1957, supplement 6, 211-219.

Ikegami, R. Psychological study of Zen posture. In Psychological Studies on Zen, Y. Akishige (ed.), Bulletin of the Faculty of Literature of Kyushu University, No. 11 (V), Fukuoka, 1970.

Kasamatsu, A., & Hirai, T. An electroencephalographic study on the Zen meditation (zazen). Folio Psychiatrica et

Neurologica Japonica, 1966, 20, 315-336 (reprinted in Altered States of Consciousness, C.T. Tart (ed.), John Wiley & Sons, New York, 1969).

Kasamatsu, A., Hirai, T., & Izawa, H. Medical and psychological studies on Zen. Proceedings of the Twenty-seventh Convention of the Japanese Psychological Association, 1963, 347 (cited by Akishige, 1970).

Miles, W.R. Oxygen consumption during three yoga-type breathing patterns. Journal of Applied Physiology, 1964, 19, 75-82.

Miller, N.E. Learning of visceral and glandular responses. Science, 1969, 163, 434-445.

Mulholland, T. Can you really turn on with alpha? Paper presented at the meeting of the Massachusetts Psychological Association, 1971.

Sargent, J.D., Green, E.E., & Walters, E.D. Preliminary report on the use of autogenic feedback techniques in the treatment of migraine and tension headaches, Unpublished manuscript, 1971.

Tart, C.T. The psychophysiology of some altered states of consciousness. In Altered States of Consciousness, C.T. Tart (ed.), John Wiley & Sons, New York, 1969.

Wallace, R.K. Physiological effects of transcendental meditation. Science, 1970, 167, 1751-1754.

Wallace, R.K., & Benson, H. The physiology of meditation. Scientific American, 1972 (February), 226 (2), 84-90.

Wallace, R.K., Benson, H., & Wilson, A.F. A wakeful hypometabolic physiologic state. American Journal of Physiology, 1971, 221 (3), 795-799.

Wenger, M.A., & Bagchi, B.K. Studies of autonomic functions in practitioners of Yoga in India. Behavioral Science, 1961, 6, 312-323.

# FREDERICK, A. N. D. & BARBER, T. X.

# 21

## *Yoga, Hypnosis and Self-Control of Cardiovascular Functions*

During the past century reports have been filtering back from India concerning yogis who can exercise voluntary control over autonomic functions. Among the more dramatic of these reports are those claiming that yogis can stop the heart and can markedly vary the temperature of the skin.

Some *S*s under "hypnotic trance" have also been said to show an increased heart rate following direct suggestions that the heart is beating faster and a decreased heart rate when given suggestions to slow the heart. It has also been claimed that "hypnotized" *S*s show changes in skin temperature when they are given the suggestion to think of cold or warmth (Barber, 1970).

The purpose of this study is to evaluate cardiac and vasomotor phenomena observed in studies with yogis and to compare these phenomena with those observed in experimental hypnosis.

### *Cardiac Functions*

Five studies have been conducted that bear directly on the claim that yogis can stop the heart (Anand & Chhina, 1961; Green, Ferguson, Green, & Walters, 1971; Hoenig, 1968; Satyanarayanamurthi & Sastry, 1958; Wenger, Bagchi, & Anand, 1961). A critical evaluation of these studies leads to the following conclusions:

1. There is no evidence that yogis can stop the heart. Sensitive measures, such as the electrocardiogram and finger plethysmograph, consistently showed that there was heart activity during the yogis' attempts at heart stopping. However, as will be seen below, some yogis were able to attenuate heart sounds and the radial pulse.

2. The ability to attenuate the heart sounds (without stopping the heart) was achieved by use of the Valsalva maneuver. During this maneuver the inhaled breath is held with the glottis closed, and the muscles of the thorax and abdomen are strongly contracted. The consequent increase in intrathoracic pressure obstructs the thin-walled veins in the thorax and interferes with the venous return to the heart. Since heart sounds are produced by the heart's contracture over the contained blood and the closure of the valves, and since there is little blood returning to the heart, the heart sounds become attenuated or inaudible. Also, the strong contractions of the thoracic muscles produce a murmur that helps to obscure the heart sounds.

3. The ability to attenuate the radial pulse is due to contractions of the pectoralis, latissimus dorsi, and other muscles of the arm, chest, and back. These contractions, together with the pressure of the arm against the side, lead to mechanical compression of the brachial artery and an attenuation of the pulse.

4. Since early workers did not use sensitive instruments, such as the electrocardiogram, they falsely concluded that yogis could stop the heart voluntarily. This invalid conclusion was derived from (*a*) the ability of some yogis to attenuate heart sounds when tested by auscultation with a stethoscope and (*b*) the ability to attenuate the radial pulse when tested by palpation. Both of these indices can be absent without a stoppage of the heart.

Although yogis do not stop the heart, some yogis have shown changes in heart rhythm that have not yet been fully explained. Wenger et al. (1961) studied a 37-yr.-old male who had about 5 yr. of yogic training. He was able to slow his heart markedly from 63 to 25 beats per min. An increase in the P-R interval and a marked decrease or disappearance of the P wave was noted for periods up to 3 sec.

Rao, Krishnaswamy, Narasimhaiya, Hoenig, and Govindaswamy (1958) and Hoenig (1968) have both discussed another instance of a yogi who showed unusual cardiac manifestations. While buried in a pit, this yogi's heart rate varied from 100 to 40 bpm. in a cyclical manner every 25 min. This cyclical variation in heart rate was not correlated with other observations such as EEG or respiratory rate. Also, this yogi showed no other cardiac abnormality.

More recently, Green et al. (1970) noted that a trained yogi produced about 17 sec. of atrial flutter when he attempted to stop the heart. The yogi stated that he produced the cardiac manifestation by a "solar plexus lock" which may have been his term for the Valsalva maneuver. Green et al. also reported that the polygraph briefly recorded a heart rate of 300 bpm. during the experiment. It is not clear whether this was a polygraph artifact or a genuine phenomenon.

The ability of some yogis to accelerate and decelerate the heart has also been noted in some hypnotic *S*s who have been given the suggestion that the heart is beating faster or slower (Barber, 1970). These changes in heart rate appear to be correlated with changes in levels of arousal or activation. Barber (1970) has summarized the studies in this area by noting that "Cardiac acceleration or deceleration can be produced in some subjects by various types of suggestions or instructions given under either hypnotic or waking conditions [p. 159]." There is also evidence indicating that voluntary control of the heart rate is more common than has at times been supposed and is not discontinuous from other known psychophysiological phenomena (Barber, 1970).

*Vasomotor Functions*

Wenger and Bagchi (1961) report the case of a yogi who was able to perspire at will on his forehead between 1½ and 10 min. after he started concentrating on warmth. This man lived in Himalayan caves during part of two winters. The intense cold disturbed his meditation and he was advised by his guru to concentrate on warmth. He was also asked to visualize himself in hot places. After 6 mo. of practice, he was able, when thinking about warmth, to produce a feeling of warmth and perspiration from the forehead. Along similar lines, Green et al. (1970) found that a trained yogi could produce a temperature difference of 2° - 7° F. on the same hand between the hypothenar and thenar eminences. The yogi did not specify how he carried out this feat but the principles involved may be similar to those following.

Localized vasoconstriction and vasodilation (and a concomitant localized skin temperature alteration) can be induced by various types of suggestions or instructions given to *S*s who have not received yogic training. Menzies (1941) demonstrated that some normal individuals show vasodilation and vasoconstriction in a limb when instructed to recall previous experiences involving warmth or cold to the limb respectively. McDowell (1959) found that a good hypnotic *S* showed erythema with vasodilation and increase in skin temperature of a leg following suggestions that the leg was immersed in warm water. Hadfield (1920) noted that localized changes in skin temperature could be induced by suggestions given to a person in the waking state. In this case, *S* had exercised vigorously before the experiment and the temperature of both hands had reached 95° F. When it was suggested that his right hand was becoming cold, the temperature of his right palm fell to 68° F. while the temperature of the left palm stayed at 94° F. Next, when it was suggested that his right hand was becoming warm, the temperature of his hand rose to 94° F. in 20 min.

More recently, Zimbardo, Maslach, and Marshall (1970) presented experimental data showing that some individuals can exercise cognitive control over skin temperature. Three trained hypnotic *S*s were first asked to relax deeply and then to make one hand hot and the other cold. The *E* suggested several images and encouraged *S*s to generate their own imagery which might be helpful in increasing or decreasing hand temperature. All three *S*s were able to lower the temperature of one hand by about 2° to 7°. Two of the three *S*s were able to raise the temperature of the other hand by about 2° C.

The above data suggest that a substantial proportion of normal individuals might be able to produce localized changes in skin temperature. Apparently, the process of vividly imagining cold gives rise to vasoconstriction and the process of vividly imagining warmth gives rise to vasodilation. Of course, vasoconstriction in turn produces a drop in skin temperature and vasodilation produces a rise in skin temperature. We venture to predict that intensive research will be conducted in the near future to develop methods for teaching individuals to manifest this type of control over skin temperature.

## REFERENCES

Anand, B. K., & Chhina, G. S. Investigations of Yogis claiming to stop their heart beats. *Indian Journal of Medical Research*, 1961, 49, 90-94.

Barber, T. X. *LSD, marihuana, yoga, and hypnosis*. Chicago: Aldine, 1970.

Green, E. E., Ferguson, D. W., Green, A. M., & Walters, E. D. *Voluntary control project: Swami Rama*. Topeka: Menninger Foundation, 1970.

Hadfield, J. A. The influence of suggestions on body temperature. *Lancet*, 1920, 2, 68-69.

Hoenig, J. Medical research on yoga. *Confinia Psychiatrica*, 1968, 11, 69-89.

McDowell, H. Hypnosis in dermatology. In J. M. Schneck (Ed.), *Hypnosis in modern medicine*. (2nd ed.) Springfield, Ill.: Charles C Thomas, 1959.

Menzies, R. Further studies of conditioned vasomotor responses in human subjects. *Journal of Experimental Psychology*, 1941, 29, 457-482.

Rao, H. V. G., Krishnaswamy, N., Narasimhaiya, R. L., Hoenig, J., & Govindaswamy, M. V. Some experiments on a "yogi" in controlled states. *Journal of the All-India Institute of Mental Health*, 1958, 1, 99-106.

Satyanarayanamurthi, G. V., & Sastry, P. B. A preliminary scientific investigation into some of the unusual physiological manifestations acquired as a result of yogic practices in India. *Wiener Zeitschrift fuer Nervenheilkunde*, 1958, 15, 239-249.

Wenger, M. A., & Bagchi, B. K. Studies of autonomic functions in practitioners of Yoga in India. *Behavioral Science*, 1961, 6, 312-323.

Wenger, M., Bagchi, B. K., & Anand, B. K. Experiments in India on "voluntary" control of the heart and pulse. *Circulation*, 1961, 24, 1,313-1,325.

Zimbardo, P., Maslach, C., & Marshall, G. *Hypnosis and the psychology of cognitive and behavioral control*. Stanford, Calif.: Stanford University, 1970.

# 22

**TIMMONS, B. et al.**

# *Abdominal-Thoracic Respiratory Movements and Levels of Arousal*

Breathing patterns are considered to be closely related to states of consciousness in the meditative disciplines of the East. European respiration therapists have observed individual differences in breathing patterns and regard them to be reliable indicators of psychological states (Proskauer, 1968). Observations from these disciplines and from clinicians (Clausen, 1951) indicate that the relative amplitude of abdominal and thoracic movements may be one of the most significant aspects of respiration with regard to psychophysiological states. This parameter of respiration has received relatively little attention from behavioral scientists.[1] Sleep researchers have indicated that the abdominal-thoracic ratio may be different during the waking state as compared to sleep, but the findings are inconsistent (Kleitman, 1963; Goldie & Green, 1961). Clausen (1951) reported differences in abdominal-thoracic relationships among groups of normal, neurotic, and psychotic Ss. Goldie & Green (1961) saw a change in abdominal-thoracic ratio during hypnosis and suggested that in the absence of other objective evidence, it could be used as the first sign of the hypnotic mode.

The present study was an attempt to elucidate the relationship between abdominal-thoracic respiratory movements and the electrophysiological state of consciousness as indicated by the EEG.

## SUBJECTS AND PROCEDURE

Eleven young adults (10 males, 1 female) with no history of sleep disturbances served as Ss. Each S participated in one recording session, which lasted approximately 45 min. The experiments were conducted during the afternoon in a semidarkened room. After the recording electrodes were applied, Ss reclined in a supine position and were instructed to relax and go to sleep.

## APPARATUS

The EEG was recorded from a left-central/left-occipital placement, and eye movements from electrodes placed at the nasion and outer canthus of the left eye. Respiratory movements were monitored with mercury thread strain gauges[2] stretched to 32 cm in length and taped at both ends to the S's body. The thoracic gauge was placed across the chest at the level of the armpits, and the abdominal gauge was placed just below the navel.

## RESULTS

As the EEG indicated a transition from the relaxed waking state to Stages 1 and 2 sleep, there were distinctive and systematic changes in abdominal and thoracic respiratory movements.

### Changes in Abdominal and Thoracic Amplitudes

The relaxed waking state, characterized by an abundance of alpha activity (8-13 Hz), was associated with a breathing pattern in which the amplitudes of abdominal movement exceeded those of the thorax in 10 of 11 Ss (Fig. 1a, Table 1).

Changes in the pattern of breathing were observed as EEG indications of drowsiness appeared, viz, vacillations in the EEG between alpha activity and a low-voltage mixed pattern with theta activity, accompanied by slow eye movements. The relation between EEG fluctuations and changes in breathing pattern were determined by comparing the amplitudes of the two breath cycles immediately preceding and following an EEG transition. Such transitions were defined as a dropout of alpha activity for a period of at least 10 sec duration (alpha-theta transition), or the return of alpha rhythm for at least 5 sec (theta-alpha transition). A reduction of the amplitude of abdominal movements occurred with 93% of the alpha-theta transitions (Fig. 1b), and an enhancement of abdominal amplitude with 81% of the theta-alpha transitions (Fig. 1c). Table 2 shows the frequency with which the succeeding abdominal cycle amplitude decreased or increased following an EEG transition. Thoracic amplitudes were not closely related to the alpha-theta transitions. In some Ss, the slow eye movements characteristic of drowsiness (Aserinsky & Kleitman, 1955) preceded the EEG-abdominal amplitude changes; in others, they were simultaneous or occurred slightly later.

Throughout the period of drowsiness and Stage 1,[3] a tonic decrease in abdominal breath cycle amplitudes and a concomitant increase in thoracic amplitudes occurred. As a result, the abdominal and thoracic excursions became virtually equal. All 11 Ss displayed this equality at times during the recording. In 9 Ss, it was present at the onset of Stage 1 (see Table 2). There was much individual variation in the amount of time Ss remained in the drowsy state and Stage 1, during which they vacillated between alpha and the low-voltage mixed pattern with theta and between abdominal-dominant and abdominal-equal-to-thoracic modes of breathing.

Thoracic amplitudes increased gradually during drowsiness and Stage 1, until finally a thoracic-dominant mode of breathing emerged (Fig. 1d). This mode generally developed in late Stage 1 or early Stage 2. It was seen in 10 Ss (although only 6 Ss attained Stage 2). EEG arousals (alpha bursts) occurring during thoracic-dominant breathing were associated with immediate

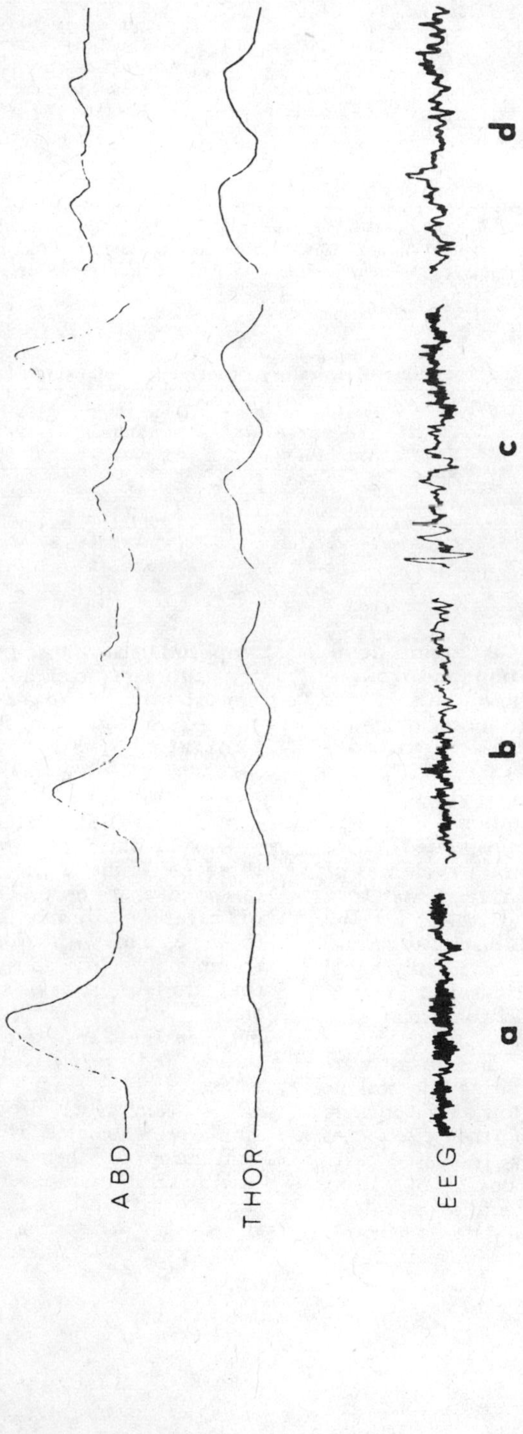


Fig. 1. Abdominal and thoracic respiratory movements at various levels of arousal.

**Table 1**
**Number of Ss Displaying Each Pattern of Respiratory Movement at Each EEG Stage***

| | Abdominal-Dominant | Abdominal Equal (or Approximately Equal) to Thoracic | Thoracic-Dominant |
|---|---|---|---|
| Initial Waking State | 10 | 1 | 0† |
| Onset Stage 1 | 1 | 9 | 1†† |
| Onset Stage 2 | 1 | 2 | 3 |

**The initial 30-sec epoch of the first appearance of each stage was observed.*
*†An additional S displayed thoracic-dominant breathing later in the wake recording.*
*††Five additional Ss showed thoracic-dominant breathing later in Stage 1 but did not progress to Stage 2.*

**Table 2**
**Incidence of Changes in Abdominal Respiratory Movements Following EEG Transitions***

| | Increase in Abdominal Amplitude | Decrease in Abdominal Amplitude | No Change in Abdominal Amplitude |
|---|---|---|---|
| Alpha-Theta | 2 | 51 | 2 |
| Theta-Alpha | 38 | 8 | 1 |

**Totals for 11 Ss*

resumption of the abdominal-dominant mode of respiration (analogous to the effect of arousal during the abdominal-equal-to-thoracic mode described above).

Changes in
Inspiratory-Expiratory
Phase Durations

In 7 of 11 Ss, the inspiratory phase of the abdominal breath cycle was of longer duration than the expiratory phase in the waking state.[4] At the onset of Stage 1, inspiratory and expiratory phases were virtually equal in 8 Ss (Fig. 1b). At onset of Stage 2, 5 of 6 Ss continued to display this equality of phases.

Thoracic phase durations were difficult to judge during the waking state because of the low amplitude and indefinite form of the cycle. As thoracic amplitudes increased with drowsiness and onset of sleep, however, a more definite waveform emerged. When the thoracic respiratory movements were of greater amplitude than those of the abdomen, the thoracic inspiratory phase was consistently of longer duration than the expiratory. Also, the form of the thoracic breath cycle generally assumed a distinctive "skewed dome" shape at this time (see Fig. 1d).

DISCUSSION

Our findings are in accord with those of Goldie & Green (1961), who observed that the predominant mode of breathing during light sleep was thoracic, and with arousal it became abdominal.[5] In addition, we found that during drowsiness and Stage 1, there was a striking parallelism between the transient changes in brain states and respiratory movements. Bülow (1963) found the transient EEG changes of drowsiness to be similarly associated with changes in ventilation[6]: "When the alpha activity in the EEG disappeared and theta waves developed, ventilation decreased. When the alpha activity reappeared sporadically, ventilation again increased [p. 31]." The present findings suggest that changes in ventilation may be effected by changes in relative dominance of abdominal or thoracic modes of breathing.

The present study also supports the contention of Goldie and Green that changes in mode of breathing may be a useful adjunct to the EEG in defining levels of consciousness. For example, our data may make possible a finer differentiation of the transitional state from the earliest signs of loss of wakefulness to the onset of sleep. Observations of respiratory parameters may also be particularly relevant to the study of meditative states and hypnagogic imagery. EEGs recorded during various types of meditation have generally shown patterns compatible with relaxed wakefulness or drowsiness (see Timmons & Kamiya, 1970). Green, Green, & Walters (1970) have observed that the hypnagogic reverie state is accompanied by a "slowed alpha-theta" pattern. In the present study, this EEG pattern (see Fig. 1b) was observed to be associated with characteristic respiratory patterns: vacillation between abdominal-dominant and abdominal-equal-to-thoracic breathing, and equality of abdominal inspiratory and expiratory phase durations.

Since spontaneous changes in consciousness, i.e., the process of sleep onset, are accompanied by specific respiratory patterns, it seems reasonable that self-manipulation of these patterns might be useful as a means of voluntarily altering states of consciousness. A precedent for this approach is found in the meditative disciplines which have traditionally emphasized breathing practices of various types. Biofeedback techniques[7] might be effective in training individuals to maintain specified respiratory patterns.[8]

## REFERENCES


PROSKAUER, M. Breathing therapy. In E. Otto and J. Mann (Eds.), *Ways of growth.* New York: Grossman, 1968

L. R., & KELLY, G. A feedback device for teaching diaphragmatic breathing. American Review of Respiratory Disease, 1969, 100, 577-578.

BULOW, K. Respiration and wakefulness in man. Acta Physiologica Scandinavica, 1963, 59, Suppl. 209, 1-110.

CLAUSEN, J. Respiration movement in normal, neurotic and psychotic subjects. Acta Psychiatrica et Neurologica, 1951, Suppl. 68, 1-74.

ASERINSKY, E., & KLEITMAN, N. Two types of ocular motility occurring in sleep. Journal of Applied Physiology, 1955, 8, 1-10.

BARACH, A. L., & SEAMAN, W. B. Role of the diaphragm in chronic pulmonary emphysema. New York Journal of Medicine, 1963, 63, 415-417.

BLOCK, J. D., LAGERSON, J., ZOHMAN,

RECHTSCHAFFEN, A., & KALES, A. (Eds.) *A manual of standardized terminology, techniques and scoring system for sleep stages of human subjects.* Washington, D.C: U.S. Government Printing Office, National Institutes of Health Publication No. 204, 1968.

TIMMONS, B., & KAMIYA, J. The psychology and physiology of meditation and related phenomena: A bibliography. Journal of Transpersonal Psychology, 1970, 2, 41-59.

GOLDIE, L., & GREEN, J. M. Changes in mode of respiration as an indication of level of awareness. Nature, 1961, 189, 581-582.

GREEN, E., GREEN, A. M., & WALTERS, E. D. Self-regulation of internal states. In J. Rose (Ed.), *Progress of cybernetics: Proceedings of the international congress of cybernetics, London, 1969.* London: Gordon & Breach, 1970. Pp. 1299-1317.

KLEITMAN, N. *Sleep and wakefulness.* (2nd ed.) Chicago: University of Chicago Press, 1963.

## NOTES

1. Physicians recognize that some types of pathology are associated with specific modes of breathing (see Barach & Seaman, 1963).

2. Parks Electronics, Beaverton, Oreg. 97005. Specially designed dc amplifiers and techniques of recording will be described in a subsequent paper.

3. EEG states were defined according to the criteria set forth by Rechtschaffen & Kales (1968). Stage 1 is characterized by a record containing less than 50% alpha combined with low-voltage activity in a 30-sec epoch.

4. Inspiration = expansion, expiration = contraction of the abdominal or thoracic region.

5. Inconsistent results in previous studies of abdominal-thoracic ratios and sleep (see Kleitman, 1963, p. 48) may be due to absence of simultaneous EEG observations, with the exception of the Goldie and Green study.

6. As measured by spirometry (L/min).

7. Such techniques augment the sensory feedback from the physiological activity and provide assistance in enhancing voluntary control of the activity.

8. Feedback training is already in use to help emphysema patients suppress thoracic breathing (see Block et al, 1969).

# 23

## GOLEMAN, D.

# *The Buddha on Meditation and States of Consciousness*

There is inevitably great difficulty in translating from noumenal experience to the realm of discourse, from raw reality to abstract concept. Experience is the forerunner of all spiritual teachings, though similar experiences may come to be articulated differently; the Vedas say, "The Truth is one, only the sages call it by different names." In any given exploration of higher states of consciousness, the version set down in words is of necessity an arbitrary, and perhaps nebulous, delimitation of states, their characteristics, and their bounds. Lao Tzu recognizes this dilemma in the *Tao Te Ching:*

> The way that can be told
> Is not the constant way;
> The name that can be named
> Is not the constant name.

*two levels of religious doctrine and practice*

Garma Chang (1970) explains that the Tibetans recognize two levels of religious doctrine and practice: "The Expedient Teaching" and "The Final Teaching."[1] The Expedient Teachings are the multitude of world religions, each shaped by and for the people who adhere to it; the variance among faiths is accounted for by these shaping factors. But the Final Teaching at the (often esoteric) core of all faiths is essentially one and the same. The typology of techniques which follows here is aimed at the level of Final Teaching, where doctrinal differences fall away, the unity of practice coming into focus. Religious systems differ by virtue of accident of time and place, but the experience that is precursor to religion is everywhere the same. The unity in Final Teaching underlying the various techniques is inevitable: all men are alike in

[1]I am grateful to Sonja Margulies for calling this distinction to my attention.

nervous system, and it is at this level that the laws governing Final Teaching operate.

*typology of meditation practices*

The Buddha's map of MSC in the *Visuddhimagga* embodies a threefold generic typology of meditation practices which undercuts ostensible distinctions in techniques stemming from differences in ideologies. Though any given system may draw on techniques from different categories, it is the specific technique that is classifiable in this typology, and not the system as a whole. As a first step in a systematic investigation of the myriad meditation practices, the *Visuddhimagga* road-maps serve here as the skeleton of a typology allowing the sorting out of techniques in terms of their mechanics, despite the conceptual overlay that accompanies them. This exercise in typology is intended to be seminal, not exhaustive. In some cases only one of numerous techniques belonging to a given system will be discussed by way of illustration. This typology is one of parts, of specific practices, rather than a taxonomy of the complex totality of religious systems and spiritual paths. In this classificatory application of the *Visuddhimagga,* I have drawn examples from among the meditation systems represented at present in the West, dealing with both their specific techniques and their antecedent roots in the schools of the East. The summaries that follow are based primarily on published sources rather than personal investigation. They may, therefore, seem incomplete or imprecise to a person on any of these paths, for each is a living tradition that presents itself differently to each person according to his needs and circumstances. The summaries are intended to discuss each technique in enough detail to show its unique flavor while demonstrating its place within the typology.

*the path of concentration and the path of insight*

In the realm of mind, the method is the seed of the goal: the state of consciousness one reaches is contingent upon how one chose to get there. Just as each meditation subject is consequential in the level of absorption for which it serves as vehicle, so does one's technique determine whether one will follow the path of insight or of concentration. If the mind merges in samadhi with the meditation subject, and then transcends its subject to even higher levels of jhana, then one traverses the path of concentration. On the path of insight, mind witnesses its own workings, coming to see finer segments of mind-moments and becoming increasingly detached from its workings to the point of turning away from all awareness in nirvana. The great traditions evolved from these two paths can be broadly distinguished by their goal: whether it be the "One" or the "Zero." The One is the path of samadhi, of mind merging with its object, of self dissolving into Self in union. The Zero is the path to nirvana, mind taking itself as object, where all phenomena, including mind, are finally known to be voidness, where ego-self dissolves into nothingness.

*a third path*

There is a third path, which combines the One and the Zero; *vipassana* as described in the *Visuddhimagga* is itself perhaps the best example of practices integrating concentration and insight. When concentration and insight are combined in a meditation system, the combination is not simply additive, but rather *interactive*. Concentration multiplies the effectiveness of insight; insight-borne detachment facilitates concentration. This interaction can occur only when concentration is held to the access level—in jhana there can be no insight. In systems that combine the two, the outcome is a nirvanic state and consequent ego reduction. In terms of the One and the Zero, the formula that best expresses this interactive dynamic is: $1 \times 0 = 0$.

*Integrated: The One and the Zero*
Concentration and insight combine and interact, ending in nirvana; $1 \times 0 = 0$.

*Concentration: The One*
Samadhi leads through the jhanas; mind merges with the object in Unity.

*Insight: The Zero*
Mindfulness culminates in nirvana; mind watches its own workings until cessation.

## A CONICAL TYPOLOGY OF MEDITATION TECHNIQUES

*Naranjo's typology of meditation techniques*

Claudio Naranjo (1971) has outlined an overlapping threefold typology of meditation techniques, which includes as its first two categories "The Way of Forms" and "The Negative Way," the paths of concentration and of insight, respectively. His third category, "The Expressive Way," includes visionary and prophetic experiences, possession states, artistic, shamanistic, and psychotherapeutic surrender and openness to impulse and intuition. From the viewpoint of the *Visuddhimagga* system this third category entails experiences within the domain of discursive thought, not within the range of MSC (though some, such as visions and prophecy, can be fruits of jhana).[2] As such, they perhaps represent a maximal ex-

[2]Fischer (1971) makes a distinction similar to Naranjo's; while he lumps the Way of Forms and The Negative Way along a "perception-meditation" continuum of trophotropic (decreasing) sympathetic nervous system arousal, he distinguishes

pansion of normal consciousness into altered states, but do not overleap its bounds into the realm of jhana or nirvana, where discursive thought stops.

*meditative states of consciousness and altered states of consciousness*

This difference in typologies demonstrates the point of divergence between altered states (ASC) and meditative states (MSC): from the perspective of normal consciousness, the Expressive Way is unquestionably a range of extraordinary mental states, but from the viewpoint of the *Visuddhimagga* these are not, strictly speaking, meditative states. It may be, in fact, that the Expressive Way is inimical to the attainment of MSC, since by acting out every impulse one may reinforce patterns of thought and desire, strengthening these habits of mind so as to enhance their power to hinder transcending the sphere of thought. Sila, a standard preparation for meditation, is exactly opposite: the conscientious denial of expressing impulse in action. A possible alternative effect, as Naranjo points out, is the arising of *vairagya*—spontaneous renunciation—brought about by consciously living through all one's desires.[3]

*emphasis: behavioral analysis of procedures and techniques*

Naranjo's typology is "beyond the forms," focusing on general similarities rather than specifics; this discussion is of the forms per se: a behavioral analysis of procedures and techniques, so that researchers will be able to interpret more appropriately the nature of results, and design and plan accordingly. Among traditional meditation schools there are perhaps few pure types save for those systems centering around a single technique—e.g., "Transcendental Meditation." Many contemporary schools are eclectic, using a variety of techniques from both paths, making allowances for individual requirements—the Sufis, for example, use mainly the *zikr,*

the Expressive Way as an opposite continuum of "perception-hallucination" with ergotropic (increasing) arousal. His trophotropic dimension includes creativity, psychosis, and mystic ecstasy; the ergotropic subsumes insight and concentration meditation. Fischer postulates increasing arousal as a path to jhana: at the peak of arousal one "rebounds" into jhana as a physiological protective mechanism.

Fischer's dichotomy is in partial agreement with Meher Baba (Donkin, 1954), who said "mind speeded is mad, mind slowed is *mast,* mind stilled is God." Meher Baba traveled throughout India identifying and aiding *masts,* "God-intoxicants," who had begun to slow their minds by focusing on God but had gone astray. *Masts* were usually wholly out of touch with the world of consensual reality and most often regarded as insane. While agreeing with Fischer's view that madness is in the direction of "mind speeded," Meher Baba distinguished between "mind slowed" in the *mast's* "divine madness" and psychosis—a distinction wholly unknown to Western psychiatry.

[3]Suzuki (1957), in comparing the spontaneity of a Zen master with that of certain Christian gnostics, shows that both share what Naranjo characterizes as Expressive behavior. But in doing so, Suzuki emphasizes the distinction between spontaneous expressiveness resulting from the loss of ego through Zen, which brings one into the eternal moment and spontaneity, and that which is itself in the service of an ego impulsively satisfying every desire. The former is the by-product of sustained meditation practice and MSC; the latter is itself an obstacle to the intensive efforts necessary for MSC.

a concentration practice, but also sometimes draw on insight techniques like *Muraqaba,* which is concentration on the flow of one's own consciousness. For purposes of typology a specific technique within each system will be emphasized by way of illustration.

*goal of all meditation systems*

The goal of all meditation systems, whatever their ideological orientation or source, and whichever of the three main types, is to transform the waking state through the fruits of practice —to die to the life of the ego and be reborn to a new level of experience. The state of consciousness gained through concentration in jhana, or through insight in nirvana, is discontinuous with the three normal states of waking, dreaming, and sleeping; it is a fourth state. The ultimate transformation sought by meditation systems is a new state still: a fifth state of consciousness mixing with and re-creating the three normal states.[4] In each school this end-state is labeled differently according to the unique perspective of the accompanying belief systems. But no matter how diverse the names, the phenomenon itself is the same. All these systems—whether concentration, insight, or integrated—propose the same basic formula in an alchemy of the self: the diffusion of the effects of meditation into the waking, dreaming, and sleep states, though each identifies this process in its distinct vocabulary.

In the Buddha's teaching, the path to the One is of subsidiary importance, useful as initial mind-training in the path to nirvana. Eliade (1969) points out that in the *Visuddhimagga* tradition, jhana is a means of access to "a suprasensible reality, and not a *unio mystico*"—the jhanic experience prepared the monk for a "super knowledge" whose final goal was nirvana. But by no means all great spiritual teachers have been in agreement with the Buddha's assessment of path and goal. The most notably polar opposite approach to HSC is that of the adherents to the various sects and schools of *bhakti,* and so this typology will begin there.

### HINDU BHAKTI

*Bhakti,* or devotion to a divine being, is perhaps the dominant popular mode of worship in contemporary world religions. In this respect a Christian gospel singer, a Hassidic Jew dancing

[4]The fifth state meets Tart's (1971) criteria for a "higher state of consciousness": (1) all functions of "lower" states are available—i.e., waking, dreaming, sleeping,— and (2) some new functions, derivative of jhana or nirvana, are present in addition. Since the fifth state has these attributes by definition, it may be the only unequivocally "higher state." Within Tart's formulation, jhana and nirvana are not HSC, but rather meditation-specific states of consciousness, or MSC.

*the essence of bhakti*

and singing at the Wailing Wall, a Sufi reciting "El Allah Hoo," a Hindu singing "Hare Krishna," and a Japanese Buddhist repeating "na-mu-a-mi-da-bu, na-mu-a-mi-da-bu," are all more or less engaged in the same process, though directed toward different objects. The essence of bhakti is making the object of devotion one's central thought. The ecstacy of the devotee is most often that borne of access concentration; in its higher reaches bhakti merges into the path of jhana.

*Hare Krishna*

Swami Bhaktivedanta's Hare Krishna group is in an orthodox Hindu bhakti tradition. In the classic *Srimad Bhagavatam,* remembering or constant chanting of Krishna's name is recommended over all other practices as the best path for this age; the *Kalisantaram Upanishad* has Brahma extol to the bard Narada as the highest or *maha*-mantra, "Hare Rama, Hare Krishna"—Hare, Rama, and Krishna all being manifestations of Vishnu. Even so, a bhakta may choose any deity or divine being as his devotional object, or ishta. Having done so, he must try to keep the thought or name of his ishta foremost in his mind at all times. Besides *kirtan* (chanting or singing) there are three main levels of *japa,* or repetition of the name: verbal, silent verbalization, and mental. Each succeeding form of japa is regarded as "ten times" more efficacious than the preceding one (Poddar, 1965).

In its beginning stage, japa is to be maintained in the midst of life's activities, until gradually the mind is occupied solely with that one thought. The *mala,* or rosary, is a common technical adjunct to japa; with the telling of each bead, the name is recited once. Other aids to japa include gearing recitation to each breadth, or to every beat of the pulse. No matter what the mnemonic device, the principle is the same: to return attention to repetition at once when the mind ceases to be engaged elsewhere. The goal of this stage of practice is to make the habit of repetition stronger than all other mental habits—i.e., one-pointedness. Poddar (1965) suggests that the neophyte practice a minimum of six hours of japa per day. If successful, the name will repeat of itself virtually every moment, day or night.

By way of social reinforcement of the initially vulnerable mental habit of constant worship through remembering, the *Bhakti-Sutras of Devarsi Narada* (Poddar, 1968) make stipulations similar to those of the *Visuddhimagga* to the would-be meditator. *Satsang,* the company of persons on the same path, is highly recommended as a counter to the pull of worldly attachments, as is the visiting of saints. The bhakta is further urged to avoid talk of "women, wealth, unbelievers, and enemies." In early stages it may be necessary to seek out a new, nonworldly reference group; as one's consciousness becomes more thoroughly imbued with the thought of the ishta worldly company may be seen as repugnant.

Another echo of the *Visuddhimagga* is in the emphasis on purity in the bhakti path. The success of the bhakta is dependent upon his own virtues; purity, says Vivekananda (1964), "is absolutely the basic work, the bedrock upon which the whole Bhakti-building rests." As in all such paths, virtue, which is in the beginning an act of will, becomes a by-product of the practice itself. As the mind becomes attached to its devotional object, it withdraws from worldly objects; by love of God, says Vivekananda, "love of the pleasures of the senses and of the intellect is all made dim." An aspect of renunciation unique to bhakti is the "giving up" of attachments in the sense of offering them up to the ishta. Thus, claims Vivekananda, the bhakta has no struggle "to suppress any single one of his emotions, he only strives to intensify them and direct them to God." Poddar (1965) observes that "compared to the joy of repeating the 'Rama nama' all other enjoyments of the world are insipid."

*unique aspect of bhakti renunciation*

Bhakti begins on the level of duality, with the devotee separate from his ishta, as from any love object. The *Bhakti Sutras,* in fact, include a typology of Divine Love which includes loving the ishta as one's friend, as one's spouse, and as one's child. Prabhavananda and Isherwood (1969) suggest that "all human relationships may be sublimated through the practice of bhakti yoga." Though this love may begin with the forms of, and energies invested in, interpersonal love, it ends in union with the state of love evoked by the love-object. Here, says Vivekananda, "Love, the Lover, and the Beloved are One." At this level the practice of bhakti merges into the path of jhana. The mergence comes in two stages: ecstasy and absorption. The fruit of japa, constant remembering at every moment of waking awareness, brings with it "love-intoxication." The feelings of bliss, rapture, and joy at this stage are characteristic of access concentration. The ecstatic devotee's behavior may be as erratic as a madman's; the *Srimad Bhagavata* (XI, ii) describes this stage:

> . . . the devotee loses all sense of decorum and moves about in the world unattached. . . . His heart melts through love as he habitually chants the Name of his beloved lord, and like one possessed, he now bursts into peals of laughter, now weeps, now cries, now sings aloud and now begins to dance.

*characteristics of devotee's behavior*

*an accomplished bhakta and samadhi*

The enraptured devotee may be on the threshold of samadhi. From the access-level that his ecstasy indicates, he can gain in meditation the first jhana through concentration on his ishta. Once this level is reached, according to Swami Muktananda (1971), there is no further need for chanting or japa: they are preludes to meditation. An accomplished bhakta can attain samadhi on the least stimulus suggesting his devotion. Sri Ramakrishna, for example, once went to a theater performance of the life of Sri Chaitanya, a seventeenth-century bhakti saint. At several points during the play, on seeing portrayals of Chaitanya's devotion to Krishna, Ramakrishna went into samadhi (M., 1928).

The psychological concomitants of this level of proficiency on the way of bhakti are tantamount to a basic personality change. As Vivekananda (1964, p. 90) puts it, "when a person loves the Lord, the whole universe becomes dear to him . . . his whole nature is purified and completely changed." Renunciation becomes effortless, all attachments save to the beloved having fallen away. From this intense and all-absorbing love comes perfect faith and self-surrender, the conviction that nothing that happens is against one: "not my, but Thy will be done." He perceives "the sacred within the secular," as Maslow (1970) describes sacralization; everything is sacred because it belongs to the Beloved. All things being His, the bhakta no longer need observe any external forms or symbols for worship. He worships in his heart, the world having become his altar. Kabir (1970, p. 40) eloquently sums up his own experience of this state:

> O Sadhu! the simple union is the best,
> Since the day when I met with my Lord,
> there has been no end to the sport of our love . . .
> I see with eyes open and smile, and
> behold His beauty everywhere;
> I utter His name, and whatever I see, it
> reminds me of Him; whatever I do,
> it becomes His worship . . .
> Wherever I go, I move round Him,
> All I achieve is His service:
> When I lie down, I lie prostrate
> at His feet.
> He is the only adorable one to me: I
> have none other.
> My tongue has left off impure words, it
> sings His glory day and night:
> Whether I rise or sit down, I can
> never forget Him; for the rhythm
> of His music beats in my ears.

> Kabir says: I am immersed in the one
> great bliss which transcends all
> pleasure and pain.

SUFISM

Kabir, himself beyond all religious forms, was from a Muslim family, though he followed a Hindu guru; the officials of his sixteenth century Benares classified him as a Sufi. Sufism is the tradition associated with Islam most closely corresponding to the form and spirit of Hindu Bhakti. The most widely known Sufi practices involve ecstatic singing and dancing. In his quest for union with the Divine Beloved, the Sufi follows a familiar pattern and path. The accent in one segment of Sufi teaching is on divine grace, which descends from above on the pure of heart and lifts him to transcendental heights. Understandably, then, there is a great emphasis on practices of renunciation and purification. In his study of Persian Sufis, Rice (1964) enumerates the stages of progressive self-purification preparatory to divine union. These stages include: acts of repentance, avoiding whatever has the least semblance of wrong, turning one's back on worldly vanities, and a "constant watch over the heart"; acts of renunciation, such as voluntary poverty, heedlessness of worldly affairs, and self-surrender to the Divine will; entrusting one's destiny to God; accepting all tribulations as tests of purification, and practicing contentment with whatever comes. The central psychological premise supporting these renunciatory acts permeates Sufi thought; Abu Said of Mineh framed that premise as (Rice, p. 34)

*self-purification and divine union*

> When occupied with self, you are separated from God. The way to God is but one step; the step out of yourself.

An auxiliary, but key, practice among Sufis is that of *zikr,* the Farsi term for japa, which literally means "remembrance." The *zikr* par excellence is *La ilāha illā 'llah:* "There is no god but God." A *zikr* always accompanies Sufi dancing, the efficacy of which is enhanced by maintaining the remembrance throughout. "The dance opens a door in the soul to divine influences," wrote Sultan Walad, Rumi's son (Rice, p. 101); "the dance is good when it arises from remembrance of the Beloved." Sufi dancing embodies a two-fold method for strengthening concentration: on the one hand there is the need to attend to the dance steps, on the other there is constant oral repetition of God's name. The bliss and ecstasy often accompanying Sufi dancing mark a concentration developed to the access level; the dance itself may, with experience,

*"remembrance"*

*"dance"*

stimulate internal cues for increasingly easy entrance to access-level bliss states.

The *zikr* is also to be practiced as a solitary meditation. At first it is an oral repetition, later a silent one; a fourteenth-century manuscript on the practice says, "When the heart begins to recite, the tongue should stop." The goal, as in all meditation systems, is to overcome one's natural state of mind—"carelessness and inattention"—and become one-pointed on God. One's original motivation may well be the realization of the truth of the Sufi comment on normal consciousness, that man is "asleep in a nightmare of unfulfilled desires"—and that with transcendence, desires fall away. Along the way the Sufi undergoes a number of states typical of progress in meditation—e.g., *qurb,* a sense of God's constant nearness induced by concentration on Him, and *mahabba,* losing oneself in contemplation on the Beloved. Among its fruits are visions and the "station of unity," where *zikr* (the remembrance), *zakir* (the one who remembers), and *mazkur* (the One remembered) become one—i.e., the first jhana. Mastery is recognized as the point when there is effortless fixed attention on the *zikr,* driving out other thoughts from the mind. This state is seen as a pure "gift of grace" where one is "lost in Truth," having achieved *fana,* or the absorption of jhana. The ultimate stage is that of *baga,* abiding in the *fana*-consciousness while in the midst of the phenomenal world (Manzani, 1928). The Sufi Idries Shah (1971) speaks of it as an "extra dimension of being" operating parallel to ordinary cognition, and calls it "Objective Consciousness." Union with God in absorbed love marks the height of attainment, but Sufis, according to Robert Graves (in Shah, 1971), "admit its value only if the devotee can afterward return to the world and live in a manner consonant with his experience."

*sequence of states*

*ultimate stage*

#### CHRISTIAN HESYCHASM

The route of the Sufi is the path of jhana, while his telling of his inner journey is in the vernacular of the gnostic: if one opens his heart to God, His grace descends on the pure of heart, and one loses oneself in mystic union. So also with Christian gnostics and mystics. The practice of japa has been a mainstay of Christian worship from the beginning, though the usual contemporary use of rosary beads is a dim remainder of more whole-hearted remembrance of God. Thomas Merton (1960) observes that what is today practiced as "prayer" in Christian churches is but one—albeit the

*Christian gnostics and mystics*

surviving one—of a range of more intensive contemplative practices. The fourth century Desert Fathers, for example, engaged in absorption aided by the verbal or silent repetition of a single phrase from the Scriptures. The most popular was the prayer of the Publican: "Lord Jesus Christ, Son of God, have mercy on me a sinner." In its short form, *Kyrie eleison,* it was repeated silently throughout the day "until it became as spontaneous and instinctive as breathing." The Desert Fathers emphasized sila, and renunciatory and expiatory acts were commonplace among them. As in the *Visuddhimagga,* sila was an adjunct to concentration; in the words of one of the Fathers, "the soul, unless it be cleansed of alien thoughts, cannot pray to God in contemplation." The hoped-for result of the Fathers' endeavors was what Merton calls a "nowhereness and nomindness"—a condition known by the name *quies,* literally "rest"—the individual having lost all preoccupation with a limited "self."

*Kyrie eleison*

The tradition stemming from the practices of the Desert Fathers, though virtually lost in Western Christendom, has been kept unchanged since the first millenium of Christianity in Eastern Orthodoxy. The practice of the Prayer of Jesus is seen as the fulfillment of Paul's injunction to "pray always"; the early Fathers called it "the art of arts and the science of sciences," which led one toward the highest human perfection. This teaching has been preserved in the collection of early Christian writings known as the *Philokalia* (Kadloubovsky and Palmer, 1971), the translation of which from Greek to Russian at the turn of the century came on the crest of a wave of revival of the practice throughout Russia (chronicled in *The Way of the Pilgrim*; French, 1970). The practice itself is designed to awaken and develop strength of attention and concentration, and as in all bhakti paths, the essential conditions enumerated for success are "genuine humility, sincerity, endurance, purity." Hesychius of Jerusalem, a fifth-century teacher of the use of the Jesus Prayer (known now in the West as Hesychasm), describes it as a spiritual art that releases one completely from passionate thoughts, words, and evil deeds, and gives a "sure knowledge of God the Incomprehensible"; its essence is purity of heart, which is the "same as guarding the mind, kept perfectly free of all fantasies" and all thoughts. The means is unceasingly calling upon Christ with perfect attention, resisting all thoughts; he describes discursive thought as "enemies who are bodiless and invisible, malicious and clever at harming us, skillful, nimble and practised in warfare," who enter in through the five senses. A mind caught in discursive thought is distant from

*the practice of the prayer of Jesus*

Jesus; to overcome sense-consciousness and attain a silent mind is to be with Him.

*instructions*

Among the "Directions to Hesychasts" is the direction that no effort be spared to find a teacher and guide who bears the Spirit within him and to devote oneself to such a master, obeying all his commands. Once the teacher is found, further aids include seclusion in a quiet, dimly lit cell, eating only as much as one needs to keep alive, silence, full performance of Church ritual, fasting, and vigils, and most important, practice of the Prayer. The *Philokalia* quotes St. Nilus: "He who wishes to see what his mind really is must free himself of all thoughts; then he will see it like a sapphire or the hue of heaven." The instructions for stilling the mind specify sitting on a low stool in the solitude of one's cell on first awakening, and for an hour (or more, if one is able), "collect your mind from its customary circling and wandering outside, and quietly lead it into the heart by way of breathing, keeping this prayer: 'Lord Jesus Christ, Son of God, have mercy on me!' connected with the breath." When with practice it becomes possible to so "pray" with perfect one-pointedness, "then, abandoning the many and the varied, we shall unite with the One, the Single and the Unifying, directly in a union which transcends reason"—presumably, in jhana. The Prayer is not to be limited to these sessions only, but practiced always without distraction in the midst of all activity. One who has mastered this phase of ongoing practice is described as himself having the stature of Christ, enjoying perfect purity of heart. St. Isaac comments that one who has attained a state of effortless, constant prayer (Kadloubovsky and Palmer, 1971, p. 213):

> . . . has reached the summit of all virtues, and has become the abode of the Holy Spirit . . . when the Holy Spirit comes to live in a man, he never ceases to pray, for then the Holy Spirit constantly prays in him. . . . In eating or drinking, sleeping or doing something, even in deep sleep his heart sends forth without effort the incense and sighs of prayer.

*from interpersonal to transpersonal love*

The initial power of bhakti—Hindu, Sufi, or Christian—is the element of interpersonal love felt by the bhakta toward his devotional object. As he progresses on this path, that love becomes transformed from an interpersonal to an "impersonal," or transpersonal, love. Said St. Bernard, "Love begins in the flesh and ends in the spirit." It is no longer the object of devotion that is experienced as bestowing bliss; rather, it is the transcendental states of which that bliss is one aspect, and these are found to exist within the devotee as a potentiality of his own consciousness. It is no longer necessary to cling to the external form of the devotional object; the states once evoked therefrom have come to be fixtures of one's own consciousness. The process of coming to identify the devotional object with an internal state is parallel to that of attaining jhanas. By becoming one-pointed on the object of devotion, keeping it ever in mind, the devotee refines his consciousness to the state of jhana. Sankaracharya noted this process when he observed that bhakti ends in a quest for the Self: what begins as an external evocation of love becomes in the end an internal absorption, delighting uninterruptedly in "pure Self"—i.e., in jhana (Poddar, 1968).

*transcending the devotional object*

The practice of bhakti, by bringing the mind to one-pointedness through constant remembrance of the object of devotion, can bring the bhakta to the level of the first jhana. But if he is to go beyond this level, he must transcend his own devotional object, for any thought of name-and-form, even that of a Deity, binds one to the lower jhana reaches. Sri Ramakrishna, for example, for many years an ardent devotee of the Divine Mother, had experienced many visions and states of bliss as Her devotee. Later he took initiation from a naked ascetic (Saradananda, 1963, p. 255):

> After initiating me . . . The Naked One asked me to make my mind free of function in all respects, and merge in the meditation of the Self. But, when I sat for meditation I could by no means make my mind go beyond the bounds of name and form and cease functioning. The mind withdrew itself from all other things, but as soon as it did so, the intimately familiar form of the universal Mother appeared. . . . But, at last, collecting all the strength of my will, I cut Mother's form to pieces with the sword of discrimination. . . . There remained no function in the mind, which transcended quickly the realm of names and forms, making me merge in samadhi.

The Visuddhimagga emphasizes the need, at the point of initial access to a new plane of consciousness, to cut ties to the preceding plane. Each plane has its special points of appeal, some exceedingly sublime. The prerequisite work for gaining the next higher level, then, is to become detached from the lower plane, as Ramakrishna did, lest the mind be pulled back to it. For bhaktas in general, this means that one's devotional object in form must finally be abandoned in favor of becoming oneself, in jhana, that manifestation of pure being for which the object of devotion is himself worshipped.

*Meher Baba: an eclectic master*

Although Meher Baba's primary teaching is devotion to a guru and the self-surrender of a bhakta—his American followers know themselves as "Baba lovers"—he is eclectic in offering a wide range of meditation techniques as complementary practices, under the guidance of one who has himself successfully completed this journey, a "Perfect Master." Meher Baba describes the ascent to HSC in terms of seven planes or states of consciousness which, reflecting his Sufi background, he calls *fanas*. The means of access to each fana is concentration. At each new plane there is a radical change in the conditions of mental life: initially one experiences the plane only in a "paralysis of mental activity"—i.e., jhana—and gradually that plane comes to characterize the mind's functioning in all phases of life. With each higher fana one undergoes a "lowering down of mental activity" and a substantial diminution of ego-life. At the seventh and last plane, mind is quiet and ego is totally and finally annihilated.

*progression of fanas*

The progression he describes through the fanas is a close parallel to that of the jhanas. The first fana is characterized by a temporary experience of bliss and loss of limited self; the second by absorption in bliss and "infinite light," the third by loss of body-consciousness, a feeling of infinite power, and withdrawal of consciousness from the external world. In terms of the *Visuddhimagga,* this is the ascension through access concentration to the first, second, or third jhana. The fourth fana is marked by the emergence of supernormal powers, just as is the fourth jhana. At the fifth plane, all worldly desires are annihilated; the tendency of jhana-consciousness overpowers the discursive mind so that thought and action in the waking state become wholly intuitive and spontaneous. Then at the sixth plane one sees "God and the Infinite" (perhaps as in the sixth jhana) as a continual perception, without any break. Reaching the seventh and last plane—"Fana-Fillah"—one no longer sees God, but merges with Him, in a "final annihilation of the self." This final stage is sahaj samadhi; God-consciousness pervades one's entire universe of experience. Meher Baba insistently warns of the danger at each new fana of thinking it to be the final destination. Attachment to each fana must be broken if one is to finally reach sahaj samadhi, "the only real awakening." He distinguishes two aspects of sahaj samadhi: *nirvana* in the sense of jhanic absorption (not necessarily identical with the *Visuddhimagga* nirvanic state), and *nirvikalpa,* the waking-state manifestation of fana-consciousness, "Divinity in Expression."

*final stage: sahaj samadhi*

The function of meditation for Meher Baba is to take one "beyond the limitations of the mind." What he calls "meditation" is the first stage of a process that gradually develops into the focused concentration of samadhi. He recommends for the object of meditation some divine person or object, or some spiritually significant theme or truth; the process should not be forced and mechanical, but rather an intensification of one's natural inclinations. Such general meditation could entail thinking about some expression of "the Divine Truth," hearing a discourse from a Master, or reading his writings, until discursive thought stops and one has an intuitive perception of its truth. But there is no set course of exercises prescribed for all comers; instead he emphasizes that a Master can best decide what technique is most suited to each aspirant at each point on the path. If, for example, one has the capacity for concentration, these meditations are unnecessary. Says Meher Baba (1967, p. 113):

> In concentration mind seeks to unite with its object by the process of fixing itself upon that object, whereas meditation consists in thorough thinking about a particular object to the exclusion of everything else.

*Meher Baba and meditation*

In other words, "meditation" for Meher Baba is in the realm of access concentration, and preliminary to what he calls "concentration," which is the means to jhana. The essence of the process is one-pointedness, for the development of which Meher Baba enumerates a broad range of techniques. For beginners, he proposes "personal meditation," where the meditation subject is a person who is a "spiritually perfect" Master—e.g., Jesus, Buddha, Krishna, or Meher Baba himself. The four stages of this technique—a form of bhakti—are: meditating on the divine qualities of the Master; concentration on the physical form of the Master; the "meditation of the heart," where one feels an uninterrupted flow of love toward Him accompanied by joy and self-forgetfulness; and finally, the "meditation of action"—a karma yoga—where one offers all one's action to the Master and tries to express the ideals He embodies in all one's acts.

The "impersonal meditations" suggested by Meher Baba begin with cultivating a habit of thought which regards "all forms as equally the manifestations of the same one all-pervading life and as nothing in themselves separately." This contemplation is to be coupled with an attitude of detachment toward one's own body. The two together prepare one for meditation on the "formless and infinite aspect of God"; he suggests one focus on a symbol of infinity such as the sky or "vast emptiness." The final phase of this exercise is to identify oneself with and merge into the infinite—very possibly as in the fifth or sixth jhana. Another variety of meditation recommended is the "quest for an agent of action," where one ceaselessly presses the query: "Who is this 'I'?" This search for an agent to one's acts is designed to lead to a detachment toward these processes of self. An alternative means recommended for cultivating detachment is similar to mindfulness techniques: regarding oneself as the witness of all physical and mental happenings. Still another range of techniques offered by Meher Baba to the aspirant are a close approximation of vipassana. These take as the object of attention the mental operations themselves, and ultimately aim at stilling the mind. The first step in this procedure is to write down one's thoughts as they come, in stream-of-consciousness fashion. A later stage is the intensive awareness of thoughts as they appear in consciousness. These prepare the way for the attempt "to make the mind blank." At this stage the practice differs from vipassana per se: the procedure is to alternate two "incompatible" forms of meditation. The example given is five minutes of concentration on the form of the Master with eyes open, in alternation with five minutes of absorption with eyes closed in the thought "I am infinite."[5] The state thereby achieved sounds much like the nirvanic state: "complete internal silence."

*a variety of techniques*

All these forms of meditation are seen as culminating in sahaj samadhi. At this "ultimate goal of life" meditation is a self-sustained spontaneous fact of existence. Stillness of mind is expressed in the world of action. One is now free of all ego ties and interests; consciousness is no longer determined by the deposits of the past. Meher Baba (1967, p. 167) describes it as "a state of full wakefulness in which there is no ebb and flow, waxing or waning, but only the steadiness of true perception." One is now a *siddha* or *sadguru,* himself a suitable object for meditation.

*stillness of mind in world of action*

#### SRI AUROBINDO

In a sense, Sri Aurobindo's yoga begins where Meher Baba's leaves off—with sahaj samadhi. Sri Aurobindo (1949, 1955,

[5]As we have seen, the former practice corresponds to access concentration, while the latter can bring one to the fifth jhana. The basic principle in vipassana practice is to use concentration borne of samadhi to witness thoughts while at the access level; it may be that the technique proposed by Meher Baba for achieving a "blank" mind is functionally the same as the vipassana path to the nirvanic state, though structurally different. He attributes the utility of this technique to a "quick alternation" between high-intensity incompatible mental operations.

1958), in his voluminous works on the "synthesis of yoga," makes use of a dynamic similar to bhakti but within a framework as eclectic as Meher Baba's. Aurobindo's concept of his Integral Yoga subsumes and overreaches other systems, and is described in a wholly original system of imagery and vocabulary. His is an evolutionary view, seeing man as a transitional being: Integral Yoga aims at a conscious collaboration in the next stage of human evolution. The means is to blend the transforming power of HSC with life's activities, making life-as-lived a divine experience while working on altering one's physiology in order to enter the next evolutionary level. The real work—physiological self-alteration—can begin in earnest only with the attainment of sahaj samadhi.

*Aurobindo's evolutionary view: Integral Yoga*

*the real work—physiological self-alteration*

The process of spiritual unfolding is as varied as individual differences, and so Aurobindo (1958) prescribes no uniform, set practice: "The spiritual life is not a thing that can be formulated in a rigid definition or bound by a fixed mental rule; it is a vast field of evolution" with a thousand variations. Thus Integral Yoga can consist in whatever technique is found to work for one at a given point in sadhana. Perhaps the central criterion for this path is described by Aurobindo as "a will for purity, a readiness . . . to subject to a divine yoke the limiting and self affirming ego." Certainly another criterion is allegiance or devotion to Aurobindo himself and to his successor and collaborator, the Mother at Pondicherry, and to their goals. Among traditional paths commonly followed by practitioners of Aurobindo's Integral Yoga are bhakti, karma-yoga—i.e., striving to act in detached self-awareness while remembering the Mother—and sitting meditation. The usual combination is the practice of one-pointedness techniques and devotion to the Mother.

*central criterion for this path*

*usual practice—one-pointedness techniques and devotion to the Mother*

The fruits of meditation in MSC are, from Aurobindo's point of view, not the final goal but "a first stage of evolution." All samadhis, including the highest jhanas, are to be reintegrated with the activities of life. These jhana states belong to the realm of the "Overmind"—when, e.g., consciousness rises to the *sahasrara*, "and one emerges into the light" (i.e., in the sixth jhana, of infinite consciousness). This is but the starting point of Aurobindo's yoga. He says (1958), "It is in the waking state that this realization must come and endure." The fundamental process is at each higher level of consciousness to "bring down" its power and perception into "mortal life," making it a constant attribute of the waking state. This

*fundamental process*

"divine life in the body"—what Meher Baba would call sahaj samadhi—is the "Supermind."[6]

After each ascent of consciousness into the realms of the Overmind (i.e., the jhanas) comes a descent which unearths "all the layers of dirt . . . throwing up all the impurities." When this period of purification is over, one can sustain a "supramental consciousness." Aurobindo describes this emergent consciousness as beyond the conceptual universe, knowing everything in all aspects, seeing "the infinite in the finite." Living in an eternal now, one's actions are natural and spontaneous, "led by an inner consciousness which is in tune with the Infinite and the Eternal." In this egoless state one is beyond becoming or striving. One has further unleashed the psychic power known as *shakti* and can mobilize its energy as the key to the final stage of Integral Yoga: transformation of being at the cellular level. Esconced in the Supermind, one is potentially ready for the ultimate step in Aurobindo's dream, conscious collaboration in the next evolutionary stage of the human species. The strategy is to re-make one's body via a structural reorganization on the molecular level altering the function of the cells. Normal organic function is to be replaced by "a dynamic functioning" of *chakras* (psychic energy centers), entirely transmuting all physiological systems. Among the effects of this transformation would be cessation of the need for nutrients as sustenance and a vastly expanded lifespan. This phase is still in its experimental stage, and is being carried on by the Mother (Aurobindo passed on in 1950) as an "adventure into the unknown." If successful, this experiment, in the words of Satprem (1970), will "create a divine supermanhood on the earth which will no longer be subject to the laws of ignorance, suffering, and decomposition."

*final stages of integral yoga*

*ultimate step in Aurobindo's dream*

## PATANJALI'S ASTANGA YOGA

The goal of bhakti is *yoga,* or union; as such it is reckoned as one of many Indian yogic paths for transcending duality. The ultimate locus of the phenomenon of duality is within the mind, in the separation between the mechanisms of experience and the object of experience. The state in which a bridge is forged between the experiencer and the object in yoga is called *samadhi,* where consciousness "merges" with its contents, and is the same as jhana. The *Bhagavad Gita* places yogic techniques at the heart of Hinduism, recommending

[6]The Overmind pertains to an MSC experienced apart from waking activity; the Supermind represents the merging of MSC with the waking state.

yoga as the means for obtaining mystical union with Krishna, a personal God; the Lord Rama himself is instructed by his guru in the *Yoga-Vasishtha* (Shastri, 1969) to "remain rooted in the consciousness: 'I am infinite,'" and so unite with Brahman. In either case, the principle is that central to all yogas: the transcendence of normal dualistic consciousness in samadhi.

*principle central to all yogas*

The most authoritative source on yoga today remains Patanjali's *Yoga Aphorisms* (Prabhavananda and Isherwood, 1969; Vivekananda, 1970), dating back more than 1500 years, to about the same period as the *Visuddhimagga.* The spiritual *zeitgeist* of that era is reflected in both—indeed the paths they outline are in large part identical. The main difference between these two manuals for HSC is Patanjali's insistence that samadhi is the highway to liberation. The royal, or *raja,* yoga outlined by Patanjali entails *ashtanga*: eight key practices, or limbs. The first two, *yama* and *niyama,* are moral training for purity—i.e., sila. The next two are *asana,* the development through physical exercises of a firm and erect posture, or "seat," and *pranayam,* exercises for controlling and stilling the breath. Both the third and fourth limbs have become intricately developed in their own right, so that some yogic schools use these practices as their main methods—and most Americans associate "yoga" with these two exclusively *hatha* practices.[7] Most detailed expositions of *hatha* and *pranayam* point out that these practices are adjuncts to the attainment of samadhi, though some focus solely on rigorous physical purifications as means to HSC. Vyas Dev (1970), for example, details 250 *asana* postures, elaborates 50 different *pranayam* exercises and 25 methods for cleansing internal organs. Before sitting in samadhi for a long time, advises Vyas Dev, one should clear the bowels completely by drawing in and expelling water through the anus, empty the bladder by drawing water and expelling it through a catheter, and purify the digestive system by swallowing and extracting about 70 feet of string made of fine yarn, swallowing two or three pints of lukewarm salt-water to induce vomiting, and swallowing and extracting a three-inch wide strip of cloth seven yards long.

*the eight limbs of ashtanga yoga*

Patanjali's stipulation about these first four limbs, however, is that they be undergone simply to the point where body and mind are stilled as preliminaries for sitting in meditation, and the obstacles to concentration such as doubt, sloth, de-

**[7]Among the systems introduced to the West which emphasize these two limbs are Yogananda's Self-Realization Fellowship, Yogi Bhajan's "3-H" Organization, and Swami Sachidananda's Integral Yoga Institute.**

spair, and craving for sensual pleasures are overcome. The second group of limbs are all steps in becoming one-pointed. The fifth, *pratyahara,* entails withdrawing the mind from sense objects, so that attention can focus on the primary object. The sixth, *dharana,* is holding the mind on the object, while the seventh, *dhyana,* involves "an unbroken flow of thought toward the object of concentration"—these two repectively correspond to initial and sustained application in the *Visuddhimagga* system. The final limb is samadhi. The combination *dharana, dhyana,* and samadhi is the state of *samyama,* what the *Visuddhimagga* calls jhana.[8]

*samadhi as heart of yoga*

The aphorisms mention that practicing samyama on "single moments and their sequence" gives discriminative knowledge, or prajna, which "delivers from the bondage of ignorance." But this foray into the path of insight is overlooked in almost every modern system based on Patanjali. It is samadhi which is seen and taught as the heart of yoga; Vivekananda (1970) says, "samadhi is Yoga proper; that is the highest means." Patanjali names any number of objects for concentration: the syllable *Om* or other mantra, the heart, a deva or "illumined soul," a divine symbol, or any object. The meditator, in merging his consciousness with the primary object, will first achieve *savichara samadhi*—access concentration, where there is identity with the primary object "mixed with awareness of name, quality, and knowledge"—and then *nirvichara* samadhi—first jhana, where there is identity without other awareness. Once the *nirvichara* level is gained, the meditator is to wipe out even the thought of the primary object, and so attain *nirvikalpa* samadhi (as in the example of Sri Ramakrishna), where all sense of duality is obliterated. When *nirvikalpa* samadhi is mastered, so that one can at will pass in and out of it repeatedly, one's consciousness differs decisively from before. Having "realized the Atman," one knows the conceptual universe to be an illusion and comes to regard all normal experience as painful. The final stage is enlightenment, "eternal existence in union with the Atman"—sahaj samadhi. Even in the waking state one now resides in samadhi, no longer identifying with the normal mind or its sense-perceptions. Being is grounded in a consciousness transcending the sensory world, and so remains detached

[8]Samyama mastery brings with it a long list of supernormal powers—virtually the same enumeration as in the *Visuddhimagga.* The procedure for using them is also the same. By "making samyama" on an appropriate object, a variety of supernormal feats become possible—e.g., samyama on the distinguishing marks of another man's body gives one knowledge of the true nature of his thoughts and moods. The list includes knowledge of the past and future and of previous lives, supernormal hearing and sight, and so on. Powers, observes Patanjali, appeal to the ego, and so are "the last temptation." One must give them up before full liberation; Sri Ramakrishna calls powers "heaps of rubbish."

from that world while operating in it. This "ideal of Yoga, the state of *jivan-mukti,*" writes Eliade (1970), is life in an "eternal present" where one "no longer possesses a personal consciousness—that is, a consciousness nourished on his own history—but a witness consciousness which is pure lucidity and spontaneity."

*a witness consciousness*

RAMANA MAHARSHI

The process of attainment via samadhi of the jhanas up to the sixth, awareness of infinite consciousness, is the basic practical teaching of Sri Sankaracharya's classical Advaitist school of Vedanta (Vimuktananda, 1966). The goal is union of mind with Brahma, infinite consciousness; the fifteen steps elucidated for "becoming Brahma" approximate those recommended in Patanjali and the *Visuddhimagga* for the jhana path. The preliminary steps are of renunciation and restraint of the senses; the sila formulation is in terms of *yama*: nonkilling, truthfulness, nonstealing, continence, and nonreceiving of gifts. The complementary practice of *niyama* is the development of one-pointedness in absorption on Brahma, i.e., "pure consciousness, where seer, sight, and seen cease." In this state there is "complete forgetfulness of all thought by first making it changeless and then identifying it with Brahman." In his succinct instructions, Shankaracharya thus telescopes the entire progression from initial concentration to what may be the sixth jhana. He echoes Buddha in warning against attachment to gross feelings of pleasure arising from lower attainments in the material jhanas, which could serve as an obstacle to achieving the formless states. He also warns against the same "mental hindrances" to concentration, such as idleness, desire for sense-pleasure, distractedness, and the "tasting of joy" resulting from the jhanas. Shankaracharya, like Buddha, is careful to emphasize the need for jhana mastery (1966, p. 66): "The aspirant should carefully practice this meditation . . . until, being under his full control, it arises spontaneously, in an instant when called into action."

*"becoming Brahma"*

Sri Ramakrishna is one contemporary being who realized these teachings; *The Gospel of Sri Ramakrishna,* recording his day-to-day life as witnessed by the anonymous author M., is an extraordinary document of life lived in sahaj samadhi. His disciple Vivekananda carried the theme of Advait Self-realization to the West, and the organization he founded carries on that tradition. Another who attained full sahaj samadhi was Ramana Maharshi. He himself reached that state spontaneously at 17 when suddenly one day he experi-

*the path of "Self-inquiry"*

enced a "death" from which he emerged a realized being (Osborne, 1964). His basic teaching is that of Advait: the goal is "the plenary experience of the non-dual self," or Brahman. The direct path he taught is "Self-inquiry," one-pointed attention to the inquiry "Who am I?" tracing the thought "I" back to its subtlest beginnings. Constant concentration on the source of the "I-thought" brings a state where the "I"-thought ceases, a wordless, illuminated "I-I" remaining. This pure consciousness, says Ramana Maharshi, "is unlimited and one, the limited and the many thoughts having disappeared"; the *Visuddhimagga* system would see it as the first jhana. Sri Ramani defines samadhi as a subtle state in which even the thought "I-I" disappears—i.e., the second jhana and above. By the continual practice of samadhi it becomes a permanent state, suffusing all other states of consciousness. This is the level of the *jivan-mukta,* the liberated man. Ramana Maharshi (1962) proposes a simple operational definition for distinguishing between one still on the path at the level of *nirvikalpa* and one liberated in sahaj samadhi: if there remains a difference between samadhi and the waking state, there is still work to do; if no difference, the goal of sahaj samadhi has been reached.

*Maharshi's operational definition for liberation*

*subsidiary practices*

All paths, according to Ramana Maharshi, end in the process of Self-inquiry. But not all aspirants are immediately ready for the intense one-pointedness required. For these others Sri Ramana recommends subsidiary practices such as japa and the breathing exercise of *pranayam,* or whatever else might aid in stilling the mind. An alternative path to Self-inquiry suitable to some is *Guru-kripa,* surrender to a Master whose grace descends on the devotee. If one's surrender is complete, all sense of self is lost. Coupled with association with the pure being of the guru, the devotee's mind thus becomes "purified" or stilled so that he is able to turn inward in meditation and find the Self. This is the guru's "grace," which is in fact immanent in the devotee as a potentiality of his own being. There is, says Ramana Maharshi, no difference between God, Guru, and Self: the external guru helps the devotee find the internal Self. Samadhi, says Sri Ramana, is your true nature; for one who dwells in it, there is no ego and there are no "others." The *jivan-mukta* has transcended body-consciousness and the conceptual universe; he does not see the world as different from himself. The state of the Realized One is described in Shankaracharya's *Vivekachudamain* (R. Maharshi, 1962, p. 92):

> He who, even when his mind is merged in Brahman, is nevertheless awake, but is at the same time free from the character-

istics of the waking state, and whose realization is free from all desire, should be considered a *jivan-mukta.*

MAHARISHI MAHESH YOGI

The teachings of Shankaracharya are a variant of the classic statement found in Patanjali's *Yoga Sutras.* Both advocate enlightenment through the path of jhana; Patanjali more fully discusses a wide range of subsidiary practices of purification. Maharishi Mahesh Yogi's widely known system of "transcendental meditation" traces its roots back to these two sources, but is a re-formulation of both in Western terms. Maharishi denies the necessity of imposing on oneself an attitude or acts of renunciation. He sees purification as an effect of MSC, but not as a cause. According to Maharishi (1971), "proficiency in the virtues can only be gained by repeated experiences of samadhi."

*"Transcendental Meditation"*

In other respects, Maharishi's technique is in the mainstream of the jhana path. Like all yogis, Maharishi sees that "duality is the fundamental cause of suffering." His technique for transcending suffering entails three major steps. The first is silent repetition of a mantra—a Sanskrit word or sound—to develop one-pointedness. Though in teaching there is emphasis in avoiding effortful concentration, the student is told to bring the mind as it wanders back to the mantra, and in effect the process is one of becoming one-pointed. The following oft-quoted description by Maharishi of the nature of the technique can be seen as a description of the focal narrowing of attention on a meditation subject and subsequent transcendence of the subject in ascending through access concentration to the second jhana (1969, p. 470):

*three major steps*

> . . . turning the attention inward towards the subtler levels of a thought until the mind transcends the experience of the subtlest state of the thought and arrives at the source of thought . . .

Maharishi describes the consequent process of progressive stillness of mind in terms of the bliss that arises. The goal of mantra is what he calls "transcendental consciousness": when mind "arrives at the direct experience of bliss, it loses all contact with the outside and is contented in the state of transcendental bliss-consciousness." That is, one achieves access-concentration or jhana. The second phase is the infusion of jhana, or "transcendental consciousness" into the waking and sleep states by alternating them with periods of meditation. In intensive courses, hatha yoga asanas alternate with sitting in meditation. The state thereby achieved is *nirvikalpa* samadhi, or "cosmic consciousness," where "no activity, however rigorous, can take one out of Being." As the meditator progresses, he is given instruction in techniques more advanced than simple use of mantra, and the periods of practice are extended; the specifics of advanced techniques are not given in published sources, but revealed to the individual only at his initiation.

While most bhakti paths end in samadhi, Maharishi's program is unique in approaching devotion through the back door, via jhana mastery. The third major step utilizes the bliss borne of samadhi, focusing it as devotion toward an external object. This step can take the form of initiating others into the technique: prior to the transmission of mantra, the initiator does *puja,* making offerings of gratitude to Maharishi's lineage of gurus, "the cherished names of the great masters of the holy tradition." Cosmic consciousness is thus transformed through devotion into "God-consciousness," where all things perceived are experienced as sacred; "everything is naturally experienced in the awareness of God." One now dwells in perfect harmony with nature and the Divine; "God-consciousness" is the resultant state. Arriving at God-consciousness, according to Maharishi, entails a physiological transformation whereby the metabolic changes characteristic of jhana permeate the waking and sleep states and one is aware of God in all aspects of creation. Beyond God-consciousness one may evolve into a state called "Unity," where consciousness is so refined that all things are perceived free of any conceptual illusion. From the viewpoint of other yoga systems, Maharishi's path ends with sahaj samadhi.

### SWAMI MUKTANANDA

*Tantric tradition and Kundalini Yoga*

A number of systems recently introduced to the West trace their roots back to the same sources as Maharishi's but emphasize still another tradition: *Kundalini Yoga,* an essentially Tantric teaching. The Tantric tradition indigenous to India is apparently a refinement of Shamanistic practices that has found its way into both Hindu and Buddhist meditation systems; its means to liberation are MSC and the arousal of energies that give rise to supernormal powers, or *siddhis* (Douglas, 1971; Eliade, 1970). Kundalini, according to Tantric physiology, is a huge reserve of spiritual energy located at the base of the spine, in the *Muladhar*. When aroused, the kundalini is said to travel up the spine through six centers, or chakras, reaching the seventh at the top of the head. As it reaches the higher centers, kundalini is said to produce experiences of MSC[9] (Sivananda, 1971).

*Swami Muktananda's siddha-yoga*

A variant of kundalini yoga is *siddha-yoga* as practiced by followers of Swami Muktananda. Swami Muktananda's system may begin with traditional practices: asana, pranayam, bhakti chanting, and japa, or meditation with mantra—e.g., "Guru Om," or with each breath "so-ham." But he emphahizes the guru-disciple relationship; the core of his teaching is the tradition of *siddha-yoga,* in which the guru is said to grant a direct, instantaneous transcendental experience to the devotee. This process, called *shaktipat diksha,* is an initiation by look, touch, or word whereby the devotee who approaches the guru with love, devotion, and faith has his *shakti*—the energy of kundalini—aroused. When this happens, all other intentional practices fall away; the action of kundalini within produces spontaneous meditation, pranayam, asanas, and mudras, without the devotee's prior training or volition. This process of purification is said to take 3 to 12 years, by which time the entire personality of the devotee is transformed, the "limited I" having been abandoned, and realization attained of "oneness with all-pervading Cosmic Intellect" (Amma, 1969; Muktananda, 1969, 1970). The imagery and terminology with which Muktananda describes this process is that of kundalini (1970, p. 54):

*initiation by the guru*

> . . . . the Kundalini, which stays in the *Muladhara,* gradually travels upwards piercing the *chakras* on her way until she reaches *Sahasrara,* the thousand-petalled lotus in the crown of the head . . . and the spiritual endeavor of an aspirant gets fulfilled.

While undergoing *shaktipat,* one experiences a wide variety of involuntary reactions: powerful moods of joy, dullness, or agitation; strange bodily postures, gestures, tremors or dancing poses; feelings of wonder or fright; a period of pain in all parts of the body; various internal stirrings, muscle throbbing, or thrills; spontaneous deep meditation; visions of lights, deities, or celestial places accompanied by a great joy and bliss; and, finally, there is a "divine light of indescribable

[9]Lama Govinda (1969) has related the chakras to specific physiological loci; Green and Green (1971)—themselves psychophysiologists—describe them in terms of an "occult physics," as "etheric organs." The physiology of kundalini seems to have few specific correlates with Western anatomical science; Ramana Maharshi (Mahadevan, 1965) says these "mystic centres" are "but products of imagination," meant for "beginners in Yoga." Their status in the West thus far seems to be on a par with, say, Freud's constructs of ego, superego, libido, and cathexes—useful conceptual tools without specific anatomical referents—though future research may verify their existence. Many organizations in the West have an orientation to kundalini yoga—e.g., Swami Sivananda's Divine Life Society and its offshoots.

lustre" or a subtle inner sound always in meditation (Muktananda, 1970). These phenomena serve to purify the meditator, so that he can more or less sustain *turiya*—jhana-consciousness—while in the three ordinary states of waking, dreaming, and sleeping. *Turiyatita* is reached when the kundalini has stabilized in the *sahasrara;* one in this state has forgotten body-consciousness, enjoys extraordinary bliss and profound tranquility, and has attained "the fruit of Yoga," remaining "ever absorbed in the Supreme State," whatever he does.

*Supreme State*

*a first-person account*

Muktananda's autobiographical *Guru* is a remarkable first-person account of the whole process. His own guru, Sri Nityananda, raised Muktananda's kundalini via *shaktipat,* "a secretly concealed means of initiation used by the great sages," and transmitted to him the power to give this *diksha* to others. Though previously he had done pranayam and mantra meditation, he finally meditated only on his guru. The process ended for Muktananda with the vision in meditation of a small blue light, which he calls "the Blue Pearl." This tiny spot suddenly extended until it was an "infinite light," filling the universe with blue rays (similar to the *Visuddhimagga* description of attaining the fifth jhana via kasina), then subsided again to a dot. After this vision, "Muktananda was bereft of consciousness and memory. The distinction 'inner' and 'outer' evaporated. He was no longer aware of his own self . . ." (p. 178). On emerging from meditation, he found that the Blue Pearl stayed in his field of vision, eyes opened or closed, in his "inner eye." To this day he always sees it; when he looks at an object, he first sees the dot of blue, then the object. Though Muktananda meditates still, he feels there is nothing more to see—the Blue Pearl signifies the merging of kundalini in *sahasrara,* marking union of self with Self in *turyatita.* From then on, says Muktananda, "I attained perfect peace and equanimity." A disciple of Muktananda, Amma (1969, p. 11), says of one in this state:

> He has nothing to do and nothing to achieve; still he does the activities of worldly life remaining a witness to them all.

#### KIRPAL SINGH

*the Path of Sound Current*

Kirpal Singh (1971) in his presentation of *Shabd* Yoga, the Path of Sound Current, does not dwell on the role of chakras, but like Swami Muktananda's *Siddha*-Yoga emphasizes the role of the guru in guidance, and offers a means for reaching from this world of form to the realm of the Formless. To do so via this system, three conditions must be fulfilled: one needs a true Master, must practice self-discipline, and must pursue the method of *Shabd,* meditation on transcendental inner sounds. A true Master, or *Satguru,* under guidance from his own teacher has himself traversed this inner path to its goal; his state of mind is free of ego and attachment, his acts virtuous and creative. He is the living embodiment of the unity of experience at the foundation of all religious creeds, says Kirpal Singh, and has the compassion of Buddha and the love of Christ. Such a *Satguru* is pivotal to success at every step in Shabd Yoga: through his initiation the disciple will experience inner light and sound, and with his guidance will finally transcend body-consciousness (in jhana) to find the "inner guru" whose "Radiant Form will appear unsought to guide him onward." Through loving and obeying the true Master, as Kirpal Singh describes the process, the "little self is forgotten," and the Master's grace descends (or emerges from within), rewarding the disciple's efforts by facilitating the requisite condition for finding the inner guru: one-pointed concentration.

*daily record*

A key adjunct in developing one-pointedness is self-discipline in the form of a simple and pure life. Kirpal Singh does not advocate an ascetic renunciation of the world and one's place in it, nor the repression of desires, but rather urges the cultivation of internal detachment and moderation. As an aid to his pupils, he has them each keep a daily log of any "lapses in thought, word, and deed" as well as a record of time spent and experiences in meditation. These records of the inner life are sent to him by his students all over the world in a monthly progress report as an aid in achieving conscientiousness and its fruit in self-discipline. Kirpal Singh sees an interaction effect between self-discipline in life and concentration in meditation: "Some discipline is necessary, but . . . it must ultimately be inspired by inner spiritual experience." The integration accruing from the meditator's self-discipline "enables him to gain greater concentration, and so higher inner experience, and this inner experience must in turn have repercussions on outer thoughts and action."

*development of concentration*

The method wherein concentration is developed begins with an initiation by the Master where the disciple, it is said, is given a first-hand experience of at least a rudimentary level of a transcendental reality. As Kirpal Singh describes the initiation, the teacher instructs his student to close his eyes and focus attention on a point between and behind the eyebrows—"the seat of the soul"—and receives a mantra "charged with the inner power of the guru" which is to be "repeated slowly and lovingly with the tongue of thought." By this means the disciple's scattered thoughts are gradually collected at a single point. As he approaches the level of access concentration, he will begin to see "shifting points of light," which cease flickering as concentration increases and which consolidate into a "single radiating point." As the light becomes a point, "inner hearing" begins, marking entry into "another world, a different realm of experience," where physical consciousness is transcended in jhana, and the inner guru emerges. Through this "divine guide" one acquires the detachment required for attaining higher levels of jhana. Just as the *Visuddhimagga* advises, from the inner guru "the soul learns to overcome the first shock of joy and realizes that its goal lies still far ahead." Exactly how far this is in terms of jhanas can't be known from printed sources, save that at last there is "naught but the Great Ocean of Consciousness, of Love, of Bliss Ineffable." The effect of this achievement as it permeates the rest of one's life, says Kirpal Singh, will make the disciple himself a true Master.

*emergence of inner guru*

### TANTRA AND TIBETAN VAJRAYANA

*tantra yoga and supernormal psychic powers*

Neither Swami Muktananda nor Kirpal Singh make much of the supernormal powers which are said by Tantrics to accrue from mastering the jhanas. Tantra yoga is unique among systems for changing consciousness in seeing the attainment of *siddhis,* or supernormal psychic powers, as marking the end of the path: "For all sadhana ceases when it has borne its fruit in siddhi" (Woodruffe, 1965, p. 14). It may be due to the high states that the possession of powers betokens that they are taken by some as symptomatic of the goal in Tantra. Certain Tantric sadhanas are devised to produce specific siddhis; the perfected Tantric master is called a *siddha,* one who has mastered powers. Meditation is the central characteristic of all Tantric practices, samadhi the means and ends, no matter the specifics of formulation.

*the essence of tantric practice*

The essence of Tantric practice is the use of the senses to transcend sense-consciousness in jhana. Though the senses are, of course, the modality of all techniques for one-pointedness, Tantrism is unique in the diversity of techniques it offers for transcending sense-consciousness: among them are the use of mantra; *yantra,* or objects for visualization exercises such as kasina and mandala; concentration on *shabd,* the super-subtle inner sounds; *pranayam* and *asanas*; concentration on the play of forces in the chakras; and *maithuna,* the arousal of shakti—kundalini energy—through controlled, ritual sexual intercourse. The key to *maithuna,* as well as the goal of all these practices, is the detachment borne of samadhi, which converts the energy of desires into higher forms. Tantric texts frequently repeat (Eliade, 1970, p. 263), "By the same acts that cause some men to burn in hell for thousands of years, the Yogin gains his eternal salvation." Practitioners of Tantric sadhana sometimes deviate from cultural proprieties—e.g., violating the Hindu tradition by taking wine and meat, meditating in ritually unclean places such as charnel grounds—especially in the Bon Marg, or "left-handed" path. Actions which from outside may seem cultural improprieties have within Tantra a special, deeper meaning, as can be seen in this description from the catalog of the Tibet House Museum in New Delhi of a *kapala,* a cup made of human skull mounted on a silver stand:

> The vessel holds the Amrit used for performing esoteric rituals. Those who have such dualistic concepts as the clean and the unclean cannot think of using a human skull. But the Tantrics, who have gained Transcendental Wisdom, have no superstitution and to them golden cups and human skulls are the same. The skulls are used to symbolize this attitude of mind.

The language of Tantra is veiled, and typically is open to many levels of interpretation.

*preliminary training for one-pointedness*

Tantric sadhanas are often intricately complex, consisting of series and combinations of many interwoven elements—e.g., gazing at a yantra, reciting mantra, and visualizing a deity or set of symbols, all in a set sequence.[10] Many of the more complicated Tantric practices are not themselves transcendental in nature, but are a preliminary training in one-pointedness and preparation for jhana. An example of one such is the following Tibetan practice of Arising Yoga, which its

[10]One such current technique is that taught by the Mahatmas of the Divine Light Mission, devotees of the teen-age Guru Maharaj Hans-ji. This teaching comes from a line of gurus including Kirpal Singh's own Master, and resembles Shabd in some ways. The first initiation entails a fourfold practice wherein the initiate visualizes a "divine light," experiences a "divine taste," hears a "divine sound"; and visualizes the guru, all accompanied by appropriate mudras. Another new proponent of Tantric spiritual practice in the West is the group called Ananda Marg, path of bliss. Ananda Marg offers the student a similarly complex array of advanced practices, including meditation on the chakras accompanied by appropriate visualizations of colors and slokas in Sanskrit describing chakra function, projecting consciousness outward from chakra points, pranayam, and mantra for use throughout the day's activities. As with most tantric schools, the specifics of practice in these two are secret, as are details of more advanced techniques.

translator, Garma Chang (1963, p. 122), explains is done with conscious effort through the "mundane mind"; he enumerates as its main features and steps:

(1) Visualizing all objects and the self-body as dissolving into the great Void.
(2) Visualizing in the Void a bija seed (i.e., mantra) transforming itself into an image of the Self-Patron Buddha.
(3) Visualizing the Self-Patron Buddha Body in its entirety, including the Three Main Channels and the Four Chakras.
(4) Visualizing the Mandala and identifying all manifestations with Buddhahood.
(5) Reciting the Mantra of the Patron Buddha and applying a specific visualization for a special yogic purpose.
(6) Visualizing all objects, including the Self-Patron Buddha Body, as dissolving into the bija in the Heart.
(7) From the Void again projecting the Self-Patron Buddha and the Mandala.

*assessment of spiritual paths difficult without participation in practices*

It is difficult to assess the true nature of any spiritual path without participating oneself in its practices. This methodological principle is especially apparent with respect to Tantric systems like Tibetan Vajrayana, where the heart of instruction is wholly esoteric. Vajrayana, the Tantric segment of Tibetan Buddhism, is veiled in secrecy; the great legendary Tantric Milarepa warns (Chang, 1970), "The teachings of Tantra should be practiced secretly; they will be lost if demonstrated in the marketplace." Though translations like Evan-Wentz' (1968, 1969) give a vivid taste of these Tibetan teachings, if one is to follow the intricacies of this path it is essential to find a teaching lama as guru, for even now the practical methods are transmitted only from teacher to student.[11]

*teaching lama essential*

*outline of Vajrayana theory in practice*

Though the techniques of Vajrayana are founded on the *Visuddhimagga* tradition, it also blends purely Tibetan elements with Indian Tantrism. In an outline of Vajrayana theory and practice by the Dalai Lama (1965), the theory of Vajrayana is seemingly identical with the *Visuddhimagga*—or as Mahayanists call it, the *Hinayana* tradition, or "Lesser Vehicle." The critical difference between the traditions is the Mahayanist "Bodhisattva Vow": to gain enlightenment not just for oneself, but for the sake of the salvation of all sentient beings. This difference in motive is seen by the Dalai

[11]Among the lamas actively teaching in the West are Tarthang Tulku in Berkeley, and Chogyam Trungpa in Colorado and Vermont. Chogyam Trungpa (1971) reiterates the need on this path for a guru or "competent guide," since "the tendency towards self-deception becomes increasingly dangerous as one progresses on the path."

Lama as decisive, producing a subsequent qualitative difference in both path and goal. The Hinayana nirvana is seen as a prior stage to the Mahayana goal of Bodhisattva. Still, the conception of the nirvanic state is the same: it is "liberation from this bondage" of *samsara* by "cessation," where the "roots of delusion are thoroughly extracted," the ego or I-thought severed.

*approximation of Vajrayana path and Visuddhimagga teaching*

The Vajrayana path as the Dalai Lama describes it is a near-perfect approximation of the *Visuddhimagga* teaching. There are three "Moral Precepts," vehicles for the realization of the "Triple Refuge"—Buddha, Dharma, and Sangha—as internal realities. The first precept is sila; the second is samadhi (Tibetan: *shiney*), fixing the mind on one object so it develops one-pointedness. The recommendations for optimal conditions to practice samadhi are as in the *Visuddhimagga*: seclusion, severing ties to worldly activities, and so on. The meditation objects resemble those of Indian Tantra, mainly figures of deities, Buddhas, and Bodhisattvas, and are portrayed in multiple aspects "so that they suit the physical, mental, and sensuous attitudes of different individuals," and arouse strong faith and devotion. The lama who is instructing will select a *yidam,* or deity, for meditation, appropriate to the student's needs. The Dalai Lama enumerates four steps in the stages of samadhi. There is an initial fixing of the mind on the primary object, then the attempt to prolong the sustained period of concentration on it. In the next stage, concentration is intermittent, diversions alternating in the mind with attention to the primary object; the experience of joy and ecstasy from one-pointedness strengthens efforts at concentration. This stage—jhana access—culminates when the mind finally overcomes disturbances, enabling concentration on the object without any interruption whatsoever—the full one-pointedness of the first jhana and above. The final stage is that of "mental quiescence," where concentration is possible with the minimum of conscious effort—i.e., jhana mastery. One can now concentrate on any object with effortless ease; psychic powers have become possible.

*"Sunyata", essential emptiness of phenomenal world, including oneself*

The significance of jhana mastery in Vajrayana, however, is not in the powers made possible, but in its potential use to realize *Sunyata,* the essential emptiness of the phenomenal world, including oneself—what the *Visuddhimagga* calls *anatta.* The means for this is the third precept, the practice of vipassana (Tibetan: *thagthong*), using the power of samadhi as a stepping stone for meditation on the "meaning of Sunyata." Though the Dalai Lama (1965) does not detail the nature of vipassana technique in Vajrayana, he mentions that the flow of the undisciplined mind can be stopped, "and the wandering or projecting mind brought to rest, by concentration on the physical make-up of one's body and the psychological make-up of one's mind"—two techniques of vipassana taught in the *Visuddhimagga*. By means of vipassana with Sunyata as focus one discards ego-beliefs, finally reaching "the goal that leads to the destruction of all moral and mental defilements."

*consequential differences between Mahayana and Hinayana*

At this final stage of the Vajrayana path, the differences in motive between Mahayana and Hinayana become consequential. If one undertook the process solely to realize the Triple Gem within and liberate himself, he will be what the *Visuddhimagga* calls an "arahant." If motivated by the "Bodhi-chitta of love and compassion," one will gain the "superior release" of the Bodhisattva, where one's state of consciousness makes him a perfect vehicle of compassion, leading others toward liberation. In either case, says the Dalai Lama, a Bodhisattva has "cleansed his mind of all impurities and has removed the motives and inclinations that lead to them," and severed ties to the conceptual world of name-and-form, the locus of normal consciousness.

*Mahamudra*

The penultimate in some Vajrayana teaching lines is *Mahamudra,* first expounded in the eleventh century by the guru Tilopa to his disciple Naropa with the fundamental instruction "Look into the mirror of your mind."[12] Chang's (1963) translation of Tilopa's "Song of Mahamudra" has these summatory lines:

> If with the mind one observes the mind
> One destroys distinctions and reaches Buddahood.
> The clouds that wander through the sky have no roots, no home;
> Nor do the distinctive thoughts floating through the mind.
> Once the self-mind is seen, discrimination stops.

The means, in theory, to the Mahamudra state is strikingly similar to the *Visuddhimagga* practice of vipassana (though the specifics of practice are given only in oral transmission). Guenther (1963) describes it as a "relaxation of the tensional pattern of the senses" which breaks up the perceptual-cognitive chain by "arriving at pure sensation"; Tilopa says, "Mahamudra is like a mind that clings to nought." Sense-

[12]There are numerous schools within Tibetan Buddhism, each with its own special emphasis and training; Chogyam Trungpa, for example, belongs to a line whose highest teaching is "*Maha Ati,*" the "Zen of Vajrayana," said to be a stage beyond Mahamudra.

perceptions are attended to with detachment, by the power of which whatever one has met with as appearance is understood to be "co-emergent awareness," i.e., mind taking an object. At this precognitive level one recognizes that "all the entities of the outer objective world are based in mind." All external objects are thus reduced in the perceptual situation to pure sensation or raw experience. One sees that all samsara is only mind-process, devoid of any self. This realization results in "securing an inner immunity which cannot be assailed by doubts, hopes, and fears."

*practices for the development of Mahamudra*

In his translation of the Mahamudra text "The Yoga of the Great Symbol" Evans-Wentz (1968) enumerates numerous practices for the development of Mahamudra, most representative of Tantra, and some clearly along the lines of the *Visuddhimagga.*[13] The Evans-Wentz version starts from the initial development of one-pointedness, "the path leading to Mahamudra." A second method is "concentration without using an object"—i.e., contemplation of the process of mind. Throughout, the text intermingles techniques for one-pointedness and vipassana-like practices. The latter include detachedly watching the "interminable flow of thoughts" until one perceives "the arising and cessation of thoughts," and letting thoughts go as they will so that "when cognitions arise . . . consciousness of them is concomitant with their arising." Such practices lead to a state where there is neither inhibition of nor reaction to thoughts, and an equanimious spontaneous cognition of thoughts arising and vanishing. These are all prior steps in what Evans-Wentz' Tilopa (1968, p. 139) describes as:

> This art of attaining Liberation by merely recognizing the thoughts, whereby one acquireth understanding of the inseparable nature of the abandoner (i.e., the mind) and of the thing to be abandoned (i.e., the thought).

*end state as non-effortful task rather than achievement*

"Abandoning the mind" has the same significance in Vajrayana as in vipassana: the realization of non-self and subsequent ego-loss. This end state of Mahamudra, says Guenther (1963), is "an ever-lasting task rather than an achievement"; it has to be "attended to by meditation and

[13]Evans-Wentz notes that this teaching was extant in India before Tilopa. The text of the teaching itself cites the *Abhidhamma,* the Therevadan collection containing the *Visuddhimagga,* as well as a wide variety of yogic sources. It may be that the core of Mahamudra is the body of techniques detailed in the *Visuddhimagga* with a Tantric admixture. The Tibetan tradition uses Therevadan sources such as the *Visuddhimagga* as a basic teaching, acknowledging their validity and utility and then amplifying upon them. In reckoning the ten *bhumis* (or stations) of the Bodhisattva Path, for example, Chogyam Trungpa says the seventh bhumi is equivalent to the *Visuddhimagga* arahant stage—there being three bhumis beyond (personal communication).

practiced." Still, this "task" cannot be said to be effortful—it is simply the ongoing process of mind in what Lama Govinda (1969) calls "the ultimate state of integration." The Ven. Lama Kong Ka, in transmitting the teaching of Mahamudra, directs one who would become a Bodhisattva through perfect Mahamudra-awareness to "stop discriminating, abandon habitual thoughts of 'accept this' and 'reject that,'" and strive to reach a state where meditation and activities become one. This meditation of the Bodhisattva, according to Chogyam Trungpa (1971), is mindfulness, albeit of an effortless and spontaneous sort: "He is awake to the situations as they are. . . . He doesn't watch himself acting or meditating, so his action is meditation and his meditation becomes action."

## Zen

Zen, like Tibetan Vajrayana, perhaps differs more on the level of theological rationale than in actual practice from the *Visuddhimagga* techniques of which it is ultimately derivative. "Zen" is, in fact, a cognate of "jhana," and both are derived from the Sanskrit "dhyana," meditation. The process of cultural diffusion culminating in Japanese Zen is historically linked to the *Visuddhimagga* tradition through the Ch'an school of China. The transitions undergone in the voyage through time and space from India of the fifth century to Japan of the present day are most evident in terms of doctrine; doctrinal differences have tended to emphasize these changes and to obscure similarities. The basic practice, zazen, remains essentially identical to vipassana, though with the addition of subsidiary trappings such as sutra chanting and manual labor. Among the changes, the focus in zazen has broadened from sitting meditation to a range of stimuli and life-situations which act as multiple motivators to overcome the ennui relentless sitting alone might bring, especially for beginners.

*basic practice: zazen*

The practice of zazen begins, as with vipassana, with a firm grounding in concentration. The accent in most Ch'an and Zen schools is on a variety of concentration techniques: the insight of prajna is seen to flow from samadhi. Of the "awakenings" in Zen, many are stages of jhana; Luk (1971) elaborates the Ch'an master Han Shan's autobiography, showing that the bulk of his major awakenings encompassed the jhanas into the formless level. To realize an "absolute nirvana," however, Luk (1966) advises that concentration and insight must be equally developed. The essential interrelatedness of the two is set forth by the Sixth Patriarch, Hui Neng, a link in the chain of transmission which the Mahayana tradition traces directly back to Gautama Buddha (Luk, 1962, p. 44):

> Dhyana and wisdom are one and not two separate things. Dhyana is the substance of wisdom and wisdom is the function of dhyana . . . They are like a lamp and its light.

Throughout its history there has been a tension within Zen and affiliated schools of Buddhism centering around maintaining a functional equilibrium between the two poles of dhyana and wisdom—i.e., concentration and insight. In the fifteenth century, for example, the Pure Land sect practice of *Nembutsu*—repetition of the name of Buddha—made inroads into Zen circles. The Zen master Huan-chi responded by warning his disciples that though there was no dispute between the two pathways, one should choose one or the other exclusively, for neither will be attained if both are attempted. Suzuki (1958, p. 168) notes that the goal of Nembutsu, "rebirth in the Pure Land," is a symbolic reference to the state of samadhi reached by its intensive practice: "The devotee is persuaded to practice the Nembutsu in order to see the Buddhas, but when he actually enters into a samadhi he sees them in quite a different form from what he might have expected." The "rebirth" is a spiritual regeneration, one and the same psychological fact as the achievement of jhana. But this is not the goal of Zen. Jhana—in Zen terminology, the "great fixation" or "a state of oneness"—is an intermediate stage in progress toward final realization. Suzuki warns (1958, p. 135):

> When this state of great fixation is held as final, there will be no upturning, no outburst of satori, no penetration, no insight into Reality, no severing the bonds of birth and death.

*koan as unique variant of devices for achieving samadhi*

Among the techniques used in Zen are some unique variants of devices for achieving samadhi. One such, the koan (used primarily by the Rinzai sect), is a puzzle utterly impervious to solution by logic or reason—its "solution" lies in transcending thought, its purpose is to liberate the mind from the snare of language (Miura and Sasaki, 1965). Assigned a koan such as "What was your face before you were born?" or "What is Mu?" the aspirant keeps the koan in mind constantly, no matter what he is doing—when other matters intrude on the mind, he immediately returns to it. As the mind discovers its inadequacy to solve the insoluble, a feverish pitch of concentration is generated accompanied by a supreme frustration, and what once was a fully stated koan reduces to an emblematic fragment—e.g., simply "Mu." When the discursive faculty finally exhausts itself, the moment of "realization" comes: thought ceases in the state of *daigi* or "fixation," and the koan "yields up all its secrets" in the attainment of jhana (Suzuki, 1958).

*fruits of joriki and "seeing into your true nature"*

Yasutani (Kapleau, 1967), a contemporary roshi, utilizes the koan for his more advanced students, while for beginners he assigns concentration on breathing. He sees the aim of zazen not as rendering the mind inactive in jhana, but "quieting and unifying it in the midst of activity." Consequently, his students work with concentration techniques until a modicum of *joriki*—strength arising from a mind unified and one-pointed—develops. The fruits of *joriki* are equanimity, determination, and a potential ripeness for *Kensho-godo,* the satori-awakening of "seeing into your True-nature." Working with a koan, for instance, the student finds that the point of samadhi-fruition comes when there is "absolute unity with Mu, unthinking absorption in Mu—this is ripeness." At this point, "inside and outside merge into a single unity." With this samadhi experience, *Kensho-godo* can take place, where one will "see each thing just as it is." This satori-awakening is seen in Zen as a waking state aftereffect of samadhi; Yasutani-roshi notes that satori usually follows a period of samadhi practice. In an autobiographical essay on his own training, D. T. Suzuki tells of his first attainment of samadhi, on the koan Mu (1969):

> But this samadhi is not enough. You must come out of that state, be awakened from it and that awakening is prajna. That moment of coming out of samadhi and seeing it for what it is—that is satori.

*"just sitting" and "bare attention"*

A given *kensho* experience may fall anywhere within a wide range of depth, degree, and clarity. *Joriki* strengthens satori; the *joriki* developed in zazen cultivates the satori-effect until finally it becomes an "omnipresent reality shaping our daily lives." When the student has gained some degree of control over his mind via one-pointedness exercises like counting breath, or "exhausted the discursive intellect" with koan, Yasutani-roshi frequently sets him to *shikan-taza,* where one marshalls a heightened state of concentrated awareness in "just sitting," with no primary object. One sits alert and mindful, free of points of view or discriminating thoughts, merely watching; the technique is markedly similar to vipassana. A connected practice is "mobile zazen," where one enters fully into every action with total attention and clear awareness—it is "bare attention" as taught by the *Visuddhimagga.* The close parallel between zazen and vipassana is striking; Kapleau (1967), in fact, cites a key sutra from the *Visuddhimagga* on mindfulness as a "prescription" for this zazen:

> In what is seen there must be just the seen;
> In what is sensed there must be just the sensed;
> In what is thought there must be just the thought.

The awakening which samadhi brings is a prior step in Zen to the final satori, the "whole of Zen." The technical Mahayana term for satori is *paravritti,* a "turning-over" at the base of the mind by which one's entire consciousness is wholly transformed. One becomes thoroughly detached from thought and sense-perception as the result of this turning over of the mind, described by Wei Wu Wei (1968, p. 78) as a transition from

*discussion of satori*

> . . . externalization to internality, from objectifying the "kingdom of the Earth" *without* to integrating the "kingdom of Heaven" *within.* . . . This is a reversion from durational thought and sensation to immediate apperceiving unextended in "space" and "time."

Suzuki (1949) describes the process as one where the facts of daily experience are taken as they come, and from them "a state of no-mind-ness is extracted"; all sense data is received and registers, but with non-reaction. This abstention from reactive thought, says Blofeld (1962, note 64), "does not mean trance-like dullness, but a brilliantly clear state of mind in which the details of every phenomenon are perceived, yet without evaluation or attachment"; Blofeld's description is the essence of the insight path as set forth in the *Visuddhimagga.* It was the Sixth Ch'an Patriarch, Hui-Neng, whose teaching set the tone for Zen practice to this day, who introduced *chien-hsing,* "to look into the nature of the mind" as the key practice of his teaching.[14] The

[14]At the time he was in the midst of a factional dispute with Shenhui (a Dharma scholar competing for successorship from the Fifth patriarch), who advocated a Zen centering on samadhi practices, with prajna relegated to mere intellectual understanding. Hui-Neng countered by affirming the equal footing (and essential sameness) of samadhi with prajna practice; the "insight" he advocated was an "abiding in the non-abiding." His instructions parallel the Buddha's for vipassana (Suzuki, 1949 p. 65):

> . . .sit in the right meditation posture, and purge your mind thoroughly of thoughts—thoughts about all things. . . . Present events are already here before you; then have no attachment to them. . . .When thoughts come and go, do not follow them. . . .When abiding with thoughts, do not tarry in them. . . .When thus freed from abiding in thoughts, you are said to be abiding with the non-abiding. . . . If you have a thoroughly clear perception as to the mind having no abiding place anywhere, this is a clear perception

master Hui Hai (in Blofeld, 1962), a successor to Hui-Neng's teaching, is succinct in his statement of the Zen principle of deliverance: "When things happen, make no response: keep your minds from dwelling on anything whatsoever." The fourteenth-century Zen master Bassui, in a sermon on attaining "One-mind," affirms that what is termed "zazen" is "no more than looking into one's own mind, neither despising nor cherishing the thoughts that arise." What the masters describe is a neutral psychological stance toward all inner and outer phenomena, which is both means and end in Zen. The coalescence of means and ends is functionally marked by a psychological continuity between sitting and the rest of one's day; Ruth Sasaki (Murai and Sasaki, 1965, p. xi) elaborates:

> The experienced practicer of zazen does not depend upon sitting in quietude on his cushion. States of consciousness at first attained only in the meditation hall gradually become continuous, regardless of what other activities he may be engaged in.

*false satori stage*

There are numerous moments of satori in zazen practice, some of which seem to be experiences of jhana, some stages in the path of insight. Yasutani warns his students, for example, to ignore *makyo,* illusory visions and sensations, which he describes as temporary mental states arising when one's ability to concentrate develops to a point within reach of *kensho* (probably indicators of the access concentration level). Kapleau mentions a "false satori" stage, sometimes called the "cave of Satan," where one experiences serenity and believes it to be a final realization; this pseudo-emancipation must be broken through, just as with the pseudo-nirvana on the vipassana path. The final drive toward enlightenment as described by Kapleau (1967, p. 13) is also a description of the psychology of the stages just prior to nirvana on the path of vipassana: one's effort is "powered on the one hand by a painfully felt inner bondage—a frustration with life, a fear of death, or both—and on the other by the conviction that through satori one can gain liberation."[15]

of one's own being. This very Mind which has no abiding anywhere is the Buddha-Mind itself.

[15]A common popular error is the view that satori comes about fortuitously, without any particular prior effort. Collections like Rep's *Zen Flesh, Zen Bones* can be misunderstood as supporting this view, enumerating case after case of the dramatic moment of final satori-breakthrough seemingly brought about by a mere word, gesture, or odd moment of perception. What is lacking, of course, is mention of the years of intensive zazen practice which has brought the aspirant to the final moment of ripeness. The underlying and invisible dynamic of these moments of sudden intuitive understanding is explained in a work on Satipatthana; its applicability to zazen is clear (Nyanaponika Thera, 1968 p. 46):

Silently and in the hidden depths of the subliminal mental processes, the

The stress in Zen practice is on the need to ripen an initial satori through subsequent practice, until it finally permeates one's life. The means to a satori is concentration coupled with insight or mindfulness; the subsequent full fruition is a state of mind stilled, beyond any further technique or practice. Kapleau describes the object of zazen as: "the cultivation first of mindfulness and eventually mindlessness." These two psychological conditions are amplified by Kapleau (1967, p. 201):

> Mindfulness is a state wherein one is totally aware in any situation and so always able to respond appropriately. Yet one is aware he is aware. Mindlessness, on the other hand, or "no-mindness" as it has been called, is a condition of such complete absorption that there is no vestige of self-awareness.

*final stage of Zen*

This final Zen stage of "no-mind" is *mujodo no taigeu,* where the spontaneity and clarity of *kensho* or satori is manifest in all one's acts. Here means and ends coalesce; the posture of mindfulness is built into one's consciousness, and so it is full awareness devoid of self-consciousness. On the way to this enlightenment one will have directly experienced, e.g., the arising, flourishing, and passing away of thoughts, and so realized the three truths of Buddha: that all things are impermanent, that "life is pain, and that all forms are *ku,* empty or voidness." One thus ceases clinging to the phenomenal world, yet continues to act in the world. Yasutani-roshi calls this "truly living Zen," when one's life and final Zen awareness are fully integrated. Among the attributes of one in this state are childlike spontaneity and simplicity, compassion, effortless grace, and the experiencing of life with immediacy and full awareness. Recognizing the depth of this transformation of personality and its pervasive effect on behavior, Zen has comparatively little emphasis on moral precepts. Rather than merely imposing precepts from the outside, Zen sees morality as emerging from within, a by-product of the change in consciousness zazen can bring. The depth and quality of this change can vary in degree and kind; it is a Zen rule of thumb that there are many satoris along the way to final, full enlightenment. Thomas Merton (1965) points out that the Ch'an and Zen teachings are the true inheritors of the thought and spirit of the Taoist Chuang

*attributes of "truly living Zen"*

*degrees of enlightenment*

work of collecting and organizing the material of experience and knowledge goes on until it is ripe to emerge as what we call an *intuition.* The breaking through of that intuition is sometimes occasioned by quite ordinary happenings which, however, may have strong evocative power. . . .Many instances are recorded of monks where the flash of intuitive penetration did not strike them when they were engaged in the meditative practice of insight proper, but on quite different occasions: when stumbling, etc.

Tzu, who wrote these words, which could be taken to summarize the path as well as the finished product in Zen (p. 112):

> No drives, no compulsions,
> No needs, no attractions:
> Then your affairs
> Are under control.
> You are a free man.

### GURDJIEFF

The system that G.I. Gurdjieff introduced to the West after extensive travel in Asia meeting "remarkable men" is, in the words of his pupil Orage (in Anderson, 1962), the religious teachings of the East disguised "in a terminology which would not alienate the factual minds of Western thinkers." Ouspensky (1971), another student of Gurdjieff, characterizes the system as an "esoteric school," not suited to mass tastes, which tells *how* to do what popular religions teach *has* to be done—i.e., raise one's consciousness. Gurdjieff himself called it The Fourth Way: not the traditional path of the fakir, monk, or yogi, but the way of the "sly man," who does not retreat from the world in solitary meditation, but works on his consciousness in the mirror of his relationships with people, animals, property, and ideas. Gurdjieff founded a school for disseminating his insights and techniques, and since at an advanced stage the student must share his acquired knowledge with others in order to advance still further, there have grown up numerous second-, third-, and fourth-generation Gurdjieff groups, each with its own style and idiosyncracies. The original school made use of a great range of techniques, so that any given latter-day group of this Fourth Way may or may not fit the Gurdjieffian system discussed here.

*most every person is "asleep"*

Gurdjieff's assessment of the human condition is that most every person is "asleep," living a life of mechanical repetition and automatic response to stimulus. "Contemporary man," writes Gurdjieff (1971), "has gradually deviated from the natural type he ought to have represented . . . the perceptions and manifestations of the modern man . . . represent only the results of automatic reflexes of one or another part of his general entirety." Like the Buddha, Gurdjieff understands the normal state to be one of suffering. The remedy he offers begins with observing oneself; Kenneth Walker (1969, p. 206), who studied with Ouspensky and Gurdjieff, puts it thus:

> We are imprisoned within our own minds, and however far we extend them and however highly we decorate them we still remain within their walls. If we are ever to escape from our prisons, the first step must be that we should realize our true situation and at the same time see ourselves as we really are and not as we imagine ourselves to be. This can be done by holding ourselves in a state of passive awareness.

*"self-remembering" and "observing I" or "Witness"*

The specific practice Walker describes is "self-remembering," a technique of deliberately dividing the attention and directing a portion back on oneself. Within the multiple and fluctuating selves which compose the normal "self" one establishes a self that is only watching all the rest: the "observing I" or the "Witness." There is initially great difficulty in coming to a stable observing "I": the beginner constantly forgets to remember himself, and self-observation surrenders to the usual full identification with whichever "I" has reign over the mind at a given moment. But, with persistence, the self-remembering process becomes self-reinforcing, for in Ouspensky's words, "the more we appreciate our present psychological state of sleep, the more we appreciate the urgent need to change it." The psychological stance required is self-directed detachment, as though one's own thoughts and acts were those of some other person with whom one is only slightly acquainted. Ouspensky (in Walker, 1969, p. 40) instructs:

> Observe yourself very carefully and you will see that not *you* but *it* speaks within you, moves, feels, laughs, and cries in you, just as *it* rains, clears up and rains again outside you. Everything happens in you, and your first job is to observe and watch it happening.

*self-remembering and mindfulness*

Self-remembering proceeds just as does the mindfulness of vipassana, which it closely resembles: with the realization of a lapse in self-observation, one returns from wandering mind to the task of watching oneself. Though the various Gurdjieff circles make use of a range of techniques for developing one-pointedness, these are subsidiary to the principal work of self-remembering; the critical skill sought is the capacity to direct attention to self-observation. Gurdjieff taught to his own groups Eastern sacred dances which served multiple functions, among them to illustrate the cosmological system he propounded and to instill a degree of one-pointedness in the dancers: Walker's experience as a dance pupil was that one or two moments of mind wandering and all coordinated movements collapsed.[16] Ouspensky (1971) em-

[16]Walker (1969 p. 69) describes another key exercise learned directly from Gurdjieff, called "body-sensing":

phatically links self-remembering to the path of insight, naming as antithetical to his goal both the samadhi trance state and the normal state of identifying which "imprisons man in some small part of himself." Just as with the practice of insight, in self-remembering the "distorting glasses of the personality" are abandoned in order to see oneself clearly. Like mindfulness, in self-remembering one acknowledges oneself in entirety without any comment and without naming what is seen; it is pre-conceptual cognition. Other examples of self-remembering practices are: to focus on one aspect of everyday behavior—e.g., movements of the hands or another body part, or facial gestures—witnessing it all day; or "wherever one is, whatever one does, remember one's own presence and notice always what one does." These instructions for developing the Witness are parallel to, e.g., those of the Buddhist monk Nyanaponika (1968) for mindfulness, though they are cast in terms of Gurdjieff's system of "psychic centers" controlling body, emotion, and thought. The similarity between systems is probably no accident; both Gurdjieff and Ouspensky traveled in lands where vipassana was taught precisely to learn such methods, and Gurdjieff was a great borrower, re-shaper, and transmitter of Eastern teachings.

*examples of self-remembering*

*multiplicity of selves*

In the course of self-remembering one comes to realize (as on the path of insight) that one's inner states are constantly flowing and fluctuating and that there is no such thing as a permanent "I" within. One comes to recognize an internal cast of characters—"principle features"—each in turn dominating the stage and adding its idiosyncracies to the shape of personality. With self-observation the multiplicity of selves becomes apparent, then falls away; through observing them these selves lose their hold as one ceases to identify with them. In the process, analytic self-awareness gives way to self-remembering, for which it is both preparatory and supplementary; this change marks a transition from a conceptual self-observation to a state of nonconceptual cognition. By strengthening the observing "I" and remaining detached from all the others, one can "wake up." In waking

> We were told to direct our attention in a predetermined order to various sets of muscles . . . relaxing them more and more as we came around to them again. . . .Whilst we were doing this we had at the same time to "sense" that particular area of the body; in other words, to become aware of it . . . with practice the attention can be thrown on to any part of the body desired, the muscles in that particular area relaxed, and sensation from that region evoked.

This exercise as described fits precisely a technique for *vedana* vipassana (insight of sensation) which I was taught in India, save that the primary task was to feel sensations and the relaxation was a side-effect. Gurdjieff sometimes alternated body-sensing with concentration-developing practices—e.g., counting, repeating strings of words—just as the *vedana* vipassana I learned is systematically alternated with concentration on breathing.

up, the existence of everyday selves is sacrificed in order to enter into a unique state qualitatively distinct from normal consciousness. Walker describes this state of continuing self-awareness as "a sense of being present, of being there, of thinking, perceiving, feeling, and moving with a certain degree of control and not just automatically." In this state the Witness is crystallized as a continuous psychological function; one can see oneself with full objectivity. The criterion for knowing oneself completely in this way is observation simultaneous with occurrence in the mind rather than in retrospect—also a key landmark on the insight path.

*highest state: objective consciousness*

Complete self-knowledge of this kind is seen as an intermediate stage, preliminary to the highest state, "Objective Consciousness." In this state one sees not only oneself but everything else as well with full objectivity. Objective Consciousness is reached by, and is the culmination of, self-remembering. Ordinary consciousness is not wholly dislodged, but full objectivity in an a-conceptual reality is superimposed upon it, adding an "inner silence" and liberating sense of distance from the continuing rumblings of the mind. One's experience of the world in Objective Consciousness is entirely altered; Walker (pp. 47–48) describes this end-state in Gurdjieff's training:

> The small limiting "self" of everyday life, the self which insists on its personal rights and separateness, is no longer there to isolate one from everything else, and in its absence one is received into a much wider order of existence . . . as the clamor of thought within dies down into the inner silence, an overwhelming sense of "being" takes its place. . . . Such limiting concepts as "yours" or "mine," "his" or "hers" are meaningless. . . . and even those old divisions of time into "before" and "after" have been drowned into the fathomless depth of an ever-present "now." So also has disappeared . . . . the division between the subject and the object, the knower and the thing known.

## KRISHNAMURTI'S CHOICELESS AWARENESS

*analysis of human predicament*

Krishnamurti's (1962) analysis of the human predicament is quite close to that of the Buddha. The mind and the world, says Krishnamurti, are in everlasting flux: "There is only one fact, impermanence." The mind clings to a "me" in the face of the insecurity of flux, but the "me" exists only through identification with the things it imagines it has been and wants to be. The "me" is "a mass of contradictions, desires, pursuits, fulfillments, and frustrations, with sorrow outweighing joy." There is constant conflict within between "what is" and "what should be." The conditioned mind, in Krishnamurti's analysis, flees from the facts of its impermanence, non-self, and sorrow, building walls of habit and repetition, pursuing the dreams of the future or clinging to that which has been, paralyzing one from living in the present moment.

*opposition to methods and techniques*

In its dissatisfaction, says Krishnamurti, the mind may try to achieve an escape from the mechanisms of conditioning, but in the very attempt simply creates another prison of methods to follow and goals to achieve. He opposes methods and techniques of every kind, urging one to put aside all authority and tradition—from them one can only collect more knowledge, while what is needed is "understanding." For according to Krishnamurti, no technique can free the mind, for any effort by the mind only weaves another net. "Freedom is not the outcome of the desire to be free," but rather desirelessness itself. He is most emphatically opposed to concentration methods for liberation (quoted in Coleman, 1971, p. 114):

> By repeating Amen or *Om* or Coca-Cola indefinitely you obviously have a certain experience because by repetition the mind becomes quiet. . . . It is one of the favorite gambits of some teachers of meditation to insist on their pupils learning concentration, that is, fixing the mind on one thought and driving out all other thoughts. This is a most stupid, ugly thing, which any schoolboy can do because he is forced to.

*"choiceless awareness"*

The "meditation" Krishnamurti advocates does not follow any system, least of all "repetition and imitation." He proposes a "choiceless awareness" as both means and end: the "experiencing of what is without naming." This meditation is not within the realm of discursive thought; all thought and all knowledge he says, belong to the past, and meditation is always the present. The mind must relinquish all the patterns and habits it has acquired out of the urge to be secure; "its gods and virtues must be given back to the society which bred them." All thought and all imagining must be relinquished; advises Krishnamurti (1962, pp. 8–10):

> Let the mind be empty, and not filled with the things of the mind. Then there is only meditation, and not a meditator who is meditating . . . the mind caught in imagination can only breed delusions. The mind must be clear, without movement, and in the light of that clarity the timeless is revealed.

Krishnamurti echoes Tilopa's *Song of Mahamudra* in advocating what sounds like an end-state only, a methodless method. But on closer scrutiny, Krishnamurti, like Tilopa, directly tells all who might hear the "how" while at the same time he insists that "there is no how; no method." He instructs one "just to be aware of all this . . . of your own habits, responses." His means is to observe all awareness, constantly watching. This mode of careful attention he calls "self-knowledge"; its essence is "to perceive the ways of your own mind" so that the mind is "free to be still" as it must be to understand. Understanding as Krishnamurti describes it comes into being when the discursive habits of thought are still. The key is "attention without the word, the name"; still, he instructs, "Look and be simple": where there is attention independent of reactive thought, reality is.

*tells "how" and insists "there is no how; no method"*

The process Krishnamurti proposes for attaining self-knowledge is a virtual duplicate of mindfulness training as described by the Buddhist monk Nyanoponika. But Krishnamurti himself most certainly would not condone such a comparison because of the danger he sees inherent in trying to achieve any goal via preformulated technique. The process he suggests for allowing the mind to become still springs from the very realization of one's predicament, for to know "that you have been asleep is already an awakened state." This very truth, he insists, will act on the mind, setting it free. Without detailing any specifics, Krishnamurti (1962, p. 60) assures that:

> When the mind realizes the totality of its own conditioning . . . then all its movements come to an end: it is completely still, without any desire, without any compulsion, without any motive. . . .

This awakening is for Krishnamurti a spontaneous, automatic process: "realization." The mind discovers, or rather is caught up in, the solution "through the very intensity of the question itself." This realization cannot be sought: "it comes uninvited." Should one somehow experience the realization of which Krishnamurti speaks, a new state of being would emerge, freed from conditioned habits of perception and cognition, devoid of self.[17] To thus understand reality in his

*awakening is spontaneous automatic process: "realization"*

[17]Given that the groundwork for (and the result of) this realization is similar to mindfulness, one sees that Krishnamurti's nontechnique may tap into the same dynamic as vipassana, where the identical realizations—of impermanence, nonself, suffering—trigger a sudden stilling of the mind in the nirvanic state. The *Visuddhimagga* system would classify Krishnamurti as a "dry-worker"—i.e., one who undertakes vipassana ("seeing things as they are") without any prior or auxiliary practice of samadhi. Though, again, he himself would undoubtedly reject any such comparisons, in his person-to-person talks he creates a situation that confronts his listener with the absurdity and futility of resolving one's dilemmas of whatever sort via the rational mind, which sets the stage for a "realization." After a dialogue with Krishnamurti, Coleman (1971: p. 91) wrote,

*"aloneness beyond loneliness"*

sense is seen by Krishnamurti as equivalent to love: "Where the self is, love is not." The state thus emergent is an "aloneness beyond loneliness," where there is no verbal movement within the mind, but rather a pure experiencing, "attention without motive." One is free from envy, ambition, and the desire for power, and is free to love with understanding and compassion. Here feeling is knowing, in a state of total attention with no watcher. Living in an eternal present, one ceases collecting impressions or experiences; the past dies in each successive moment. The sleep state becomes one of complete rest and renewal where one does not dream at all. With choiceless awareness, one is free to be simple; as Krishnamurti (Coleman, 1971, p. 95) puts it:

> Be far away, far away from the world of chaos and misery, live in it, untouched. . . . The meditative mind is unrelated to the past and to the future and yet is sanely capable of living with clarity and reason.

## MEDITATION RESEARCH: FOOTHOLDS AND STRATEGIES

*problems in terminology*

The differing names used among meditation systems to describe one and the same way and destination are legion. Sometimes the same term is used in special, but very different, technical senses by various schools. "Void," for example, is used by Indian yogis to refer to jhana states, and by Mahayana Buddhists as signifying the realization of the essential emptiness of all phenomenon; the former usage denotes a mental state *devoid* of contents (e.g., the formless jhanas), the latter refers to the *voidness* of mental contents (i.e., *anatta*). Another example of the confusion in naming: Phillip Kapleau (1967) distinguishes between zazen and meditation, saying that the two "are not to be confused"; Krishnamurti (1962) says *only* "choiceless awareness" is really meditation. Only the recognition that both zazen and choiceless awareness are insight techniques, and that by "meditation" Kapleau means concentration (while Krishnamurti denies that concentration practices are within the province of meditation at all), allows one to see that these seemingly unrelated remarks are actually emphasizing the same distinction: that between concentration and insight. In using the Buddha's map and vocabulary as a template for viewing diverse reports from within the mind, we can gain

*distinction between concentration and insight*

"I believe he . . . deliberately leads his listeners nowhere, frustrates them to the point where they seek the answers within themselves"; like a Ch'an or Zen koan master, he baffles his listener with sometimes elliptical and seemingly fruitless intellectual mazes.

a foothold in these otherwise shifting sands, regardless of the overlay of jargon and cosmology.

*criteria for classification of 15 meditation systems*

In Table 1 a representative spectrum-wide sample of 15 meditation systems is classified according to the threefold typology developed here. The principle criteria for classification are (1) the mechanics of technique: whether mind concentrates on a fixed mental object, or mind observes itself, or both operations are present in integrated combination; and (2) internal consistency in description: if a concentration technique, whether other characteristics of the jhana path are mentioned—e.g., increasingly subtle bliss accompanying deepened concentration, loss of sense-consciousness; or if an insight technique, whether other characteristics of insight practices, such as the realization of the impersonality of mental processes, are present; or if combined, whether, e.g., concentration techniques are adjuncts at the access level to insight (as in vipassana). Inclusion in this classification is restricted to those cases where both criterion (1) and (2) are clearly met in the literature pertaining to each of the fifteen systems.

*strategies of spiritual masters and Western scientists compared*

The "findings" on the topography of consciousness by the Buddha and other spiritual masters of the East are in the empirical-experiential mode; scientists in the West tend to attack these (or any) areas of knowledge in the empirical-experimental mode. These are not, of course, opposite strategies, but rather an interacting duality. The experiential gives rise to hunches, hypotheses, constructs; the experimental investigation refines and amends, feeding back new data. Each is an essential adjunct to the other, and both are essential elements in the spiral process whereby solidly grounded theory is generated. The Buddha and other masters can be seen as taking the first tentative steps into a psychic *terra incognita,* laying the experiential groundwork that would subsequently prompt others to follow in their own style.

*trans-personal research may require a trans-methodology*

Transpersonal psychology researchers may discover that their discipline requires at certain points a trans-methodology: the psychological safety and distance afforded by traditional behavioral-science tools and the accompanying conceptual superstructure—e.g., the notion of "subjects"—may prevent contact with beings who are in the fifth state. Their teaching and being seems to center in inner realities, and may evaporate for those who need at every step to objectify and cross-validate these transpersonal aspects. For ages the communi-

TABLE 1
APPLIED TYPOLOGY OF MEDITATION TECHNIQUES

| TEACHER, SYSTEM, OR SCHOOL | TECHNIQUE | TYPE | NAME OF FIFTH STATE |
|---|---|---|---|
| Hindu Bhakti | Japa | Concentration | Union |
| Sufi | *Zikr* | Concentration | *Baga;* Objective Consciousness |
| Hesychasm | Jesus Prayer | Concentration | *Quies;* Purity of Heart |
| Meher Baba | Varied spectrum of meditations | Integrated | Sahaj Samadhi; Sadguru |
| Sri Aurobindo | "Bringing down the Overmind" | Concentration | Supermind |
| Patanjali's Ashtanga Yoga | Samadhi | Concentration | Sahaj Samadhi |
| Ramana Maharshi | Self-inquiry | Concentration | *Jivan-mukti* |
| Maharishi Mahesh Yogi | Transcendental Meditation | Concentration | God-consciousness; Union |
| Swami Muktananda | *Shaktipat-diksha* | Concentration | *Turyatita* |
| Kirpal Singh | *Shabd* Yoga | Concentration | True Master |
| Tantra Yoga | *Yantra, maithuna,* mantra, visualization, etc. | Concentration | Siddha |
| Tibetan Vajrayana | Mahamudra: *shiney* and *thagthong* | Integrated: concentration and insight | Bodhisattva |
| Zen | Zazen: koan, breath, and *shikan-taza* | Integrated: concentration and insight | "No-mind" |
| Gurdjieff | Self-remembering | Insight | Objective Consciousness |
| J. Krishnamurti | Self-knowledge | Insight | Choiceless Awareness |

cation and transmission of fifth-state qualities have been within a master-student, guru-disciple paradigm, and by their very nature may not be feasible in any other structure; the work of Carlos Casteñada (1971) demonstrates this dynamic. In short, perhaps one may *know of* these beings and their qualities, but not *share in* those qualities, as long as they are approached within the confines of Western research strategies. Guenther (1963), in his introduction to the life of Tilopa, who resigned his position as head of the eleventh century Nalanda University to seek out his guru and devote himself wholly to meditation practice, comments:

> Throughout the years he had been engaged in intellectual activities which are essentially analytic and thereby become oblivious to the fact that the human organ of knowledge is bi-focal. "Objective" knowledge may be entirely accurate without, however, being entirely important, and only too often misses the heart of the matter.

Ouspensky (1971) cautions that it is difficult, if not impossible, to judge the level of consciousness of a person higher than oneself, and that one can only recognize with any certainty beings on one's own or a lower level. For a researcher, this means that it may be hard to recognize the most fruitful subjects for studies of HSC, especially those in the fifth state. A further complication is the possibility that we do not yet accurately perceive the most crucial parameters of HSC. It may be, for example, that the dimensions of physiology—e.g., EEG patterns—which are testable at present are *not* the critical variables in levels of consciousness, or that they are only peripherally and not particularly systematically related to HSC. One possibility is that the gross changes in psychophysiology—heart rate, blood pressure, alpha, etc.—show up largely in the early stages, marking the distinction between the waking state and the MSC "fourth state" (i.e., jhana). When one has made the transition into the fifth state, the key changes may have more subtle indicators. It may be that in the fifth state indicators other than psychophysiological measures are more appropriate indices, e.g., the quality of "loving kindness" or of "open-heartedness"—the degree one loves others without attachment—may be more central a variable than brain-wave patterns.

*differences*

A sample of meditation masters would show striking behavioral differences and idiosyncracies, some stemming from life history, some attributable to training, some cultural, and so on. These differences may be passed on in their own teaching as unique styles and practices: Kirpal Singh, e.g., is a celibate, a strict vegetarian, and a teetotaler, while Chogyam Trungpa is married, eats meat, and drinks liquor; Maharishi Mahesh Yogi is the proponent of a single set series of techniques for all pupils, while Meher Baba suggests a varied spectrum of practices depending on individual requirement. There may well be an innate hierarchy within HSC, but even though it is tempting to draw judgments of relative attainments among masters and teachers, by what criterion such a hierarchy might be ordered is by no means clear from the vantage point of normal consciousness. In evaluating these behavioral differences among masters and among the various meditation paths, the researcher should heed the advice in a Sufi tale retold by Idries Shah (1971, p. 75):

> Yaqub, the son of the Judge, said that one day he questioned Bahaudin Nawshband in this manner:
>
> When I was in companionship with the Murshid of Tabriz, he regularly made a sign that he was not to be spoken to, when he was in a condition of special reflection. But you are accessible to us at all times. Am I correct in concluding that this difference is due to your undoubtedly greater capacity of detachment, the capacity being under your dominion, rather than fugitive?
>
> Bahudin told him:
>
> No, you are always seeking comparisons between people and between states. You are always seeking evidences and differences, when you are not you are seeking similarities. You do not really need so much explanation in matters which are outside such measurement. Different modes of behavior on the part of the wise are to be regarded as due to differences in individuality, not of quality.

The fifth state, borne of the consequences of meditation practice, at its highest level means the displacement of the personal ego as the basis for behavior.[18] In its initial phase the

[18]One conceptual model applicable to an understanding of the fifth state is Arthur Deikman's (1971) theory of "bimodal consciousness." Deikman describes two primary modes of psychophysical organization: an "action" mode and a "receptive" mode. The action mode is geared to manipulating and acting on the environment, its agencies are the striate muscle system and the sympathetic nervous system, and it is associated with beta waves, an increased baseline muscle tension, focal attention, object-based logic, heightened boundary perception, striving toward achieving personal goals—in sum, what we usually consider the active waking state. By contrast, the receptive mode is (p. 481):

> a state organized around intake of the environment rather than manipulation. The sensory-perceptual system is the dominant agency rather than the muscle system, and parasympathetic functions tend to be most prominent. The EEG tends toward alpha waves and baseline muscle tension is decreased. Other attributes of the receptive mode are diffuse attending, paralogical thought processes, decreased boundary perception, and the dominance of the sensory over the formal.

The receptive mode is typically maximal in infancy; as we progress developmentally into egohood, the striving activity of the action mode comes to dominate. The receptive mode can, however, predominate briefly in adult life in such activities as making love or in relationships of the sort Buber calls "I-thou." One's choice of mode is tied to one's basic motive for action: these are simply different strategies for engaging in the world. As Deikman points out, an "enlightened monk" would operate in the action mode to the minimal extent necessary to conduct his work in the world, and while doing so, the receptive mode would still predominate in his awareness. Deikman further notes that meditation techniques are geared to take the meditator out of the action mode—if only for a time—and shift his awareness to the receptive mode in a process he calls "deautomatization, an undoing of the automatic psychological structures that organize, limit, select, and interpret perceptual stimuli"—i.e., those habits of mind the *Visuddhimagga* terms "hindrances to concentration." In the case of concentration techniques this shift focuses on disattending to these usual ways of thinking and perceiving, which come to be seen as distractions to one-pointedness. With in-

fifth state seems to be an act of effort, albeit subtle, and is contingent upon the emergent ability to maintain prolonged meditation awareness in the midst of other activities. As the state produced by meditation melds with waking activity, the fifth state comes into being, lastingly changing one's experience of the waking state. Fifth-state reality is seemingly discontinuous from our normal experience of ourselves and our universe. Though the *Visuddhimagga* would draw distinctions at the level of enlightenment according to the path of access, it may be that at this point all paths merge, or that from our perspective the similarities far outweigh the differences. A fifth-state being transcends his own origins; e.g., persons of any faith can recognize him as exceptional or "perfect," or—if so inclined—revere him as a saint. Elsewhere (1971) I have made a beginning in relating the fifth state to Western psychology. A more precise and detailed phenomenology of the fifth state would be more fittingly drawn from studies of those rare beings in that state now alive. Suffice it to say here that from the perspective of Western psychology an enlightened being defies classification or understanding within the framework of traditional psychodynamic theory. From an Eastern perspective he is what every person should strive to become. Contemporary research approaches to meditation have focused for the most part on the changes occurring within the meditation session per se. But to focus there and ignore the global effects of meditation practice on the meditator's life as a whole is to misunderstand the central aim of the whole process and to underestimate the grand design of which sitting in meditation is only a part.

*similarities far outweigh differences*

*enlightened beings defy classification by traditional Western terms*

GLOSSARY[19]

*Abhidhamma*—lit., "the nature of now," a lengthy treatise on consciousness attributed to Gotama Buddha and included among the oldest of Buddhist scriptures in the Pali language.

*anagami*—lit., "non-returner," the third of four levels at which nirvana can be realized.

*ananda*—subtle and exquisite feelings of bliss.

sight techniques the shift comes in withdrawing from the cognitive level of thought and perception and holding attention at the level of bare percepts, thus undercutting mental manipulation of reality through mechanisms like categorization. When these meditative skills are carried over into all life situations they produce the fifth state, one attribute of which is the receptive mode.

[19]The meanings given are for the terms as used in the context of this paper and are not to be considered definitive.

*anatta*—lit., "not-self," the Buddhist doctrine that all phenomena, including "one's self," are devoid of any indwelling personality; the realization that there is no abiding entity within one's mind or being.

*anicca*—lit., "impermanence," the Buddhist doctrine that all phenomena are transitory; the realization that one's world of reality is continually arising and disappearing every mind-moment.

*arahant*—lit., "saint," the final of four stages of realizing nirvana, at which the last vestige of selfish motivation has disappeared; the end of the path in the Visuddhimagga system of psychospiritual development.

*asubhas*—decaying corpses used as objects for meditation in their natural state in burial or burning grounds, classified according to their state of decomposition and including a skeleton.

*bardos*—intermediate states between life and death; realms of reality representing mind states.

*chakra*—one of seven psychic energy centers distributed from the base of the spine along the spine to the top of the head.

*Dharma language*—the esoteric, spiritually oriented, or symbolic sense of ordinary words and their meanings.

*dukkha*—lit., "suffering," the Buddhist doctrine that the world of consensual reality is the source of all woe; the realization of the unsatisfactory nature of all mental phenomena.

*fana*—Sufi term for a state of full absorption, equivalent to jhana.

*HSC*—Higher states of consciousness; a state where functions of "lower" states are available in addition to new functions of other, altered states of consciousness.

*jhana*—a degree of absorption on a continuum beginning with a full break with normal consciousness marked by one-pointed concentration on a meditation object to the exclusion of all other thoughts or awareness of external sensory inputs, and ending in a state of ultrasubtle residual perception.

*kasina*—a visual meditation object, usually a foot or so in diameter, circular or square, consisting of a single color or light, which may be concrete or imagined.

*loca*—a realm of reality existing in mental or supramental dimensions, spoken of as a "world" as real as our own, and typifying a distinct mental state.

*MSC*—meditation-specific states of consciousness; a state attained through meditation which transcends normal sensory awareness and cognition.

*mudra*—a ritual physical gesture, posture, or pose expressing a specific state of mind or consciousness.

*Nikaya*—lit., "collection," a compilation of Southern Buddhist sutras.

*nirodh*—the state of total cessation of awareness attained through meditation.

*nirvana*—the state in meditation of awareness of no consciousness at all, the experience of which diminishes the ego as a subsequent effect; the unconditioned state.

*nirvichara samadhi*—a state of concentration where there is only awareness of the primary object; equivalent to first jhana.

*nirvikalpa samadhi*—a state of concentration where all thoughts, even awareness of the meditation subject, cease altogether; equivalent to second jhana and above.

*Pali*—the North Indian dialect spoken by Gotama Buddha in preference to Sanskrit, and the sacred language of scriptures in Southern Buddhism (as Latin is used in Catholicism).

*prajna*—lit., "insight," also, "wisdom," the ability to perceive phenomena simply as they exist rather than in terms of a meaning derived from a learned personal, group, or cultural belief system or other consensual notion of reality.

*pranayam*—techniques for altering consciousness by controlled breathing patterns.

*sadhana*—any system of spiritual practice; a path for psychospiritual evolution.

*sahaj samadhi*—the stabilization of jhana-consciousness in the midst of the ordinary state of waking, dreaming, and sleeping.

*sakadgami*—lit., "once-returner," the second of four levels of realizing nirvana.

*samadhi*—the technique of one-pointed concentration in meditation; also, in Sanskrit sources, a psychophysiological state of absorption in a single object of concentration to the exclusion of all awareness of any other sensory inputs or thoughts (see *jhana*).

*sangha* (Pali) or *satsang* (Sanskrit)—technically, those who have attained the nirvanic state, and generally speaking, the community of seekers on a spiritual path.

*satipatthana*—lit., "mindfulness," a technique of constant bare attention to all sensory perceptions or thoughts, so that the mind is not stimulated by them into thought chains, but witnesses them all without reaction; when mastered, satipatthana develops into vipassana.

*savichara samadhi*—a state of concentration on a meditation subject where awareness is mixed with thoughts relating to the object; equivalent to access concentration.

*sila*—lit., "virtue," the practice of moral precepts for the purpose of clearing the mind of preoccupations which would distract one from spiritual practice, especially concentration in meditation.

*sotapanna*—lit., "stream-enterer," the first of four levels of attainment of nirvana.

*sukha*—a state of intense pleasure and well-being.

*sutra*—a literary form used for most Hindu and Buddhist sacred scriptures.

*varagya*—the falling away of desires as a side-effect of spiritual growth.

*vipassana*—lit., "seeing things as they are," a meditation technique where attention is turned to constant scrutiny of each successive unit in the thought-continuum.

*Visuddhimagga*—a summary of the Abhidhamma sections

on meditation and consciousness, done in the fifth century A.D. by Bhuddaghosa.

REFERENCES

AKISHIGE, Y. (ED.). *Psychological studies on Zen.* Tokyo: Zen Institute of Komazawa Univ., 1970.

AMMA. *Dhyan-yoga and kundalini yoga.* Ganeshpuri, India: Shree Gurudev Ashram, 1969.

ANAND, B., CHHINA, G., SINGH, B. Some aspects of EEG studies in Yogis, EEG *Clin. Neurophysiol.*, 1961, *13*, 452–56. Also in C. Tart (Ed.), *Altered states of consciousness.* New York: Wiley, 1969.

ANDERSON, M. *The unknowable Gurdjieff.* London: Routledge & Kegan Paul, 1962.

ASHBY, W. R. *Design for a brain.* London: Science Paperbacks, 1970.

AUROBINDO, SRI. *The life divine.* New York: Sri Aurobindo Library, 1949.

AUROBINDO, SRI. *The synthesis of yoga.* Pondicherry, India: Sri Aurobindo Ashram Press, 1955.

AUROBINDO, SRI. *On yoga II, tome two.* Pondicherry, India: Sri Aurobindo Ashram Press, 1958.

BABA RAM DASS. *Be here now.* New York: Crown, 1971.

BAGCHI, B. K., WENGER, M. A. Electro-physiological correlates of some Yogi exercises. Reprinted in T. X. Barber et al. (Eds.), *Biofeedback and Self-Control.* Chicago: Aldine-Atherton, 1971.

BHIKKU SOMA. *The way of mindfulness.* Colombo, Ceylon: Vajirama, 1949.

BLAKNEY, R. B. *Meister Eckhart.* New York: Harper & Row, 1941.

BLOFELD, J. *The Zen teaching of Hui Hai.* London: Rider, 1962.

BROWN, B. B. Recognition of aspects of consciousness through association with EEG alpha activity represented by a light signal. *Psychophysiology,* 1970, *6,* 442-52.

BUCKE, R. M. *Cosmic consciousness.* New Hyde Park, NY: University Books, 1961.

BUDDHADASA, BHIKKU (Ariyananda Bhikku, Transl.). *Two kinds of language.* Bangkok, Thailand: Sublime Life Mission, 1968.

CASTAÑEDA, C. *A separate reality.* New York: Simon & Schuster, 1971.

CHADWICK, A. W. *A sadhu's reminiscences of Ramana Maharshi.* Tiruvannamali, India: Sri Ramanasram, 1966.

CHANG, G. C. C. *Teachings of Tibetan yoga.* New York: New York Univ. Press, 1963.
CHANG, G. C. C. *The hundred thousand songs of Milarepa.* New York: Harper Colophon Books, 1970.
CHOGYAM TRUNGPA. *Meditation in action.* London: Stuart & Watkins, 1969.
CHOGYAM TRUNGPA. *Garuda,* 1971, *I*:1.
COLEMAN, J. E. *The quiet mind.* London: Rider & Co., 1971.
CONZE, E. *Buddhist meditation.* London: Allen & Unwin, 1956.
DALAI LAMA, THE FOURTEENTH. *An introduction to Buddhism.* New Delhi: Tibet House, 1965.
DALAI LAMA, THE FOURTEENTH. *Short essays on Buddhist thought and practice.* New Delhi: Tibet House, n.d.
DALAL, A. S., BARBER, T. X. Yoga, "yogic feats," and hypnosis in the light of empirical research. *Amer. J. Clin. Hypnosis,* 1969, *11,* 155-66.
DEIKMAN, A. J. Bimodal consciousness, *Arch. Gen. Psychol.,* 1971, *25,* 481-89.
DHAMMARATANA. *Guide through Visuddhimagga.* Varanasi, India: Mahabodhi Society, 1964.
DONKIN, W. *The wayfarers.* New York: Dodd, Mead, & Co., 1954.
DOUGLAS, N. *Tantra yoga.* New Delhi: Munshiram Manoharlal, 1971.
ELIADE, M. *Yoga: immortality and freedom.* Princeton, N.J.: Princeton Univ. Press, 1970.
EVANS-WENTZ, W. Y. *Tibetan yoga and secret doctrines.* London: Oxford Univ. Press, 1968.
EVANS-WENTZ, W. Y. *The Tibetan book of the great liberation.* London: Oxford Univ. Press, 1969.
FISHER, R. A cartography of the ecstatic and meditative states. *Science,* 1971, *4012,* 897-904.
FRENCH, R. M. (Transl.) *The way of the pilgrim.* New York: Seabury Press, 1970.
GOLEMAN, D. Meditation as meta-therapy: hypotheses toward a proposed fifth state of consciousness. *J. Transpersonal Psychol.,* 1971, *3*(1), 1-25.
GOVINDA, LAMA ANAGARIKA. *The psychological attitude of early Buddhist philosophy.* London: Rider, 1969.
GOVINDA, LAMA ANAGARIKA. *Foundations of Tibetan mysticism.* London: Rider, 1970.
GREEN, E. E., GREEN, A. M., WALTERS, E. D. Voluntary control of internal states: psychological and physiological. *J. Transpersonal Psychol.,* 1970, *2*(1), 1-26.
GREEN, E. E., GREEN, A. M., WALTERS, E. D. Biofeedback for mind-body self-regulation: healing and creativity. Pa-

per delivered at symposium on "The Varieties of Healing Experience," Cupertino, California, October, 1971.
GUENTHER, H. V. *The life and teaching of Naropa*. London: Oxford Univ. Press, 1963.
GURDJIEFF, G. I. *Meetings with remarkable men*. New York: Dutton, 1969.
GURDJIEFF, G. I. *The herald of coming good*. New York: Samuel Weiser, 1971.
KABIR (R. Tagore, Transl.). *Poems of Kabir*. Calcutta: Macmillan, 1970.
KADLOUBOUSKY, E., PALMER, G. E. H. *Writings from the philokalia on prayer of the heart*. London: Faber & Faber, 1971.
KAMIYA, J. Operant control of the EEG alpha rhythm and some of its reported effects on consciousness. In C. T. Tart (Ed.), *Altered states of consciousness*. New York: Wiley, 1969, 507-17.
KAPLEAU, P. *The three pillars of Zen*. Boston: Beacon Press, 1967.
KASAMATSU, A., HIRAI, T. An EEG study of Zen meditation, *Folia Psychiat. Neurol. Jap.*, 1966, *20*, 315-36. Also in C. Tart (Ed.), *Altered states of consciousness*. New York: Wiley, 1969.
KASHYAP, J. *The Abhidhamma philosophy*, Vol. I. Nalanda, India: Buddha Vihara, 1954.
KRISHNA PREM. *Yoga of the Katopanishad*. Allahabad, India: Ananda Publ. House, 1958.
KRISHNAMURTI, J. (D. Rajagopal, Ed.). *Commentaries on living: Third series*. London: Victor Gollancz Ltd., 1962.
LAO TZU (D. C. Lau, Transl.). *Tao te ching*. Baltimore: Penguin Books, 1968.
LEDI SAYADAW. *The manuals of Buddhism*. Rangoon, Burma: Union Buddha Sasana Council, 1965.
LUK, C. *Ch'an and Zen teaching, third series*. London: Rider, 1962.
LUK, C. *Secrets of Chinese meditation*. London: Rider, 1966.
LUK, C. *Practical Buddhism*. London: Rider, 1971.
M. *Gospel of Sri Ramakrishna*. Mylapore, India: Sri Ramakrishna Math, 1928.
MAHADEVAN, T. M. P. (Transl.). *Self-inquiry of Bhagavan Sri Ramana Maharshi*. Tiruvannamalai, India, 1965.
MAHARISHI MAHESH YOGI. *On the Bhagavad Gita*. Baltimore: Penguin Books, 1969.
MAHASI SAYADAW (Nyanaponika Thera, Transl.). *The process of insight*. Kandy, Ceylon: The Forest Hermitage, 1965.
MAHASI SAYADAW. *Buddhist meditation and its forty subjects*.

Buddha-gaya, India: International Meditation Center, 1970.

MAHATHERA, P. V. *Buddhist meditation in theory and practice.* Colombo, Ceylon: Gunasena, 1962.

MANZANI, R. P. *The conference of the birds: a Sufi allegory.* London: Oxford Univ. Press, 1928.

MASLOW, A. Theory Z. *J. Transpersonal Psychol.,* 1970, *2*(1), 31-47.

MASLOW, A. New introduction: Religions, values, and peak experiences (New Edition), *J. Transpersonal Psychol.* 1970, *2*(2), 83-90.

MCCLURE, C. Cardiac arrest through volition. *California Med.,* 1959, *90,* 440-41.

MEHER, BABA. *Discourses I, II, III.* San Francisco: Sufism Reoriented, 1967.

MERTON, T. *The wisdom of the desert.* New York: New Directions, 1960.

MERTON, T. *Mystics and Zen masters.* New York: Farrar, Straus & Giroux, 1967.

MERTON, T. *The way of Chuang Tzu.* London: Unwin, 1965.

MIURA, I., SASAKI, R. F. *The Zen koan.* New York: Harcourt, Brace & World, 1965.

MUDALIAR, A. D. *Day by day with Bhagavan.* Tiruvannamalai, India: Sri Ramanasram, 1968.

MUKTANANDA PARAMAHANSA, SWAMI. *Soham-japa.* New Delhi: Siddha Yoga Dham, 1969.

MUKTANANDA PARAMAHANSA, SWAMI. *Gurukripa.* Ganeshpuri, India: Shree Gurudev Ashram, 1970.

MUKTANANDA PARAMAHANSA, SWAMI. *Guruvani Magazine.* Ganeshpuri, India: Shree Gurudev Ashram, 1971.

MUKTANANDA PARAMAHANSA, SWAMI. *Guru.* New York: Harper & Row, 1972.

NARADA THERA. *A manual of abhidhamma, I & II.* Colombo, Ceylon: Vajirarama, 1956.

NARANJO, C., ORNSTEIN, R. E. *On the psychology of meditation.* New York: Viking, 1971.

NIKHILANANDA, SWAMI. *Drg-drysa-viveka: an inquiry into the nature of the 'seer' and the 'seen.'* Mysore, India: Sri Ramakrishna Ashram, 1964.

NYANAPONIKA THERA. *Abhidhamma studies.* Colombo, Ceylon: Frewin, 1949.

NYANAPONIKA THERA. *The heart of Buddhist meditation.* London: Rider, 1962.

NYANAPONIKA THERA. *The power of mindfulness.* Kandy, Ceylon: Buddhist Publication Society, 1968.

NYANATILOKA. *The word of the Buddha.* Colombo, Ceylon: Buddha Publishing Committee, 1952(a).

NYANATILOKA. *Path to deliverance*. Colombo, Ceylon: Buddha Sahitya Sabha, 1952(b).

OSBORNE, A. *Sri Ramanasramam*. Tiruvannamalai, India: Sri Ramanasram, 1964.

ORME-JOHNSON, D. Autonomic stability and transcendental meditation. Unpublished manuscript.

OUSPENSKY, P. D. *The fourth way*. New York: Vintage, 1971.

PODDAR, H. P. *The divine name and its practice*. Gorakhpur, India: Gita Press, 1965.

PODDAR, H. P. *The philosophy of love: Bhakti sutras of Devarsi Narada*. Gorakhpur, India: Gita Press, 1968.

PRABHAVANANDA, SWAMI. *Srimad Bhagavatam*. Mylapore, India: Sri Ramakrishna Math, 1964.

PRABHAVANANDA, SWAMI, ISHERWOOD, C. *How to know God: Yoga aphorisms of Patanjali*. New York: Signet, 1969.

PRABHAVANANDA, SWAMI, ISHERWOOD, C. *Crest-jewel of discrimination*. New York: Mentor, 1970.

RAMANA MAHARSHI. *Maharshi's gospel, I & II*. Tiruvannamalai, India: Sri Ramanasram, 1962.

RICE, C. *The Persian Sufis*. London: Allen & Unwin, 1964.

REPS, P. *Zen flesh, Zen bones*. New York: Doubleday, 1961.

SARADANANDA, SWAMI. *Ramakrishna the Great Master*. Mylapore, India: Sri Ramakrishna Math, 1963.

SATPREM (Tehmi, Transl.). *Sri Aurobindo: The adventure of consciousness*. Pondicherry, India: Sri Aurobindo Society, 1970.

SCHACHTER, S., SINGER, J. Cognitive, social, and physiological determinants of emotional state, *Psychol. Rev.* 1962, *69*, 379.

SHAH, I. *The Sufis*. London: Jonathan Cape, 1970.

SHAH, I. *Wisdom of the idiots*. New York: Dutton, 1971.

SHAPIRO, D. *Neurotic styles*. New York: Basic Books, 1961.

SHASTRI, H. P. *Yoga-vasistha: the world within the mind*. London: Shanti Sadan, 1969.

SINGH, K. *The crown of life*. Delhi: Ruhani Satsang, 1971.

SIVANANDA, SWAMI. *Kundalini yoga*. Sivanandagar, India: The Divine Life Society, 1971.

SULLIVAN, H. S. *The interpersonal theory of psychiatry*. New York: Norton, 1953.

SUZUKI, D. T. *The Zen doctrine of no-mind*. London: Rider, 1949.

SUZUKI, D. T. *Mysticism: Christian and Buddhist*. New York: Macmillan, 1957.

SUZUKI, D. T. *Essays in Zen Buddhism (second series)*. London: Rider, 1958.

SUZUKI, D. T. In C. Humphreys (Ed.), The field of Zen. *Contributions to the Middle Way, the Journal of the Buddhist Society*. London: The Buddhist Society, 1969.

TART, C. Scientific foundations for the study of altered states of consciousness. *J. Transpersonal Psychol.* 1971, *3*(2), 93-124.

TAUSSIG, H. B. "Death" from lightning and the possibility of living again. *Amer. Sci.* 1969, *57*(3), 306-16.

THOMAS À KEMPIS (R. Whitford, Transl.). *The imitation of Christ.* Garden City, New York: Image Books, 1955.

TULSI DASS (M. Growse, Transl.). *Ramayana.* Gorakhpur, India: Gita Press, n.d.

VENKATARAMIAH, M. (Transl.). *Advaita Bodha Deepika: Lamp of non-dual knowledge.* Tiruvannamalai, India: Sri Ramanasram, 1967.

VIMUKTANANDA, SWAMI. *Aparokshanubhuti: Self-realization of Sri Sankaracharya.* Calcutta: Advaita Ashrama, 1966.

VIVEKANANDA, SWAMI. *Bhakti-yoga.* Calcutta: Advaita Ashrama, 1964.

VIVEKANANDA, SWAMI. *Raja-yoga.* Calcutta: Advaita Ashrama, 1970.

VYAS DEV, SWAMI. *First steps to higher yoga.* Gangotri, India: Yoga Niketan Trust, 1970.

WALKER, K. *A study of Gurdjieff's teaching.* London: Jonathan Cape, 1969.

WALLACE, R. K. *Physiological effects of TM: A proposed fourth major state of consciousness.* Los Angeles: Students International Meditation Society, 1970.

WALLACE, R. K., BENSON, H., WILSON, A. E. A wakeful hypometabolic state. *Amer. J. Physiol.,* 1971, *224*(3), 795-99.

WEI WU WEI. *Posthumous pieces.* Hong Kong: Hong Kong Univ. Press, 1968.

WENGER, A. M., BAGCHI, B. K., ANAND, B. K. Experiments in India on "voluntary" control of the heart and pulse. *Circulation,* 1961, *204.*

WOODROFFE, J. *Hymn to Kali.* Madras, India: Ganesh, 1965.

YOGANANDA. *Autobiography of a yogi.* Los Angeles: SRF Publishers, 1946.

# 24

## WATTS, A.

# *Selections from In My Own Way: An Auto-Biography, 1915-1965*

We regularly attended meetings of the Buddhist Lodge together, and worked at their meditation sessions. At that time I was practicing the method of holding one's consciousness in the present moment, being—as Krishnamurti puts it—choicelessly aware of what is, or—as Gurdjieff expressed it—in a state of constant self-remembering. This was also in line with George Woodhouse's idea of mind flowing with melody, for if the attention lags or overanticipates, the melody is lost, and it is the same with dancing. It should be the same with the rhythms of life. Do this, and you actually feel yourself one process with the whole energy.

One evening, when Eleanor and I were walking home from a meditation session, I began to discuss the method of concentration on the eternal present. Whereupon she said, "Why try to concentrate on it? What else *is* there to be aware of? Your memories are all in the present, just as much as the trees over there. Your thoughts about the future are also in the present, and anyhow I just love to think about the future. The present is just a constant flow, like the Tao, and there's simply no way of getting out of it." With that remark my whole sense of weight vanished. You could have knocked me down with a feather. I realized that when the Hindus said *Tat tvam asi*, "You ARE That," they meant just what they said. For a whole week thereafter I simply floated, remembering Spiegelberg's telling me of the Six Precepts of Tilopa:

> No thought, no reflection, no analysis,
> No cultivation, no intention,
> Let it settle itself.

This was doubtless a premature *satori*, for I was unable to resist the temptation to write, think, and intellectualize about it. Yet when I am in my right mind I still know that this is the true way of life, at least for me. Conscious thought, reflection, analysis, cultivation, and intention are simply using the mind's radar or scanning beam for purposes which the mind as a whole can do of itself, and on its own, with far more intelligence and less effort.

1 I am assuming that most of my readers have at least some basic information about Zen. For those who do not, it should be said that Zen—or, in Chinese, Ch'an—Buddhism is a school which arose in China between the sixth and eighth centuries, and passed on to Japan in the twelfth. It continues, in its own way, the general practice of Buddhism, which is to free the mind from its habitual confusion of words, ideas, and concepts with reality, and from all those emotional disturbances and entanglements which flow from this confusion. Thus the ego, time, the body, life, and death are all viewed as concepts having neither more nor less reality than abstract numbers or measures, such as inches or ounces. The Zen school holds that this freedom has to be found by an intuitive leap rather than a gradual and cumulative process of learning, although this leap may not be possible until one has tried through long periods of meditation to let the mind settle into calm clarity, silencing the perpetual chatter in the skull. The *koan* are based on anecdotes about the question-and-answer teaching of the old masters, and are problems designed to tease one out of thinking. Zen monks (or, rather, seminarists) were prolific artists, poets, architects, and gardeners, and left a strong mark on Chinese and Japanese culture. Zen training has always been open to both men and women, and is now available at at least six centers in the United States.

Personal prayer simply got in the way of my fundamental mystical feeling that God is what there is and all that there is. It is obviously difficult to feel this if you suppose that the universe is a work of pottery, wherein the Divine Will has given form and order to some gross and basic stuff known as matter. But any such stuff has escaped the detection of scientists as much as spirit, since all scientific descriptions of the world are in terms of form and structure, process and pattern, and never in terms (could they be found) of any primordial, unstructured, inert, and stupid sludge—which would, of course, be something quite other than God. Yet the ghosts of material and spiritual stuffs or substances still haunt our common sense, and these obsolete metaphors from ceramics and metallurgy render it hard to see that there is no such *thing*, no such definable object, as reality. We cannot classify what is common to all possible classes, and yet we know very well that it is there! And it has been obvious to me, for as long as I can remember, that whatever it is, I am that, and whatever I am is also what stars and galaxies, space and energy are.

My whole work in religion and philosophy has been to convey this feeling to others, and to show that our apparent separateness from what there is and all that there is arises, in the main, from our failure to notice space as a vital reality, which is just as important as the negative pole in an electric circuit. Although this feeling has not protected me from a vast amount of folly and confusion, just as it would not restore sight to a blind man, it has nevertheless delivered me from basic, existential anxiety. It is simply that I think people would be much happier and more at home in this world if they felt as I do, that I have no other self than this whole universe. I am not controlling it volitionally any more than I am controlling my autonomic nervous system, and at the same time it is not befalling or happening to any separate me as its observant victim. There is simply the whole process happening of itself, spontaneously, and with every pair of eyes it takes a fresh look at itself. This happening is what I call God, and what it is essentially is beyond all possible conception. I feel it most intensely in a stillness of mind where words and ideas are not running around in my brain.

I am therefore ill at ease with people who earnestly abstain from such things as smoking, drinking, and sex, to the point of making their squeamishness militant. Obviously, there are forms and degrees in which these pleasures can be unhygienic, as also can be driving cars, climbing mountains, and nursing the sick. There are points of view from which almost everything can be seen as bad for one's health, and Jung once remarked in jest that life itself is a disease with a very bad prognosis: it lingers on for years and invariably ends with death. And in this connection I might also quote Freud, writing to Dr. Fleisch: "As to your injunction to give up smoking, I have decided not to comply. Do you think it such a good thing to live a long and miserable life?" So Freud contracted a horrible cancer of the mouth, as did Aldous Huxley, who never smoked at all. I have no wish to defend my "vices" with propaganda, making out that they are in fact virtues which others should follow. I am only saying that I distrust people who show no sign of naughtiness or self-indulgence.

My vocation in life is to wonder about at the nature of the universe. This leads me into philosophy, psychology, religion, and mysticism, not only as subjects to be discussed but also as things to be experienced, and thus I make an at least tacit claim to be a philosopher and a mystic. Some people, therefore, expect me to be their guru or messiah or exemplar, and are extremely disconcerted when they discover my "wayward spirit" or element of irreducible rascality, and say to their friends, "How could he possibly be a *genuine* mystic and be so addicted to nicotine and alcohol?" Or have occasional shudders of anxiety? Or be sexually interested in women? Or lack enthusiasm for physical exercise? Or have any need for money?

Such people have in mind an idealized vision of the mystic as a person wholly free from fear and attachment, who sees within and without, and on all sides, only the translucent forms of a single divine energy which is everlasting love and delight, as which and from which he effortlessly radiates peace, charity, and joy. What an enviable situation! We, too, would like to be one of those, but as we start to meditate and look into ourselves we find mostly a quaking and palpitating mess of anxiety which lusts and loathes, needs love and attention, and lives in terror of death putting an end to its misery. So we despise that mess, and look for ways of controlling it and putting "how the true mystic feels" in its place, not realizing that this ambition is simply one of the lusts of the quaking mess, and that this, in turn, is a natural form of the universe like rain and frost, slugs and snails, flies and disease. When the "true mystic" sees flies and disease as translucent forms of the divine, that does not abolish them. I—making no hard-and-fast distinction between inner and outer experience—see my quaking mess as a form of the divine, and that doesn't abolish it either. But at least I can live with it.

Perhaps all this is a way of saying that I see the same problems in being natural, genuine, or authentic as the saints have found in their efforts to be truly humble, contrite, and in love with God. You can't make it without faking it, for the real thing is a grace not of your own making, which comes upon some people as involuntarily as their lovely eyes or golden hair. It is thus that by grace or nature (take your choice) I am a mystic in spite of myself, remaining as much of an irreducible rascal as I am, as a standing example of God's continuing compassion for sinners or, if you will, of Buddha-nature in a dog, or of light shining in darkness. Come to think of it, in what else could it shine?

These rather self-conscious observations may help to explain the point from which I began: that I find it hard to take myself and my work seriously, even though I am dealing with what are supposed to be the most serious subjects. I am sincere but not serious, and one of my most sincere convictions is that God is not serious. Irreverent and idolatrous as it may be, it is sometimes useful to speak of God anthropomorphically, as a person. I cannot conceive any zealous earnestness or missionary dedication, much less solemnity or pomposity, in the mind of One who has created the hippopotamus, the toucan, the giraffe, and the Brazilian bell-bird. (The latter creature, about the size of a pigeon, puffs itself up into a complete sphere, opens its beak, and returns suddenly to normal shape with a high, penetrating "Dong!") And when I contemplate such ordinary creatures as pigs, chickens, ducks, lazy cats, sparrows, goldfish, and squids,

I begin to have irrepressibly odd notions as to the true shapes of angels.

For this very reason I take an intense dislike to the use of humor, jocosity, or good clean fun as sugar upon some religious pill, because this is a reversal of the true situation. The outward and superficial aspect of religion should rather be ascetic and solemn, to conceal the guffaws in the inner sanctum. My feelings here have been greatly influenced, since my twenties, by the work of Gilbert Keith Chesterton—that Catholic equivalent of Hotei, the "laughing Buddha"—who, though neither a great poet nor a great theologian, had the sort of bewitched imagination from which great poetry and theology can be made. He shone as an essayist and fantast, and of all his many essays the most profound and provoking was "On Nonsense," the peculiarly British kind of nonsense represented by Edward Lear and Lewis Carroll, which is something of a much higher and subtler order than mere twaddle, gibberish, poppycock, or balderdash. So much higher, indeed, that it would take a better literary critic than I to define its precise spirit, for it has in it something waywardly ineffable, which Chesterton invoked to unravel the problem of Job.

That problem is, of course, why the righteous should suffer if God is truly just, and the deeper problem is why Job should have been satisfied with God's answer, given in a long speech at the end of the book. For God's speech is a series of riddles in the course of which he asks Job why it rains on the desert "where no man is," and whether he can bind the influences of the stars or catch a whale with a fishhook. Is it stretching things too much to believe that this is like asking

> Why the sea is boiling hot,
> And whether pigs have wings?

Not if Chesterton was right in feeling, as I do, that if *le rire est le propre de l'homme,* that humor is uniquely human, and that if, furthermore, man is made in God's image, then, as Chesterton suggested, we should not be surprised at the verbal similarity of cosmic and comic. One thinks of *The Divine*

*Comedy* in which Dante likened the song of the angels to the laughter of the universe. Chesterton finished his essay by observing that those who think that faith is nonsense may have the tables turned on them when it comes back in the form that nonsense is faith.

But I part company with Chesterton so long as he must insist, as a Catholic, that man is only a creature of God, for then I cannot imagine God as laughing while children are sprayed with napalm. But what if—and only if—those children are God himself in disguise, incognito, dreaming the most horrible dream imaginable for the convulsive shock of waking up divine? In a time when we can entertain notions of the curvature of space and the paradoxes of quantum theory, might not this constitute a relatively reasonable theory of what life is about? So long as I, too, am God dreaming, and dreaming so well that it all seems vividly real, I am not, however, going to spray children with napalm, for in my half-awake state I suffer from the knowledge that I am those children, and that they feel the "quaking mess" of self-consciousness as strongly as I.

Basically, my own laughter at myself has something to do with the incongruity of such a clown being God in disguise, of the "big act" called Alan Watts being a manifestation of the infinite energy of the universe. For behind the scenes you see all the string, tacks, wire, and masking tape that prop up the show, and as I witness the universe getting away with me I wonder what other uproarious deceptions it will perpetrate. I say this mainly so that you—dear reader—possibly ashamed of your own string and wire, may have the courage to go on with your show.

During this interlude I applied myself to the art of cooking, for in cold weather the kitchen was the only tolerable room in the farmhouse—one of those archaic rural structures whose rooms are severe closetless boxes with small window-frames decaying from much painting. Dorothy and I would pore over recipes and challenge ourselves to increasingly ambitious feats of gourmetism, so that by the time Christmas came we were ready to stage a gastronomic house party which is not to be forgotten, both for the fare and the combination of guests. Why is it that in America a *charcuterie* is hardly to be found? In France every village has at least one shop for the sale of cold meats, and more especially, of sausages, galantines, and *pâtés* in crusts of pastry. Even in England the cold pork pie is to be found in most pubs, and since childhood I have been unable to resist this type of fare. We therefore prepared an ample *pâté de veau en croûte,* a long loaf-shaped pie stuffed with veal, ham, truffles, and pistachio nuts, and encased in glazed pastry lined with small French pancakes. There was also a roast turkey dressed with a parsley forcemeat that I had learned from my mother, with chestnuts added, and before being put into the oven the skin was treated with a mysterious alchemy of spices put together by one of our guests—Luisa, widow of the fabulous Ananda Coomaraswamy.

The party was somehow in his honor. Though I had never met him, I was at that time much under the influence of his writings, for he had exemplified my own vision of the complete man as both mystic and sensualist, and he had gone before me in the work of discussing Christian scholastic theology in a global context which included Hindu, Buddhist, and Islamic metaphysics and iconography, being a religious man who had transcended religions. Yet he was at the same time an antiquarian, art historian, linguist, botanist, lover, and fisherman; so gifted in the latter art that it was said that with one cast of his line into the Atlantic off the coast of Massachusetts he would hook a fish only to be found along the coasts of France. Like my present wife's father, he would fish with unbarbed hooks and give the impression that fish actually wanted him to catch them.

From the beginning, I was never interested in being "good at Zen" in the sense of mastering a traditional discipline, as for example, in studying the piano with Schnabel to the point where my recordings of the Beethoven sonatas would be indistinguishable from his. I had already done that kind of thing, and the point here is not to boast but to explain the real nature of my interest in Zen. For I had, without any formal teacher, unquestionably mastered the art of public speaking, and in the church had become as expert a liturgist as anyone. What I was after was, therefore, not so much discipline as understanding, in the way suggested by the British mathematician G. Spencer Brown in his amazingly mystical treatise, *Laws of Form*:

> To arrive at the simplest truth, as Newton knew and practised, requires *years* of *contemplation*. Not activity. Not reasoning. Not calculating. Not busy behaviour of any kind. Not reading. Not talking. Not making an effort. Not thinking. Simply *bearing in mind* what it is one needs to know. And yet those with the courage to tread this path to real discovery are not only offered practically no guidance on how to do so, they are actively discouraged and have to set about it in secret, pretending meanwhile to be diligently engaged in the frantic diversions and to conform with the deadening personal opinions which are being continually thrust upon them.[2]

And, so far as I was concerned, the formal study of Zen was "busy behaviour." To sit hour after hour and day after day with aching legs, to unravel Hakuin's tricky system of dealing with *koan,* to subsist on tea, pickles, and brown rice, or to master Dogen's ritual style of life was—although as good in its own way as learning to sail—not what I needed to know.

What I saw in Zen was an intuitive way of understanding the sense of life by getting rid of silly quests and questions. The archetypal situation was when Hui-k'e asked Bodhidharma how to attain peace of mind. Bodhidharma said, "Bring your mind out, and I will pacify it." "But when I look for it," said Hui-k'e,

2 G. Spencer Brown, *Laws of Form* (London: George Allen & Unwin, 1969), p. 110.

"I can't find it." "In that case," the master concluded, "it's pacified already." Wittgenstein put it this way:

> We feel that even if *all possible* scientific questions be answered, the problems of life have still not been touched at all. Of course there is then no question left, and just this is the answer. The solution of the problem of life is seen in the vanishing of this problem. (Is not this the reason why men to whom after long doubting the sense of life became clear, could not then say wherein this sense consisted?)[3]

It is thus that almost every morning, when I first awaken, I have a feeling of total clarity as to the sense of life, a feeling of myself and the universe as a matter of the utmost simplicity. "I" and "That which is" are the same. Always have been and always will be. I could say that what constitutes me is the same jazz that constitutes the cosmos, and that there is simply nothing special to be achieved, realized, or performed. And so also Emerson, in his essay on "Self-Reliance":

> These roses under my window make no reference to former roses or to better ones; they are for what they are; they exist with God today. There is no time for them. There is simply the rose; it is perfect in every moment of its existence. . . . But man postpones or remembers; he does not live in the present, but with reverted eye laments the past, or, heedless of the riches that surround him, stands on tiptoe to foresee the future. He cannot be happy and strong until he too lives with nature in the present, above time.

Sokei-an Sasaki told me that reading this passage touched off his first experience of *satori*. The point made sounds negative or nihilistic only because the words are saying, as they must say of being in love or of sexual ecstasy, that they are speechless. One could say it with music, but this is expressive, not descriptive, and the trouble with industrially civilized people is that they have no gift for spontaneous music. Our music is so counted out, scaled, metered, and trickily calculated that no one but an ex-

3 *Tractatus Logico-Philosophicus* (New York: Humanities Press, 1961) 6:52, 6:521.

pert may have the nerve to indulge in it lest he be accused of making a nasty noise. But we would understand the sense of life if we would sing more and say less.

I have for years been trying to show people that it is extremely important to chant spontaneously, or at least to hum, and also to dance. I have offended people who, on attending seminars to hear an internationally famous philosopher, were simply encouraged to breathe effortlessly and allow their voices to hum along a line of least resistance, like water. I have dismayed dancing partners because I would not go

> One, two, one, two, three and four,
> Over to the window and back to the door—

but would instead use liquid and unpremeditated rhythms which my daughter Ann can follow as if she were my shadow. Chanting, flute or drum playing, and dancing in demilitarized patterns are ideally natural forms of yoga-meditation, because they silence the hypnotic chattering of thought and give one a direct feeling of *shabda*—the basic energy or vibration of the universe. This is why Gregorian chant, for example, gives the sense of eternity so absent from metered hymns.

# 25

CLARK, W. H.

# *Selections from Religious Experience: Its Nature and Function in the Human Psyche*

## Psychedelic Drugs

In the early years of the 1960's, certain religious scholars began to be aware of a superlative instrument for the study of religious experience. This was the psychedelic or "mind-revealing" drugs. They are mind revealing in the sense that people who ingest them nearly always become aware of capacities they did not know they possessed, the most surprising being their mystical potentialities. I have written about this subject in my *Chemical Ecstasy* (1969). Some self-styled experts have labeled the religious effects of the drugs illusory, a kind of religious fake. I have carefully and critically studied the subject for 10 years through firsthand investigation and self-experimentation and have come to the conclusion that if this is fake religion, then the fake is frequently better than the real thing. There are many well-attested cases on record of dramatic, lasting conversions and religious growth of a profound nature following use of LSD-type drugs.

The study of the religious agency of the drugs, at least in America, was initiated chiefly by Dr. Timothy Leary at Harvard, who gave psilocybin to convicts. Most of these volunteers reported intense religious experiences. I have carefully followed up some of them and can substantiate Leary's contentions. One of Massachusetts' most dangerous criminals had a vision of Christ which, since that moment in 1962, has completely kept him from crime.

I have just completed a survey of 100 users of LSD-type drugs, randomly selected and many of them hippies, and 20 users of *Cannabis* drugs. All reported at least some of the elements of profound religious experience, though not all of these users could be said to have had the well integrated and clearly formed religious experience of the majority. Of the users of LSD-type drugs, 76 per cent reported experience of the Holy, 61 per cent to an intense degree; 78 per cent reported psychological rebirth; while 32 per cent reported that their experience of God had been "beyond anything ever experienced or even imagined." Only one wished he had not taken the drugs, while 77 per cent reported the significance of their experience as intense, and half of the sample rated its significance as "beyond anything ever experienced or imagined." A teaching fellow at the State University of New York stated that since his experience, he has found a greatly increased sensitivity to religious values with particular openness to the wisdom of the mystics.

Responses such as these help us to understand certain very resistant aspects of the counterculture and "the green rebellion" along with the commune movement (cf. Hedgepeth and Stock, 1970 and Houriet, 1971).

But to return to the value of the drugs to the study of religious experience, let me say something of what is the most rigorously controlled and clearest in its conclusions of all experiments with religious experience with which I am familiar. Dr. Walter N. Pahnke, in a doctoral study done at Harvard, 1964) gave 10 theological students psilocybin under double-blind conditions with another 10 receiving a placebo and then sent all 20 to a Good Friday service. Nine of the 10 experimental subjects reported some of the characteristics of mystical experience, while only one of the control group did so. The results were statistically significant to a very high degree at the .001 level of confidence (cf. Clark, 1969, pp. 77-80).

In various investigations, I have confirmed Pahnke's results. I have increased the depth of my understanding of religion, whether released by the psychedelics or otherwise, through interviews and the study of religious documents produced by users (cf. Huxley, 1963 and Metzner, 1968). Such studies have persuaded me that at the very least, the conservative statement is justified as follows: *In some situations and with some people, and especially when both subject and guide intend it, the psychedelic drugs release very profound religious experience of a mystical nature.*

## MYSTICISM

I now turn to what is probably the most captivating and transforming experience of which human nature is capable. I am referring to mystical experience. We cannot precisely separate mysticism from conversion, for mysticism tends to be equally sudden. And it reaches down to an even deeper layer of the soul. Furthermore, most mystical experiences mark a conversion involving perceptions that lead to a radical change of values. As I have continued my studies in the psychology of religion through the years, more and more I have shifted my earlier interest and belief in conversion to a more recent concern with mysticism because I have come to realize its richer possibilities. It represents a riper and more penetrating form of spiritual awakening and growth.

I have no illusions about there being anything very original in my stand. William James gave his opinion that mysticism is the "root and center" of personal religion (1958, p. 292). Evelyn Underhill, a mystic herself, has written several scholarly volumes on the subject, while Princeton's late professor of Philosophy, W. T. Stace, has been only the most distinguished recent American scholar to treat the subject systematically with an enlightening and thoroughly scholarly rigor.

There has always been a strong and healthy tradition of mysticism within Christianity, stemming originally from neo-Platonism and particularly marked in the Medieval church. It is probably the mystical element which, more than any other single feature, explains the amazing and perennial vigor of Catholic Christianity. But it has always had to contend with the even stronger tradition of rationalism, in all branches of Christianity, to which I have already referred in my first lecture. This has led to its neglect, which helps to explain the thinness, blandness, and harmlessness of much that passes for Christianity in many of our churches.

There is a sense in which, as we approach these areas of conversion and mysticism, the student on such sacred ground may be felt to be an intruder. For those who experience religious ecstasy are not in the slightest degree interested in an analysis of the process they are undergoing. If they were it would only be as an interference and a hindrance. The initiative does not seem to come from within themselves but from God, or some source far beyond themselves. Like Paul confronted by Jesus on the Damascus road, or Francis Thompson, as he so beautifully described his pilgrimage in "The Hound of Heaven" (Manly 1926), the convert may feel relentlessly though lovingly pursued by an awesome power greater than himself. To study such experiences may appear almost blasphemous. To attempt to analyze them with rational tools may seem like trying to study the beauty of a snowflake armed with a blowtorch and iron tongs. We may be skirting perilously the borders of reductionism, about which I have already warned you.

However, if the reason and rationality is to have any place in directing the religious life, we must have knowledge to help guide us. If I thought it blasphemous to study religious experience I would not be talking about the subject. My intent is to approach my subject with as much knowledge and intelligence as I can muster at the same time that I must acknowledge that the roots of these experiences reach far beyond my sight in the infinite depths and recesses of the holy. In dealing with mysticism I will simply try to describe the experience so that it can be recognized, even though never completely understood, within yourselves or in other people, and then say something of conditions that favor its appearance.

## MYSTICISM: ITS PHENOMENA

One of the characteristics of mysticism, universally recognized, is the difficulty one has in describing it. For this reason most people look on it as foggy, dubious, and even esoteric. This presents any scholar who wishes to describe it with a dilemma. He is asked to describe the indescribable, to utter the unutterable. Great Eastern mystics have been known to recommend total silence on the subject. But Western scholars have nevertheless attacked the subject in characteristic Western fashion. Probably the most successful and incisive of these has been W. T. Stace in his *Mysticism and Philosophy* (1960). Much of my description is dependent on him.

To prepare for his analysis, Stace studied the literature of mysticism in all ages and all faiths. From this he abstracted seven characteristics which appeared over and over again in widely scattered and largely unrelated sources. These seven characteristics he called "the universal core" of mysticism. They appeared in accounts given by Christians, Hasidic Jews, Mohammedan Sufis, Hindus, Buddhists, and Taoists. It would seem that the capacity for mysticism is a natural gift of God, possessed probably by all men though, as with other gifts, not in equal abundance in all.

The first and probably the most essential of Stace's characteristics is the experience of unity, in which all sense impressions and specific awareness of the sensible world drops away and the mystic feels himself to have encountered what may be variously described as "the Void," "the boundless Sea," "the white light," or simply "Infinity." In a well-known couplet the English mystic Henry Vaughan wrote:

I saw Eternity the other night
Like a great Ring of pure and endless light

The effect of such experiences is to give the mystic a feeling of his identity with all things. Consequently he knows that every man is his brother; he experiences directly the feelings that he and his enemy are one and so becomes capable of loving him. It is out of such knowledge that the often noted compassion of the mystic springs. It is significant that it was a mystic who wrote the lines, "Never send to enquire for whom the bell tolls; it tolls for thee."

Derived from the experience of unity comes the next characteristic, the experience of timelessness and spacelessness. Our sense of time comes from the perception of a series of images or events, while space derives from a sense of self set amongst the perception of objects and images surrounding one. Consequently the sense of time and space are closely intertwined. When the conception of these images melt into an undifferentiated oneness, it follows that any perceptions dependent on them will fall away also. It is in such a way that not the reasoned concept of time and space but the immediate experience of them will melt away. It was after a mystical event that solved his problems and taught him compassion for his neighbor that Thomas Carlyle, in his fine spiritual autobiography *Sartor Resartus* declared:

> On the roaring billows of Time, thou art not engulfed, but borne aloft into the azure of Eternity. Love not pleasure; love God (1896, 174-175).

To the nonmystic this last quotation may seem a dark saying, but it leads us to Stace's third characteristic. It is the sense of having been in touch with some sort of objectivity or ultimate reality. In Christianity the name for this reality is God, and the Christian mystics have nearly always identified this reality as the Father, or one of the other members of the Trinity, or the Trinity itself, as with Saint Teresa of Avila on one occasion. It is such a reality that gives meaning to life and along with this a fortitude, strength, and courage that to those standing by are sources of amazement. Such steadfastness on the part of Stephen helped to convert Paul; the spectacle of Christian martyrs meeting death in the forum with singing were seeds of the early Church; while the sight of heretics being burned alive to the glory of God by the Inquisition in later days touched the minds of many and helped bring about the Reformation.

The effects of these encounters with unity and reality are also such as to leave the mystic with feelings of blessedness, joy, and peace – the fourth characteristic. "The peace of God which passes all understanding" is a phrase all of us have heard at the end of a religious service and have been impressed with its beauty, though few of us have ever ascribed it to a mystic. Also this characteristic will help us better to understand the many references to joy in the Bible, a characteristic of religion that many of our churches seem to have forgotten.

Closely associated with all of the foregoing characteristics is Stace's fifth category of the feeling of holiness, the sacred, or the divine. Otto would round out this feeling with allusions to the terror and awe often associated with the presence of the divine, as when the Lord approached Abram, who felt himself overcome by "an horror of great darkness" (Genesis 15:12), or the statement of the writer of Hebrews to the effect that "it is a fearful thing to fall into the hands of the living God" (Hebrews 10:31). More than any of the other categories this is the most specifically religious.

A further characteristic is the claim by the mystics that their experiences are unutterable or ineffable. They have often likened their dilemma to that of one trying to describe the experience of sight to a race born blind. The stuttering attempts of the sighted to convince his hearers that there really does exist a sense transcending those that they have would only mark him as peculiar and queer, a laughing stock to the uncomprehending ones. He would either give up the attempt and remain silent, or with a frustrated eloquence vainly reiterate the perceptions so wonderfully vouchsafed to him whose eyes had been illumined. The latter is the lot of many mystics who cannot help believing that God wishes to illumine with his Presence all those to whom He has granted human life.

The fact that there is no literal way adequately to convey to a nonmystic the essence of the mystical consciousness requires that the mystic use riddles, figures of speech, and other out-of-the-way means to suggest his meaning. Thus the mystics become the poets and artists of the religious life. To convey the beauty of the sunset to him who has been born blind, one might liken it to the effect of a symphony. The imaginative blindman would get the point even though he could never experience directly the sight of the sunset itself. Thus the value of the simile.

The most common figure of speech or riddle through which the mystics attempt to resolve their frustration is paradox – and this is the last of Stace's seven characteristics of mysticism. Logically inconsistent, paradox, nevertheless, often conveys more perceptively and movingly than everyday speech the essence of the experience toward which it points. Thus if the mystic refers to his perception as "the Void," he may also describe it as a "full void." In the literature of mysticism we find very common such expressions as "dazzling darkness," "teeming desert," "wayless path," or "dark silence."

It will be instructive here to contrast the method of the

theologian and that of the mystic to convey the meaning of the word "God." The theologian might present a list of adjectives, such as "omnipotent, omniscient, just, merciful, loving, etc." But listen to a mystic's attempt to convey his immediate perception of God. The words are those of Jan Van Ruysbroeck, a Medieval Dutch brother:

> The abysmal waylessness of God is so dark and so unconditioned that it swallows up within itself every Divine way and activity, and all the attributes of the persons within the essential unity . . . .This is the dark silence in which all lovers lose themselves. But if we would prepare ourselves for it . . . we should strip ourselves of all but our very bodies, and we should flee forth into the wild sea, whence no created thing can draw us back again (cf Stace, 1960, p. 97).

Both the method of the theologian and the mystic have their own value, but any of you who to any degree found yourselves moved by the poetic beauty of the Ruysbroeck passage can know that this testifies to the mystic sleeping deeply within yourselves and that in essence you too are mystics.

I have not the time to review the analyses of mysticism listed by two other keen students of the mystical life, namely William James and Evelyn Underhill, though I will mention one or two of their points in passing. James refers to the transiency of the mystical state. Though Gautama averred that an achievement of perpetual Nirvana, the Buddhist name for the mystical consciousness, was possible, and certain Eastern mystics have claimed they have attained it, it seems extremely unlikely that a constant high level of spiritual bliss could be attained in this life. Though the essence of the state may be a perception, nevertheless the resulting emotion attendant on the attainment of a state of consciousness so different, delightful, and new could hardly be expected to last indefinitely without fluctuation. Furthermore the demands of everyday life, at the very least of clothing and housing and feeding oneself would be apt to interrupt the state of vision. Practically speaking, I think we can expect these states normally not to exceed more than two hours at most, while a half hour or less would seem more usual. However, the aura of the experience may last for many days, and its influence for a lifetime.

On another point James and Underhill are at odds. James

mentions passivity as a characteristic of the mystical state while Underhill marks the fact that "true mysticism is active and practical" (1955, p. 81 ff.). Doubtless the difference can be resolved if we separate the state of mind during ecstasy, which must be totally accepting and, as Underhill states herself, "an act of surrender," from the attitude afterward. Many mystics, like Teresa of Avila, have lived confused and ineffective lives before their visions, while afterward their lives have become marvels of practical activity. It is true that there is the danger of what the Catholic Church has branded "quietism," when the attainment of ecstasy may become a form of self-indulgence with few constructive results. But more often the state will mark a person's coming to himself and achieving what Erik Erikson might call his essential "identity."

## MYSTICISM: ITS TRIGGERS

To ask the question "What causes mysticism?" would involve us in theological and metaphysical issues far beyond my scope as a psychologist. The religious mystic sees the cause of his moving experience as God, and nothing that the psychologist will say can controvert this perception and commitment of faith. I will simply point out conditions which seem to favor the mystical state. Perhaps we can best talk of these conditions as "triggers" which set off a chain of internal events physiological and neurological in character to heighten perceptivity and so make ready sensitivity to respond to these conditions. What then are some of these triggers?

But before we turn to the subject of triggers let me call your attention to what Stace calls "The Principle of Causal Indifference" (1960, pp. 29-31). Stace refers to what I have called "triggers" as "causes" of mystical experience. We are both referring to what I think we would both agree are favoring circumstances. There is a tendency for some people to hold that if the trigger is trivial, artificial, or contrived, then the resulting experience cannot be "genuine," whatever that may mean. Stace's principle states that no matter what the trigger, if the phenomena fits the definition of mysticism it is just as "genuine" as any other mystical experience. My experience in the use of drugs to evoke religious experience causes me to agree.

One of the best discussions of triggers for mystical experience is to be found in Marghanita Laski's *Ecstasy* (1962, pp. 176-277). Not all of the cases of ecstasy reviewed in her excellent study are religious, but many are, and her general comments refer to both types. Her discussion will illustrate most of my following generalizations. A further feature of the Laski study is that she points out what she calls "anti-triggers," the sights and symbols of mundane, crass, and practical living that tend to "turn off" ecstasy.

Probably one thing that prepares a person for a mystical experience is to know that there is such a thing. The purpose of much religious liturgy is to suggest it, from the rich Catholic Mass to the simple Quaker silence. In this way the reading of scripture can be a general trigger as well as spiritual biography and even the hearing of a lecture such as this, as I hope it may in many of you. I have known of several people who have reported that ecstasy was preceded by the reading of the sympathetic pages of William James' *Varieties of Religious Experience* (1958). It is also a favorable condition for a potential mystic to know that mysticism is approved of. Otherwise these holy impulses will be mistaken for oddity or even signs of oncoming mental illness. In such cases they will be repressed and spiritual growth hindered.

Typical triggers are found in abundance in the world of nature, as mystical poets so often remind us. William Blake wrote:

> To see the world in a grain of sand
> And a heaven in a wild flower
> To hold Infinity in the palm of your hand
> Eternity in an hour (Yeats, no dat, p. 90).

Clouds, sky, violent storms, green grass, and tender flowers may initiate impulses or, as Shakespeare put it,

> . . . antres vast and deserts idle
> Rough quaries, rocks, and hills whose heads touch heaven (1879, p. 51).

A trigger related to some of the foregoing is sensory deprivation. Agnostic psychologists who have confined subjects in dark, silent rooms to see what would happen have been surprised, not to say even frightened, when some have reported religious visions and experiences. This throws light on the preference of some ecstatics for the "antres vast" (dark caves), silence, or other monotonous surroundings like the desert, the wilderness, or the vast wastes of the sea. Moses met Jehovah in the burning bush on the wild slopes of Horeb, while St. Anthony came to his spiritual majority in his encounter with visions in the depths of a cave. This is one of the purposes of the Gregorian chant or plainsong, otherwise a stumbling block to the literal-minded.

Another is the attitude of complete surrender, the willingness to accept whatever may come in utter passivity and open-mindedness. "Here am I," said Isaiah following his vision, "Send me" (Isaiah 6:8). Often the mystical state is completely unintended and accompanies a period of exhaustion or enforced relaxation following an illness, as with St. Francis and St. Ignatius of Loyola. This may help to explain why mystical experience sometimes follows childbirth or other trauma. Exhaustion is sometimes brought on deliberately for religious purposes not just in previous times or in primitive religious ceremonies but contemporaneously among the Penitente sects in the southwest and Mexico, the snake-handling sects of the southern back-country, or the marathon worship in some Pentecostal services (cf. Sargant, 1961, Chapters 5-8). Exhaustion makes possible complete relaxation and willingness to accept whatever experience comes without fighting it or trying to control it. Thus perfect surrender might be called one of God's hand maidens.

A final trigger is biochemical change within the body. Doubtless some people probably are more susceptible to mysticism due to their physiological makeup, just as others are conditioned by their makeup to be poets or musicians. Others deliberately manipulate biochemical changes by fasting or the use of a special diet, like the macrobiotic. Still others, more directly, either inject or ingest certain drugs, the most popular currently being the psychedelics. At this point Stace's Principle of Causal Indifference is helpful to us in calming the stormy sea of controversy surrounding this troublesome area. Dr. Walter N. Pahnke, in a Harvard experiment carried out on Good Friday with Christian theological students as subjects, mentioned in my first lecture, clearly showed that psilocybin greatly enhanced the phenomena of mysticism in a favorable environment. I have confirmed this in my own experiments (cf. Clark, 1969, p. 77). Breathing exercises, chanting, incense, in part are means of biochemical intervention, whether realized or not, while inadevertent changes in diet, fasting, or other unconscious production of bodily change may release the mystical. However, the conscious aiming at religious experience seems always to make it more likely though not inevitable.

The foregoing discussion of the triggers of mystical experience, of course, must be considered as the merest of introductions to what is a wide, complicated, fascinating and important field both for the theoretical and practical understanding of the religious life.

## THE MODERN COUNTERCULTURE

Despite the dubiousness and dangers of the drug culture, I have been particular in referring to the psychedelic drugs (to be distinguished from other varieties of drugs), since I believe we can learn much by studying their effects carefully and critically. They are certainly an important element in the religious movement among our youth, which I see as the most dynamic expression of religion of our times. In their rebellion against the established traditions of middle-class America, many youth have gone far beyond the churches in their pursuit not only of the mystical values of the East but also of these same values embedded in the mystical traditions of the West, and probably, as I believe, in all of human nature. It is on this probability, and on this probability alone, that we can rest any hope there is of building a new and harmonious world. From such a vantage point, religious experience takes on an importance far beyond that of a mere academic or religious exercise.

Yet the hippies in their "green rebellion" would seem a slender reed on which to base any hope for a better world. Youth in revolt against their elders are too ready to reject tradition and the wisdom of the ages. Drug-using communes like the Manson family would seem like the very reverse of that on which any kind of stable base could be founded, unless it were a demonic one. Perhaps one thing that has to be said about the counterculture and the hippie movement is that it is often confused.

This, it must be admitted, is one of the shortcomings of the contemporary cult of youth. Many of the hippies *are* confused, if for no other reason than the fact that in their rejection of reason and the social structures of their parents, they tend to reject that part of the collaborative team of the rational and the nonrational that supplies guidance, structure, and criticism. But on the other hand, they tend to supply that vitality, power, and energy that radically can change human nature.

How can we say that this is so? Their human nature does not seem to be changed but only bent on what they themselves celebrate as "tuning in, turning on, and dropping out." Almost as by common consent, we of the older generation brand this sort of thing as escape. The use of drugs seems only to underline this interpretation. There is no doubt that one can select examples that will support this case.

But one can also support the case for the exact opposite – that these young people have somehow sensed deeply within themselves a basic hunger for that which will make some sense of their lives. This hunger goes much deeper and is more pervasive than the desire for drugs, which most come to realize are not ends in themselves but simply one means to awaken in some persons a perception of a larger world. Many youth are either not interested in the drugs or have gone beyond them to other methods of achieving the same thing. The interest in meditation, in Zen, in other Eastern forms of religious disciplines, in new experimental forms of Christian worship tinged with encounter methodology along with ecstatic celebration symbolized by the appearance of the guitar and the talk of love – all point to these deeper, mystical forms of religion of which I have been speaking. In Judaism we are hearing more of Hasidism, while some young people are even reviving interest in Sufism, the Muslim mystical tradition.

Along with these activities, some of them faddish and superficial but others deeply sincere, there go the radical changes of values that so often is seen in the mystics. For long years many of us have gone to church and been told to lay not up treasures on earth where moth doth corrupt and thieves break through and steal. Our ready assent to such pious sentiments, nevertheless, hardly ever carry over into any kind of effective action. The reaction that most of us have to treasure upon earth is that we are not enabled to lay up half enough of it. It is the hippies and the Zen enthusiasts who, after an overwhelming encounter with what they themselves will identify as beauty, ultimate reality, or the Holy, will reject the crass, materialistic values of middle-class culture. Forsaking all, many of them, even if not point by point following scriptural instruction, have in effect come too close to the spirit of Christ's teaching for their parents to feel quite comfortable about it.

But there is no doubt that for many of our youth, their religious experiences have marked a sharp and visible break with the kind of lives in which they have grown up. This has come largely from their change in values perceived through mysticism, however achieved. Success, competition, college degrees, getting ahead, acquiring the status symbols of prosperity – all of these things have taken a lower rank in their scale of values. The bizzarrely festive clothing of the hippies are largely messages to their middle-class parents that they have discarded the old values of neatly trimmed respectability. Through the smoking of marijuana or the use of stronger psychedelics they have been introduced to experiences of beauty and religious depth which they may not know what to do with but which they feel their parents would never understand. This is the explanation of many runaways and the reason why there are hundreds of communes or extended family groups to be found in city and country throughout the land. (For an account of representative communes, see reference to Hedgepeth, Stock, and to Houriet in the first lecture.)

It is in these communes that one can see most visibly the changes in behavior that have been brought about through modern religious experience. You must not get the idea from my references to drugs that these communes are all devoted to continuing drug use. Many have given it up and forbid the use of drugs within the community. But the great majority of residents have at least tried the drugs and have found an opening to vast reaches of inner space and the beginning of a spiritual quest that will take many of them far beyond the drugs. As one "graduate" of drug use put it, the drugs supply a door to a new life but not a room to live in. This generalization, however, might be applied to nearly all forms of religious experience.

Many of these communities have collapsed when faced with some of the realities of self support and the maintenance of personal relations. The life with like-minded idealists that in summer weather seemed so attractive may lose its appeal under winter's blasts when living together harmoniously becomes an achievement rather than a pleasant holiday. Also, neighbors and the police have often proved inhospitable, particularly when the commune has not developed some sense of responsibility for those around them, as indeed some of the more stable communities have done. Those that have survived have learned that they could not do without a modicum of the organization they despised in "the Establishment," while rejected middle-class cleanliness is found a necessity if communities are to avoid crippling illnesses and epidemics. In other words, just as ecstasy requires the structure supplied to it by the rational, so does the transcendental community require the support of organization and hard work if the communes are to become the monastic movement of the twentieth century, as has been suggested.

But the point I am making is that for many youth there has been a radical break with their past lives and their families that has been far from a fad with all of them. Their religious experiences have given them some taste of that sympathy and warmth of fellowship that we call love, and they have set out whether with their friends or with the strangers within their gates, to meditate, to experiment, and to find those spiritual exercises that will lead them toward a more significant existence than they have observed among their elders.

The rise of this counterculture raises many questions but none of more importance to the churches than what its final disposition is to be religiously. To the extent that it is only a passing fad, it can be dismissed, like the flowers with which the hippies adorn their hats, as a phenomenon that is here today and gone tomorrow. On the other hand, there are many who, like Timothy Leary, are ready to be harrassed and imprisoned rather than to renounce what to them are the means through which they approach God. Leary's former colleague, Richard Alpert, now called Baba Ram Dass and graduated from drug use, has joined a

Hindu spiritual community on the slopes of the Himalyas in India and has a sizable following in this country. Such people constitute the hard core of this modern monasticism, and any movement with a hard core capable of such devotion is bound to have an impact. I have attended a service led by Baba Ram Dass at a Unitarian church in Boston with pews filled and young people crowded on the floors. Alternatively, they listened attentively to remarks of religious wisdom and to songs accompanied by the sitar, then chanted, then meditated in perfect silence. It is this kind of religious dynamic which the churches can ill afford to lose.

It cannot be said that expressions of youth's interest in religious experience have had no influence on the churches, but in general a youth's visit to his church or synagogue will impress on him more sharply what he has already sensed as the generation gap. For the most part, however, the type that will hear Ram Dass or Timothy Leary will not otherwise bother even to step inside the churches. Yet these youth have nearly as much need of the church as the church has need of them with their hunger for celebration and their acquaintance with the nonrational. The Roman Catholic Bishop Cletus O'Donnell of Madison, Wisconsin, commenting on the gap between younger and older members of the Church, observed, "It is certainly curious that many young people are searching out the mystical and the sacred and do not find it in their churches" (1970). It is probable that many who run the churches have either never known profound religious experience or, if they have, have forgotten it.

Let me try to put what I have said in perspective by telling you the story of a runaway Italian kid named Frank. Perhaps I might preface the story by asking you what the average American small village would think of a visit from Jesus and his twelve disciples. Would they be arrested as vagrants or just invited to leave town?

I read the story of Frank in a psychiatric publication in an account of hippies in San Francisco (Allen and West, 1968, p. 369).

> Frank was a real cool guy – he grooved on trees, on birds, and on people. But his parents were worried and embarrassed. They had worked hard and now had a good life, and here Frank was running around with a bunch of dropouts. He didn't bathe too often, he went

barefoot, he even panhandled for food.

Finally Frank was discovered breaking into his father's warehouse and giving things out free – the first Digger store. His old man took him to court. In a fit of pique, Frank stripped off his clothes, threw them at his father's feet, and stomped out of the courtroom, stark naked. Well, Frank didn't run away to Haight-Ashbury, for there was no San Francisco then, but he has become a patron saint to the hippies . . . .

For that is the story of the person *after whom* San Francisco was named!

SECTION VII

# DREAMS AND SLEEP

# 26

**RECHTSCHAFFEN, A.**

## *The Psychophysiology of Mental Activity During Sleep*

Why might sleep research have some special contribution to make to the psychophysiology of thinking?

1. Sleep studies permit examination of the generality of psychophysiological relationships determined during wakefulness. Do the relationships of wakefulness reflect necessary links between physiological measures and

Preparation of this paper was supported by Grants M-4151 and K5-MH-18,428 from the National Institute of Mental Health, U.S. Public Health Service, and Grant 148-13-RD from the Department of Mental Health, State of Illinois.

the kinds of responses which are generally taken to reflect mental activity? If they do, we would expect the relationships to obtain during sleep as well. If, on the other hand, the relationships of wakefulness reflect only one specific kind of psychophysiological organization rather than necessary causal or isomorphic relationships, then we would not necessarily expect to find the same psychophysiological relationships during sleep.

2. Any search for correlations is enhanced by variability in the parameters studied. Although there are exceptions, notably in autonomic measures such as heart and respiratory rates, there is generally greater physiological and psychological variability during sleep than during wakefulness. For example, the EEG of wakefulness is fairly uniform in amplitude and fluctuates mostly between alpha and low voltage fast activity. The EEG of sleep, by contrast, can range from less than 10 $\mu$V to over 200 $\mu$V, and from less than .5 Hz to over 25 Hz. Between these limits there is a rich display of distinctive waveforms during sleep, such as 2–3 Hz "sawtooth" waves, 4–6 Hz "theta" activity, biparietal humps, K-complexes, and 12–14 Hz sleep spindles. During wakefulness the eyes move intermittently throughout the day, depending on the task at hand. During sleep there are well-defined long periods with little or no rapid eye movement and well-defined periods with a wealth of eye movement activity.

The enhanced variability of mental activity during sleep is even more apparent. Certainly wakefulness has its ups and downs—its more emotional moments and its less emotional moments—its more attentive moments and its less attentive moments. On most days, however, there is a fairly stable level of consciousness with few or no extended periods that we would describe either as completely blank or fantastically stimulating and exciting. By contrast, during each night of sleep we fluctuate many times between apparent mental voids and a sort of low-keyed mental idling on the one hand, and the vivid, highly emotional, absorbing material of vivid dreams on the other. Thus sleep provides the pronounced variability of physiological and psychological activity that should be opportune for revealing correlations between the two.

3. Sleep permits evaluation of psychological–physiological correlations under conditions of reduced responsivity to external stimuli. Where the focus of study is on the "spontaneous" covariation of psychological and physiological parameters, the lower responsivity of sleep aids the cause by reducing the error variance contributed by nonexperimental stimuli. Where the focus of interest is a comparison of physiological and psychological responses to given stimuli, then sleep studies suffer from the limited range and intensity of stimuli that can be introduced.

4. Finally, as with any new area of investigation, the study of sleep permits the discovery of new relationships and phenomena which could not have been anticipated from studies of wakefulness. It has been almost 20 years since Aserinsky and Kleitman (1953) first reported on the eye movement–dreaming relationship that started the boom in psychophysiological sleep research; it may be mostly verbal habit that still makes us refer to this sleep research as a new area. Nevertheless, the past two decades have provided a flow of stimulating discoveries that were not anticipated by the psychophysiology of wakefulness.

This paper will review research on relationships between physiological and psychological measures during sleep to see how well the potentials listed above have been realized. Reliance will be placed on reports elicited on awakenings as the indicators of mental activity during sleep. Several variables other than sleep mentation can influence waking reports including verbal style, memory, and alertness upon awakening. But the verbal report is probably the best available indicator of sleep mentation so researchers stay with it and try to hold the nonexperiential factors which influence reports relatively stable with respect to the physiological measures. Even with an attempt to achieve this kind of control, correlations between a report and a physiological variable could result from a relationship of the physiological variable to the *recall* process rather than to the sleep mentation. Therefore, the terms "recall" or "sleep mentation" in this review, strictly speaking, refer to the verbal production. In spite of all controls, there is always a residue of uncertainty about how much of verbal production was determined by sleep mentation. For example, some studies aim at the physiological correlates of how much mental activity there was during sleep. But we cannot be certain whether the amount reported reveals the amount of mental activity that was present or the amount that could be remembered. The problem of using awakening reports as indicators of sleep mentation has been reviewed in greater detail in another paper (Rechtschaffen, 1967).

## I. DESCRIPTION OF THE STAGES OF SLEEP

As a subject passes from wakefulness to sleep, there is a gradual slowing of EEG activity. The waking EEG, be it alpha or low voltage–fast activity, gradually subsides and is replaced by a relatively low voltage, mixed frequency pattern with increased activity in the 2–7 Hz band. This pattern is called Stage 1. After 5–10 min of Stage 1, bursts of 12–14 Hz sinusoidal waves called sleep spindles and isolated higher voltage biphasic waves called K-complexes appear and define the presence of Stage 2. After varying amounts of Stage 2, high voltage, slow "delta waves" signal the appearance of Stage 3. This delta activity increases gradually so that it dominates the record, which is then called Stage 4. Stages 1–4 collectively are called NREM, or *no* rapid eye movement sleep, because it was once believed that there were no rapid eye movements during these periods. Recently, more refined recording techniques have revealed the intermittent occurrence of small rapid eye movements during NREM sleep, and more will be said about that later. For the moment we need note only that these eye movements are much less plentiful than in the now well-known REM, or rapid eye movement periods of sleep. Sometime during the second hour of sleep, large amplitude eye movements occur episodically during periods when EEG activity is very similar to the Stage 1 observed at sleep onset. These REM periods may last from a few minutes to over a half-hour. They reappear at about 90-min intervals during sleep so that typically there are about four REM periods a night, comprising altogether about one-fourth of total sleep.

The EEG stages of sleep and their associated eye movement patterns are shown in Fig. 5.1. These stages should not be construed to represent a

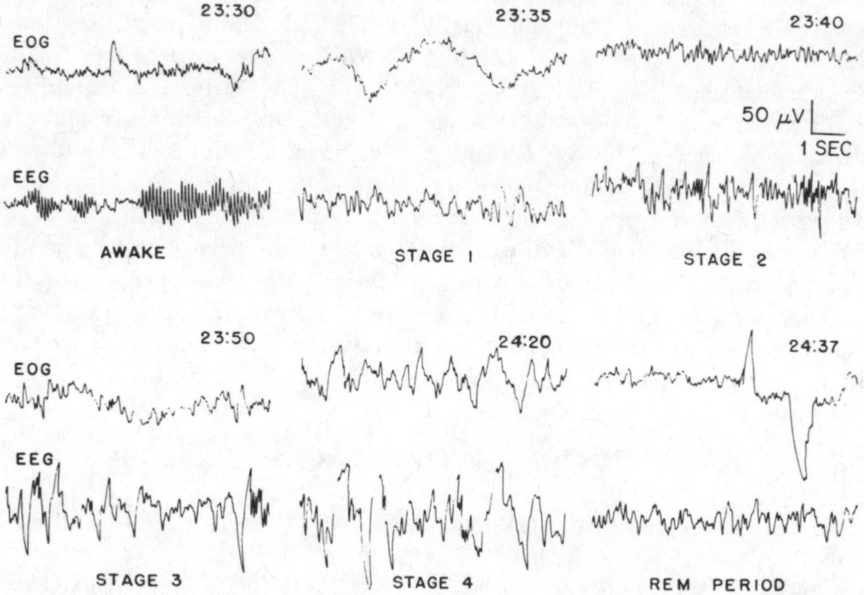


**Fig. 5.1.** Illustration of the eye movement (EOG) and EEG patterns in the different stages of sleep. The potentials in the EOG tracings of Stages 2, 3, and 4 represent EEG activity in prefrontal areas rather than eye movements.

continuum of light to deep in the general sense that the brain, body, or nervous system is more active in one stage than another—as common sense or our wish for order might dictate. Rather, the stages represent different neurophysiological organizations of activity. As we shall see, some measures may be elevated and others depressed within a stage. For example, it is usually most difficult to awaken a subject from Stage 4 (Rechtschaffen, Hauri, & Zeitlin, 1966), yet heart rate and spontaneous GSR activity may be at their highest levels of the night during this stage.

Figure 5.2 illustrates the progression of stages through the night during the last 7 of 15 consecutive nights which one subject (the author) spent sleeping in the laboratory. As is true of most subjects who are relatively

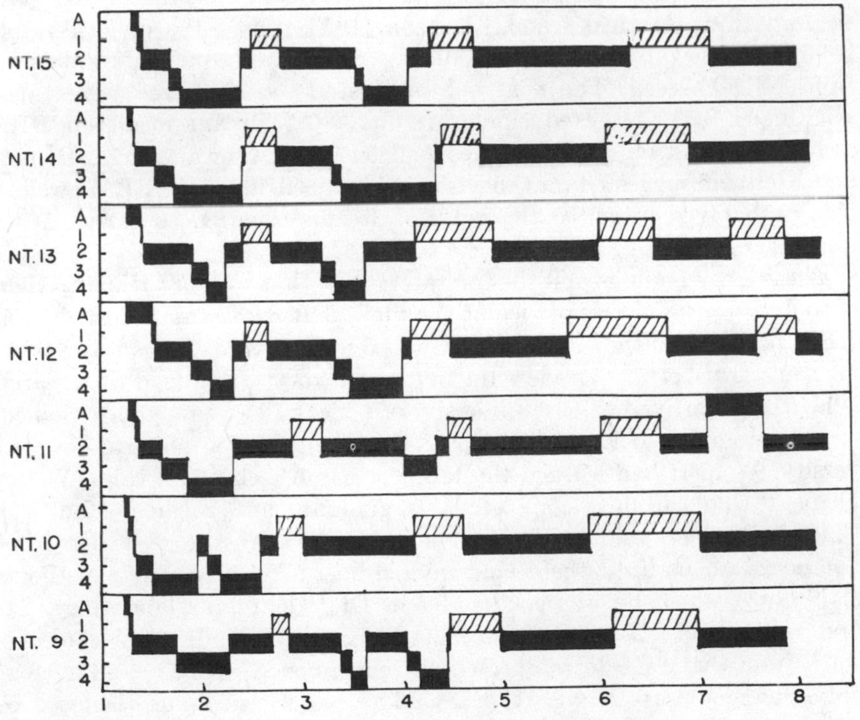


**Fig. 5.2.** Progression of sleep stages during seven consecutive nights in one subject. Designations of 1–4 along the ordinate indicate the respective sleep stages; "A" indicates awake. REM periods are shown by the bars with diagonal markings. Very brief stage changes were omitted for purposes of schematic clarity.

good sleepers and accustomed to the laboratory, the sleep pattern remains relatively stable from night to night, e.g., the first REM period occurs at about the same time each night, as does the second and third. Note that Stages 3 and 4 appear mostly during the early part of the night.

## II. RELATIONSHIP OF MENTAL ACTIVITY TO SLEEP STAGES

To venture an historical interpretation, it now seems fortunate that some of the earliest work on this area suffered from a certain crudeness of data collection, data analysis, and, very likely, a very fortuitous selection of subjects. Were it not for the overly simplified but attractive generalizations which resulted, sleep research might not have gained the popularity that it did during the next 15 years, and most of the substantial discoveries which resulted from this research might not have been made.

The great interest in psychophysiological dream research started with the report by Aserinsky and Kleitman (1953) that 74% of awakenings from REM sleep produced dream recall, as compared to 9% of awakenings from NREM sleep. The next published study in this area (Dement & Kleitman, 1957) reported similar results: 80% dream recall on REM awakenings and only 7% dream recall on NREM awakenings. Dement and Kleitman suggested that the dream reports elicited on NREM awakenings probably represented the recall of dreams experienced earlier in the night.

These early findings and the interpretations that were attached to them encouraged general acceptance of the view that dreaming occurred in all REM periods and that NREM sleep was a mental void. Indeed, it was my own initial belief in this view that attracted me to this field of research. When I first arrived at the University of Chicago 14 years ago, I chanced to be introduced to Edward Wolpert, then a medical student at the University. Wolpert had learned the REM research techniques from William Dement who had just completed his graduate and medical studies at Chicago. Wolpert told me a bit about this field of research—which I had not heard about until then—and invited me to observe an experiment of his own which he was conducting in Dr. Kleitman's laboratory. My first evening of observing Wolpert's experiment decided my choice of work from that time to the present. I remember Wolpert poised over an old 4-channel Grass Model III EEG. (This historic machine was used by Aserinsky, Kleitman, Dement, Wolpert, Kamiya, Foulkes, and myself—in short, the whole first generation of Chicago REM researchers. The same machine is still in use in Chicago.) Wolpert showed me the rapid eye movements as they were traced on the moving paper and told me that when he awoke the subject we would hear a vivid dream report; that is exactly what happened. About a half-hour later, Wolpert pointed out the spindles and lack of eye movements of Stage 2. He said that this time the subject would have nothing to report upon awakening, and that is just what happened. At that point, I said to myself something like, "My God, here is the mind turning on and off during sleep, and we actually have a physiological indicator of when it is happening. What better opportunity is there to study how the mind and body are related?"

As it turned out, my initial impressions and the interpretations of the early REM researchers were, as we might expect in the early phases of almost any research, overly simplified. Most of the sleep studies which followed revealed more recall on NREM awakenings than was reported in the first wave of this research. The first of the reports in the "second wave" came from Goodenough, Shapiro, Holden, and Steinschriber (1959) who found that 35% of NREM awakenings led to the report of a dream. These authors were inclined to follow the earlier interpretation that the NREM reports might represent the recall of dreams experienced earlier in the night. Encouraged by a popular press which did not even try to explain inconsistent observations the way the original researchers had, the lay public as well as scientists began to refer to REM and NREM as "dreaming" and "nondreaming" sleep, respectively.

The first to seriously question the exclusive assignment of dreams to REM sleep was Foulkes (1962). Foulkes found that 74% of NREM awakenings produced recall of some mental activity and that 54% produced "dreams" by the criteria that the reported mental experiences contained some sensory imagery, or that in the experiences the subject assumed an identity other than his own or felt that he was in a physical setting other than the laboratory. Five years later, in a review of research on NREM mental activity, Foulkes (1967) would report on nine studies subsequent to the original reports of Aserinsky and Kleitman and Dement and Kleitman. The incidence of NREM recall in these studies ranged from 23 to 74. Obviously, the numbers were now too large to permit dismissal of NREM recall as infrequent products of faulty memory.

Although Foulkes (1966, 1967) has reviewed many of the reasons why NREM reports had not been recognized and accepted as indicative of mental activity during sleep, the reasons are worth a brief review here, since much of our discussion will concern NREM mental activity.

One reason relates to qualitative differences between REM and NREM reports. Foulkes (1962) first reported on these differences as follows: "Reports obtained in periods of REM activity showed more organismic involvement in affective, visual, and muscular dimensions and were more highly elaborated than non-REMP reports. REMP reports showed less correspondence to the waking life of the subject than did reports from spindle and delta sleep. The relatively frequent occurrence of thinking and memory processes in spindle and delta sleep was an especially striking result." Rechtschaffen, Verdone, and Wheaton (1963) reached similar conclusions: ". . . as compared with REM mentation, subjects report NREM mentation as more poorly recalled, more like thinking and less like dreaming, less vivid, less visual, more conceptual, under greater volitional control, more plausible, more concerned with their contemporary lives, occurring in lighter sleep, less emotional, and more pleasant. Our impression is that NREM mentation resembles that large portion of our waking thought which wanders in seemingly disorganized, drifting, nondirected fashion whenever we are not attending to external stimuli or actively working out a problem or a daydream."

Two reports from consecutive awakenings—the first NREM, the second REM—from a subject studied by Rechtschaffen, Vogel, and Shaikun (1963) illustrate the most typical differences between REM and NREM reports.

NREM report: "I had been dreaming about getting ready to take some type of an exam. It had been a very short dream. That's just about all that it contained. I don't think I was worried about them."

REM report: "I was dreaming about exams. In the early part of the dream I was dreaming I had just finished taking an exam, and it was a very sunny day outside. I was walking with a boy who's in some of my classes with me. There was a sort of a, a break, and someone mentioned a grade they had gotten in a social science exam. And I asked them if the social science marks had come in. They said yes. I didn't get it, because I had been away for a day."

Clearly, the second report contains much more of the perceptual vividness and thematic organization that is ordinarily associated with dreaming but the decision about how much of such vividness and thematic coherence a report should contain before it is labeled a dream is arbitrary. Most important, the discovery of wide-variations in mental activity during sleep with widely varying degrees of "dreaminess," underlines the importance of specifying reproducible operations by which the distinction between dream and nondream is made. For example, Dement and Kleitman indicated only that, "The *S*s were considered to have been dreaming only if they could relate a coherent, fairly detailed description of dream content." It is doubtful that reliabilities of dream-nondream discriminations would be very high given that criterion alone. Thus, it is very possible that Dement and Kleitman found much less NREM dreaming than the vast majority of subsequent investigators largely because they required more dreaminess[2] of a report before they were willing to call a report a dream. By the criteria imposed by the majority of subsequent investigators, there is much more dreaming in NREM sleep than one would have imagined from the early papers in this area.

Another variable which could have caused different results in different studies is the subject variable. Whereas young adults, the favorite subject of REM type dream content studies, report dreams (by almost any criterion) with high frequency on REM awakenings, the incidence and quality of NREM reports varies widely from subject to subject (Foulkes & Rechtschaffen, 1964). Thus any study with few subjects is susceptible to a sampling error which might bias the results against NREM mentation. (The bulk of data from the original Dement and Kleitman study came from five subjects.)

It did not take very long for sleep researchers generally to accept that NREM reports were more frequent than they had believed. Now the focus of skepticism shifted to how accurate the NREM reports reflected the mental activity of the subject while he was asleep. Foulkes (1966, 1967) has reviewed the major arguments against the acceptance of NREM reports and has effectively, we believe, countered them, therefore we need review this issue only briefly here.

The argument that NREM dream reports might represent dreams experienced in earlier REM periods is countered by several studies which showed that NREM reports, including NREM dream reports, may be elicited on awakenings made before any REM periods have occurred. Another argument has been that NREM reports may refer to mental activity elicited in the process of waking up, i.e., hypnopompic mentation, rather than to what was happening during sleep. Goodenough *et al.* (1965) compared the content elicited after abrupt awakenings with the content elicited after awakenings which were induced gradually, thus increasing the length of the awakening process. More reports of "thinking" were

[2] A factor analysis of dream reports elicited on REM awakenings (Hauri, Sawyer, & Rechtschaffen, 1967) revealed a "vivid fantasy" factor which reflected primarily three correlated variables: (a) unreality—imagination, distortion; (b) intensity of experience—dramatization, clarity, emotion; (c) productivity—length of dream report. As these authors put it, "These three elements—the extent of a dream, its unreality and intensity—are central to what is commonly referred to as a 'good dream' (a lot of strange and wonderful things seem really to be happening). It is the combination of these components—with the unreal seeming real—that most distinguishes dreams. . . ." We use the term "dreamy" in the present paper as a conversational and shorthand way of referring to these qualities.

elicited on the gradual NREM awakenings, which lends credence to the argument that some NREM reports of thinking may represent hypnopompic rather than sleep experiences. However, many NREM thinking reports were elicited on abrupt awakenings, and these are not so easily explained as products of the awakening process. Furthermore, there was no relationship between the incidence of NREM dream reports and the abruptness of the awakening.

Another argument against the acceptance of NREM reports has been that many of them might represent confabulations designed to meet the presumed expectations of the experimenter. Foulkes and Rechtschaffen (1964) found virtually no correlation between the MMPI L scale, which has been used to measure the tendency toward such confabulation, and the amount of recall on NREM awakenings. Rechtschaffen, Verdone, and Wheaton (1963) and Foulkes (1967) have recorded several instances in which NREM awakening reports indicated an apparent incorporation of external stimuli into an ongoing stream of NREM mental activity. Evidence of a similar significance comes from the studies of sleep talking. Arkin *et al.* (1970) and Rechtschaffen, Goodenough, and Shapiro (1962) found that the content of NREM sleep-talking incidents frequently corresponded with the content of reports elicited on awakening shortly after the talking. These two types of evidence—the incorporations and the sleep talking—provide temporal landmarks to which the content elicited on subsequent awakenings can be reasonably assigned. Thus these lines of evidence indicate that NREM reports cannot be completely dismissed as confabulations, hypnopompic reveries, or memories of mental activity experienced at a much earlier time.

It now appears that the early research underestimated the absolute amount of NREM mental activity and too quickly rejected the evidence for NREM dreaming. But as it turns out, this early work did not overestimate the degree of relationship between mental activity and sleep stages. Dreaming does seem to occur in NREM as well as in REM sleep, and individual subjects may report mental activity on as many as 70% or more of their NREM awakenings. However, fewer reports of mental activity are elicited on NREM awakenings, the proportion of reports which are labeled thinking rather than dreaming is higher for NREM, and even the NREM reports which are labeled dreams tend to be less dreamy than REM reports. The net result is that REM and NREM are highly discriminable on the basis of the amount and quality of mental activity that they yield.

The degree of discriminability between REM and NREM was shown in a study by Monroe *et al.* (1965) who asked two judges to postdict whether reports had been elicited on REM or NREM awakenings on the basis of the amount and quality of the content reported. A postdiction made simply on the basis of whether any mental content had been elicited on the awakening yielded 70% correct identifications of sleep phase (assuming that REM awakenings would yield recalled content and NREM awakenings would not). When judges were asked to consider both the amount and quality of content, postdiction accuracy rose to 80% (average of two judges). When REM and NREM reports were matched for other variables which are associated with sleep mentation (subjects, night, and time of night) discriminability rose to 89%. These figures—discriminability ranging from about 70 to 90%—probably represent one of the best correlations ever discovered between psychological and physiological variables.[3]

To what extent the association between sleep stage and mental activity was enhanced by the variability in psychological and physiological activity during sleep, by the reduction of responsivity to external stimuli, or by the emergence of distinctive psychological and/or physiological phenomena during sleep cannot be determined here. But in general, at least some of the potential promise of sleep research for yielding correlations between psychological and physiological responses has certainly been realized.

Sleep researchers have not rested content with the wonderful correlations that have been established between sleep stages and mental activity. At least two major problems have remained. Perhaps encouraged by earlier successes, sleep researchers have pursued these problems with vigor. The first problem is that considerable variance in sleep mentation

[3] The high discriminability of REM and NREM reports does not premit the convenient generalization that the mental activity of REM sleep is dreaming and the mental activity of NREM sleep is thinking. Subjects describe their NREM mentation more often as dreamlike (see review by Pivik & Foulkes, 1968), and extremely vivid, bizarre, emotional, highly organized reports which would qualify as dreams by almost anyone's definition may be elicited on NREM awakenings. In fact, if there is any question about the validity of NREM awakening reports as indicators of sleep mentation, that question has to be asked more seriously about the NREM thinking reports than about the NREM dreaming reports. As noted earlier, Goodenough *et al.* (1965) found that gradual awakenings produced more NREM thinking reports than abrupt awakenings, which supported the possibility that some NREM thinking reports reflect hypnopompic rather than sleep mentation. The evidence on temporal landmarks for NREM mentation simply indicates that *not all* NREM thinking reports can be so explained; an unknown number of NREM thinking reports may actually represent hypnopompic activity rather than thoughts experienced *during* the NREM sleep. By contrast, the NREM dream reports do not appear related to abruptness of awakening; apparently, they are much less likely to represent hypnopompic artifacts. In our own experience, subjects appear to be much more certain about what had been going on in their NREM dreams than in their NREM thoughts.

remains unrelated to sleep stages. But this is the relatively smaller problem. Even if all of the variance in sleep mentation could have been related to sleep stages, the second problem would have still remained. This second problem is the determination of the most "intimate" physiological correlates of sleep mentation. A sleep stage is a complex organization of several physiological variables. To this point, we have attended only to the EEG and eye movement patterns which are the defining characteristics of sleep stage. But the stages have other physiological correlates as well—including muscle tone, cardiorespiratory, and metabolic variations. Which of the defining characteristics and correlates of stages are most intimately correlated with sleep mentation?[4]

In reviewing this question, several strategies can be used. Most important, is to examine within-stage empirical correlations between physiological measures during a period of sleep and reports of mental activity which presumably occurred during the same period. For some physiological measures, evidence on the relationship between the measures and reports is either absent, sparse, or conflicting. In these cases, one might gain some impression of the likelihood of a correlation between the report and the psychological variable by observing how each is related to a third variable. For example, given the known relationships of awakening reports to stage, one might expect a good physiological correlate of reports to vary with stage as the reports do. (Although it is possible that each stage has its own best physiological correlates of reports, a first parsimonious guess would be that the most intimate correlates of the mentation remain stable across stages.) Also, there are certain temporal correlates of reported sleep mentation independent of stage (see next section) and one might expect good correlates of sleep mentation to vary with time parameters in the same manner that reports do.

[4] Hidden behind this relatively humble question is a more pretentious hope. Might it be possible eventually to find such a precise psychophysiological correlation that we can feel either that the perfect mirror-image ideal of isomorphism has been achieved or that we are knocking on the door of causality. Even if such a glorious correlation were achieved, however, empirical proof of causality might not be demonstrable. The empirical demonstration of causality is usually defined by the effect of an *experimentally* introduced stimulus. Naturally occurring responses certainly act as stimuli and may be reasonably *interpreted* as such, but one could not be certain of their causal role. Even when such responses precede and are highly correlated with presumed effects, the possibility exists that an undetected stimulus causes both the initial response and its presumed effect. One can speak of the causal effect of experimentally manipulated *external* stimuli on responses which are defined as psychological or physiological. But the causality now in question is between *internal* psychological and physiological responses, which cannot, by virtue of being internal, be directly manipulated themselves.

## III. TEMPORAL CORRELATES

In the search for the best physiological correlates of amount and quality of mental activity during sleep, certain temporal correlates of this mental activity may be of assistance. Reports tend to be more detailed and more emotional (but not more bizarre) on awakenings made late in a REM period than on awakenings early in a REM period. There is a similar increase in detail and emotionality on REM awakenings made later in the night than on REM awakenings made early in the night, with most of the variance accounted for by the relatively mundane quality of the first REM report of the night (Foulkes, 1960; Verdone, 1963).

The data on temporal correlates of NREM mentation are more equivocal. Hauri and Rechtschaffen (1963) found no substantial difference in amount of recall on NREM awakenings made 15 min after sleep onset as compared to NREM awakenings made 45 min after sleep onset. However, only two points in NREM sleep were sampled and only three subjects were studied, so the possibility of some yet undetected within-cycle temporal correlate of NREM mentation cannot be firmly excluded. Pivik and Foulkes (1968) reported that NREM mentation became more dreamlike later in the night. However, their time-of-night variable was partially confounded with NREM stage differences, and their conclusion was based largely on the results of only seven reports from the first Stage 2 awakening of the night. Therefore, time-of-night effects for NREM mentation are not so firmly established as one might wish.

## IV. EEG CORRELATES

Since EEG is one of the defining characteristics of sleep stage, the opportunities for correlating EEG with sleep mentation independent of stage are limited. Nevertheless, there are enough data to indicate that EEG-mentation correlations during sleep are not particularly strong. Within NREM sleep, the EEG patterns of Stages 2 and 3 appear quite different. Stage 2 has a relatively low voltage, mixed frequency pattern with periodic sleep spindles and K-complexes. During Stage 3 there is a marked increment in high amplitude, slow wave activity along with the sleep spindles and K-complexes. Yet the amount and quality of recall elicited on Stage 2 and Stage 3 awakenings are quite similar (Pivik & Foulkes, 1968). The EEG of Stage 4 differs even more dramatically from the EEG of Stage 2, but Stage 4 is so strongly related to time of night that uncontaminated comparisons of mental activity in Stages 2 and 4 are difficult to make.

It is doubtful that the EEG pattern of Stage REM is most responsible for the quality of mental activity in that stage. The EEG of Stage REM and the Stage 1 EEG pattern which occurs at sleep onset are very similar. Both consist of relatively low voltage, mixed frequency activity. There are some differences. In Stage REM, distinctively notched 2–3 Hz sawtooth waves tend to occur in conjunction with bursts of rapid eye movement; activity resembling sawtooth waves may appear in Stage 1, but the waves are not so clearly formed nor nearly so plentiful as in Stage REM. High voltage vertex sharp waves are more abundant in Stage 1 and sometimes do not appear at all in Stage REM. Although there are differences in episodic EEG events as noted, the tonic, background EEG activity of Stage 1 and Stage REM are virtually indistinguishable. Vogel, Barrowclough, and Giesler (1970) asked judges to postdict whether reports had been elicited on REM awakenings or on awakenings from sleep onset Stage 1. They found that the judges could do this with much better than change accuracy. Therefore, stages with very similar EEG patterns seem to yield discriminable reports.

Finally, there is the obvious point that within stages there is much variation in the amount and quality of mental activity reported on awakenings. For example, Pivik and Foulkes (1968) found that 71.6% of awakenings from Stage 2 produced recall, which means that 28.4% of awakenings from the same stage—with the same EEG—did not.

To summarize: stages with different EEG patterns may produce similar awakening reports; stages with similar EEG patterns may produce discriminable awakening reports; and within a single stage—with a single EEG pattern—there is marked variation in the reported content. Evidently, the EEG alone is not a very good indicator of sleep mentation. But all of the studies cited above refer to "tonic" EEG patterns, i.e., gross patterns which persist over extended periods of at least several minutes. Perhaps more productive of correlations with mental activity would be a focus on specific EEG waveforms—especially where hypotheses for such specific relationships exist. Later we will review some studies of this type in relation to phasic events during sleep.

## V. MOTOR ACTIVITY

That mental activity during sleep may have motor correlates is dramatically demonstrated by the correspondences between sleep talking and sleep mentation noted earlier. But sleep talking does not occur very frequently. Therefore, the question progresses to whether there are any less overt motor correlates which regularly accompany sleep mentation.

There is very conclusive evidence from the work of Wolpert (1960) and Stoyva (1965) that there are many more fine movements of the extremities in REM than in NREM sleep. In this crude sense there is definitely a relationship between fine motor twitches and dreaming. However, these fine motor twitches might represent some expression of stage physiology which is not specifically related to the mental activity of the stage. To attack this question, one must consider the relationship between the twitches and mental activity within stages. Wolpert (1960) found a relationship between the specific electromyographic activity recorded just before REM awakenings and specific dream content which was reported to have occurred just prior to the awakening, e.g., dreams of using the hand associated with EMG potentials at the wrist, but the relationship obtained only for some subjects. A recent report by Grossman, Gardner, Roffwarg, Fekete, Beers, and Weiner (1971) also offers evidence that twitches of the extremities may be associated with REM dream content. McGuigan and Tanner (1970), in a study of one subject, found a relationship between conversation in REM dreams and lip and chin EMG potentials.

Thus there is little doubt that the psychological events of the dream may be reflected in motor discharges. But it is also clear from the data of the reports cited above that not all of the fine muscle twitches are accompanied by dreams of correlated motor activity, nor are all the hallucinated motor acts in dreams reflected in the recorded EMG potentials. Stoyva (1965) found that deaf subjects, who presumably would dream of moving their fingers more often than normals, had no more frequent finger twitches in REM sleep than control subjects—contrary to the historic report of Max (1935).

Apart from the relationship of the EMG twitches to specific dream content, are the twitches diagnostic of dream activity per se? There is not very much data on this question, but the report of Stoyva that the finger twitches of his deaf subjects were not correlated with reports of NREM dreaming would argue against such a possibility.

Apart from discrete motor responses, are higher levels of psychological activity during sleep accompanied by higher tonic levels of muscle activity? Here there is a clear answer which illustrates a dramatic departure from waking psychophysiological correlations. During REM sleep, when psychological activity is at a peak, tonic electromyographic activity in the head and neck region is drastically reduced (Berger, 1961; Jacobson *et al.*, 1964). Trunk and limb muscles do not show the same decrease in tonic activity during Stage REM. Except for increases in tonic activity associated with occasional body movements, the tonic activity of the limb and trunk muscles remains stable in the transition from NREM to REM sleep. Thus the increased fine muscle twitches of REM sleep discussed above occur against a background of stable tonic EMG activity of limb and trunk muscles and a decreased level of tonic EMG activity in the head and neck region.

In the cat it has been shown that the decrease in tonic EMG activity in the neck muscles during REM sleep results from an active supraspinal inhibitory control, since this decrease is not seen in Stage REM after prebulbar transections of the brain stem (Jouvet, 1967). In fact, the structure responsible for the inhibition of neck muscle tone has been localized by Jouvet to the area of the nucleus locus coeruleus.

In view of the evidence in the cat for a cerebral structure which actively participates in the inhibition of muscle tone during REM, it becomes reasonable to ask whether the decreased muscle tone also signals the emergence of active processes responsible for dreaming. Larson and Foulkes (1968) took advantage of the fact that the chin EMG frequently decreases just prior to Stage REM to investigate the relationship between EMG suppression and reported content in NREM sleep. (Since the tonic EMG suppression is maintained throughout most of REM sleep, the association with mental activity has to be studied during NREM sleep where the suppression occurs only occasionally.) Contrary to the expectation that the NREM EMG suppression might be a positive dream indicator, Larson and Foulkes found a trend toward fewer and less dreamlike reports on awakenings made from periods of EMG suppression than on control awakenings.

To summarize, apart from the increased muscle twitches of Stage REM and the relationship of some of these twitches to specific mental content, muscle activity during sleep does not appear to be a very promising indicator of mental activity. There are two additional aspects of muscle activity during sleep which are of potential importance, phasic EMG inhibitions and the activity of the extraocular muscles. These two topics can be more meaningfully discussed in a later section on phasic events during sleep.

## VI. CARDIAC AND RESPIRATORY ACTIVITY

Heart rate per se does not appear to be related to sleep mentation. Several investigators have failed to detect significant relationships between heart rate during Stage REM and emotionality of the subsequent awakening dream reports (Fahrion, Davison, & Breger, 1967; Hauri & Van de Castle, 1970; Knopf, 1962; Verdone, 1963). Shapiro, Goodenough, Biederman, and Sleser (1964) found no relationship between REM period heart rate and whether dreaming, thinking, or no content reports were elicited on the awakening. There are some indications, however, of a relationship between heart rate variability and the content of REM dreams. Fahrion *et al.* found that heart rate variability was significantly related to REM dream emotionality in one subject but not in another. Hauri and Van de Castle (1970) found that heart rate variability prior to a REM awakening was significantly related to emotionality and other content parameters in the subsequently reported dreams.

The data on respiration show mixed results. Knopf (1962) found no significant relationships between respiratory rate in REM sleep and several parameters of dream content. Hauri and Van de Castle (1970) found that the respiratory rate during the last minute of REM sleep just prior to awakening was related to emotionality of the whole REM dream reported on awakening. There were no significant relationships between emotionality and respiratory rate for the whole REM period, respiratory rate during the last 6 min of the REM period, or any measure of respiratory variability. Respiratory variability in the last minute before awakening was negatively related to "involvement" of the subject in the dream.

Shapiro *et al.* (1964) found no significant relationship between REM period respiratory rate and whether a dreaming, thinking, or no content report was elicited on awakening, but they found that high respiratory irregularity was significantly related to the incidence of dream reporting. Hobson, Goldfrank, and Snyder (1965) related respiratory measures to a "total content rating," a combined estimate of physical activity, emotion, and vividness which should correlate highly with what we have called dreaminess. In their study, the relationship of the total content rating to respiratory variability fell short of significance, but there was a significant relationship between respiratory rate and total content rating both within REM and NREM sleep.

Although the reports on respiration and dream content in REM sleep represent a somewhat mixed bag of data, there are definite indications of a relationship between respiratory activity and what we have called dreaminess which is of theoretical significance. But the significance might be quite different from the traditional conception of a heightened autonomic response to an exciting mental content. Later we will find cause to question whether the respiration-content correlations might not be "secondary" to more fundamental relationships between respiration and certain "phasic" events of sleep.

## VII. ELECTRODERMAL ACTIVITY

One of the favorite responses of psychophysiologists, electrodermal activity, does not show up very well as an indicator of mental activity during sleep. On the basis of stage-related changes in mental activity, one might expect a decrease in basal skin resistance and more spontaneous electrodermal changes in Stage REM than in NREM sleep. No such results have been reported. One early study of stage-related changes in skin resistance (Hawkins *et al.*, 1962) reported an increase in basal skin resistance during Stage REM over the level during the preceding NREM sleep, but subsequent studies have revealed no consistent relationship of basal electrodermal levels to sleep stages (Johnson, 1966; Koumans, Tursky, & Solomon, 1968; Tart, 1967). None of the above studies has shown any consistent skin resistance decline in Stage REM.

With respect to spontaneous electrodermal responses, several investigators have reported the initially surprising result that these responses were by far most frequent during Stages 3 and 4 (Asahina, 1962; Broughton, Poire, & Tassinari, 1965; Burch, 1965; Hauri, 1968; Johnson & Lubin, 1966; Lester, Burch, & Dossett, 1967). These electrodermal fluctuations are so vigorous during Stages 3 and 4 that they have been called "GSR storms" (Burch, 1965). Broughton *et al.* (1965) have suggested that the appearance of these storms ". . . when psychological activity is apparently least developed . . . would appear to be another reason for discarding the term 'psychogalvanic reflex'." Lester, Burch, and Dossett (1967) reported that nonspecific GSRs increased in all sleep stages on nights following daytime stress. Whether these GSR increments following stress are associated with distinctive mental activity during sleep, or whether they represent some delayed chemical response to stress that does not have immediate psychological correlates remains to be determined. Hauri and Rechtschaffen (1963) found no relationship between spontaneous or evoked skin potential changes and mental activity during NREM sleep. Verdone (1963) found no relationship between basal skin resistance and several content features of REM reports.

Hauri and Van de Castle (1970) did report one specific association between psychological and electrodermal activity during sleep. In a study of REM period reports, they found that skin potential activity during the last minute preceding the awakening was significantly related to the judged emotionality of the reported dream. Broughton *et al.* (1965) had noted that skin potential responses were relatively infrequent in Stage REM, but that when they did occur they tended to appear with bursts of rapid eye movements. Therefore, one has to question whether the skin potential changes associated with Stage REM emotionality might not depend upon the relationship of emotionality to other phasic changes during sleep. We will return to this issue later.

In general, there is not much evidence for a close association between electrodermal and mental activity during sleep. Broughton *et al.* and

Johnson and Lubin have suggested that the storms of electrodermal activity during Stages 3 and 4 might result from the liberation of electrodermal excitatory centers in the upper brain stem from the inhibiting influences of corticothalamic systems. Johnson and Lubin have suggested that the paucity of electrodermal activity in Stage REM might result from the activation of electrodermal inhibitory systems in the lower brain stem. These hypotheses suggest that major rearrangements of excitatory and inhibitory activity along the neuroaxis, such as occur with sleep, can alter the relationships between peripheral indicators and mental activity that obtain during wakefulness. As Johnson (1970) has pointed out "Instead of using our autonomic and EEG measures to define state, the reverse appears more appropriate. We must first determine the state before we can interpret our physiological measures." Furthermore, the data on GSR storms during NREM sleep indicate that the failure to observe usual waking relationships is not simply the result of a general depression of the response during sleep.

## VIII. PENILE ERECTIONS

It has been well established that penile erections regularly accompany REM sleep. Fisher, Gross, and Zuch (1965) reported that full or partial erections were recorded in 95% of REM periods; 60% of REM periods showed full erections and 35% showed partial erections. Erections rarely occurred in NREM sleep. Similar results were reported by Karacan *et al.* (1966). They found that 80% of REM periods were accompanied by erections; 42% of REM periods had sustained erections which reached and maintained a maximal level, and 37% of REM periods had erections which had fluctuating amplitudes or were interrupted by detumescence. Only 19 erections were recorded during NREM sleep compared to 191 during REM sleep; thus the association of penile erections and REM sleep is quite specific. Of most immediate interest to us is the relationship of the erections to mental activity during sleep.

The data on the penile erections lend themselves to several different kinds of analyses. First, one can ask whether the regularly occurring erections of REM sleep are associated with sexual content. Here the answer is a clear "no," at least insofar as we deal with manifest content and with everyday definitions of what is sexual. If we were to predict sexual content on the basis of penile erections, we would have to predict that 80–95% of REM dreams should have the kind of manifest erotic content that is usually associated with erection—not just speaking with a member of the opposite sex, but engaging in expressly sexual physical contact or at least having explicit sexual fantasies. There is just not that much sexuality in dreams. For example, Hall and Van de Castle (1966) reported that sexual interactions occurred in only 12% of the dreams of their male subjects. The observation of most sleep researchers that nocturnal emissions are very rare in the laboratory is more consistent with the paucity of sexual content in dreams than with the frequency of penile erections. Fisher, Gross, and Zuch have reviewed the possible bases for the disassociation of erections and sexual content in dreams.

One could argue from a psychoanalytic orientation that there is something intrinsically sexual in all dream content, that is, the inferred libidinal energy which the dream theoretically is supposed to discharge in a disguised way so as to prevent awakening. But unless one specifies reliable empirical criteria for inferring sexuality, then the designation of all dreams as sexual is made a priori on a theoretical basis rather than on observable distinguishing features of the dream content.

Although the regularly appearing erections of REM sleep are not regularly accompanied by manifest sexual content, there are some indications of occasional specific associations between erection and sexual content within REM periods. Fisher (1966) was able to successfully postdict a sudden, sharp increase in tumescence in five of six instances mainly on the basis of highly erotic sexual content. In 17 episodes with no or partial erections, there were no indications of overtly sexual content, whereas in 30 episodes of full or moderate erection there were eight instances of overtly erotic content. There is also evidence from both Fisher and Karacan, *et al.* (1966) that the failure of erections to occur in REM sleep as well as detumescence in REM sleep are associated with dysphoric content, e.g., anxiety, aggression, etc.

To attempt a summary of these data, it appears that the very high frequency with which erections appear in REM sleep is not associated with a correspondingly high frequency of manifest sexual content. In this respect, the erections are not diagnostic of dream content. On the other hand, variations in tumescence during REM are somewhat diagnostic of variations in REM dream content. There has been no specific study reported on the relationship of NREM erections to the incidence of NREM dream reports. However, the very infrequent occurrence of NREM erections would at least suggest that most NREM dreams occur in the absence of erections.

Two additional relationships involving REM erections are of interest. Karacan *et al.* (1966) found that 95% of awakenings from REM periods with sustained erections produced recalled content as compared with 85% of awakenings from REM periods with no or interrupted erections. (The difference was statistically significant.) Karacan *et al.* (1966) also found that sustained erections were associated with greater amounts of eye movement activity.

## IX. TEMPERATURE

One might guess that an increase in general systemic arousal as reflected in body temperature might be positively correlated with psychological arousal. It is well established, for example, that several different kinds of waking performance are at their best when body temperatures are relatively high (Kleitman, 1963). It turns out, however, that body temperature is negatively correlated with several types of psychological arousal in dream content. Verdone (1963) examined the relationships between rectal temperatures recorded during REM periods and several content parameters of the dreams reported on awakenings from the REM periods. Rectal temperature was negatively related to the subjects' ratings of goodness of recall, vividness, and emotionality of the dream. Once again, however, the possibility arises that these relationships might be secondary to a more intimate relationship between the psychological variables and phasic events. In Verdone's study, there was a significant negative relationship between rectal temperature and amount of eye movement activity, which, in turn, was positively related to goodness of recall, vividness, and emotionality. The relationship of eye movement activity to recall and vividness were stronger than the relationship of rectal temperature to those two variables.

There was one psychological variable to which rectal temperature related that eye movement activity did not. Lower rectal temperatures were associated with dream content that referred to life experiences from the subjects' more distant past. Neither eye movement activity nor rectal temperature were significantly related to the implausibility of the dream content.

Finger and forehead skin temperatures did not relate in any consistently convincing way to the psychological variables.

## X. SYMPATHETIC AROUSAL

Of course, we have dealt with several indicators of sympathetic arousal throughout our review. There are, however, a few studies which deal with sympathetic arousal in a more general sense and therefore deserve special attention. There is one report on sympathetic arousal which is unfortunately brief but noteworthy for the clarity of its theoretical formulation and the significance of its findings. Hersch *et al.* (1970) hypothesized that

"... the level of autonomic activity is a precondition which determines how the sleeper interprets impinging stimuli and memories; i.e., if the sympathetic nervous system is reasonably quiescent, ongoing cognition may be experienced as thought, but it may be experienced as dreams if the sympathetic nervous system is comparatively active." This formulation suggests that it is the sympathetic arousal of REM sleep that is responsible for REM mentation being experienced as dreams. To test the hypothesis that it is sympathetic arousal which is responsible for NREM mentation being experienced as dreams, epinephrine was injected subdermally during Stage 4, and the subjects were awakened 10 min later for reports. These reports were compared with reports elicited on awakenings made 10 min after control injections of saline. The postepinephrine reports were rated significantly more vivid, emotional, and perceptual than the control reports. The postepinephrine reports also tended to be more bizarre.

The "activation" of NREM mentation by norepinephrine stands as an important empirical result. It is certainly consistent with the report of Hobson *et al.* (1965) that respiratory rate is positively related to emotionality and vividness of NREM reports. What seems to require more discussion, however, is the original hypothesis that it is the sympathetic arousal of REM sleep which is responsible for the high incidence of dreaming in that stage.

Several lines of evidence suggest that Stage REM is not characterized by markedly elevated levels of sympathetic arousal. Baust, Weidinger, and Kirchner (1968) reported that in the cat sympathetic tone, defined as the tonic discharge of pre- or postganglionic sympathetic neurons, is regularly decreased in REM sleep from the preceding NREM level. Of course, it may be dangerous to generalize from the cat to the human, so a review of sympathetic activity during sleep in the human seems indicated.

Snyder *et al.* (1964) studied the changes in respiration, heart rate, and systolic blood pressure during human sleep. They found that there were increases in each of these variables during REM periods as compared to the preceding NREM level, but the magnitudes of these increases were quite small: 6% for heart rate, 7% for respiratory rate, and 4% for systolic blood pressure. Kamiya (1965) obtained similarly low REM period increments in his study of heart and respiration rates. The reduction of electrodermal responses during REM periods noted earlier could be taken to indicate a decrease in sympathetic activity during REM sleep. Are the increases in autonomic level great enough to account for the marked shifts in mental activity with REM sleep? Probably not. For one thing, the data of Snyder *et al.* show that heart and respiratory rates tend to fall in successive REM periods of a night, which is inconsistent with the increase in dreamlike quality of REM periods later in the night. (Blood pressure did tend to increase in later REM periods.)

An even more compelling argument against the sympathetic arousal–dreaming hypothesis is the evidence reviewed earlier on the absence of a relationship of heart rate and respiratory rate to sleep mentation. In the case of respiration the results were mixed.

Overall, the results indicated better relationships of dreamlike quality to heart and respiration rate variability than to rate per se. Considering these results, one might expect marked increases in the variability of autonomic indicators in the passage from NREM to REM sleep. This is exactly the case. In contrast to the meager increases in autonomic level, Snyder *et al.* (1964) reported increases in a variability measure of 55, 55, and 50% for pulse, respiration, and blood pressure, respectively. Johnson (1966) has also reported minimal changes in baselevels of autonomic activity with Stage REM but massive changes in variability. Furthermore, in contrast to the decrease in heart rate in successive REM periods of a night, Snyder *et al.* (1964) showed substantial increases in heart rate variability in successive REM periods—just as one might expect on the basis of correlations of dreaming with time of night.

What does a relationship of autonomic variability to mental activity during REM periods mean for the sympathetic arousal hypothesis? The hypothesis of Hersch *et al.* (1970) is addressed to the issue of autonomic level, not autonomic variability. Further theoretical work on the relationship of autonomic variability to sleep mentation seems indicated.

Finally, we must consider whether the autonomic variability of REM sleep represents variability in sympathetic or parasympathetic activity. This question is again prompted by the work of Baust and his collaborators in the cat. Their findings are perhaps not generalizable to humans, but they represent the best available data on the issue. Baust, Bohmke, and Blossfeld (1971a) found that reflex discharges of the cervical sympathetic nerve in response to sciatic nerve stimulation were reduced during NREM sleep as compared to wakefulness, and then *further* reduced during REM sleep. These results left open the question of whether the reduction of sympathetic response might have resulted from reduced sensory input. Therefore, Baust, Bohmke, and Blossfeld (1971b) directly stimulated the reticular formation. Similar results were obtained; evoked sympathetic activity was reduced during NREM sleep and then further reduced during REM sleep. Evoked responses in the vagal nerve were reduced in NREM sleep as compared to wakefulness, but in contrast to the sympathetic responses, the vagal responses during REM sleep were increased over those of NREM sleep and approximated the waking responses.

Baust and Bohnert (1969) also studied the phasic changes in heart rate associated with bursts of eye movements in REM sleep. The usual pattern was for heart rate to increase from 1–2 sec prior to the REM burst. Then there was a decline in heart rate which began during or at the end of the REM burst, reached a maximum in 5–8 sec, and was absent after 10–15 sec. Sympathetic and parasympathetic contributions to this pattern were evaluated by various heart denervations. Baust and Bohnert concluded that the initial 1–2 sec rise was caused mostly by decreases in parasympathetic activity, and that the later brachycardia was produced by a combination of increased vagal and decreased sympathetic activity. Therefore, the cat data show that during REM sleep there is not only a decreased tonic sympathetic discharge, but also a decreased sympathetic response to stimulation as well as phasic decreases in sympathetic activity in conjunction with bursts of eye movement. It remains to be considered how much of the phasic autonomic activity during REM in humans is associated with eye movement activity. We will return to this issue later. In the meantime, the cat data should raise some caution about the interpretation of the autonomic changes during sleep in humans.

## XI. EYE MOVEMENT ACTIVITY

There are two types of relationship between eye movements and mental activity during sleep to be considered. One is the content-specific relationship or the so-called scanning hypothesis which proposes that the eyes move in REM sleep as the dreamer scans the dream scene and follows the movements of objects in the scene. This hypothesis predicts that the amount of eye movement activity will be related to the amount of visual scanning and that the direction of recorded eye movements will correspond to the direction of scanning in the dream. The second major type of relationship may be called nonspecific. It has to do with how the eye movements may relate to the amount and quality of reported mental activity. Although scanning activity may enter into the determination of such relationships, it is not crucial to them. Nonspecific relationships could obtain because the eye movements are a peripheral expression of central events which are correlated with mental activity, that is, the eyes might move during certain types of brain activation even when they are not engaged in the scanning of the dream imagery.

The most specific evidence on the content-specific relationships is the data on the relationship between dream imagery and eye movement direction, but first we will review some of the other evidence which has been brought to bear on the question.

Dement and Wolpert (1958) classified REM dreams as "active" or "passive" without knowing the amount of eye movement activity which had been recorded polygraphically. Active dreams were those "... in which the dreamer was an active participant in the events of the dream," that is, where many eye movements might be expected. Passive dreams were "... those in which *S* was quietly reflecting upon an event, talking quietly to another person, or watching an event occur, often from a distance, in which he took no active part," that is, dreams in which relatively less eye movement activity might be expected. There was a very highly significant relationship of this active–passive dichotomization of dreams to the amount of eye movement activity independently judged from the polygraph records. These results have been replicated by Berger and Oswald (1962).

The above results are certainly consistent with the scanning hypothesis, but of themselves they are not very convincing in view of a reasonable alternative interpretation. As Aserinsky (1965) has suggested, the eye movements might reflect heightened activity in parts of the central nervous system which are also responsible for active dreams rather than reflect a response of the oculomotor system to the dream imagery. In other words, the correspondence of amount of dream activity and amount of eye movement activity could be an example of what we have called a nonspecific correspondence.

There is evidence which shows that the amplitude, density, velocity, stereotypy, predominant direction, sequential pattern, temporal distribution, or organization of eye movements during REM sleep is different from those of eye movements during wakefulness (e.g., Aserinsky, 1971; Fuchs & Ron, 1968; Gabersek & Scherrer, 1970; Jacobs, Feldman, & Bender, 1971; Jeannerod, Mouret, & Jouvet, 1965; Oswald, 1962; Spreng, Johnson, & Lubin, 1968). Such evidence of differences in waking and REM eye movements has been used to argue against the scanning hypothesis (Aserinsky, 1971; Moskowitz & Berger, 1969; Oswald, 1962). Certainly these data do not speak for the scanning hypothesis, but neither do they doom it. First, we must allow for the possibility that peculiarities in the way the succession of dream images unfolds and peculiarities of the images themselves might account for some of the features of REM period eye movements. Second, we must allow for the possibility that peculiarities of oculomotor organization during Stage REM account for some unique features in Stage REM eye movements, even though a scanning correspondence is maintained. (A subject with impaired extraocular muscles might have abnormal eye movements during wakefulness, even though those eye movements are in the service of scanning.) Third, there is certainly more than one type of eye movement during sleep (Jeannerod *et al.*, 1965). Perhaps some types of eye movement are related to scanning whereas others are not. For example, Jeannerod *et al.* (1965) distinguished between isolated or small groups of eye movements and dense bursts of eye movement in the cat during REM sleep. Total decortication caused almost complete disappearance of the isolated eye movements but an increase in the number of bursts. Frontal decortication caused an increase in the ratio of burst to isolated movement, whereas occipital decortication caused a decrease in the ratio. Isolated and small group movements appeared during wakefulness, whereas the dense bursts appeared only in REM sleep. Pompeiano and Morrison (1965) found that bilateral lesions of the medial and descending vestibular nuclei abolished the bursts of rapid eye movements in REM sleep, but the isolated eye movements persisted. These results suggest that the isolated eye movements might be involved in scanning, whereas the burst activity is not. But the particulars of which eye movements might be involved in scanning is not crucial at this point. The major issue is that the hypothesis that all the eye movements of REM sleep represent scanning activity is just one of several possible scanning hypotheses. In one sense it is an impossible hypothesis to study. The complexity of eye movements in REM sleep, the need to account for such factors as head movement and compensatory eye movements in the scanning process, and the viscissitudes of dream recall make it virtually certain that we would never be able to muster conclusive support for this scanning hypothesis even if it were true.

Another approach to the scanning hypothesis has been to observe whether eye movements are present during REM sleep in subjects who do not have scanning activity. One such group is the congenitally blind or people who have been blind for so long that they no longer have visual imagery during wakefulness or sleep. Offenkrantz and Wolpert (1963), in a study of a congenitally blind subject, reported only a single instance of eye movements during "emergent Stage 1," the cyclically appearing EEG pattern which is usually accompanied by eye movements. In other words, their subject appeared to have "REM periods" without eye movements. Awakenings from these emergent Stage 1 periods produced reports of dream imagery in all the nonvisual modalities. Offenkrantz and Wolpert interpreted these results "... as supporting the hypothesis that while Stage 1 EEG is a physiological concomitant of dreaming, REMs (rapid eye movements) only reflect visual activity in the manifest content of dreams." Berger, Olley, and Oswald (1962) found that three congenitally blind subjects and two subjects who were blind for many years and no longer experienced visual imagery showed no eye movements during emergent Stage 1. Three subjects who had become blind more recently and still had visual images showed normal eye movements in REM sleep. Although Berger *et al.* conceded that their results were consistent with the scanning hypothesis, they also suggested the possibility that "... owing to non-use, nervous pathways involved in the execution of conjugate eye-movements are poorly developed in those with life-long blindness, or, once established, suffer through disuse during prolonged blindness."

Very different results were observed in two other studies of blind subjects. Amadeo and Gomez (1966) studied eight subjects with lifelong blindness. Seven of the eight showed eye movements during REM sleep although the eye movements appeared less frequently and were smaller than in sighted subjects. Noting the "disorganized, often asynchronous EOG records" of their subjects, Amadeo and Gomez suggested that the eye movements "... could be interpreted as indicative of a lack of those maturational processes normally underlying the close association between dream imagery and REMs." Gross, Byrne, and Fisher (1965), who used a ceramic strain gauge transducer to record eye movements,[5] recorded eye movements in the REM periods of five subjects blind since birth. These authors proposed, however, that this result had no necessary bearing on the scanning hypothesis. They proposed that the eye movements of the blind and sighted subjects had a similar "physiologic substratum," but that in the sighted subjects the eye movements might have become coordinated with the visual imagery of dreams. By analogy, they reasoned that the presence of mouth movements in infants did not preclude a later specific coordination of mouth movements with speech.

It is obvious that the data on blind subjects does not resolve the issue of the scanning hypothesis. Not only are the data conflicting, but the various plausible interpretations render any result ambiguous. For

[5] The use of the ceramic strain gauges arises from a methodological problem. Gross, Byrne, and Fisher (1965) argued that the failure to record eye movements from the blind in some studies might result from the EOG (electrooculographic) method of recording eye movements. This method could fail to register eye movements when there is a diminished or absent corneofundal potential, which could be the case in many blind subjects. The ceramic strain gauge method (Baldridge, Whitman, & Kramer, 1963) detects the mechanical rotation of the eye and does not depend on a normal corneofundal potential. Berger (1967) countered that his blind subjects, who showed no eye movements by the EOG method during emergent Stage 1, showed good EOG potentials when they voluntarily moved their eyes during wakefulness. Berger suggested that the deflections recorded in emergent Stage 1 in blind subjects with the strain gauge technique might have represented eyelid blinks rather than eye movements. This issue could be resolved by direct observation of blind subjects sleeping with their eyelids taped open. Rechtschaffen and Foulkes (1965) were able to observe the eye movements of sighted subjects during Stage REM with this technique.

example, for the two studies that showed no eye movements in the blind, the authors of one interpreted their results as favorable for the scanning hypothesis, whereas the authors of the other were inclined against the hypothesis. In both studies which showed eye movements in the blind, the authors were inclined toward the scanning hypothesis.

A similar diversity of interpretations befalls other studies which demonstrate the presence of eye movements during emergent Stage 1 in subjects who are not likely to scan visual images. Moskowitz and Berger (1969) cited several studies which showed that rapid eye movements are present in the REM periods of neonates as casting doubt on the scanning hypothesis. However, we have already noted the argument that eye movements might occur as a purely physiological expression of Stage REM in the absence of visual imagery, but might become linked to the imagery with maturation. Berger (1967) has countered this argument by citing evidence of Stage REM period eye movements in decorticate cats and humans. He has proposed this evidence as indicating that if there is a maturation linkage of the eye movements and dream imagery, the linkage has not rendered the two phenomena mutually dependent. I suppose one could respond to this point by suggesting that decortication interferes with the mature linkage pattern.

The ambiguities reviewed above seem to result from the uncertainty of generalizing to eye movement–imaginary relationships in normal, sighted subjects from data on other kinds of subjects. To show how inconclusive all of the above arguments are, consider that they would all fall by the wayside if there were strong, replicable evidence that the direction of recorded eye movements corresponded to the direction expected from the reported imagery. This would be the most direct test of the scanning hypothesis because this is what is meant by scanning—moving the eyes in the direction required to inspect the visual environment.

Unfortunately, such direct tests of the scanning hypothesis have produced conflicting results. In the first "directional" test of the scanning hypothesis, Dement and Kleitman (1957) awakened subjects after 1 min of one of four predominant EOG patterns: (1) mainly vertical eye movements, (2) mainly horizontal movements, (3) both vertical and horizontal movements, (4) very little or no movement. Unfortunately, only three periods of purely vertical and only one period of purely horizontal movement were seen. In each of these four instances, the correspondence between the imagery and EOG direction was very good. Periods with little movement generally produced reports of less active dreams than periods of mixed movement, but such a difference might also be expected on the basis of nonspecific relationships.

Dement and Wolpert (1958) concentrated on the correspondence between the very last eye movement before awakening and the very last fixation reported in the dream. Only 23 of 39 reported dreams were clear enough to differentiate the last fixation in the dream. In 17 or 74% of these 23 cases the report and the eye movement corresponded—far beyond chance probability. These data appear as strong support for the scanning hypothesis. Unfortunately, there was little discussion of the criteria for rejecting reports as insufficiently detailed or of guarantees against bias in judging the correspondence of dream reports and eye movements.

Roffwarg *et al.* (1962) conducted an elaborate study in which an independent interrogator who was not aware of the recorded eye movements carefully questioned the subject upon awakening and then made a blind prediction of the pattern of eye movements recorded in the last 10–20 sec before awakening. Two judges then rated the correspondence between the predictions and the paired EOG records as good, fair, or poor. "Good correspondence" was judged for 75–80% of the pairs in which subjects had confidence in their recall of the dream. The problem with this study is that there may not have been a reliable operational definition of good correspondence. What these investigators called good correspondence might not have been called "good" by judges less friendly to the scanning hypothesis.

Moskowitz and Berger (1969) improved on the method of Roffwarg *et al.* (1962) by having a judge who was naive about the pairing of reports and EOG recordings try to match the two on the basis of the scanning hypothesis. In this way, the number of successful matchings of reports and eye movements could be evaluated against the probability of making successful matches by chance alone. Eighteen of 56 matches were correct, which was not significantly different from the 14 expected by chance. This improved methodology eliminates the effects of a bias for the scanning hypothesis. But prior to the actual matching procedure, a bias for the scanning hypothesis could help provide the fairest test of it. For example, the report of Moskowitz and Berger gives no indication of the kind of pretraining in recognizing waking scanning movements or of the kind of care in interviewing subjects that was exercised by Roffwarg *et al.* (1962). It might be productive to have investigators who are enthusiastic about the scanning hypothesis try to establish evidence for it by the rigorous methodology of Moskowitz and Berger.

Jacobs, Feldman, and Bender (1971) reported that recorded eye movements matched the dream action in only 18% of awakenings. However, the description of their methodology was very brief, and it is difficult to evaluate the study.

We have perhaps spent too many words in reviewing the data on the scanning issue. But the scanning hypothesis was one of the cornerstones on which modern psychophysiological dream research was built. Perhaps it requires a detailed review to demonstrate that the issue is still in doubt.

The evidence for nonspecific relationships between eye movements and mental activity during sleep indicates more dreamlike content associated with an abundance of eye movements. Verdone (1963, 1965) found that impressionistic ratings of amount of rapid eye movement activity in a REM period related significantly to the amount of recall, vividness, and emotionality of the awakening report. The implausibility or amount of bizarreness in a dream was not significantly related to judged amount of eye movement in the REM period, but the trend was in a positive direction. Hobson, Goldfrank, and Snyder (1965) found a highly significant relationship between amount of eye movement activity and their total content ratings, which combined estimates of physical activity, emotion, and vividness.

A recent series of experiments on the moment-to-moment relationships between eye movement activity and variations in dream quality will be considered in the next section on phasic events.

## XII. PHASIC EVENTS

In the past few years, attention has been drawn to the "tonic–phasic model of sleep" (Grosser & Siegal, 1971). This model emphasizes the distinction between the long-lasting phenomena of sleep such as stages and the short-lasting discrete events such as eye movements. The model recognizes the inhomogeneity of the tonic periods and seeks to understand it in terms of phasic changes within the tonic periods. For the psychophysiologist, the model means greater attention to short-term covariations between mental experiences and phasic events. Of course, this kind of approach is not entirely new; it has been about 15 years since Dement and Wolpert tried to relate single eye movements to specific dream images. Apparently, enough of this kind of research has now transpired that it has earned the distinction of "model." The phasic–tonic model also suggests that similarities across different tonic periods might be understood in terms of similar phasic events in the different tonic periods. This is the kind of thing that Hobson, Goldfrank, and Snyder (1965) tried to do by relating respiratory activity to dreaminess both within REM and within NREM sleep.

To judge from the nonspecific relationships between eye movement activity and dream quality for the REM period as a whole, it is a reasonable hypothesis that moment-to-moment variations in dream quality might coincide with the presence or absence of eye movements. Aserinsky (1967) hypothesized such a relationship, and Molinari and Foulkes (1969) looked for it by having subjects describe their very last experience immediately prior to awakening. The experimenters then related the presence or absence of eye movements immediately prior to awakening to ratings of the report quality. REM period reports were evaluated for presence of "secondary cognitive elaboration," that is, cognitive activity such as thinking, interpreting, or comparing. Only 12% of reports from awakenings with eye movements contained secondary cognitive elaboration as compared to 80% of reports after intervals of ocular quiescence within the REM period. Secondary cognitive elaboration was about as frequent on Stage 2 awakenings as on awakenings after intervals of ocular quiescence during REM periods.

As Molinari and Foulkes pointed out, the results of their content classification required cross-validation ". . . since not all of the dimensions finally employed in that analysis were anticipated in advance of data collection." A cross-validation study was begun in Foulkes' laboratory by Medoff and Foulkes (1971). In two subjects intensively studied by them by the time of his preliminary report, there was no confirmation of the Molinari and Foulkes result. In contrast to the method of Molinari and Foulkes, in which secondary cognitive elaboration was judged from the reports, Medoff specifically asked his subjects about the presence of secondary cognitive elaborations. It is possible, therefore, that the failure of Molinari and Foulkes (1969) to obtain secondary cognitive elaboration on eye movement awakenings could have resulted from their occlusion in the reporting process by more salient features of the mental activity associated with eye movement activity. Evidence of such salient features will be noted later. Medoff also noted a tendency for a decrease in auditory imagery in association with eye movements as compared to awakenings from quiet intervals or intervals with sawtooth waves. Perhaps it was the relatively reduced auditory activity associated with eye movement awakenings that gave these reports the appearance of having less cognitive activity in the Molinari and Foulkes study.

Medoff also found a greater incidence of recall on sawtooth and eye movement awakenings than on quiet awakenings. In the one subject with enough data on the question, he did not find, as Molinari and Foulkes had, a greater incidence of visual imagery on eye movement than on quiet awakenings.

Moving to studies of phasic events during NREM sleep, Weisz (1971) investigated whether there were any psychological differences in reports elicited after K-complexes and those after sleep spindles. There were no significant differences on any of a large number of psychological variables, including recall, imagery, dreamlike fantasy, and secondary cognitive elaboration.

Pivik (1971) studied the association of phasic events in both REM and NREM sleep to the incidence and quality of recall of mental activity immediately preceding the awakening. For phasic events during REM sleep, Pivik used the eye movements. For phasic events during NREM sleep, Pivik used the phasic inhibition of the electrically induced spinal H reflex. In the major analysis (of a complex, multifactor study) there was no significant relationship of phasic activity to recall. From among a host of mental quality variables studied (including dreamlike fantasy, sexuality, orality, thought, emotion, etc.) only increased hostility and auditory imagery were significantly related to the phasic events.

The study of Pivik was notable for his deliberate attempt to examine, in both the NREM and REM sleep of humans, a peripheral manifestation of a cerebral event called the ponto–geniculate–occipital spike (PGO).

Bursts of high voltage (200–300 $\mu$V) monophasic potentials of about 100 msec duration were first reported to occur in the pons of the cat in conjunction with bursts of rapid eye movement during REM sleep (Jouvet, Michel, & Courjon, 1959). Shortly afterward, similar spikes were observed in the lateral geniculate nucleus (Mikiten, Niebyl, & Hendley, 1961) and then in the occipital cortex (Mouret, Jeannerod, & Jouvet, 1963). The spikes appear almost synchronously in the three structures and appear to originate from a common neural generator, probably in the pons. Their initial discovery in the three structures noted above accounts for the term ponto–geniculate–occipital spike. Later, the spikes were observed in several additional structures as well.

From almost the time they were discovered, the PGO spikes have been considered by many sleep researchers as excellent candidates for a very intimate correlate of dream activity for several reasons. Their prominent appearance in the visual system (Michel, *et al.*, 1964b) was consistent with dreams as very visual phenomena. The increase in unit firing rates in many areas of the brain in conjunction with spiking (see Hobson & McCarley, 1971) is consistent with expectations that the brain is probably very active during dreaming. The PGO spikes are most dense during REM sleep when dreaming is most reliably present. Within REM sleep, the spikes are closely, although not exclusively associated with eye movements—and we have already reviewed some evidence which indicates that amount of eye movement activity is positively related to the dreamlike quality of reports elicited on REM awakenings. (Most of the eye movement activity of REM sleep is accompanied by PGO spikes, but many spikes appear independent of eye movement. Usually, there is a build-up of spike activity for a second or two in advance of a burst of eye movements, and then the spikes continue through the burst. Frequently, isolated spiking appears without any correlated eye movement activity.) Although the spikes are most plentiful during REM sleep, where they occur at the rate of about 50–70/min, isolated or short bursts of spikes appear intermittently throughout NREM sleep, which allows for the possibility that they could correlate with mental activity in both REM and NREM sleep. Finally, PGO spikes are normally (except for special drug or surgically induced states) a phenomenon of sleep—just as dreaming normally is. Spike activity appears in the lateral geniculate nucleus during wakefulness in association with eye movements, but the waking spikes follow the eye movements, whereas the sleep spikes precede the eye movements (Delorme, Jeannerod, & Jouvet, 1965).

There has been no dearth of reasons for hypothesizing PGO spikes as correlates of dream activity. The problem has been one of recording some manifestation of PGO activity in the human which could then be correlated with reports of mental activity. The search for a PGO indicator in the human hinges on a willingness to extrapolate from correlates of PGO activity in cats. Pursuing this rationale, bursts of eye movement actvity during REM sleep in humans are almost certainly indicative of PGO spike activity, which explains Pivik's use of eye movements as phasic indicators in REM sleep. The problem with this indicator, however, is that it would miss the PGO spikes of Stage REM that occurred in the absence of eye movements. Nevertheless, the eye movements should constitute a partial PGO indicator, since there are many more spikes in association with the eye movements than without them.

The problem of a PGO indicator in NREM sleep is more acute. The use of sensitive measuring techniques, multielectrode dc electrooculography by Jacobs, Feldman, and Bender (1971) and the ceramic strain gauge technique by Rechtschaffen *et al.* (1970), has revealed the presence of small but definite rapid eye movements in NREM sleep. In our experience, however, these NREM eye movements are very infrequent and do not begin to approach the incidence of PGO spiking in feline NREM sleep.

The solution to the NREM–PGO problem selected by Pivik was the phasic suppression of a spinal reflex, because it had been shown that such phasic suppressions were highly correlated with the eye movement bursts of REM sleep in the cat and in the human (Baldissera, Broggi, & Mancia, 1966; Gassel, Marchiafava, & Pompeiano, 1964; Hodes & Dement, 1964; Shimizu *et al.*, 1966). Furthermore, Pivik and Dement (1970) found that in the human, phasic suppressions of the H-reflex were coincident with phasic inhibitions of the chin muscle during NREM sleep. In the cat, phasic inhibitions of the neck musculature are frequently coincident with PGO spikes in NREM sleep, although there are many more spikes than phasic inhibitions.

Our own approach to the problem of a PGO indicator in the human was to proceed from observations that spikes recorded from the electrodes in the extraocular muscles of the cat frequently coincide with both REM and NREM–PGO spikes recorded in the brain (Gadea-Ciria & Jouvet, 1971; Michel, Rechtschaffen, & Vimont-Vicary, 1964; Rechtschaffen, Michel, & Metz, 1971). We attempted to record from surface electrodes near the orbit of the human some manifestation of the electrical activity of the extraocular muscles (Rechtschaffen *et al.*, 1970). By using very high amplification and integrating the activity to "stretch" it out enough

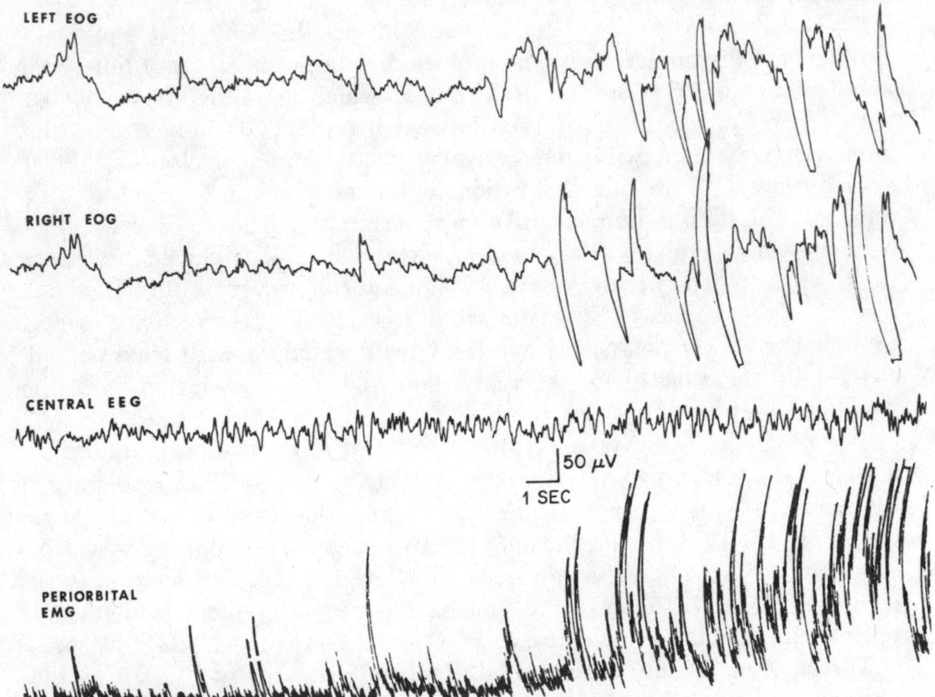


**Fig. 5.3.** Illustration of PIPs (in periorbital EMG tracing during Stage REM). Note the occurrence of PIPs both in the presence and absence of distinctive eye movements. In the latter part of the tracing there is a marked increase in tonic periorbital EMG activity along with the marked increase in PIP activity.

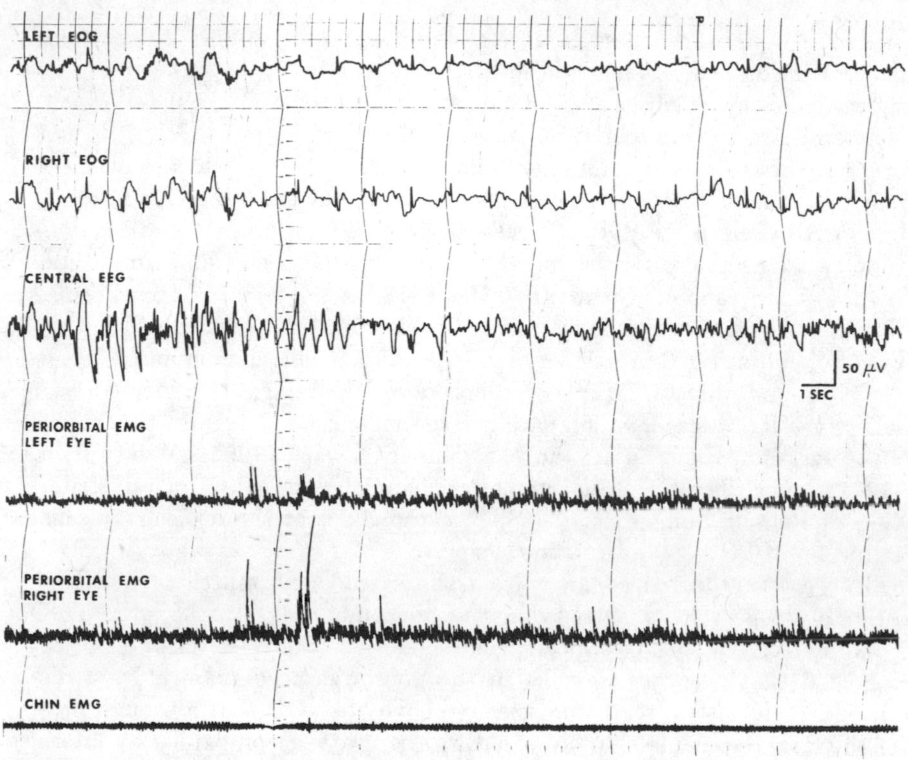


**Fig. 5.4.** Illustration of a short burst of PIP activity in the periorbital EMG tracing during Stage 2. Note the indication of a phasic suppression of the chin EMG about the time of the PIPs. Note the appearance of sawtooth waves in the EEG tracing at the time of the PIPs.

in time so that it could be monitored by the galvanometers, we recorded spike potentials which resembled those we had recorded from the extraocular muscles of the cat. These periorbital phasic integrated potentials (PIPs as we called them) regularly appear in conjunction with the rapid eye movements of REM sleep, but are also plentiful in REM sleep in the absence of eye movements (see Fig. 5.3). (Waking eye movements are generally accompanied by much smaller phasic potentials.) The PIPs also appear intermittently during NREM sleep, sometimes in conjunction with phasic inhibitions of the chin muscle and sawtooth waves (see Fig. 5.4).

We cannot be sure that the periorbital PIP signals originate in the extraocular muscles, because we have not recorded from electrodes directly in these muscles in the human. Many of the PIPs undoubtedly originate in the orbicularis muscles, and these probably represent false positive PGO spikes, since the orbicularis muscle of the cat sometimes shows spikes in the absence of PGO activity, but fortunately these orbicularis spikes are relatively rare. Most likely the periorbital PIPs do not originate in the masseter muscle. Spikes recorded from electrodes over the masseter muscle frequently accompany periorbital PIPs in NREM sleep, but in REM sleep the PIPs increase dramatically in frequency and amplitude, whereas the masseter spikes decrease in frequency and amplitude. Although we cannot be sure that the PIPs originate in the extraocular muscles, they do tend to be distributed in sleep like PGO spikes. Also, they have some functional properties of PGO spikes. Rechtschaffen and Chernik (1971) found that REM period deprivation increased the incidence of PIPs in NREM sleep, which parallels the increase in NREM PGO spikes after REM deprivation in the cat (Vimont-Vicary, 1965). Wyatt *et al.* (1971) found that the drug parachlorophenylalanine caused a redistribution of PIPs in human sleep similar to the effect of the drug on the distribution of PGO spikes in feline sleep.

If the PIPs do indeed arise from the extraocular muscles, then they probably reflect PGO activity in the pons more closely than the PGO spike activity in the lateral geniculate nucleus. Gadea-Ciria and Jouvet reported that every PGO spike in the pons was accompanied by a discharge in the lateral rectus muscle. We have observed that although most of the lateral geniculate spikes of REM sleep were accompanied by lateral rectus spikes, only about half of the NREM lateral geniculate spikes were accompanied by lateral rectus spikes. It appears that, at best, some false negative as well as false positive detection is involved in the use of periorbital PIPs as PGO spike indicators. Nevertheless, there appeared to be sufficient similarity between the two phenomena to venture studies of the relationship of PIPs to mental activity during sleep.

Two studies on the relationship of mental activity to PIPs have just been completed in our laboratory. The data analysis has just begun, and to date only the analyses on "distortion" (lack of correspondence to everyday life) have been completed. In the first study (Rechtschaffen, *et al.*; paper submitted for presentation at the 1972 annual meeting of the Association for the Psychophysiological Study of Sleep) we investigated the PIPs in NREM sleep. Ten subjects who slept in the laboratory for 10–22 nights each were awakened after 3–5 sec of PIP activity in Stage 2 and from control periods in Stage 2 without PIP activity. Subjects were asked to describe their experience just prior to awakening. PIP awakenings produced significantly more reports with distortion than control awakenings. The relationship was most pronounced for instances of "extreme distortion" as rated by independent judges. In this analysis, only 5% of control awakenings produced reports with extreme distortion. Awakenings from intervals with a mixture of PIPs and tonic periorbital activation produced extreme distortion in 27% of reports. Awakenings from intervals with PIP activity alone produced extreme distortion in 50% of the reports. Eye movement activity (recorded by the strain gauge technique) in association with the PIPs did not increase the incidence of distortion in the reports.

Watson (paper submitted for presentation to the 1972 meeting of the Association for the Psychophysiological Study of Sleep) followed-up this study with an investigation of PIP activity in the REM sleep of four subjects. Watson employed three kinds of awakenings: control awakenings—made after at least 15 sec of quiescence (no PIPs or eye movements); PIP awakenings—made after about 3–4 sec of PIPs in the absence of detectable eye movements; PIP–REM awakenings made after about 3–4 sec of PIPs accompanied by rapid eye movements. PIP and PIP–REM awakenings were preceded by at least 12 sec of quiescence. Both PIP and PIP–REM awakenings produced subjects' ratings of very bizarre or moderately bizarre for the last experience on 55% of reports as compared to 24% for control awakenings. Only 7% of control awakenings, as compared to 61% of PIP and 41% of PIP–REM awakenings produced reports of an increase in bizarreness from the next-to-last to the very last experience. Only 9% of control awakenings, compared to 34% of PIP and 37% of PIP–REM awakenings produced reports in which the very last experience did not fit into the context of the next-to-last experience.

Taking the two studies together, it appears that PIPs, with or without eye movements, are associated with bizarreness or unreality in the stream of sleep mentation. This association obtains within Stage 2 sleep, and within REM sleep. Considering the much greater frequency of PIPs in REM sleep, PIP activity is very likely related to many of the differences between REM and NREM mentation as well. It should be emphasized that PIPs do not appear responsible for dreaming per se. Rather, they are associated with the appearance of the bizarre in the dream. Whether this appearance results from the active intrusion of discordant mental engrams or from the loosening of associative connections remains to be determined.

Following are excerpts from two PIP awakening reports from Watson's study which illustrate the intrusion of bizarre content into the dream, presumably coincident with PIP onset.

In the next to the last experience, the dreamer, a female, was talking with an older woman who said, "If I could get you to work better." During the last experience, which the subject estimated as about 5 sec in duration, she suddenly felt she was both women: "There was two of me." She spoke a confused sentence to herself: "To keep those two days free, I'll probably surround the weekend." (PIPs started 6 sec before the awakening; there were no eye movements.)

In the next-to-the last experience, the dreamer was listening to his girl friend talk about a problem she was having and was feeling concerned and wondering what he could do for her. The girl was crying. At some point within the last 5 sec by the subjects' estimation, he noticed that her tears were running down in four straight vertical lines from each eye. (PIPs started 5 sec before awakening; there were no eye movements.)

## XIII. PHASIC EVENTS AND OTHER PHYSIOLOGICAL VARIABLES

For several of the instances in which we have noted a relationship between a psychological and physiological variable, there was evidence that one or both of the variables were also related to eye movements (and by inference to PGO activity). Dreamlike mentation was related to low rectal temperature; both of these variables were related to amount of eye movement activity in the REM period. In fact, dreamlike quality tended toward stronger relationships with eye movements than with rectal temperature. There was some evidence of an association of skin potential activity in REM sleep to dream emotionality; other evidence indicated that the skin potential fluctuations of REM sleep tended to appear with bursts of rapid eye movement. Sustained erections in REM sleep were associated with more recall of content on awakening; sustained erections were also associated with more eye movement activity in the REM period—which in turn had been related to more recall in other studies. There are some indications that heart rate variability is related to dream emotionality, as well as suggestions from the work of Aserinsky (1965) and Baust and Bohnert (1969) that the heart rate tends to vary at the time of rapid eye movement bursts. Respiratory rate is related to dreaminess in Stage REM; in the same study (Hobson, Goldfrank, & Snyder, 1965) the correlation of dreaminess to eye movement activity was even greater, and Aserinsky has noted a stereotyped increase of respiratory rate in conjunction with eye movement bursts in REM sleep. Respiratory rate was also related to dreaminess of NREM mental activity; one can only wonder whether both these variables are related to undetected NREM phasic events.

What we are getting at is that the psychophysiology of sleep research is at the point where we should think about unconfounding our physiological variables in the search for the specific variables which are most intimately related to sleep mentation. Of course, we will also need to unconfound the psychological variables, but this seems to be the less pressing problem at the moment. Most recent psychophysiological studies of sleep have measured several dimensions of the mental activity—which at least permits a statement about the dimensions that do relate to a physiological variable and the dimensions that do not. (Where more than one psychological dimension has related to a physiological variable, there has not been much effort to determine the dependence of one dimension on another.) On the physiological side, the attempts at a multidimensional approach have been fewer. The difference is understandable. Once a verbal report has been elicited, it can be rated on a number of dimensions. By contrast, there are limits to the number of channels on a polygraph and the amount of gear that can be attached to a subject and still allow him to sleep comfortably. Furthermore, the amount of work in a study begins to escalate geometrically. I already regret having raised this issue.

Nevertheless, sleep researchers will have to proceed with some unconfounding. Partial correlation techniques may help. Making awakenings after different combinations of physiological activity is another tactic.

The confusion which seems most bothersome at the present is between the phasic events which reflect PGO activity and the systemic variables—mostly the autonomic measures. Are the correlations between autonomic variability and sleep mentation epiphenomenal to the correlations between phasic events and sleep mentation? Phrased another way, can we find autonomic-content correlations when there are no PGO indicators associated with the autonomic changes. Johnson and Karpan (1968) have reported that autonomic changes are regularly associated with K-complexes but not with isolated sleep spindles, whereas Weisz (1971) could find no psychological differences in reports after K-complexes and reports after sleep spindles.

Or perhaps, following a James–Lange approach, the phasic event–mental activity correlations are epiphenomenal. Are there any such correlations when autonomic changes do not accompany the phasic events?

Perhaps the phasic events and the autonomic changes are largely inseparable because they arise from a common generator. Morrison and Pompeiano (1970) have reported that the lesions of the medial and descending vestibular nuclei which abolish the bursts of rapid eye movement in the REM sleep of the cat also abolish many of the phasic vegetative variations of REM sleep. On the other hand, Spreng, Johnson, and Lubin (1968) have reported that autonomic variability in human REM sleep is not significantly related to the amount of eye movement burst activity.

But one then has to wonder about possible relationships to the phasic events which are not associated with eye movements.

Back to the laboratory!

## REFERENCES

Amadeo, M., & Gomez, E. Eye movements, attention and dreaming in subjects with lifelong blindness. *Canadian Psychiatric Association Journal*, 1966, **11,** 501–507.

Arkin, A. M., Toth, M. F., Baker, J., & Hastey, J. M. The degree of concordance between the content of sleep talking and mentation recalled in wakefulness. *Journal of Nervous and Mental Desease*, 1970, **151,** 375–393.

Asahina, K. Paradoxical phase and reverse paradoxical phase in human sleep. *Journal of the Physiology Society of Japan*, 1962, **24,** 443–450.

Aserinsky, E. Periodic respiratory pattern occuring in conjunction with eye movements during sleep. *Science*, 1965, **150,** 763–766.

Aserinsky, E. Rapid eye movement density and pattern in the sleep of normal young adults. *Psychophysiology*, 1971, **8,** 361–375.

Aserinsky, E., & Kleitman, N. Regularly occurring periods of eye motility, and concomitant phenomena, during sleep. *Science*, 1953, **118,** 273–274.

Baldissera, F., Broggi, G., & Mancia, M. Monosynaptic and polysynaptic spinal reflexes during physiological sleep and wakefulness. *Archives Italiennes de Biologie*, 1966, **104,** 112–133.

Baldridge, B. J., Whitman, R. M., & Kramer, M. A simplified method for detecting eye movements during dreaming. *Psychosomatic Medicine*, 1963, **25,** 78–82.

Baust, W., & Bohnert, J. The regulation of heart rate during sleep. *Experimental Brain Research*, 1969, **7,** 169–180.

Baust, W., Bohmke, J., & Blossfeld, U. Somato-sympathetic reflexes during natural sleep and wakefulness in unrestrained cats. *Experimental Brain Research*, 1971, **12,** 361–369. (a)

Baust, W., Bohmke, J., & Blossfeld, U. Reflex responses in the sympathetic and vagal nerve evoked by reticular stimulation during sleep and wakefulness. *Experimental Brain Research*, 1971, **12,** 370–378. (b)

Baust, W., Weidinger, H., & Kirchner, F. Sympathetic activity during natural sleep and arousal. *Archives Italiennes de Biologie*, 1968, **106,** 379–390.

Berger, R. J. Tonus of extrinsic laryngeal muscles during sleep and dreaming. *Science*, 1961, **134,** 840.

Berger, R. J. When is a dream is a dream is a dream? *Experimental Neurology, Suppl.* 1967, **4,** 15–28.

Berger, R. J., & Oswald, I. Eye movements during active and passive dreams. *Science*, 1962, **137,** 601.

Berger, R. J., Olley, P., & Oswald, I. The EEG, eye movements and dreams of the blind. *Quarterly Journal of Experimental Psychology*, 1962, **14,** 183–186.

Broughton, R. J., Poire, R., & Tassinari, C. A. The electrodermogram (Tarchanoff effect) during sleep. *Electroencephalography and Clinical Neurophysiology*, 1965, **18,** 691–708.

Burch, N. R. Data processing of psychophysiological recordings. In L. D. Proctor & W. R. Adey (Eds.), *Symposium on the analysis of central nervous system and cardiovascular data using computer methods.* Washington, D.C.: National Aeronautics and Space Administration, 1965. Pp. 165–180.

Delorme, F., Jeannerod, M., & Jouvet, M. Effects remarquables de la reserpine sur l'activite EEG phasique ponto-geniculo-occipitale. *Comptes Rendus des Seances de la Societe de Biologie*, 1965, **159,** 900–903.

Dement, W., & Kleitman, N. The relation of eye movements during sleep to dream activity: An objective method for the study of dreaming. *Journal of Experimental Psychology*, 1957, **53,** 339–346.

Dement, W., & Wolpert, E. A. The relation of eye movements, body motility, and external stimuli to dream content. *Journal of Experimental Psychology*, 1958, **55,** 543–553.

Fahrion, S. L., Davison, L., & Breger, L. The relationship of heart rate and dream content in heart-rate responders. Paper presented at the meeting of the Association for the Psychophysiological Study of Sleep, Santa Monica, California, April 1967.

Fisher, C. Dreaming and sexuality. In R. M. Lowenstein, L. M. Newman, M. Schur & A. J. Solnit (Eds.), *Psychoanalysis—a general psychology.* New York: International Universities Press, 1966. Pp. 537–569.

Fisher, C., Gross, J., & Zuch, J. Cycle of penile erection synchronous with dreaming (REM) sleep. *Archives of General Psychiatry*, 1965, **12,** 29–45.

Foulkes, D. Dream reports from different stages of sleep. Unpublished doctoral dissertation, University of Chicago, 1960.

Foulkes, D. *The psychology of sleep.* New York: Scribner, 1966.

Foulkes, D. Nonrapid eye movement mentation. *Experimental Neurology, Suppl.*, 1967, **4,** 28–38.

Foulkes, D., & Rechtschaffen, A. Presleep determinants of dream content: Effects of two films. *Perceptual and Motor Skills*, 1964, **19,** 983–1005.

Foulkes, W. D. Dream reports from different stages of sleep. *Journal of Abnormal and Social Psychology*, 1962, **65,** 14–25.

Fuchs, A. F., & Ron, S. An analysis of the rapid eye movements of sleep in the monkey. *Electroencephalography and Clinical Neurophysiology*, 1968, **25,** 244–251.

Gabersek, V., & Scherrer, J. Les mouvements oculaires pendant la phase pardoxale du sommeil. *Acta Neurologia Latinoamerica*, 1970, **14,** 40–50.

Gadea-Ciria, E., & Jouvet, M. Corticofugal control of pontine PGO activity in the cat. Paper presented at the meeting of the Association for the Psychophysiological Study of Sleep, Bruges, Belgium, June 1971.

Gassel, M. M., Marchiafava, P. L., & Pompeiano, O. Tonic and phasic inhibition of spinal reflexes during deep, desynchronized sleep in unrestrained cats. *Archives Italiennes de Biologie*, 1964, **102,** 471–499.

Goodenough, D. R., Shapiro, A., Holden, M., & Steinschriber, L. A comparison of "dreamers" and "nondreamers": Eye movements, electrocephalograms, and the recall of dreams. *Journal of Abnormal and Social Psychology*, 1959, **59,** 295–302.

Goodenough, D. R., Lewis, H. B., Shapiro, A., Jaret, L., & Sleser, I. Dream reporting following abrupt and gradual awakenings from different types of sleep. *Journal of Personality and Social Psychology*, 1965, **2,** 170–179.

Gross, J., Byrne, J., & Fisher, C. Eye movements during emergent stage 1 EEG in subjects with lifelong blindness. *Journal of Nervous and Mental Disease*, 1965, **141,** 365–370.

Grosser, G. S., & Siegal, A. W. Emergence of a tonic-phasic model for sleep and dreaming: Behavioral and physiological observations. *Psychological Bulletin*, 1971, **75,** 60–72.

Grossman, W., Gardner, R., Roffwarg, H., Fekete, A., Beers, L., & Weiner, H. Relations of dreamed to actual limb movement. Paper presented at the meeting of the Association for the Psychophysiological Study of Sleep, Bruges, Belgium, June 1971.

Hall, C. S., & Van de Castle, R. L. *The content analysis of dreams*. New York: Appleton, 1966.

Hauri, P. Effects of evening activity on early night sleep. *Psychophysiology*, 1968, **4,** 267–277.

Hauri, P., & Rechtschaffen, A. An unsuccessful attempt to find physiological correlates of NREM recall. Paper presented at the meeting of the Association for the Psychophysiological Study of Sleep, New York, March 1963.

Hauri, P. & Van de Castle, R. L. Dream content and physiological arousal during REMPs. Paper presented at the meeting of the Association for the Psychophysiological Study of Sleep, Santa Fe, March 1970.

Hauri, P., Sawyer, J., & Rechtschaffen, A. Dimensions of dreaming: A factored scale for rating dream reports. *Journal of Abnormal Psychology*, 1967, **72,** 16–22.

Hawkins, D. R., Puryear, H. B., Wallace, C. D., Deal, W. B., & Thomas, E. S. Basal skin resistance during sleep and "dreaming". *Science*, 1962, **136,** 321–322.

Hersch, R. G., Antrobus, J. S., Arkin, A. M., & Singer, J. L. Dreaming as a function of sympathetic arousal. *Psychophysiology*, 1970, **7,** 329–330.

Hobson, J. A., & McCarley, R. W. *Neuronal activity in sleep. An annotated bibliography.* Los Angeles: Brain Research Institute Publications Office, 1971.

Hobson, J. A., Goldfrank, F., & Snyder, F. Respiration and mental activity in sleep. *Journal of Psychiatric Research*, 1965, **3,** 79–90.

Hodes, R., & Dement, W. C. Depression of electrically induced reflexes ("H-reflexes") in man during low voltage EEG "sleep". *Electroencephalography and Clinical Neurophysiology*, 1964, **17,** 617–629.

Jacobs, L., Feldman, M., & Bender, M. B. Eye movements during sleep. I. The pattern in the normal human. *Archives of Neurology*, 1971, **25,** 151–159.

Jacobson, A., Kales, A., Lehmann, D., & Hoedemaker, F. S. Muscle tonus in human subjects during sleep and dreaming. *Experimental Neurology*, 1964, **10,** 418–424.

Jeannerod, M., Mouret, J., & Jouvet, M. Etude de la motricite oculaire au cours de la phase pardoxale du sommeil chez le chat. *Electroencephalography and Clinical Neurophysiology*, 1965, **18,** 554–566.

Johnson, L. C. Spontaneous and orienting responses during sleep. *Navy Medical Neuropsychiatric Research Unit Report* #66–9, 1966.

Johnson, L. C. A psychophsiology for all states. *Psychophysiology*, 1970, **6,** 501–516.

Johnson, L. C., & Karpan, W. E. Autonomic correlates of the spontaneous K-complex. *Psychophysiology*, 1968, **4,** 444–452.

Johnson, L. C., & Lubin, A. Spontaneous electrodermal activity during waking and sleeping. *Psychophsiology*, 1966, **3,** 8–17.

Jouvet, M. Neurophysiology of the states of sleep. *Physiological Review*, 1967, **47,** 117–177.

Jouvet, M., Michel, F., & Courjon, J. Sur un stade d'activite electrique cerebrale rapide au cours du sommeil physiologique. *Comptes Rendus des Seances de la Societe de Biologie*, 1959, **153,** 1024–1028.

Kamiya, J. Behavioral, subjective, and physiological aspects of drowsiness and sleep. In D. W. Fiske & S. R. Maddi (Eds.), *Functions of varied experience*. Homewood, Illinois: Dorsey Press, 1965. Pp. 145–174.

Karacan, I., Goodenough, D. R., Shapiro, A., & Starker, S. Erection cycle during sleep in relation to dream anxiety. *Archives of General Psychiatry*, 1966, **15,** 183–189.

Kleitman, N. *Sleep and wakefulness.* (2nd ed.) Chicago: University of Chicago Press, 1963.

Knopf, N. B. The study of heart and respiration rates during dreaming. Unpublished master's thesis, University of Chicago, 1962.

Koumans, A. J., Tursky, B., & Solomon, P. Electrodermal levels and fluctuations during normal sleep. *Psychophysiology*, 1968, **5,** 300–306.

Larson, J. D., & Foulkes, D. EMG suppression during sleep and dream activity. *Psychophysiology*, 1968, **4,** 371.

Lester, B. K., Burch, N. R., & Dossett, R. C. Nocturnal EEG-GSR profiles: The influence of presleep states. *Psychophysiology*, 1967, **3,** 238–248.

Max, L. W. An experimental study of the motor theory of consciousness: III. Action-current responses in deaf mutes during sleep, sensory stimulation and dreams. *Journal of Comparative Psychology*, 1935, **19,** 469–486.

McGuigan, F. J., & Tanner, R. G. Covert oral behavior during conversational and visual dreams. *Psychophysiology*, 1970, **7,** 329.

Medoff, L., & Foulkes, D. "Microscopic" studies of mentation in stage REM: A preliminary report. Paper presented at the meeting of the Association of the Psychophysiological Study of Sleep, Bruges, Belgium, June 1971.

Michel, F., Jeannerod, M., Mouret, J., Rechtschaffen, A., & Jouvet, M. Sur le mecanismes de l'activite de pointes au niveau du systeme visuel au cours de la phase paradoxale du sommeil. *Comptes Rendus des Seances de la Societe de Biologie*, **1964, 158,** 103–106. (a)

Michel, F., Rechtschaffen, A., & Vimont-Vicary, P. Activite electrique des muscles oculaires extrinseques au cours du cycle veille-sommeil. *Comptes Rendus des Seances de la Societe de Biologie*, 1964, **158,** 106–109. (b)

Mikiten, T., Niebyl, P., & Hendley, C. EEG desynchronization during behavioral sleep associated with spike discharges from the thalamus of the cat. *Federation Proceedings*, 1961, **20,** 327.

Molinari, S., & Foulkes, D. Tonic and phasic events during sleep: Psychological correlates and implications. *Perceptual and Motor Skills*, 1969, **29,** 343–368.

Monroe, L. J., Rechtschaffen, A., Foulkes, D., & Jensen, J. Discriminability of REM and NREM reports. *Journal of Personality and Social Psychology*, 1965, **2,** 456–460.

Morrison, A. R., & Pompeiano, O. Vestibular influences during sleep. VI. Vestibular control of autonomic functions during the rapid eye movements of desynchronized sleep. *Archives Italiennes de Biologie*, 1970, **108,** 154–180.

Moskowitz, E., & Berger, R. J. Rapid eye movements and dream imagery: Are they related? *Nature*, 1969, **224,** 613–614.

Mouret, J., Jeannerod, M., & Jouvet, M. L'activite electrique du systeme visuel au cours de la phase paradoxale du sommeil chez le chat. *Journal de Physiologie*, 1963, **55,** 305–306.

Offenkrantz, W., & Wolpert, E. A. The detection of dreaming in a congenitally blind subject. *Journal of Nervous and Mental Disease*, 1963, **136,** 88–90.

Oswald, I. *Sleeping and waking. Physiology and psychology.* New York: Elsevier, 1962.

Pivik, R. T. Mental activity and phasic events during sleep. Unpublished doctoral dissertation, Stanford University, 1971.

Pivik, T., & Dement, W. C. Phasic changes in muscular and reflex activity during non-REM sleep. *Experimental Neurology*, 1970, **27,** 115–124.

Pivik, T., & Foulkes, D. NREM mentation: Relation to personality, orientation time, and time of night. *Journal of Consulting and Clinical Psychology*, 1968, **37,** 144–151.

Pompeiano, O., & Morrison, A. R. Vestibular influences during sleep. I. Abolition of the rapid eye movements of desynchronized sleep following vestibular lesions. *Archives Italiennes de Biologie*, 1965, **103,** 569–595.

Rechtschaffen, A., & Chernik, D. A. The effect of REM deprivation on periorbital spike activity in NREM sleep. Paper presented at the meeting of the Association for the Psychophysiological Study of Sleep, Bruges, Belgium, June 1971.

Rechtschaffen, A., & Foulkes, D. Effect of visual stimuli on dream content. *Perceptual and Motor Skills*, 1965, **20,** 1149–1160.

Rechtschaffen, A., Goodenough, D. R., & Shapiro, A. Patterns of sleep talking. *Archives of General Psychiatry*, 1962, **7,** 418–426.

Rechtschaffen, A., Hauri, P., & Zeitlin, M. Auditory awakening thresholds in REM and NREM sleep stages. *Perceptual and Motor Skills*, 1966, **22,** 927–942.

Rechtschaffen, A., Michel, F., & Metz, J. T. Relationship between extraocular and PGO activity in the cat. Paper presented at the meeting of the Association for the Psychophysiological Study of Sleep, Bruges, Belgium, June 1971.

Rechtschaffen, A., Verdone, P., & Wheaton, J. V. Reports of mental activity during sleep. *Canadian Psychiatric Association Journal*, 1963, **8,** 409–414.

Rechtschaffen, A., Vogel, G., & Shaikun, G. Interrelatedness of mental activity during sleep. *Archives of General Psychiatry*, 1963, **9,** 536–547.

Rechtschaffen, A., Molinari, S., Watson, R., & Wincor, M. Extraocular potentials: A possible indicator of PGO activity in the human. *Psychophysiology*, 1970, **7,** 336.

Roffwarg, H. P., Dement, W. C., Muzio, J. N., & Fisher, C. Dream imagery: Relationship to rapid eye movements of sleep. *Archives of General Psychiatry*, 1962, **7,** 235–238.

Shapiro, A., Goodenough, D. R., Biederman, I., & Sleser, I. Dream recall and the physiology of sleep. *Journal of Applied Physiology*, 1964, **19,** 778–783.

Shimizu, A., Yamada, Y. Yamamoto, J., Fujiki, A., & Kanedo, Z. Pathways of descending influence on H reflex during sleep. *Electroencephalography and Clinical Neurophysiology*, 1966, **20,** 337–347.

Snyder, F., Hobson, J. A., Morrison, D. F., & Goldfrank, F. Changes in respiration, heart rate, and systolic blood pressure in human sleep. *Journal of Applied Physiology*, 1964, **19**, 417–422.

Spreng, L. F., Johnson, L. C., & Lubin, A. Autonomic correlates of eye movement bursts during stage REM sleep. *Psychophysiology*, 1968, **4**, 311–323.

Stoyva, J. M. Finger electromyographic activity during sleep: Its relation to dreaming in deaf and normal subjects. *Journal of Abnormal Psychology*, 1965, **70**, 343–349.

Tart, C. T. Patterns of basal skin resistance during sleep. *Psychophysiology*, 1967, **4**, 35–39.

Verdone, P. Variables related to the temporal reference of manifest dream content. Unpublished doctoral dissertation, University of Chicago, 1963.

Verdone, P. Temporal reference of manifest dream content. *Perceptual and Motor Skills*, 1965, **20**, 1253–1268.

Vimont-Vicary, P. *La suppression des differents etats de sommeil: etude comportementale, EEG, et neuropharmacologique chez le chat.* Lyon, France: Imprimerie L.M.D., 1965.

Vogel, G. W., Barrowclough, B., & Giesler, D. D. Similarity of REM and sleep onset Stage 1 reports. Paper presented at the meeting of the Association for the Psychophysiological Study of Sleep, Santa Fe, New Mexico, March 1970.

Watson, R. Mental correlates of periorbital PIPs during REM sleep. Paper presented at the meeting of the Association for the Psychophysiological study of Sleep, Lake Minnewaska, New York, May 1972.

Weisz, R. Phenomenal correlates of discrete events in NREM sleep. Paper presented at the meeting of the Association for the Psychophysiological Study of Sleep, Bruges, Belgium, June 1971.

Wolpert, E. A. Studies in psychophysiology of dreams. II. An electromyographic study of dreaming. *Archives of General Psychiatry*, 1960, **2**, 231–241.

Wyatt, R. J., Gillin, J. C., Green, R., Horwitz, D., & Snyder, F. Measurement of phasic integrated potentials (PIP) during treatment with parachlorophenylalanine (PCPA). Paper presented at the meeting of the Association for the Psychophysiological Study of Sleep, Bruges, Belgium, June 1971.

# 27

**BARBER, T. X. et al.**

# *Effect of Hypnotic Induction and Suggestions on Nocturnal Dreaming and Thinking*

Seventy-seven subjects participated in a 2 × 3 factorial experiment which examined the effects of hypnotic induction and types of suggestions on sleep mentation. Immediately before going to sleep at night, half of the subjects were exposed to a hypnotic induction and half were not, and all subjects were given either authoritative, permissive, or no suggestions to think and dream that night on a specific topic. Subjects reported their thoughts and dreams when awakened at sleep onset and during rapid-eye-movement (REM) and non-REM periods. The intricate findings indicated that hypnotic induction and types of suggestions exerted complex effects on nocturnal thinking and dreaming. The contents of the dreams were affected by an interaction between hypnotic induction and types of suggestions, and the hypnotic induction increased the number of nocturnal thoughts which pertained to the specified topic.

In 1911, Schroetter exposed subjects to a hypnotic induction procedure and then suggested that they would dream on a specific topic that night. Upon awakening the next morning, the subjects typically told Schroetter that they had dreamt about the suggested topic. Although this and other studies (Fisher, 1953; Nachmansohn, 1925; Newman, Katz, & Rubenstein, 1960) indicated that suggestions given under "hypnosis" may affect the manifest contents of nocturnal dreams, the results were not conclusive since the subjects gave their dream reports not at the time they were dreaming but many hours (or days) later.

More recent studies indicated that dreams occur at night when the sleeper shows rapid eye movements (REMs) together with a "Stage 1" electroencephalographic (EEG) pattern (low-voltage, mixed-frequency, nonspindling EEG; Dement & Kleitman, 1957a, 1957b). This discovery enabled researchers to study more directly the effects of suggestions upon nocturnal dreams. Three major studies were conducted (Stoyva, 1961; Tart, 1964; Tart & Dick, 1970) in which highly hypnotizable subjects were exposed to a hypnotic induction procedure and to suggestions to dream that night about particular events. The subjects then went to sleep and were awakened during or immediately after REM periods and asked to report their dreams. Stoyva (1961) reported that a large proportion of the nocturnal dreams were influenced by the suggestions that he gave to the subjects prior to sleep (e.g., "You will dream in every dream tonight that you are performing in a circus"). He also found that suggestions given together with a hypnotic induction procedure had a greater influence on dreams than suggestions given without a hypnotic induction. Similarly, Tart (1964) and Tart and Dick (1970) found that when awakened at night during REM periods, at least 50% of the highly hypnotizable subjects reported dreams that pertained to the suggested topic.

Although the recent studies (Stoyva, 1961; Tart, 1964; Tart & Dick, 1970) provide useful data pertaining to the effects of suggestions on nocturnal dreams, they have four general limitations:

1. It was not clearly determined whether a hypnotic induction procedure (or "hypnosis") was a necessary or helpful factor in eliciting responsiveness to the suggestions. Tart (1964) and Tart and Dick (1970) gave suggestions

to dream about particular events only to selected subjects who had been exposed to a hypnotic induction procedure. They did not attempt to ascertain if the same suggestions would also have influenced the dream reports if they had been given to subjects who had not been exposed to a hypnotic induction (nonhypnotic subjects). Stoyva (1961) used a comparison group of nonhypnotic subjects. However, he gave the suggestions to dream about particular events in a markedly different way to the hypnotic and nonhypnotic subjects. With regard to the hypnotic subjects, Stoyva repeated emphatically six times, "You will dream in every dream tonight that you are 'performing in a circus'." In contrast, the nonhypnotic subjects were simply told once, in a "by-the-way manner," "Now, then, tonight I want to make use of waking suggestions, and I want you to dream in every dream that you are 'riding a horse.' O.K.?" Although the hypnotic subjects reported more dreams on the suggested topic than the nonhypnotic subjects, it is not clear whether this difference was due to the former group being in "hypnosis" when they received the suggestions or to the fact that the hypnotic subjects were given repeated, emphatic suggestions, whereas the nonhypnotic subjects were given a simple, nonemphatic suggestion.

2. A second deficiency in this area of research is that the wording or phrasing of the suggestions has been ignored. In each of the studies cited above the hypnotic subjects were given an authoritative suggestion worded as a command, for example, "You will dream tonight on a certain topic." However, research pertaining to the wording or phrasing of suggestions (Barber, 1970; Barber & Calverley, 1966; Barber & De Moor, 1972) suggests the hypothesis that permissively worded suggestions (e.g., "Try to dream tonight on a certain topic") are more effective than authoritatively worded suggestions. This hypothesis should be tested in further research.

3. A third deficiency is that the recent studies focused on dream reports solicited during REM awakenings. However, a separate series of investigations (Foulkes, 1962; Foulkes & Vogel, 1965; Goodenough, Lewis, Shapiro, Jaret, & Sleser, 1965; Kamiya, 1961; Rechtschaffen, Verdone, & Wheaton, 1963) showed that when awakened during REM periods *and also during periods of non-REM*, some subjects stated that they were "dreaming" and others stated that they were "thinking" while they were asleep. Although subjects more often described their mental processes as dreaming during REM sleep and as thinking during non-REM sleep, both types of reports are obtained during REM and non-REM awakenings (Foulkes, 1962; Foulkes & Vogel, 1965). The hypothesis that suggestions may affect reports of thinking in a manner different from reports of dreaming needs to be tested in further research.

4. A fourth deficiency is that studies in this area used selected "highly hypnotizable" subjects. We do not know whether suggestions to dream at night on a selected topic are effective only with highly hypnotizable subjects or if they also affect the dreams of subjects who are medium or low on hypnotizability. Clearly, further studies should look more closely into the relationship between hypnotizability and responsiveness to suggestions to dream on a particular topic.

In light of these considerations, the present study was designed to answer four questions:

1. Are suggestions to think and dream on a specified topic more effective in changing the contents of nocturnal thoughts and dreams when the suggestions are given with rather than without a preceding hypnotic induction procedure?

2. Does an authoritatively worded suggestion ("You will think and dream on a specified topic") have a more potent effect on nocturnal thinking and dreaming than a permissively worded suggestion ("Try to think and dream on the specified topic")?

3. Do suggestions to think and dream on a particular topic, given with or without a hypnotic induction procedure, affect nocturnal thinking differently from nocturnal dreaming?

4. Are suggestions to think and dream on a specified topic more effective with subjects who are high, rather than medium or low, on hypnotizability?

## Method

### *Subjects*

Seventy-seven female student nurses (ages 17–22), who were receiving training in psychiatric nursing at Medfield State Hospital, volunteered to serve as subjects in a two-night sleep study. They were paid $8.00 for their participation. The students had not previously participated in experimental studies at Medfield.

## *First Night (Adaptation to the Laboratory)*

To become familiar with the general experimental situation and with sleeping in the laboratory, each subject slept in a private room in the research building for one night, one week prior to coming back for a second (test) night. On the first (adaptation) night, a subject reported to the laboratory around 10 p.m. and was exposed to a tape-recorded statement which described the nature of the recording electrodes that would be attached to her face and head during the two nights she would be sleeping in the laboratory. After the subject went to bed, a research assistant, a girl of her own age, entered the room and attached electrodes around the eyes and on the vertex and occipital area. The experimenter and polygraph operator (K. W. H.) then entered and played the following tape:

> In this experiment, we will study psychological processes, mental processes, that go on during sleep. An alarm clock will ring several times during the night. When you hear it ring, give a report of your mental processes. State first if anything was going through your mind immediately before the alarm. Think carefully and try to remember if anything was going through your mind. If something was going through your mind, please state in detail what it was. Next, state if it was a dream or if you were thinking about it. Then state if, at the time the alarm went off, you were awake, drifting off to sleep, lightly sleeping, or deeply sleeping. Please give your report loudly and clearly so that it can be recorded by this tape recorder.

The reporting procedure was then rehearsed with the subject; that is, the female research assistant entered the room, the alarm rang, and the subject was shown a printed card which reminded her of the information sought. Upon demonstrating that she understood the reporting procedure, the subject was left alone to sleep. She was awakened twice during the night—two hours and four hours after going to bed—and reports were taken.

After the subject was awakened in the morning, around 6:30 a.m., she was asked to make any possible associations to the thoughts and dreams she had reported during the night, and to sign a printed statement agreeing that she would not discuss the experiment with any other student nurse.

## *Second (Test) Night*

One week later, the subject returned for a second (test) night. The preliminary instructions were the same as in the first (adaptation) night and the subject was again informed of the reporting procedure. During the second night, EEG and REM were recorded continuously from the time the subject went to bed until she was awakened in the morning. The EEG was recorded bipolarly from two Grass silver disk electrodes, one over the occipital area and the other over the vertex. Eye movements were also recorded bipolarly from the following electrode placements: horizontal, from outer canthus of one eye to outer canthus of the other; and vertical, from right supraorbital to right infraorbital.

For the second (test) night, subjects were randomly assigned to one of six groups, four experimental and two control, that constituted the cells of a 2 × 3 factorial design, as shown in Table 1.

As illustrated in Table 1, half of the subjects were exposed to a hypnotic induction procedure and half were not, and then all subjects were given one of three types of suggestions. These experimental procedures were implemented as follows.

*Hypnotic induction versus no induction.* Soon after going to bed, half of the subjects (Groups 1, 3, and 5) were told by the experimenter (K. W. H.) that they were to be hypnotized. A standardized tape-recorded hypnotic induction procedure (Barber, 1969, Appendix B) was then administered individually to each of these subjects for a period of 10 minutes. Immediately following the hypnotic induction, subjects assigned to Groups 1, 3, and 5 were assessed on responses to five test suggestions. Four of these test suggestions (arm heaviness, arm levitation, thirst hallucination, and verbal inhibition) were from the Barber Suggestibility Scale (Barber, 1969, Appendix A), and one test suggestion (mosquito hallucination) was from the Stanford Hypnotic Susceptibility Scale (Weitzenhoffer & Hilgard, 1959). Immediately following the hypnotic induction and the test suggestions, and without a break in the continuity of presentation, each subject in Groups 1, 3, and 5 was given one of three suggestions pertaining to thinking and dreaming (authoritative suggestions, permissive suggestions, or no suggestions), which are described below.

Subjects in Groups 2, 4, and 6 were not exposed to the hypnotic induction procedure or the test suggestions. Instead, they were immediately given one of the following three suggestions pertaining to thinking and dreaming.

*Authoritative suggestions* ("You will think and dream about . . ."). Subjects allocated to Groups 1 and 2 were given the following authoritatively worded suggestions:

> The final instructions for the experiment tonight are as follows. You will think about and dream about one topic tonight. You will consciously and unconsciously think about and dream about the assassination of President Kennedy. You will think about and

TABLE 1

2 × 3 Factorial Design

| Type of suggestions | Hypnotic induction | No induction |
|---|---|---|
| Authoritative ("You will think and dream about . . .") | Group 1[a] | Group 2[a] |
| Permissive ("Try to think and dream about . . .") | Group 3[a] | Group 4[a] |
| None (control) | Group 5[b] | Group 6[a] |

[a] $n = 13$.
[b] $n = 12$.

dream about the assassination of President Kennedy all through the night. Consciously and unconsciously, you will think about and dream about President Kennedy's assassination all through the night. Nothing else will be on your mind. Now please repeat the instructions back to me ... Good. Now I will leave and you can go to sleep. All through the night you will think about and dream about President Kennedy's assassination.[3]

*Permissive suggestions* ("Try to think and dream about ..."). Subjects assigned to Groups 3 and 4 were given permissively worded suggestions as follows:

> The final instructions for the experiment tonight are as follows. I want you to try to think about and dream about one topic tonight. I want you to try very hard and to the very best of your ability, consciously and unconsciously, to think about and to dream about the assassination of President Kennedy. The entire experiment will depend on your willingness to exert all of your will power, to control your thoughts, and to limit your thoughts to the assassination of President Kennedy. Please try very hard all through the night consciously and unconsciously to think about and to dream about President Kennedy's assassination. Now please repeat the instructions back to me ... Good. Now I will leave and you can go to sleep. I am depending on you to exert all of your will power throughout the night to think about and dream about President Kennedy's assassination.

*No suggestions to think and dream (control).* The subjects allocated to Groups 5 and 6 went to sleep with no further instructions.

*Nocturnal awakenings.* A maximum of five times during the night, the subject was awakened by means of an alarm and was asked, by the research assistant, to give a report pertaining to (*a*) what was going through her mind at the time of awakening, (*b*) whether she was thinking or dreaming, and (*c*) whether, at the time of awakening, she was awake, drifting off to sleep, lightly sleeping, or deeply sleeping. When the subject had apparently answered the first question pertaining to what was going through her mind at the time of awakening, the research assistant also asked, "Is that all?" and "Can you remember anything else?" The research assistant did not know which of the experimental treatments the subject had received.

The maximum five awakenings were at the following times:

1. Ten minutes after the initial onset of sleep (as indicated by slow, rhythmical, side-to-side movements of the eyeballs and by loss of the alpha EEG rhythm).
2. Ten minutes after the beginning of the first REM period.
3. During a period of non-REM which came 45 minutes after the beginning of the first REM period.
4. Ten minutes after the beginning of the second REM period.[4]
5. During a subsequent non-REM period (45 minutes after the beginning of the second REM period).

Following the aforementioned awakenings, the subject was permitted to sleep until 6:30 a.m.

After awakening in the morning, each subject was asked to make any possible associations to the thoughts and dreams she had reported during the night and to sign a statement stating that she had actually dreamt (or thought) about what she had reported during the night and that she "did not report this for such reasons as to please the experimenter or to comply with what was expected of [her]."

In addition, the subjects who had been exposed to the hypnotic induction procedure (Groups 1, 3, and 5) were asked to complete an item which asked whether, before going to sleep, they felt they were deeply, moderately, lightly, or not hypnotized. (The item was scored 3, 2, 1, and 0 for the four possible answers.)

## *Scoring of Nocturnal Reports*

A typed transcription was made of each subject's nocturnal reports which had been recorded on tape. Two judges,[5] who worked independently and who did not know to which group the subjects belonged, rated each report as to (*a*) whether the subject considered herself to be awake, drifting off to sleep, lightly sleeping, or deeply sleeping when the awakening occurred, (*b*) whether the subject labeled her report as a thought or a dream, and (*c*) whether the content of the report referred to the suggested topic in one or more of the following ways: mention of the name Kennedy, a U.S. President, Dallas, Oswald, Ruby, Texas, death, funeral, cemetery. The foregoing items were chosen, after all reports were carefully read, as covering all direct or indirect references in the reports to the assassination of President Kennedy. These direct and indirect references to the assassination of President Kennedy are henceforth termed *suggested elements*.

The two judges agreed on 98% of the ratings pertaining to subjects' statements of how deeply they were

[3] Since this experiment was conducted in 1964, less than one year after President Kennedy's death, the subjects were very familiar with the details of the assassination. The subjects were asked to dream about the assassination of President Kennedy because it was an event that they were all acquainted with and that had emotional meaning for them.

[4] All subjects were awakened at sleep onset and during the first REM and non-REM periods, and 55 of the 77 subjects (71%) were also awakened a fourth and fifth time (during the second REM period and the subsequent non-REM period). The 22 subjects (29%) who were not awakened a fourth or fifth time did not have a clear-cut second REM period, although they had brief bursts of REM. As will be seen later, since an analysis of variance showed that the number of awakenings did not differ for subjects who were and those who were not exposed to the hypnotic induction and for subjects who received the three types of suggestions, the fact that some subjects were awakened fewer times than others does not affect the conclusions from this study.

[5] The judges were Constance Ledoux Taylor and Karl W. Hahn, Jr. We are indebted to Mrs. Taylor for serving as a judge.

TABLE 2

NUMBER OF AWAKENINGS AND NUMBER OF DREAMS AND THOUGHTS RECALLED

| Type of suggestions | Hypnotic induction | No induction | Total |
|---|---|---|---|
| | Group 1 | Group 2 | Groups 1 + 2 |
| Authoritative | | | |
| Awakenings | 59 | 61 | 120 |
| Dreams | 22 | 14 | 36 |
| Thoughts | 23 | 18 | 41 |
| | Group 3 | Group 4 | Groups 3 + 4 |
| Permissive | | | |
| Awakenings | 50 | 54 | 104 |
| Dreams | 9 | 18 | 27 |
| Thoughts | 21 | 11 | 32 |
| | Group 5 | Group 6 | Groups 5 + 6 |
| None | | | |
| Awakenings | 50 | 54 | 104 |
| Dreams | 10 | 12 | 22 |
| Thoughts | 8 | 11 | 19 |
| | Groups 1, 3, 5 | Groups 2, 4, 6 | Groups 1-6 |
| Total | | | |
| Awakenings | 159 | 169 | 328 |
| Dreams | 41 | 44 | 85 |
| Thoughts | 52 | 40 | 92 |

asleep, on 100% of the ratings concerning whether subjects labeled their reports as thoughts or dreams, and on 99% of the ratings concerning the number of suggested elements. The few disagreements in the ratings made by the two judges were resolved by a third judge (T. X. B.) who did not know the ratings made by the first two.

The effects of the suggestions on the nocturnal reports were scored in two ways. One score referred to the number of thought or dream reports proffered by each experimental group that contained at least one suggested element. This score, which used the number of *reports* as the unit of measure, provided an index of the "extensiveness" of the effects of the suggestions. A second score referred to the number of suggested elements in the thought or dream reports proffered by each experimental group. This score, which used the number of *suggested elements* as the unit of measure, provided an index of "density." These two scores will be referred to as follows: (*a*) extensiveness, *the number of thought or dream reports* from each experimental group that contained at least one suggested element, and (*b*) density, *the number of suggested elements* (in the thought or dream reports) from each experimental group.

## RESULTS

### *Effects of Suggestions on Recall of Dreams and Thoughts*

Table 2 presents the number of awakenings and the number of dreams and thoughts recalled by subjects in each of the six groups. The data in this table refer to the number of dreams and thoughts that were recalled during the nocturnal awakenings regardless of whether or not they pertained to the suggested topic. As can be seen from this table, the subjects reported some type of mental activity (a thought or a dream) during 54% of the awakenings (177 reports of thoughts or dreams were given during 328 awakenings). Fifty-two percent of this mental activity was described by the subjects as thinking and 48% as dreaming (92 reports of thinking and 85 of dreaming).

Three 2 × 3 analyses of variance (ANOVA) were performed on the data summarized in Table 2 to determine whether the independent variables and their interaction affected the number of awakenings or the number of dreams or thoughts that were recalled.

The first ANOVA, which pertained to the number of awakenings, showed no main effects and no interaction. That is, the number of awakenings did not differ significantly for subjects who had and those who had not been exposed to the hypnotic induction procedure and for subjects who were given the three types of suggestions.

TABLE 3

NUMBER OF SUBJECTS PRESENTING TWO, ONE, AND NO DREAM REPORTS CONTAINING SUGGESTED ELEMENTS

| Group | Two | One | None | Total no. Ss presenting one or more |
|---|---|---|---|---|
| 1 (hypnotic induction–authoritative suggestions) | 2 | 1 | 10 | 3 |
| 2 (no induction–authoritative suggestions) | 1 | 1 | 11 | 2 |
| 3 (hypnotic induction–permissive suggestions) | 0 | 2 | 11 | 2 |
| 4 (no induction–permissive suggestions) | 3 | 3 | 7 | 6 |
| 5 (hypnotic induction–no suggestions) | 0 | 0 | 12 | 0 |
| 6 (no induction–no suggestions) | 0 | 0 | 13 | 0 |

The second ANOVA, which pertained to the number of dreams that were recalled by the subjects, also showed no main effects and no interaction. It should be noted that this analysis pertained to the number of dreams that were recalled regardless of whether the dreams contained suggested elements. Thus, the analysis indicated that (*a*) subjects who had been exposed to the hypnotic induction procedure did not recall significantly more dreams than those who had not been exposed to the induction, and (*b*) subjects who had been given authoritative or permissive suggestions did not recall significantly more dreams than the control subjects who were not given suggestions.

A third ANOVA, pertaining to the number of thoughts that were recalled, showed a main effect for types of suggestions ($F = 3.8$, $df = 2/71$, $p < .05$) and no effects for hypnotic induction and for the interaction. Further analyses of the significant main effect for types of suggestions, by means of *t* tests, showed that (*a*) subjects who were given the permissive and authoritative suggestions recalled significantly more thoughts ($p < .05$) than the control subjects who were not given suggestions; and (*b*) subjects given the authoritative suggestions and those given the permissive suggestions did not differ significantly in the number of thoughts recalled. These data indicate that presleep suggestions to think and dream on a specified topic give rise to a greater number of thoughts that are recalled during the night. However, whether or not these thoughts pertain to the suggested topic is another matter that is discussed next.

*Number of Subjects Presenting Dream and Thought Reports Containing Suggested Elements*

Table 3 lists the number of subjects in each experimental group presenting dream reports containing suggested elements. This table shows that no subject presented more than two dream reports that pertained to the suggested topic. The last column of Table 3 shows that the 13 subjects who presented one or more dream reports containing suggested elements were distributed as follows: 3, 2, 2, 6, 0, and 0 in Groups 1–6, respectively ($\chi^2 = 13.4$, $df = 5$, $p < .02$).

Table 4 lists the number of subjects in each experimental group presenting thought reports containing suggested elements. As can be seen from this table, one subject (in Group 1) consistently reported, each of the five times she was awakened, that she was thinking about the assassination of President Kennedy. The

TABLE 4

NUMBER OF SUBJECTS PRESENTING FIVE, THREE, TWO, ONE, AND NO THOUGHT REPORTS CONTAINING SUGGESTED ELEMENTS

| Group | Five | Three | Two | One | None | Total no. Ss presenting one or more |
|---|---|---|---|---|---|---|
| 1 (hypnotic induction–authoritative suggestions) | 1 | 0 | 1 | 6 | 5 | 8 |
| 2 (no induction–authoritative suggestions) | 0 | 0 | 1 | 1 | 11 | 2 |
| 3 (hypnotic induction–permissive suggestions) | 0 | 1 | 3 | 4 | 5 | 8 |
| 4 (no induction–permissive suggestions) | 0 | 1 | 0 | 3 | 9 | 4 |
| 5 (hypnotic induction–no suggestions) | 0 | 0 | 0 | 0 | 12 | 0 |
| 6 (no induction–no suggestions) | 0 | 0 | 0 | 0 | 13 | 0 |

TABLE 5

NUMBER OF DREAM REPORTS CONTAINING SUGGESTED ELEMENTS (EXTENSIVENESS) AND NUMBER OF SUGGESTED ELEMENTS IN THE DREAMS (DENSITY)

| Type of suggestions | Hypnotic induction | No induction | Total |
|---|---|---|---|
| | Group 1 | Group 2 | Groups 1 + 2 |
| Authoritative | | | |
| Extensiveness | 5 | 3 | 8 |
| Density | 16 | 3 | 19 |
| | Group 3 | Group 4 | Groups 3 + 4 |
| Permissive | | | |
| Extensiveness | 2 | 9 | 11 |
| Density | 3 | 21 | 24 |
| | Group 5 | Group 6 | Groups 5 + 6 |
| None | | | |
| Extensiveness | 0 | 0 | 0 |
| Density | 0 | 0 | 0 |
| | Groups 1, 3, 5 | Groups 2, 4, 6 | Groups 1–6 |
| Total | | | |
| Extensiveness | 7 | 12 | 19 |
| Density | 19 | 24 | 43 |

last column in Table 3 shows that the 22 subjects who presented one or more thought reports containing suggested elements were distributed as follows: 8, 2, 8, 4, 0, and 0 in Groups 1–6, respectively ($\chi^2 = 25.0$, $df = 5$, $p < .001$).

The data in Tables 3 and 4 refer to the number of subjects in each experimental group who were affected by the suggestions to think and dream about the death of President Kennedy. The data can also be analyzed in another way: we can look at the results for each experimental group with regard to the number of dreams and thoughts containing suggested elements (extensiveness) and the number of suggested elements in the dreams and thoughts (density). Let us now turn to this type of analysis, which deals with the experimental group, instead of the individual subject, as the unit, and let us first look at the extensiveness and density measures with respect to dreams.

*Effects of Suggestions on the Contents of Dreams*

Table 5 presents, separately for each of the six groups, the number of dream reports containing suggested elements (extensiveness),[6] and the number of suggested elements in the dreams (density). It should be noted that the control subjects (Groups 5 and 6), who were not given suggestions to think and dream about Kennedy's assassination, did not report any dreams containing suggested elements. This outcome indicates that nothing about the experimental situation per se gave rise to dreams about Kennedy. In contrast, of the 63 dream reports proffered by the experimental subjects (Groups 1–4), 19, or 30%, contained suggested elements pertaining to Kennedy's assassination (extensiveness). This outcome indicates that suggestions to think and dream on a specified topic have a relatively strong effect on dreams, affecting nearly one third of the dream reports of unselected subjects.

Excluding the control subjects (Groups 5 and 6) who did not report any dreams containing suggested elements, 2 × 2 analyses of variance were performed on the extensiveness

[6] The number of subjects in each experimental group contributing to the extensiveness scores in Table 5 can be derived from Table 3. For instance, Table 5 shows that Group 1 had an extensiveness score of 5; that is, five dream reports from Group 1 contained suggested elements. Table 3 shows that these five dreams with suggested elements were contributed by three subjects in Group 1: two subjects in this group each contributed two dreams with suggested elements (totaling four dreams with suggested elements) and a third subject contributed the fifth dream with suggested elements.

TABLE 6

NUMBER OF THOUGHT REPORTS CONTAINING SUGGESTED ELEMENTS (EXTENSIVENESS) AND NUMBER OF SUGGESTED ELEMENTS IN THE THOUGHTS (DENSITY)

| Type of suggestions | Hypnotic induction | No induction | Total |
|---|---|---|---|
| | Group 1 | Group 2 | Groups 1 + 2 |
| Authoritative | | | |
| Extensiveness | 13 | 3 | 16 |
| Density | 36 | 10 | 46 |
| | Group 3 | Group 4 | Groups 3 + 4 |
| Permissive | | | |
| Extensiveness | 13 | 6 | 19 |
| Density | 36 | 18 | 54 |
| | Group 5 | Group 6 | Groups 5 + 6 |
| None | | | |
| Extensiveness | 0 | 0 | 0 |
| Density | 0 | 0 | 0 |
| | Groups 1, 3, 5 | Groups 2, 4, 6 | Groups 1–6 |
| Total | | | |
| Extensiveness | 26 | 9 | 35 |
| Density | 72 | 28 | 100 |

and density scores presented in Table 5. Although these analyses showed no main effects for hypnotic induction and for types of suggestions, they showed a significant interaction between these variables ($F = 3.4$, $df = 1/48$, $p < .10$ for extensiveness scores and $F = 6.2$, $df = 1/48$, $p < .05$ for density scores). Further breakdown of the significant interaction by means of $t$ tests showed that Group 4 (no induction–permissive suggestions) reported more dreams containing suggested elements (extensiveness) than Groups 2 and 3, and Group 1 (hypnotic induction–authoritative suggestions) did not differ significantly from Group 4. With respect to the density measure, Groups 1 and 4 did not differ from each other, but both of these groups had a larger number of suggested elements in their dreams than Groups 2 and 3. These data indicate that (*a*) overall, suggestions to dream on a specified topic are equally effective with hypnotic subjects and nonhypnotic subjects in affecting the contents of dreams, but (*b*) the most potent effects on the contents of dreams are produced when authoritative suggestions ("You will dream . . .") are given to hypnotic subjects and permissive suggestions ("Try to dream . . .") are given to nonhypnotic subjects.[7]

*Effects of Suggestions on the Contents of Thoughts*

Table 6 presents the extensiveness and density scores for the thought reports.[8] As can be seen from this table, all four experimental groups (Groups 1–4) reported more thoughts containing suggested elements (extensiveness) and a greater number of suggested elements in

[7] Another way of analyzing the same data is to consider the percentage of the total number of dreams reported by each group that contained suggested elements. (These percentages can be derived from Table 2, which lists the total number of dreams reported by each group, and from Table 5, which lists the number of dreams containing suggested elements.) The percentages of the total number of dream reports from each group that contained suggested elements were: 23% for Group 1 (hypnotic induction–authoritative suggestions); 21% for Group 2 (no induction–authoritative suggestions); 22% for Group 3 (hypnotic induction–permissive suggestions); and 50% for Group 4 (no induction–permissive suggestions). This method of analyzing the data indicates that the most potent effect on dream contents was produced by the permissive suggestions given without a hypnotic induction procedure.

[8] The number of subjects in each experimental group contributing to the extensiveness scores in Table 6 can be derived from Table 4. For instance, Table 6 shows that Group 2 had an extensiveness score of 3; that is, three thought reports from Group 2 contained suggested elements. Table 4 shows that these three thought reports with suggested elements were contributed by two subjects in Group 2: one subject contributed two thought reports with suggested elements and the third thought report containing suggested elements was contributed by a second subject.

their thoughts (density) than the control groups (Groups 5 and 6) who reported no thoughts containing suggested elements. Since the control groups did not report any thoughts pertaining to the suggested topic, it appears that nothing about the experimental situation per se gave rise to thoughts about President Kennedy.

As Table 2 shows, 73 thoughts were reported by the experimental groups (Groups 1–4). Of these 73 thoughts, 35, or 48%, contained suggested elements pertaining to Kennedy's assassination (see extensiveness scores in Table 6). This outcome indicates that suggestions to think and dream on a specified topic have a relatively strong effect on nocturnal thinking, affecting nearly one half of the nocturnal thought reports proffered by unselected subjects.

Dropping the control subjects who did not report any thoughts containing suggested elements, 2 × 2 analyses of variance were performed on the extensiveness and density scores for the thoughts. These analyses showed no main effect for types of suggestions and no interaction. However, the analyses showed a significant main effect for hypnotic induction, indicating that the presence of a hypnotic induction procedure gave rise to higher extensiveness scores ($F = 5.6$, $df = 1/48$, $p < .05$) and also higher density scores ($F = 3.4$, $df = 1/48$, $p < .10$). These results indicate that regardless of the wording of the suggestions, subjects exposed to the hypnotic induction procedure reported more thoughts containing suggested elements and also reported more suggested elements in their thoughts than subjects who were not exposed to the hypnotic induction.

*Relationship of Hypnotizability to Suggested Elements*

Subjects who were exposed to the hypnotic induction and who received suggestions to dream on the specified topic (Groups 1 and 3) rated their own depth of hypnosis and also were assessed on response to five test suggestions. Correlation coefficients were computed between these subjects' self-rated depth of hypnosis, their scores on the test suggestions, and the extensiveness and density measures for their dreams and thoughts.

The two indices of hypnotizability—scores on the test suggestions and self-ratings of depth of hypnosis—were significantly correlated ($r = .80$, $p < .01$) in Group 1 (hypnotic induction–authoritative suggestions) but not significantly correlated ($r = .30$) in Group 3 (hypnotic induction–permissive suggestions).

Neither of the two indices of hypnotizability were significantly correlated with the number of dreams containing suggested elements (extensiveness) or the number of suggested elements in the dreams (density). These data indicate that subjects who were high on hypnotizability did not *dream* more about the suggested topic than subjects who were low on hypnotizability.

With regard to Group 1, subjects' self-ratings of depth of hypnosis were significantly correlated ($p < .05$) with the number of thoughts containing suggested elements ($r = .64$) and with the number of suggested elements in the thoughts ($r = .60$). Also, with regard to both Groups 1 and 3, consistently positive but nonsignificant correlations were obtained between scores on the test suggestions and the extensiveness and density measures for the thoughts. These data seem to indicate that subjects who were high on hypnotizability tended to report more *thoughts* about the suggested topic than those who were low on hypnotizability.

*Relationship between Time of Awakening and Nocturnal Reports*

Table 7 presents the number of dreams and thoughts that were recalled at each awakening. This table shows that more thoughts than dreams were reported during the sleep onset awakening (73% of the reports were labeled

TABLE 7

Number of Thoughts, Dreams, and Suggested Elements in Thoughts and Dreams at Each Awakening

| Awakening | Thoughts | Dreams | Dreams and thoughts | Suggested elements in dreams and thoughts |
|---|---|---|---|---|
| Sleep onset | 30 | 11 | 41 | 61 |
| First REM | 17 | 25 | 42 | 20 |
| First non-REM | 20 | 18 | 38 | 26 |
| Second REM | 9 | 20 | 29 | 19 |
| Second non-REM | 16 | 11 | 27 | 17 |

as thoughts). During both REM awakenings, there were more dreams reported than thoughts and during both non-REM awakenings there were more thoughts reported than dreams.

The total number of dreams and thoughts reported at each awakening are presented in Table 7, column 3, and the number of suggested elements in the dream and thought reports are presented in Table 7, column 4. As can be seen by comparing these two columns in the table, the proportion of suggested elements to the number of dream and thought reports is also at its highest during the sleep onset awakening.

As Table 8 shows, whether or not a subject reported thinking or dreaming about a suggested element at a later awakening was related significantly to whether or not she reported thinking or dreaming about a suggested element at the first awakening during sleep onset.

## Discussion

Hypnotic and nonhypnotic subjects receiving presleep suggestions to think and dream about the assassination of President Kennedy thought and dreamed about the specified topic more often than the control subjects (who never thought or dreamed about the topic). If we focus on the number of subjects in the experimental groups (Groups 1–4) who were affected, we find that the presleep suggestions, given with or without a hypnotic induction procedure, altered the contents of nocturnal dreams in 25% (13 of 52) of these unselected subjects (Table 3) and altered the contents of nocturnal thoughts in 42% (22 of 52) of these subjects (Table 4). If we look at the total number of dreams and thoughts that were proffered by the experimental subjects (Groups 1–4) during the nocturnal awakenings, we find that the presleep suggestions influenced 30% (19 of 63) of their dream reports (Table 5 and Table 2) and 48% (35 of 73) of their thought reports (Table 6 and Table 2). This investigation thus extends previous studies (Stoyva, 1961; Tart, 1964; Tart & Dick, 1970) by showing that presleep suggestions exert an effect not only on nocturnal dreaming but also on nocturnal thinking, and not only on subjects who have been exposed to a hypnotic induction, but also on nonhypnotic subjects.

TABLE 8

Congruence between Suggested Elements at Sleep Onset Awakening and Later Awakenings

| Suggested elements present at sleep onset awakening | Suggested elements present in one or more later awakenings | |
|---|---|---|
| | Yes | No |
| Yes | 12 | 9 |
| No | 5 | 26 |

*Note.* $\chi^2$ (with Yates correction) = 7.8; $p < .01$.

### *Complex Effects of Hypnotic Induction and Types of Suggestions*

A major finding of this investigation is that the independent variables (presence or absence of hypnotic induction and types of suggestions) gave rise to complex effects when both nocturnal dreaming and thinking are taken into consideration.

Overall, the presleep suggestions were equally effective in altering the contents of nocturnal dreams when they were given with or without a hypnotic induction procedure. However, the significant interaction between hypnotic induction and types of suggestions indicated that the presleep suggestions had the greatest effect on dreams when they were given authoritatively to the hypnotic subjects and permissively to the nonhypnotic subjects. It thus appears that suggestions can affect the contents of dreams in subjects who have and also those who have not been exposed to a hypnotic induction but certain types of suggestions are more effective with hypnotic subjects and other types of suggestions are more effective with nonhypnotic subjects.

The effects of the independent variables on the thought reports were different from their effects on the dream reports. With respect to the nocturnal reports of thinking, the interaction effect was not significant, but the hypnotic induction procedure per se was effective in increasing the number of suggested elements in the thoughts. Thus it appears that subjects who have been exposed to a hypnotic induction think about (but do not dream about) the suggested topic more often than subjects who have not been exposed to an induction.

It is difficult at this point to interpret these

complex results. Why should authoritative suggestions have a greater effect on dream reports when they are given with a hypnotic induction procedure? Why are permissive suggestions more effective in altering the contents of dream reports when they are given without a hypnotic induction? One possible explanation is that authoritative suggestions ("You will think and dream about . . .") are more congruent with a hypnotic situation or, stated otherwise, they are the types of suggestions that are expected by hypnotic subjects while permissive suggestions ("Try to think and dream about . . .") are more congruent with a nonhypnotic situation. However, this explanation runs into a serious problem: Although one set of suggestions was more effective with hypnotic subjects and another set of suggestions was more effective with nonhypnotic subjects in influencing *dream* reports, the wording of the suggestions did not affect the *thought* reports. The same kind of problem is found in trying to explain why subjects reported more thoughts (but not more dreams) about the suggested topic when they were given the presleep suggestions in the context of a hypnotic induction procedure. In other words, it is difficult to explain why the independent variables had different effects on nocturnal dreams and on nocturnal thoughts, and further research is needed to clarify the problem.

Previous studies in this area can be reinterpreted in light of the complex results obtained in the present investigation. For instance, Stoyva (1961) reported that suggestions were more effective with hypnotic subjects than with nonhypnotic subjects in altering the contents of dreams. Similarly, we found that authoritative suggestions were more effective with hypnotic subjects. However, we also found that permissive suggestions were more effective with nonhypnotic subjects than with hypnotic subjects in affecting dream contents. If we had used only the permissive suggestions, we would have concluded that suggestions have a greater effect on the contents of dreams when they are given without a hypnotic induction procedure. On the other hand, if we had used only the authoritative suggestions, we would have concluded, in the same way as Stoyva, that suggestions are more effective when given with a hypnotic induction. The results clearly indicate that future research pertaining to the effects of suggestions and hypnotic induction should seriously consider the wording of suggestions as an important independent variable.

The present investigation also has broader implications for interpreting earlier work in this area. Previous studies (Stoyva, 1961; Tart, 1964; Tart & Dick, 1970) used only highly hypnotizable subjects, gave authoritative suggestions, awakened subjects only during REM periods, and asked only for reports of dreams. It is now clear that these studies missed many of the complexities of research in this area. For instance, by awakening subjects only during REM periods and by asking subjects to report their dreams, these studies avoided the complex fact that subjects report *both dreams and thoughts at both REM and non-REM periods*. Further studies are needed that (*a*) use subjects who are high and also those who are medium or low on hypnotizability, (*b*) give suggestions that are worded permissively and also authoritatively, (*c*) administer the suggestions in the context of a hypnotic induction procedure and also without a hypnotic induction, (*d*) give suggestions to think about the suggested topic and also to dream about it, (*e*) awaken subjects during REM periods and also during non-REM periods, and (*f*) consider both reports of nocturnal thoughts and also reports of nocturnal dreams.

### *Effects of Hypnotizability*

The subjects who were given the presleep suggestions together with a hypnotic induction (Groups 1 and 3) were examined to see if the more hypnotizable subjects reported more suggested elements in their nocturnal dreams and thoughts. Hypnotizability was indexed by the subjects' responses to the five test suggestions and by their self-ratings of hypnotic depth. Hypnotizability, as measured by these variables, was not related to dreaming about the suggested topic. However, the more hypnotizable subjects tended to report more nocturnal thoughts that pertained to the suggested topic. These results indicate that hypnotizability is not as important as has been previously assumed (Stoyva, 1961; Tart, 1964; Tart & Dick, 1970) in eliciting positive responses to the suggestion to dream about a specified topic, even though it is important in eliciting positive responses to the suggestions to think about it.

It appears that factors other than the subjects' hypnotizability may play a crucial role in determining whether suggestions will affect the contents of dreams. These factors may include characteristics of subjects with regard to dreaming and sleeping such as whether or not they are "light" sleepers or "deep" sleepers, whether their dreams are more or less vivid, and whether they recall their dreams with difficulty or with ease (Zimmerman, 1967).

*Effect of Time of Awakening*

The suggestions to think and dream on the specified topic had their greatest effect during sleep onset rather than later at night. More suggested elements were present in the dream and thought reports at the sleep onset awakening rather than at later REM and non-REM awakenings. Of course, the sleep onset period was closest in time to the administration of the suggestions. Also, Foulkes and Vogel (1965) have described the mentation at sleep onset as more volitional in nature than the mentation at REM. The larger number of suggested elements that were reported during the sleep onset awakening may thus be due to the fact that the subjects had received the presleep suggestion just a few minutes previously and to the possibility that subjects had more voluntary control over their thoughts during the onset of sleep.

However, at sleep onset, some subjects reported neither thoughts nor dreams on the suggested topic. The data were examined to see the relationship between presence or absence of suggested elements at sleep onset and at the awakenings later at night. If a subject reported thinking or dreaming on the suggested topic at sleep onset, it was likely that she would also report thinking or dreaming on the suggested topic at later awakenings. This particular time period at sleep onset, therefore, appears to be a crucial one for tracing the effects of suggestions given prior to sleep.

The above considerations, taken together with two additional sets of data summarized below, indicate a provisional answer to the question, How did the suggestions to think and dream about the specified topic alter the contents of the nocturnal dreams?

1. As indicated in the present investigation, and also in many previous investigations, thought processes do not stop when we are asleep. In fact, it appears that we continue to think, in a loose fashion, much of the time that we are asleep, and these mental processes that occur during sleep are related to those that went on during the day and also during the period immediately preceding sleep onset (Foulkes, 1966).

2. The dreams that occur during sleep "do not arise *sui generis* as psychologically isolated mental productions but emerge as the most vivid and memorable part of a larger fabric of interwoven mental activity during sleep [Rechtschaffen, Vogel, & Shaikun, 1963, p. 546].

With the above data in mind, we can postulate that the suggestions to think and dream about a specified topic affected the contents of the nocturnal dreams as follows: (*a*) Most of the subjects who were given suggestions to think and dream on the specified topic thought about the topic immediately before falling asleep. (*b*) The mental processes that occurred during sleep onset were related to those that occurred immediately prior to sleep. (*c*) In some subjects, the contents of the dreams occurring later at night were related to the mental contents present immediately before sleep and during sleep onset.

The above postulates suggest a somewhat different method for influencing the contents of nocturnal dreams. Instead of giving elaborate suggestions to think and dream about a specified topic, subjects could be told simply, "Before going to sleep tonight, try to focus your thoughts on [a particular topic]." It appears possible that this simple statement may be as effective as involved suggestions in producing dreams later at night which pertain to the particular topic.

*Limitations of Investigation and Suggestions for Further Research*

The results of the present investigation point to a fruitful area for further research. It appears likely that careful research in this area may be able to trace how mental contents during sleep are related to preceding events and to the mental contents that are present immediately prior to sleep. Further studies can also determine the kinds of suggestions or instructions that are most effective in altering the contents of nocturnal thinking and dreaming. There is no compelling reason to believe that the types of suggestions used in the present investigation or in other recent investigations are maximally effective. Other kinds of procedures and other kinds of instructions or suggestions may have more potent effects. For instance, a greater effect on the contents of dreams may be produced if subjects are given the suggestion to dream on a specified topic when they are in Stage 1 sleep (Evans, 1972). Also, it appears possible that subjects can learn to influence their own dreams by giving themselves suggestions before going to sleep at night. A potent effect on dream contents might also be produced if subjects purposively think about a particular topic immediately before going to sleep. Clearly, further research is necessary which delineates methods for maximizing control of dreams.

Further studies in this area could provide data with broader implications if they could overcome three limitations of the present investigation:

1. The present investigation focused on the "manifest contents" of dreams.[9] Further studies that probe into the "latent contents" might enhance our understanding of how presleep suggestions influence nocturnal dreams. Further research should look more closely at the subjects' associations to their dreams, at their experiences during the day preceding the sleep session, and at their biographies and personality characteristics.

2. In the present investigation, subjects were simply asked to state what was going through their minds at the time of awakening. Further studies could probe more thoroughly into the details of the dreams and the subjects' emotional reactions to their dreams. The procedures used by Witkin would be useful. Witkin (1969) instructed the subject, on awakening,

> to include in his running report of the dream a description of the surroundings; including other persons; any feelings in himself and others; his own activity; activity going on around him; manner of representation of the self in the dream; color and sound; and extent of vividness of the dream experience [p. 298].

3. The data obtained in the present investigation and also in other recent investigations (Stoyva, 1961; Tart, 1964; Tart & Dick, 1970) are valid only to the extent that the subjects truthfully reported what was passing through their minds when they were awakened during the night. To what extent did the subjects present honest reports and to what extent did they state that they were thinking or dreaming about the specified topic in order to be "good" subjects or to comply with the suggestions they had received? Of course, there is no way of definitely answering this question. Although all of the subjects in the present investigation signed statements in the morning testifying that they had truthfully reported their experiences, the possibility remains that at least some of the subjects some of the time elaborated or even fabricated their reports to harmonize with the suggestions they had received (Barber, 1962). An indication that the subjects were truthfully reporting their experiences is that, with one exception, the subjects did not consistently state that they were thinking or dreaming about the suggested topic at every awakening. If they were simply trying to please, we may have expected more subjects to report suggested elements whenever they were awakened. The detailed contents of the subjects' reports, which seemed to us to have the "flavor" of nocturnal thoughts and dreams, also suggest that the subjects' were honestly reporting what was "going through their minds" when they were awakened. However, this is only our subjective impression and certainly cannot stand as scientific data. Further studies in this area could use "demands for honesty" (Bowers, 1967; Spanos & Barber, 1968; Spanos, Barber, & Lang, 1969) and other techniques to ascertain more reliably the truthfulness of the subjects' reports.

[9] Before the subjects left the laboratory in the morning, they were asked to make any possible associations to the dreams and thoughts they had reported during the night. These sparse reports provided no useful data pertaining to the "latent contents" of the nocturnal dreams.

## REFERENCES

Barber, T. X. Toward a theory of "hypnotic" behavior: The "hypnotically induced dream." *Journal of Nervous and Mental Disease*, 1962, **135**, 202–221.

Barber, T. X. *Hypnosis: A scientific approach.* New York: Van Nostrand Reinhold, 1969.

Barber, T. X. *LSD, marihuana, yoga, and hypnosis.* Chicago: Aldine, 1970.

BARBER, T. X., & CALVERLEY, D. S. Toward a theory of "hypnotic" behavior: Experimental analyses of suggested amnesia. *Journal of Abnormal Psychology*, 1966, **71**, 95–107.

BARBER, T. X., & DE MOOR, W. A theory of hypnotic induction procedures. *American Journal of Clinical Hypnosis*, 1972, **15**, 112–135.

BOWERS, K. S. The effect of demands for honesty on reports of visual and auditory hallucinations. *International Journal of Clinical and Experimental Hypnosis*, 1967, **15**, 31–36.

DEMENT, W., & KLEITMAN, N. Cyclic variations in EEG during sleep and their relation to eye movements, body motility, and dreaming. *Electroencephalography and Clinical Neurophysiology*, 1957, **9**, 673–690. (a)

DEMENT, W., & KLEITMAN, N. The relation of eye movements during sleep to dream activity: An objective method for the study of dreaming. *Journal of Experimental Psychology*, 1957, **53**, 339–346. (b)

EVANS, F. J. Hypnosis and sleep: Techniques for exploring cognitive activity during sleep. In E. Fromm & R. E. Shor (Eds.), *Hypnosis: Research developments and perspective*. Chicago: Aldine-Atherton, 1972.

FISHER, C. Studies of the nature of suggestion: Part 1. Experimental induction of dreams by direct suggestion. *Journal of the American Psychoanalytic Association*, 1953, 1, 222–255.

FOULKES, W. Dream reports from different stages of sleep. *Journal of Abnormal and Social Psychology*, 1962, **65**, 14–25.

FOULKES, D. *The psychology of sleep*. New York: Scribners, 1966.

FOULKES D., & VOGEL, G. Mental activity at sleep onset. *Journal of Abnormal Psychology*, 1965, **70**, 231–243.

GOODENOUGH, D., LEWIS, H., SHAPIRO, A., JARET, L., & SLESER, I. Dream reporting following abrupt and gradual awakenings from different types of sleep. *Journal of Personality and Social Psychology*, 1965, **2**, 170–179.

KAMIYA, J. Behavioral, subjective, and physiological aspects of drowsiness and sleep. In D. W. Fiske & S. R. Maddi (Eds.), *Functions of varied experiences*. Homewood, Ill.: Dorsey Press, 1961.

NACHMANSOHN, M. Ueber experimentell erzeugte Traeume nebst kritischen Bemerkungen ueber die psychoanalytische Methodik. *Zeitschrift Neurologie und Psychiatrie*, 1925, **98**, 556–586. In, *Organization and Pathology of thought*. (Trans. by D. Rapaport) New York: Columbia University Press, 1951.

NEWMAN, R., KATZ, J., & RUBENSTEIN, R. The experimental situation as a determinant of hypnotic dreams. *Psychiatry*, 1960, **23**, 63–73.

RECHTSCHAFFEN, A., VERDONE, P., & WHEATON, J. Reports of mental activity during sleep. *Canadian Psychiatric Association Journal*, 1963, **8**, 409–416.

RECHTSCHAFFEN, A., VOGEL, G., & SHAIKUN, G. Interrelatedness of mental activity during sleep. *Archives of General Psychiatry*, 1963, **9**, 536–547.

SCHROETTER, K. Experimentelle Truaeme. *Zentr. Psychoanal.*, 1911, **2**, 638–648. In, *Organization and pathology of thought*. (Trans. by D. Rapaport). New York: Columbia University Press, 1951.

SPANOS, N. P., & BARBER, T. X. "Hypnotic" experiences as inferred from subjective reports: Auditory and visual hallucinations. *Journal of Experimental Research in Personality*, 1968, **3**, 136–150.

SPANOS, N. P., BARBER, T. X., & LANG. G. Effects of hypnotic induction, suggestions of analgesia, and demands for honesty on subjective reports of pain. Unpublished manuscript, Boston University, Department of Sociology, 1969.

STOYVA, J. The effects of suggested dreams on the length of rapid eye movement periods. Unpublished doctoral dissertation, University of Chicago, 1961.

TART, C. T. A comparison of suggested dreams occurring in hypnosis and sleep. *International Journal of Clinical and Experimental Hypnosis*, 1964, **12**, 263–289.

TART, C. T., & DICK, L. Conscious control of dreaming: I. The posthypnotic dream. *Journal of Abnormal Psychology*, 1970, **76**, 304–315.

WEITZENHOFFER, A., & HILGARD, E. R. *Stanford Hypnotic Susceptibility Scales: Forms A and B*. Palo Alto, Calif.: Consulting Psychologists Press, 1959.

WITKIN, H. A. Influencing dream content. In M. Kramer (Ed.), *Dream psychology and the new biology of dreaming*. Springfield, Ill.: Charles C Thomas, 1969.

ZIMMERMAN, W. Psychological and physiological differences between "light" and "deep" sleepers. Unpublished doctoral dissertation, University of Chicago, 1967.

(Received January 16, 1973)

SECTION VIII

# PARAPSYCHOLOGY AND PSYCHIC RESEARCH

# 28

SCHMEIDLER, G.

## *Respice, Adspice, Prospice-On ESP*[1]

IF YOU'VE NEVER heard a talk that was based on a college seal, today's will at least have some novelty value for you. Our seal at CCNY seems to have seeped into my thinking, and it gives me today's directive. It shows three faces, joined at the neck like Janus's two. They look backward, about and forward and tell us to do the same: "Respice, adspice, prospice." I'll try to do what they say, to look at where we seem to have come in parapsychology and then put to you a model of where we might go—a model which in some ways is so different from the usual one that I don't know how you'll like it or how much I trust it myself.

But the first part, where I think we've come, troubles me. It's so likely to bore you if you agree with me or annoy you if you don't. I'll try to take some of the curse off it (and help my own education at the same time) by asking you for feedback on the questionnaire that my friends will pass out to you now.[2] It's a different way of "draining off the psi-missing"—you can show me where I am missing in talking about psi.

[1]This paper is the Presidential Address presented at the Fourteenth Annual Convention in Durham, North Carolina, on September 10, 1971.

[2]See Appendix for questionnaire. The results have been analyzed and reported in Schmeidler, 1971. Some of these are mentioned in footnotes in the present paper.

While they're giving you the papers, I'll fill the time by telling you why I wish I could have seen your answers three months ago. They would have gotten me out of an embarrassing spot. What happened was that last June, at City College, a couple of us were walking downstairs to a committee meeting. I mentioned this convention of parapsychologists, and my colleague came out with a question that stopped me cold. He said, "What do they think about it now?"

That was a tough one. There was so much to say that it was hard to say anything, and my mind stopped moving, though luckily the rest of me kept walking down the stairs. I gave him some feeble answer; and then began to wonder what the right answer was.

What *do* we think now about parapsychology? The Parapsychological Association as such has no official stand, but surely as individuals we have some areas of agreement—otherwise we couldn't talk to each other. The trouble is that what we agree on is probably what we don't talk about. (I've always enjoyed the paradigm of this: that if you ask a fish to describe his surroundings, the last thing he'd mention would be water.) Still, among the things we *don't* talk about, there may well be some where we disagree without realizing it. This made me feel that part of what I should do today was to air my own impressions of "what we think" and let you respond on these questionnaires. You can agree by checking the first column, or tell me "No, Gertrude, you can't say that!" by checking the second or third columns, or else at the end say, "You should have put *that* in" for some place where I had a blind spot.

We'll see what consensus there is. Where we disagree, some of us might be interested enough to start new research. And the results could be of historical interest, a generation from now, by showing which sound ideas we've taken told of, in 1971; and which false ideas we've agreed on (if any); and which important ideas we haven't caught onto yet.

Let's begin with ESP. We're all agreed, aren't we, that some kind of ESP has been so firmly established that any clear-thinking, informed person must accept ESP as he accepts gravitation or electromagnetism? that it's only the uninformed—of whom there are so many—and the bigots who could question it. I'll suggest to you my touchstone for finding what we've agreed on: almost an operational definition of consensus. It's whether we feel interest in new research. Any experiment to find if ESP occurs would (I think) only bore us.[3] It's been done already. Neither positive nor negative results would matter, really, except as they cast light on how or when ESP occurs.

What about the three or four subcategories of ESP? I'll go down the list. It seems to me that clairvoyance is an inescapable concept. Some of the arrangements in Dr. Rhine's Parapsychology Laboratory, like the "chutes" technique (Humphrey & Pratt, 1941), my experiment where a computer selected pseudorandom targets and scored responses but never printed the targets for anyone to see (Schmeidler, 1964), and perhaps other experiments like Tyrrell's (1938), which used a machine, have all shown target-response relations without anyone ever having direct knowledge of the targets or grounds for inference about them; in other words, "pure" clairvoyance.

Telepathy too. Experiments of the McMahan (1946) type, where the subjects' ESP calls are symbols but their written targets are random numbers, and the written targets are translated into symbols only by a code which the experimenter thinks but never writes or speaks—these experiments seem to me to demonstrate "pure" telepathy: extrachance relations between an individual's mental or brain processes and the subject's responses, without any other target possibilities.

Precognition. It's less tidy. It seems to me always possible to explain away precognition as due to PK. The argument is that when you have a correspondence between the subject's calls —given first—and the targets—chosen later—the correspondence can be due to someone's choosing (or influencing) the targets so as to make them correspond to the calls. However, I'm willing to dismiss this argument, and I think there's probably consensus among us that it should be dismissed. My own reasoning goes this way.

Consider the experiments where many subjects try to make precognitive calls. Before the targets are selected, no one looks

[3]I was wrong. Of the 39 Parapsychological Association members who answered the questionnaire, four indicated that such research would interest them (Schmeidler, 1971).

at what the subjects have written and therefore any one person knows only a negligible fraction of the data. The whole series of targets is selected by a single entry point in a random number table. To produce extrachance results by PK, someone would have to use clairvoyance or telepathy to learn the subjects' calls and also to learn the random number sequence, then use PK to throw his ten-sided dice for an appropriate entry point in the random number table. But clairvoyance and telepathy are generally weak, and PK is generally weak. This means that PK which works by clairvoyance or telepathy would be a multiple of two weak factors. Thus if precognition were due to PK it should give lower scores than either GESP or PK. But usually precognition scores are not lower; we've been finding that they are at about the same level as GESP scores (and both tend to run higher than PK). Therefore I'd conclude that our empirical evidence opposes explaining away precognition as merely a secondary effect of PK, and that we need to consider it separately established.

And retrocognition. The logical argument for it is that, if time relations are symmetrical, it is the mirror image of precognition. Accepting one implies accepting the other. But are past and future time symmetrical? We've no reason except ignorance (I think) to say that they are. We know that simple symmetry doesn't always occur in nature. I would say that the logical argument for retrocognition is feeble.

What about empirical evidence? So far, it seems to have come only from checking historical records that show a person's glimpse of the past was accurate—but since the records exist, obviously clairvoyance is enough to account for the correspondence. The retrocognitive spontaneous cases usually add colorful details that cannot be checked out, but they may be only imaginative dramatizations, like Koko's adding "a touch of verisimilitude to an otherwise bald and unconvincing narrative." I think the only research that could offer good evidence for retrocognition would come from some variant of the cipher method. For example, if Cretan Linear B had not yet been deciphered it would have been a good test, because there's no Rosetta Stone (so far as we know) to give clairvoyant information about the script. In short, a test for retrocognition could be to turn to undeciphered archeological records; and find if subjects can put order into checkable material although no present statement of that order exists. Until such research is done, I think we must consider retrocognition to be plausible but not demonstrated.

PK. Do we by now all agree that it occurs? It seems to me that convergent lines of evidence force us to. In spontaneous cases there are many well-supported accounts of poltergeists and of other sporadic physical occurrences, like those Jung reported after his stormy interview with Freud in Freud's office, where Oedipal emotions seemed to be causing actual physical disturbances (Fodor, 1963). In laboratory work there have been several experiments with positive results in which experimenter bias was controlled because recordings were blind; and there have been many experiments—some done by careful research workers—in which the two-experimenter method makes gross scoring errors seem unlikely. There is also the strong evidence of the Quartile Decline effect (Rhine & Humphrey, 1944). Some experiments with mediums like Palladino (Feilding, Baggally, & Carrington, 1909) and Schneider (Hope *et al.*, 1933) seem well controlled. There are the impressive recent reports of Ted Serios (Eisenbud, 1967) and Mme. Kulagina (Ostrander & Schroeder, 1970). There are Crookes's (1874) classic observations that D. D. Home used PK to make a pointer shielded from air currents track curves on smoked glass.

We can add a similar massive case of laboratory PK recently reported by Elmer Green (1971) at Menninger. Just last year he had a swami, wearing a face mask to shield both nose and mouth, sit in the lotus position while a committee of scientists was watching. Several feet in front of the swami was a long aluminum knitting needle, mounted on a pivot with a friction bearing. The swami had agreed to try to make the needle move toward him. Three times he gave the "word of command" and on two of those times the needle moved toward him, through about ten degrees of arc each time. This seems fully as striking as the Crookes report. Crookes and Green are certainly good research men; conditions were stringent (as indeed they were in many of the other projects) and I think that with all these independently strong lines of evidence we must, like it or not, agree in accepting PK.

And what of the other big classification within parapsychology, the variants of the spiritistic hypothesis that involve survival after death, or reincarnation, or possession, or discarnate entities, or out of the body travel? We agree, I think, that there are enough provocative findings to justify further research, but that at present they can all be explained away as some combination of PK and ESP. And I think we agree to differ amicably on whether each of us personally prefers a parsimonious theory which accepts only PK and ESP and then by complicated, strained *ad hoc* hypotheses accounts for all the other effects, or whether our personal preference is for a less parsimonious but more elegant theory which accepts some variant of the spiritistic hypothesis and then accounts for the effects more simply and directly.

Our next question is, how do ESP and PK function? And the first subquestion is whether we need one model or more; whether telepathy, clairvoyance, precognition and PK are separate processes or only one process which we describe for our convenience by various terms.

There's been absurdly little work on this basic issue, though those of you who were at last year's convention surely remember Dean's (1970) report, indicating that precognition and clairvoyance have different intraserial effects. With this possible exception, and perhaps a few others, it's my opinion that telepathy, clairvoyance, precognition and PK have shown no differences in either scores or correlates except those that seem due to the subjects' preferences or other personality factors. Dean's report was provocative and impressive, but I'd like to see it replicated with careful attention to similarity in instructional set and to counterbalancing order effects before generalizing from it. As of now, the empirical evidence does not seem to me to compel us to call the processes different. If you disagree, tell me why, at the end of the questionnaire!

Theoretically, it's possible to see all of these processes as basically unitary. I'll give a quick rundown. J. B. Rhine (1946) has pointed out that telepathy from a living person can be described as only clairvoyance of that person's brain events. This lets us collapse clairvoyance and telepathy into a single process. Certain theories of time, like Orme's (1969), describe clairvoyance and precognition as differing only in their experimental arrangements; that is to say, according to some theories of time the difference between precognition and clairvoyance is merely quantitative, comparable to the difference between precognition of the near and more distant future; and thus these two can be collapsed into one process. What of PK? On the face of it, there ought to be some difference between ESP, where information comes into the individual, and PK, where action goes out—but this may be only a matter of looking at the same relationship from opposite perspectives. They may be two aspects of the same basic process of interaction between parts of the universe. Telepathy, for instance, might be a PK effect of one individual upon another. If a psi field of the kind that Roll (1964) describes can be implanted upon an inanimate object, then clairvoyance could be a PK influence from the target's psi field upon the subject. So far as I know, there's no clear basis yet for a firm opinion about whether they are all one process or more, and therefore of whether we need one model for them or more than one. I'll tentatively opt for one.

What should be built into the model? Let's start at the outside: the ESP target. To define it we must say what it is not; we must describe its limits—but we can't. No research on its physical concomitants has given satisfying results. One series of Osis's recent work shows no attenuation with terrestrial distance. Data from his two other series indicate a faint attenuation, but in my opinion this can be attributed to changes in the experimenters' feelings or moods (Osis, Turner, & Carlson, 1971). Further, Commander Mitchell's (1971) data involving far greater distances tend to discount distance effects. Electromagnetic shielding by a Faraday cage seems not to affect ESP unless the subject expects it to (Vasiliev, 1963). No physical barriers have yet been found which cut out ESP success.

But even if we can't state a cutoff point for the ESP stimulus, the zero point for no ESP stimulation, can we describe any functional relations between more or less effective physical factors? I think not. I think work with physical variables has shown preferential effects but not stimulus effects. My touchstone question (like an operational definition of how much we know) is: if a newcomer to experimentation asks for advice about the best physical conditions for ESP success, what can we tell him with certainty? I think all we can say is that the conditions should be congenial to him and his subjects. Some subjects feel the need to be close to the target, or to have a psychometric object they can hold, or to know the experimenter is thinking of the right answer. Others do not. And the scores correspond to the subject's need better than to the physical condition.

I'll add one more negative item. A few years ago I played with the idea that if ESP is transmitted across distance, it might work like radar or sonar: the subject might scan a wide field, get feedback when he came near the target, then use that feedback to home in on it. I did three separate experiments to look for this and all came out negative, though they all gave evidence of other ESP effects (Schmeidler, 1968; Schmeidler & Lewis, 1968; Schmeidler & Lewis, 1969). Both Eastman (1967) and Osis, Turner and Carlson (1971) have also found negative results when they looked for this kind of homing in. I therefore propose to you as the first part of my model that we should discard the whole concept of ESP transmission over distance, just as physicists discarded the "luminiferous ether" after the report of Michelson and Morley's negative findings. Like the physicists, we need to reformulate our problem; to put it in other terms. I propose a geometrical statement instead: that the universe in which ESP or PK is effective has an extra dimension and that this dimension permits topological folding. It thus permits immediate contact between two areas which in an Einsteinian universe would be separated. The analogy would be to the parallel edges of a sheet of paper. In our everyday two-dimensional space, parallel lines don't intersect; but of course they can if they are moved through a third dimension.

We need, I think, a new geometry or physics to work out what stresses are associated with such folding over of distance. But even without the geometry, this model lets us raise new experimental questions. For example, suppose one gifted subject gives an accurate ESP response to some complex target; i.e. produces a fold. Could his fold make it easier for others associated with him to give successful ESP responses to the same target? If so, are their responses only those which the gifted subject made, or are additional details given? Evidence of group telepathic or PK effects would be relevant also, since groups might conjointly supply whatever energy is necessary for folding.

To investigate this, of course, it would be necessary to build into the experimental design an answer to the psychological question of which individuals are truly associated so that they are working members of a group, as opposed to being present but not participating in the group effort or even working at cross-purposes with it. We can also ask experimentally whether such hypothetical folding leaves after-effects upon the target: whether a target becomes more accessible to ESP after a gifted subject has responded accurately to it than it was before he responded. Research on the generalizability of Ryzl and Pratt's focusing effect (1963) is obviously relevant here.

Now let us turn back to the stimulus properties of the ESP target. Physical stimulus variables seem unimportant unless they relate to the subjects' preferences. Rao (1963), as you all know, has used target words in a language unknown to the subjects, and found the subjects responded with words of the same meaning in their own language. I've similarly had subjects give extrachance scores when they tried to call ESP cards, although the targets were only unfamiliar symbols designating the cards. And I'm still baffled by the significant data when my subjects were calling colored ESP cards, like green star or red wave, but the targets were only changes within a computer, never printed out and therefore never translated back into those colored cards (Schmeidler, 1964). The subjects' calls of red wave or blue circle somehow corresponded to internal computer changes. In short, target-response relations do not seem to depend on the physical characteristics of the target. Our data, I think, force us to conclude that the ESP target is not an object but instead is something like the meaning of an object, or an informational pattern.

If therefore we shift from the physical to the informational aspects of the ESP target, the data look more orderly (though they're in short supply). Suppose we inquire, as Cadoret (1961) and Scott (1961) did, how much information comes through ESP. We can compare complex targets with simple ones, binary targets with those where the odds are longer, and so on. We all agree, I imagine, on one answer to this question: that the percentage of extrachance hits shows a rough decrease as the odds get longer.[4] In the crudest case, a hundred calls with binary targets (odd or even, white or green) should give more extrachance hits than a hundred calls on the ten digits. The shape of the function has not been mapped, nor have its extremes, but at least we know the direction of its slope in the middle range. The Psi Quotient has been developed, of course, because this effect seems so consistent (Schmidt, 1970b).

This immediately gives us what seems to me one basic, important fact about ESP. It is not an all-or-none type of event. If it were, if it gave complete information whenever it appeared, targets with odds of thousands to one would give the same number of extrachance hits as would ESP cards. I'll put the same thing affirmatively. Our data tell us that ESP gives partial information; that errors can be admixed with accuracy, in the same response. In my model, then, the ESP stimulus is a pattern of partial information transferred by a fold of the space-time matrix.

What kinds of errors occur? Not entirely random ones. Sometimes there is a displaced correspondence to the target, so that it's often useful to allow for temporal (serial) displacement in the research design. We all know that Carington (1944) used ten randomly chosen words (each with a drawing) as his targets for ten days, one for each day, and found most hits on the correct day, next most hits on the days before and after the correct one, and so on. Because of Carington's findings, Soal set up research with a gifted subject in which he predicted, on the basis of pretests, success not on the target displayed at the time of the call, but on the target that would follow it; then found striking confirmation of this predicted displacement (Soal & Goldney, 1943). My own hunch is that with achievement-oriented subjects who are both impatient and friendly, there will be a psychological tendency to hurry ahead which results in +1 displacements (Schmeidler, Friedenberg, & Males, 1966; Schmeidler & Lewis, 1969). So far as I know, no one else has ever tried to check out my findings, or this generalization from them.

That was serial or temporal displacement. Content displacement also occurs. Predictably, with some subjects, a particular "incorrect" response is substituted for a particular correct

[4]Far from it! There was less than 50 percent agreement with this point among the Parapsychological Association members (Schmeidler, 1971).

one, as with the person who repeatedly dreamed of feces just before receiving money in the mail (Dommeyer, 1955; 1956). Predictably, with hostile or negativistic subjects, there is psi-missing, the extreme case of content displacement that shows up as target avoidance. Predictably, with the Fisk and Mitchell clock cards (where the target is one of twelve positions on a circle) there is a scatter of responses which center upon the correct position, so that weighted credit for near misses results in extrachance scores (Mitchell & Fisk, 1954). Predictably, with eager subjects, oscillation between psi-missing and psi-hitting gives extrachance large variances. From these observations we have, I think, learned one substantive point for agreement in 1971 and also one procedural point. The substantive point is that the partial information of ESP may be systematically gated, in a direction different from what the instructions call for, without the subject's being aware that the gating occurs. From this follows the procedural point: that good ESP research should increase its scoring repertoire beyond looking for direct hits. If there is appropriate evidence from related research or from pretests, it should incorporate into the experimental design the scoring of displacement effects (including psi-missing) and variance changes as evidence of unconsciously misdirected ESP.

But one apparently contradictory finding needs statement here: the extraordinary precision of some matchings of target and response. Spontaneous cases often show it. And Carington (1944) found repeatedly, using R.A. Fisher's formula to score his data, that pinpoint precision occurred more dependably than blurred near precision. If his target was an elm tree, for instance, the advantage of his experimental over his control group was greatest if he counted only "elm" as a hit instead of counting any tree, or any leafy plant. This in a way contradicts the scatter pattern of near misses with clock targets. And this apparent contradiction seems to me to give us a particularly interesting and potentially informative research lead. Where the probability of the target is very low or high, at the extremes, there may be some complex, nonlinear relation between probability of success and precision in response, perhaps because of what Murphy (1958) has called "potentiation." Another possibility is that there may be some interaction among the components of a complex target which leads to more precision than with a simple target which has the same chance probability of success. I won't ask for agreement here, though maybe there is some. But my own feeling is that this is a problem where careful research could yield basic information about the functioning of ESP. We need to compare simple with complex targets that have the same probability, to find the effect of redundant information; and we need to explore extreme P's as well as the middle range, to find the shape of the function.

On the next point, I will with some uncertainty ask if you concur. I would not have done so a few years ago. It is the statement made first, I think, by Taetzsch (1962) that the basic tenet of quality control applies to ESP: where some information is available, proper control methods can increase the yield to whatever level of accuracy is demanded. Dean and Taetzsch's work (1970), and the work of Fisk and West (1957), Brier and Tyminski (1970), Ryzl (1966), and Carpenter (1970) seem to me by now to have shown that repeated attempts to identify a target, if conducted in a sophisticated way (for example, utilizing psi-missing as well as psi-hitting data) will refine the crude information, reduce the noise, and permit specification of even a multi-digit number through a modified "majority vote" technique. I therefore put it to you that accurate communication by ESP is possible. It may be expensive; it may take many man-hours; but it can be done. Suppose someone asked us, "If we give you a large budget to pay for the transmission, can this short message be transmitted by ESP?" I suggest that by now our answer should be "Yes. We know how to do it."

Let's move further in, from the informational content which ESP provides to the biology of the organism that responds to ESP or produces PK. On animal research, do you all agree with me, especially after the last few years of affirmative reports from FRNM (Levy, Mayo, André, & McRae, 1971; Levy & McRae, 1971; Morris, 1970; Schmidt, 1970a), that by now the evidence for ESP or PK from non-human animals is so strong that we must accept that ESP or PK is not an exclusively human ability? But on plants, do you agree that the data can rather readily be explained away as PK from the experimenter, so that our opinion of plant ESP (Backster, 1968) is "Not proven"? And further, that so little has been learned about ESP or PK from non-human animals that we do not know of any distinctive ways it functions, different from the ways it functions in humans? Watkins's (1971) dominance-submission data on lizards look very like Kanthamani's (1966) dominance-submission data on high school youngsters. Since we know so little about animal psi, we must restrict our conclusions about biological concomitants to the work on human subjects.

With humans, I'll start with one point which used to be a live issue, but on which there's now (I think) such general concurrence that I almost forgot to put it on your list.[5] It's the question of whether ESP ability is restricted to a rare few, like flaming red hair, or is widespread, like red hair pigment. Research with unselected subjects has given extrachance scores in so many projects, from the Andhra University ones (Kanthamani & Rao, 1971; Rao, Kanthamani, & Sailaja, 1967) and Bhadra's (1966) in India, to Van Busschbach's (1959) in Holland or Carington's (1944) and Fisk and West's (1956) in England, and of course very many in the United States, that it now looks as if we have all, as it were, voted with our feet. Most of us have chosen to work at times with any moderately large group that comes our way, because we expect to find extrachance patterns if we set up reasonably agreeable or challenging conditions. Further, no evidence shows clearly that we should exclude any special subgroup of age or sex or physical characteristics from our subject sample. The expectation now is that some more or less weak ESP or PK ability is available in anyone or almost anyone (though it may take research skill to tap it).

Now onward to biological questions. Where is ESP received, or PK produced? We have, I think, not even a hint about PK; but for ESP we have some specifications and perhaps a pointer toward an answer.

ESP input needs a receptor sufficiently versatile to process both specific, detailed information and also those vague, nonsensory impressions which seem to yield a low grade of ESP information. It sounds as if the ESP receptor must have as detailed

[5]Questionnaire returns show the issue is still alive. One Parapsychological Association member disagreed with the statement, and half a dozen considered it premature (Schmeidler, 1971).

an internal structure as the eye or ear or brain. Perhaps we should look first at the sensory projection areas of the brain. Here I think we have an important pointer: the errors made by gifted psychics. Their mistakes sometimes sound as if they'd had an accurate auditory impression but then misinterpreted it as a homonym—and sometimes look as if they'd had an accurate visual impression but misinterpreted it as something of similar shape or color. These errors imply that either the visual or auditory brain area may be an input channel for ESP, but that neither is the exclusive channel. How I wish we had studies of subjects with localized brain injuries, or localized small areas of excitation, to tell us if some particular type of brain cell or some small locus was the receptor for ESP! We need systematic research with careful modern methods, to give us a guideline. However, what we might find after such research, as Gardner Murphy put it to me years ago, is that ESP sensitivity is nonspecific; that it's a kind of general protoplasmic sensitivity, and thus that many parts of the nervous system (or other cells) can be stimulated by ESP input. Some support for this—weak support—shows as we go down the biological scale and find evidence for ESP in animals whose brains are different than ours. Hardy (1950) among others has proposed that intraspecies ESP is common or universal. It may be that different specialized receptors have evolved in different species, or that there is no specialized receptor. No one has tried to find out.

But in spite of this ignorance, it's time to build up the model a little more. For human ESP, I propose that a relational pattern of partial information can come directly to some brain processing center or centers, and that it typically bypasses the periphery. It comes by means of a topological fold in the space-time matrix, so that there is no transmission across space. It may come directly into different areas: if into the visual, it gives visual information; if into some other, it gives auditory, or affective, or other qualitatively different information. If it bypasses the sensory projection areas it may produce only a cognitive change, more like an idea or a meaning than an image. If it comes into the limbic or other noncortical areas it may alter ongoing processes to produce autonomic nervous system changes such as those that a plethysmograph registers (Dean & Nash, 1967). Such changes may provide a mechanism for psychic healing—for which there's increasingly good evidence these days (Grad, 1965; Onetto & Elguin, 1966; Smith, 1968; Watkins & Watkins, 1971). And if nonneural tissue can act as a receptor, then ESP might directly modify the ongoing processes in any part of the body. At this point ESP informational input has merged into PK input; they would be two different descriptions of the same event. Such direct input could be another mechanism for psychic healing. If Hardy's description of intraspecies ESP effects is validated (I don't know its current status among biologists) I suppose we would have to include mutations as another possible effect, and genes as another input locus.

Let's leave localization and turn to body processes. Almost all we have here, I think, is a sort of negative: that no body changes which a doctor would call unhealthy have produced reliable, consistent improvement in ESP or PK. You might cite as exceptions the rather high ESP scores that I found in concussion patients (Schmeidler, 1952), and in women who had not yet recovered from childbirth (Gerber & Schmeidler, 1957), but these seem to me irrelevant because the high scores looked like a side effect of the mood or attitude changes in these patients, who were resting comfortably and passively. Another apparent exception comes from Ehrenwald (1947) and Ullman (1952), who have independently reported that patients about to sink into a frank psychosis give flashes of unusually accurate ESP; but both psychiatrists attribute this also to changes in need or motivational patterns. Stimulants perhaps give a higher than normal variance of ESP scores (Rogers & Carpenter, 1966); but this may be due to loss of control, which is not equivalent to an increase in ability. Hallucinogens may sometimes be associated with erratic ESP success (Cavanna & Servadio, 1964); but the data are not firm. Depressants seem in some research to give marked extrachance low scores (Cadoret, 1953; Huby & Wilson, 1961); but in other research they give chance scores (Huby & Wilson, 1961; Rhine, 1935). The two findings taken in conjunction imply again that it is not ESP ability which is affected but only mood or attitude. Many cultures describe fasting or other abstinence as conducive to heightened ESP success, but the evidence is anecdotal and it is uncontrolled, especially for cultural expectations. Bhadra's

(1968) research with Sheldon's constitutional types, indicating that endomorphs have more ESP success, is as yet unconfirmed by others. So is Hyslop's suggestion (made in conversation one day) that women with anterior pituitary hyperfunction have strong ESP ability, or Eysenck's (1967) hypothesis that the ratio of cerebral inhibitory to excitatory processes relates to ESP success, or any other physiological theory that I know. Buess, a student of mine who is studying breathing patterns, has so far found only the familiar preferential effect: that some type of breathing seems conducive to high scores in a particular person but not in the next person (Buess, 1971). Genetic transmission of ESP ability has been suggested but never adequately examined. Autonomic nervous system changes seem to be one mode of ESP response (Tart, 1963; Dean & Nash, 1967), and perhaps are ESP concomitants, but have not been demonstrated to affect ESP functioning. Research on brain changes, such as alpha waves, is provocative but as yet inconclusive. My feeling about body relations to ESP is that we have hints but no conclusions. We must keep on looking.

When we turn to psychological processes, the story is different. The "hard" areas, like perception and learning, give us no hard findings; but the "soft" areas like personality give us many somewhat softer ones. (Perhaps the last letter of "ESP" should change its significance from "perception" to "personality.") In any event, the traits, moods, attitudes, needs—those vaguely defined intervening variables of contemporary personality work—seem to me to relate as clearly to ESP responses as they do to any other responses in psychology. Time is growing short, and I will give you only a few generalizations and a single example here, instead of a list of specifics.

The first generalization is that measurement of personality variables is difficult. Anxiety, aggression, affiliation and achievement needs cannot be measured directly; they must be inferred from test scores, or introspective comments, or observers' reports, or body processes. Often scores must be corrected, or subjects discarded, because of some response bias such as answering in terms of social desirability, or defensiveness, or lying. When the independent variable (need, mood, etc.) is measured with so much uncertainty, it is likely to show only a weak relation to any dependent variable, such as ESP score.

And yet these weak relationships have, by and large, appeared rather consistently in ESP research. I'll take as my one example the sheep-goat effect because then when I criticize it, I'll be treading on no one's toes except my own. It's been tested in different ways, but according to Palmer (1971; 1972), who recently reviewed dozens of sheep-goat experiments, it stands up pretty well. Palmer found that the mean sheep-goat differences of the various experiments shaped up to a distribution centering rather near the mean of the original research. Many experiments came out in the predicted direction and a sizable handful of them were significant; only a few came out in the opposite direction and (he told me this morning) he found none of those to be significant.

But does this mean that accepting the possibility of ESP success in a particular task facilitates ESP hitting in that task? I must say "No" to that, even if it makes me sound like an unnatural mother denying her own child. Consider the procedure. An experimenter has typically been making either a hard sell or a soft sell for ESP. He then asks his subject if ESP is possible in the procedure that he, the experimenter, has set up. What will the subject say? Probably the answer depends as much on his attitude toward the questioner as toward the question. He might say, "Yes, it's possible" because of respect for authority, or general good will, or need for conformity, or being willing to try anything once, or of course because of belief that ESP is possible. He might say "No" because of resenting the experimenter, or from lively, counteractive mischief, or from fear of failure, or of course from cognitive appraisal that ESP is impossible in this situation. Probably the yesses converge on friendly acceptance and willing participation, while the noes converge on hostility or withdrawal. I interpret the high proportion of successful sheep-goat replications as much to the question's tapping socially oriented moods as to intellectual appraisal of ESP's possibility.

Beloff's supersheep question ("Do you think that you yourself can succeed because of your ESP ability in this task?") separates out the achievement-oriented, ego-involved expectation of personal success, and is a fine step toward specifying one of the subclasses in this conglomerate of sheep attitudes (Beloff

& Bate, 1970). We need more such separations. In general, for this or any other personality score, we should identify the factors that led a particular subject to produce his score before we make predictions about that subject's performance. Two subjects can make the same personality test score for quite different reasons.

But does this bring us into such a fuzzy area that we can't find our way? My opinion (and I put it on your questionnaire to find if it was your opinion too) is that by now so many different methods of inquiry have converged on two specific underlying variables that—even though no single inquiry specifies those variables unequivocally—we have a right to draw at least one pair of conclusions about them. In my own thinking I fuse with the sheep-goat findings Johnson and Kanthamani's (1967) lower ESP scores from their more defensive subjects, Shields's (1962) lower scores from her more withdrawn children, Rao's (1965) lower scores when his subjects used non-preferred targets, along with the Nicol-Humphrey (1953; 1955), Anderson-White (1958), Osis-Dean (1964), and Mihalasky (1970) findings. These and many others all seem to me to point toward the association of lower ESP scores with defensive, negativistic withdrawal from the task situation as the subject sees it, and of higher ESP scores when the subject has an interested, friendly acceptance of the task situation and its demands. Decline effects and variance changes seem to me to fit under this generalization also; they would belong in the special subclass of intrasession shifts between interest and withdrawal. I should add that the two personality variables I proposed obviously influence many other forms of behavior in essentially the same way as they influence ESP responses.

All this applies to run-of-the-mill, unselected subjects. What special patterns do we find in the gifted subjects who have produced extraordinary extrachance success? It troubles me that though so many of these subjects have been studied, the only generally accepted statement about them that I can find is that they're likely to make poor scores if they're unhappy with the procedure; and this is hardly distinctive. Descriptions vary; Stepanek, for example, seems to need the support of a familiar method (Ryzl, Freeman & Kanthamani, 1965; Ryzl & Pratt, 1962), but Mrs. Garrett seemed to need the challenge of frequent novelties in the procedure (Birge & Rhine, 1942). We have

White's (1964) brilliant proposal that gifted subjects go through the stages of relaxation, engaging the conscious mind, waiting, tension and release; but though this seems not to have been denied, it seems also not to have been widely affirmed. Let me propose to you an idea which I am playing with now but have not yet had time to test: a variant of Eysenck's theory.

Subjects who call correctly a deck of 25 ESP cards usually say afterwards that they found it an intense strain. Psychics after a prolonged and particularly successful sitting often report that they too were strained by it, that they feel washed out. We can try to generalize about this in terms of the two chemical processes that act at nerve centers to produce excitation or inhibition. If excitation had been extremely strong during the prolonged period of ESP success we would, I think, expect it to spread; to result in jerky muscles and reports of intense, rapidly varying sensations, floods of memories, interlocking ideas. Some of this is reported, but not much. Now consider the alternative. If inhibition had been extremely strong, we would expect it too to spread and produce subsequent lethargy; and this is what seems typical. It looks as if some localized excitation was present, along with very strong inhibition. Suppose we take as a working hypothesis that the extremely gifted subject must be a good inhibitor.

Masses of other material seem to support this hypothesis (but of course this is common among untested ideas). According to Eysenck (1957) extraverts are good inhibitors; and extraversion scores tend to correlate with ESP (Humphrey, 1951) and perhaps PK (Van de Castle, 1958) success. In neurosis, the symptom choice is hysterical or psychasthenic for good inhibitors, but obsessive-compulsive or neurasthenic for weak inhibitors (Eysenck, 1957); and several independent series from Bender's (Rasch, 1955; Sannwald, 1961-1962) and Tenhaeff's (Tenhaeff, 1962) laboratories indicate that the psychics they studied fall on the psychasthenic rather than the neurasthenic side. Introspections from psychics typically report a "stilling of the mind" (White, 1964), and this sounds like inhibition of potential conflicting impulses. Trance, including hypnotic trance, is often associated with marked ESP success; and trance seems an extreme example of a stilled mind and of inhibition. The disciplines imposed by Yoga and Zen are traditionally associated with developing psychic ability; and both these disciplines look like paradigms of encouraging inhibition rather than excitation. The in-between or drowsy or sleep states that Murphy tells us are typically associated with spontaneous phenomena (Murphy, 1945; Murphy & Dale, 1943) are inhibitory rather than excitatory. In short, it seems not unreasonable to suggest that individuals with extremely high ESP or PK ability have a high ratio of inhibition to excitation. I like the idea partly because it can be tested so easily, if the gifted subjects are available. It requires only comparing their reminiscence in pursuit or other motor learning, or their performance on sensory tasks such as the one for negative time error or spiral afterimage with the previously published norms of the general population.

Now back to my model. We've brought ESP information into the brain. What happens to it when it gets there? It finds other ongoing brain events, and some are compellingly strong. Which will be prepotent, so that it determines a response? I suggest that to rough out our answer we make an analogy between ESP and incidental or subliminal stimulation, and ask the same question there. An answer—a rough answer, at least—is that there seem to be three conditions in which incidental stimuli elicit a response.

One is the "cocktail party" effect. You all know that in a crowded room there may be such a buzz of conversation that a person seems unable to hear anyone who is not addressing him directly—until someone else off to the side mentions his name, and that comes through loud and clear. For ESP as for incidental stimuli, what's relevant to a person's needs—or in Klein and Holt's (1960) words, what resonates with the drive cathexes that are active—is likely to "come through" either by facilitating ESP hits, as in Fisk and West's (1955) subject who responded so well to erotic stimuli, or, with defensive subjects, by facilitating psi-missing (Johnson & Kanthamani, 1967).

The second condition which seems effective for both incidental and subliminal stimuli is the use of an indirect measure of response instead of direct recall. Projective tests (as in Louwerens's ESP work in Utrecht, 1960), dream recall (as in the Ullman-Krippner work on dream telepathy or precognition, 1970), and free association (as in a psychic's "reading") have shown effects of subliminal stimulation where demands for direct statement failed to do so. Such is especially the case in the forced choice method of signal detection with instructions to guess among the choices (like ESP cards). This also is a part of the Klein and Holt arguments, since indirect measures permit a fusion of the subliminal or incidental input with other ongoing processes. The fusion permits either immediate retrieval, as in guessing, or delayed retrieval, as in dreams. The analogy to ESP seems clear.

A third condition is an increase in the strength of the incidental or subliminal stimulus until it becomes focal, or to have repeated presentation of subliminal stimuli. In ESP we do not know how to increase stimulus strength (though perhaps batteries of agents can do so); but the repeated guessing technique described by Taetzsch (1962) is analogous to the repeated presentation of a subliminal stimulus, which eventually makes it supraliminal. A related method of increasing stimulus effectiveness for incidental material is of course to attend selectively to the stimulus so as to try to make it focal and clear; and perhaps this is like the stilling of the mind, the inhibition of other input, which seems a characteristic of gifted ESP subjects.

I left our model with the ESP information in the brain, and asked how it is processed in relation to other ongoing brain events. There must, I think, be a list of answers. It may be completely blocked and disappear without a trace. It may be partially blocked. It may be shunted into long-term memory and retrieved later in dreams or waking, just as other incidental stimuli are. Like them, it may fuse with ongoing related processes, which distort it. It may be prepotent over the other processes, if they can be inhibited by a stilled mind or a trance state. It may move up to consciousness. It may influence an effector system, producing autonomic changes or motor automatisms (or perhaps psychic healing—or psychic injury). The personality factors—moods, needs, and so on—that relate to ambiguous perceptual input apparently relate in similar ways to ESP input. The model thus predicts that whatever psychological laws apply to the processing of ambiguous sensory material will apply also to the processing of ESP information.

The model, in short, bypasses the problem of how ESP or PK is transmitted and calls instead for relevant topological concepts. It proposes a folding of the space-time matrix, and suggests research which could support or contraindicate this proposal. It states that the basic units for ESP are relations and meanings, i.e., are informational units, and states that ESP ordinarily gives only partial information. It treats PK as it does ESP, in terms of informational, patterned relations. It points to the need for research on whether there are special brain cells or brain processes which determine ESP receptivity, and proposes in the absence of such research that any part of the body may act as ESP receptor, though reception typically occurs in brain centers. It suggests that inhibition of competing brain events is a condition for accurate processing of ESP information, and proposes that gifted subjects are good inhibitors. And it attempts to integrate our findings about ESP responses and personality factors with similar findings in other fields of psychological research.

## REFERENCES

ANDERSON, M., & WHITE, R. A. A survey of work on ESP and teacher-pupil attitudes. *Journal of Parapsychology,* 1958, 22, 246-268.

BACKSTER, C. Evidence of a primary perception in plant life. *International Journal of Parapsychology,* 1968, 10, 329-348.

BELOFF, J., & BATE, D. Research report for the year 1968-69. *Journal* S.P.R., 1970, 45, 297-301.

BHADRA, B. R. The relationship of test scores to belief in ESP. *Journal of Parapsychology,* 1966, 30, 1-17.

BHADRA, B. R. Physique in relation to ESP performance. *Journal of Parapsychology,* 1968, 32, 131. (Abstract)

BIRGE, W. R., & RHINE, J. B. Unusual types of persons tested for ESP: I. A professional medium. *Journal of Parapsychology,* 1942, 6, 85-94.

BRIER, R. M., & TYMINSKI, W. V. Psi application: Part I. A preliminary attempt. Part II. The majority vote technique—analyses and observations. *Journal of Parapsychology,* 1970, 34, 1-36.

BUESS, L. M. The effects of breathing upon ESP—A systematic investigation. 1971, unpublished ms.

CADORET, R. J. The effect of amytal and dexadrine on ESP performance. *Journal of Parapsychology,* 1953, 17, 259-274.

CADORET, R. J. Some applications of information theory to card-calling performance in ESP. *Journal of General Psychology,* 1961, 65, 89-107.

CARINGTON, W. Experiments on the paranormal cognition of drawings. *Proceedings* A.S.P.R., 1944, 24, 3-107.

CARPENTER, J. Facilitation of psi communication by the use of run score variance effects, index sampling, and the repeated-guessing technique. *Proceedings of the Parapsychological Association,* 1970, 7, 13-14. (Abstract)

CAVANNA, R., & SERVADIO, E. ESP experiments with LSD25 and Psilocybin; a methodological approach. *Parapsychological Monographs* No. 5. New York: Parapsychology Foundation, 1964.

CROOKES, W. *Researches in the phenomena of spiritualism.* London: J. Burns, 1874.

DEAN, D. Can subjects differentiate clairvoyance from precognition? *Proceedings of the Parapsychological Association,* 1970, 7, 31-32. (Abstract)

DEAN, D., & NASH, C. B. Coincident plethysmographic results under controlled conditions. *Journal* S.P.R., 1967, 44, 1-14.

DEAN, D., & TAETZSCH, R. Psi in the casino: Taetzsch method. *Proceedings of the Parapsychological Association,* 1970, 7, 14-15. (Abstract)

DOMMEYER, F. C. Some ostensibly precognitive dreams. *Journal* A.S.P.R., 1955, 49, 109-117.

DOMMEYER, F. C. Another veridically significant dream. *Journal* A.S.P.R., 1956, 50, 162-163.

EASTMAN, M. The relationship of ESP scores to knowledge of target location, and to birth order and family size. *Journal of Parapsychology,* 1967, 31, 168-169. (Abstract)

EHRENWALD, J. *Telepathy and medical psychology.* London: Allen, 1947.

EISENBUD, J. *The world of Ted Serios.* New York: William Morrow, 1967.

EYSENCK, H. J. *The dynamics of anxiety and hysteria.* London: Routledge and Kegan Paul, 1957.

EYSENCK, H. J. Personality and extra-sensory perception. *Journal* S.P.R., 1967, 44, 55-71.

FEILDING, E., BAGGALLY, W. W., & CARRINGTON, H. Report on a series of sittings with Eusapia Palladino. *Proceedings* S.P.R., 1909, 23, 309-569.

FISK, G. W., & WEST, D. J. ESP tests with erotic symbols. *Journal* S.P.R., 1955, 38, 1-7.

FISK, G. W., & WEST, D. J. ESP and mood: Report of a "mass" experiment. *Journal* S.P.R., 1956, 38, 320-328.

FISK, G. W., & WEST, D. J. Towards accurate predictions from ESP data. *Journal* S.P.R., 1957, 39, 157-162.

FODOR, N. Jung, Freud, and a newly-discovered letter of 1909 on the poltergeist theme. *Psychoanalytic Review,* 1963, 50, 119-128.

GERBER, R., & SCHMEIDLER, G. R. An investigation of relaxation and of acceptance of the experimental situation as related to ESP scores in maternity patients. *Journal of Parapsychology,* 1957, 21, 47-57.

GRAD, B. Some biological effects of the "laying on of hands": A review of experiments with animals and plants. *Journal* A.S.P.R., 1965, 59, 95-129.

GREEN, E. Report to the Third Interdisciplinary Conference on the Voluntary Control of Internal States, Council Grove, Kansas, 1971.

HARDY, A. C. Telepathy and evolutionary theory. *Journal* S.P.R., 1950, 35, 225-238.

HOPE, C., *et al.* Report of a series of sittings with Rudi Schneider. *Proceedings* S.P.R., 1933, 41, 255-330.

HUBY, P. M., & WILSON, C. W. M. The effect of centrally acting drugs on ESP ability in normal subjects. *Journal* S.P.R., 1961, 41, 60-67.

HUMPHREY, B. M. Introversion-extraversion ratings in relation to scores in ESP tests. *Journal of Parapsychology,* 1951, 15, 252-262.

HUMPHREY, B. M., & PRATT, J. G. A comparison of five ESP test procedures. *Journal of Parapsychology,* 1941, 5, 267-292.

KANTHAMANI, B. K. ESP and social stimulus. *Journal of Parapsychology,* 1966, 30, 31-38.

KANTHAMANI, B. K., & RAO, K. R. Personality characteristics of ESP subjects: I. Primary personality characteristics and ESP. *Journal of Parapsychology,* 1971, 35, 189-207.

KLEIN, G. S., & HOLT, R. R. Problems and issues in current studies of subliminal perception. In J. G. Peatman and E. L. Hartley (Eds.), *Festschrift for Gardner Murphy.* New York: Harper, 1960.

JOHNSON, M., & KANTHAMANI, B. K. The Defense Mechanism Test as a predictor of ESP scoring direction. *Journal of Parapsychology,* 1967, 31, 99-110.

LEVY, W. J., MAYO, L. A., ANDRÉ, E., & MCRAE, A. Repetition of the French precognition experiments with mice. *Journal of Parapsychology,* 1971, 35, 1-17.

LEVY, W. J., & MCRAE, A. Precognition in mice and jirds. *Journal of Parapsychology,* 1971, 35, 120-131.

LOUWERENS, N. G. ESP experiments with nursery school children in the Netherlands. *Journal of Parapsychology,* 1960, 24, 75-93.

MCMAHAN, E. A. An experiment in pure telepathy. *Journal of Parapsychology,* 1946, 10, 224-242.

MIHALASKY, J. The influence of sex dominance in group precognition experiments on the relationship between the hare-tortoise categories. *Proceedings of the Parapsychological Association,* 1970, 7, 60-62. (Abstract)

MITCHELL, A. M. J., & FISK, G. W. Clock cards and differential scoring techniques. *Journal of Parapsychology,* 1954, 18, 153-164.

MITCHELL, E. D. An ESP test from Apollo 14. *Journal of Parapsychology,* 1971, 35, 89-107.

MORRIS, R. L. Psi and animal behavior: A survey. *Journal* A.S.P.R., 1970, 64, 242-260.

MURPHY, G. Field theory and survival. *Journal* A.S.P.R., 1945, 39, 181-209.

MURPHY, G. Progress in parapsychology. *Journal of Parapsychology*, 1958, 22, 229-236.

MURPHY, G., & DALE, L. A. Concentration versus relaxation in relation to telepathy. *Journal* A.S.P.R., 1943, 37, 2-15.

NICOL, J. F., & HUMPHREY, B. M. The exploration of ESP and human personality. *Journal* A.S.P.R., 1953, 47, 133-178.

NICOL, J. F., & HUMPHREY, B. M. The repeatability problem in ESP-personality research. *Journal* A.S.P.R., 1955, 49, 125-156.

ONETTO, B., & ELGUIN, G. H. Psychokinesis in experimental tumorogenesis. *Journal of Parapsychology*, 1966, 30, 220. (Abstract)

ORME, J. E. *Time, experience and behaviour*. New York: American Elsevier, 1969.

OSIS, K., & DEAN, D. The effect of experimenter differences and subjects' belief level upon ESP scores. *Journal* A.S.P.R., 1964, 58, 158-185.

OSIS, K., TURNER, M. E., & CARLSON, M. L. ESP over distance: Research on the ESP channel. *Journal* A.S.P.R., 1971, 65, 245-288.

OSTRANDER, S., & SCHROEDER, L. *Psychic discoveries behind the Iron Curtain*. Englewood Cliffs, New Jersey: Prentice-Hall, 1970.

PALMER, J. Scoring in ESP tests as a function of belief in ESP. Part I. The sheep-goat effect. *Journal* A.S.P.R., 1971, 65, 373-408.

PALMER, J. Scoring in ESP tests as a function of belief in ESP. Part II. Beyond the sheep-goat effect. *Journal* A.S.P.R., 1972, 66, 1-26.

RAO, K. R. Studies in the preferential effect: II. A language ESP test involving precognition and intervention. *Journal of Parapsychology*, 1963, 27, 147-160.

RAO, K. R. The bidirectionality of psi. *Proceedings of the Parapsychological Association*, 1965, 2, 37-59. (Presidential Address, Eighth Annual Convention)

RAO, K. R., KANTHAMANI, B. K., & SAILAJA, P. Dissonance hypothesis and some incongruent ESP results. *International Journal of Parapsychology*, 1967, 9, 128-133.

RASCH, W. D. Psychodiagnostic examination of sensitives. *Proceedings of the First International Conference of Parapsychological Studies*. New York: Parapsychology Foundation, 1955.

RHINE, J. B. *Extra-sensory perception*. Boston: Bruce Humphries, 1935.

RHINE, J. B. A digest and discussion of some comments on "Telepathy and clairvoyance reconsidered." *Journal of Parapsychology*, 1946, 10, 36-50.

RHINE, J. B., & HUMPHREY, B. M. The PK effect: Special evidence from hit patterns. I. Quarter distributions of the page. *Journal of Parapsychology*, 1944, 8, 18-60.

ROGERS, D. P., & CARPENTER, J. C. The decline of variance of ESP scores within a testing session. *Journal of Parapsychology,* 1966, 30, 141-150.

ROLL, W. G. The psi field. *Proceedings of the Parapsychological Association,* 1957-1964, 1, 32-65. (Presidential Address, Seventh Annual Convention, 1964)

RYZL, M. A model of parapsychological communication. *Journal of Parapsychology,* 1966, 30, 18-30.

RYZL, M., FREEMAN, J., & KANTHAMANI, B. K. A confirmatory ESP test with Stepanek. *Journal of Parapsychology,* 1965, 29, 89-95.

RYZL, M., & PRATT, J. G. Confirmation of ESP performance in a hypnotically prepared subject. *Journal of Parapsychology,* 1962, 26, 237-243.

RYZL, M., & PRATT, J. G. The focusing of ESP upon particular targets. *Journal of Parapsychology,* 1963, 27, 227-241.

SANNWALD, G. Beziehungen zwischen parapsychischen erlebnissen und personlichkeitsmerkmalen. *Zeitschrift für Parapsychologie und Grenzgebiete der Psychologie,* 1961-1962, Bd. 5 (No. 2-3), 81-119.

SCHMEIDLER, G. R. Rorschachs and ESP scores of patients suffering from cerebral concussion. *Journal of Parapsychology,* 1952, 16, 80-89.

SCHMEIDLER, G. R. An experiment on precognitive clairvoyance. Part I. The main results. *Journal of Parapsychology,* 1964, 28, 1-14.

SCHMEIDLER, G. R. A search for feedback in ESP: Part I. Session salience and stimulus preference. *Journal* A.S.P.R., 1968, 62, 130-142.

SCHMEIDLER, G. R. Parapsychologists' opinions about parapsychology, 1971. *Journal of Parapsychology,* 1971, 35, 208-218.

SCHMEIDLER, G. R., FRIEDENBERG, W., & MALES, P. Impatience and ESP scores. *Journal of Parapsychology,* 1966, 30, 275. (Abstract)

SCHMEIDLER, G. R., & LEWIS, L. A search for feedback in ESP: Part II. High ESP scores after two successes in triple-aspect targets. *Journal* A.S.P.R., 1968, 62, 255-262.

SCHMEIDLER, G. R., & LEWIS, L. A search for feedback in ESP: Part III. The preferential effect and the impatience effect. *Journal* A.S.P.R., 1969, 63, 60-68.

SCHMIDT, H. PK experiments with animals as subjects. *Journal of Parapsychology,* 1970, 34, 255-261.(a)

SCHMIDT, H. The Psi Quotient (PQ): An efficiency measure for psi tests. *Journal of Parapsychology,* 1970, 34, 210-214.(b)

SCOTT, C. Models for psi. *Proceedings* S.P.R., 1961, 53, 195-225.

SHIELDS, E. Comparison of children's guessing ability (ESP) with personality characteristics. *Journal of Parapsychology,* 1962, 26, 200-210.

SMITH, J. Parnormal effects on enzyme activity. *Proceedings of the Parapsychological Association,* 1968, 5, 15-16. (Abstract)

SOAL, S. G., & GOLDNEY, K. M. Experiments in precognitive telepathy. *Proceedings* S.P.R., 1943, 47, 21-150.

TAETZSCH, R. Design of a psi communications system. *International Journal of Parapsychology,* 1962, 4, 35-70.

TART, C. T. Physiological correlates of psi cognitions. *International Journal of Parapsychology,* 1963, 5, 375-386.

TENHAEFF, W. H. C. *Proceedings of the Parapsychological Institute of the State University of Utrecht,* 1962, 2, 1-79.

TYRRELL, G. N. M. The Tyrrell apparatus for testing extrasensory perception. *Journal of Parapsychology,* 1938, 2, 107-118.

ULLMAN, M. On the nature of resistance to psi phenomena. *Journal* A.S.P.R., 1952, 46, 11-13.

ULLMAN, M., & KRIPPNER, S. Dream studies and telepathy: An experimental approach. *Parapsychological Monographs* No. 12. New York: Parapsychology Foundation, 1970.

VAN BUSSCHBACH, J. G. An investigation of ESP in the first and second grades of Dutch schools. *Journal of Parapsychology,* 1959, 23, 227-237.

VAN DE CASTLE, R. L. An exploratory study of some personality correlates associated with PK performance. *Journal* A.S.P.R., 1958, 52, 134-150.

VASILIEV, L. L. *Experiments in mental suggestion.* Church Crookham, Hampshire, England: Institute for the Study of Mental Images, 1963.

WATKINS, G. K. Possible PK in the lizard *Anolis sagrei. Proceedings of the Parapsychological Association,* 1971, 8, 23-25. (Abstract)

WATKINS, G. K., & WATKINS, A. M. Possible PK influence on the resuscitation of anesthetized mice. *Journal of Parapsychology,* 1971, 35, 257-272.

WHITE, R. A. A comparison of old and new methods of response to targets in ESP experiments. *Journal* A.S.P.R., 1964, 58, 21-56.

**BRAUD, W. G. & BRAUD, L. W.**

# 29

# *Preliminary Explorations of Psi-Conducive States: Progressive Muscular Relaxation*

ABSTRACT: Subjects in states of deep muscular and mental relaxation (induced by a modified Jacobson's progressive relaxation technique) were tested for psi perception of randomly selected target pictures in a series of seven exploratory experiments. The first two studies, one involving repeated testing of a single subject and the second involving individual tests of six subjects, yielded highly significant hit and direct hit rates of 100 per cent. An attempt to duplicate these results in a group setting was equally successful. Four confirmatory group experiments were conducted: two were successful, two were not. Overall analyses, using subjects as the basic unit of observation, yielded highly significant hit (86 per cent as opposed to 50 per cent chance expectation) and direct hit (59 per cent as opposed to 17 per cent chance expectation) rates. A much more conservative statistical test (conducted to counter a possible "stacking effect" criticism) yielded 16 hits in 17 individual tests (binomial $P < .001$). Overall results suggest that a state of deep muscular relaxation may be conducive to some forms of psi and justify continuation of research using more sophisticated experimental designs in which muscular relaxation and its co-varying factors (mood, attitudes, expectancies, physiology) are more directly assessed.

## Introduction

Considerable progress in psi research might result from the discovery, exploration, and more frequent utilization of psychological and physiological states conducive to the occurrence of psi. Several independent lines of evidence suggest that physical and mental *relaxation* may be quite favorable to the occurrence of several psi phenomena.[3] The converging lines of evidence include the following:

1. Relaxation seems to be a reliable characteristic of the percipient in a majority of cases of spontaneous psi phenomena (15).
2. Reference to the importance of relaxation (both physical and mental) is found in the writings of and about nearly all gifted psychics.
3. Rhea White, in her classic study (20) of the introspective

[3] Excluded from this discussion of "receptive" psi are certain "output" forms of psi (e.g., PK) in which a state other than relaxation might be important.

reports of gifted subjects which have appeared in the experimental literature, has pointed to the critical role attributed by these subjects to deep physical and mental relaxation, reduction of strain, increase in passivity, and stillness of mind.

4. Autonomic nervous system state measures which have been found to accompany facilitated psi (12) closely resemble physiological syndromes traditionally associated with relaxation.

5. EEG indications sometimes associated with enhanced ESP performance suggest an electrical correlate of the subjective state of relaxed awareness and of the physiological state of muscular relaxation (5, 10, 14).

6. The dream state so successfully exploited as a psi-favorable condition by the Maimonides group in recent years (18) is characterized by extremely low muscular tension (4, p. 410).

7. Slowed alpha (alphoid) rhythms characterized two out-of-the-body experiences (which are sometimes accompanied by psi) studied in the laboratory (16, 17).

8. Alpha predominance characterizes certain meditative states (1, 8, 19) which have traditionally been associated with heightened psychic sensitivity.

9. Hypnosis, which has been reported to facilitate psi performance (6), would seem to have a strong relaxation component (2).

10. Schmeidler (13) obtained good psi results in her studies of relaxed and passive maternity and concussion patients.

Although no single source mentioned is completely convincing, taken together the evidence is strikingly consistent and highly suggestive of the important role of relaxation in successful psi functioning. This report describes our preliminary explorations of deep muscular relaxation as a possible psi-conducive state. A relaxed state was produced in our subjects according to a standardized procedure. Psi functioning in these subjects was then assessed through the use of a free-response procedure similar to that used so successfully by the Maimonides group (18).

## Experiment 1: Repeated Tests of a Single Subject

### *Subject*

The subject in this first pilot study was a twenty-seven year old male assistant (now associate) professor of psychology at the University of Houston. He had no history of unusual psychic experiences (i.e., he had had several, but they were not particularly striking), but was firmly convinced of the reality of psi and enthusiastically felt that he would perform well under the conditions of the experiment.

*Procedure*

A session began with the subject sitting in a comfortable armchair with eyes closed. He was instructed to relax his entire musculature, using an abbreviated version of Jacobson's progressive relaxation procedure (7). This procedure (see Appendix 1) involves alternately tensing then relaxing each part of the body in turn until a profound state of muscular relaxation is produced. The subject then attempted to "mentally" relax, at first employing imagery of pleasant and relaxing scenes (e.g., fields, forests, bodies of water, clouds, etc.), then "blanking" his mind and becoming as passive as possible. Before achieving this relaxed state, he had been instructed to "keep somewhere in the back of his mind" the fact that a particular target picture would be transmitted and that he was to try to receive impressions about that picture. He had been instructed to verbalize his impressions in as much detail as possible. Permanent tape recordings were made of these verbalizations. At the end of a session, the subject was instructed to return to his normal state of consciousness and was asked to record his impressions in writing and also to make drawings of any visual impressions he might have had while in the relaxed state. The subject was urged to distinguish true impressions from associations elicited by those impressions; i.e., he was urged not to interpret, intellectualize, analyze, or synthesize impressions. He was also asked to attempt to distinguish target-relevant impressions from the sort of images evoked by the state itself (i.e., conventional meditation imagery). The resulting protocols for that session were marked for later identification. Marking was done by affixing already numbered pressure-sensitive labels to the protocols in a random manner to be described below; such a procedure prevented any order cues or conscious or unconscious cues which might otherwise have been produced in the process of marking. A session lasted approximately thirty minutes.

While the subject was relaxing, an agent in another room seventy-eight feet away and on another floor (separated by a closed door, a stairway, and another closed door) randomly selected a visual target from a pool of 150 postcard-sized art reproductions and pictures clipped from magazines, without seeing any of the targets not selected. The random selection procedure was accomplished through the use of a table of random numbers which contained pairs of digits arranged in 40 rows and 40 columns. To gain an entry point in the table, a deck of 40 $3 \times 5$ index cards (each card containing a single number from 1 through 40) was shuffled five times, cut, and the number appearing on the cut card recorded. This process was then repeated to yield a second number. The two numbers thus generated provided the row and column designation of the entry point. A coin was then tossed to determine which number corresponded to the row and which to the column. "Heads" indicated that the first number referred to the row; "tails" indicated that the first number referred to the column. The agent entered the random number table at the appropriate intersection. Since the target pool consisted of 150 items (contained in individual envelopes and already numbered from 001 through 150 by means of removable pressure sensitive labels), a pair of digits in the table was coupled with the first digit of the adjacent pair to provide the three digits needed for selecting an item. If the three digits at the entry point yielded a number between 001 and 150, the picture labeled with that number was chosen as the target. If the entry number did not fall between 001 and 150, the agent moved vertically downward through the table until he encountered the first number which did fall within that range; this number directed him to the appropriate item in the target pool. The target pool had been established by a person who had no contact with any of the subjects or agents who participated in any of the experiments reported here. All pictures used in these experiments were later replaced with new pictures so that the target pool always contained 150 items.

The agent concentrated upon the selected target picture in terms of its "raw sensory information" (shapes, colors) and avoided "intellectualizing" the picture (i.e., he did not attempt to put the parts of the picture into words, did not try to associate to the picture, etc.). In addition to looking at the picture, the agent traced the outlines of the major shapes in the picture with his finger and also attempted to hallucinate textures, tastes, odors, and sounds that were portrayed in the picture but could not be directly sensed. This was done in an effort to involve all sensory modalities, not merely vision. When he had concluded his attempt to send, the agent marked the target (with an already prepared pressure sensitive label containing a letter from A through F) for later identification and sent the target to a naive judge.

Sessions were run at a rate of one per day until six targets had been transmitted and six protocols had been collected from the subject. The protocols were labeled with already prepared pressure sensitive labels bearing the digits 1 through 6. The numbers assigned to the six protocols were determined using a random process similar to that described above, but using only the numbers 01 through 06 and moving vertically downward through the random number table until all six numbers had been assigned. Thus, any original correspondences were adequately concealed from the judge. The agent then randomly (using the procedure just mentioned) ordered the six subject protocols and sent these to the naive judge. Each protocol consisted of a typewritten transcript of the tape recording augmented where necessary by the subject's own written comments and drawings for a given session. It was the judge's task to attempt to force-match the six protocols with the targets to which they most closely corresponded. The judge was told that each protocol matched one and only one target, and that each target matched one and only one protocol.

### *Results*

Comparison of the judge's pairings of targets and protocols with the list of correct pairings (which had been kept in the possession of the agent) yielded six out of six correspondences. Such a perfect matching has an associated probability (3, Vol. 1, pp. 97–99) of .0014. To convey to the reader something of the qualitative nature of the "hits" obtained in this pilot study, we include excerpts from the six protocols. For convenience, the protocols have been re-identified to match the identifying letters of the targets shown in Figures 1 and 2. Since space is limited, examples are taken from only two protocols:

> Excerpts, Protocol B: " . . . *two crossed* . . . *lines* . . . the '*X*' appeared . . . in the center upper left. . . . I vividly saw a *glass, a frosted glass filled with Coca-Cola.* This *glass* appeared to be in the *upper right-hand area.* . . . Some secondary images: . . . a *road* in the *center* of the photo. . . . Dominant colors: *brown, green, tan, white,* and *silver.*"

> Excerpts, Protocol F: " . . . a *silver* utensil. Saw what looked like a *yellow cornucopia* (*horn of plenty*) . . . like a *yellow calabash pipe* . . . small girl *happily* playing in a garden, touching *brightly colored flowers* . . . what appeared to be a *silver bell* or *horse's stirrup.*"

## Experiment 2: Individual Tests of a Small Number of Additional Subjects

Encouraged by the results of the pilot study, a second experiment was conducted in which six subjects were tested once and only once in the state of profound muscular relaxation, rather than testing one subject repeatedly as was done in the first study.

### *Subjects*

The subjects were three male and three female advanced undergraduate and graduate students from the University of Houston.

FIG. 1. Target picture "B." Dominant colors are brown, green, tan, white, and silver. Reproduced by permission of the Coca-Cola Company.

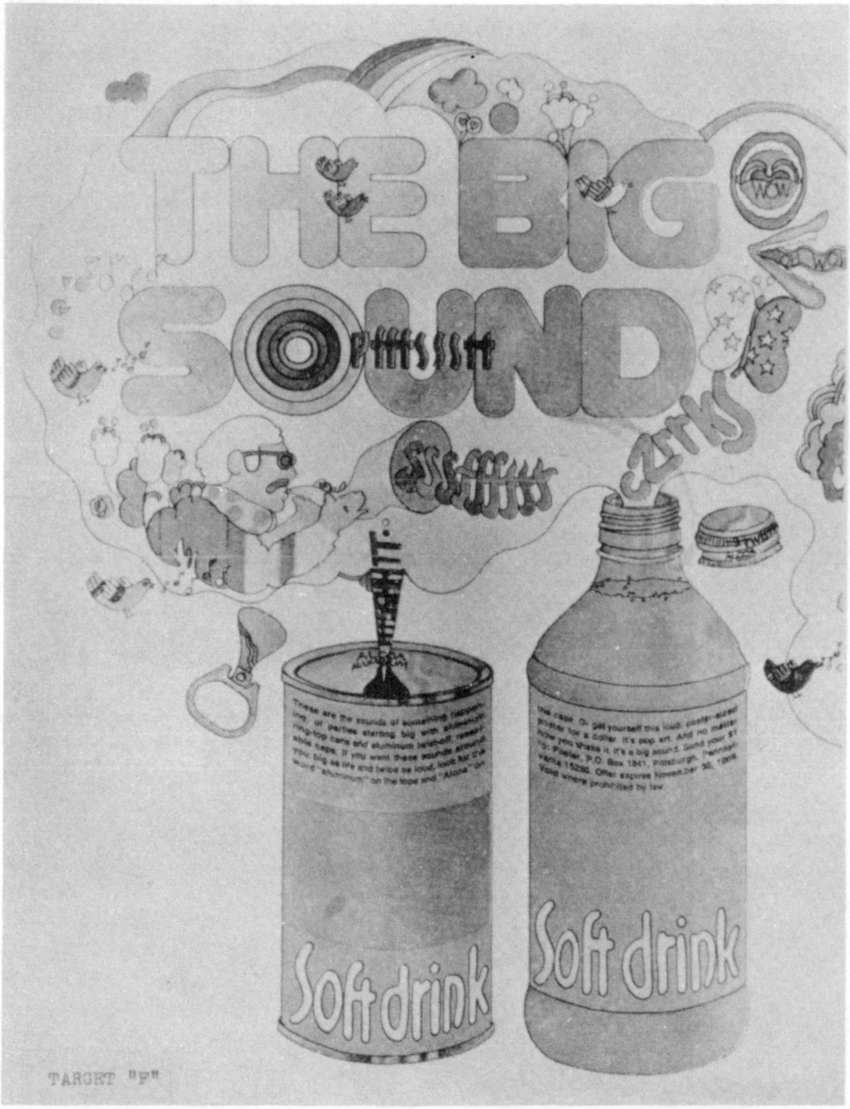


FIG. 2. Target picture "F." The horn is yellow and the metal snap-top from the can is silver. Reproduced by permission of the Aluminum Company of America.

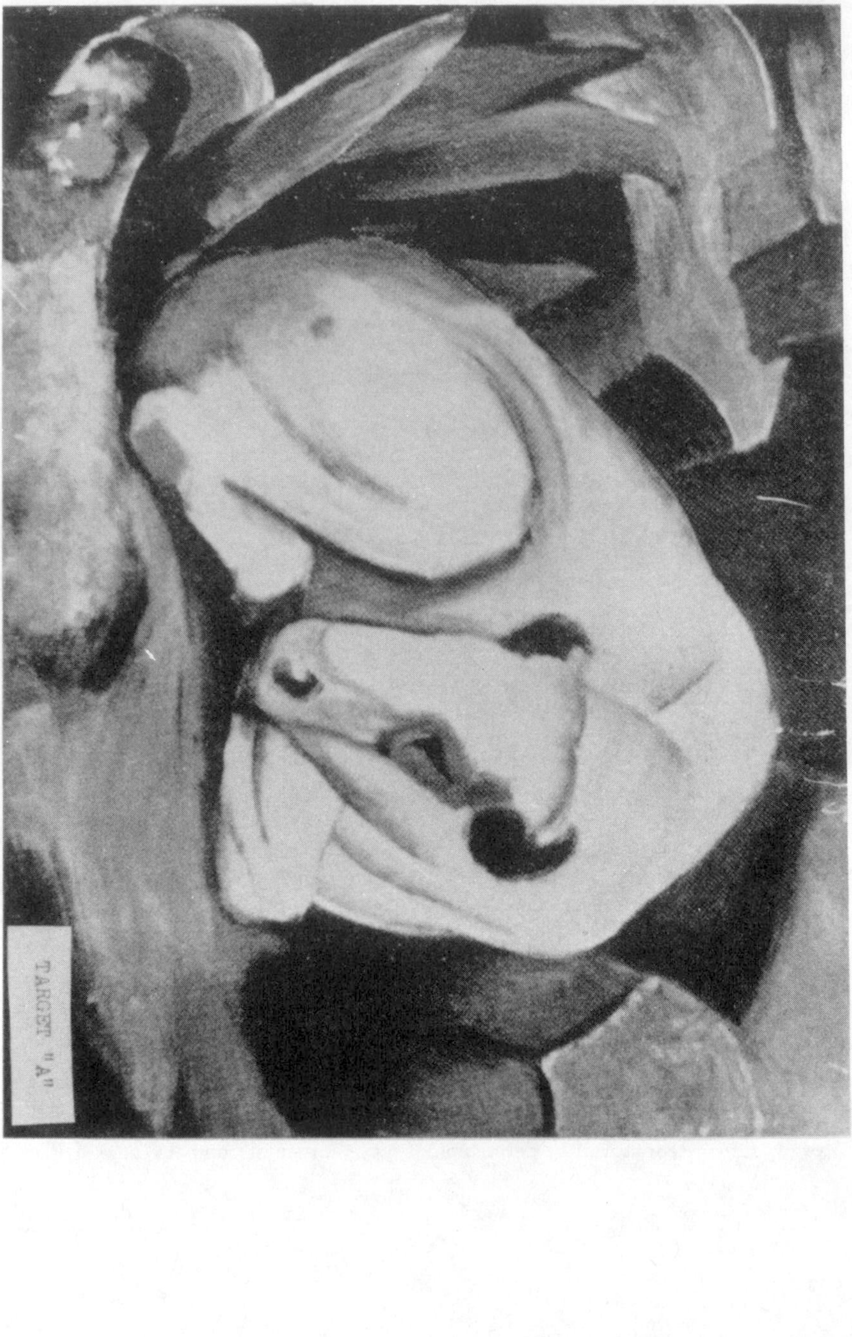


FIG. 3. Target picture "A." Dominant colors are green, white, and gray. The crescent-shaped mark at the cow's rear end is reddish. Reproduced by permission of the Solomon R. Guggenheim Museum, New York City.

FIG. 4. Target picture "D." The outfit is red, the fur is very light gray. Reproduced by permission of White Stores, Inc.

All subjects would be classified as "sheep." Four had had no unusual previous psychic experiences. One female had several psychic experiences involving a close friend at the approximate age of fourteen years. One male had practiced the formal discipline of yoga for a period of seven years. All subjects were anxious to participate and were convinced that they would perform well.

### *Procedure*

The procedure was identical to that described in Experiment 1, except that each subject participated in only one session. A different agent was used with each subject: agents were spouses of the subjects. Targets were selected randomly as before. The experimenter collected each target and each protocol as completed, accumulated these until six had been collected, then marked them for later identification (using already prepared pressure sensitive labels and the random number table procedure described above), scrambled their orders through the use of the randomizing procedure just described, and sent them to a naive judge. The judge used the same procedure as before, force-matching the six targets with the six protocols.

### *Results*

Again, a comparison of the judge's matchings with the correct matchings (in the experimenter's possession) yielded six out of six correct correspondences. The probability associated with this perfect matching is .0014. Again we present excerpts from some of the six protocols (see Figures 3 and 4):

> EXCERPTS, PROTOCOL A: " . . . there appeared one and then *two* structures which looked like the *claws of a crab* . . . then they became *horns* with a *cow's head* attached . . . a *cow's head with horns* on it . . . a *moon-crescent slice* . . . a *skinny crescent moon* . . . *rolling background* . . . *fringes* like a Christmas tree . . . maybe *green* . . . *not the whole tree, only the fringes on the side. . . .*"
>
> EXCERPTS, PROTOCOL D: "I saw a vodka bottle . . . a woman (Czech or Slovak) in a *red winter outfit* . . . *boots, gray fur trim* . . . *gray hat* . . . *foot elevated with knee bent.*"

## EXPERIMENT 3: GROUP TEST OF A LARGER NUMBER OF SUBJECTS

Greatly encouraged by the results of the first two exploratory studies, we planned a third experiment. Thus far, we had used a single naive judge to rate the protocol-target correspondences.

The hits were so striking that virtually anyone would have had no difficulty matching the protocols and targets. However, it was anticipated that correspondences might not always be so striking, and that the idiosyncrasies of the naive judges might become important. It was therefore decided to allow the subjects themselves to judge their own protocols. This would require a larger group of subjects. This decision was prompted in part by the formation of a Psychic Research Group by the authors at about this time. It was also decided to try testing in a group context, rather than individually as before. This section of the report describes our first group experiment. It is also the first employing the new scoring technique. Another innovation is the use of a tape-recorded relaxation induction procedure.

*Subjects*

Ten subjects participated in this third experiment: six females and four males. Six of the subjects were members of the newly formed Psychic Research Group. The remaining subjects were spouses and friends of some of the group members. Nine subjects were "sheep"; one was a "goat." All participated enthusiastically.

*Procedure*

The procedure differed somewhat from that of the first two experiments. The instructions for mental and physical relaxation were tape recorded (see Appendix 1) and this recording was played to the group of subjects to induce the appropriate state. Instructions were identical to those used before and included the abbreviated version of Jacobson's progressive relaxation technique as well as instructions for mental relaxation. The instructions played for fifteen minutes. There followed a five-minute "reception" period, indicated on the tape by a very low intensity "white noise." Following the soft white noise, the tape provided instructions for returning to normal consciousness. The tape also contained instructions regarding reception and recording of impressions. Subjects were to remember their impressions and record them on specially prepared sheets which were to be used in later judging. At the beginning of this session, the tape was played once so that the subjects might become familiar with its contents. The scoring procedure was then explained (see below). The subjects were told that at the end of the reception period, the agent would silently place on the table an envelope containing six art reproductions, one of which was the correct target which he had just sent. The position of the correct target among the alternatives was randomly determined using the technique described in Experiments 1 and 2. Immediately after placing the sealed envelope on the table, the agent was to leave the room, not to return until the subjects had signaled him that they had completed their judging. One subject was to open the envelope and spread out the six targets (lettered "A" through "F") on the table. The subjects were then to rank the six targets in terms of their correspondence to the subjects' individual protocols. The target most closely matching the protocol was to be ranked "1," that corresponding least to be ranked "6." After all subjects had ranked their protocol-target correspondences, the agent would return to the room and collect the protocols. He would record the number of times the correct target was assigned ranks of "1," "2," and "3"—these were considered "hits." Ranks of "4," "5," and "6" were considered "misses." Ranks of "1" were considered "direct hits." Frequencies of hits and direct hits could then be compared with chance expectations ($p = 1/2$ and $p = 1/6$, respectively) to yield a probability value for the session.

After giving the instructions just mentioned, the agent (W.G.B.) further instructed the subjects to become comfortable, turned down the lights, started the tape recorder for the actual run, then left the room. When he reached the second room (distance, etc. described above), he randomly selected six art reproductions from the pool, without looking at them. The random selection procedure was as described in Experiment 1. From these six, he selected one, randomly, as the correct target for that session. To select the one correct target, the agent entered the random number table using the card cuts and coin toss and moved vertically downward in the table until he encountered a two-digit number between 01 and 06; that number defined the correct target for that session. The remaining five prints served as the control alternative prints later to be judged. The agent attempted to "send" the contents of the target print in a manner identical to that described in Experiment 1. Following sending, he returned to the "reception" room and the judging proceeded as indicated above.

*Results*

As defined above, there were ten hits and no misses; seven direct hits occurred. A binomial test applied to the hits and misses yielded a probability of .001. A binomial test applied to the direct hits frequency yielded a probability of .0002.

## EXPERIMENT 4: SECOND GROUP TEST

This was the first of four confirmatory experiments carried out in an attempt to duplicate the results of Experiment 3.

### *Subjects*

Eleven subjects participated in this study: six males and five females. Five of the subjects were members of the Psychic Research Group. The remaining subjects were spouses and friends of some of the members. Nine subjects were "sheep," two were "goats."

### *Procedure*

With the exception of the change in number and nature of the subjects, the procedure was identical to that described in Experiment 3. The agent was again W.G.B. Subjects were again tested once and only once in a group setting, with tape-recorded instructions.

### *Results*

There were ten hits and one miss; six direct hits occurred. The subject scoring the miss was a goat. A binomial test applied to the frequencies of hits and misses yielded a probability of .006. A binomial test applied to the direct hits data yielded a probability of .004. Thus, in this first confirmatory experiment, the significant results of Experiment 3 were replicated.

## EXPERIMENT 5: THIRD GROUP TEST

This was the second of four confirmatory experiments carried out in an attempt to duplicate the results of Experiment 3.

### *Subjects*

Ten subjects participated in this study: five males and five females. Six of the subjects were members of the Psychic Research Group. The remaining subjects were spouses and friends of some of the members. Nine subjects were sheep; one was a goat.

### *Procedure*

The procedure was identical to that described in Experiments 3 and 4. Again, the agent was W.G.B.

*Results*

There were four hits and six misses; two direct hits occurred. A binomial test applied to the hits vs. misses yielded a nonsignificant probability of .377. Direct hit frequency yielded a binomial probability of .291, which is nonsignificant. The significant results of Experiments 3 and 4 were not replicated in this fifth experiment.

## Experiment 6: Fourth Group Test

This experiment differs somewhat from those just reported, but is included nonetheless because we wish to report *all* of our studies, whether the conditions under which they were undertaken were optimal or not. While the three group experiments described above were conducted during regularly scheduled meetings of the Psychic Research Group, this fourth group test (Experiment 6) occurred during a hastily called and poorly attended meeting.

*Subjects*

A reporter from a local newspaper wished to interview members of the group and a special impromptu meeting was called for that purpose. Since several persons who had participated in previous experiments were away on holiday, attendance was small. Only six subjects participated: five group members and the reporter. Four subjects were female, two male. All subjects were sheep.

*Procedure*

The procedure was identical to that of experiments 3, 4, and 5. The agent was W.G.B.

*Results*

There were four hits and two misses; there was one direct hit. A binomial test applied to the hits vs. misses yielded a nonsignificant probability of .344. Direct hit frequency yielded a nonsignificant binomial probability of .402.

## Experiment 7: Fifth Group Test (Long Distance)

This fourth attempt to confirm the results of Experiment 3 differs from all others reported in this series in that the agent and the subjects were separated by a distance of approximately

1400 miles at the time of the testing session. One of our group members was visiting in Los Angeles and we took advantage of this to conduct a Los Angeles to Houston long-distance study. We were not testing the effects of distance on psi efficiency in this experiment because the subjects and agent were not "blind" with respect to distance and because a host of confounding subjective factors (of both agent and subjects) were not assessed and statistically accounted for as in the distance studies of Osis and his co-workers (11). The experiment was conducted because the opportunity presented itself and because we felt that the motivational boost of a distance experiment might revitalize our psi processes.

### *Subjects*

Eleven subjects participated: six males and five females. Ten subjects were sheep; one was a goat. Six subjects were members of the Psychic Research Group. The remaining subjects were spouses and friends of some of the group members.

### *Procedure*

The procedure was identical to that described in Experiment 3, with the following exceptions: (*a*) a group member (D.W.) other than W.G.B. served as agent, (*b*) the distance separating agent from subjects was increased from 78 feet to 1400 miles, and (*c*) the targets were selected by agent D.W. while she was 1400 miles away. The subjects recorded their impressions at a time previously agreed upon. The six targets (the correct target and the five controls) were then mailed from Los Angeles to Houston and upon being received, correspondences were rated. (The labels and order of targets, of course, were randomly determined using the randomizing techniques of the experiments reported above.) When agent D.W. returned, the correspondences were scored.

### *Results*

In this long-distance experiment, eleven hits and no misses occurred. Four direct hits were obtained. A binomial test applied to the hits vs. misses yielded a probability of less than .001. The binomial probability resulting from the direct hit frequency was .07 and was not significant. Thus, the significant results of Experiments 3 and 4 were again replicated, and this time at a distance of 1400 miles.

## ADDITIONAL QUALITATIVE MATERIAL

In this section, we report excerpts from the protocols of subjects in the five group tests just described. The correct target art print for Experiment 3 was "Praying Hands" by Albrecht Durer: two hands, palms together in a prayerful posture, extend to the upper left corner of the picture; dominant color is a somber grayish-green. The following are sample comments extracted from the protocols for this session:

SUBJECT 1: This subject drew two multi-pointed structures having precisely the same orientation as the hands in the Durer reproduction.

SUBJECT 2: " . . . dominant color was *greenish-gray*. . . ."

SUBJECT 3: " . . . *dark, cave-like, leaning, pointed* . . . three to *five post-like forms*. . . ."

SUBJECT 4: This subject drew a *five-pronged* pitchfork.

Nearly all subjects drew forms closely resembling hands and fingers; all subjects reported subdued colors or lack of color.

The correct target for Experiment 4 was "Sleeping Gypsy" by Rousseau. This painting depicts a dark-skinned human figure robed in a long coat having many brightly colored vertical stripes and reclining horizontally on colorful striped pillows on what appears to be brown desert sand. Standing just above the human figure and apparently looking into the latter's face is a large brown lion with a full mane and a long outstretched tail. In the background are pinkish mountains and a dusky blue sky. A bright full moon appears in the upper right. Beside the reclining figure is a stringed musical instrument and a tall water jar. Here are representative protocol excerpts:

SUBJECT 1: " . . . thought it was a *laughing bear*. . . . Strong impression of *death*."

SUBJECT 2: "Next, I got the song '*Hey, Look Me Over, Lend Me an Ear*'—just that line."

SUBJECT 3: " . . . a fleeting *horse's head*. . . ."

SUBJECT 4: " . . . reminding me of a *brown animal* sitting on a fence with its *tail* hanging down . . . like *at night* . . . *figure looked down* . . . fence . . . black . . . crescent *moons facing one another*. . . ."

SUBJECT 5: " . . . *elephant* . . . *drums* . . . *jungle feelings* . . . *water jar*. . . ."

The correct target print for Experiment 6 is Manet's "Soap Bubbles." The painting depicts a young boy standing behind what looks like the flat top of a waist-high brick wall which resembles a brown stone table. In his left hand, held against his body is a white bowl (shallow) containing soapy water. In his right hand he holds a long tube to his lips and is blowing a bubble about the size of his fist. Parts of the protocol of one subject for this session read as follows:

> SUBJECT 1: "Thoughts of a picture I once saw called 'Picasso as a *Boy*' . . . I pictured *the boy* . . . a single *eye* . . . a *rounded object with a very long handle* . . . like a pot with a *long handle* . . . again, a view of Picasso as a *boy* . . . saw a *shallow bowl* with pointed ends . . . saw a *table top, only the top*. . . ."

As a final illustration of the group experiment protocol-target correspondences, we present excerpts from the long-distance Experiment 7 protocols. The correct target was a color photo clipped from a magazine (probably *National Geographic*) featuring a tall giraffe, large brown irregular spots on a white body. Many trees are visible in the background. In the foreground are two tall straight trees. The giraffe's extended neck and one tree form a "Y" shape. Dominant colors are green, blue sky, gray ground, and the giraffe's numerous brown spots.

> SUBJECT 1: ". . . *orchard* or *vineyard* . . . *tree with Y-shaped branches* . . . *jungle greenery*. . . ."
>
> SUBJECT 2: "*Spots* . . . *spotty black and white dog* . . . *brown* swirly *caramel* . . . marshmallows, mushrooms, confetti . . . *spots*. . . ."
>
> SUBJECT 3: "*Dark dots on a white background* . . . become punched paper tape which is moving. The *spots* move from the tape to become the *spots* on dominoes, then dice. *Dots* become darkened windows on *skyscrapers*."
>
> SUBJECT 4: ". . . maybe a *tall tree* . . ."

## OVERALL ANALYSES

Between November, 1969, and January, 1972, a total of 60 protocols were collected from a total of 22 persons. Some of these subjects participated once, others repeatedly. Since testing conditions were almost identical in the 17 sessions generating these 60 protocols, it was decided to pool all data collected and do an overall statistical analysis of the combined results. So that the subject could be used as the basic unit of observation, all sessions past the first (for each subject) were discarded for the purpose of this overall analysis. This procedure reduced the number of analyzable protocols to 22. In all, there were 19 hits and 3 misses, producing a significant binomial probability of less than .001. In the 11 cases in which males served as subjects, there were 8 hits and 3 misses, yielding a binomial probability of .113. In the 11 cases in which females served as subjects, there were 11 hits and no misses, yielding a significant binomial probability of less than .001. When the data from these sessions were subjected to analysis in a 2 × 2 table (sex of subject vs. hits and misses), a nonsignificant Fisher's exact probability was obtained; thus, the scores of males and females did not differ reliably.

Direct hits (rank of "1" for the correct target) were also analyzed over all sessions. In all, there were 13 direct hits, producing a significant binomial probability of .000007. In the 11 cases in which males served as subjects, there were 5 direct hits, yielding a binomial probability of .019. In the 11 cases in which females served as subjects, there were 8 direct hits, yielding a binomial probability of .00006. A Fisher's exact probability test on direct hits subjected to a 2 × 2 analysis (sex of subject vs. hits and misses) yielded nonsignificant results. Again, success was not significantly related to sex of the subject.

A summary of the results of the entire preliminary series of seven relaxation experiments is presented in Table 1.

One final statistical comment is in order. In evaluating the trials of the subjects in the group tests, one might question the assumption that all the trials were independent. There is, in other words, the possibility of a "stacking effect" here, since any factor that might conceivably have influenced the subjects' rating of the protocol against the targets might have tended to influence most of them in the same way. Such conceivable factors are the position of the target picture among the six, the content of the target picture in relation to outstanding public events of the day, picture content in relation to conversation of group members before matching, etc. (*N.B.* What if the common factor responsible for the "stacking effect" is psi?) Some might argue against evaluation of the data of group experiments as if each protocol represented an independent trial, as has been done in this paper. Rather than argue for or against the likelihood of a stacking effect in these group data and for or against the independence assumption, we have re-analyzed the data in a manner which is not subject to criticism on the basis of a possible stacking effect. In this final analysis, each group experiment is counted as a single trial with the members of the group and their individual protocols treated as "votes" regarding which of the six pictures was the correct target. On the basis of a "majority vote" criterion, the first, second, fourth, and fifth group tests (i.e., Experiments 3, 4, 6, and 7) are scored as "hits." These four hits from the group tests may be added to the hits scored in the individual tests (12 individual hits) to yield a total of 16 hits out of 17 sessions. A binomial test applied to 16 hits vs. 1 miss yields a probability of less than .001. This method of treating the group results is a highly conservative one and quite wasteful of data, but would appear to deal effectively with the stacking effect criticism.

Table 1

SUMMARY OF RESULTS OF FIRST SEVEN PRELIMINARY RELAXATION EXPERIMENTS

| Experiment | Condition | Cases | Hits | Misses | % Hits | P | Direct Hits | % Direct Hits | P |
|---|---|---|---|---|---|---|---|---|---|
| 1 | Repeated tests of single *S* | 6 | 6 | 0 | 100 | .001 | 6 | 100 | .001 |
| 2 | Individual tests of six *S*s | 6 | 6 | 0 | 100 | .001 | 6 | 100 | .001 |
| 3 | First group test | 10 | 10 | 0 | 100 | .001 | 7 | 70 | .0002 |
| 4 | Second group test | 11 | 10 | 1 | 91 | .006 | 6 | 54 | .004 |
| 5 | Third group test | 10 | 4 | 6 | 40 | n.s. | 2 | 20 | n.s. |
| 6 | Fourth group test[1] | 6 | 4 | 2 | 67 | n.s. | 1 | 17 | n.s. |
| 7 | Fifth group test[2] | 11 | 11 | 0 | 100 | .001 | 4 | 36 | n.s. |
| Noncorrected Total | (see text) | 60 | 51 | 9 | 85 % | | 32 | 53 % | |
| Corrected Total | (see text)[3] | 22 | 19 | 3 | 86 % | .001 | 13 | 59 % | .000007 |

[1] Smaller group with reporter present. — [2] Long-distance experiment (Los Angeles to Houston). — [3] These figures are not corrected for a possible stacking effect. See p. 39 for this correction.

## Discussion

Subjects in states of profound muscular and mental relaxation were tested for psi perception of randomly selected target pictures in a series of seven experiments carried out over a two-year period. Two exploratory studies, one involving repeated testing of a single subject and the second involving single individual tests of six subjects, yielded highly significant hit and direct hit rates of 100 per cent. An attempt to duplicate these results in a group setting (Experiment 3) was equally successful. Four confirmatory group experiments were conducted: two were successful (Experiments 4 and 7), two were not (Experiments 5 and 6).

Why did Experiments 5 and 6 fail? It appears likely that three factors may have been important in yielding the chance performance levels in those two studies: (*a*) The presence of the newspaper reporter in Experiment 6, (*b*) the agent's (W.G.B.) poor mood immediately before Experiment 5, and (*c*) the beginning of a decline effect even in these otherwise striking results. We recognize that these notions are completely speculative and that they must be either disconfirmed or not by future research. Having completed the preliminary series, we are in fact in the process of testing notions (*a*) and (*b*) in a number of much more formally designed laboratory studies (see below).

In spite of the chance results of Experiments 5 and 6, the results of the series as a whole are strikingly significant. The overall hit rate is quite high (86 per cent as opposed to 50 per cent chance expectation), as is the direct hit rate (59 per cent as opposed to 17 per cent chance expectation). Group testing was as successful as individual testing. It did not seem to matter whether the protocols were scored by naive judges or by the subjects themselves. Tape-recorded relaxation-inducing instructions were as effective as personal instructions. Although female subjects tended to score slightly higher than male subjects, statistical analyses did not yield significant sex differences. Krippner (9) has found, in his studies of psi in dreams, that the only agent-subject pairings to produce significant results were male agent with male subject and female agent with male subject. While we have not yet collected protocols under enough agent-subject sex pairing conditions to make a complete analysis, the data already in indicate that female subjects do score significantly when paired with a male agent in our relaxation paradigm. A complete study of agent-subject pairings is nearing completion and will be described in a later report. We mention these preliminary findings here only to indicate that sex differences do not appear to play a major role in the relaxation paradigm.

We have exploited the state of deep physical and mental relaxation in an attempt to increase the probability of the occurrence of psi. Psi did indeed occur quite reliably in this preliminary series. We have certainly not shown that relaxation is definitely a factor which facilitates psi in and of itself. Such a demonstration would involve experimentally unconfounding relaxation from a number of co-varying factors such as concommitant mood and attitude changes, heightened expectancies of success in subjects, heightened success expectancy in the agent, etc. These factors have obviously not been disentangled in the preliminary research just described. However, a formal study is under way in which these confounding factors and others are being controlled and their effects evaluated. Physiological measures are being taken to determine objectively the degree of physical relaxation. Individual tests are being done in order to avoid possible stacking effects.

The mechanism through which relaxation facilitates psi (if indeed formal experiments indicate that it does) is quite unclear at present and might be determined only through considerably more experimentation.

## References

1. Anand, B. K., Chhina, G. S., and Singh, B. Some aspects of electroencephalographic studies in Yogis. In C. T. Tart (Ed.), *Altered States of Consciousness*. New York: Wiley, 1969. Pp. 503-506.
2. Barber, T. X. *Hypnosis: A Scientific Approach*. New York: Van Nostrand Reinhold, 1969.
3. Feller, W. *An Introduction to Probability Theory and its Applications*. New York: Wiley, 1957. 2 vols.
4. Hartmann, E. *Sleep and Dreaming*. Boston: Little, Brown, 1970.
5. Honorton, C., Davidson, R., and Bindler, P. Feedback-augmented EEG alpha, shifts in subjective state, and ESP card-guessing performance. *Journal* A.S.P.R., 65, 1971, 308-323.
6. Honorton, C., and Krippner, S. Hypnosis and ESP: A review of the experimental literature. *Journal* A.S.P.R., 63, 1969, 214-252.
7. Jacobson, E. *Progressive Relaxation*. Chicago: University of Chicago Press, 1929.
8. Kasamatsu, A., and Hirai, T. An electroencephalographic study of Zen meditation (Zazen). In C. T. Tart (Ed.), *Altered States of Consciousness*. New York: Wiley, 1969. Pp. 489-501.

9. KRIPPNER, S. Electrophysiological studies of ESP in dreams: Sex differences in seventy-four telepathy sessions. *Journal* A.S.P.R., 64, 1970, 277-285.
10. MORRIS, R. L., AND OTHERS. EEG patterns and ESP results in forced-choice experiments with Lalsingh Harribance. *Journal* A.S.P.R., 66, 1972, 253-268.
11. OSIS, K., TURNER, M. E., JR., AND CARLSON, M. L. ESP over distance: Research on the ESP channel. *Journal* A.S.P.R., 65, 1971, 245-288.
12. OTANI, S. Relations of mental set and change of skin resistance to ESP score. *Journal of Parapsychology*, 19, 1955, 164-170.
13. SCHMEIDLER, G. R., AND MCCONNELL, R. A. *ESP and Personality Patterns*. New Haven: Yale University Press, 1958.
14. STANFORD, R. G., AND STANFORD, B. E. Shifts in EEG alpha rhythm as related to calling patterns and ESP run-score variance. *Journal of Parapsychology*, 33, 1969, 39-47.
15. STEVENSON, I. Telepathic impressions: A review and report of thirty-five new cases. *Proceedings* A.S.P.R., 29, 1970, 1-198.
16. TART, C. T. A second psychophysiological study of out-of-the-body experiences in a gifted subject. *International Journal of Parapsychology*, 9, 1967, 251-258.
17. TART, C. T. A psychophysiological study of out-of-the-body experiences in a selected subject. *Journal* A.S.P.R., 62, 1968, 3-27.
18. ULLMAN, M., AND KRIPPNER, S. *Dream Studies and Telepathy: An Experimental Approach*. New York: Parapsychology Foundation, 1970.
19. WALLACE, R. K. Physiological effects of transcendental meditation. *Science*, 167, 1970, 1751-1754.
20. WHITE, R. A. A comparison of old and new methods of response to targets in ESP experiments. *Journal* A.S.P.R., 58, 1964, 21-56.

*Department of Psychology*
*University of Houston*
*Houston, Texas 77004*

*Department of Psychology*
*Texas Southern University*
*Houston, Texas 77004*

## Appendix 1

*Transcript of Taped Muscular and Mental Relaxation Procedure*

The purpose of this tape is to induce a state of physical and mental relaxation. We will begin with muscular relaxation. Relaxation is the elimination of all muscular tension. Get as comfortable as you can; loosen any clothing that may be too tight. When you relax, do not think about the instructions. Just follow them passively and automatically. When tensing any part of your body, remember to leave all other muscles completely relaxed. Begin by curling your toes downward into a tense position. Tense up more and more and notice the discomfort. Hold this tension while I count from 10 to 1, letting go at the count of 1. (*Count*) Relax. Now relax your toes completely, and feel the difference. Instead of curling your toes, arch them up towards your face and feel the tension and discomfort all along your shins. Hold this . . . (*Count from 10 to 1*) . . . relax. Feel the relief in your legs. Next, curl your toes again and tense up your entire legs and calves, making sure the rest of your body is completely relaxed . . . (*Count*) . . . relax. Enjoy the feeling of relief that accompanies the removal of muscular tension. Relax all tension, release all pressures, place your body in a state of deep relaxation, going deeper and deeper every time. Next, tense your stomach muscles as tightly as you can as I count . . . (*Count*) . . . relax. Let go completely. Relax. Arch your back now, and feel the tension all along your spine . . . (*Count*) . . . relax. Settle down comfortably again. Let go of all of your weight; let go of all of the tension in every muscle of your body. Now focus your attention on your arms and fists. Relax the rest of your body completely. Tense your fists and bend your arms at your elbows, flexing your biceps. Hold this as tightly as you can . . . (*Count*) . . . relax. Let your arms flop to your sides. Relax completely. Now, take in a deep breath, fill your lungs, feel the tension all over your chest. Hold it . . . exhale. Feel the relief as you exhale. Relax. Make sure that all of the body parts that we have concentrated on are completely relaxed. If there is any tension, relax those muscles completely. Now, press your head back as far as it will go. Feel the tension in the muscles of your neck . . . (*Count*) . . . relax. Bend your head forward now . . . touch your chest with your chin . . . (*Count*) . . . relax. Relax completely. Tightly squinch up all the muscles of your face and around your eyes, making a face. Hold this . . . (*Count*) . . . relax. Remove all strain and tension. Relax your neck . . . your throat . . . mouth . . . relax your scalp . . . smooth out the muscles of your forehead . . . relax your eyes, and all of your facial muscles. Relax . . . relax . . . relax. Relax every muscle of your body. Focus on that area which is most relaxed and imagine that same pleasant, positive, relaxing feeling to spread, engulfing your entire body in one comfortable, warm, pleasant feeling of relaxation. Relax totally and completely.

We will now begin mental relaxation. Hold your head straight and lift your eyes upward in order to strain the eyes. Do not blink.

Your eyelids will become heavy; your eyelids will become tired. While waiting for this effect, take a deep breath, and while exhaling, imagine yourself becoming more deeply relaxed. Imagine relaxing more and more with each breath. When your eyes feel heavy and tired, do not force them to remain open. Close your eyes when they become tired. Take deep breaths, and with each exhalation, become more deeply relaxed. Now, concentrate again on relaxing . . . relaxing your whole body. Relax all tension . . . release all pressures. Place your body in a state of deep relaxation, going deeper and deeper. Make certain that all muscles are completely relaxed. It feels so good to be completely and totally relaxed. Noises and sounds will not distract you, but will help you to become more mentally at ease and more relaxed. Now concentrate on relaxing your mind. To do this, visualize a pleasant, passive scene. Visualize your ideal place of relaxation. Visualize waves rolling slowly over your body, or a walk through the woods, or a peaceful island, or trees, or a gentle breeze, or an easy chair, or a hammock, or clouds . . . visualize *your* favorite place of relaxation . . . (Pause) . . . relax. With each breath, imagine yourself becoming more deeply relaxed. To relax even more deeply, count with me backward from 25 . . . with each count, feel yourself going deeper and deeper into a profound relaxed state, a state ideal for the functioning of the psychic process. With each count, feel yourself becoming more deeply relaxed . . . deeper and deeper with each count . . . (*Count from 25 to 1, slowly*) . . . relax. Take a deep breath, and go deeper. You are now in a very relaxed, peaceful state. This is the optimal level for psychic functioning. Your entire body . . . your entire brain . . . your entire being . . . has been adjusted . . . has been adjusted to its optimal level of functioning. You will function psychically in a perfect manner in this state.

Now, relax completely . . . rid your mind of mundane problems . . . and try to make your mind blank. You might concentrate on a circle of blankness . . . a circular fence to keep out thoughts that keep trying to come in like stray sheep. When a thought strays in, you must be very patient . . . like a shepherd . . . and shove the stray out. No matter how many times it strays back . . . gently push it out. When your mind is stilled . . . and the circle is blank . . . quietly await impressions of the target picture. Don't try to force it . . . just relax and wait . . . and then the impressions will come. They may be visual, auditory, olfactory, taste, or feeling impressions. You'll be completely aware of all impressions. You will remember these perfectly, so that you'll be able to describe your impressions at the end of the session. When I snap my fingers, you are to begin . . . (*Snap*).

(*There follows a five-minute period of soft white noise on the tape at this point.*)

The impression part of the session is now over. We will now return to the normal state of consciousness. To do this, we will count mentally . . . slowly . . . from 1 to 5 . . . when you reach the count of five, you will be wide awake, feeling fine, feeling better than you've ever felt . . . (*slowly count 1 to 5*) . . . open your eyes . . . you're now wide awake . . . in your normal state of consciousness.

# 30

**PALMER, J.**

# *Scoring in ESP Tests as a Function of Belief in ESP*

ABSTRACT: This is the second part of a two-part review dealing with the effect of belief in ESP on ESP test performance. Having tentatively accepted the existence of a genuine positive relationship between belief and ESP deviation scores (the "sheep-goat effect," or SGE), attempts to determine the boundary conditions of the SGE are reviewed and possible theoretical interpretations explored. Several experiments relating belief in ESP to the variance of ESP deviation scores (both between subjects and within subjects) are reviewed in detail. In discussing these results, it is suggested that the subjects who manifest the largest and most reliable deviation scores may be those who are most emotionally involved with the issue of the existence of ESP. This is followed by a discussion of one experiment relating belief in ESP to scoring patterns within the run. Finally, a distinction is made between "belief" and "attitude" regarding ESP. A few experiments dealing specifically with attitude toward ESP as a predictor of ESP scores are reviewed, but the results are found to be inconsistent. Because of the need to understand ESP from a psychological standpoint and the desirability of pursuing those research traditions that appear most promising, it is concluded that the sheep-goat question is certainly a candidate for continued intensive study.

## INTRODUCTION

Part I of this review attempted to answer the question whether the suggested positive relationship between belief in ESP and ESP test scores (the so-called "sheep-goat effect," or SGE) is supported by the data. It was concluded that "... the data presently available support the hypothesis of a genuine SGE, although the relationship is very slight and difficult to demonstrate with small samples" (22, p. 405). Part II will deal with a potpourri of issues related in some way to belief in ESP and its effect on ESP test performance. At the empirical level, this will include discussions of the relationship of belief in ESP both to other independent variables and to ESP scores expressed in terms other than deviation from mean chance expectation. Possible theoretical interpretations of the SGE and these other relationships will also be discussed.

*Monetary Incentive*

A final example of research designed to discover the boundary conditions of the SGE is an unpublished experiment (23) conducted by one of my students, Mr. Avrum Miller.

Four groups of McGill University undergraduates (total N = 47) were each given two clairvoyance runs. Two of the groups were told that the person(s) receiving the highest total number of hits would receive (or share) a ten dollar prize (monetary condition). The other two groups were told nothing about a reward (control condition).

*S*s were given a three-item sheep-goat questionnaire developed by Stanford (35). *S*s scoring above the theoretical midpoint of the scale were labeled sheep, *S*s scoring below the midpoint were labeled goats, and *S*s scoring at the midpoint were eliminated from the analysis.[4] Half of the *S*s in each condition received the questionnaire before taking the ESP test and the rest received it afterwards, but before knowing their scores.

The results revealed rather sharp differences between the monetary and control conditions. In the control condition, twelve sheep had a mean of 5.79 while nine goats had a mean of 4.06. In the monetary condition, however, the SGE was wiped out. Eleven sheep had a mean of 4.82 and nine goats had a mean of 4.89. Analysis of variance revealed a significant ($P < .05$) interaction between incentive and sheep-goat, and internal analyses revealed that the SGE in the control condition was independently significant ($P < .01$). Subsequent post hoc analyses indicated that the interaction was due primarily to those *S*s scoring in the midrange of the sheep-goat questionnaire.

An interpretation of these findings can perhaps be best articulated by referring to an earlier quote by Schmeidler, which I discovered after the present experiment had been completed:

> Another factor in the ESP experiments is that no reward was ever offered other than the intrinsic interest of the task and perhaps my implicit concern for high scores. This might have been the reason for the significant sheep-goat differences: in the absence of other stronger rewards, theoretical concern with the rationale of ESP would be relatively important, weak though it was for many. It would therefore not be surprising if no sheep-goat difference were found in experiments where strong rewards were offered, or if with stronger rewards, a sheep-goat difference were found only for subjects who had considerable concern with the sheep-goat problem (30, p. 58).

Incidentally, the subject who won the ten dollars was a goat.

---

[4] This scheme was adopted by the reviewer after the data had already been analyzed using a less straightforward criterion. The results reported in the text from the revised classification were *less* significant than those from the original classification.

## Explaining the SGE

One finding in parapsychology that literally begs for a theoretical interpretation is the SGE. While it has received a greater amount of theoretical attention than most empirical relationships in parapsychology, interpretation still has been restricted to a few somewhat vague suggestions which have never been subjected to rigorous definition and test. One frequently heard explanation of the SGE is that sheep are more interested or involved in the ESP test than are goats. As Rao has put it, "[the sheep] is more likely to react favorably to the test and is less easily bored than the goat" (24, p. 43). I am aware of no experimental evidence indicating that sheep do in fact take a more favorable attitude toward the test than do goats, although it is certainly an intuitively appealing notion. Of course, even if such evidence did exist, it would not in itself demonstrate that the SGE occurs because of these differences. The case for this hypothesis would be more compelling if it could also be demonstrated that sheep and goats, taken separately, score best on ESP tests they enjoy and which engage their motivation. However, Stanford's finding (36, 37) that above-chance scoring sheep and goats rated his multiple-calling ESP test *less* favorably than below-chance scorers is inconsistent with this prediction. Finally, one might expect that if this hypothesis is valid, sheep and goats, again considered separately, would score more positively when they are in the mood to take an ESP test than when they are not. The evidence here, however, indicates that while mood affects run-score variance it does not affect deviation scores (5, 25, 26). Although the evidence may not be sufficiently conclusive to rule out the "reaction to the test" hypothesis, it does suggest that there may be greener pastures.

A slightly different interpretation is that while both sheep and goats are motivated, they are motivated toward different ends. Commenting on her impressions from extensive testing of sheep and goats, Schmeidler observes that "Sheep, who in general were interested, friendly, and cooperative, could be expected to be motivated toward high scores. Goats, who in general rejected the plan of the research . . . could be expected to be motivated against high scores, since failure to hit the targets seemed, to many of them, to prove their thesis that the assigned task was an impossible one" (30, p. 5). She goes on to suggest that the negativism of at least some of the goats may be unconscious, thus requiring projective tests to uncover it.

Unfortunately, Schmeidler's Rorschach data (30), interesting as they are in other respects, do not deal directly with this hypothesis. No measures of *S*s' motives in the test situation itself were included. Even if some of the Rorschach measures are considered relevant to *S*s' motives in the test situation, no data were reported indicating whether sheep as a group differed from goats on any of these indices.

At this point I would like to introduce my own interpretation of the SGE, not because I consider the evidence for it to be particularly compelling, but because I consider it only fair to put my own head on the chopping block, and it also gives me an opportunity to talk about a pet theory of mine. Actually, the interpretation is quite similar to Schmeidler's, but there are a few refinements that may be of interest. I recently proposed a motivational construct which I labeled the "need for vindication" and defined as "the need to defend the validity of one's previously formed opinions on important social, moral, and political issues" (21). Although ESP is perhaps neither a social, moral, nor political issue (at least not yet), it is clearly an "important" issue as I was using the term. I suggested in the paper that disagreement, particularly if it comes from a "competent" person, is threatening because it implies the possibility that *S* is incompetent in the sense that he failed to reach the "correct" conclusion on the issue. He therefore seeks to defend his opinion as a means of defending or vindicating his competence. This conceivably could be a factor in the motivation of sheep and goats to score above and below (or at) chance, respectively, on ESP tests, because their scores provide a sort of evidence about the validity of their previously formed opinions. One prediction implied by this interpretation is that those *S*s who conform most closely to the sheep-goat hypothesis should be the ones most defensive about their attitudes in general, and attitudes toward ESP in particular. Schmeidler's suggestive finding that theoretically-oriented *S*s tended to manifest the strongest SGE fits in nicely with this notion, as having wrong opinions might be most ego-threatening to theoretically oriented persons.

The interpretations presented thus far have assumed that belief in ESP affects performance in ESP tests. It could just as easily be the case that it is performance in ESP tests that determines belief. More specifically, persons who had previously participated in ESP tests, either formally or informally, may have been converted to a belief or disbelief in ESP or in their own ESP ability as a result of their success or failure in these tests. Even a few such *S*s in a random sample could bias results in favor of the sheep-goat hypothesis. Of course, psychic ability manifested in ways other than test performance could also lead to a belief in ESP, and if this more general ability is reflected in test scores, a similar bias would result.

Some experimental psychologists consider theorizing to be useless or even harmful until there exists a rather large and diverse body of data to theorize about. This body of data is often called a *data base*. While theories are likely to be more fruitful if they evolve from attempts to integrate a data base, I see no harm in theorizing prior to the existence of such a base so long as such theorizing is not taken too seriously at first. Data gathered as a result of testing "ad hoc" theories are as likely to be useful guides for subsequent theorizing as are data collected by a random selection of variables, if such is really possible. Moreover, hypothesis testing at the early stages of investigation, in addition to speeding up this all important process, encourages the selection of experimental variables that are the most likely to contribute to an understanding of the problem at hand.

Be that as it may, the data base for explaining the SGE is rather meager. Although there have been a fairly large number of sheep-goat experiments, the great majority have done nothing more than demonstrate (or fail to demonstrate) the SGE itself. A relatively easy and surprisingly neglected means of generating this data base is to determine the personality correlates of belief in ESP. Carpenter (6) has reported a significant difference between sheep and goats on "sex guilt" as defined by the Mosher Guilt Scale, with goats showing the greatest guilt. He speculates that "... persons who are relatively high in guilt about experiences as unavoidably human as sexual feelings and ideas would feel more need than others to keep such experiences to themselves, and hence would be less comfortable in a world in which ESP is a real possibility than one in which it is impossible by fiat" (6, p. 213).[5] Data of this type will most certainly prove valuable as a guide to further theorizing about the SGE.

## Concluding Remarks

The length of this two-part review is a testimony to the large amount of research parapsychologists have devoted to the sheep-goat question. Has it been worth it? Or perhaps a more timely question would be whether it is worth pursuing further. In a field such as ours with limited resources, research priorities must be set. For one thing, we have yet to achieve the all-important "repeatable experiment," which is another way of saying that we have yet to learn how to control and elicit psi reliably except perhaps from a few

[5] The inclusion of this example is in no sense intended to insinuate that persons who do not believe in ESP are more socially maladjusted than are believers. As data of this type accumulate, flattering and unflattering adjectives of various types will come to be applied to both believers and non-believers.

highly gifted subjects. It is becoming increasingly obvious that parapsychology cannot really move forward as a science until this objective is reached. The real question is whether the best way to achieve this objective is through a direct frontal attack or through attempting to understand the processes underlying what psi we can extract from both unselected and gifted subjects. The nature of this review perhaps reflects my own belief that such understanding is necessary for achieving this end, although it is probably not sufficient.

One road to this understanding is to find out what kinds of people perform well on what kinds of ESP tests—and why. However, this road is hardly the proverbial primrose path. One implication of our inability to produce reliable ESP is that any relationships between psychological variables and currently available ESP tests can only be confirmed by using large samples in repeated experiments preferably conducted by different experimenters—an expensive and time-consuming undertaking, to say the least. This state of affairs would seem to dictate that we cannot continue to perform just any experiment that happens to strike our fancy at the moment and hope to make meaningful contributions to our knowledge about ESP. While some exploratory work is obviously necessary to provide new leads, we must nevertheless focus the brunt of our efforts on pursuing those variables which show the most promise of yielding meaningful results. Since the sheep-goat variable is one of the most, if not the most, consistent and potentially meaningful predictors of ESP yet discovered, it certainly is a candidate for continued intensive study.

## References

1. Allport, G. W., Vernon, P. E., and Lindzey, G. *Manual For Study of Values*. Boston: Houghton-Mifflin, 1960. (3rd ed.)
2. Anastasi, A. *Psychological Testing*. New York: Macmillan, 1968. (3rd ed.)
3. Brehm, J. W., and Cohen A. R. *Explorations in Cognitive Dissonance*. New York: Wiley, 1962.
4. Buzby, D. E. Subject attitude and score variance in ESP tests. *Journal of Parapsychology*, 31, 1967, 43-50.
5. Carpenter, J. C. Two related studies on mood and precognition run-score variance. *Journal of Parapsychology*, 32, 1968, 75-89.
6. Carpenter, J. C. The differential effect and hidden target differences consisting of erotic and neutral stimuli. *Journal* A.S.P.R., 65, 1971, 204-214.

7. Casper, G. W. A further study of the relation of attitude to success in ESP scoring. *Journal of Parapsychology*, 15, 1951, 139-145.
8. Dana, R. H. Review of the Rorschach. In O.K. Buros (Ed.), *The Sixth Mental Measurements Yearbook*. New Jersey: Gryphon, 1965. Pp. 492-495.
9. Eilbert, L., and Schmeidler, G. R. A study of certain psychological factors in relation to ESP performance. *Journal of Parapsychology*, 14, 1950, 53-74.
10. Festinger, L. *A Theory of Cognitive Dissonance*. Stanford, California: Stanford University Press, 1957.
11. Fishbein, M., and Raven, B. H. The AB scales: An operational definition of belief and attitude. In M. Fishbein (Ed.), *Readings in Attitude Theory and Measurement*. New York: Wiley, 1967. Pp. 183-189.
12. Jones, J. N., and Feather, S. R. Relationship between reports of psi experiences and subject variance. *Journal of Parapsychology*, 33, 1969, 311-319.
13. Kahn, S. D. Studies in extrasensory perception: Experiments utilizing an electronic scoring device. *Proceedings* A.S.P.R., 25, 1952.
14. Levy, L. H. *Conceptions of Personality*. New York: Random House, 1970.
15. Moss, T. ESP effects in "artists" contrasted with "non-artists." *Journal of Parapsychology*, 33, 1969, 57-69.
16. Moss, T., and Gengerelli, J. A. ESP effects generated by affective states. *Journal of Parapsychology*, 32, 1968, 90-100.
17. Munroe, R. L. Prediction of the adjustment and academic performance of college students by a modification of the Rorschach method. *Applied Psychology Monographs*, No. 7, 1945.
18. Nash, C. B., and Nash, C. S. Checking success and the relationship of personality traits to ESP. *Journal* A.S.P.R., 52, 1958, 98-107.
19. Nash, C. B., and Nash, C. S. Relations between ESP scoring level and the personality traits of the Guilford-Zimmerman Temperament Survey. *Journal* A.S.P.R., 61, 1967, 64-71.
20. Osis, K., and Dean, D. The effect of experimenter differences and subjects' belief level upon ESP scores. *Journal* A.S.P.R., 58, 1964, 158-185.
21. Palmer, J. Vindication, evaluation, and the effect of the stranger's competence on the attitude similarity-attraction function. Doctoral dissertation, 1969. University Microfilms, Ann Arbor, Michigan. Order No. 69 - 21, 868.

22. PALMER, J. Scoring in ESP tests as a function of belief in ESP. Part I. The sheep-goat effect. *Journal* A.S.P.R., 65, 1971, 373-408.
23. PALMER, J., AND MILLER, A. Monetary incentive and the sheep-goat effect. Brief presented at the 1970 Convention of the Parapsychological Association.
24. RAO, K. R. *Experimental Parapsychology*. Springfield, Illinois: Thomas, 1966.
25. ROGERS, D. P. Negative and positive affect and ESP run-score variance. *Journal of Parapsychology*, 30, 1966, 151-159.
26. ROGERS, D. P. Negative and positive affect and ESP run-score variance—Study II. *Journal of Parapsychology*, 31, 1967, 290-296.
27. RYZL, M. Precognition scoring and attitude. *Journal of Parapsychology*, 32, 1968, 183-189.
28. SCHMEIDLER, G. R. Comparison of ESP scores with Rorschachs scored by different workers. *Journal* A.S.P.R., 43, 1949, 94-97.
29. SCHMEIDLER, G. R. Personal values and ESP scores. *Journal of Abnormal and Social Psychology*, 47, 1952, 752-762.
30. SCHMEIDLER, G. R. ESP in relation to Rorschach test evaluation. *Parapsychological Monographs No. 2*. New York: Parapsychology Foundation, 1960.
31. SCHMEIDLER, G. R. An experiment on precognitive clairvoyance. Part I. The main results. *Journal of Parapsychology*, 28, 1964, 1-14. Part V. Precognition scores related to feelings of success. *Ibid*. 1964, 109-125.
32. SCHMEIDLER, G. R., AND LINDEMANN, C. ESP calls following an "ESP" test with sensory cues. *Journal* A.S.P.R., 60, 1966, 357-362.
33. SCHMEIDLER, G. R., AND MCCONNELL, R. A. *ESP and Personality Patterns*. New Haven: Yale University Press, 1958.
34. SCHMEIDLER, G. R., NELSON, M. J., AND BRISTOL, M. Freshman Rorschachs and college performance. *Genetic Psychological Monographs*, 59, 1959, 3-43.
35. STANFORD, R. G. Differential position effects for above-chance scoring sheep and goats. *Journal of Parapsychology*, 28, 1964, 155-165.
36. STANFORD, R. G. A further study of high- *versus* low-scoring sheep. *Journal of Parapsychology*, 29, 1965, 141-158.
37. STANFORD, R. G. A study of high- *versus* low-scoring goats. *Journal of Parapsychology*, 29, 1965, 159-164.
38. VAN DE CASTLE, R. L. Differential patterns of ESP scoring as a function of differential attitudes toward ESP. *Journal* A.S.P.R., 51, 1957, 43-61.

39. Van de Castle, R. L., and White, R. R. A report on a sentence completion form of sheep-goat attitude scale. *Journal of Parapsychology*, 19, 1955, 171-179.
40. Woodruff, J. L., and Dale, L. A. Subject and experimenter attitudes in relation to ESP scoring. *Journal* A.S.P.R., 44, 1950, 87-112.
41. Young, R. K., and Veldman, D. J. Heterogeneity and skewness in analysis of variance. *Perceptual and Motor Skills*, 16, 1963, 588.

*Division of Parapsychology*
*Department of Psychiatry*
*School of Medicine*
*University of Virginia*
*Charlottesville, Virginia 22901*

# 31

TART, C. T.

# *Concerning the Scientific Study of The Human Aura*

I AM going to discuss primarily the methodological problems of trying to study the human aura. I shall not try to review the literature about the aura, but take a basic position that although there is a lot of nonsense in this area, there may be some genuine, important phenomena. Given that, how do we begin to collect some hard data about this problem? How do we get *reliable* and *valid* types of observation that can enable us to understand what the aura is, how we might use it, and so on? I am going to define the aura in a very minimal way as simply a *something* that is perceived by human beings, and is perceived as a something that surrounds a person. We will call that latter person the target person.

Figure 1 shows an observer who sees this aura surrounding the target person. Thus the aura is minimally defined as a something, associated with the space immediately surrounding a target person that an observer[1] can see.

[1] The terms 'sensitive' and 'psychic' are commonly used to describe people ostensibly possessing psychic abilities, and will be used in this paper to describe an observer who believes he can see the human aura fairly often.

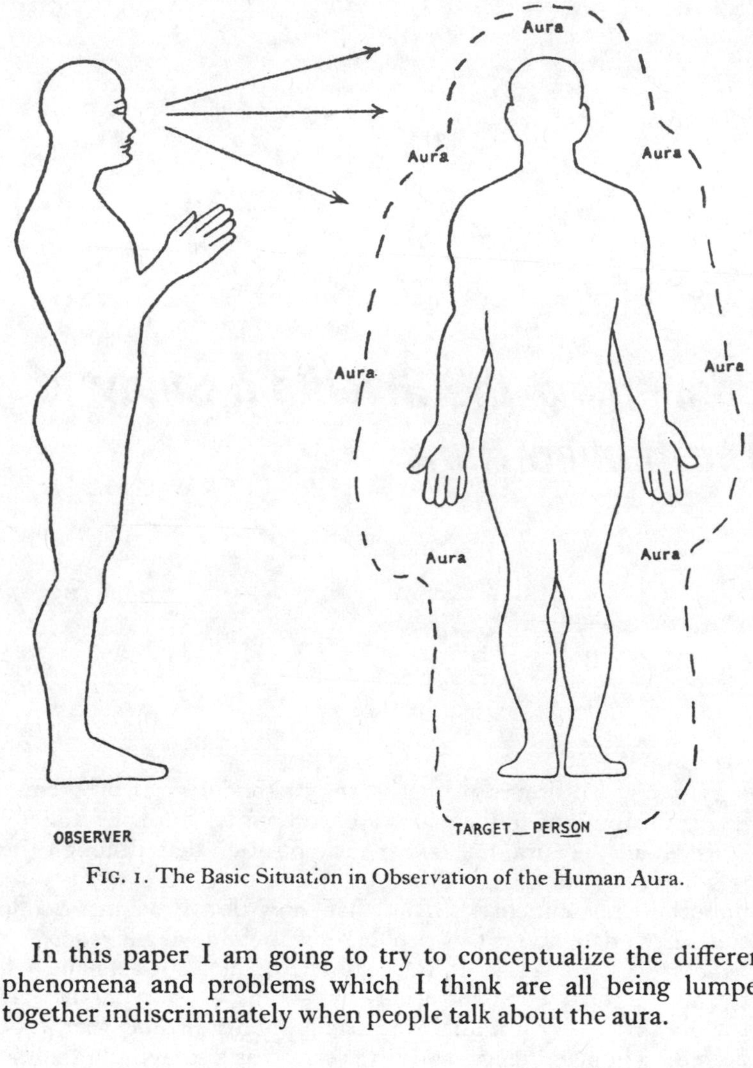


FIG. 1. The Basic Situation in Observation of the Human Aura.

In this paper I am going to try to conceptualize the different phenomena and problems which I think are all being lumped together indiscriminately when people talk about the aura.

## Confounding of Physical and Aural Information

To begin with, in talking about the target person's aura we have to remember that in practically all cases we hear of not only is the observer presumably looking at the target person's aura, he is also looking at the target person. The physical appearance of the target person comprises a large body of information. You can see a great deal about people simply by looking at them, their posture, the way they move, the way they dress, the way they groom themselves, etc. This leads to a great confounding when someone gives an aura reading[1] because you do not know how much of the information that is being produced is information that actually exists in some sense 'in' the target person's aura, and how much comes from physically observable characteristics of the target person, whether static characteristics or behaviour. At one extreme, for instance, an observer ostensibly doing an aura reading may say a number of valid things about the target person, but they may have nothing to do with any such thing as an aura. They are characteristics that a good observer of human beings can pick up from their outward physical characteristics.

The first methodological problem that has to be dealt with then, is, how do you separate out these two sources of information so that you know when you are dealing with the aura? The way that it *should* be done, and which has practically never been done in the research that I know of, is that all sensorily perceivable information from the target person himself must be blocked. So there is no *sensory* information to pick up, and the only information available is in the hypothetical aura. How do you do this?

## The Doorway Test

I developed an appropriate test many years ago, which I have never had a chance to apply for lack of good aura readers. I call it the 'doorway test.' First; to optimize conditions, you let your sensitive find a target person who has a *big* aura, one that sticks out a lot and is stable over time. It is not something that fades out every couple of minutes, or something like that, it is a steady, big surround.

Second; you then block the target person's physical characteristics by the simple expedient of having the target person stand behind the edge of a doorway. His shoulders should be just behind it, so that none of his physical body is visible to the sensitive, *but his aura sticks out several inches beyond the doorway*. The basic setup is shown in aerial view in Figure 2. More elaborate shields could be used, but doorways are generally available.

[1] An 'aura reading' is a term used to cover a description of a target person (personality, habits, problems, etc.) supposedly inferred from the perceived characteristics (colour, form, density, etc.) of his aura by a sensitive.

Third; you set up a random trial schedule, where sometimes the target person does stand *immediately* behind the doorway, sometimes he stands ten feet further back from the doorway. On each of these trials an experimenter, who is with the sensitive, asks: 'Is the aura protruding beyond the doorway or not?'

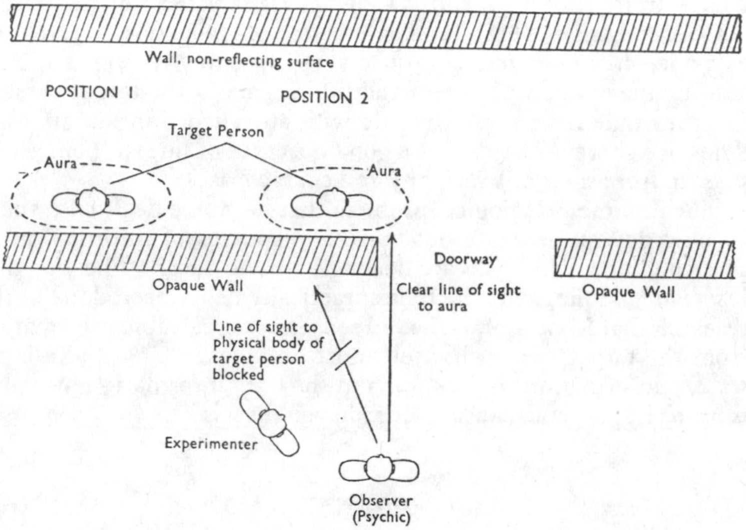


FIG. 2.

If the sensitive is objectively perceiving the aura, there should be practically one hundred percent success in saying that either the person is right by the doorway or that the person is *not* right by the doorway.

This is a simple, straightforward test in theory. In practice you have to eliminate all sensory cues, such as reflecting surfaces. You can't use noisy target people who clump their way back and forth to the doorway. The experimenter with the sensitive should not know where the target person is on any given trial, etc. But it is relatively easy at present to eliminate these sorts of cue.

This test will deal with the first methodological problem, separating out the target person's *physical* characteristics from information that might be 'located' in this aura that surrounds the target person. What I am saying, in another way, is that we have to be careful not to ascribe to the *aura* characteristics which are picked up from sensory observation of the target person himself.[1]

## The Physical Aura

The next point I want to make is that we have to distinguish between several distinct types of aura, and make it clear which one we are trying to study at any given time, which one we are talking about. Otherwise we are going to get into a lot of confusion. The first kind of aura is what I shall call the *physical aura*. By 'physical,' I mean physical in the ordinary sense of the word[2], matter or energy fields that immediately surround the target person. This means that, in principle, the physical aura should be detectable by known physical instruments.

Now we know that there *is* a physical aura. For instance, a person is sweating: this means that there are a variety of organic molecules mixed with water vapour in the immediate vicinity of his body. A person is usually warm with respect to his surroundings, so there are thermal gradients and resultant air currents in the air immediately around him. Thermal (infrared) energy is being radiated from the body. There is an electrostatic field around a person, and electrical ion fields (ionized particles and gases) surround him. Electromagnetic radiation (radio waves) in the microwave region of the spectrum is emitted at a low level,[3] as well as low frequency electromagnetic radiation of up to one hundred kilocycles being generated by muscle action and possibly radiated (Volkers, 1960). At any given time, any or all of these possible 'auras' may exist in a complex mixture around a person's body.

Now, one of the first research questions that we have to deal with is: is this physical aura actually detectable either by instruments or human observers? It is quite possible that while *in principle* this physical aura exists, in practice it exists at such a

[1] The outcome of the doorway test cannot be simply interpreted as 'proving' or 'disproving' the reality of the aura for the tested sensitives, as will become clear in the following discussion of types of auras. A negative outcome (the sensitive cannot guess correctly beyond chance expectancy) may be interpreted to mean that whatever it is that sensitive claims to perceive, it is *not* something physically localized in the space immediately surrounding the target person. Interpretations of positive outcomes will be discussed later.

[2] I should also add the disclaimer that I talk about known physical matter and energy; but what is known today may appear very ignorant from the viewpoint of tomorrow.

[3] C. Maxwell Cade, personal communication, 1971.

weak level of intensity that you cannot detect it; that atmospheric noise is so great that you cannot really detect the physical aura.

In practice, instruments can detect some things around the human body. For instance if you have a sensitive water vapour detector and put it up close to the human body you will get a reading on this, because atmospheric water molecules will tend to be denser immediately in the vicinity of the skin. Electrostatic fields, electrical ion clouds, thermal radiation,[1] (exceptionally weak) magnetic fields, and microwave radiation have been detected around humans under special circumstances. The important question with respect to the physical aura, however, is whether observers can detect the physical aura. Are human beings' known sensory mechanisms sensitive enough, under *any* kinds of condition, actually to detect the physical aura? Could a person for instance, see the air turbulence around another person rising from the thermal radiation? By and large, we would say no, or find only trivial cases: we are not amazed that a human can sense the warmth of another's body a few inches away.[2] But suppose a sensitive passed the doorway test, reliably indicated whether the target person was close to the doorway edge or not? Would this indicate that the physical aura was detectable by known human senses, such as vision?

Unfortunately, the interpretation is not quite so simple, because you also have the possibility of *clairvoyant* detection, or detection of the physical aura by extrasensory means. While we have an immense amount of evidence for the reality of something like clairvoyance, we have little information on what the *limits* of this kind of faculty are. No one could authoritatively say, for instance, that you could *not* detect an ionic cloud around a person by using clairvoyance, even though you may be able to put up a good argument on theoretical grounds, or show practically, that the *known* human senses are not sensitive enough to pick up this aspect of the physical aura.

Another research problem with the physical aura is whether the characteristics of the physical aura show a variation over time, or

[1] Important variations in infrared radiation from the surface of the human body are now used in medical diagnosis, using sensitive instruments developed by Cade (Cade, 1968). A distinct layer of hot air between the skin and convection currents around the body can be photographed with a process known as Schlieren photography (Lewis, 1969).

[2] Some persons apparently have optical sensitivity to the infrared portion of the spectrum far exceeding that of others, so some can see what is invisible to others. Personal communication from C. Maxwell Cade, 1971.

are a permanent structure that correlates only with the long-term characteristics of the target person. At one extreme, the physical aura might be a rather static phenomenon—it is there if you are alive and gone if you are dead, and that is about the maximum amount of information you can get from it. On the other hand, there may be variations in these various components of the physical aura which would relate to changes in physiological activity, mental activity, etc. If this were so, they might be of interest not only in and of themselves, they might provide practically useful information. There might be an advantage in observing the physical aura of a person through appropriate instrumental or clairvoyant means in order to tell something about the person.

Or there might not be. This is an empirical question. For instance, you might devise a hundred thousand dollar instrument that could measure a person's body temperature by focusing on his aura alone. But why should you do that when a clinical thermometer would do the trick for you? So the question of the *usefulness* of the kind of information you can pick up from the physical aura is an empirical question that we simply have to work out.

With respect to the possible correlation of physical aura characteristics with the target person's internal state, another interesting research question arises: can a person learn volitional control over his physical aura? Can he learn to do things which will alter its characteristics, such as intensify it to make it more accessible for observation, or to perform better some of the functions that have been hypothesized for the aura? For instance, in some of the occult literature the aura is described as acting as a protective barrier to incoming stimuli. Somehow it protects a person from the shock of stimulus input. Might the physical (or other types of) aura perform such a function? I'm interested in this possibility because of my own research in the area of biofeedback, where all sorts of biological and physiological processes that were formerly considered involuntary and totally beyond human control can now be brought under volitional control by giving people appropriate feedback signals through the right kinds of instruments.

Another important research question with respect to the physical aura is: how does the environment (both the physical and psychological environment) affect the physical aura? May it change its detectability, for instance? For example, from known physical principles we would predict that clothing would dissipate or disorganize the physical aura. You can't build up much of a layer of sweat-saturated air while leaving layers of cloth under your arms. What are the things that will shield the physical aura?

Will atmospheric turbulence have major effects on this sort of aura? Is there any way of varying environmental conditions that will deliberately affect the physical aura? Increase its detectability? Kirlian[1] photography, e.g., seems to be a way of environmentally affecting the physical aura.

Another important research question is: can the environmental conditions that an experimenter can alter deliberately change the correlation of the physical aura with physical and psychological characteristics of the person? That is, if we hypothesize the physical aura as depicting information about the internal state of the target person, might some environmental conditions wash out a particular correlation, so that the aura could no longer give you a valid reading of that particular information? These are all sorts of things that we need to know.

Now I have talked so far as if people were rather static and you could go in and examine them at any time. If there is one thing we do know about people from psychology, it is that a given person varies a great deal from time to time, and that when you look at more than one person there is a tremendous variability between persons. I cannot stress enough how important it is to begin to study the sources of variability between people, the dimensions of differences, and what causes these particular sorts of differences.

The physical aura would be detectable in this kind of doorway test that I talk about. If you can find some kind of physical emanation around a person that sticks out you should, with the proper instruments or a person whose sensory mechanisms are keen enough, be able to do extremely well in predicting when a person is right around the corner and when he is not.

## The Psychological Aura

There is an entirely different type of aura that we can talk about, which I shall call the *psychological aura*, or the phenomenological aura. By this I mean that there is no physical or psychical 'thing' of any sort that actually occupies the space around the person. Rather, the target person has a *mental concept* that 'something' occupies the space immediately around him. That is, a psychological

[1] My knowledge of Kirlian photography, while limited to a popularized account, (Ostrander & Schroeder, 1970), suggests that the basic technique is the application of very high potential radio frequency energy to the body. The electrical energy added in this way seems to potentiate the matter and field structure of the physical aura sufficiently to result in some light emission, which may then be photographed.

aura is a mental construct *concerning* the immediate space around the target person, and it exists only in the target person's mind. It has no existence independent of the target person's mental state.

This concept may be conscious, semi-conscious, or even unconscious. Many people act as if they possess a psychological aura, but if you ask them if they have an aura, is there something special in the space around them, they give you a blank look: what are you talking about? They do not sense it themselves, so clearly this sort of thing can exist on an unconscious level.

A typical reaction, in our culture, to the idea of a psychological aura is to say that it is *subjective*. Subjective has quite negative connotations. Subjective means it is not real, you cannot study it, and it is unreliable. But that is not the case with the psychological aura: it is quite amenable to study, even though it does not have an existence independent of the target person's own conscious or unconscious concepts. You can study the psychological aura by observing a person's behaviour and/or by asking him about his feelings. From this data you can infer what his psychological aura is like.

For instance, consider the target person depicted in Figure 1. At any given time, there are various sensory stimuli coming in to him which are affecting his experience and his behaviour. Added to these are various internal factors: his thought, his fantasies, his feelings, etc. which are also affecting his behaviour. These result in some external behaviour and some internal behaviour (inferred from his report of what he is experiencing). Our observer can observe these sorts of thing, and might say, from a long series of observations, 'This person is acting *as if* he has a field 3 feet wide around him, and as if that field is bigger in the front than it is at the sides," or something like that.

I am not speaking hypothetically here, and I am going to illustrate in a minute actual research that has been carried out on the psychological aura.

For the sake of completeness, I want to note that the same sorts of problem can be thought about with respect to the psychological aura as to the physical aura. For instance, what about its detectability? What kinds of observation are best for inferring the psychological aura? What sorts of thing does a person do which are most revealing about his concept of the aura? What kinds of instruments[1] would record a person's psychological aura? The

[1] By *instruments* here I would include not only mechanical instruments, but the use of trained observers who are both good psychological observers and maybe psychics, who may be able to see rather unusual things about a person's behaviour that are not apparent.

correlations of the psychological aura with the person's own inner characteristics are again a fertile area for investigation. If you go to the trouble of observing these characteristics, and you infer a psychological aura from them as an explanation of the target person's behaviour, what will that tell you about other aspects of the person's behaviour?

Is it useful? Again, we have the possibility that we may develop an elaborate scheme for observing people under certain conditions inferring what their psychological aura is like, then trying to predict what they will do next. But you may get a very low level of predictability.[1] So there is a real question here of acquiring useful measures in a practical sense.

As with the physical aura, we can look at the effect of environments on the detectability of the psychological aura, its correlates, etc. We can ask research questions about the function of the psychological aura. If a person has a psychological aura of such and such characteristics, *why* does he have it? What does it do for him? What does he gain from it? What does he lose from it? How does it affect his transactions with the world, etc.? How does it affect his personality, his self-concept, and various things like that?

We might also take up a related research question. How could you train the target person to sense his own psychological aura, and would this be a useful thing for him to do, to be aware of what this psychological construct is that he is carrying around with him, and of its effect on his behaviour?

Now let me illustrate that I am not just talking hypothetically at this point. A number of psychologists have done research on the psychological aura, although they have not done it under the name of aura research: after all, they're respectable people and to use a bad word like that. . . . They've done it under the concept of 'personal space.' It has been observed that people act *as if* there is something special about the space immediately around them, and that the space may be quite sharply defined.

A number of investigators have done what we might call *invasion* studies. They have mapped out a target person's personal space by invading it and seeing at what distance he moves away or reports feeling uncomfortable. One of my colleagues (Sommer, 1969) has done many invasions of personal space in libraries, e.g., he has an experimenter pick out target people who have been studying alone. The experimenter will then sit down at various

[1] In spite of the theoretical nicety of learning a person's behavioural patterns and predicting what he's going to do, it is still true in psychology that the best way to predict what a person is going to do next is ask him 'What are you going to do next?'

distances from the target persons, and note how close he has to sit to get people to flee within various time limits.

You can study this another way by simply explaining the idea to a person, explaining that: 'Sometimes when people get very close to you, you get uncomfortable. Okay, we want to map this sort of thing. You stand here, and I'm going to walk toward you, very slowly, and tell me at what point you get uncomfortable.' People have been found to have differently shaped personal spaces this way. A person's personal space is usually much bigger in front. It may stick out a foot, two feet, something like that. In general, you can get much closer in on the side before he gets uncomfortable, closer in on the back than you can on the front.

This kind of mapping can be affected by psychological effects. If you walk toward a person with a knife in your hand, I suspect his personal space will become somewhat larger! But allowing for these sorts of thing, you still find that for many people there's a stably defined area, immediately around them. They act as if it is a very special kind of area, and if people, except under very special circumstances, penetrate into that personal space, they generally become uncomfortable.

The size and shape of the psychological aura gotten by this mapping technique will vary with the type of invasion. It will vary with whether it is a person or a material object invading it. You can put a hatrack closer to a person without his feeling uncomfortable, in many instances, than you can another person. The janitor can come further into your personal space than your boss. There are fairly stable differences among individuals here. This research is in its infancy.

There are considerable cultural differences: the personal space of South Europeans tends to be smaller than the personal space of Americans. One of the things that you frequently find at a cocktail party, shall we say, is a South European backing an American across a room. As the South European moves to the limit of his personal space, the American backs away, but the South European has not had his smaller personal space violated.

The uncomfortableness of invasion has been put to practical use. In some police interrogation manuals, they tell you that the interrogator should sit directly across from the suspect, with no table or anything in between, and at first should sit a few feet away. But as the interrogation proceeds, the interrogator keeps moving in until he's just about touching the suspect. This will get the suspect nervous enough to be more likely to confess!

Another study I have carried out on the psychological aura is also quite interesting (Tart, in preparation). Several years ago I began to wonder if you could take the personal space construct and not make it just an inferred thing, but teach people to "sense it" directly while hypnotized. I first began experimenting in some group situations, with untrained subjects who had various degrees of hypnotizability. Before hypnotizing the group, I would explain the psychological concept of personal space. After hypnotizing them, I would tell them: 'All right, over the next minute or two something is going to happen, so you're going to *directly* experience this personal space around you. I don't know *exactly* how *you* will experience it. You might *see* it. You might *feel* it. You might *smell* it. You might do something I couldn't possiby conceive of, but in the next minute you're going to begin to sense your personal space.' I've done this same sort of thing with well-trained hypnotic subjects in a more systematic manner also.

I found that most hypnotic subjects, even those who do not have a great deal of talent for hypnosis, who can only get into light to medium levels of hypnosis, will consciously detect their personal space after this procedure. Some of them will say they see something very dimly. Others will say there is something that feels 'elastic' right around them, and they can tell when somebody bumps into it. They are bumping this tenuous elastic thing. Others will say it's a 'vibration' feeling. Their eyes can be open, if they can still maintain hypnosis, without disturbing this 'sensing' of the psychological aura.

Some people, once I've explained the idea of personal space, can begin to 'sense' it without being hypnotized. Just to know that there is something they can look for is sufficient to let them 'sense' this psychological aura.

Some other very interesting things can be done with the psychological aura under hypnosis. One of the things I did was to give subjects suggestions systematically to vary the size of their personal space. For instance, I would tell them their personal space was going to shrink until it did not extend beyond the boundaries of their skin. With practically every subject I have done this with, they report that this is a very unpleasant state. They feel pains, they feel unprotected, they get nervous, they feel off-balance. They don't like this kind of condition at all. On the other hand, I have also suggested that they expand their personal space to three times its original size. Almost all subjects report they really like this. It's euphoric, they feel cushioned, happy. If I tell them to expand it to the size of the whole room, most subjects report that when this happens their perception of it just fades out completely, and it's no longer there.

One of the interesting possibilities here is that while we talk about the psychological aura, a purely *inferential* construct, perhaps the person is not simply carrying around the mental construct, but actually detecting to some extent his own psychical aura or his physical aura.

Now, again, for investigating the psychological aura, I'd stress the importance of individual variability, which tends to be overlooked. I suspect there may be very different types of people with respect to the personal space they have.

## THE PSYCHICAL AURA

Now let us turn to a third type of aura, which I will call the *psychical aura*, to use the old-fashioned term. By this I mean a 'thing' (without committing myself to what the thing is) that 'exists' in the space immediately surrounding the target person. This thing is not built of any known physical energies, yet it has a more 'substantial' or 'objective' kind of existence than simply a psychological construct that the person carries around. Another way of saying this might be to say that it exists on a different 'level' or a different 'plane.' I am hesitant to use those words, since they tend to be popularly used in such ambiguous ways.

Again we have the same research questions as with respect to other kinds of aura. How is it detectable, what kind of conditions optimize detectability? Can you detect by any kind of instruments?[1] What are the factors affecting the detectability of this sort of thing? Not only environmental factors, that will make it easier or harder to see, but psychological factors. Do some people have practically undetectable kinds of aura? Do other people have auras that are very easily detectable? What kind of people show this kind of variation? These are all questions that we eventually have to do research on.

Also, what are the characteristics of the observer that make possible the detection of this? How does the psychic detect it? This is one of the main things that I am going to come back to later because it's a very difficult problem. Again, the correlation of the psychic aura with the target person's characteristics is another large area that we are going to have to begin investigating.

[1] By 'instruments,' I mean not ordinary instruments but the whole class of so-called 'psionic machines,' devices that do not work in terms of known physical principles but which are reputed to produce results when used by a psychically talented person. I will not comment upon the validity of such claims at present. Note too that it is conceivable that the psychical aura may, at times, produce a physical energy derivative that might be detectable by known physical instruments.

We might ask questions also eventually about the *function* of the psychical aura. If it exists, what does it do for the person? What good is it? What disadvantages, if any, might we have? How do you train people to sense their own aura, possibly to enhance its functions? Or to eliminate undesirable functions, etc.?

In studying the psychical aura we come to a very difficult methodological problem. Since you must postulate some kind of extrasensory ability to detect it, how do you keep that extrasensory ability from picking up other, non-auric, characteristics of the observer which may be falsely attributed to the aura?

Going back to this doorway test, a way of starting to get at some of these problems, the *physical* aura would be instrumentally detectable in the doorway test, and the *psychical* aura should also be detectable by a talented psychic. The *psychological* aura would not: it is only a construct in the mind of a person, so it is not going physically to occupy the space around the edge of a doorway. The target person's position could be clairvoyantly detected, however, so it is conceivable that a psychic could reliably tell you when a person was and was not at the edge of that doorway, but falsely attribute it to seeing the psychical aura. As we do not know how to eliminate clairvoyance at any given time, we do not know how to deal with this possible confounding.

## The Projected Aura

The fourth kind of aura I will call the *projected* aura. I use *projected* in the psychological and psychiatric sense of the term projection, meaning that you have an experience which exists only *within* your mind but you (falsely) classify it as a *perception* of the outside world. You project this thing into the outside world: nothing is out there, but you think it is there. This is quite distinct from the psychical aura: the psychical aura *is* there in some fashion.

We then can define the projected aura as something which is not out there at all: it exists only in the mind of the *observer*. The psychological aura, by contrast, existed only in the mind of the *target person*, although it could exist in other people's minds if he convinced them of it through persuasion.

The immediate reaction of many people to the concept of a projected aura is usually to think: 'Oh, it's just an *error*. It's just a hallucination.' But that is not the point I want to emphasize about it. The projected aura may or may not be a very *useful* source of information for the observer, even though it has no 'objective' existence.

The way we might think of this process of experiencing the projected aura is this. The observer looks at the target person, and picks up various physical, and behavioural characteristics from seeing him. He may also receive an information input, to varying degrees, from his own *psychic* faculties, which may range from zero information to a great deal of information. Then, somewhere on an unconscious level, these inputs are transformed into a mental image and delivered to consciousness so that he 'sees' an aura surrounding the target person. This projected aura may have 'valid' characteristics. Depending on how good his observation of the target person's physical characteristics was, and/or the quality of the psychical information input, this projected aura may be a very *useful* and *valid* indication of the status of the target person.

We can thus treat the projected aura as an *information display system*. It may be a way in which certain kinds of information are presented to, 'sensed' by an observer. It is an arbitrary way. Another person might never see auras: he might have an image, when he looks at a target person, of a scroll over their heads with things written on it. So one of the questions, in studying the projected aura, is, how *good* is the information coming through? At one extreme, if there is no psychical input, no clairvoyant input giving you extrasensory information about the person, and the only information the observer has is the physical and behavioural characteristics of the target person, then we are dealing with an interesting display but one that cannot really add any information over and above what you could get from simply carefully observing the actual target person. On the other hand, if there is psychical information input, there may be considerable information brought to the observer's consciousness in this fashion which might not be available otherwise. This is the observer's way of expressing himself.

The observer is, however, making an error in attributing his own information display process to something that exists in the outside world. A good example of this, for instance, with respect to 'instruments,' is the Kilner goggles (Kilner, 1965). These are a pair of lenses coated with an organic dye which supposedly allows one to see auras. Ellison measured the optical transmission characteristics of the Kilner goggles (Ellison, 1962). He found that the transmission was very good in the *far* red and the *far* violet. Since the human eye is not a perfect optical instrument, it will not focus the extreme ends of the visible spectrum perfectly, so there is an optical fringe created around anything viewed because these two extremes are being focused at slightly different places on the retina, and you don't have the information in the middle range of the visible spectrum to mask this lack of focus. So persons who put on Kilner goggles and see a fringe around people and say, 'I see the aura,' are seeing the *projected* aura. They are mistaking the malfunctioning of their visual system for something that exists in the environment.[1]

Another instance of the projected aura, that is now occurring quite commonly in today's culture, occurs with people taking psychedelic drugs. I well remember the first time I took mescaline. I saw beautiful auras around people. And then I noticed that not only were they around people, but they were around objects, and then pretty soon they just came loose from everything and floated off through the air! It became rather clear to me that what I was seeing were changes in my optical system that were producing fringes of coloured lights everywhere, rather than something that could be attributed to the external visual objects.

Along this line, I have been studying the effects of marijuana intoxication among a group of 150 experienced marijuana users (Tart, 1970; 1971). Table 1 shows results of some phenomena of interest to us here. Note that 8% of the users see fringes of coloured light around *objects* very often when intoxicated, 20% see them sometimes, 21% rarely. Only 1% report them as a usual phenomenon. 46% have never seen them. Fringes of coloured light around people, the human aura, are reported almost as frequently. These are both phenomena that occur primarily at the higher levels of marijuana intoxication. Feelings of energy flowing in the body, which some sensitives have said constitute the aura, are reported more frequently and at lower levels of intoxication than perceiving auras *per se*.

Probably the drug effect is producing a projected aura by altering the nature of visual information processing. Possibly it is increasing the user's sensitivity to other types of aura. In any case, psychedelic drugs may provide an interesting avenue of research on the aura.

## The Observer

Let us now consider the opposite end of the process, the observer himself. We tend naively to take our perception for granted. We

[1] This does not necessarily mean that there is *nothing* to the Kilner goggles, because while that may explain some of the effect, it does not explain all the effects reported by Kilner. For instance, why does an aura, as seen with the goggles, seem to expand or contract with the application of an electrical charge? That's not going to affect the transmission characteristics of the goggles, so the Kilner goggles still have something to be looked at.

TABLE I

EXPERIMENTAL EFFECTS OF MARIJUANA INTOXICATION
RELEVANT TO 'SENSING' AURAS

| | Frequency of Occurrence | | | | | Minimal Level of Intoxication | | | | |
|---|---|---|---|---|---|---|---|---|---|---|
| *Description of Effect* | *Usl* | *VyO* | *Smt* | *Rly* | *Nvr* | *Max* | *VyS* | *S* | *Fly* | *Jst* |
| I see fringes of coloured light around objects | 1% | 8% | 20% | 21% | 46% | 13% | 10% | 15% | 4% | 1% |
| I see . . . auras . . . around people | 1% | 5% | 19% | 23% | 50% | 15% | 12% | 9% | 2% | 3% |
| I get feelings in my body that are best described as energy, force, power . . . flowing | 9% | 21% | 35% | 12% | 21% | 7% | 26% | 25% | 10% | 4% |
| I get a vibration or tingling . . . that is not an actual muscle tremor | 7% | 17% | 32% | 15% | 27% | 7% | 25% | 24% | 10% | 1% |
| I become very much aware of my spine and feel energy flowing through it | 3% | 2% | 14% | 17% | 59% | 7% | 14% | 7% | 4% | 3% |

Abbreviations Used:

Usl = usually
VyO = very often
Smt = sometimes
Rly = rarely
Nvr = never

Max = maximum
VyS = very strong
S = strong
Fly = fairly
Jst = just perceptible

all walk around thinking that we see what's out there. If there is one thing we have learned from modern research in this area, it is that perception is one of the most complicated processes imaginable. We take tremendous numbers of physical energies of various sorts, perform an immense number of mental operations on them, and end up with a mental construct that may be fairly far removed from the actual physical world.

This process provides a reasonable approximation of the real world for our ordinary life. We can see this blur of sensations coming down the street, we realize that it is a car, and we should not step out in front of that. Our mental construct is quite useful, it keeps us from getting run over.

Because of the complexity of perception, I suspect that in beginning to study the processes of the observer we may be reaching the most difficult area of study in this whole process of talking about seeing the aura. We know there are immense differences between people as observers in just the general sense of 'observer.' Some people are very poor observers in the sense that their observational processes are very much controlled by their needs, their past histories, etc. They pretty much see what they want to see. If they want to see the world as an unfriendly place, they see unfriendly actions all round them. If they are optimistic, they see people doing nice things all the time. Good observers tend to be people who have most of their needs satisfied so that these needs no longer interfere with their perception. They tend just to respond to what is there, they do not have to label it good or bad, pleasant or unpleasant. They can be more passive about it, simply reporting what they see.

Most of us, of course, are neither terribly bad observers with most of our perceptions determined by our needs, or good observers who can function without this. We are somewhere in between. Still, to a large extent, especially in marginal areas of perception, where the stimulus is not obvious, it is very easy to see what you want to see. It is very easy to take the multitude of stimuli coming into yourself and all of us and to organize them into a pattern which fits your belief system, whatever your belief system may be.

Now when we deal with someone looking at the aura, this problem is very important: how do we know when we are getting a good report of what is 'out there,' and how do we know when we are primarily getting a report of the person's experience which reflects mainly his own belief system, his own special way of processing information which has only a tangential or zero relationship to whatever might or might not be 'out there?' This is the problem of evaluating the usefulness of the aura reading. How valid is the information?

I think it would be very worthwhile at this time if I took a couple of minutes to describe a technique which has been developed in parapsychology, to give you an *objective* assessment of how much paranormal information you get from a psychometric reading, since it is directly applicable to evaluating the usefulness of aura readings. How do you objectively evaluate this?

The first thing that should be clear is that a single person cannot make an objective evaluation. His own belief system will alter what he wants to do. Some people, if they want to believe in a psychic, might hear the psychic say, 'This man is a human being,' and if the person wants to believe he'll say: 'Yeah, right on, what fantastic psychic powers!' Another psychic might say, correctly: 'You have a brother with two heads who lives in Hong Kong.' And someone who doesn't want to believe may say: 'Well, a lot of people have brothers with two heads who live in Hong Kong: it's probably coincidence.' What is a reasonable assessment for one person is absolutely ridiculous to a second person. A given person's judgments on the accuracy of a psychic reading this way, the paranormality of the information, is usually going to be terribly subjective.

There was a technique, developed some years ago, but still not widely used, called the Pratt-Birge technique, (Pratt-Birge, 1948) which gets around the problem of subjectivity of evaluation entirely. To evaluate the paranormality of *any* kind of psychic reading, be it aura reading, psychometry reading, or the like, you start with a *sample* of persons who will each have a reading. To describe a typical experiment, you might start with locks of hair. Something like this eliminates one problem: there is no physical contact with the person, so you have eliminated the problem of valid information about the person arising from their physical characteristics alone. A lock of hair in an envelope presents very little useful *physical* information to a sensitive about what kind of person that human being is. So you start essentially with only some kind of token object, or just a name of a person, or an aura sticking around the doorway, or something like that, and you use, let's say, ten different persons, and your sensitive gives you a reading on each one of these. He says, 'This is a man of such and such an age. He does such and such for a living.' He gives various kinds of information. Some of it will be rather specific, and it might be right or it might be wrong.

Now if you simply gave those readings to each of the ten people and say: 'This is what was said about you. How accurate is it?' you would still be dealing with a purely subjective evaluation.

Instead, what you do is to take *all* the information from all ten readings, and put it together in one big heap. You just type it all out into single statements of information, with no indication that this was intended for this person and this was intended for that person. You take the whole battery of information, you give this to all the people, and you say, 'Some of these statements were intended to be about you. Some of them were intended to be about others. I'm not telling you which. But you should treat every statement *as if* it were intended to be a description of you, and rate it as true or false.' You can use a more elaborate rating system if you want to, to allow for the improbability of various kinds of thing.

You then get all this information back, and you break the code showing which statements were intended for which people and which were not and you can then statistically assess whether, at one extreme, the readings are equally right for everybody. Such a result is most simply interpreted on a null hypothesis of chance, that you are dealing essentially with generalities, there is really no specific information. Or, you can assess at the other extreme, whether statements specifically intended for a given person were right more frequently for that person than they were for other people. And you end up with a statistical figure on this that tells you whether you are dealing with paranormal information.

The beauty of this technique, and the refinements that could be done on it, is that you can find out when you have a 'good' sensitive, in the sense of someone who is really giving you information about what is out there, and when you have a poor sensitive who is primarily telling you about his own belief system. Again, this assumes you can filter out the information from the physical characteristics of the person. If you're doing an aura reading and the sensitive is looking at the target person, you're clearly going to get very significant scores with a Pratt-Birge analysis, but these are going to be a matter of what you can tell about a person simply from looking at his physical characteristics. But this sort of technique can begin to tell us how much paranormal information there is in the phenomena we study. Then, once you can develop a number of good sensitives who are giving you primarily paranormal information, then you can begin to use them in a calibrated way, or as a known good observer, and begin to study other kinds of auric properties.

## SUMMARY

Let me just summarize by saying that if you ask a question, 'Is the aura real?' you are asking much too simple a question. Which aura? The physical one? The psychical one? The psychological one? The projected aura? Under what kinds of condition, with what kinds of observers? Real to *whom*? To an instrument, to a human being, to an animal which you might train as an observer?[1] So, you cannot just ask whether an aura is 'real.' You have got to specify what kind of aura you are talking about, under what kinds of condition, etc. What I have tried to do here is to indicate some of the methodological and logical complexities in the field we have been discussing and to point out the need for distinguishing these things, as well as to suggest some methods we can begin to use to get at these phenomena.

## References

Ellison, A., Some recent experiments in psychic perceptivity. *J. Soc. Psych. Res.*, 1962, **41**, 355–365.

Cade, C. M., Seeing by heat waves. *Proc. Roy. Instn.*, 1968, **42**, No. 196, 170–192.

Kilner, W., *The hunan aura*. New Hyde Park, NY: University Books, 1965.

Lewis, H., (Photograph of thermal boundary layer of human body). *New Scientist*, 1969, **42**, No. 649, 15 May, 342.

Ostrander, S., & Schroeder, L., *Psychic discoveries behind the iron curtain*. Englewood Cliffs, New Jersey: Prentice-Hall, 1970.

Pratt, J., & Birge, W., Appraising verbal test material in parapsychology. *J. Parapsychology*, 1948, **12**, 236–256.

Sommer, R., *Personal space: a behavioral basis of design*. Englewood Cliffs, New Jersey: Prentice-Hall, 1969.

Tart, C., Marijuana intoxication: common experiences. *Nature*, 1970, **226**, 701–704.

Tart, C., *On being stoned: a psychological study of marijuana intoxication*. Palo Alto, California: Science & Behavior Books, 1971.

Tart, C., The body as experience: III. Hypnotic explorations of personal space. In preparation.

Volkers, W., Detection and analysis of high frequency signals from muscular tissues with ultra-low-noise amplifers. Institute of Radio Engineers Convention Record, 1960.

[1] I want to toss that out as a research possibility. We have a lot of folklore that animals are very sensitive to paranormal effects, and now we have a lot of psychological techniques which essentially enable you to train an animal so he can tell you what he's experiencing, in a limited kind of way. And the possibility of developing animals as bio-detectors, of a sort, that will give you an objectively measurable physical output in terms of their behaviour is intriguing.

**TART, C. T.** 32

# *Out-Of-The-Body Experiences*

I'm going to talk about out-of-the-body experiences today and about scientific approaches to what is really a very difficult subject. I'll start out by asking the question, "Do you have a soul that survives death?"

You know, of course, the scientific answer to that: the idea of a soul is nonsense. You're a product of the physics and chemistry of your body and when the physics and chemistry of your body stop functioning, that's it...

Nevertheless, working within modern science itself, you can come up with phenomena that suggest that this current physical view, that says the idea of a soul is ridiculous, is actually a very incomplete view, and that you have to allow for something else within this world view. The kind of data that upset the current world physical view are the phenomena of extrasensory perception (ESP). Things like clairvoyance or telepathy or precognition or psychokinesis simply don't fit within the current framework. That doesn't mean that the current framework isn't any good: it just means that it's quite incomplete, and it's going to have to be supplemented or expanded in very vital and basic ways.

I'm not going to talk about ESP in general today. There are many other good sources of information on that. What I want to talk about is the specific kind of psychic experience called an out-of-the-body experience, a phenomenon which requires us to take the idea of a soul fairly seriously...

An out-of-the-body experience feels like this. If you know right now, for a fact, that you're not here, you're really at home in bed asleep; but nevertheless you seem to be as sane as you ordinarily are, your mind seems to have all its critical faculties, you can reason about the fact that it looks very real here even though you know you're not really here, and in five minutes you wake up in bed, that would be what an out-of-the-body experience feels like. It's the experience of being somewhere other than where your physical body is, but it doesn't feel like a dream. You're not in some state of consciousness where you can't critically reflect on your experience. You can really think about it and try to do things, tell yourself it's impossible, even though you can't really deny your immediate experience.

You may or may not have a "second body" of some sort if you have an out-of-the-body experience. Most experiencers do, but just feel that they're "perceiving" from some point in space that's different from where their physical body is.

Now as I've defined an out-of-the-body experience, I've defined it strictly in terms of your experience. You feel that you're in a normal state of consciousness, but that you're somewhere else than where your physical body is. Now suppose you recognize the distant place that you're at, and afterwards, on coming back to your physical body, you check to see if that's actually what things look like there and if the events you saw while out were really happening. If your description of the distant location was correct and it's not the sort of thing that you could guess at, it's not the sort of thing you've seen pictures of or otherwise have normal knowledge of, then you have had more than just an interesting psychological experience. Then you have had a parapsychological experience. You have a problem in explaining how you knew about what was going on at a distant place...

What I mainly want to talk with you about today is what you might think of as the opening of a new approach to out-of-the-body experience. That approach is to find talented individuals who can produce this experience and try to study them under laboratory conditions where you can really get a good look at what's going on and decide if this phenomena is genuine, what happens, etc.

The possibility of a new approach came about through luck, my luck in meeting a young woman; I'll call her Miss Z to protect her identity, who had out-of-the-body experiences several times per week. She had had several per week from as early in her childhood as she could remember. The experience would generally consist of her coming awake for a few seconds during the night and finding that she was floating near the ceiling over her bed. She could look down and see her physical body sleeping in bed. Nothing else generally happened, and she would fall back asleep in a few seconds. She assumed it was "normal," that this sort of thing happened to everybody, and so never bothered to mention it to anyone until she was in high school. Then she mentioned it and quickly found out that it wasn't normal, and she'd better keep her mouth shut if she didn't want people to think she was odd!

I suggested to Miss Z that she do a little experiment at home to determine for herself whether the experience was "real" in the sense of her really perceiving things from a position near the ceiling over her bed, or whether it was an interesting kind of dream experience or altered state of consciousnes, but not paranormal. I told her to take ten slips of paper, number them 1-10, and put them in a box. After she went to bed, she was to shuffle the slips, draw one without looking, and put it on her bedside table, in a position where anyone floating near the ceiling could read it, but no one lying in bed could. If she floated out she should memorize the number that she saw and check it for accuracy in the morning.

I saw her a couple of weeks later and asked her if she had tried this experiment. She reported that she'd done it seven times, she was always right when she checked the number in the morning, and was there anything else interesting we could do.

You can imagine that my answer was yes!

Over the next few weeks, before she moved from the area where my laboratory was located, she spent a total of four nights in my sleep laboratory, sleeping through the night and attempting to float out as many times as she could, while I measured her brain waves and other aspects of her bodily functioning to see what happened to her when she had these brief, out-of-the-body experiences.

She slept on a comfortable bed, just below an observation window where I could peek through and see that she wasn't up to any "no good" at any time. Parapsychologists are very paranoid about people being up to "no good," so it's standard procedure to be able to take a look if you have to.

There were electrodes glued to her head, to measure her brain waves, and then up above her, about seven feet off the floor, was a shelf, and above the shelf was a clock. The clock was so that if she should float up toward the ceiling, she could note what time it was by looking at the clock.

After she was wired up for the evening and ready to go to sleep (and couldn't get out of bed because of the delicate connections), I would go off to my office and randomly select a five-digit number from a table of random numbers, write it in big letters on a sheet of paper and come in and slip it flat on the shelf, so that nobody in the room, especially down on her bed, could read it, but anybody floating up near the ceiling could read the five-digit number right off. Then her instructions were to go ahead and go to sleep. If she could "float out," great, then try to read the number, read the clock and try to wake up soon afterwards and tell me that it happened so I could make something of it...

By monitoring Miss Z's brain waves through the night and trying to compare them with when she had the experience, I could get some kind of answers to questions like: Does this occur in a dream state? A non-dream state? Does she actually wake up in order to do it? What sort of thing goes on in her body?

The three of the four nights she spent in the lab she at no time felt that she was able to see the target number. She said she floated out several times, and she usually woke up within a minute or so and told me about it, but she found she had very little control over where she could go when she floated out. So she simply wasn't in a position where she could see the target number. She did frustrating things, such as one night, when it was very hot in the lab, she repeatedly floated out of her body and tried to turn on the air conditioner in the room, but with no luck. I haven't been able to decide whether I would have enjoyed her succeeding or not. It might have rather startled me to have the air conditioner turn on "by itself!" So she had a number of out-of-the-body experiences, but on none of them would she make a guess as to what the target number was because she felt she hadn't seen it.

She usually woke up within a few seconds to a minute or two afterwards and she would say, "About a minute and a half ago I had an experience which seemed to last about half a minute," or the like. Then I could make some rough correlations with her brain wave pattern and other bodily measures. I found, for example, that her out-of-the-body experiences were not associated with the stage 1--REM dreaming pattern...

It's a pattern that looks somewhat like the dreaming pattern, somewhat like the waking pattern. It is superimposed on a stage 1 pattern that was dominated by a slowed down alpha rhythm. It was definitely slower than a normal awake pattern, and I don't know what this pattern means. I consulted with several other experts in the field of sleep, and they all agreed that it was never seen in normal sleep records and they didn't know what it meant!

It was a distinctive kind of pattern associated with her out-of-the-body experiences. She shows slowed alpha rhythm during them. There are no rapid eye movements, and judging from some of the other physiological measures, she was in no sense on the point of death either. Her heart rate was quite normal, her skin resistance wasn't showing anything unusual. So this was a unique physiological state of her body, but neither deathlike nor dreamlike. Nor could you say that she was simply asleep, nor could you say that she was simply awake. Rather she was showing a unique kind of physiological pattern.

On the fourth night in the laboratory, she woke up at one point and said, "I woke up; it was stifling in the room. Awake for about five minutes. I kept waking up and drifting off, having floating feelings over and over. I needed to go higher because the number was lying down." She had expected it to be propped up and then said, "Between 5:50 and 6:00 a.m. that did it." She was able to see it. She correctly told me what this five-digit number was.

Now the odds by chance of guessing a five-digit number correctly are 100,000 to 1 if you only guess at it once. So this was obviously not coincidence. Now you can draw three possible conclusions here, depending upon your level of paranoia. One is that she really did have an out-of-the-body experience, she was able to perceive from a point near the ceiling and correctly read the five-digit number by some kind of extrasensory perception.

The second one, just to be cautious about this, is that she was quite skilled at fraud and she cheated. For instance, we weren't on such intimate terms that I could search her thoroughly, so perhaps she had a mirror and collapsible rod hidden in her pajamas and, hoping that I wouldn't be looking through the window, she attached the mirror to the rod and pushed it up the wall and read the number. I think that was pretty unlikely, but it could happen.

The third alternative is that I'm lying and I'm part of the international conspiracy of parapsychologists who are trying to put one over on the rest of the world. You can judge that one for yourself.

The main thing I think this particular study demonstrated was that it's possible to take a really exotic phenomena like what seems to be your soul leaving your body, study it in the laboratory, have it actually happen there, and get some idea about what goes on in the brain and nervous system while this is happening. That kind of information may be very useful in attempting to produce this kind of phenomena later. And you may also take it as proof that out-of-the-body experiences can be "real" in the sense that you really can perceive (extrasensorially) from a location different from your physical body. Whether you buy the last one or not, as I say, depends on your level of paranoia.

I worked with a second subject who has since published a fascinating book about his hundreds of out-of-the-body experiences (Monroe, 1971). His four, brief out-of-the-body experiences in the lab took place in conjunction with a stage 1 dreaming state. Apparently his out-of-the-body activity has taken over the physiological state ordinarily associated with dreaming, and replaced it. He wasn't able to read any five-digit numbers though. During the few out-of-the-body experiences he had, he just didn't feel in enough control to be able to see the numbers. Details are reported in the original journal article (Tart, 1967) and summarized in the foreward to Monroe's book.

These were the only two out-of-the-body laboratory studies for several years, but just recently Dr. Karlis Osis and Miss Janet Mitchell of the American Society for Psychical Research in New York City have tested another talented subject, Ingo Swann who's able to have out-of-the-body experiences at will. Mr. Swann sits in a comfortable chair where he's wired up for measuring his physiology during attempts to leave his body. He doesn't have to go to sleep for it; he can do it more directly. I think it's a different type of out-of-the-body experience. They found somewhat similar brain wave changes as those of Miss Z. when he leaves his body, but not identical.

Mr. Swann didn't feel his out-of-the-body vision was acute enough to read a number, so what they did was suspend a box near the ceiling. The top was open, but had sides and a bottom, so anybody floating up near the ceiling could see what's in the box quite readily. Then they would randomly put some kind of object in the box, a different object each time. They did eight different sessions with him that way, and he would attempt to verbally describe the object as well as make a drawing of it. Then they gave his drawings to judges who didn't know which object was supposed to go with which drawing and they would try to match them up. If his descriptions were just imagination, kind of random, you'd only expect to get one or two out of the eight drawings and targets correctly matched up. Instead the judges correctly matched all eight drawings and descriptions against all eight objects, leaving no doubt that he was using some kind of extrasensory perception, as if he were really perceiving from a point up near the ceiling looking down into this box...

I think out-of-the-body experiences, then, are very important in telling us something about the nature of man. If there really is some separate realm we could think of as "mind," and some totally separate one we could think of as "body," then it may very well be the case that out-of-the-body experiences give us a way of investigating these separate realms. And, if we really do have a soul, if we really do have something that our consciousness functions in that can leave the physical body and survive independently of it, that makes a big difference. It means, for instance, you give religion a much more serious consideration than if you're convinced that the stuff that they talk about has to be impossible. You have a very different world view if the only end in store for you is death, than if you should seriously look at the idea that there's something more than that.

Now I'm trying to be a conservative scientist, so don't quote me as saying the soul has been scientifically proven to exist! I wouldn't make that big a jump yet. I'm saying the scientific evidence we've collected now, this parapsychological study I've explained to you here, says that while out-of-the-body experience is an improbable thing in terms of the rest of our scientific world view, we should look very seriously at this then and the idea of soul. Soul is not "just" a word.

**JOHNSON, r. V. II.**

# 33

# *Letter to the Editor - on Cleve Backster and Plant Perception*

To the Editors:

This letter is in reference to a research article published in the (now discontinued) *International Journal of Parapsychology*, Vol. X, Winter 1968, No. 4, pp. 328-48 entitled "Evidence of a Primary Perception in Plant Life" by Cleve Backster. I became interested in Backster's work with plants in September of 1969 and decided to repeat it to get a better understanding of the phenomena. I too connected a Wheatstone bridge to a philodendron leaf, amplified the output, and plotted it on a strip chart recorder. I was pleased to get the same sudden changes in the leaf's resistance that Backster reported. However, I found that the correlation between threats to the plant, the killing of brine shrimp, or the destroying of other plants and these changes of resistance were lacking. The resistance of the plant would just change significantly and then return in 3 to 10 seconds to its original value. For a month or more I observed these fluctuations with no positive correlations. I even tried using more sophisticated equipment which was available, with the same results.

At this time, it was recommended to me to try a controlled environment to eliminate the number of uncontrollable variables in an open room. Well, the controlled environment eliminated more than that. All sudden unexplainable variations ceased when the temperature and humidity were held constant. The slightest variation in either temperature or humidity caused immediate variations in the leaf's resistance. I carefully checked, to prove that the variations were not due to any effects of the electrodes applied to the leaf. Now I could get exact reproductions of the changes I observed in an open room by fluctuating the temperature 1 or 2 degrees centigrade or the humidity 10% to 15%. In an open room, both the temperature and the humidity change this much or more with heating, drafts, dumping shrimp into boiling water, etc.

I wrote Mr. Backster, reporting my results, in June of 1971. I have never received a reply.

I did my research under the careful scrutiny of the electrical engineering and botany departments at the University of Washington and received my Master's degree based on my work. I feel it is important that Mr. Backster either repeat his work in a controlled environment or that the fact that his results are questionable be made public. I would appreciate your help. I would be more than willing to send you a copy of my research work if desired. I personally am deeply interested in parapsychical phenomena, but feel that careless research and sensational reports do a great deal of harm.

REX V. JOHNSON II

*3407 Thirty-eighth Ave. S.W.*
*Seattle, Wash. 98126*

# 34

SMITH, E. L.

# *The Raudive Voices — Objective or Subjective?*

IN his book *Breakthrough* Raudive claims to receive spoken messages from the dead on a tape recorder. If the claim could be sustained, and if the voices said anything of importance, then it would be justifiable to speak of a 'breakthrough in a new dimension'. In the earliest days of wireless telegraphy it was a miracle to receive any message at all however trivial, but development was swift. With the 'Raudive voices' this stage of uncritical wonder at brief banal messages has already lasted over 7 years. A critical analysis of the phenomenon seems overdue. The following analysis is based mainly on the ample internal evidence of the book. I have not had an opportunity to listen to Raudive's recordings, but I have made a few myself.

The work devotes nearly three quarters of its 400 pages to setting down the actual words recorded from some of the 72,000 voices that have been heard, and trying to catalogue them by the content of the messages. But the technical details needed to make an assessment of the phenomenon are scattered in a haphazard unscientific manner through pages of chat and numerous appendices by colleagues.

## TECHNIQUES

The basis of the technique is to set up a tape recorder with a source of background noise from which, on playback, voices emerge faintly and indistinctly, speaking very brief telegraphic messages, at great speed and often in a mixture of languages. Two fairly mundane ways by which the voices might arise will be suggested here. If the author can refute these hypotheses then no harm is done, for Raudive's case will be strengthened by the need to defend it.

Five different set-ups are described for producing the recordings, but the method used is frequently omitted from the transcription of messages in the text.

(1) Microphone. The usual microphone is plugged in to the tape recorder, which is set to record at maximum volume.

(2) Radio. A radio receiver is connected directly to the input socket of the recorder (not via the microphone) but the radio is tuned to some frequency on which no station is transmitting, usually in the medium wave band.

(3) Radio microphone. As (2) but the microphone is plugged in and placed close to the loud speaker of the radio which is not otherwise connected to the recorder.

(4) Frequency-transmitter recording. From the brief description it appears that this method is also like (2) but an unmodulated carrier frequency is generated by a small transmitter in the room.

(5) Diode. A germanium diode rectifier connected to a simple circuit is plugged in to the radio input of the tape recorder. The circuit resembles that of the old crystal set unsharply tuned to a fixed wave length (unstated but by implication in the medium wave band) but the aerial is only a few inches long, suitable only to receive much higher frequencies.

An essential feature of the technique seems to be that the voices emerge from a background of so-called 'white noise' recorded on the tapes. As tabulated below, numerous sources of noise are present, and they would not in fact combine to produce white noise, which technically means noise uniformly distributed over the aural frequency range.

### Sources of Noise

| | |
|---|---|
| Mechanical noise from motor and tape; mains hum; electronic noise in circuits. | All methods |
| Noise in room picked up by microphone. | Methods 1 and 3 |
| Static and mush; interference between radio stations. | Methods 2, 3 and 5 |

The microphone voices are said to be very soft, quick as lightning, and to comprise only very short statements. Three grades of audibility are listed but it is not clear whether this classification is general or only for the microphone voices.

These grades comprise:

(*a*) Voices that can be heard and identified by anyone with normal hearing and a knowledge of the language. (Nevertheless it is mentioned elsewhere that (*a*) type voices have been missed even by experienced operators on first replay.)

(*b*) Voices that speak more rapidly and softly but are still quite plainly audible to a trained and attentive ear.

(*c*) Voices that can only be heard in fragments even by a trained ear. These are the most interesting because they sometimes give information and paranormal data.

The book does not make it clear that the departed entities could inject their voices into the system in three basically distinct ways. With methods 1 and 3 that include a microphone ordinary speech would serve, i.e. sound vibrations in air which the microphone would convert into electrical impulses to be recorded on the magnetic tape. Alternatively corresponding electrical currents could be injected somehow into the lead between microphone and recorder; indeed such electrical impulses could be used with all the methods. Thirdly, with methods 2–5 voice-modulated radio-frequency waves could be injected into the input side of the radio or diode, or voice modulation could be superimposed on the available radio frequency waves. I shall not attempt to suggest how disembodied entities could perform any of these three feats, for I am not at all convinced that they do. This part of the analysis is intended to serve a different purpose, as will appear later.

## Characteristics of the Voices

The very peculiar characteristics of the voices should tell us something about how they are produced. They all have a characteristic rhythm, not further described, they have about twice the speed of normal speech and most of them are quite indistinct. Indeed it is said that it may take months of practice in listening to the tapes before the voices can be distinguished. One may wonder how anyone could find the patience to spend months hopefully listening to meaningless rushing and hissing noises, and in fact many of the accounts suggest a much speedier recognition of at least some of the voices on a tape. Perhaps the statement about 'months of practice' is a protective device, a sort of insurance; if sceptics fail to hear the voices, it is because they lack patience; but if believers hear then quickly they can be complimented on their acute hearing. What tends to happen even with an experienced listener is that he plays a tape until he hears a segment that sounds something like a voice; then he plays and replays that segment many times until at last it falls into a recognizable pattern of words. One collaborator lists the following stages in deciphering a message:

My sense of hearing reacted usually in a set pattern:

A. Hearing a noise.
B. Isolating it from other noises.
C. Detecting a definite rhythm.
D. Differentiating the vowels.
E. Differentiating the consonants.
F. Understanding the word or words.

G. A re-examination; that is, a conscious effort to determine whether a different psychological attitude whilst listening may produce a different result.
H. Interpretation of the utterances.

This is cited in full to emphasize how difficult it is to distinguish the messages and what scope this provides for imagination to play a part. With Raudive himself the messages are often in Latvian or even in the Latvian dialect of his district, but some words may be in any of the several other languages he knows. A brief message can have each word in a different language. Even so, invented words and abbreviations are sometimes included; also incorrect endings proper to a different language. The messages often include place names and proper names only some of which are recognized. With the help of a name, and sometimes even without, a voice is sometimes recognized as that of a departed relative or friend. Other experimenters however receive messages in their mother tongue only, or with a few words of another language they know. The messages usually make some sort of sense but they are seldom grammatical sentences; the style is that of an abbreviated telegram with every superfluous word omitted. Another listener may reinterpret part of the message, hearing a different word sometimes in another language, which alters the sense of the message.

The author recommends that messages should be re-recorded on to another tape, not just once, but four or five times, giving no reason for the procedure. It is understandable that the messages should be edited away from the much longer periods of unintelligible mush on the tape; also they can doubtless be amplified, but it seems unlikely that they would become clearer by straightforward copying. A colleague states however that intelligibility can be improved by using a band-pass filter.

## Objective Voices

There is much discursive talk about the unconscious mind in the book, intended for the most part to discount the anticipated criticism that the 'messages' arise in Raudive's unconscious mind. Even if they did, the argument goes, how would they get on to the tape? To spiritualistic believers it seems more credible that discarnate entities can somehow get them there, using Raudive as a medium. However, a number of other people have succeeded in recording messages and there is no suggestion that they are all mediums. Moreover two colleagues mention in passing that messages have been received on a tape recorder set up in an empty room. It must be concluded therefore that the presence of a medium is not essential.

I can suggest a means by which the experimenter's unconscious mind could put voices on to the tape, with or without the guidance of spirits. I will call this method 'subliminal ventriloquism'. First it should be recalled that the commonest form of mediumistic communication consists of the entranced medium speaking in a voice different from his normal speech and often recognized as that of a departed relative or friend. What I now suggest is that Raudive and the other mediums may go into a light trance and whisper the messages through nearly-closed lips, using the characteristic rhythm and high speed that blends in with the recorded noise, and so is not noticed by other persons who may be present. No suggestion whatever of deliberate fraud is implied; the medium is presumed to be quite unaware of what he is doing just as a normal medium seldom knows what he has said in trance.

I consider this hypothesis may explain some of the voices. However, it cannot be a general explanation because it could only apply to methods 1 and 3 in which a microphone is used. Voice sounds would not affect recordings by the other methods, as Raudive confirms by permitting general conversation during such recordings. Also of course it could not explain successful recordings made in an empty room.

## Subjective Voices

Although I cannot conceive any means by which a human entity living or dead could either consciously or unconsciously insert electrical impulses into a circuit or modulate existing currents generated by noise or a radio carrier wave, I would not presume to deny the possibility altogether. But I reject it personally until someone can suggest a convincing mechanism. Therefore any general hypothesis I may present to cover all five ways of producing Raudive voices must perforce be one that denies their objective reality. I do have such a hypothesis which I will call 'audible tealeaves'. Just as the clairvoyant stares at the tealeaves till pictures appear before her inner eye, so I suggest do Raudive and his colleagues listen intently to the rushing noises on their tapes until they turn into voices. The idea is not so improbable as it may sound at first. Who has not listened to the howling of the wind on a dark night and heard ghostly voices and sinister happenings? A squeegee rubbed on wet glass 'talks' most persuasively. Many people fit words to bird songs; some are generally accepted and get published in books on bird-watching. The rhythmic chattering of train-wheels also suggests words; the very term we use, 'chattering', has a verbal connotation. I recall lying in an hotel bed early one morning wondering where distant music was coming from and trying to identify the composition; some time elapsed before I realised it was nothing but water gurgling in the pipes.

There is background noise on the tapes and it would not be surprising if it occasionally chanced to produce a succession of sounds with some resemblance to voices; this might especially be expected with the radio methods, since interference between stations on the crowded wave band often yields fragments of highly distorted speech. The radio methods are said, in fact, to give a high yield of messages. After all, the tealeaves do sometimes fall into a pattern that almost anyone can recognize as a tree, castle or whatever, especially if he is told what to look for.

From another angle, it is in accord with statistical law that a long succession of random events should include the occasional brief ordered sequence. When random numbers are produced electronically, (e.g. to guide scientific sampling procedures), disconcerting sequences of the same number or of consecutive numbers turn up from time to time, though they are usually removed before the lists are published. A tape recording lasting ten minutes may contain a dozen brief messages taking on average only around one second apiece with the rapid speech used. This is only about 2 per cent of the total time so it would in fact be surprising if there were *not* something like this proportion of ordered fragments present. Thus it is conceded that there can, by chance, be objective sounds of verbal character on the tapes, sounds which imagination can construe into words.

The credulous investigator, striving to discover some meaning in these chaotic sounds, is wide open to the promptings of his unconscious mind, whether it is operating on its own or is in turn prompted by disembodied entities. Either way, the investigator has in effect handed over his judgment to the unconscious and becomes unaware of its deceptions.

It must be emphasized that the nature of the messages provides strong support for this hypothesis. First, their polyglot character gives plenty of scope for fitting a word in some language or other to amost any vague sound pattern. Then their non-grammatical construction removes any limitation on the next word, which in normal speech would often need to be one of a fairly restricted range of verbs. Most messages contain no more than ten syllables, so the fragment of sound used to construct them does not need to be very complex. Another indication that the words originate in the unconscious mind is the fact noted by one expert that certain errors that Raudive habitually makes in his German also appear in his transcribed messages. One can agree with Raudive that the speed and rhythm of the voices is imposed by the set-up; I suggest however that the explanation is not that the electronics somehow impose restraints upon the manifesting entities, but that the nature of the imagined message is constrained by the quality of the chance pseudo-verbal sounds within the noise.

The message should preferably make some sort of sense and bear some relation to preceding ones, but even these limited requirements are frequently not fulfilled. The messages in fact most closely resemble dream conversations, which again suggests that they arise as a mere effervescence of the unconscious mind.

Once a message is 'decoded' there is a tendency for the accepted interpretation to reinforce itself at each repetition, so that one can hardly imagine why it was not clearly heard sooner. The situation recalls those picture puzzles with a picture hidden in extraneous patterning; once discerned one wonders how one could have missed seeing the picture at once. Since however these are real pictures, a better analogy would be with imagined pictures in the fire or in the clouds.

Raudive states that a typical ten-minute recording may require as long as ten hours for complete analysis of the messages it contains. Allowing for rewinding this is equivalent to playing the recording through about fifty times. Such a marathon performance of listening intently to material on the border of audibility (if not beyond) must induce a condition bordering on hypnotic state, in which anyone might well hear voices.

## Confirmations by Other Listeners

The obvious objections to this hypothesis is that other people hear the same words as the experimenter does, and that they all declare belief in the objective reality of the voices. But of what value are their protestations? The book says that the wording of many messages has been confirmed by other listeners, but it is clear that they have been given not just the tape but also a transcript of the messages; that is to say they were told in advance what they ought to hear. This wholly unscientific procedure seems hardly credible, yet it is repeatedly stated or implied in the book that this is what was done. It is confirmed by one of the experts, who suggests that totally independent auditioning of the tapes *ought* to be arranged as a test—from which it is fair to assume that this has in fact never been done.

Thus the other listeners hear plausible noises on the tape recording. They are also told what words they represent, but that these are difficult to hear without long practice. Being inclined to believe the claims anyhow, they are in a highly suggestible condition, and naturally they play and replay the tape until they persuade themselves they can actually hear the messages. Even if they were not told the words, this is a situation in which telepathy is quite likely to operate.

In fact, some people cannot discern the words even when they do know what they are supposed to hear. Others suggest alternative renderings, of which two examples may be given, the first version in each instance being Raudive's.

> Sava Kungs Atis
> Ça va, tas kungs Atis ('tas kungs' appears to be Latvian for 'the Mr.')
>
> Te Macloo, may—dream, my dear, yes
> Mark you, make believe, my dear, yes

The messages are not particularly illuminating in either version but they are fairly typical examples.

## Speech Analysis

The frequency profiles of speech sounds are now well established and segments of the tapes could be submitted to this analysis to check if the claimed words of the message are objectively present. The possibility is indeed mentioned by two of the many 'experts' whose testimony occupies the last quarter of the book, but it is dismissed as expensive and unnecessary. Though it seems to be the only way to settle the issue, it may not be worth attempting, as an inconclusive result is probable. Such admittedly indistinct words are bound to yield correspondingly diffuse frequency profiles, difficult to analyse; and again the recording and assessment of the tapes would need to be done under the supervision of the laboratory involved. There is little doubt that any resulting messages would be of low audibility, unsuitable for analysis, and that this would be explained as the result of sceptical scientists scaring off the spirits!

## Own Experiments

Having suitable equipment available, it seemed proper to supplement this analysis of Raudive's book with some practical tests. Accordingly I made a few short recordings by methods 1,

2 and 3 using three different tape recorders, two of them battery-operated. On playback, I did indeed hear on some recordings sounds emerging from a background noise, some of them startlingly voice-like in quality. Nevertheless, I had to listen repeatedly before actual words suggested themselves. I have no doubt that the sounds themselves were objective; they reappeared without fail at the position on the tape previously noted, and sounded the same as before; moreover they have the characteristics Raudive describes. Some of them, from radio recordings, might have been actual distorted voices from a distant foreign radio station that had faded out but became faintly audible for a few moments. However I am reasonably certain that the words I eventually fitted to the sounds were not recognized but imagined, i.e. they were subjective. They have no significant meaning for me and do not seem worth setting down, except perhaps for one amusing example. I had crumpled a plastic bag beside the microphone, to indicate a change of method. On playback I had no difficulty in persuading myself that the resulting rustle was a voice saying, 'What's all this then—eh?'! I spent only a few hours at this work, not months as Raudive considers necessary. If I had listened repeatedly to my recordings I have little doubt that other faint sounds noticed would have resolved themselves into messages, but I believe I should have remained sceptical of their paranormal origin and indeed of their objectivity.

## Discarnate Entities or Unconscious Mind?

There finally remains the all-important question as to whether the voices arise in the listener's own unconscious mind, or whether all or some of them come from discarnate entities. Those who accept the validity of other forms of mediumistic communication will do so for the Raudive voices also, while those who invoke the dramatizing power of the unconscious will explain these voices in the same way. I do not see that Raudive's work[1] throws any new light on this controversy, but I should like to suggest that the issue is not as clear cut as some think, for I believe our unconscious minds are by no means completely segregated one from another; they are undoubtedly open in some degree to the thoughts of others, so that if minds survive death there seems to be nothing to preclude unconscious communication with the departed.

[1] K. Raudive, *Breakthrough* (English translation), Colin Smythe 1971.

## SECTION IX

# TOWARD A BROADER AWARENESS IN SCIENCE

# 35

MUSES, C.

## *Altered States of Consciousness in Science*

Altered states of consciousness have been responsible for all great successful scientific discoveries. Science really has its genesis in the phenomena of intimate, immediate and even normally inaccessible states of consciousness. Nikola Tesla's induction motor was born early in this century out of a spontaneous vision of incredible exactitude. F. A. Kekulé was similarly struck in his discovery of the idea of the benzene ring, which began modern organic chemistry. So much so that he published an account of his *ouroboros*-type revelation in the 1890 proceedings of the German Chemical Society, ending with the memorable sentences: "As though from a flash of lightning I awoke [and] occupied the rest of the night in working out the consequences of the hypothesis . . . . Let us learn to dream, gentlemen."

Henri Poincaré similarly left us a record of his ultraconscious finding of automorphic functions—so important in modern mathematics. The discovery of the laser by an American scientist in a visionary experience in a park at dawn is a well-known twentieth century addition to the evidence.

---

Finally, the quantum physicist Max Born, in a letter of his of 1967, wrote that he had experienced during his lifetime "perhaps a dozen flashes of ideas which proved to lead to scientifically significant . . . results." He compared the quality of his experience to that of Kekulé and added that "I know for certain that in the few cases where I have discovered something of importance it came like a flash, and a minute before I knew nothing of it."

Among the findings thus made, Born lists the important quantum formula $qp - pq = ih/2\pi$ and the relation between wave mechanics and probability.

The evidence adduced by Coxeter in the following chapter provides other cases in point.

Science is verifiable knowledge integrated by key concepts that render the data intelligible. The beginnings of such knowledge come from ordinarily inaccessible levels of awareness. In this sense, the genesis of all science lies in noetics—the master science of the knowledge of consciousness and the release of its potentialities.*

The latter half of this century has seen enormous breakthroughs in understanding and we may expect more—especially in psychology and biology—as men bring these largely untapped and tremendous possibilities into use.

* The term "noetics" was first used by the present author to denote the science of states, changes, structures and processes of consciousness, this usage having been introduced at the First International Conference on Consciousness and Creativity, held in October 1967 at the St. Vincent Medical Center in New York City, and in the subsequent first issue of the Journal for the Study of Consciousness in January, 1968. The term was later adopted by astronaut Edgar Mitchell, a subscriber to the Journal, when he formed his Institute of Noetic Sciences.

## Evolutionary Theory in the DNA Era

At the core of the new breakthroughs will be a deeper grasp of the ways consciousness manifests itself. In particular, evolutionary theory, we surmise, will shift markedly to a less reductive view than the present too rigid and too inadequate notion of natural selection—so useful up to a point and yet insufficient to render intelligible all that can be observed. The explanatory inadequacy of natural selection, instances of which will follow, has become especially noticeable in the DNA-RNA era ushered in by Wilkins' brilliant X-ray photography of the molecular double helix and the subsequent relating by Crick and Watson of his photographs to the key genetic molecule and the process of cell division, mutation, and hereditary transmission.

The weakest point in present mutation theory is the notion that mutations are *wholly* undetermined and unpredictable, a view comparable to the outdated idea of "spontaneous generation."

## Random Mutation Is Not Enough

The curious fact remains that even in the view of evolution that depends on natural selection (the dying out of forms that are unable to survive, by the deaths of individuals before sexual maturity), there is a persistent theoretical and observable need to assume the constant occurrence of mutations. The trouble is that the mutation induced by all the heretofore supposed agents—that is, radiation and cosmic rays, undirected chemical or micro-mechanical shock or microscopic lesion—is insufficient to explain the arising of the tailor-made mutations necessary to explain the observed amazing patterns of species differentiation, for the mutations produced through random shocks are known not to be patterned, to be at best neutral, and in fact mostly harmful or even lethal to the organism.

## Patterning Mutations

The observed differentiation in species is quite different from the simplistic schemes based on randomness and natural selection, and is highly, often most intricately and complexly patterned. Thus the harmless Bolivian moth *Pseudosphex ichneumoneus*, has become mutated so as to depart almost completely from the normal lepidopteran form (the antenna being the one noticeable external exception), and the insect has come to appear almost exactly like a poisonous wasp. Blind natural selection certainly had a hand in this, but also some very patterned mutation process was needed. In other cases, like certain extinct elephants and the saber-toothed tiger, the mutation pattern was persisted in and even developed by the species in complete defiance of natural selection, until the species literally put itself out of business and became extinct because of the anti-survival effect of its extreme and finally unusable appendages—the incisives in this case.

Darwin, as with many originators, was far ahead of the school that codified him as "Darwinism." In his early writings, he had called attention to the astounding and varied devices of certain orchids to achieve pollination. These devices—far from being original necessities to survival—are extremely involved and often bizarre in character and have not been found necessary by any other flowering plant, even in those cognate with the orchids. For example, a lovely Javanese orchid flowers in a form that seems, with amazing exactitude, to be a bevy of butterflies above the branch. Another orchid native to the Peruvian highlands apes exactly the genital appearance of a female fly of the same region. The male fly, completely seduced by the ersatz Mata Hari, pollinates the orchid when he attempts intercourse with the shamelessly exhibitionist "female fly"—the wily orchid in lurid disguise. Other equally exotically evolved orchids temporarily drug their victims with specially exuded substances, making the pollination process easier.

A small field orchid of Northeastern United States, though not so colorful as its tropical sisters, exhibits the same morphological ingenuity. The *labellum* (literally "lip" or "small basin"), or largest of the three petals of an orchid, is here startlingly modified into resembling a pollen-laden group of stamens, but is really a trap door, on which an unsuspecting bee lands (to collect the mirage-pollen) and falls through the door into a one-way passage in the orchid that thus forces the victim to pollinate it.

Plant hormone (enzyme) controls operate in all these phenomena and in some cases very obviously, as in those orchid flowers that begin to wilt only after they have been pollinated, sometimes having to wait as long as a dozen weeks or so—far longer than the bloom period of most flowers. Pollination changes the enzyme pattern with remarkable swiftness—similar to the mammalian shift from estrogenic to luteal hormones after fertilization.

### The Role of RNA-DNA in Patterned Mutation

In a 1962 lecture given before the Cybernetics Group of the Institute for Theoretical Physics of the University of Naples (published at Rome, 1965, by the National Research Council of Italy in the volume edited by Prof. E. Caianiello, "Cybernetics of Neural Processes," pp. 189-190), we voiced the proposition that the *central nervous system* is "the source of modification of the DNA-RNA through the organism's choice of adaptation to its environment" via—to explain the precise technical procedure—"mutant genetic RNA-DNA patterns which are biochemically coupled with a tagging hormone directed to the gonads for mutant penetration into selective target areas in the formative germ plasm." In short, decision—deep in the unconscious in most cases—is involved.

Six years later Carl C. Lindgren, professor emeritus of the Biological Research Laboratory of Southern Illinois University, voiced the same proposal: that the brain, by its interaction with the environment, could influence the DNA patterns of the germ cells, resulting in a new kind of pangenesis worked through a feedback control of the nervous system on the germ cells.*

The recent work of the molecular biologist Thomas H. Jukes and the geneticist R. King at the NASA-sponsored Space Sciences Laboratories at the University of California at Berkeley now demands mention. Drs. Jukes and King found that there were "Darwinianly neutral" mutations, formed independently of the process of natural selection and oblivious to its censoring power. Previously in 1967, under NASA grant NsG-479, Jukes had written that "a major point in the evolution of the [genetic] code had been played by mutations that are transcribed into the various transfer RNA molecules." He was

**Cold War in Biology*, Ann Arbor, Michigan, Planarian Press, 1968.

referring here to adaptive and non-pathological mutations.

It is only time before full verification of the thesis first voiced in 1962 will be established; namely, that the brain (or its lower life-form analogue)—the central organ of environmental interaction—mediates adaptive changes in animal or plant germ plasm via modified RNA, doing so whenever a brain reaction is forced to be repeated enough by the environment in token of some constantly re-arising situation. Then a new era in evolutionary theory—now only adumbrated—will be at hand.

Awareness, consciousness on some level, is always the touchstone of nature's ways. Details surrounding the investigation of the foregoing facts demonstrate that richly, carrying this seminal concept even into the foundations of modern science: physics and mathematics. More on these matters will be available in our forthcoming volume Language of the Gods (now in press with The Julian Press).

C. Musès, M.A., Ph.D.

# 36

## TAYLOR, A.

# *Meaning and Matter*

Man's approach to truth through science during the last few centuries has been, as we all know, a spectacular success. The way of scientific research now overshadows all other methods of obtaining knowledge of man and the universe.

It is difficult to estimate the full extent of what science has accomplished in the relatively brief period it has grown to dominate society. Knowledge has been obtained that gives man a measure of control over his environment. Bodies, thoughts and things are moved with great speed over the surface of the earth and into the stratosphere. Manpower has been multiplied by machine power. We are able to produce more food, more habitations, more health than ever before. The average life span has been greatly extended. In every aspect of material welfare, science has been a source of accomplishment.

Yet we must admit, too, that along with positive values, serious problems have arisen because of the misuse of scientific knowledge. Chemical research, for example, enables man to synthesize myriads of new chemical compounds, but some of these compounds in the form of certain pesticides, detergents and other products have brought about serious ecological disturbances, poisoning, among other things, the birds of the air and the fishes of the sea. Scientific achievement has resulted, on the one hand, in great benefits for mankind, and on the other hand, in conditions that now menace human welfare and survival. It is said that every good thing can become a bad thing in the hands of those who proceed with selfish interests and ignorance.

The theme of this paper is concerned with a misuse of scientific knowledge not usually recognized. Modern man has peppered the landscape with chemicals that are not only anti-pest, but also anti-life, and in many other ways misapplied the fruits of the scientific method. However, the "crowning" achievement, in this regard, may be the way he has darkened the human mind with the delusion of materialism. The idea that matter, in the sense that this word is used in physical science, is the source of all values, including human intelligence, has become as much of a dogma as any of those charged to religious thought. The materialistic hypothesis, though beginning to be challenged, is often considered to be beyond discussion. Scientists, so free and mentally independent in most respects, are, with outstanding exceptions, generally emotionally committed to a materialistically oriented line of thought. No paper has the slightest chance of being accepted for publication in a recognized scientific journal that deviates from orthodox materialism and its corollary, "randomization"—the notion that blind chance lies at the heart of things.

We would assume that such dedicated devotion to an idea by scientists must be based on weighty and compelling evidence. Yet a careful consideration of scientific data discloses not only no support for the materialistic concept, but reveals it to be incompatible with the findings of science and with ordinary human experience.

Why then has the materialistic hypothesis become so widely accepted among scientists? The answer to this question is not simple. A number of factors are involved. Scientists in their laboratory research must be careful to have clear-cut criteria and objective representations of their results. Where quantities and their relationships are concerned, the data must be free of subjective influences. Another element contributing to materialism is man's over-emphasis of sensory data. (This tendency is just as evident, but in a different way, among the followers of religion as it is with the workers in science.)

At present, due to the success of scientific research, the speculations of scientists are given special weight by the public. Accordingly, what might be called a scientifically flavored materialism has become a most potent influence in human affairs. The scientist who accepts the materialistic hypothesis prides himself on being most realistic. He tends to be skeptical of philosophic values and casts metaphysics into outer darkness.

Yet scientific research itself is based on an assumption that cannot be reconciled with the materialistic concept. The research scientist *assumes* an intelligently ordered world. Otherwise research would be impossible. As he progresses, he discovers nature to be made up of complexes of energy systems, actions and reactions, and changing forms of a degree of complication only slightly within the understanding of the human mind at its present evolutionary stage. In a living form, for every second of time, trillions of linked events occur, forming patterns necessary for the organism to proceed in the normal sequences of its life cycle. Any break in the rhythm of these ordered operations means the death of the body. But materialism—the notion that life is merely the collocation of inanimate individual units—cannot account for the incredible organization it assumes, and indeed finds.

The cult of materialism appears to arise because of a confusion of the values existing in all forms. For example, a book is obviously made up of physical materials such as paper and ink. But no one would suggest that the primary value of the book is in its physical form. We know that the material aspect of a book serves to transmit a message, and the message is the book's reason for existence. If we observe all man's productions from this viewpoint, we discover, as in the case of the book, a combination of plan, design, meaning, or message, communicated by materials. An automobile has its source in human thinking and can be summarized in a set of blueprints. The plan contained in the blueprints, when embodied in suitable materials, provides us with a car. It follows from this, that all man's productions, whether a machine, a cathedral or a symphony, always manifest a duality—meaning (or mind) and matter.

Further, the material aspect of a book or a machine is in dimensional space and time, and so wears out or ages, while the meaning or mind element, not in physical dimensional space or time, is not affected by the passage of the years. It is obvious that if we remove the ideation or mind from any human creation—take away its organization—a pile of materials with no sign of human intervention remains.

As far as human artifacts are concerned, then, the duality of meaning and matter is beyond question. But does this principle of meaning and matter, which all will agree characterizes human constructions, apply to the forms and systems of nature?

The materialist accepts the fact of human intelligence, even though he considers it to be a product of nerve cell physiology, and so would admit that ideation or mind is the primary value in the matter of human activity. But he considers naturally occurring forms to be in a *different* category. However, as we study this issue, we note that the same characteristics prevail in the works of man and those of nature. Actually, we would expect this to be so since the advance of science has revealed a cosmos unified in law and basic principles. In any case, there is no evidence that meaningful forms of human creation involve laws or principles that do not apply to those of naturally occurring bodies.

We will all agree that living forms are the most complex of any known to us in nature. There is, as we know, unthinkably more meaning, more information, more of the qualities which in human experience arise only through the intelligent manipulations of materials, in a plant or animal body than is present in any human fabrication. Yet all this intricate organization comes from a tiny cell that contains no obvious trace of what will develop from it. The only reasonable assumption is that a germ cell is analogous to the blueprint of a machine. A microfilmed blueprint for a jet liner is as to the giant machine that can emerge from it as an acorn is to an oak tree. If we dissect either the acorn or the blueprints, no part of what they produce is discovered, because they contain meanings not yet materialized.

Taking the argument a step further, we can draw on an analogy between the evolution of the automobile and the evolution of plants and animals. The first primitive models of cars appeared around the beginning of this century. They were the embodiment of the "car ideation" of that time. As a result of experience, plans were modified and reembodied in new cars. In this manner, car ideation has been passed through millions of car bodies. And so, cars have evolved from the early stage to today's sophisticated models. An automobile wears out and is scrapped, but the information necessary to produce a new car remains separate and independent of any particular machine, and so new cars are manufactured. But in nature the body of an organism is propogated by germ cells before it ages and dies.

Everything points to the idea that evolution is a process of the accumulation of meaning. In embryological development we note the rapid expression of the qualities evolved through eons of time. A chick germ cell develops so rapidly that in twenty-one days, the yolk and white of the egg has been transformed into a lively, active animal of such complexity as to be far beyond the understanding of the human mind. The chicken has taken millenia, however, to evolve to this point. Analogous to this is the rapid production of a present-day automobile, which has taken some seventy years to evolve. The point is that meaning is cumulative and grows through experience. The scientist accepts the law of the conservation of energy-matter. Conservation of experience or learning is also an obvious and necessary postulate that arises from scientific data. This conservation is expressed in evolutionary change.

In biology, there is the principle that ontogeny recapitulates phylogeny. In other words, in embryological development the embryo goes through past stages of evolution. Thus, biological memory, as it has been called, is in evidence as the organized form (DNA-coded in the germ cell) comes into manifestation. This phenomenon is direct evidence for the conservation of the meanings that have been evolved in past ages. (It seems to be a reasonable assumption that not only the biological forms but also the minerals carry with them traces of their past history; otherwise, evolution from lighter to heavier chemical elements would be impossible. It is known that the heavier nuclei were formed later.)

Animals and plants evolve in a similar manner. The reptile type, for example, has evolved from the small-brained lumbering forms of the dinosaur age to the relatively improved models of today. In all this evolution, reptile ideation, as contained in the germ cells, has been the source of countless generations of reptilian bodies. Gradually through the ages, relatively better forms emerge, marked particularly by greatly increased brain size.

The materialist will admit the presence of information in the germ cells, but also postulates it as a secondary product of biochemical processes. Also, it is assumed that the evolution of plant and animal forms results from random mutations and natural selection. Is this so?

Actually natural laws are limiting, but not determining. The principle of natural selection eliminates the unfit, but it is quite evident that it cannot determine whether a man or an elephant emerges from an evolutionary sequence. Man constructs an edifice. In doing so, he must conform to such limiting laws as gravity and proportion in the building operation. But certainly these laws do not decide whether a house or a cathedral comes forth from the work. The same is true where the principle of mathematical probability is concerned.

The materialist assumes that values or ideation not present in a situation can arise as a result of random actions and reactions. Bertrand Russell speaks of man as having evolved from the "accidental collocations of atoms." Now, it is true that where the potentiality for various meanings or organisms exists in an evolving matter-energy complex, the process of natural selection will determine which of the various possibilities will be realized. But this does not mean that any degree of random manipulations of matter and energy could create meaningful forms not present potentially from the beginning. It is obvious that a particular organism evolves in a manner analogous to the development of a germ cell. There must be the requisite information or plan and intelligent utilization of matter and energy in bringing the plan or meaning into objective manifestation.

The whole basis of the materialistic hypothesis rests on the assumption that ordered sequences can evolve out of materials, solely by random play of forces. We need no special knowledge to realize the unreality of such a belief. It is as if a group of monkeys, through mindless play with a pile of bricks and other building materials, could build a house or some other meaningful structure. (Actually, random forces not only do *not* construct forms of value, but they destroy those already in existence, or, as it is more technically said, increase the entropy of a system.)

The relationship of meaning to matter is brought out very clearly through the principles set forth first by Maxwell and Lorentz and then developed in the quantum physics launched by Max Planck at the turn of the century and developed by Einstein and others. One of these principles especially pertinent to this discussion is the demonstration that the basis of matter is light or electromagnetic energy. All that we perceive has its roots in invisible, imperceptible energy that can be contacted only indirectly through the use of suitable apparatus. We do directly sense light, but visible light is not ultimate energy. Light (as has been predicted already by Newton-Maxwellian theories) responds to gravitational fields. The same is true for other frequencies of radiation known to be associated with certain of the elementary particles of atomic physics. Energy free of differentiation, or pure energy, cannot be contacted by scientists since there is no way to bring it into observable manifestation. In other words, undifferentiated energy could not affect a Geiger counter or any such apparatus. The assumed existence of energy, unassociated with manifestation, is based on the fact that the elementary particles can be transformed from one type into another. They are therefore transitory phenomena. Hence, back of the elementary particles—and this means the constituents of the physical world—it is necessary to postulate an ultimate basic reality about which nothing is known directly. This hypothetical substance is termed "energy" or "vacuum" or "electromagnetic wave medium"—a conclusion generally accepted by atomic physicists, and indeed mandatory in modern quantum physics, pioneered by Dirac.

A consequence of the principle that all manifestation, all matter, whether in the category of minerals or as the tissues and organs of living creatures, is derived from a common source-substance leads directly to the notion that the quality of meaning—or noumenon, consciousness as such—is as the basis of phenomenon. Since all forms have their origin in one source, we are forced to the conclusion that *organization* is the determining factor, whether energy appears as hydrogen or lead, as a daisy or a man. Something must distinguish one from the other, and that something is organization, meaning, consciousness.

Just as the pen's scratches in a written letter must be arranged so as to convey the message in the mind of the writer, so matter evolves in formations and relationships that convey meaning to an intelligent observer. It is this element of organization that is too neglected in the theoretical speculations of scientists. The reason for this neglect is due apparently to the fact that organization, in human experience—and what other experience can we utilize?—is associated with intelligence. And the materialist has no place for the principle of intelligence in his evaluations of evolution.

When organization is considered, it is mostly to attempt to reduce it to random forces. (As mentioned earlier, organization, or meaning, is not in either physical space or clock time. Consequently, on the basis of the assumption that there is nothing in the universe other than matter-energy, organization or meaning must be dogmatized to be a product of matter.) We are asked to accept then, that by *random* action and reaction over a sufficient period of time, light, with its energy of 186,000 miles per second, could be condensed and precisely organized into the state of matter designated as hydrogen. In like manner, so it is maintained, the higher elements came into existence, followed by the tremendous complexity of the organic compounds associated with the kingdoms of life. The strained logic of the materialistic position is emphasized by the idea that all this could come about by chance.

We can, however, look at the relation of meaning to matter from another aspect. A human body, which represents the highest level of evolution on this planet earth, contains more information, meaning or organization, than any other matter known to man. And in this body, the cerebral cortex of a human being represents matter in its most organized or meaningful state. When such highly organized matter is subjected to a certain concentration of heat, all the values resulting from human evolution are destroyed. The tissues and organs are reduced to mineral matter. If a sufficiently high temperature could be maintained long enough, the mineral matter itself would be reduced to electromagnetic energy (radiation) and finally to unmanifest energy. In this process, there would be no change in the *quantity* of energy present before the body was subjected to these disintegrating temperatures. But the degree of organization would decrease sharply. The organization is therefore demonstrated to have a nonquantitative relationship to the matter-energy that made up the living body.

It is a striking fact, though techniques are not yet available to accomplish it fully, that a human or any other form, by the removal of its organization, is transformed into the completely mysterious, imperceptible state of no-thingness, or energy. The very quality that is given so little attention by the materialist as he speculates about the beginning of the world–life and evolution–is the factor without which there cannot be a beginning to anything.

Organization, as noted already, is not in the three-dimensional space of the world we perceive directly or indirectly through the sense organs. The quantity of mass-energy in relation to the weight of a form is unaffected by the concentration of information it contains. Matter-energy itself is, however, deeply related to organization or meaning, both as we have seen and as follows.

According to the relativity theory, the total energy of the steady-state universe is constant and is measured in terms of the speed of light. Some of this energy is potentially present in the chemical elements and all the forms arising from them as given in the equation, $E = MC^2$, where E is energy, M the mass of matter, and $C^2$ the square of the speed of light.* At any particular moment in the evolving of the universe there is an equilibrium between free energy as light or electromagnetic energy and energy organized into denser matter. Only as the energy of radiation or light is *ordered* into particular energy points and systems does it become reduced to gas, liquid and solids. Thus all manifestation is centered, not in matter or energy, but in meaning. Just as the message of a book is not in the paper and printing itself, but is in the way the printing is organized to express meaning. Matter-energy is essential in order to communicate or objectify meaning, as the physical book is necessary to convey the author's ideation.

Further evidence for the primary value of meaning in material forms is available through studies on the turn-over of matter in living tissues of man and animals.** It has been discovered that the material basis of tissues is constantly changing. This appears to occur as a normal accompaniment of living. By the use of radioactive isotopes, or "tagged" atoms, it is possible to learn how long elements remain in tissues, and so obtain data on the flow of matter through a living body. The turn-over of matter goes on at a higher rate in healthy, young individuals as compared with older persons. Since the matter aspect of the body is constantly changing, this fact alone discredits the idea that matter is the primary value, since something clearly controls the matter and its changes. The turn-over of materials is such that the total matter of the body changes many times during a normal life span. How then can consciousness or intelligence be a mere product of the functioning of the nervous system, when this system is compounded of transitory materials? The *meaning* of the form transcends

*This equation is derivable from Maxwell's non-relativistic electromagnetic field theory, using simply the electromagnetic energy and momentum vectors (the Poincaré and Poynting vectors), i.e. using retarded potentials. *C.M.*

**Meaning, in modern scientific thinking, is closely linked with what is called "negative entropy", a characteristic of living forms. *C.M.*

matter-changes. The same being continues, but not the same materials.

It is interesting to note that in the Einsteinian relativity concept, the concern is with mass in *relative* motion and time. Absolute motion and time are assumed to be nonexistent. Motion and time are viewed as free from any organized body or system. But it is obvious that organisms, or meaningful forms and systems, are the realities of the universe. It is possible to consider physical phenomena below the level of form or systems, but in doing so, we are concerned with abstractions that leave out the essential values of nature. The universe, according to scientific data, is an organized system. This is true whether applied to a galaxy, such as the Milky Way, the solar system, the planet earth, or the various kingdoms of nature. All around us are ordered dynamic systems of matter and energy evolving towards more meaning, more information, or ever-increasing complexity of organization.* The principle of progressive increase in meaning is evident in both organic and mineral evolution.

Thus, the world as an ecological organism necessitates, in contrast to Einstein's concept, some absolute time and motion. For example, time in relation to a developing form, such as the body of a child, is not the clock-time of relativity, but biological time. It is absolute in that it is tied to an individual form that has no exact counterpart in the universe. The same is true with the motion or dynamics of the developing organism. Obviously the same principle applies to the evolution of all forms and systems. Each individual group in its evolvement has its own time and motion, and these cannot be relative to time and motion of other evolutions. Mineral and rock formation time, for example, is enormously slower than plant or animal time, and motion or energy of mineral forms is just as decidedly greater. Motion and time serve to communicate the meaning that emerges from a germ cell in embryological development or through evolution. To neglect absolute time and motion, as is

*It is a characteristic of living forms that this complexity is *hierarchical* in nature. This fact imposes even greater organization on the structure. *C.M.*

done in present-day theories, is to neglect the true source of reality in man and nature. This concept is expressed by Goethe:

> Thus at the roaring loom of time I ply,
> And weave for God the garment thou see'st Him by.

Another factor contributes to the quality of uniqueness in forms and systems. The solar system or galaxy constitutes an organized or systemic entity. Similarly each evolving form, by virtue of position in its space and time, must occupy a particular and individual relationship to the forces of the universe. If we think of a living form or any organized whole, it is self-evident that points in it must have a certain uniqueness. In a dynamic, developing organization, points in time must also be individual. In our solar system, it is obvious that the complex of gravitational and magnetic forces, radiations and possibly undiscovered energies, must be such that points in solar space and time cannot be duplicated. Each entity evolves in conditions that are original or unique to some degree. No two leaves on the trees are identical and, in the mineral world, a study of thousands of snowflakes has failed to discover two exactly alike. A world made up of random elements and forces would not be characterized by such design relationship.

To accept meaning, intelligence or information as the reality in beings and things would not at all negate the objectivity of the scientific approach to truth. Rather, the strange, unrealistic idea that meaning can emerge from chaos by random changes of matter and energy would be exchanged for a concept in accord with reason and experience. Research workers are very much concerned with meaning and order in all their investigations. Physics is necessarily becoming more metaphysical as its research progresses. Chemistry is based on elaborate theoretical organizations of chemical elements and associated energies. And the life sciences are primarily involved with the quality of organization. The materialistic hypothesis certainly does not add to the objectivity of scientific research, but rather brings to it a quality more weird than a tale from the Arabian Nights.

There can be no deterioration of research standards as a result of accepting things as they are. On the contrary.

In this connection, it is well to remind ourselves that the seemingly realistic world we contact through our sense organs is not a primary experience. All forms are the result of organization or meaning, and so can be perceived only by mind, not sense organs. We look at a rose and are under the illusion that the idea of it in our minds is what we receive through the sense of physical sight. But, of course, this is not so. A rose is a meaning, a value, that can be appreciated only by an intelligent observer. Our eyes bring to us only different qualities of brightness and color. No sense organ can possibly react to meaning or significance, since these qualities are not in physical space or time. In verbal communication with each other, we know the message is carried by the vocal sounds, and so, we do not make the mistake of thinking our sensc of *hearing* interprets the sound vibrations. But animals, plants, houses, scenery, and so forth, seem to be actually brought to us as they are by the sense of sight. We are not so clearly aware that just as much interpretation is going on here.

It is now evident that as we view the world through the sense organs our minds respond to the meaning qualities implied in the sensory data we perceive. The sense organs bring to us appearances by means of sounds, odors, tastes, and sights; and as intelligences we decipher the meanings those data convey. Man is an intelligent being, first and foremost. Even emotions or feelings are forms of intelligence, since they have the quality of meaning. We are centered in intelligence and can contact only ordered, organized, meaningful situations. This fact in itself irreparably discredits the whole basis of the materialistic hypothesis.

Scientific knowledge has revealed a universe of meaning, plan, ideation, intelligence. The more that scientists are able to translate the book of nature, the more astounding is the wisdom revealed. We can be confident that the previous emphasis on materialism will soon be discarded. Further, it will in fact be through even better science that the strange aberration of materialism will be removed from human affairs, leaving man that much more able to develop his intelligence in ways far beyond our present scope.

## SECTION X

# HUMAN POTENTIALITIES

## RORVIK, D. M.

# *Jack Schwarz Feels No Pain*

The brightly lighted room seems an unlikely setting for what is about to happen. One expects candles, perhaps even a little incense, certainly hushed tones. Instead there is a clatter of electrical equipment, an explosion of flashbulbs, the whir of a video-tape recorder, loud voices, even some joking. The subject, seated in an ugly but comfortable chair in the center of the room, emanates an uncanny calm. He has sharp, penetrating eyes, heavy brows, straight black shoulder-length hair and a silver goatee. He is wearing a wide tie and plaid bell-bottoms. One of his sleeves is rolled to just above the biceps. A p.r. man hovers over him intently asking questions. A scientist makes the final adjustment on wires attached to his scalp, fingers and forearms. The subject drops a six-inch darning needle on the floor, rolls it around with his foot and then picks it up. "All right," he says, "now I'll put it through the biceps."

Without hesitation he begins pushing the dirty needle into his right arm. His eyes are open, trained on the needle. It pierces the skin, penetrates the tough muscle tissue, passes through a vein and comes out the other side of the arm. The subject has not so much as flinched, though he has had to push very hard to skewer the arm. The look on his face can only be described as that of *intense* detachment and nonchalance. It is obvious that he feels no pain.

As the subject begins to pull the needle out, Dr. Elmer Green, who is conducting this experiment at The Menninger Foundation in Kansas, asks him if the wound will bleed. Immediately, blood spurts out both sides of the wound for about fifteen seconds. Still there is no look of alarm on the subject's face. "Now it stops," the subject says abruptly, and it stops instantly. More incredible, within seconds the holes that were clearly visible during the bleeding close up, as if drawn tight by some invisible purse strings, and disappear. Dr. Green asks the subject if he can repeat the demonstration, this time with no bleeding whatever. The subject pauses for a few seconds and then pushes the needle through his arm again. This time Dr. Green squeezes the arm as though it were a wet dishrag but fails to get even a tiny drop of blood. Again the subject shows no hint of pain.

The subject is Jack Schwarz, a forty-eight-year-old Dutchman who emigrated to the United States in 1957. He and his wife and their six children (ages two to twenty) now live in Selma, Oregon, but are building a house on 118 acres of unspoiled woodland in mountainous southern Oregon, called Gold Hill. There, he hopes to establish a "Metaphysical Liberal Arts College" dedicated, among other things, to teaching everyday mortals the same voluntary control over supposedly "involuntary" processes that he has demonstrated at

Menninger. Clearly, he is the man for such a venture, for, as Dr. Green, head of Menninger's Voluntary Controls Project, says, "Jack Schwarz has, in the realm of voluntary controls, one of the greatest talents in the country and probably the world."

There have been many reports of yogis and others who can prance through burning coals and pass swords through their bodies without passing out or on, but Jack Schwarz is one of the first to have his mind-over-body capabilities scientifically evaluated in a leading research institute. While I am aware that the mind of the average reasonable man resists admitting that such things can happen—perhaps even resents being faced with the fact that such things *do* happen—nevertheless I think the story is an important one. The Menninger study of Jack Schwarz provides some of the most reliable data in this domain to date.

In addition to sticking needles through his arm, Schwarz burned himself several times with cigarettes while at Menninger. On two occasions he held the burning ash against his skin for periods of ten seconds. On another occasion, the burning ash fell onto his arm and glowed red-hot there for about half a minute. The instrumentation indicated that during these demonstrations Schwarz was as calm inside as he was outside. A galvanic skin-reflex monitor showed that there was no particular variation in stress, for example, before, during or after the experimental episodes. Heart rate, similarly, remained remarkably constant, increasing by only a couple of beats during the needle demonstrations. Thermistors attached to the fingers revealed that hand temperatures were high, a physiological indication of deep relaxation.

Most remarkable were the electroencephalograph (EEG) readings from the brain. At the moment Schwarz began pushing the needle into his arm, fast-paced beta waves, associated with normal wakeful activities, began to give way to slower alpha waves, which have come to be associated with a sort of alert detachment and which generally can be produced only with the eyes *closed*. At one point during the experiment, Schwarz produced as much as eighty-percent alpha.

Inevitably, the question arises: "Is Jack Schwarz some kind of physiological freak, a man whose sensory apparatus is so dysfunctional that he can't feel pain, a man whose blood or skin is so unusual that he can't bleed?" This same question was going through Dr. Green's mind when he conducted the first experiment. "I was worried," he recalls. "So when I asked him if the wound was going to bleed and it did, I was more relieved than disappointed. This enabled me to see that there was nothing peculiar about his skin or blood, after all. By asking him whether there would be any bleeding I introduced a possibility that he had obviously shut out of his mind. This upset him a little; he went back into beta, and the bleeding began. Still, he demonstrated his control by stopping the bleeding instantly. And the second time there was no bleeding at all." As for the possibility that Schwarz is simply *incapable* of feeling pain, Dr. Joseph Sargent, a specialist in internal medicine at Menninger, says this is so remote as to be out of the question. Without the protective warning system that pain provides, he says, no one can live very long without suffering severe damage.

Schwarz was observed for nearly two weeks to see whether any infections would set in. None did. "In fact," says Dr. Green, "there weren't even any black-and-blue marks, nor the slightest evidence of any subdermal bleeding. Jack said, 'Okay, so there are germs crawling all over those needles; I'm telling the body not to let any of them grow.' He says he's done this hundreds of times, and I have no reason to doubt him. Apparently there's *never* been any infection."

Schwarz professes to find nothing very remarkable about what he does. Pain, he says, is "man's servant." He thinks of it as an "alarm clock that wakes you when something goes wrong in the body that you should know about. But if you're doing something to the body of your own free will, something that you know is not really going to hurt you, then there's no reason for the alarm to go off, is there?"

Word of Schwarz's unusual abilities quickly spread from The Menninger Foundation to the nearby Veterans Administration Hospital, which is also a psychiatric training and research center. Dr. Walter Bruschi, Chief of Psychiatry at the hospital and a specialist in psychosomatic medicine, invited Schwarz to give similar demonstrations for the hospital staff. Again Schwarz stuck an unsterilized needle through his upper arm without detectable pain or bleeding. "It was quite astonishing," Dr. Bruschi recalls. "I watched him push the needle through a vein, and it was not a small vein, either. It was a medium-sized vessel and there was no bleeding, nor any sign of pain. I'm convinced there was no trick to any of this; it was all genuine." Dr. Bruschi and his colleagues were so impressed with Schwarz that they have invited him to return to the hospital both as a consultant and as a subject in further experimentation.

Schwarz stood out at an early age. When he was nine, he was practicing mesmerism, easing the pains of others simply by passing his hands over their bodies. His mother attributed her partial recovery from suspected tuberculosis to his healing touch, and friends and neighbors called upon him to heal everything from frogs to nephews. He claims no spectacular cures, but reports that he was able to alleviate pain in many cases.

At twelve he began studying metaphysics—"the Indian and Oriental philosophies, Wilhelm Reich, Rudolph Steiner, the books of Theosophy, the Rosicrucians, whatever I could get my hands on." From all of these he began to devise his own philosophy and, out of it, a meditative exercise he continues to the present day. In his teens he discovered that he could match some of the feats of the Indian fakirs he had read so much about. He was working in a clothing store, in the Dutch town of Dordrecht. He kept his lapel full of pins, and one day one of the shopgirls came up to him and playfully slapped him on the chest. The pins penetrated his flesh, but he found he could easily shut out the pain. He ran to the rest room to pull the pins out.

"There were little holes," he recalls, "but almost no blood. So, I thought, maybe I'm a fakir. To find out, I selected one of the largest pins and pushed it straight into my wrist, right through one of the veins. It went in about two inches, right down to the head. There was no pain. I was an egotistical little brat then, just sixteen, and I wanted to show everybody I could control the bleeding, too. So I went out and called the shopgirls over to watch me pull out the pin. And I managed to do it without any bleeding.

"I was so excited by all of this that I ran home and asked my father to build me a bed of nails just like the ones I'd seen in some of the books. He refused, so I got a carpenter friend to do it. Meanwhile, my friends and I put up signs all over town giving notice that in two weeks I would lie on a bed of nails. I asked the carpenter not to bring it to the hall where I was going to perform until five minutes to eight. So when the curtain opened I was seeing it for the first time, just like the audience. That way I didn't have any chance of losing my nerve.

"The thing was a piece of wood six feet long with little legs. The nails protruded up through it about four inches and were spaced seven or eight inches apart. There were about forty nails altogether, and my body rested on about fifteen of them. They were large nails but very sharp. I am told that with my body weight of one hundred fifty pounds, there would be about thirty-three pounds of pressure per square inch. But since the nail points are much smaller than a square inch, the actual pressure over each nail was much greater than that. That, of course, was with no weight on me. Then I would invite members of the audience to come up and stand on me. Once I had a man who weighed four hundred five pounds. I'd also put a fifty-five-pound rock on my stomach while I was on the nails and invite members of the audience to come up and hit it as hard as they could with a large sledgehammer. I never felt any pain during any of this."

There were wounds perhaps half an inch deep, but there was little or no bleeding, even in the beginning, and over the years, he says, "The holes became less and less deep with each new performance so that, finally, they were only about an eighth of an inch deep. There was no infection, and my skin today is as smooth as a newborn baby's. The holes closed up rapidly and usually weren't visible fifteen minutes after I got up from the bed of nails."

Then he adds quickly, "I never really was on the bed of nails. Not mentally. I left my body, became detached from it. If, for a moment even, I had said to myself that I was really stretched out on a bed of nails I would have suffered like anyone else. But, you see, my real goal was not to lie on a bed of nails but to show people that if they were in an accident they could stop pain and bleeding through detachment. The average person has to be reeducated, reoriented, because he has been taught to believe that these nails are dirty and will therefore give him an infection, that they are sharp and will therefore cause him pain. By gradually teaching yourself detachment you can shut these things out. What you must do is put a goal before you that fills you with excitement. My goal was to bring something to these people that could help them. That alone brought me tremendous energy, tremendous joy, and carried me away from the bed of nails."

Just as he says he never *really* was on the bed of nails, so he says he never *really* sticks needles through his arms. "It's very simple," he explains. "I do it by changing a single word. I don't stick a needle through *my* arm; I stick it through *an* arm. I move outside my body and look at the arm from a distance; with that detachment it becomes an object. It is as though I am sticking the needle into the arm of a chair. I have taught myself to move as easily outside my being as inside it. The Swami Rama [a particularly accomplished yogi] has a saying that is a favorite of mine: 'All of the body is in the mind, but not all of the mind is in the body.' There is a part of your being that can move beyond the body. Sometimes when I'm lecturing I get into these completely detached states, and suddenly I am walking around myself, quite literally looking at and listening to what this guy is saying. And I can control what is said from out there at a distance much better, sometimes, than when I am all in one package." (This same talent for detachment, Schwarz says, saved him when he was captured and tortured by the Nazis during World War II.)

After lecturing throughout Europe on what he calls "self healing" and what scientists like Dr. Green call "voluntary controls," Schwarz moved to the United States in 1957, eager to take his message to new audiences. He was supporting himself and his family by working in an Army surplus store in San Pedro, California, when he met Dr. Kurt Fantl, a psychiatrist. Dr. Fantl witnessed one of his bed-of-nails demonstrations in San Pedro and was so impressed that he began an association with Schwarz that has continued to this date. One of the first things Dr. Fantl did was to arrange for Schwarz to perform before a gathering of psychiatrists.

"Some of the skeptics," Dr. Fantl remembers, "checked to make sure he wasn't using some sort of concealed shields for protection against the nails. They failed to find anything. There was no trick to it. We also tested him for abnormalities of circulation, blood flow, clotting and the like. There was nothing abnormal. In addition to the bed of nails, he ran skewers through his arms and mouth and burned himself with cigarettes. The skewers through the cheeks were particularly impressive because this is an area where it is so easy to develop infection. He did this time after time and there was never any infection, despite the fact that he often rolled the needles around in dirt to demonstrate that he wasn't afraid of it. He never showed any sign of discomfort during any of these demonstrations, and the healing of the wounds was extremely rapid, a matter of minutes or hours at most."

Dr. Fantl also attests to Schwarz's ability to "diagnose" illness on some occasions simply by making passes over the body with his hands. "He is sometimes remarkably accurate," he says. "I tested him on a few occasions; once, for example, when I had just had some immunizations he knew nothing about. I asked him to see whether he could locate anything unusual on my body, and his hand stopped precisely over the spot where the needle had gone in. There was nothing visible, but he said he could 'feel' discomfort there. Usually he said that he felt a sort of 'stickiness' whenever his hands passed over a diseased or hurt area."

Though I personally saw no evidence of Schwarz's diagnostic powers, I did get a taste of what Dr. Fantl calls his "uncanny perceptions." There were several times during my interview with Schwarz when I became uncomfortable with the notion that he was reading my mind, and on at least one occasion he scared the hell out of me. It may have been mere coincidence that he answered some of my rather specific questions seconds before I asked them, but what about the goatee? I was taking a mental inventory of his features, while, of course, politely avoiding any direct stares, so that I could describe him later on, when suddenly I was stymied by his beard. It was one of those ludicrous mental blocks on par with forgetting where your head is. "What do you call that type of beard?" I distinctly remember asking myself. And at that precise moment, Schwarz looked directly at me with what must have been a smile and abruptly changed the subject to sheep and how we've got to stop emulating them. "As for me," he said, "I'd rather be a goat." And tugging his beard, he added, "You see, I've even got the symbol of stubbornness—a goatee." Then, just as abruptly, he returned to the subject he had so unaccountably tossed aside a few seconds before.

When I asked Schwarz about extrasensory perception (ESP), he scoffed. "When people ask me if I have ESP, I tell them I must have left it on the bureau. There is nothing special about these things. We all have the potential for direct, nonverbal communications. The trouble is, we've let this ability atrophy. As for ESP, however, I abhor the term; it makes it sound like this is something supernatural, something outside our understanding. One of the main reasons I'm subjecting myself to study at places like The Menninger Foundation is to try to dispel some of the occult, mystic nonsense people become hung up on. There are so many fantastic things that are *real*; why dwell on these other things? These occult fads are so incredibly banal."

But what evidence does he have that we are really capable of nonverbal communications? First, he says, I must understand that man is the expression of three forces: soul, mind and body, all unified in one totality. "To me, the soul is nothing other than a capacity of energy that is directed by the mind. This mind, in turn, creates a body, a vehicle by which we can operate in what we call the physical world. The soul is the battery, the store of energy itself. Soul energy cannot express anything, however, without an intelligence; thus you might think of the mind as a set of jump wires leading from the battery, generating and giving direction to the body, which is then set into motion." The cosmic energy that powers us is ultimately measurable, he believes, and thus may someday become more accessible as a means of expressing our totalities directly and nonverbally. A portion of this soul energy is already visible to some people, he says, in the form of "auras."

"I am convinced that everyone can be taught to see auras, to see the emanation of energy, the light coming from the human body and, through this, to come to understand the individual better, perhaps even to merge with that individual through merging auras, to embrace the periphery of the individual directly rather than to attempt communication through sterile verbalization. We must learn to *feel* about other people, rather than talk about them or think about them."

*"Grok,"* I suggest, for I have been thinking for some time about Robert A. Heinlein's fictional stranger in a strange land, Valentine Michael Smith, who communicates without words ("groks"), surfaces during an era of charlatan Christers, phony miracle men, and rampant occultism much like our own, performs real miracles on the stage and is impervious to physical pain.

"Exactly," he says. "And by learning to see auras we move in that direction." There is serious investigation of auras proceeding now at the scientific level, and the Soviets are claiming some preliminary photographic evidence of these mysterious emanations. Schwarz says that he has seen them since an early age, though his parents tried to discourage him from talking about them "for fear that some men in little white suits would come and take me away." All very young children, he believes, see auras at some level of consciousness, "but because society does not believe that such things exist, they suppress what their brains are registering and soon their capacities to see them become dormant." He believes their capacities can be revitalized, however.

The auras that Schwarz says he sees emanate in a variety of colors from all parts of the body. They fluctuate, he says, with brain and body rhythms, reflecting states of mind, health and emotion. Thus, apart from providing a new and perhaps better means of communications, he claims they can be valuable in medical diagnosis. (Dr. Donald Stewart, of Vancouver, B.C., has already invited him to help out in the examining room.) Occasionally, however, they get in the way. "When I'm facing a large audience it can become a confusing whirlpool of colors. Then I sometimes have to tune them out." Over the years he says he has gradually learned how to "read" auras, so that he can now associate certain colors and light fluctuations with specific feelings and even thoughts, which is as close as he comes to saying he can read minds.

"Of course," he adds, "I can only speak of my own experiences with these things. We must still demonstrate scientifically the reality of auras." He hopes to set up an experiment at Menninger in which he will read the auras of individuals whose brain waves are being monitored by EEG. He believes, and Dr. Green agrees, that if he can make reproducible readings that correlate well with the brain-wave data (as, for example, consistent reports of blue auras about the head during periods of high alpha), a significant first step will have been taken in establishing auras as proved phenomena.

In the meantime, Schwarz has not been reluctant to have his ability to "read" auras challenged and tested by skeptical scientists. While he was at the V.A. Hospital in Topeka, two psychiatrists asked him on the spur of the moment to "interpret" some aspect of their auras. The first, Dr. Sanford Pomerantz, was told without hesitation that he is indecisive, that he swings from a rigid analytical stance in which he is unwilling to consider anything that has not been scientifically established to the opposite end of the spectrum in which he becomes deeply involved with the mystical and metaphysical aspects of being. Asked to comment on this analysis, Dr. Pomerantz, who had just then met Schwarz for the first time, said it was "essentially correct; it's true what he says. This is one of my most pronounced characteristics." Later he added that he was "impressed" with the reading. "I don't know that there is actually such a thing as an aura, but it seems possible that Schwarz is able to pick up information about people psychically, after which his brain *projects* an aura, presenting the incoming data in a sort of visual configuration."

Then Dr. Peter Schram, the second doctor to have his aura read, said the Pomerantz reading "rang true, but I wanted more evidence. In order to get at more specific things I asked for a physical rather than a psychological reading." This time Jack Schwarz's performance was even more remarkable. First he saw a difficulty that he said had arisen in the abdominal area two years before. He surmised that it had been a difficulty in the large bowel. "Actually," Dr. Schram says, "it was a renal problem but it was in the abdomen and it *was* two years ago. I was hospitalized at the time when this problem was discovered." Some of the doctors present at the reading report that Schwarz accurately named the season (spring) as well as the year of the abdominal difficulty, but Dr. Schram says he was able to recall only the year.

"He also suggested," Dr. Schram continues, "that I have a cerebral dysfunction of some sort. Actually it's a spinal dysfunction, but they're connected, so, again, he was close. He said he could see some congestion in my upper lungs and this is essentially accurate. He also stated I have a small lesion in one of the upper lungs that developed with a lung infection eight years ago. I don't remember any specific lung infection eight years ago; but I'm sure I wouldn't remember it even if I'd had one. It's true that I'm prone to lung infections. As for the lesion I intend to have that checked out.

"Another thing he pointed out was that there is sometimes a delay between what I hear and the time at which this registers in my brain. Again, this is true to a minor extent, and he said that it was worse with my right ear than with my left. I think I do hear better with my left ear than with my right."

One thing that didn't immediately connect was "pain" that Schwarz saw behind Dr. Schram's eyes. "I've never had any pain behind my eyes," he says, "but then I remembered that I had an operation on my eyes as a child so, again, he was in the ball park." After these impressive "insights," Dr. Schram was surprised that Schwarz made no comment on his atrophic arm and leg, the result of polio. "Still, it seemed to all of us that he made a very good showing, particularly since he was challenged and under duress. I feel that he is definitely experiencing something in the area that is affected or was affected, but that he sometimes has a little trouble interpreting specifically what the difficulty in each area was." Dr. Schram agrees with Dr. Pomerantz that the aura may be "a translation of intuited information into visual imagery that the brain can work with."

Another scientific investigator who has had an aura reading is Dr. Arthur Deikman, a psychiatrist in San Francisco. A cautious scientist, understandably concerned about "preserving credibility," Dr. Deikman was initially circumspect when questioned about Schwarz but opened up as the interview advanced. "There were aspects of the reading he did for me that were quite startling," he admitted. "He talked specifically about a certain period of change in my life beginning a certain number of years ago. He correctly named the year that this change began to take place; he also gave a general description of the change. He said that he could tell by certain patterns in the aura that there were certain marked changes occurring in my life beginning at a specific time and that these were continuing. He also made a prediction as to when these things would be resolved. Everything he said about this fit very well. On some other matters, however, it seemed to me that he missed on occasion. There is definitely something to all of this. Whether he's actually seeing an aura or perceiving these things psychically, it's remarkable. I am convinced that he is neither a charlatan nor a con man. I think that he is a good person who endeavors to be helpful. But remarkable as he is, Jack Schwarz has human needs like all the rest of us. I think it would be unfair to expect perfection of the phenomenon, the performance or the man."

Yet another reading was performed on the wife of a Menninger scientist. In this reading Schwarz was able to pinpoint to within a few weeks "a very happy event" that presaged a fundamental change in the life of the subject. When questioned about this later, the woman indicated that the date named by Schwarz coincided with her engagement to be married several years before. Schwarz observes that he relies upon "rings" in the aura to "count back" to events that occurred in the past. Thus, in his interpretation of what he sees, the aura or "energy body" keeps a record of everything that happens to the physical body.

Dr. Peter Phillips, a physicist and parapsychologist on the staff of the physics department at Washington University in St. Louis, is convinced that there "are forces and energies the nature of which are still unexplained. I think that people like Jack Schwarz use some of these energies, either by natural gift or extensive training or both. I'm quite convinced these energies are real, though at this point I'm at a loss to tell you much about them. It seems apparent, however, that telepathic phenomena require some sort of energy."

When it comes to auras, Dr. Phillips disagrees with Schwarz in one respect. "I'm skeptical about these things being a function of the retina. I've talked to several people who apparently have this facility and have come to the conclusion that auras are a very controlled, stable sort of hallucination. My personal opinion is that the person picks up valid information, telepathically or whatever, and then the mind records and perceives this information in this special way. Why this should be so I have no idea. About Schwarz's sincerity I have no doubt; about the mechanisms involved in these phenomena I have many, many questions."

By now one fully expects the extraordinary of Jack Schwarz. He is a man who feels and sees differently; little wonder that he should also eat and sleep differently. *Less* is the word: two hours a night for sleep, sometimes only one or two meals a week for food. He became accustomed to little sleep during his years in the Dutch underground resistance (some of that time spent masquerading as a Nazi officer, some of it in prison camps) and still finds plenty to keep him awake. He attributes much of his need for so little sleep to his system of "cosmic accounting."

Each evening (actually, early morning) before he meditates, he spends about half an hour watching a movie of the day's events. "It's all a true visualization," he says. "It is as though I am really seeing every event of the day passing before me on a movie screen. I can speed up the action a great deal and still focus on it, slow it down at troublesome spots and even freeze a frame. When I come to something that is a negative—and of course what one regards as negative is subject to change as one grows—I must come to terms with it before I move on. In this way I do not permit anything to settle into my subconscious that could give me trouble later on. And so I take no difficulties into meditation or sleep with me."

Dr. Green at Menninger finds this explanation persuasive, noting that Schwarz, Swami Rama and other unusual individuals who require little sleep seldom dream. Apparently, he says, systems like Schwarz's "cosmic accounting" are a means of handling dream material, in effect, while wide awake, consciously sorting the material of the day that normally gets filed perhaps far less efficiently, speedily and accurately during sleep and particularly the dreaming phase of sleep.

As for his spartan eating habits, Schwarz learned to get along on very little as a child. "We were very poor," he says; "I would sometimes go out and steal a sugar beet, and my parents, my sister and I would make our whole meal of that." Though he often eats a meal a day (his maximum intake), he says he has gone for a week on a single meal without experiencing hunger or enervation. "I believe that you can get energy directly from the cosmos. The secret is to be always joyful, never to have a moment of letdown. To give people what they have need of gives me such a feeling of exuberance that I emanate energy. And we know by the law of resonance that whatever you send out you attract, as well. So, in a way, I am feeding myself with joy." His weight, he claims, never fluctuates, regardless of diet. Even during those periods when he eats only a single meal a week, he says, "I still continue to have a good bowel movement twice a day. So it's apparent to me that I'm taking in energy. Somehow it becomes chemical and is processed by normal metabolism."

I found it somehow incongruous for a man who eats almost nothing and hasn't touched any sort of medication in twenty years to be smoking cigarettes. "Everyone asks me about this," he says, "but I enjoy it; I don't get anything negative from it. And I know that it won't harm me. If I can stick infected needles through my arms. . . ."

That others can do what Schwarz does, at least to some extent, was demonstrated recently at the V.A. Hospital in Topeka. During one of Schwarz's exercises in pain and blood-flow control, a young psychiatrist in attendance, Dr. Stuart Twemlow, was so infected by Jack Schwarz's confidence that he announced he would try to stick a needle through his own arm. "It was a strange thing," Dr. Twemlow recalls. "I felt his extraordinary confidence, and it seemed that there was a transference of some of it to me. I was teetering on the verge. Would I or wouldn't I? And then I looked at him and knew that I would."

At first, he says, "I was very apprehensive. I thought that it would hurt and in fact it did. I got it through the skin and I thought that perhaps I'd gone far enough. Yet, at a deeper level I believed that what Schwarz had said was true, that it is possible to do this sort of thing if you can detach yourself sufficiently. At this point he told me to close my eyes, to concentrate on some flowers that were blooming outside the building, to see only these flowers in my mind. I succeeded in doing this but I was still unable to push the needle through. I think Schwarz somehow perceived my state of mind at this point, that I had achieved sufficient detachment to get the needle through, but that certain of my conscious processes wouldn't permit me to do this. So he got up and pushed the needle through my arm. Then he told me to open my eyes. I was surprised to see the needle completely through my arm. I hadn't felt a thing or even been aware of the fact that he had got up, gripped my arm and pushed the needle through."

This experience, apart from suggesting that Schwarz possibly has some extraordinary hypnotic powers, again also presupposes some uncanny perceptions. How would he dare push a needle through another man's arm unless he were fully cognizant of that man's state of mind? Dr. Twemlow agrees that it is almost as though Schwarz had got "inside my head" and "acted for me—in a way that I would have acted if I had had full confidence." This cerebral interaction or transference seemed to carry over beyond the experiment itself. Dr. Twemlow suddenly found himself in the same "high state of mental arousal" that he had observed in Schwarz throughout the demonstration. "After the experiment, when I opened my eyes, I felt very high. I couldn't figure out what had happened. I actually thought someone had brightened the lights somehow."

It might be argued that Schwarz somehow momentarily projected his powers into Dr. Twemlow, negating the idea that these abilities can actually be learned by others. The day after this experiment, however, Dr. Twemlow reported to his dentist to have a tooth capped; despite the fact that he has "a low toleration for dental pain," he decided to forego anesthesia in order to see whether he could control the pain. "By turning my mind to other things," he notes, "I felt no sensation of pain, even though the tooth was drilled right down to the gum and despite the fact that surgery was performed on the gums themselves." Bleeding, however, was profuse. "The dentist said the bleeding was interfering with his work and asked me to try to control that as well as the pain. I failed to do this at first. Then I got an idea. I asked for a mirror so that I could see the bleeding. With this I was able to somehow stop the bleeding, too."

Dr. Bruschi, chief of the department in which Dr. Twemlow works, says that Schwarz is "tapping into" processes which, in most of us, are dormant from lack of use. "We don't understand these things because we don't want to. Even the most conservative in the medical profession today will hesitate to call Schwarz a charlatan. They don't dare because too much convincing data is turning up in this field, relating to altered states of consciousness, voluntary controls, biofeedback and so on. Then, too, the more knowledgeable have heard of the rather convincing work in the Soviet Union where a very hard-nosed scientific establishment is paying a great deal of attention to people like Schwarz. Personally, I'm compelled to investigate these things, to seek answers that are scientifically satisfying. If, in the process, I have to give up the scientific framework in which I have worked my entire life, I will do that. I can't smile the way some do, say, 'Well, this Schwarz fellow is certainly an interesting person,' and then walk away."

At Menninger, Dr. Green and his associates have taught dozens of "ordinary" mortals to voluntarily control some of their internal states. The tool they use is biofeedback instrumentation, which enables the individual to "see" what is happening inside his brain and body. With brain-wave feedback, for example, an individual can begin to make associations between specific states of mind and specific EEG patterns and thus can gradually begin to produce specific brain waves, such as alpha or theta, at will, altering his state of consciousness in the process.

None of these individuals has yet attained the incredible control of a Swami Rama or a Jack Schwarz, but a beginning has been made. Eventually, Dr. Green and many others are convinced, such serious maladies as migraine head aches, hypertension, ulcers, psychosomatic ills of all descriptions and even cancers can be treated and perhaps cured through voluntary control of physiological processes.

Dr. Green says that the key to voluntary control is the integration of the upper, thinking parts, and the lower, automatic or "involuntary" parts of the brain. "If you can get the two parts in agreement," he maintains, "there is very little you cannot do with the body." This agreement, when it occurs, is perhaps mediated by a midbrain structure called the reticular formation. "This," Dr. Green explains, "acts like a sort of bias control on all of the sensory systems. It's almost as though you had a whole bunch of little knobs in there, potentiometers that you can turn up and down in volume. By turning the volumes way down, you can shut out things like pain." (This dovetails with the gate-control theory of pain posited some years ago by Dr. Ronald Melzack of McGill University. In place of "knobs" he sees a "gate" that can be opened to allow pain impulses to pass through or, under a variety of circumstances, closed to prevent these impulses from reaching the higher levels of the brain.)

Yogis expend years of intense concentration trying to get their fingers on those knobs and/or gates; a few others, like Jack Schwarz, seem to be able to reach them almost at birth. Now, with biofeedback, the average person, who doesn't have the patience of a yogi or the seemingly innate abilities of a Schwarz, has a means of grabbing some of the controls in a relatively short period of time.

But even with biofeedback those who aspire to fully match the skills of Jack Schwarz may, for all his protestations to the contrary, find the task very nearly impossible. Dr. Fantl, obviously troubled by the question I pose, says, "Well, with biofeedback it's possible that many more people may be able to master some of these things and in much shorter periods of time. But Jack is a terribly unusual person, dedicated, amazingly selfless. There is no ego involvement there at all, and that makes a tremendous difference. So, no, I don't think many of us can be like him. I'm afraid that Jack comes as close to being a saint as anyone I've ever encountered."

My own evaluation, as I've already indicated, is that Valentine Michael Smith of the groks, or a close cousin, is alive and well in Selma, Oregon. ###

PEPER, E.

38

# Voluntary Pain Control: Psychological and Physiological Correlates

Different techniques of pain control resulted in different EEG patterns in two subjects who had learned voluntary control over pain and bleeding. Each subject had trained himself since childhood in specific meditative modes, and both appeared to have normal pain sensitivity as shown in the response to touch and pinching. They volunteered with the hope that the physiological findings would set guidelines for biofeedback training to enable other people to rapidly acquire control over pain.

In May 1971, I studied R.C.T., a 24-year old Ecuadorian, who has repeatedly placed swords through his body and had previously been suspended in air from hooks inserted under his shoulder blades. He had also walked through fire; all without damaging his flesh or reporting pain. In the laboratory, he pushed sharpened bicycle spokes through one cheek - through the center of his mouth - and out through the other cheek and also through the sides of his body while physiological parameters were measured.

Occipital and frontal EEG's were recorded. When S (R.C.T.) pierced and pushed the unsterilized, sharpened spoke through the skin, the presence of occipital alpha activity increased to 100% time in his EEG and the amplitude increased 73% over the eyes-closed baseline. He stayed relaxed, reported no pain, and did not bleed even when the spokes were removed. The puncture wounds healed rapidly and there was no infection. Even though he has done this many times, he has few scars on his body. He reported: "that pain is mainly the fear of pain and one's attention to pain. Anyone can learn to control the pain and bleeding by quickly relaxing and then detaching his awareness (consciousness) away from the insertion point or body - preoccupied with a simple distraction task". He enters this meditative state rapidly and upon command, which results in a rapid unfocusing, relaxation, and dissociation from any stimuli.

Later, in July 1972, with Marjorie and Herschel Toomim, I had the opportunity to study another subject, J.S.L., a 31-year old Korean karate expert, who placed a sharpened spoke through a fold of skin on his forearm and suspended from it a 25 lb. bucket of water (1). He showed alpha activity in his EEG during baseline recording. However, when he placed a bicycle spoke through the fold of skin on his forearm and hung a bucket of water from it, his occipital EEG consisted mainly of beta activity with some low amplitude alpha; the frontal leads showed some slowing; the EKG increased from 81 to 100 beats/min. The subject, using a karate meditation, reported that instead of passively detaching his attention from his body, he focused totally upon a small point of energy which he subjectively moved upward from the bottom of his abdomen to a point where he inserted the needle. "Once you concentrate on that square, you can allow the energy to flow into any part of the body. The concentrated mind can be applied to anything it does, and when it is applied, it no longer feels, the concentrated mind is the activity itself, it does not exist in the world," the S reported.

When a subject gives total attention to internal sensations (responses to internal sensations) EEG alpha is usually blocked, as alpha disappears when efferent commands are given. A similar record to R.C.T. was obtained by Green, Green and Walters (2) in their study of J.S., who placed a needle through his biceps and controlled both bleeding and pain. During baseline recording, his EEG (left occiput relative to left ear) showed almost no alpha activity (predominantly beta). However, when he inserted the needle for the first time through his biceps, alpha was present 10% of the time, while during the second trial it was present 60% of the time. He controlled the bleeding and pain by becoming detached: he thought of his arm as an object, not attached to him, and he pushed the needle through it as if it were the arm of a chair.

The EEG recordings of R.C.T., the yogi studied earlier, and Green, et al, indicate that increase in alpha occurred when the subjects felt no pain. If the subject does not respond to external or internal stimuli, such as pain, alpha should not block. These voluntary pain control studies suggest that EEG alpha feedback training may be used as a technique to teach pain control and might be explored for the relief of phantom pain, neuralgia, pre- and post-operative pain and bleeding, and during dentistry.

One of my subjects was trained to keep alpha ON while a pin was inserted through the flesh on the back of his hand. He reported no pain and there was no alpha blocking. Similarly, another subject reported neither pain nor anxiety when she kept alpha ON during dental work without novacain - surprising both herself and her dentist. (3)

Self-control of pain and bleeding seems to occur when a subject allows this to occur and does not respond in an active sense. The process is similar, if not identical, to the way we allow ourselves to balance on a bicycle - one can learn balance; the moment one analyzes and tries to describe it, one loses one's balance. This is similar to the reports of subjects who have learned to control their EEG alpha by feedback, and who have described the sustaining of an alpha rhythm as pleasant, a feeling of passive alertness, absense of looking, boring, and even anesthetic. (4)

Similarly, some yogis claim that during their meditation they are oblivious to their external and internal environment. No alpha blocking occurred during studies of meditation (Samadhi) when the yogis were either touched with a hot glass tube or kept their hands in cold water ($4^{o}$ for 55 min.), although during the baseline, they had showed prominent alpha activity and alpha blocking when stimulated. (5)

Although the subjects used different meditation techniques to attain pain control, there is a similarity. The first S totally dissociated himself from somatic sensations by giving no inward responses and allowing alpha to occur in the EEG. The second S totally focused upon an internal feeling of energy. This reaffirmed the well-known situation in which prolonged attention to something else may diminish or abolish pain perception.

Pain and bleeding were controlled by both methods and each S healed rapidly. They pointed out that most individuals who possess average patience and fortitude can stick pins through their flesh and control their own healing process. This exploratory study reaffirms that it is possible to have self-control over many body functions (6). If we can have self-control over internal states, then we should also have self-control over our own health. The study suggests one possible application of EEG alpha feedback training for pain control, but meditation, karate, autogenic training, hypnosis, etc., may be equally effective.[7]

## References and notes

1. I thank Marjorie Toomim and Hershel Toomim for inviting me to study their subject and the use of their equipment.


2. E.E. Green, A.M. Green, E.D. Walters, A demonstration of voluntary control of bleeding and pain, Research Department, The Menninger Foundation, Topeka, Kansas 66601 (1972).

3. L. Gannon, R.A. Sternbach, Behav. Ther. and Exp. Psych. 2, 209-213 (1971) E. Peper, Developing a biofeedback model: alpha EEG feedback as a means for pain control, in preparation.

4. E. Peper, Kybernetik, 9 (6), 226-231 (1971).

   T.B. Mulholland, E. Peper, Psychophysiology, 8 (5), 556-575, 1971.
   B.B. Brown, Psychophysiology, 7, 451-464, 1971.
   J. Kamiya, Psych. Today, 1, 57-60, 1968.

5. B.K. Anand, G.S. Chhina, B. Singh, Electroenceph. clin. Neurophysiol. 13, 452-456 (1961).

6. Many articles on voluntary control have been reprinted in, Biofeedback and Self-Control, Reader, 1970, 1971, T. Barber, L.V. DiCara, J. Kamiya, L.E. Miller, D. Shapiro, J. Stoyva, Eds. (Aldine-Atherton, Chicago, 1971, 1971, 1972).



7. The author is indebted to Jack Martz, Hershel Toomim, Marjorie Toomim for the opportunity to do these studies and Gay Luce for valuable comments and discussions.

MURPHY, M. & BRODIE, J.

# "I Experience a Kind of Clarity": Two Explorers Fathom the Psychic Unknowns of Football

*John Brodie has played quarterback for the San Francisco 49ers for 16 years. He is second only to John Unitas in the number of yards he has gained passing during his career in the National Football League. In 1970 he was given the Jim Thorpe trophy as the league's most valuable player, the most respected award in professional football. During the 1970 and 1971 seasons he led his team to the championship of the Western Division of the National Football Conference. He is also a championship golfer and played on the professional golf tour for a year.*

*Michael Murphy is president and cofounder of the Esalen Institute in California. He is the author of* Golf in the Kingdom, *a metaphysical sports fantasy that explores what Murphy calls the "hidden side of sport" [ID, April 1972]. In his book he demonstrates the possibility that games often become "theaters of the occult."*

*Brodie and Murphy are now collaborating on a book about football and sport in general that will explore some of the issues the two of them discuss here...*

**Murphy:** There are hundreds of thousands, maybe millions of words written about football. There is a huge amount of talent assembled to describe the game on TV and radio and in sports magazines and newspapers. Supposedly, the best sports writers are analyzing what the game means. Recently, there has been an abrasive and "realistic" approach like Howard Cosell's or in books like Jim Bouton's *Ball Four.* But it seems to me, from my seat on the five-yard line, that there is a lot to the game that has *not* been described by all these talented sportswriters and analysts. All of these people are missing something.

**Brodie:** Many fans feel the way you do. A great many football players do. I certainly do. There is a side to the game that really hasn't been described yet—that "hidden" side of sport you talk about in your book, things having to do with the psychological side of the game, with what we might call "energy flows," and the extraordinary states of mind performing athletes sometimes get into. I've been reluctant to talk to sportswriters about these things because I'm afraid they would reduce them to categories they were more familiar with.

**Murphy:** What are these writers and analysts looking at when they describe football?

**Brodie:** People tend to look at life—and at sport—through their own experience and mental categories. When a person looks at a game of football, he tends to see a reflection of his own life. If it's mainly violence and getting ahead and winning at all costs, he'll tend to see that in the game. Or if life is mainly statistics and numbers and measurements, he'll tend to see that—many people have an incredible interest in football statistics. People look at the game and project their own reality onto it.

**Murphy:** You could say that the two images that dominate our understanding of football now are the Beast and the Computer.

**Brodie:** But many of the players—most of the ones I know—resent those images. They know there is more to the game than that. And I think there are many fans who see past those images and get glimpses of something more.

**Murphy:** Can you give me some examples of the aspects that usually go unrecorded, some examples of the game's psychological side or what you call "energy flows"?

**Brodie:** Often, in the heat and excitement of a game, a player's perception and coordination will improve dramatically. At times, and with increasing frequency now, I experience a kind of clarity that I've never seen adequately described in a football story. Sometimes, for example, time seems to slow way down, in an uncanny way, as if everyone were moving in slow motion. It seems as if I have all the time in the world to watch the receivers run their patterns, and yet I know the defensive line is coming at me just as fast as ever. I know perfectly well how hard and fast those guys are coming and yet the whole thing seems like a movie or a dance in slow motion. It's beautiful.

**Murphy:** What happens to your performance in moments like that? Do you actually see what's happening more clearly?

**Brodie:** Yes. Of course, some of the players on the other team may be in a similar state! Then the game moves up a level.

**Murphy:** Are these things contagious? Sometimes it looks as if a whole team catches fire and starts doing things it couldn't do ordinarily. In the Washington Redskins game last year, something seemed to happen to the 49ers in the third quarter after you threw that touchdown pass to Gene Washington.

**Brodie:** We had to *make* something happen then. That's why I went with that play. With third down and one yard to go on your own 22-yard line in a close game—and a playoff game, which leaves you with no second chances—you wouldn't usually go with the particular call I made. After I came to the line of scrimmage and started my snap count, I saw the defense shift into a position that might not happen in the game again. I gave the team a basic pass audible and gave Gene a little signal we had worked out, faded back and threw him that pass. When I threw it I *knew* it was going to connect.

**Murphy:** When the play began it looked for a moment like the safety would make an interception. But then it seemed as if the ball went through or over his hands as he came in front of Washington.

**Brodie:** Pat Fischer, the cornerback, told the reporters after the game that the ball seemed to jump right over his hands as he went for it. When we studied the game films that week, it *did* look as if the ball kind of jumped over his hands into Gene's. Some of the guys said it was the wind—and maybe it was.

**Murphy:** What do you mean by *maybe*?

**Brodie:** What I mean is that our sense of that pass was so clear and our *intention* so strong that the ball was bound to get there, come wind, cornerbacks, hell or high water.

**Murphy:** In *Golf in the Kingdom* I discuss the "energy streamers" that a golf ball rides on its way toward the hole. I mean those lines of force that seem to emanate from the golfer when he can visualize and execute his shot in a moment of high clarity. Is that the kind of thing you are talking about? I know there are golfers who have had the experience.

**Brodie:** I would have to say that such things seem to exist—or emerge when your state of mind is right. It has happened to me dozens of times. An intention carries a force, a thought is connected with an energy that can stretch itself out in a pass play or a golf shot or a base hit or during a 30-foot jump shot in basketball. I've seen it happen too many times to deny it.

**Murphy:** Is this something you can practice or develop? Can you learn to develop clarity during a game? Can you strengthen your intentions?

**Brodie:** Yes. Pressures that used to get me down don't affect me to the same extent now. I've learned to shed certain destructive attitudes when a game is under way. A player's effectiveness is directly related to his ability to be right there, doing that thing, in the moment. All the preparation he may have put into the game—all the game plans, analysis of movies, etc.—is no good if he can't put it into action when game time comes. He can't be worrying about the past or the future or the crowd or some other extraneous event. He must be able to respond in the here and now. This is an ability we all have potentially. I believe it is our natural state. But because most of us lose it as we grow up, we have to regain it.

**Murphy:** This sounds very much like Zen or other spiritual disciplines. It seems to me that in many ways sport is like a Western Yoga. I have heard mountain climbers, surfers, sky divers and skiers who talk a language that is almost mystical, and now I hear you talking the same way.

**Brodie:** Call it mystical if you like. For me it is simply one of the elementary facts of experience. Here-and-now awareness, clarity, strong intention, a person's "tone level"—these are things a lot of people who don't know anything about Yoga or mysticism talk about. The trouble is, people don't make them operative in their life as often as they could.

**Murphy:** But some of the things you seem to suggest, like a ball jumping over a defender's hands or time slowing down, go beyond ordinary experience. In the East, and in our Western religious traditions, there have been disciplines to develop these extraordinary powers and states of mind. But the modern Western world, for the most part, is lacking in such disciplines. They seem esoteric and alien to most of us. Maybe that is one of the reasons sportswriters and sports commentators find it difficult to comprehend the kinds of things you are talking about.

**Brodie:** Not only reporters find it difficult, but oftentimes coaches do too. If a player begins to develop methods for tuning in to these deeper levels, many coaches are likely to criticize or disregard them. A player often has to be big enough to transcend his coaches' limitations. But then a coach has to deal with the team's owners and even with the fans and the media to some extent. The whole system works to build up certain attitudes about the way in which a team should be run. Take the computer for example: the way some teams worship it in the selection of their players and the creation of their game plans, you would think it was God. But computer-made game plans often lead a team away from the game itself. A team with a fixed game plan can be a brittle team, if it can't relate to the here and now of a game. The computer *can* be a helpful tool, as long as you don't expect too much from it. The same thing is true for certain programs of physical exercise: exceptions have to be made for the experienced athlete who has discovered training methods suited to his own makeup. A good coach will let him use those methods, even if they deviate from the fixed procedures the coaching staff has set up.

**Murphy:** One of the problems coaches and players have—and it's a problem all of us have in talking about these things—is that our language about unusual powers and states of mind is so limited. We don't have commonly understood words to describe "energy flows" or what you call "being clear." These expressions don't make sense to a lot of people. I think the time has come to begin creating a language and an understanding about these dimensions of life.

**Brodie:** Athletics could be a place

where this kind of insight is developed. Sport is one of the few activities in which many Americans spend a great deal of time developing their potentialities. It influences character, I think, as much as our schools and churches do. But, even so, it falls far below what it could be. It leaves out so much. I would love to see a sports team developed with a more fulfilling purpose.

One place in which you see the principle of self-knowledge work most clearly is with injuries. Two years ago I had a problem with my arm; I couldn't lift it above my shoulder—which is not good for a quarterback. Dealing with that sore arm led me into a process of self-discovery. Getting well meant *more* than getting the soreness out of my shoulder. I found out that my arm's condition was related to a very limited notion I had about myself and life. It wasn't enough anymore to simply play a better game of football. I had to change the way I perceived the world, the way I thought and felt, and the way I treated others. Life was a larger and more interesting affair than I had ever dreamed.

**Murphy:** Why do you still play football? Sixteen years is a long time.

**Brodie:** I play because I enjoy the game. After 16 years there is still an enormous satisfaction in it.

**Murphy:** And yet so many people see football only in terms of winning at any cost, knocking the hell out of the other guy. Is that the only reason you enjoy the game?

**Brodie:** No. It's important to win—there's nothing quite like it. It's important to go all out during a game. But there is a lot more to football than that. Involving yourself wholeheartedly, in the way we have been discussing, is a satisfaction in itself.

**Murphy:** I get the idea that you and Gene Washington have a special kind of communication when a game is under way. Can you say anything about that?

**Brodie:** Well, we room together, and we are good friends. We've worked out a series of signals that can change even after I've begun my snap count. But most of all, I guess, is that we read each other so well. He knows where I want him to be on a given pass play. Sometimes he will run a set pattern, but at other times he has to get to a place in the field any way he can.

**Murphy:** Could that place be marked with a set of coordinates, say at a particular yard line? Or is it better to say that you meet somewhere in the field of existence, in the field of your relationship, amidst all the flux on the playing field?

**Brodie:** I think the more poetic way says it better—it's a highly intuitive thing. Sometimes we call a pass for a particular spot on the field, maybe to get a first down. But at other times it's less defined than that and depends upon the communication we have. Sometimes I let the ball fly before Gene has made his final move, *without* a pass route being set exactly. That's where the intuition and the communication come in. But then we don't know what the other team, what those cornerbacks and safety men, might do next. That's part of the fun of the game, not knowing what they are going to do. The game *never stops.* You can never really take anything for granted—at least in most games in the NFL. And that's what's wrong with game plans so often—because you don't know where those guys are going to be a second before something happens. You have to be ready for the sudden glimmer.

**Murphy:** Do you ever get the idea after one of these incredible pass completions that there was some destiny to the play, something more than skill involved? To me, as a slightly lunatic fan, there are times when it seems as if the script for a game has been written by God himself—or that it springs from someplace in the collective unconscious.

**Brodie:** I know the feeling, but I don't know that we should call that kind of explanation an objective fact.

**Murphy:** But isn't there a kind of communication, a kind of artistry, a kind of Being, if you will, that emerges during an inspired game? Something that isn't measured by grids or coordinates or statistics? Doesn't bringing forth this kind of quality depend upon something that one is not ordinarily aware of?

**Brodie:** Yes, that's a good way to say it. I was reading a statement by Alan Page [defensive tackle for the Minnesota Vikings, the NFL's most valuable player for 1971] the other day in which he described the comedown when a game is over. He said it was a weird feeling adjusting back to reality, to sanity—having to be a person again. I understand that feeling. Life can feel like a box after a game. You can get into another order of reality when you're playing, a reality that doesn't fit into the grids and coordinates that most people lay across life—including the categories coaches, fans and sportswriters lay on the game.

**Murphy:** When you are in a state like that you must be tuned in to an incredible number of energies and patterns, to all those players on both teams, to the crowd. In fact, when you begin your first offensive sequence, you seem to be deliberately tuning in to all of this. I sometimes get the sense that you are probing the situation before you work out your plan of attack. Are those opening minutes a time when you are learning what a game is going to be like?

**Brodie:** Yes, we are tuning into the situation. And centering ourselves, dropping the nervousness, getting the feel of the game. We may have to drop useless emotional buildup and other distractions.

**Murphy:** So you are saying you have to be both focused and sensitive. An effective quarterback has to have his radar working.

**Brodie:** I equate creativity with awareness. It's a matter of simple knowledge. The more I know, the more I can do.

**Murphy:** But knowing like this is more than the kind of knowing we are supposed to learn in school, more than verbal knowing or book knowing. It involves a tuning in to subtle energies and feelings and forces we can only come to through direct awareness. It involves the emotions and the spirit as well as the intellect—and the here and now, the complexities and subtleties of a given situation rather than preconceptions about it, or your rehearsals of it or what has been written in a book about it. It seems to me that this sort of knowing leads to a new kind of being.

**Brodie:** You might say that. Football players and athletes generally get into this kind of being or beingness—call it what you will—more often than is generally recognized. But they often lose it after a game or after a season is over. They often don't have a workable philosophy or understanding to support the kind of thing they get into while they are playing. They don't have the words for it. So after a game you see some of them coming down, making fools of themselves sometimes, coming way down in their tone level. But during the game they come way up. A missing ingredient for many people, I guess, is that they don't have a supporting philosophy or discipline for a better life.

**Murphy:** After hearing you talk I gather that top athletes are people who are accustomed to altering time, who are accustomed to a higher state of focus and concentration, who are accustomed to altered perceptions of many types and to going with the inner flow of things. But I don't see any of this on the sport pages. Or in the sport books you hear about, or on the radio and TV programs. Our culture seems to screen it all out, even though such experience is at the very heart of a game so many of us love.

**Brodie:** That's right. It's a case of experience being ahead of what we can say about it. Maybe if we could talk about it more clearly we could make it happen more. Sport is so important in creating values in America, it would be great if it could open up these inner dimensions for people. It's really what many coaches and players want to do, after all. They want sport to be more than winning at any cost, more than beating people up and making money and getting ahead over somebody else's dead body. But we have got to break out of this conspiracy to belittle sport and human nature.

**Murphy:** Some critics of the game would say that its violence destroys the very things you hope for.

**Brodie:** Violence is not the game's basic intention, even though some people think it is. The idea is not to hurt or damage somebody. But there is an intensity and a danger in football—as in life generally—which keep us alive and awake. It is a test of our awareness and ability. Like so much of life, it presents us with the choice of responding either with fear or with action and clarity.

**Murphy:** I have heard some people say that all of this talk about "higher possibilities" and building character is fine, but that you don't need football to do it, that the game is a poor instrument in fact for accomplishing these things.

**Brodie:** But that wouldn't stop us from playing or enjoying football. It is better to improve the game, I think, than to indulge in a lot of idle criticism of it. And when you look at its history you see that it has already gone through enormous changes. It is a much different game than it was in the 1920s or 30s. It's a more complex and artistic game now, with all the offensive and defensive plays, with the game plans and the variety of skills involved. Why shouldn't the game go on changing? I see no reason why we should fix the game of football where it is, after the change it has gone through already. Why shouldn't it be a place to develop the mental and spiritual dimensions we have been talking about?

40

**BURR, H. S.**

# *An Adventure in Science*

1

We live in troubled and difficult times. There are wars and dangers of war. In many parts of the world there are revolts, protests, crime and lawlessness in ceaseless eruption. And over this age hangs the Sword of Damocles of possible nuclear destruction.

More and more people ask themselves despondently whether life has any sense or purpose. Many are tempted to believe that man is an accident, left to grapple with his lonely fate on an insignificant planet in a harsh and lawless Universe.

In a materialistic, scientific age many find it hard to accept those religious beliefs that sustained their forefathers in times which—to them—seemed as troubled and perilous as the present. They would like to believe that man is no accident and that the Universe in which he lives is one of law, order and purpose. But, dazzled by the methods and triumphs of science, they are unwilling to take anything on trust; they demand some 'scientific' proof or evidence.

Until some forty years ago this demand could not be met because the necessary electronic instruments and techniques had not been developed. When these became available, however, an entirely new approach to the nature of man and his place in the Universe became possible. For these instruments revealed that man

—and, in fact, *all* forms—are ordered and controlled by electro-dynamic fields which can be measured and mapped with precision.

Though almost inconceivably complicated, the 'fields of life' are of the same nature as the simpler fields known to modern physics and obedient to the same laws. Like the fields of physics, they are a part of the organization of the Universe and are influenced by the vast forces of space. Like the fields of physics, too, they have organizing and directing qualities which have been revealed by many thousands of experiments.

Organization and direction, the direct opposite of chance, imply purpose. So the fields of life offer purely electronic, instrumental evidence that man is no accident. On the contrary, he is an integral part of the Cosmos, embedded in its all-powerful fields, subject to its inflexible laws and a participant in the destiny and purpose of the Universe.

This book is an account of the adventure in science —of the long, step-by-step exploration—that wrested from Nature the answer to the question which so many in these times are asking so anxiously:

## 2

Electro-dynamic fields are invisible and intangible, and it is hard to visualize them. But a crude analogy may help to show what the fields of life—L-fields for short—do and why they are so important:

Most people who have taken high-school science will remember that if iron-filings are scattered on a card held over a magnet they will arrange themselves in the pattern of the 'lines of force' of the magnet's field. And if the filings are thrown away and fresh ones scattered on the card, the new filings will assume the same pattern as the old.

Something like this—though infinitely more complicated—happens in the human body. Its molecules and cells are constantly being torn apart and rebuilt with fresh material from the food we eat. But, thanks to the controlling L-field, the new molecules and cells are rebuilt as before and arrange themselves in the same pattern as the old ones.

Modern research with 'tagged' elements has revealed that the materials of our bodies and brains are renewed much more often than was previously realized. All the protein in the body, for example, is 'turned over' every six months and, in some organs such as the liver, the protein is renewed more frequently. When we meet a friend we have not seen for six months there is not one molecule in his face which was there when we last saw him. But, thanks to his controlling L-field, the new molecules have fallen into the old, familiar pattern and we can recognize his face.

Until modern instruments revealed the existence of the controlling L-fields, biologists were at a loss to explain how our bodies 'keep in shape' through ceaseless metabolism and changes of material. Now the mystery has been solved, the electro-dynamic field of the body serves as a matrix or mould, which preserves the 'shape' or arrangement of any material poured into it, however often the material may be changed.

When a cook looks at a jelly-mould she knows the shape of the jelly she will turn out of it. In much the same way, inspection with instruments of an L-field in its initial stage can reveal the future 'shape' or arrangement of the materials it will mould. When the L-field in a frog's egg, for instance, is examined electrically it is possible to show the future location of the frog's nervous system because the frog's L-field is the matrix which will determine the form which will develop from the egg. (See page 61.)

Inspection of L-fields is done with special voltmeters and electrodes—to be described shortly—which reveal different patterns or gradients of voltages in different parts of the L-field.

To return to the cook, when she uses a battered mould she expects to find some dents or bulges in the jelly. Similarly, a 'battered' L-field—that is, one with abnormal voltage-patterns—can give warning of something 'out of shape' in the body, sometimes in advance of actual symptoms.

For example, malignancy in the ovary has been revealed by L-field measurements before any clinical sign could be observed. Such measurements, therefore, could help doctors to detect cancer early, when there is a better chance of treating it successfully. (See page 54 and Dr. Langman's paper in Part II.)

Nature keeps an infinite variety of electro-dynamic 'jelly-moulds' on her shelves with which she shapes the countless different forms of life that exist on this planet. L-fields have been detected and measured not only in men and women but also in animals, trees, plants, seeds, eggs and even in one of the lowest forms of life, slime-moulds.

Of these L-fields, those of trees can tell something that others cannot because trees do not move about, live to a great age and can be hitched up to recording instruments for long periods of time. For many years a maple tree in New Haven and an elm in Old Lyme were continuously connected to recording voltmeters—something which, obviously, cannot be done with men and women.

These long records showed that the L-fields of trees vary not only with sunlight and darkness but also with the cycles of the moon, with magnetic storms and with sunspots. (See page 97 and Mr. Markson's paper in Part II.)

If such extra-terrestrial forces can influence the relatively-simple L-fields of trees we would expect them to have an even greater influence on the more complex

L-fields of men and women; and there is evidence that they do.

These sturdy Connecticut trees, then, have helped to answer the question which philosophers have disputed for centuries and which many ask so anxiously today. For they have shown that life on this planet is not isolated from the Universe but a part of it—susceptible to those irresistible forces that exert their influence across the vast distances of space.

## 3

L-fields are detected and examined by measuring the difference in voltage between two points on—or close to—the surface of the living form. In men and women L-field voltages can be measured by placing one electrode on the forehead and the other on the chest or the hand. Alternatively, the index finger of each hand is dipped into bowls of saline solution connected to the voltmeter. In special cases voltage readings may be taken by applying the electrodes to some specific organ or part of the body.

In trees, the electrodes are in contact through salt bridges with the cambium layer, one about two feet above the other.

These voltage measurements have nothing to do with the alternating electrical currents which doctors find in the heart and the brain. They are pure voltage *potentials* which can yield only an infinitesimal amount of *direct* current. That is why L-fields could not be detected before the invention of the vacuum-tube voltmeter, which requires virtually no current for its operation. An ordinary voltmeter needs so much current to swing the needle that it would drain away the L-field potentials and make any reading useless if not impossible.

When Sir John Fleming, an Englishman, discovered that electrons flow from a heated wire in a vacuum and Lee DeForest, an American, found out how to use them with a grid, it is unlikely that either of them ever imagined that the vacuum tube which resulted from their discoveries would one day make possible a new approach to the mystery of life. And it was many years before the vacuum tube had been sufficiently perfected to make the vacuum-tube voltmeter a reliable instrument.

In the early days of his researches, some forty years ago, the author spent three years developing his own instruments. Today highly sensitive and reliable vacuum-tube voltmeters are available commercially and are to be found in most physics laboratories and electronic factories.

There is nothing mysterious, then, about the instruments required to measure L-field voltages. But these are harder to measure than those of a car or transistor-radio battery. Special electrodes must be used and the methods outlined in Chapter 2 must be followed rigidly and explicitly for successful results. But it will be no more difficult to train doctors and their assistants to read and interpret L-field voltages than it was to train them to use electro-cardiographs or electro-encephalographs.

Extensive medical use of L-field readings, however, may not be seen for some time. For it took over thirty years before electro-cardiograph techniques were perfected to the point where they were useful in doctors' offices.

## 4

In the case of L-fields there is no technical reason why their use by doctors should take so long. Modern instruments are reliable; and any intelligent man or woman can learn the techniques of taking and interpreting L-field readings in a short period of intensive instruction. It is to be hoped that many will do so because L-fields can be helpful to doctors, psychiatrists and others in various ways.

Immediate and practical results, in fact, can stem from this adventure in science—quite apart from the assurance that human life has purpose and that man is not isolated from the Universe—which have made the adventure even more worthwhile.

As mentioned earlier, abnormalities in L-field voltages can give advance warning of future symptoms before these are evident. This does not apply only to the early detection of cancer. As more research is done and L-fields are better understood, it is probable that they will be used to give early warning of a variety of physical problems in time to tackle these effectively. And they have already been used to forecast certain psychological and psychiatric troubles. (See page 18 and Dr. Ravitz' paper in Part II.)

Among the physical events which can be predicted by measuring the voltage-gradients is the precise moment of ovulation in a woman. This is possible because ovulation is preceded by a steady and substantial rise in voltage, which falls rapidly to normal after the egg has been released.

Such measurements have revealed that some women may ovulate over the entire menstrual period, that ovulation may occur without menstruation and menses without ovulation. The potential importance of this knowledge to gynaecology, family-planning and birth-control is obvious; and it helps to explain why the 'rhythm method' of birth-control is inadequate.

A patient of the author's, a married woman, made good use of her L-field. For years she and her husband had longed in vain to have children. So, over a period of weeks, she made regular visits to the author's office and herself measured the voltages in her own L-field by dipping her fingers into bowls of solution connected to a voltmeter. When, one day, she saw her voltages rising rapidly, she knew that ovulation was imminent and went to her husband. A longed-for child was the result.

Wounds—even a small cut on the finger—will change the voltages in the L-field and, as the wound heals, these will return to normal. This offers surgeons a simple, reliable way to measure the rate of healing, which will be specially useful with internal wounds from operations. (See page 82.)

L-field measurements are not only useful in diagnosing local conditions; they can also be used to assess the general state of the body as a whole. For these pure voltage-differences—independent of any current flow or changes in skin-resistance—reveal the state of the whole human force-field. Such conditions, then, as ovulation or malignancy can be detected by measuring changes in the L-field of the body *at a distance from the affected organs*. And, as the force-field extends beyond the surface of the skin, it is sometimes possible to measure field-voltages with the electrodes a short distance from the surface of the skin—*not* in contact with it. *This shows that it is a true field that is measured and not some surface potential.*

*This, too, is additional evidence that L-fields have the same qualities as the simpler fields of physics because they can produce an effect across a space or gap, without any visible intervening means.*

Since L-fields reveal the state of the body as a whole they can be used to assess the general effects of drugs, sleep or hypnosis. Dr. Leonard R. Ravitz, Jr., has not only measured the depth of hypnosis with a voltmeter but has also found that strong emotions recalled during hypnosis can cause a voltage-rise of as much as from 15 to 20 millivolts. (See page 87 and Dr. Ravitz' paper in Part II.)

This suggests the fascinating possibility that psychiatrists of the future will be able to measure the intensity of grief, anger or love electrically—and as easily as we measure temperature or noise-levels today. 'Heartbreak', hate, or love, in other words, may one day be measurable in millivolts.

Good doctors have always known how important it is to consider the patient as a whole—to take into account his mental or emotional state as well as his physical symptoms—because many human ills have a 'psychosomatic' cause. Business worries or an unhappy marriage are often the real cause of, say, headaches or ulcers. Since L-field voltages reveal both physical and mental conditions they can offer doctors a new insight into the state of both body and mind.

When the effects on the human L-field of extraterrestrial forces are established and understood, this knowledge will be important in the study not only of human health and behaviour but also of medical problems which may arise in long space explorations. The fields of space may have unforseen effects on the L-fields of astronauts if they are exposed to them for long periods.

## 5

This adventure in science promises still further 'dividends' in the form of a better understanding of the human mind.

Dr. Ravitz has discovered that the voltages of the L-fields of healthy people are not constant but vary in steady rhythms over periods of weeks—whatever the cause may be. From plotting over 50,000 measurements on 500 human subjects he has found that these rhythms show how the subjects feel. When they feel 'on top of the world' their voltages are high; when they feel 'below par' their voltages are low.

For healthy, normal people these voltage rhythms can be plotted as steady regular curves which alter little over long periods. From these curves, then, it is *possible to predict in advance* when the individual will be at his best and when he will be feeling 'below par'.

This knowledge could be of vital importance to those engaged in hazardous duties, especially in the Armed Forces. If commanding officers had advance knowledge of the 'low' periods of, say, combat pilots, they could try to avoid sending them on dangerous missions at times when their alertness and efficiency would be reduced. If operational necessity made that impossible, at least this knowledge might warn the men to use special vigilance and care.

Intelligently used, warnings offered by the state of the L-fields could save valuable lives and equipment not only in the Armed Forces but also in dangerous industrial occupations.

With emotionally-unstable people the voltage variations cannot be plotted as steady regular curves. They display an erratic pattern which, in many cases, can be detected within a few days. By purely objective, electronic means, therefore, it will be possible for the Armed Forces quickly to detect and weed out emotionally-unstable personnel before time and money are spent on training them for duties for which they are not fitted.

Similarly, industry will be able not only to avoid hiring personnel who might 'crack' under responsibility but also to find those best qualified to assume greater responsibilities.

Since L-field voltages reflect mental and emotional states they can also be useful in the handling of mental patients because they offer doctors an objective measurement of progress. Thus they can help to prevent the release of patients who might be a danger to the public; they can also help doctors to decide when it is safe to release others—with a great saving of hospital space and taxpayers' money.

Voltage measurements used in this kind of psychological testing are completely impersonal and reproducible. There is no need to question the patient; the technician who takes the readings need not open his mouth.

In the medical laboratories of the future, it is probable that trained technicians will take the voltage-readings and then submit these to a doctor qualified to interpret them, in much the same way as technicians take X-ray photographs and submit them to a radiologist. 'Voltage-interpreters', however, need not be as specialized as radiologists; and many doctors in the future will be their own interpreters.

## 6

Since L-fields have been found in all living forms examined so far, their potential usefulness is not limited to medical diagnosis.

In measuring the L-fields of plants, for instance, it has been found that the change of a single gene in the parent stock produces profound changes in the voltage-pattern. This phenomenon could be of great importance in the study of genetics in plants and in animals. (See page 70.)

By measuring the L-fields of seeds it is possible to predict how strong and healthy the future plants will be. To have advance knowledge of the future vitality of living forms could be useful in many fields. (See page 71.)

Since the fields of life are dominant and control the growth and development of all living forms, medical science may one day find ways directly to treat the health of the patient electrically before the onset of physical symptoms.

Agricultural scientists of the future may, perhaps, find ways to stimulate the growth of crops electrically and to eliminate defects in their L-fields which render them prone to pests or diseases. It has long been known not only that sunlight—a form of electro-magnetic radiation—is essential to the growth of most plant life but also that different species require different 'dosages' of sunlight. It is known, too, that certain frequencies or colours of light are beneficial in specific cases. It may one day be discovered, then, that other and invisible electro-magnetic frequencies have beneficial effects on the L-fields of plants.

Since animals and plants possess—and are controlled by—their characteristic L-fields, like man they are an integral part of the Universe and subject to its laws. So the human race and the animal and vegetable kingdoms are component parts of the same whole. You and I, our pets, our trees and our plants are all subject to the same universal laws.

This is borne out by the mutual interdependence of species. Plants depend for their existence on sunlight—an extra-terrestrial force; plants nourish man and animals; animals feed on each other. So when we remember that we should starve without sunlight from some ninety-three million miles away, it is not hard to accept that we are subject to the other great forces of space.

# 41

## KRIPPNER, S. (ED.)

# *The Plateau Experience: A. H. Maslow and Others*

*A. H. Maslow:* There are two matters to bring up. One of them is something I'm interested in, and the other is something I have less interest in, but would like to bring up anyway. The second matter concerns a preface to a new edition of a little book that I did some time ago called *Religions, Values, and Peak-Experiences*. In it, I make various warnings about misinterpretations of my thesis. In the first edition of the book I had warned about the dangers in overemphasizing the legalistic, organizational, institutional, and traditional aspects of religion. In the preface to the new edition, I speak of the dangers of overemphasizing the mystical aspects of religion; some people run the danger of turning away from the world and from other people to search for anything that will trigger peak experiences. This type of person represents the mystic gone wild.

*two kinds of religious overemphasis*

To this preface, I added a footnote in which I speak about astrology, the *I Ching*, numerology, Tarot cards, and fortune-telling, which—so far as I know—have no empirical support at all. In the footnote, I use these approaches to illustrate the point I make that a person with a truly scientific attitude can even be open—although skeptical—regarding them. I have never examined any of these, my attitude being one of benevolent disinterest. But I do have friends I respect who do take these things seriously.

*Maslow's attitude toward the occult*

What I say to my friends and my readers in the footnote is not that these things are necessarily wrong or false, but that I just don't know about them because there is no evidence. I also ask them, if they have the hunch that there is something to numerology, Tarot cards, etc., why don't they put it to the test?

However, I began to reconsider this footnote during our conversation this morning when Stan Krippner mentioned that there were personal experiences involving the *I Ching* which had not been published. I would hold that some of these experiences, if written down and verified, might be part of the literature of science. You see, my conception of evidence is very inclusive. I write about "degrees of knowledge," and would say that one person whom I trusted, telling me that he has had an unusual private experience, would constitute evidence for me. True, it is a little teeny bit of evidence; even so, it is above zero. In these instances, I would not insist on the experimental model with all the usual controls.

*"degrees of knowledge"*

So what I am asking you is whether or not I should include this footnote in my book. Is there any evidence, even in the realm of private experience, to support the claims of astrology and these other approaches? If some evidence does exist, I am not justified in stating that these approaches have no empirical support at all.

*James Fadiman:* There was a recent study which eliminated my disbelief in astrology. It was done with Stanford University freshmen, using Strong Vocational Interest Blank data. There were significant correlations among certain astrological signs and certain vocational interest scales. As for some of the other areas Abe mentioned, I have had a number of personal experiences I have found to be convincing.

*a study in astrology*

*Maslow:* I would take some of these personal testimonials rather seriously.

*Charles T. Tart:* There is another type of evidence that should be mentioned, and that is the laboratory work on extrasensory perception or ESP. Sometimes people seem to receive information through channels totally unknown to us at the present time. The evidence for ESP is overwhelming.

*evidence for ESP*

*Maslow:* I agree with you and wasn't even talking about laboratory ESP in my footnote.

*Fadiman:* This is an important distinction because there is something unique about astrology and palmistry that isn't accounted for by the assumption of ESP phenomena. You could explain the astrology experiment by claiming that ESP influenced the experimenters to select just the right Stanford students so that their vocational interest scores would correlate with the astrological signs. But the data seem to go beyond that possibility.

*Maslow:* Stan, are there other examples of this type of research?

*Stanley Krippner:* There is some evidence from a study dealing with several thousand people over two generations. Jonas, a European investigator, found that the ability of a woman to conceive tends to occur under exactly that phase of the moon which prevailed when she was born. Furthermore, the time of a woman's maximum fertility in each lunar month was at the point at which the moon reached exactly the same relationship with the sun, in degrees and minutes, as it had at the time of her own birth. Jonas noted that the two days previous to this point would be the times when sexual intercourse would be most likely to result in conception. He has applied his data to the areas of birth control, selection of the unborn child's sex, and the prevention of birth defects.

*fertility and astrology*

*Tart:* There are also the studies people have made of the relationship between months of the year in which people have been born and the eminence they attain. There appear to be certain months of the year that are more closely related to future eminence than others. Presumably this involves being carried in the womb during that time of the year when the mother is most likely to be in good health.

*correlations of eminence and dates of birth*

*Krippner:* A French husband and wife team, Michel and François Gauquelin, reported a relationship between 576 members of the French Academy of Medicine and their dates of birth. In another study of 25,000 professional workers, they found statistically significant results when they compared types of profession to the "rising" and "culminating" position of the moon and certain planets. For example, there was a significant association between the births of writers and politicians after the "rise" and "culmination" of the moon. They suspect that there is some force produced by the moon or planet which affects the embryo.

*other correlations*

*Tart:* There is a very interesting book on environmental influences, although nobody reads it any more. It is *Main-*

*springs of Civilization* by Ellsworth Huntington and has an especially worthwhile section on ionization of the air.

*Andrew Weil:* I think that all of these influences from the environment might tie in with astrology. Has anybody here read the book by Goodavage called *Astrology: The Space Age Science?*

*Krippner:* Yes, I have.

*prediction of solar flares*

*Weil:* Goodavage claims that RCA uses astrology to predict solar flares. It has something to do with the position of the center of gravity of our solar system. For example, when Mercury, being close to the center of gravity, moves toward the sun's surface, there are quite often huge flares. Robert Becker, in the Veterans Administration Hospital at Syracuse, became interested in this and began to study the relationship between the body's electric potentials and illness. He found that the voltages from head to toe change as a person gets ill. He later discovered that small voltage changes impressed on a person would change that person's mood. This got him to thinking that there might be a relationship between solar flares and the rates of admittance into mental hospitals. He checked this out at several New York hospitals and found a striking association between the two events.

*solar flares and hospitalization*

*Maslow:* All of these data indicate that man is a part of his environment—which I think is more miraculous than the astrological system.

*Krippner:* This is the point of view taken by Michel Gauquelin in his book *The Cosmic Clocks,* in which he takes a skeptical point of view on astrology as it is traditionally conceived. However, Gauquelin does present evidence that man is related to what happens in his environment, even to events on the sun, the moon, and the planets.

*phenomena and alternative explanatory systems*

*Maslow:* Could I suggest something? Some of us have learned the hard way that there is no necessary relationship between phenomena and systems which try to explain the phenomena. For example, I have no doubt that ESP exists and I have read about 42 different attempts to explain it. All 42 systems look equally good, or equally lousy. As for astrology, it's quite conceivable that these relationships occur because there are more negative ions or sun spots or whatever, when somebody is born in April than when someone else is born in May. In the meantime, the world is being flooded with crap about astrology, Tarot cards, and the rest of this stuff.

It's certainly 99 percent crap, if not more. If you are interested in it, then I would like to make a suggestion. Why don't you do some research on it?

*Weil:* I think that is a very basic question. I believe in astrology and in Tarot, but have no intention of doing research on them. And I want to tell you why. I think there is a basic difference in outlook as to whether you require proof in advance of believing in something or whether you believe in something because you rely on your own intuition and on personal evidence. Now I'll give you a personal testimonial. I am a very profound skeptic and I also rely entirely on private experience. The fact that a scientific journal has printed an article about what astrological predictions were confirmed on Stanford students is a low quality of evidence for me. If the predictions were confirmed or were not confirmed, it would not make much difference to me in terms of my own interest in astrology. The way that I became interested in these things was with the Tarot cards. Tarot is a system of organizing one's experiences. Since the Tarot was based on astrology, I began to take an interest in astrology. In the past two years, I have found that my experiences have been sorting themselves out along the lines suggested by Tarot and astrology. In my day-to-day life, I'm able to make more sense of phenomena that I encounter than I ever did before. With Tarot, I've been able to make more deductions and inferences about human health and disease—and to test and confirm them in everyday experience—than according to any system I was ever given in my formal medical training.

*Weil's reliance on personal experience*

This is what has happened in every field that I've looked into, when I've systematized the field according to the arrangements given in Tarot. These systems have two very important aspects, the exoteric and the esoteric. Exoteric astrology means very little as it is mechanistic and is concerned with the external connections between the signs and the personality. However, most of what one sees in the media is basically exoteric astrology. I use esoteric astrology as a system because it is internally consistent, it's available to anyone, and it includes the infinite. Any system which meets these criteria can be used as a system for organizing most of our perceptions. Tarot is a similar system that is internally consistent, highly ordered, interesting, and beautiful. It explains the meaning of every incident. In other words, it works. These systems work better than any other system that I've seen. So that's my personal testimony.

*exoteric and esoteric aspects of astrology*

*Maslow:* And you're not interested in research?

*Weil:* I'm not interested in research. I don't need to be convinced. I'm aware now that these systems are right, that they work, and that any research I do would confirm them.

*Maslow:* You know, if we had a transcript of this conversation, and if I changed the words from "Tarot cards" to "Roman Catholicism," you wouldn't have had to change another word. In the meantime, it is apparent that we have our own ways of organizing material.

*Weil:* We should always be on the lookout for better ways of organizing reality.

*comments on traditional and new models of science*

*Maslow:* Yes, that is true. But in the meantime, our discussion demonstrates how the traditional model of science irritates some people. During the last few days, I've heard science being attacked—and that makes me bristle a little bit. The science that has been attacked is crappy science, but there's a whole new model of science which is available. I would certainly urge you to read Michael Polanyi's *Personal Knowledge.*

*a major lack in traditional science*

*Fadiman:* One problem with science and one reason that people who look beyond science are suspicious of it is that it has not very well taken account of the infinite. Therefore, it's inherently less of a system than some of these other systems.

*Maslow:* But science is beginning to do that.

*Krippner:* How does our discussion affect your footnote for the book?

*aging process and peak experiences*

*Maslow:* Well, I am still skeptical about astrology and these other things, but I am neutral, so I won't make any attack on them. I'll probably drop the footnote. At the beginning of our discussion, I said that there were two matters I wanted to talk about. One of these was my footnote. The other is the experience of transcendence. I found that as I got older, my peak experiences became less intense and also became less frequent. In discussing this matter with other people who are getting older, I received this same sort of reaction. My impression is that this may have to do with the aging process. It makes sense because to some extent, I've learned that I've become somewhat afraid of peak experiences because I wonder if my body can stand them. A peak experience can produce great turmoil in the autonomic nervous system; it may be that a decrease in peak experiences is nature's way of protecting the body.

Also, I've discovered that there is a difference between me and other people who are growing older. For me, part of the loss of peak experiences was the loss of newness and novelty. Last night, we were listening to music. When I discovered music, I had kind of a love affair with each new piece and I could remember them very vividly. I had that experience the first time I heard Stravinsky's "Firebird," for example. You know, it's like the first kiss, the first sexual experience, the first writing of poetry, or something like that. What's happened to me now is that the whole standard repertory is gone. I mean, I don't get the shaking and the tears any more. I can get great pleasure only from music that I haven't heard too often. By now, I've heard the standard repertory six million times. I am not a professional musician, but I have been told by professionals that a peak can continue, that you can get the same pleasures from an old war horse like Beethoven's "Fifth Symphony" over and over again. Perhaps a professional musician can do this, but I can't. So there is a difference between people in this regard.

*loss of newness and novelty*

*possible individual differences*

As these poignant and emotional discharges died down in me, something else happened which has come into my consciousness which is a very precious thing. A sort of precipitation occurred of what might be called the sedimentation or the fallout from illuminations, insights, and other life experiences that were very important—tragic experiences included. The result has been a kind of unitive consciousness which has certain advantages and certain disadvantages over the peak experiences. I can define this unitive consciousness very simply for me as the simultaneous perception of the sacred and the ordinary, or the miraculous and the ordinary, or the miraculous and the rather constant or easy-without-effort sort of thing.

*a definition of unitive consciousness: simultaneous perception of miraculous and ordinary*

I now perceive under the aspect of eternity and become mythic, poetic, and symbolic about ordinary things. This is the Zen experience, you know. There is nothing excepted and nothing special, but one lives in a world of miracles all the time. There is a paradox because it is miraculous and yet it doesn't produce an autonomic burst.

This type of consciousness has certain elements in common with peak experience—awe, mystery, surprise, and esthetic shock. These elements are present, but are constant rather than climactic. It certainly is a temptation to use as kind of a model, a paradigm for the peaking experience, the sexual orgasm, which is a mounting up to a peak and a climax, and then a drop in the completion and its ending. Well, this other type of experience must have another model. The words that I would use to describe this kind of experience would be "a high plateau." It is to live at a constantly high level in the sense of illumination or awakening or in Zen, in the easy or miraculous, in the nothing special. It is to take rather casually the poignancy and the preciousness and the beauty of things, but not to make a big deal out of it because it's happening every hour, you know, all the time.

*peak experience and "high plateau" experience*

This type of experience has the advantage, in the first place, that it's more voluntary than peak experience. For example, to enter deeply into this type of consciousness, I can go to an art museum or a meadow rather than into a subway. In the plateau experiences, you're not as surprised because they are more volitional than peak experiences. Further, I think you can teach plateau experiences; you could hold classes in miraculousness.

*comparison of peak experience and plateau experience*

Another aspect I have noticed is that it's possible to sit and look at something miraculous for an hour and enjoy every second of it. On the other hand, you can't have an hour-long orgasm. In this sense, the plateau type of experience is better. It has a great advantage, so to speak, over the climactic, the orgasm, the peak. The ascending to a great height sort of implies the descending into a valley, and living on the high plateau doesn't imply this. It is much more casual.

*serenity and emotionality*

There are some other aspects of this experience. There tends to be more serenity rather than an emotionality. Our tendency is to regard the emotional person as an explosive type. However, calmness must also be brought into one's psychology. We need the serene as well as the poignantly emotional.

*possibility of measuring plateau experience*

My guess is that the plateau experience one day will be observed on psychophysiological instruments. I believe that peak experiences have something to do with automatic discharge, which we should be able to catch easily enough if the instrumentation is available. Brain wave measurement techniques and biofeedback sound very much like a possibility for measuring, detecting, and teaching serenity and calmness and peacefulness. If so, we should be able to work with it, which means that we may be able to teach serenity to our children and pass it on.

Oh yes, the big thing, for me anyhow, is that the peak experience seemed, when I first worked with it, to be a type of cognition. For example, I wrote a paper called "Cognition of Being in a Peak-Experience." And then slowly I learned that this was not always the case. There were peak experiences which seemed to be empty of cognitive content. They were just emotional bursts, very happy and ecstatic, but passive. My attention was called to this partly by the fact that if you witness heaven in a peak experience, why the hell isn't everybody getting better all the time? We should soon turn into a race of angels. Well, very obviously I was able to get reports of peak experiences from extremely sick people and from sons-of-bitches. So this peak experience is not an exclusive possession of "nice guys."

*cognitive and non-cognitive peak experiences*

Let's say that certainly there is something you can call angelic in everybody. There is also something devilish, in varying proportions and different mixes. For example, everybody that I've been able to dig into deeply enough can be vengeful and cruel. Also, everybody that I've been able to dig into very deeply can be very generous and kind and affectionate. The nastiest people I've ever been able to find do have peak experiences, but they are generally few in number and lack cognitive content.

The important point that emerges from these plateau experiences is that they're essentially cognitive. As a matter of fact, almost by definition, they represent a witnessing of the world. The plateau experience is a witnessing of reality. It involves seeing the symbolic, or the mythic, the poetic, the transcendent, the miraculous, the unbelievable, all of which I think are part of the real world instead of existing only in the eyes of the beholder.

*plateau experience as witnessing of reality*

There is a sense of certainty about plateau experience. It feels very, very good to be able to see the world as miraculous and not merely in the concrete, not reduced only to the behavioral, not limited only to the here and now. You know, if you get stuck in the here and now, that's a reduction.

Well, it's very easy to get sloppy with your words and you can go on about the beauty of the world, but the fact is that these plateau experiences are described quite well in many literatures. This is not the standard description of the acute mystical experience, but the way in which the world looks if the mystic experience really takes. If your mystical experience changes your life, you go about your business as the great mystics did. For example, the great saints could have mystical revelations, but also could run a monastery. You can run a grocery store and pay the bills, but still carry on this sense of witnessing the world in the way you did in the great moments of mystic perception. Again, this implies a cognitive experience, and it feels like a witnessing of something that's there rather than something that you produce yourself. Therefore, you have a feeling of reality and can make a claim about the nature of reality.

*Tart:* Could you elaborate slightly on the way you are using the phrase "witnessing the world"?

*Maslow:* You just see things, but you can see them well. I had a vision once at Brandeis University. It was Commencement. I had ducked Commencement for years, but this one I couldn't duck. I was corralled and I felt there was something sort of stupid about these processions and these idiotic and medieval caps and gowns. I really felt ridiculous. Well, this time as the faculty stood waiting for the procession to begin, for some reason, and I don't know why—there was suddenly this vision. It wasn't an hallucination. It was as if I could imagine very vividly a long academic procession. It went way the hell into the future, into some kind of a misty, cloudy thing. The procession contained all my colleagues, all the people I like, you know—Erasmus, Socrates, etc. In fact, Socrates was at the head of the procession. Then, behind me the procession extended into a dim cloud in which were all sorts of people, not yet born—and these were also my colleagues. I felt very brotherly towards them, these future ones. Well, you can do that all the time when you attain the plateau experience. It's the transcending of time and space which becomes quite normal, so to speak.

*plateau experience and transcendence of time and space*

*Fadiman:* Like the shadow of the archetypal that's always just on the fringe of your vision or just around the corner.

*Krippner:* You can do that all the time?

*Maslow:* Whenever I wish.

*Richard Katz:* How about other people? You talk about peak experiences very frequently which you had in the past, and now that you're getting older, not as much. How about all the people who have never had peak experiences? Or plateau experiences?

*Maslow:* My impression is that whenever I talk with anybody about them, they see what I'm talking about.

*Katz:* It's probably a developmental process. In my work with the African Bushmen, as well as in my own experiences, there's a continuous sort of return to peak experiences, like a recharging of the batteries. The issue is not so much attaining the bursts, but what you do with them once you've gotten them. I'm not sure in the model you're presenting whether there is this kind of developmental stage, or is it recurring?

*continuous return to peak experiences*

*Maslow:* I don't know. All I can do is report one life experience. My impression is that it involves a compression of a thousand experiences. It also involves the books I've read, all the compositions I've heard, so that it is possible for me to have a walk on the prairie and see the buffalo and the Indians and the pioneers. These wagon tracks that we were walking along out here in Kansas inspire these impressions. So does the surf you see when walking along the ocean.

Another aspect of the experience is the confrontation with mortality—this whole death business. The death experience makes life much more precious and poignant and more vivid, and you're required to appreciate it and you hang on to it. With surf, you sense a contrast between your own temporary nature and the surf's eternity—the fact that it will be there always, was there always, and that you are witnessing something that's a million years old and will be there a million years from now. I pass, and my own reaction to that is one of sadness on the one hand, and of great appreciation on the other hand. It seems to me that the surf is more beautiful to me now than it used to be, and more touching. That would be perhaps an example of the simultaneous perception of the temporal and the eternal which, in that sense of witnessing, is apocryphal. In thinking of the surf, I realize that I am mortal, and the surf is not. This makes a strong contrast.

*confrontation with mortality*

*Katz:* Each time you relate a description I hear duality and also a kind of synthesis of that duality. It sounds as if the plateau experience is taking what is ordinarily polarized and synthesizing it into a single unity.

*plateau experience: synthesis of polarity*

*Maslow:* Well, it can be very deep. It can be very, very touching. This whole business of witnessing eternity means you are mortal and your mortality produces a fear of the witnessing. It is happy and also sad. It's a mixture, and very beautiful.

*Walter Pahnke:* One of the most important things that you're

*plateau experience and growth of individual*

saying is that the plateau experience perhaps has more to do with the growth of the individual, while the peak experience could serve, like an LSD experience, as an opener.

*Maslow:* The whole relationship of peak experience to death fascinates me. The peak experience is frequently reported as a death, you know, as a death and rebirth. So many people say, "I'm so happy, I could die."

*coping with the problem of death*

*Pahnke:* I got the feeling when you were describing some of your plateau experiences that you really have to be in a sense unconcerned about whether you're going to live the next minute or die the next minute in order to let them happen that way. You were stepping out of personal identity, in a way, and just letting go. I was thinking of an old folks' home I visited; the people were all coping with the problem of death. I think the people in this room have, by and large, chosen to handle that situation by widening their focus, widening the scope of their consciousness, whereas a lot of other people cope with it by narrowing their focus, and keeping out other dimensions of life.

*Maslow:* But as a consequence, they lead a pretty drab life.

*Pahnke:* Yes. Yes.

*Maslow:* I wonder if it would be of any help to people in that stage of life, to be more alive and enjoy music more.

*Pauline McCririck:* I think that's a different point. For instance, I have a patient who is an extremely obsessive woman. She can't seem to feel anything. And in this sense, of course, I've thought about the LSD experience. With such people, it seems to me, if you can have one good breakthrough, that this in itself might be sufficient to open up the ability to feel. There are extreme obsessional people who just can't feel anything.

*Maslow:* I understand it's less likely that they will have a response to LSD. It's very difficult for obsessionals to get a peak experience, to melt in ecstasy.

*Weil:* Is there an alteration in sexual behavior during the plateau experience?

*Maslow:* It seems to me that it's possible that the aging process makes sex less imperative. You can take it or leave it, and that this uncovers something which is precious. I can report that women look better to me now than they did when I was young because when I was young, sex was demanding. It was ego; I could be attracted to women that I despised, and then feel not good about myself. Now it seems to be possible to admire only women whom I like, which feels good. It feels cleaner and purer.

*plateau experience in relation to sex*

Some older people push too hard for a revival of sexual interest. They obtain a wild stimulation only to give a feeble response.

The plateau experience is paradoxical because of the mixture of permanence and mortality, you see. You feel sorry for yourself and sad over the passingness of things, while at the very same moment you're more poignantly enjoying the things that other people ignore. This is an easy thing to grasp when you're working with dying people, and I've speculated if it were possible to give an experience of death and then a reprieve that people might enjoy life more. My heart attack brought about a real confrontation with death. Ever since then, I've been living what I've been calling to myself "the post-mortem life." I've already gone through the process of dying, so everything from then on is gravy.

*paradoxes in plateau experience*

If you've gone through this experience, you can be more in the here and now than with all the spiritual exercises that there are. It's just a kind of spontaneous exercise in hanging on to the moment, because the moment is precious. Competition and life planning disappear. The dominance hierarchy, the competition, the competitiveness and glory, certainly become foolish. There is certainly a shifting of values about what's basic and what's not basic, what's important and what's not important. I think if it were possible for us to die and be resurrected, it might then be possible for more people to have this post-mortem life.

*consequences of confrontation with death*

Also, if you want to read a very good description of it, look at Arthur Koesteler's autobiography. He had a confrontation with death. It was in Spain during the Civil War. He had been caught and was going to be executed before a firing squad the next morning. He was imprisoned, and so he fell asleep. He woke up in an ecstasy, partly because of the fact he was to be executed. He saw for the first time how blue the sky was.

*Walter Clark:* We spoke about how little some people make of their experience, whether under LSD or otherwise. I deplore the way young people use LSD because I believe it maximizes the dangers and minimizes the values. I think the most tragic aspect of it isn't so much that it maximizes

*misuse of peak experiences by young people (under LSD or otherwise)*

the dangers, but it minimizes the great benefits. That is, these young people are wasting something that is precious beyond words and half the time they have no idea of it. That judgment does not hold true for all of them because some young people recognize the values. I'm thinking of a student who came up to me after I'd spoken at his college. He had taken LSD perhaps a hundred times, and is just now beginning to realize how valuable this was and how much he might have made out of it. And now he wants to develop the religious aspects of it and maybe he will, but the time to make the most of it would have been in the first few trips when it is still fresh and still novel. I'm very pessimistic about his being able to get a small fraction of what he might have gotten if he had gone into it with the right guide and the right setting and the right attitude.

*responsibility for misuse*

*Maslow:* Well, I feel we're partly to blame for the misuse of LSD. I feel that my work has been misinterpreted by youngsters sometimes. Also, this peak experience stuff can be misused, especially by youngsters. They think that's the only kind of life. The ordinary life becomes devalued altogether. The whole history of psychoanalysis is a good testimonial to this. Freud stressed both insight and "working through." Decade by decade, the psychoanalysts came to emphasize more insight and less "working through" the implications of the insight. It's a struggle.

*"insight" and "working through"*

*Clark:* So often just because a person has one of these LSD experiences, he thinks he has it made. One of my subjects in an LSD experiment put it to me. He said, "I thought that when I got through with this experiment that it would be over. But now from the perspective of the year, I can see that once I got through the experiment, it was just beginning."

*Maslow:* It happens that frequently in looking for the high, a young man and a young woman meet and they have a very good sexual experience. It's a party atmosphere, you know, a high. It's wonderful. And then they say they fall in love. The first time she gets a cold and her nose dribbles, the whole thing is lost, because they expected the relationship to stay at that high.

*Too many young people delude themselves with the "Big-Bang" theory of self-actualization. One of our tasks is to communicate better with young people and give them a greater appreciation of patience and for the miraculous elements in ordinary existence.*

# 42

SMITH, B.

## *On Self-Actualization: A Trans-Ambivalent Examination of a Focal Theme in Maslow's Psychology*

Somewhere Abe Maslow observed that self-actualizing people manage to transcend their ambivalences. Over many years–essentially the full course of my life as a psychologist thus far–I have been profoundly ambivalent about Maslow's contributions. There is much in his writings that appeals to me strongly. There is much else that sets my intellectual teeth on edge and makes me squirm in discomfort or withdraw in impatience or disagreement. When I am most annoyed I typically find that if I read on, in his great tolerance for ambiguity–indeed, his evident delight in the intellectually inchoate and disordered–Abe has anticipated my objections and said something sensible to mollify me (though usually not to put in order the problems that bothered me). My personal relationship with Abe was small but delightful; my intellectual relationship with his writings has been ambivalent to the core.

This essay is an attempt to penetrate and transcend my ambivalence by focusing on a theme that is recurrent and central in Maslow's writings, that is, self-actualization. It is a theme that he shares with other spokesmen of humanistic psychology (e.g., Rogers, 1961), and it is central to the rationale of the personal growth movement (see Back, 1972) of Esalen-style centers and encounter groups with which humanistic psychology is linked. I have to come to terms with it, if I am to make further headway with my private agenda (Smith, 1969a, 1972b), to advance a psychology that is both *humanistic* (germane to man's experience and distinctive concerns) and *scientific* in a sense that is more self-critical, more abstractive, and hence, I believe, more potentially self-corrective and cumulative than Maslow's "Taoistic" version of science (Maslow, 1966; Smith, 1966). The time is ripe for me to face the problem head-on–and a difficult, weighty problem it is. As Maslow (1971) has noted, "the notion of self-actualization gets to be almost like a Rorschach inkblot [p. 41]"–a test of a psychologist's fundamental conceptions of human nature.

## SOME PERSONAL AGENDA

I have been worrying about aspects of the problem ever since I wrote a sophomoric paper in college on "Nietzsche, Ibsen, and Shaw" that helped to resolve my major adolescent identity crisis by formulating an ideal of authentic yea-saying selfhood that creates human meaning in an otherwise bleak and Godless universe. (The Ibsen I examined was *Peer Gynt*; the Shaw, *Man and Superman*.) Reading and rereading Maslow for the present purpose, I realized with a shock how significant Nietzsche also must have been to him (e.g., Maslow, 1954, p. 201; 1971, p. 37). Not only does he share Nietzsche's concern about a nontheological basis for human values, but the Superman reappears in the guise of the self-actualizing person. There are even echoes of Nietzsche in the aphoristic style of Maslow's later, less self-censored writings. Be that as it may, over the years I have been drawn again and again to the problem of the psychological status of values, how to avoid the twin perils of ethnocentric (or theological) *absolutism* with its vulnerable dogmas and of a *relativism* that undercuts the significance of human choice. (Self-actualization in its various meanings is intrinsically concerned with values. For Maslow, the doctrine bridged the gulf between value and fact.)

As I came to focus these persisting concerns in an attempt to clarify the nature and criteria of psychological well-being or "positive mental health," I arrived at a skeptical view that nevertheless seemed to me to be liberating. I argued (Smith, 1969a, pp. 179-190) that "mental health" is not a scientific concept at all, but more in the nature of a chapter heading under which any and all evaluative perspectives on human personality can be placed. Proposed criteria of mental health—like the ability to love and work, realistic perception, integration, and active mastery—are values in terms of which personality may be appraised. Scientific psychology cannot settle *which* values people should live by, and psychological arguments about criteria of mental health are therefore fruitless. But psychologists make a distinctive contribution to the discussion when they discover developmental and situational conditions under which particular values can be realized and consequences or side effects of pursuing particular values. This was not quite a relativistic position, since I assumed that in the light of such evidence and of human experience people's value choices might converge. My plea to those concerned with "mental health" was to be explicit about which values they had in mind, and not to use the global concept as a cover to impose their own idiosyncratic values in the name of science. This still seems to me good advice, and, as I will shortly make clear, it underlies a major bone that I have to pick with Maslow.

As it turned out, I could not remain comfortable with this uncommitted, skeptical position, since it gave me no help with my sociopolitical concerns for human betterment (another point where I feel a strong resonance with Maslow). (He too was a basically optimistic reformist.) In the moral atmosphere of the War on Poverty, it appeared that the public interest in mental health criteria dictated a primary focus on human effectiveness as a successor to the gross value of not-illness (appropriate to the institutional psychiatry of an earlier day) or that of personal adjustment and fulfillment (appropriate to the private client in the consulting room) (Smith, 1969b). I drew upon Robert White's (1959) motivationally based concept of competence for the key to a reformulated conception of "positive mental health" that seemed more adequate to the needs of the times.

Mulling over what seemed to me the requirements for survival at our critical juncture in human history, my own direct experience with Peace Corps volunteers and college youth, and directly cogent new research by Rotter (1966) and De Charms (1968), I came to refocus my thinking about "competence" upon processes of *self-determination* (Smith, 1972a). Some people more than others seem to be in charge of their lives—to be Agents or "Origins" of personal causation rather than Pawns. The unprecedented human situation with its headlong trends toward multiple disaster sets a high premium upon Agency, upon the rearing of people who will not passively take these trends for granted. A view of self-determination as an empirical variable in which people differ also appealed to me as cutting through the philosophical deadlock between determinists and voluntarists in psychology. If, in the realm of the reflexive self, the "self-fulfilling prophecy" is a causal mechanism, then people's causally rooted conceptions of themselves as Origins or as Pawns may make the crucial difference as to whether they actively *live* their lives or merely suffer them. Many people who were previously not self-determining–blacks and Chicanos, former colonials, women, even students–were demanding self-determination as against external constraint, and achieving the inner basis of self-determination through redefinition of their identities. A scientific social psychology of personality could help to understand this humanly important process and perhaps to advance it.

These considerations still strike me as compelling. (Incidentally, they do not appear to fit very easily with Maslow's [1954] otherwise attractive hierarchical conception of human motivation. Events have shown that people who are still suffering from gross Deficiency [D] motivation are capable of acting to promote self-determination for themselves and the groups with which they identify [though their leaders, to be sure, are unlikely to be dominated by D-motives]. Maslow's D-motive of Respect is related to the quest for self-determination, but does not seem to encompass it.) I have come to realize, however, that a specialized focus upon self-determination, understandable and appropriate as it may be for minority activists or radical feminists, is a one-sided, biased perspective for the psychologist who is concerned with optimal human functioning.

Even in the essay (Smith, 1972a) in which I developed these ideas, I noted as an afterthought that they probably reflect a male bias. The Promethean, instrumental, "coping" emphasis of what I had to say about competence and self-determination has a characteristic flavor of male aspirations and hangups (some self-analysis here!). It probably requires some modulation to fit the ways that females, on the average, will find most fitting to live their lives as the cultural pressures that limit them are relaxed. Reflection on my own experiential sources of value and protracted discussions with Santa Cruz students in seminar (a majority of whom had biases complementary to my instrumentalism) convinced me that the one-sidedness is more fundamental. In the terms of Rollo May's (1969) provocative book, for one thing, I had been focusing single-mindedly on Will. What about Love? But Maslow had long been asserting the insufficiency of coping and competence as criteria of the "fully human." A long, close look at the inkblot of self-actualization, under which he dealt with the criterion problem, thus takes high priority on my agenda.

## LARGE DETAILS IN THE INKBLOT

Among the many contexts in which Maslow discusses self-actualization, I find three major ones, which of course are closely interrelated. Initially, and throughout his subsequent writings, Maslow (1950) talked about *self-actualizing people* as rare specimens of psychological health who can be used as a kind of touchstone to explore human potentialities. He refers repeatedly to the examination of *peak experiences* of transcendent value, which he finds common among self-actualizing people. For more ordinary humanity, these may be regarded as moments of self-actualization. He also refers to a self-actualizing *growth process* governed by "metamotives" that take over when deficiency motivation is satisfied. As a basis for subsequent discussion, I will briefly (because of the familiarity of Maslow's writings) characterize each of these nodes of meaning.

### *Self-Actualizing People*

In a very modestly presented informal study (Maslow, 1950, 1954)—regrettably informal considering the speculative weight it was subsequently called upon to support—Maslow examined the characteristics that he discerned as shared among 51 public or historical figures, contemporaries, and carefully screened young people who seemed to him to exemplify or to approach the ideal of psychological health. (Later [e.g., Maslow, 1971, p. 34], he preferred to substitute "full or diminished humanness" for the medical terminology of health and illness.) Maslow (1954) wrote that

> the positive criterion for selection was positive evidence of self-actualization (SA), as yet a difficult syndrome to describe accurately. For the purposes of this discussion, it may be loosely described as the full use and exploitation of talents, capacities, potentialities, etc. Such people seem to be fulfilling themselves and to be doing the best that they are capable of doing, reminding us of Nietzsche's exhortation, "Become what thou art [pp. 200-201]!"

The following, in brief, are the characteristics of Maslow's self-actualizing people:

> superior perception of reality; increased acceptance of self, of others and of nature; increased spontaneity; increase in problem centering; increased detachment and desire for privacy; increased autonomy, and resistance to enculturation; greater freshness of appreciation, and

> richness of emotional reaction; higher frequency of peak experiences; increased identification with the human species; changed (the clinician would say, improved) interpersonal relations; more democratic character structure; greatly increased creativeness; certain changes in the value system [Maslow, 1968, p. 26].

Many of his later statements elaborate upon and add to the traits listed in this summary. Maslow is explicit that self-actualization in this defining sense is an uncommon achievement attained only in late maturity.

*Peak Experiences*

As just noted, Maslow found that his self-actualizers were especially likely to report transcendent, even ecstatic or mystical experiences that they regard as imbued with the greatest intrinsic value, in which awareness of the self and its boundaries is eclipsed by immersion in larger meanings. Not all self-actualizers are "peakers," as Maslow later (1971) observed. Many people who fall short of attaining his criterion of self-actualization nevertheless have peak experiences, which Maslow suggests are transient moments of self-actualization, of "Being." Because they involve a transcendence of the self, they also provide the link for him to a "transpersonal" psychology.

*Growth Process*

Self-actualization can be viewed not only as a life achievement and as a momentary state, but also as the normal process of psychological growth that occurs (in Maslow's [1954] theory of a hierarchy of motives) when a person's deficiency motives are satisfied and his defenses are not mobilized by present threats. "Self-actualization is not only an end state but also the process of actualizing one's potentialities at any time, in any amount [Maslow, 1971, p. 47]." Maslow (1968) suggests:

> that growth takes place when the next step forward is subjectively more delightful, more joyous, more intrinsically satisfying than the previous gratification with which we have become familiar and even bored; that the only way we can ever know what is right for us is that it feels better subjectively than any alternative. The new experience validates *itself* rather than by any outside criterion. It is self-justifying, self-validating . . . . This is the way in which we discover the Self and answer the ultimate questions Who am I? What am I [p. 45]?

> Of course this formulation of growth-through-delight commits us to the necessary postulation that what tastes good is also, in the growth sense, "better" for us. We rest here on the faith that if free choice is *really* free and if the chooser is not too sick or frightened to choose, he will choose wisely, in a health and growthward direction, more often than not [p. 48].

It is here that Maslow espouses what the critic Kurt Back (1972) identifies as the central model upon which the whole personal growth movement is based,

> the model of a prisoner in a cage. Underlying most of the thought is the idea of man (or whatever the essential man is) as being imprisoned by different layers of circumstances which do not allow him to reach his full potentialities. Allied to this image is also the supposition that, if he could escape, everything would be good, and he would only use his potentialities for creative and beneficial results [p. 110].

My quotation of Back suggests that I see problems in this faith. It is time to turn to the difficulties that I encounter with Maslow's formulations.

## DIFFICULTIES

The difficulties that make Maslow's doctrine of self-actualization stick in my craw, much as I would like to swallow it whole, touch upon central and perennial issues concerning human nature. Since I generally agree with him about which is the side of the Angels, since I entirely agree with him (and with Chein, 1972) in espousing an Image of Man as an actor, not a mechanism, and since most of the bones that I have to pick bear on other humanistic psychologies as much as Maslow's, I hope that a vigorous argument about points of disagreement may contribute to a reconstruction of humanistic psychology along lines that preserve the humanism but improve the changes for a rapprochement with science.

### *Methodological Difficulty*

First I have to note a petty methodological problem that seriously affects my reading of Maslow's study of self-actualizing people. Maslow is so modest about its inadequacies and technical flaws and so informal about reporting it that it seems quite unfair to criticize—like turning a howitzer on a butterfly. But it is necessary, since the study provides the foundation for so much of what Maslow has to say about self-actualization.

The crucial flaw, one that I noted in 1959 (Smith, 1969a, p. 169), and so far as I am aware Maslow never acknowledged, has to do with the boot-straps operation by which he selected his "sample" of self-actualizing people. In effect, Maslow eliminated people with gross pathology—the Dostoyevskis and Van Goghs—and selected people for whom, after close scrutiny, he had the highest admiration as human specimens. His empirical definition of psychological health or self-actualization thus rests, at root, on his own implicit values that underlie this global judgment. The array of characteristics that he reports must then be regarded not as an empirical description of the fully human (the value-laden facts that he claims to have established), but rather as an explication of his implicit conception of the fully human, of his orienting frame of human values. This is still interesting because of our respect for Maslow's discriminations of human quality, but it is not the factual foundation for humanistic values that he claims it to be.

The trouble is apparent when we look at the names of his seven cases of "fairly sure" or "highly probable" public and historical figures: Abe Lincoln in his last years, Thomas Jefferson, Albert Einstein, Eleanor Roosevelt, Jane Addams, William James, and Spinoza. Why not also George Washington in *his* later years, Casanova in his earlier years, Napoleon, Thomas Edison, or Lenin? All of these could equally be said to be making, in the phrasing of Maslow's criterion statement of self-actualization, "the full use . . . of talents, capacities, potentialities, . . . , to be fulfilling themselves and to be doing the best they were capable of doing, reminding us of Nietzsche's exhortation, 'Become what thou art!' " In the inherent nature of the case, the dice are loaded toward Maslow's own values. I like them, but that is beside the point.

### *The Problem of Potentialities*

The methodological point shades into a theoretical one. How, indeed, are we to understand the "human potentialities" that get actualized? The term is most at home in an Aristotelian, finalistic conception, in which development is conceived as the realization of potentialities that are in some sense uniquely predetermined. As I subsequently suggest, that is not so bad a fit to the biological facts when we are dealing with the adaptive products of long-term evolution (even though most biologists do not regard it as a viable theoretical formulation). Maslow (1968) stretches the biological analogy to cover the case of human psychology, as in the following:

> Man demonstrates *in his own nature* a pressure toward fuller and fuller Being, more and more perfect actualization of his humanness in exactly the same naturalistic, scientific sense [sic] that an acorn may be said to be "pressing toward" being an oak tree, or that a tiger can be observed to "push toward" being tigerish, or a horse toward being equine . . . . The environment does not give him potentialities or capacities; he *has* them in inchoate or embryonic form, just as he has embryonic arms and legs [p. 160].

This will hardly do. Except for some universals of the human species like language and symbolization, constructiveness, interdependence, and maybe reactive aggression that have an entrenched evolutionary status and probably fit the acorn-oak tree model as well as the plant itself does (which is to ignore the complex interactive processes of epigenesis), the young person has an extremely broad range of multiple potentialities. The course of life, including the choices of the emerging self, excludes some of them, sets limits on others, and elaborates upon still others. Vice and evil are as much in the range of human potentiality, I would argue, as virtue; specialization as much as "well-rounded" development. Our biology cannot be made to carry our ethics as Maslow would have it.

I see that I am resorting here to sheer assertions to counter Maslow's. But the burden of proof is upon him. The kinds of people that he excludes from his self-actualizing sample, its bias toward Maslovian values undermine his case for the *distinctive* humanness of the particular human potentialities that his sample exemplifies. These are among the attractive possibilities of human existence; its interest, its tragedy, and I think its glory lie in the fact that they are not "built in" but exist as possibilities among a range of very different ones, any of which can be regarded as an actualization of potentiality, though trivially so, when it occurs.

Generally, I think the doctrine of potentiality is more misleading than helpful (see also Chein, 1972).

### *Self-Actualization: What is the Self?*

The difficulties that I have just examined lead me to reject (unambivalently) a part of Maslow's doctrine. Now I come to a matter that remains a problem for me, though I think it can be clarified beyond the point where

Maslow leaves it: How do our conceptions of the *self* affect our view of self-actualization?

Although conceptual attention to the Self as actor, as reflexive object, and in its relations to other selves is a hallmark of humanistic psychology, our theories about the self remain primitive and underdeveloped. Plausible fragments from Schilder, G. H. Mead, Jung, Erikson, Allport, and others lie scattered and unintegrated. My own thinking about the self is not in good order, and so far as I can tell, Maslow's is mainly implicit. Yet one attractive meaning of self-actualization, as experience or action that is in deep accord with the self or carries forward its projects, depends entirely on what we assume about the self. Two radically contrasting versions are current, with many variants.

One version can be identified with the Socratic dictum, "The unexamined life is not worth living." Selfhood from this perspective inheres in the uniquely human gift of reflexive *self*-awareness. Actions "actualize" the self when they are done reflectively and responsibly to correspond to the value priorities that comprise the core of the person's self-accepted identity. Self-actualization is the cumulative product of such action, and is accompanied by self-understanding.

Quite a contrary version of the self can be identified with Jung who has elaborated it most richly: an "iceberg" conception according to which the true, essential self, the source of creativity, of authenticity and value, lies mostly outside of awareness. Only partly can one aspire to know and understand the self, but one can still be sensitive to and guided by the self's dictates. Self-actualizing *experience,* from this perspective, erupts for the prepared person if he is properly receptive to it–as in "peak experiences." Action is likely to be self-actualizing if it is spontaneous and *un*reflective. Thus the term self-actualization can be employed to designate empirical phenomena and ethical prescriptions that are diametrically opposed. The growth movement in humanistic psychology, and Maslow with it, seems heavily committed to the iceberg version.

I see no need to negotiate between these contrasting interpretations of selfhood, which I would rather understand as partial accounts of what it is to be human, that reflect competing realms of human value. I am sympathetic to what Maslow (1971, Appendix A) says, in a slightly different context, about Apollonian (orderly) and Dionysian (impulsive) versions of self-actualization. As he puts it, the current Dionysian excesses of the encounter movement and the counter-culture counterbalance the massive Apollonian emphasis of our technological society. But if I agree with this, I must also note that the major drift of Maslow's theoretical and quasi-empirical writings about self-actualization is one-sidedly Dionysian. Taken as a new, "scientific" gospel, it is open to the charge of anti-intellectualism and romantic impulsivity.

Human nature *is* multipotential. A dazzling choice of options is available. There is no cosmic requirement, nor biological necessity, that our choices be well balanced. But they have consequences, all the same, in the inner world of experience and the outer world of practical affairs.

## *Self-Actualization and Transcendence*

What I have just said about Maslow's Dionysian bias (an emphasis on the *daimonic,* in May's [1969] terms, though for May the daimonic carries more multivalent, potentially tragic overtones than the Dionysian in Maslow's optimistic, rather sanguine version) has implications for the meaning of "peak experiences" as glimpses or criteria of self-actualization. Peak experiences belong on the nonrational, Dionysian side; if one grants the co-reality of the more Apollonian forms of self-actualization, their authority diminishes. In a purportedly general "Psychology of Being," it seems to me questionable to give as much weight as Maslow does to insights "validated" by the content of such experiences. Maslow notes that among his self-actualizing sample, Eleanor Roosevelt was a "non-peaker." Had his sample been drawn to follow his explicit criterion more faithfully, less according to his implicit value preferences, peak experiences would figure less prominently as a characteristic of self-actualization. In question, particularly, is the raising of mysticism to a more honored status than rationality among the possible competing realms of value between which human choice historically has oscillated.

For myself, I think I understand what Maslow is talking about when it comes to peak experiences in love, nature, and music. They contribute very much to the personal richness and value of life, to the feeling that life is worthwhile and that one could die knowing that one had lived fully. They remain great mysteries that make religion imaginable to me. I wish a scientific psychology could encompass them; they surely reflect something unique to man and exceedingly important to him. It is to Maslow's great credit that he has brought them back into psychology. But the high value that I set upon these experiences does not persuade me to regard the "gut feel" as more enduringly valid than the considered thought, the passively eruptive as "higher" and "truer" than the actively sought. There are many *varieties* of human experience, religious and otherwise, all of which deserve respect and study. In a warranted pendulum swing against the prevailing emphasis in psychology, Maslow has opted for inspiration over perspiration. But a pendulum swing should not be mistaken for the revelation of a higher truth.

Peak experiences "transcend" ordinary selfhood, which they temporarily obliterate. Another of the senses in which Maslow employs the term "transcendence" I can only applaud. In an introduction to "Being-values," Maslow (1971) writes:

> Self-actualizing people are, without one single exception, involved in a cause outside their own skin, in something outside themselves. They are devoted, working at something, something which is very precious to them–some calling or vocation in the old sense, the priestly sense . . . so that the work-joy dichotomy in them disappears [p. 43].

This, of course, is only a restatement of the Christian wisdom that he who would find his life must lose it–that happiness is a by-product that eludes direct pursuit. I think the observation has validity beyond Maslow's biased sample, and I conjecture that it will remain as an enduring truth about selfhood and its fulfillment. It needs to be fitted into a conceptually articulated self-psychology.

*Self-Actualization: Biology or History?*

In my earlier discussion of the doctrine of potentiality, I questioned Maslow's biologism, that projects a determinate course of self-actualization as rooted in man's biological nature. Here Maslow is faithful to his mentor, the holistic neurologist Goldstein (1939), who wrote:

> *Normal behavior corresponds to a continual change of tension, of such a kind that over and again that state of tension is reached which enables and impels the organism to actualize itself in further activities, according to its nature. Thus, experiences with patients* teach us that we have *to assume only one drive, the drive of self-actualization,* and that the goal of the drive is not a discharge of tension [p. 197].

Goldstein anticipated the current trend in motivational theory in his attack on the principle of tension-reduction. But his concept of self-actualization according to the *nature* of the organism seems to me to have limited applicability at the level of human action. What is the *nature* of the human "organism" or, better, of the human person? Perennial problems of philosophy and psychology are involved.

The member of a subhuman animal species, stably adapted to a well-defined ecological niche as the result of long evolutionary process, *has* a nature the fulfillment of which is likely to result in adaptation and the survival of the individual (until reproduction). As a higher primate that also passed through a long evolutionary period of stable adaptation, man too has a biological nature, though what it is and what constraints it puts upon present human action are just now important controversial questions. The chances are that it has to do with such problematic matters as male enjoyment of hunting and a good fight, such essential safeguards as mothers' irresistible attraction to babies (embarrassing to the new feminists), and such important but motivationally neutral propensities as preprogrammed readiness to learn the elaborate symbol system of a human language. The "further reaches of human nature," in Maslow's phrase, are still beyond the reach of evolutionary process: historical time is so short. All the more so must this be the case because (according to Maslow's hierarchical theory of motivation) "B-" or "Metamotives," the sphere of self-actualization, take over only after Deficiency motives have been satisfied.

Maslow's is a psychology for the affluent, postindustrial society. The eons of protohuman evolutionary history must all have been lived mainly at the lower Deficiency levels when life was indeed nasty, brutish, and short. Protopeople were in ecological equilibrium with their resources (which means the edge of hunger) and with their internal parasites (which does not mean health). How, indeed, could a biological human nature of "instinctoid" metamotives of the kind Maslow regards as inherent in self-actualization get established in evolution?

These considerations raise questions as to whether the "wisdom of the body" (and of the untutored mind) is sufficient for the valid guidance of significant human choice, as Maslow's faith would have it. Just as our gut reactions of pleasure may mislead us about saccharine and more dangerous drugs that had no part in our evolution, so they may lead us astray or, what amounts to the same thing, into difficult and destructive conflicts in the human relations of an interdependent urban society. In evolutionary terms, these are almost as new as saccharine.

The trouble is, I think, that in this respect Maslow's psychology is pseudo-biologistic; it is inadequately humanistic in the sense long defended by spokesmen for the humanities. Maslow neglects the discontinuity in the biological record that came with language, culture, self-consciousness, and the accompanying moral order of society. What a humanist would regard as historical human action he persists in regarding as the instinctoid expression of biological propensities. His misguided attempt to arrive at a naturalistic basis for human values rules out any serious consideration of the ethics and politics of human action.

Darwin's principle of natural selection provides the equivalent of an Unseen Hand that gradually (though cruelly) shapes biological nature toward adaptiveness. In history and culture there is no Unseen Hand; there is human action. Human action can succeed or fail, it can be constructive or destructive of self and others, it creates a miraculous variety of values and must choose among them. This is the essence of human hope, of human tragedy, of human dignity. "Becoming fully human" is a personal-cultural-historical adventure. The biological metaphor is ill-suited to grasp it, but a humanistic psychology should.

### *Self-Actualization and the Common Good*

If an Unseen Hand is absent in human history, then self-actualization in the sense of growth process does not inevitably lead to the common good. "Doing what comes naturally" is not enough. The emphasis in Maslow's writings is on the fulfillment of the individual, and the encounter movement that draws upon his writings has become much more flagrantly individualistic.

Yet Maslow's (1971) own view is more complex. Not only do self-actualizing people tend to be altruists, but he notes that "the basic needs can be fulfilled *only* by and through other human beings, i.e., society [p. 347]." Further, societies differ in the extent to which they make it possible for people to transcend the conflict between selfishness and altruism. Maslow (p. 202) adopts from Ruth Benedict the concept of "synergy" for this characteristic of societies according to which the social institutions either tend to make virtue pay or, instead, tend to structure social life as a zero-sum game. The concept plays a central role in his Utopian (or "Eupsychian") thinking.

There is a suggestive basis here for political and ethical analysis and empirical inquiry. In spite of Maslow's preoccupation with humane institutions and management in his later writings (see especially Maslow, 1965), however, his thought was essentially unpolitical. He was an optimist about the extent to which "Eupsychian" arrangements could indeed provide the equivalent of an Unseen Hand. Maslow did not actually deny the irreducible reality of conflict, either in the unconscious psyche or in society, but he was not disposed to dwell upon it or to take it very seriously.

## TOWARD RECONSTRUCTION

I have dealt severely with several aspects of Maslow's doctrine of self-actualization because I think it deserves to be taken seriously. For my own use, I should like to salvage the *process* conception of self-actualization. I would interpret it as characterizing a person's actions or experiences when they are in congruence with his existing self (rather than dictated by external constraint or conformity, or driven by inner compulsions that are alien to the self). Such actions or experiences feed back in their consequences to enrich the self, to express its values, or to further its enterprises. This, I take it, is the crux of Maslow's concept. It is also a major part of his rationale for psychological growth. I think that it is important, and a more adequate psychology of the self can build upon it.

I would insist, however, upon an open conception of selfhood until our personological knowledge is more firmly based and better formulated–one with a place both for the creative depths of the "iceberg" theory and for the reflective commitments emphasized by a view that sets greater stock on rational consciousness. Therefore, I would stress the many routes that are open to self-actualization (corresponding to the rich variety of human nature and its personal and cultural expressions). I would not expect, however, to find a single syndrome of virtues in the "self-actualized people" who are nearing the end of the journey.

Self-actualization, so conceived, seems to me a precious psychological value, but I would want to appreciate it in the context of other psychological and social realities. Since I do not believe that self-actualizing action can dependably be counted upon to produce the common good (short of Eupsychia, which I fear would be as dull as Walden II or the classless society), I see it as in necessary and desirable interplay with social norms and sanctions, on the one hand, and with internalized principles and perhaps even taboos, on the other. These are essential if a degree of social and psychological order is to be attained which people need and which does not "come naturally." For both individuals and societies the pendulum swings between order and expressiveness. Individual differences in personal priorities (Apollonian and Dionysian) are to be expected and valued.

Because social realities are at best imperfectly synergic in Maslow's sense, conflict will remain; there is need for politics. And because "gut-feeling" and delight can be misleading guides to the common good (though valuable if fallible ones to individual self-actualization), ethics is needed as well. Neither ethics nor politics is bestowed upon man by any instinctoid biology, though workable versions of ethics and politics have to take his biological nature as well as his historically developing situation into account. Both ethics and politics are the emergent, historical creations of conscious actors who by their new human nature—a "nature" that is transformed in the dialectics of human action—are interdependent and have to take one another into account. They involve human choices about difficult matters with uncertain outcomes.

A psychology is humanistic to the extent that it takes serious account of man as an experiencing actor. We know from man's history and from appreciative acquaintance with his cultural products that even a minimally adequate account must be very complex. Maslow's corpus of writing certainly goes far toward evoking this complexity. But some of his ideas about self-actualization seem to me to purvey a one-sided, though admirable, vision of human potentiality and to fall short of full justice to the distinctively human nature of the historical domain of human choice.

## REFERENCES

BACK, K. *Beyond words. The story of sensitivity training and the encounter movement*. New York: Russell Sage Foundation, 1972.

CHEIN, I. *The science of behavior and the image of man*. New York: Basic Books, 1972.

DECHARMS, R. *Personal causation*. New York & London: Academic Press, 1968.

GOLDSTEIN, K. *The organism*. New York: American Book, 1939.

MASLOW, A. H. Self-actualizing people: A study of psychological health. In *Personality Symposia: Symposium No. 1 on Values*. New York: Grune and Stratton, 1950.

MASLOW, A. H. *Motivation and personality*. New York: Harper, 1954.

MASLOW, A. H. *Religions, values, and peak-experiences*. Columbus, Ohio: Ohio State University Press, 1964.

MASLOW, A. H. *Eupsychian management: A journal*. Homewood, Ill.: Irwin-Dorsey, 1965.

MASLOW, A. H. *The psychology of science: A reconnaisance*. New York: Harper & Row, 1966.

MASLOW, A. H. *Toward a psychology of being*. (2nd ed.) Princeton, N.J.: Van Nostrand, 1968.

MASLOW, A. H. *The farther reaches of human nature*. New York: Viking, 1971.

MAY, R. *Love and will*. New York: Norton, 1969.

ROGERS, C. *On becoming a person*. Boston: Houghton Mifflin, 1961.

ROTTER, J. B. Generalized expectancies for internal versus external control of reinforcement. *Psychological Monographs*, 1966, **80** (1, Whole No. 609).

SMITH, M. B. Review of A. H. Maslow, The psychology of science: A reconnaissance. *Science*, 1966, **153**, 284–285.

SMITH, M. B. *Social psychology and human values*. Chicago: Aldine-Atherton, 1969. (a)

SMITH, M. B. Competence and "mental health": Problems in conceptualizing human effectiveness. In S. B. Sells (Ed.), *The definition and measurement of mental health: A symposium*. Washington, D.C.: National Center for Health Statistics, USPHS, 1969. (b)

SMITH, M. B. Normality: For an abnormal age. In D. Offer and D. X. Freedman (Eds.), *Modern psychiatry and clinical research: Essays in honor of Roy R. Grinker, Sr.* New York: Basic Books, 1972. (a)

SMITH, M. B. Toward humanizing social psychology. In T. S. Krawiec (Ed.), *The psychologists*. Vol. 1. New York: Oxford University Press, 1972. (b)

WHITE, R. W. Motivation reconsidered: The concept of competence. *Psychological Review*, 1959, **66**, 297–333.

Reprint requests: M. Brewster Smith, University of California, Santa Cruz, California 95064.

43

# ROGERS, C. R.[1]

# *Some New Challenges*

I appreciate being invited to address psychologists. It has been a long time indeed since I have attended an APA convention. I have a temptation to reminisce, to think and talk about the 45 years I have been engaged in clinical psychology or work that is related to it: helping troubled individuals, conducting research in this field, promoting personal growth and development in individuals and groups, endeavoring to work with organizations such as our educational systems, even voicing my concerns about our very sick society and the near fatal illnesses of our culture.

Such reminiscences would cover such things as the strenuous effort necessary to make a place for that small infant, clinical psychology, in the APA—a struggle that seems ludicrous now—the struggle to prove that psychologists could actually and legally carry on psychotherapy, involving various professional struggles with psychiatry; the attempt to open up therapy to detailed scrutiny and empirical research; the effort to build a theoretical formulation that would release clinical work from the dying orthodoxy of psychoanalytic dogma and promote diversified and creative thinking; the efforts to broaden the scope and the vision of clinical and other psychologists; and perhaps finally the effort to help psychologists become true change agents, not simply remedial appliers of psychic Band-Aids. Each one of those phrases could be a long story in itself.

But I do not wish to yield to this temptation. I prefer to look ahead, to try to describe some of the challenges that are currently facing us or will, in my judgment, face us in the near future.

I am afraid that these challenges have little or no logical sequence. They are the dilemmas that I perceive as most significant. For this reason what follows may seem disjointed, just as I think life rather ruthlessly presents us with many divergent issues, some of which we would sweep under the rug if we conveniently could. Here are some that I think cannot be wished away.

### *Dare We Develop a Human Science?*

The first challenge I wish to mention is not particularly new, but is definitely unmet. It is this: Does our profession dare to develop the new conception of science which is so necessary if we are to have a true *psychological* science? Or will we continue as a pseudoscience? Let me explain my meaning, in terms that are full of personal meaning to me.

Psychology, for all of its thousands of experiments, its multitudes of white rats, its vast enterprises involving laboratories, computers, electronic equipment, highly sophisticated statistical measures, and the like, is in my estimation slipping backward as a significant science. We have failed dismally to heed Robert Oppenheimer's (1956) warning, addressed to the APA in 1956, when he pointed out that the worst thing psychology might do would be "to model itself after a physics which is not there anymore, which has been outdated [p. 134]." But we have determinedly tied ourselves to this old Newtonian conception of science, seemingly unaware of the changes in the views of science that have been taking place in theoretical physics and in various other "hard" as well as "soft" sciences. I and others have endeavored to spell out some of these changes (Koch, 1959; Rogers, 1955, 1964; Schultz, 1970), and I do not wish to repeat those formulations here. For me the heart of the change is best summed up in a paragraph by my friend Michael Polanyi (1958). It is a complex thought:

> To say that the discovery of objective truth in science consists in the apprehension of a rationality which com-

---

[1] This article was an invited address presented at the annual meeting of the American Psychological Association, Honolulu, Hawaii, September 2, 1972.

Requests for reprints should be sent to Carl R. Rogers, Center for Studies of the Person, 1125 Torrey Pines Road, La Jolla, California 92037.

mands our respect and arouses our contemplative admiration; that such discovery, while using the experience of our senses as clues, transcends this experience by embracing the vision of a reality beyond the impressions of our senses, a vision which speaks for itself in guiding us to an ever deeper understanding of reality—such an account of scientific procedure would be generally shrugged aside as outdated Platonism: a piece of mystery-mongering unworthy of an enlightened age. Yet it is precisely on this conception of objectivity that I wish to insist . . . [p. 5].

A beautiful example of Polanyi's view of a man being pulled, by his subjective vision, into a deeper and more significant view of reality is contained in the account of how he became a scientist by none other than B. F. Skinner (1959). It is a human, private, inner view. It is full of the use of such subjective clues as "when you run onto something interesting, drop everything else and study it [p. 363]." It is unfortunate that Skinner now regards this beautiful personal account as no more than an epiphenomenon, insignificant in itself. Yet, I have had the same kind of story from prominent scientists at Cal Tech—the dream, the vision, the hunch as to the structure of the nucleus of the atom or some other mystery, and the valuable work that has been guided by that informed but vaguely transcending dream. Reichenbach (Schlipp, 1959) reported a conversation with Einstein: "When I, on a certain occasion, asked Professor Einstein how he found his theory of relativity, he answered that he found it because he was so strongly convinced of the harmony of the universe [p. 292]." He had, in other words, a subjectively formed guiding vision.

I myself (Coulson & Rogers, 1968) have tried to sum up this newer view:

All of this which we [psychologists] have known as science becomes but one modest *part* of science. It can be seen as imbedded in an impressive personal context in which personal and group judgment of plausibility becomes as important as statistical significance. The model of a precise, beautifully built, and unassailable science (which most of us hold, consciously or unconsciously) becomes, then, a limited and distinctly human construction, incapable of precise perfection. Openness to experiences can be seen as being fully as important a characteristic of the scientist as the understanding of research design. And the whole enterprise of science can be seen as but one portion of a larger field of knowledge in which truth is pursued in many equally meaningful ways, science being one of those ways [p. 8].

These quotations indicate the kind of challenge that faces psychologists if they are to develop a science of man. (See also Dagenais, 1972, and Schultz, 1970.) It will become a science based on careful observation of inner cognitive processes, such as we find in Piaget. It will involve the exploration of inner, personal emotionalized meanings, such as I and my colleagues have pioneered. It will be based on understanding the phenomenological world of man, as well as his external behavior and reactions. This trend toward convergent lines of confirmation has been evident in research in psychotherapy. It also shows up dramatically in the increasingly sophisticated work on dreams by numerous investigators, tying together the completely subjective irrational dream world of the individual with his responses on various electronic measuring devices. Here, indeed, one of the most ancient subjective realities, the dream, is linked to the most modern technology. It is to be noted that in all of these trends toward a newer science we do not push the individual into some contrived situation to investigate some hypothesis we have imposed on him. We are instead opening our minds and our whole selves to learning *from* him.

Why is this important? Because, otherwise, man becomes but an object to us. Hanna (1971) stated it well:

Man *uses* that which he perceives to be *unlike* himself, but he searches for a *common understanding and common harmony* with that which he perceives to be *like* himself. The former perception leads to manipulation and authentic technology; the latter perception leads to understanding and authentic science.

I believe that until we develop this authentic human science, we are but developing a technology for the use of planners and dictators, not a true understanding of the human condition. Perhaps our graduate departments, those bastions of traditionalism, have kept us from bringing about this change. The PhD thesis has, in most universities, become a travesty of its true purpose. To follow one's informed curiosity into the mysteries of some aspect of human nature, and out of that rigorous, personal, independent search to come up with a significant contribution to knowledge—this is the true picture of the PhD, but this is *not* an accurate description of most doctoral dissertations today. We have settled for safe mediocrity and have frowned on creativity. If our concept of science is to change, our departments must change. If that change does not come about, psychology will become more and more irrelevant to the search for the truth of man.

## *Do We Dare to Be Designers?*

Another great challenge of our times to the psychologist is to develop an approach which is focused on constructing the new, not repairing the old; which is designing a society in which problems will be less frequent, rather than putting poultices on those who have been crippled by social factors. The question is whether our group can develop a future-oriented, preventive approach, or whether it will forever be identified with a past-oriented remedial function.

Let me take a few examples. Will the school psychologist be content with the attempt to diagnose and remedy the individual ills created by an obsolete educational system with an irrelevant curriculum, or will he insist on having a part in designing an opportunity for learning in which the student's curiosity can be unleashed and in which the joy of learning replaces the assigned tasks of the prisons we now know as schools?

To work in such a way demands that the psychologist be a radical in the true sense of that word. It means that he leave his secure little office and work—often at great risk, I know—with school administrators, teachers, and community leaders to plan and design a learning environment. His task will no longer be to try to assuage the pain of the victims of the old system, for whom failure has become a daily experience; he will have embarked on the broader task of building a flexible institution—if such is possible—with students as the core and all others as the servants of the learners. As clinicians we have seen our task in such degrading ways that I do not know whether we can lift our view enough to see the function we might be serving.

Why are psychologists not at the heart of designing environments—cities, schools, homes, cultures—which enhance rather than degrade, which utilize technology rather than becoming its slaves? To their credit let it be said that there are a few psychologists so employed, but they are *very* few.

Take one example of which I have some knowledge. A psychologist—I suppose he would be termed a consulting psychologist—is working with a large firm in its efforts to design an enormous new plant. He is working to plan for the satisfactoriness of human relationships in that plant, so he deals with the architects, with the technicians designing the automation, with the labor union leaders, with the production line specialists, with teams of all of these. His effort is not simply to modify or soften the deadening human effect of such a plant. He sees his job as putting the person at the heart of the whole enterprise, trying to discover whether a large modern unit of production can be so constructed and so organized as to enhance the human spirit and to enrich the lives of the persons involved. I believe he is engaged in an attempt to build a system that is first of all human. To the extent that the whole team can be successful, we will not need to speak of the dehumanizing effects of modern industry, of the enormous damage done to the human psyche. To be sure, he may lose, or he may win. But he is engaged in the preventive effort to *construct* a human enterprise. Would that more psychologists were similarly engaged.

The same comment applies if we are thinking of developing whole new communities from the start. The one with which I have some familiarity is Columbia, Maryland. To build a community for persons without regard to their race, cultural background, or economic level is an exciting experiment. I know they have already made mistakes, and will undoubtedly make more, but it is an attempt to build for persons, not simply to make profits for the developer. How many social scientists were involved I do not know, but not enough. How much attention is being given to building continuing relationships within the community? Far too little. But this is the kind of area in which, in my judgment, there lies a real place for psychologists if they can be creative as well as down to earth, if they can free themselves from their traditionalism as well as their professionalism, and work imaginatively with others from all pertinent fields—physicians and architects and plumbers and educators—to build a new unit of a new society.

In another area, can we be significant in the relationships between minority groups—blacks, Chicanos, Indians, women—and the so-called Establishment? Here is the kind of relevant, risky field which offers great opportunities. I know, and I am sure you do too, of individual psychologists, black, white, Chicano, and female, who have been highly influential in bringing about improved communication in crucial interface situations. Some have worked with ghetto members and police, some with the health-consuming poor and the medical establishment, and some with the drug culture and the community. We, as psychologists, have available many of the skills for facilitating communication and problem-solving procedures between these often bitter and alienated groups and the culture that has mistreated them. We can help both sides to find solutions that constitute a quiet revolution without violence. Will we do so? Will we receive any backing whatsoever from our university roots, our professional societies, our governmental agencies set up to serve the public, when we do engage in such activities? It is too soon to know, but it is not too soon to make a concerted gamble.

## *Dare We Do Away with Professionalism?*

The third challenge I wish to raise, especially for clinical and social psychologists, is the radical possibility of sweeping away our procedures for professionalization. I know what heresy that is, what terror it strikes in the heart of the person who has struggled to become a "professional." But I have seen the moves toward certification, licensure, attempts to exclude charlatans, from a vantage point of many years, and it is my considered judgment that they fail in their aims. I helped the APA to form ABEPP (as it was then known) in 1947 when I was president of the APA. I was ambivalent about the move then. I wish now I had taken a stand against it.

I am not in any way impugning the motives or the integrity and effort of those who aim toward certification and all that follows from it. I sympathize deeply. I wish there were a way to separate the qualified from the unqualified, the competent worker from the opportunist, the exploiter, and the charlatan. But let us look at a few facts.

As soon as we set up criteria for certification—whether for clinical psychologists, for NTL group trainers, for marriage counselors, for psychiatrists, for psychoanalysts, or, as I heard the other day, for psychic healers—the first and greatest effect is to freeze the profession in a past image. This is an *inevitable* result. What can you use for examinations? Obviously, the questions and tests that have been used in the past decade or two. Who is wise enough to be an examiner? Obviously, the person who has 10 or 20 years of experience and who therefore started his training 15–25 years previously. I know how hard such groups try to update their criteria, but they are always several laps behind. So the certification procedure is always rooted in the rather distant past and defines the profession in those terms.

The second drawback I state sorrowfully. There are as many *certified* charlatans and exploiters of people as there are uncertified. If you had a good friend badly in need of therapeutic help and I gave you the name of a therapist who was a Diplomate in Clinical Psychology, with no other information, would you send your friend to him? Of course not. You would want to know what he is like as a person and as a therapist, recognizing that there are many with diplomas on their walls who are not fit to do therapy, lead a group, or help a marriage. So, certification is *not* equivalent to competence.

The third drawback is that the urge toward professionalism builds up a rigid bureaucracy. I am not personally aware of such bureaucracy at the national level, but it certainly occurs frequently at the state level. Bureaucratic rules become a substitute for sound judgment. A person is disqualified because he has 150 hours of supervised therapy, while another is approved because he has the required 200. No attention is given to the *effectiveness* of either therapist, or the quality of his work, or even the quality of the supervision he received. Or another person is disqualified because his excellent psychological thesis was done in a graduate department that is not labeled psychology. I won't multiply the examples. The bureaucrat is beginning to dominate the scene in ways that are all too familiar, setting the profession back enormously.

Then there is the other side of the coin. I think of the "hot-line" workers I have been privileged to know in recent years. They handle, over the phone, bad drug trips, incipient suicides, tangled love affairs, family discord, all kinds of personal problems. Most of these workers are college students or just beyond this level, with minimal intensive "on-the-job" training. And I know that in many of these crisis situations they use a skill and judgment that would make a professional turn green with envy. They are completely "unqualified," if we use conventional standards. But they *are,* by and large, both dedicated and *competent.*

I think also of my experience in groups, where the so-called "naive" member often has an inner wisdom in dealing with difficult individuals and situations which far outclasses that of myself or of any other professional facilitator. It is a sobering experience to observe this. Or when I think of the best leaders I know for dealing with groups of married couples, I think of a man and woman, neither of whom has even a beginning of satisfactory paper credentials. So, very well qualified people exist outside the fence of credentials.

But you may protest, "How are you going to stop the charlatans who exploit persons psychologically, often for great financial gain?" I respect this question, but I would point out that the person whose purpose is to exploit others can do so without calling himself a psychologist. Scientology (from which we might have learned some things had we been less concerned about credentials) now goes its merry and profitable way as a religion. It is my considered judgment that tight professional standards do not, to more than a minimal degree, shut out the exploiters and the charlatans. If we concentrated on developing and giving outstanding personal help, individuals would come to us, rather than to con men.

In my estimation, we must face the fact that in dealing with human beings, a certificate does not give much assurance of real qualification. If we were less arrogant we might also learn much from the "uncertified" individual who is sometimes unusually adept in the area of human relationships.

I am quite aware that the position I am taking has disadvantages and involves risks, but so does the path to certification and licensure. And I have slowly come to the conclusion that if we did away with "the expert," "the certified professional," "the licensed psychologist," we might open our profession to a breeze of fresh air, to a surge of creativity, such as it has not known for years.

In every area, medicine, nursing, teaching, bricklaying, or carpentry, certification has tended to freeze and narrow the profession, has tied it to the past, and has discouraged innovation. If we ask ourselves how the American physician acquired the image of being a dollar-seeking reactionary, a member of the tightest union in the country, opposed to all progress and change, and especially opposed to giving health care where it is most needed, there is little doubt that the American Medical Association has slowly, even though unintentionally, built that image in the public mind. Yet the primary initial purpose of the AMA was to certify and license qualified physicians and to protect the public against the quack. It hurts me to see psychology beginning to follow that same path.

The question I am humbly raising, in the face of what I am sure will be great shock and antagonism, is simply this: Can psychology find a new and better way? Is there some more creative method of bringing together those who need help and those who are truly excellent in offering helping relationships?

I certainly have no answer, but I would point to one suggestive principle, first enunciated for me by Richard Farson (personal communication, 1966): "The population which has the problem possesses the best resources for dealing with the problem." This has been shown to be true in many areas. Drug addicts, or former drug addicts, are most successful in dealing with individuals with drug problems; similarly, ex-alcoholics help alcoholics, ex-convicts help prisoners—all of them probably more effectively than professionals. But if we certify or otherwise give them superior status as helpers, their helpfulness declines. They then become "professionals," with all of the exclusiveness and territoriality that mark the professional.

So, though I know it must sound horrendous, I would like to see all of the energy we put into certification rules, qualifications, licensure legislation, and written and oral examinations rechanneled into assisting clinical psychologists, social psychologists, and group leaders to become so effective, so devoted to human welfare, that they would be chosen over those who are *actually* unqualified, whether or not they possess paper credentials.

As a supplement to guide the public, we might set up the equivalent of a consumer protective service. If one complaint comes in about ineffective or unethical behavior, it might well be explained away. But if many complaints come in about an individual's services to the public, then his name should be made available to the public, with the suggestion "Let the buyer beware."

Meanwhile, let us develop our learning processes in psychology in such new ways that we are obviously of more service to the public than the "instant gurus," the developers of new and untried fads, the exploiters who feed on a public obviously hungry to be dependent on someone who has "the" answer to all human problems. When our own lasting helpfulness is clearly evident, then we will have no need for our elaborate machinery for certifying and licensing.

### *Can We Permit Ourselves to Be Whole Men and Women?*

Now I wish to move on to a quite different, yet perhaps not unrelated, challenge. Most of us spent 20 or more years in educational institutions where the intellect was *all*. Anything that counted, anything of any importance, occurred above the neck—in absorbing and memorizing, in thinking and expression. Yet, in life, in therapy, in relationships with the opposite sex, in marriage, in parent–child relationships, in encounter groups, in university faculty meetings, we were forced to learn that feelings were an equally important part of living. But, due largely to our education, we still tend to dichotomize these two aspects. I have observed this so strongly in groups. If the group is assembled for an intellectual task, feelings are denied, though they are often painfully evident. If the group is assembled for personal encounter, ideas are often strongly rejected as having no place in such a group. It seems that we live on an either–or basis. We are aware of, and express, what we think; or we are aware of, and express, our emotional reactions. Almost never are the two sides of our life brought together.

Clinical psychology is an interesting indication of the depth of this division. Training is usually separated into courses—the straight intellectual effort—or practicum experience, in which one deals with the emotions of others, and occasionally with one's own. But the rift is most clearly indicated if I present a hypothetical example. One student states that for his dissertation he wishes to measure, with all sophisticated precaution, the differences between Group A and Group B. He believes he will find this intellectually stimulating and valuable. Another states that for his dissertation he wishes to present, in appropriate form and thoughtfully viewed, the most important learning in all his graduate years: the deeply insightful self-learning in his relationship with a difficult client with whom he discovered mutual growth, bringing about lasting changes in his own and his client's behavior. We all know that the first plan would be accepted without question. The second would not only be rejected, but probably angrily and summarily rejected. Who does the student think he is, trying to bring in his feelings, his understanding of his and his client's gut-level reactions, together with his thoughts about these? This would be regarded as a ridiculous subject for a dissertation.

Although this seems only normal educational procedure to the older generation, the present younger generation is more and more frequently refusing to accede. I think of a weekend encounter between faculty and students at a strife-torn university. It ended inconclusively. I thought one student summed up the dilemma accurately when he finally told the faculty: "I don't know if our two worlds can *ever* meet; because our world has feelings in it." For me, this said it.

Why are so many of our best students leaving universities? Because they find no place there for the whole person. Why are so many young people finding life perplexing and without meaning? Partly because they do not know that it is possible to live as a person of thought united with passion, of feeling suffused with intellect and curiosity. Thomas Hanna (1970), in his excellent book *Bodies in Revolt,* puts up a strong plea for the soma, a beautiful unity of the pulsing human organism in all of its manifestations. Among many other things, he has this to say about the feeling of many young people about our "absurd" world: "The experience of 'meaninglessness' is a living accusation of that hypertrophy of one aspect of our somas: namely conscious attention and rational effort [p. 227]." I could not agree with him more. It is the overstress on the conscious and the rational and the underestimation of the wisdom of our total reacting organism that prevent us from living as unified, whole human beings.

Yet, I can testify from personal experience that it is not easy for people whose lives have been dichotomized for decades to achieve this unity. I have conducted courses in which the whole group, including myself, have agreed that our feelings are as important a part of the curriculum as our ideas. Yet, if a member starts exploring some highly emotionalized experiences into which he is beginning to gain understanding, other members hesitate to bring up anything but feeling reactions. And if one person starts a class meeting excitedly propounding the ideas involved in a budding theory he is just beginning to develop, that session tends to be intellectual in focus. Only occasionally has a group been able to *be* whole persons in the experience. Yet, when they have achieved this, the results are unforgettable. Some members turn in highly original and scholarly papers; another expresses his deepest learnings in a poem; still another brings to the final meeting a painted wooden "construction" in which he has tried artistically to set forth what his learnings have been; still another has written a sardonic and dramatic play, very pertinent to the course. For the traditional grade-bound instructor, this would be chaos. For one who is interested in expressions of learning by the total and unified person, this is heartwarming.

But in spite of such innovative efforts—and they are increasingly frequent—dichotomized persons are still an overwhelming majority. We still go to our universities for ideas, and to encounter groups or therapy to emit any "primal scream" of our pent-up emotions.

Yet if we are truly aware, we can hear the "*silent* screams" of denied feelings echoing off of every classroom wall and university corridor. And if we are sensitive enough, we can hear the creative thoughts and ideas that often emerge during and from the open expression of our feelings. Most of us consist of two separated parts, trying desperately to bring themselves together into an integrated soma, where the distinctions between mind and body, feelings and intellect, would be obliterated.

Who can bring into being this whole person? From my experience I would say the least likely are university faculty members. Their traditionalism and smugness approach the incredible. I remember with something approaching horror the statement of a Columbia University professor shortly after buildings were seized and campus turmoil erupted among the students who could not be heard in any other way. This professor told me, "There's no problem of communication at Columbia. Why, I speak to students almost every day." He sounded like a southern slaveholder in the 1850s.

No, I think if change is to come about in dealing with ourselves and others as complete somas with thought and feeling intertwined, it will be the younger generation who achieves it. They are throwing off the shackles of tradition. They have largely discarded the religious dogmas that proclaimed the body evil and only the mind and spirit capable of good. They are a strong hope against the dichotomized, dehumanized being who can drop bombs on Vietnamese civilians and handle this quite comfortably at the intellectual level. He has not murdered people, or torn flesh from bone. He has only engaged in "a protective reaction strike." Only the younger generation, I believe, can help us to see the awful dehumanization we have bred in our educational system by separating thoughts, which are to be approved, from feelings, which are somehow seen as animal in origin. Perhaps the young can make us whole again. God knows we need once more to be unified organisms, responsive to *all* of ourselves and *all* of our environment.

## *Is This the Only Reality?*

Finally, I must mention a challenge that is, I believe, the most dreadfully threatening to psychologists. It is the very strong possibility that there is more than one "reality," that there may indeed be a number of "realities." This is far from a new thought. William James (1928), in saying that "our normal waking consciousness is but one special type of consciousness," argued that "parted from it by the filmiest of screens there lie potential forms of consciousness entirely different," and that the facts then available to him, "forbid our premature closing of accounts with reality."

Now with knowledge of many types of drug-induced states of expanded consciousness and changed reality, with all the years of careful study of ESP, with the international studies of psi phenomena, with serious theorists such as LeShan (1969), we will have a harder and harder time closing our eyes to the possibility of another reality (or realities), operating on rules quite different from our well-known commonsense empirical reality, the only one known to most psychologists.

I would like to make this a bit more personal. I have never had a mystical experience, any type of experience of a paranormal reality, or any drug-induced state that gave me a glimpse of a world different from our secure "real" world. Yet, the evidence grows more and more impressive. One can pass off as most inadequate reporting such books as *Psychic Discoveries Behind the Iron Curtain* (Ostrander & Schroeder, 1971), yet there are some aspects of that which are hard to brush aside. One can regard James's thinking as just an aberration of an otherwise great psychologist. One can try to dismiss the mystics of many ages and countries, were it not for remarkable similarities in their accounts, quite separate from the religious views they held. One has a harder time with the closely reasoned arguments of LeShan (1969), in which, starting out to destroy the myth of other realities, he gradually found himself building a theory that points in the opposite direction. He shows the astonishingly close relationship of the person "sensitive" to paranormal phenomena; the mystic of all periods; and surprisingly enough, the modern theoretical physicist. A reality in which time and space have vanished, a world in which we cannot live, but whose laws we can learn and perceive, a reality that is based not on our senses but on our inner perceptions is common to all of these. The fact that he has devised and is devising ingenious ways to test his theory adds to his credibility.

Yet, I would have to say that for me personally, the most vividly convincing documents I have read come from one man, Carlos Castaneda. Beginning with a thoroughgoing skepticism worthy of a university-trained anthropologist, his excursion into a new way of knowing as practiced by a wise old Yaqui Indian becomes a truly exciting and hair-raising adventure. Then his attempt to reduce all of this to acceptable rational ways of thinking (probably to obtain his PhD) is simply ludicrous (Castaneda, 1968). Obviously, he was too frightened to admit, as he does in his second book, that there is "a separate reality" (Castaneda, 1971).

Why is this whole idea of another reality so threatening to psychologists? I believe it is for the reasons given before, that we are one of the most insecure of the sciences. We do not *dare* to investigate the mysterious. Yet, I think of a notably prominent physicist, very well read in psychology, who was thinking of transferring his interest and changing his profession to the field of psychology because he felt he was too old to make further contributions to theoretical physics (he was 32!). The major question he wished to consult me on was as to the areas of "greatest mystery" in psychology, since it was to those he would wish to devote his time. I could not help but think that I had never heard of a psychologist aiming his work toward areas of "greatest mystery." It is only the secure scientist who can do that.

I am not suggesting in any of this that we "know" there is a separate reality (or realities). What I am saying is that we would not be demeaning ourselves if we became open-minded to such a possibility and started investigating it, as the Russians and British are doing.

To be sure, much more study is needed. I would wish to see a replication of the experiment on the mother rabbit and her litter. The mother rabbit, her brain hooked up to electrodes, was kept on shore. Her infants, far off at sea in a submarine, were killed one at a time at varying periods, by the investigators. The mother rabbit, at each synchronized instant of the death of one of her babies, reportedly showed clearly registered electronic reactions (Ostrander & Schroeder, 1971, pp. 33–34). What do we make of this?

When a clairvoyant woman picks up an envelope which she has never seen before (containing a fragment of an ancient cuneiform tablet) and begins to describe "a girl associated with this," she gives completely the portrait and life history of a secretary who had assisted in packing the object. The report was so detailed that not one other woman in a thousand would have matched her report. Yet, she said not one word that could be construed as having anything to do with the tablet. Here is a double kind of mystery which LeShan (1969, pp. 53–54) thinks he begins to understand. Yet, similar studies and the testing of his theory are obviously necessary.

And what of the various instances of precognition or simultaneous cognition of the pain or death of a loved one far away? Or telepathic communication by which a hypnotist, out of sight and at a distance, can put to sleep a trained hypnotic subject simply by concentrating on the message he wishes to get across to her (Ostrander & Schroeder, 1971, p. 104)? And finally what do we make of the strange and unearthly experiences of Carlos Castaneda (1968, 1971)?

Perhaps in the coming generation of younger psychologists, hopefully unencumbered by university prohibitions and resistances, there may be a few who will dare to investigate the possibility that there is a lawful reality which is not open to our five senses; a reality in which present, past, and future are intermingled, in which space is not a barrier and time has disappeared; a reality which can be perceived and known only when we are passively receptive, rather than actively bent on knowing. It is one of the most exciting challenges posed to psychology.

## *Final Comment*

When I began this discussion, I stated that the various issues I was raising had little logical connection, but were simply diverse challenges. As I have worked over the material, I do see—from my own bias, I am sure—a certain unity to the questions I have raised. I am far from sure I have raised the most important issues. I may be greatly deceived in the way I perceive these challenges. But let me try to restate them in fresh ways and then indicate the thread that, for me, binds them together.

I have raised the question as to whether psychology will remain a narrow technological fragment of a science, tied to an outdated philosophical conception of itself, clinging to a security blanket of observable behaviors only; or whether it can possibly become a truly broad and creative science, rooted in subjective vision, open to all aspects of the human condition, worthy of the name of a mature science.

I have raised the question of whether we dare to turn from being a past-oriented remedial technology to a focus of future-oriented planning, taking our part in a chaotic world to build environments where human beings can choose to learn, where minorities can choose to remake the establishment through relating to it, where innovative communities can learn to live together. Will we continue to be peripheral to our society, or will we risk the dangers of being a significant social factor?

I have pointed out that perhaps the safety, the prestige, and the vestments of traditionalism that can be earned through certification and licensure may not be worth the cost. I have wondered aloud if we would dare to rest our confidence in the quality and competence we have as persons, rather than in the certificates we can frame on our walls.

I have questioned—a bit despairingly, I fear—whether we could possibly see the day when faculty and students and psychologists in general could function as whole persons—not as minds walking around on stilts, or headless feelings muttering wild cries to each other. Could we accept ourselves as total organisms, with wisdom in every pore—if we would but hear and be aware of that wisdom?

I have hesitantly pointed out that the reality we are so sure of, the reality so plainly shown to us by our senses, may not be the only reality open to mankind. I have raised the query as to whether we would ever be willing to take the frightening risk of investigating this possibility, without prejudgment.

As I mull over these issues, I believe that if psychology—as a science and a profession—gave a clear affirmative answer to each of these questions, gave a positive response to each of these challenges, it would be moving forward.

So the thread that I see in the issues I have raised is that each one represents a possible move toward the enhancement, the deepening, the enrichment of our profession. Each one, in a word, represents for psychology a step toward self-actualization. If my perceptions have been even approximately correct, then the final question I would leave with you is, Do we dare?

## REFERENCES


Castaneda, C. *The teachings of Don Juan: A Yaqui way of knowing.* New York: Ballantine Books, 1968.

Castaneda, C. *A separate reality: Further conversations with Don Juan.* New York: Simon & Schuster, 1971.

Coulson, W. R., & Rogers, C. R. (Eds.) *Man and the science of man.* Columbus, Ohio: Merrill, 1968.

Dagenais, J. J. *Models of man.* The Hague, Netherlands: Nimhoff, 1972.

Hanna, T. *Bodies in revolt: A primer in somatic thinking.* New York: Holt, Rinehart & Winston, 1970.

Hanna, T. The project of somatology. Paper presented at the annual meeting of the Association for Humanistic Psychology, Washington, D.C., September 1971.

James, W. *The varieties of religious experience.* London: Longmans, Green, 1928.

Koch, S. Epilogue. In S. Koch (Ed.), *Psychology: A study of a science.* Vol. 3. *Formulations of the person and the social context.* New York: McGraw-Hill, 1959.

LeShan, L. *Toward a general theory of the paranormal.* New York: Parapsychology Foundation, 29 W. 57th Street, New York, New York, 1969.

Oppenheimer, R. Analogy in science. *American Psychologist,* 1956, **11**, 127–135.

Ostrander, S., & Schroeder, L. *Psychic discoveries behind the Iron Curtain.* New York: Bantam Books, 1971.

Polanyi, M. *Personal knowledge.* Chicago: University of Chicago Press, 1958.

Rogers, C. R. Persons or science? A philosophical question. *American Psychologist,* 1955, **10**, 267–278.

Rogers, C. R. Toward a science of the person. In T. W. Wann (Ed.), *Behaviorism and phenomenology: Contrasting bases for modern psychology.* Chicago: University of Chicago Press, 1964.

Schilpp, P. A. (Ed.) *Albert Einstein: Philosopher-scientist.* New York: Harper Torchbooks, 1959.

Schultz, D. P. (Ed.) *The science of psychology: Critical reflections.* New York: Appleton-Century-Crofts, 1970.

Skinner, B. F. A case history in scientific method. In S. Koch (Ed.), *Psychology: A study of a science.* Vol. 2. New York: McGraw-Hill, 1959.

# Subject Index

# Name Index

E



F



G



H



I



J



K